W9-AEI-004

Kinship and Culture

Kinship and Culture

Edited by Francis L. K. Hsu
Northwestern University

Aldine Publishing Company / *Chicago, Illinois*

First published 1971 by
Aldine Publishing Company
529 South Wabash Avenue
Chicago, Illinois 60605

Library of Congress Catalog Card Number
72–75050
ISBN 202-01078-3
Designed by Chestnut House
Printed in the United States of America

Editor's Preface

Briefly, the hypothesis seeks to find a more definitive link, on a comparative basis, between kinship system and psychocultural characteristics. The hypothesis, in skeletal form, is: The dominant attributes of the dominant dyad in a given kinship system tend to determine the attitudes and action patterns that the individual in such a system develops toward other dyads in this system as well as toward his relationships outside of the system. For purposes of this hypothesis, kinship is treated as the independent variable and psychocultural characteristics as the dependent ones. Its primary concern is not, however, with this distinction, but with locating forces in the nuclear kinship group and translating them into categories that can be seen to express themselves variously in the kinship system and in the larger society. This is explained in Chapter 1.

The aim of the contributors to this volume is to discuss, develop, revise, or challenge this hypothesis from different points of view; this has been done with reference to theory (for example, the defensibility of its underlying assumptions and implications), to area (for example, the extent to which the hypothesis is applicable to specific cultures widely separated by geography), to methodology (for example, how to locate dominance in any one kinship system), and to cultural development (for example, the relevance of kinship systems to cultures through time). The parts into which the body of the book is divided roughly follow these four lines of inquiry (Chapters 2 through 19).

These divisions are, obviously, not inclusive. To take but one example: The chapter by Fernandez (Chapter 15) is an ethnographical exploration as much as a demonstration of a particular method for determining kinship dominance in any particular society.

The concluding chapter (Chapter 20) sets forth the main concerns and views of each contributor, some unsolved problems, and possible lines for future exploration.

Most of the contributions were first presented at a symposium on Kinship and Culture, held at Burg Wartenstein, Austria, August 20–29, 1966, under the sponsorship of the Wenner-Gren Foundation for Anthropological Research, New York City. They were then more or less revised by each contributor in light of the discussions at the symposium.

The editor is indebted to Mrs. Lita Osmundsen, Director of Research at the Wenner-Gren Foundation, for her encouragement and support, and to the contributors who agreed to spend the time and energy to educate him on his shortcomings. Conrad Arensberg participated in the conference at Burg Wartenstein, but was not able to complete his written paper in time. His comments at the concluding session of the symposium are included in Chapter XX because of their pertinence.

Throughout the symposium three young anthropologists (William M. O'Barr, Thomas P. Rohlen, and Dirk van der Veen) served as *rapporteurs*. They have helped me immeasurably with the organizational activities and by their intellectual support. In fact, they are independent contributors to the volume as well (Chapters 8 and 17). His impending departure for field work in East Africa prevented Mr. O'Barr from completing his paper in time for inclusion in this volume.

Finally, the editor is indebted to his several helpers: Mrs. Adele Andelson, Mrs. Rita Mendelsohn, and Mrs. Andrea Sherwin.

Contents

Introduction

ONE

FRANCIS L. K. HSU

A Hypothesis on Kinship and Culture

The concept of kinship extension was first explained by Radcliffe-Brown. He observed "the tendency" among the Bantu tribes and Nama Hottentots of South Africa to develop patterns for the mother's brother and the father's sister by regarding the former as somewhat of a male mother and the latter to some extent a female father (Radcliffe-Brown, 1924, reprinted 1952:19). He concludes: "In primitive society there is a strongly marked tendency to merge the individual in the group to which he or she belongs. The result of this in relation to kinship is a tendency to extend to all members of a group a certain type of behavior which has its origin in a relationship to one particular member of the group" (1952:25).

Radcliffe-Brown's use of the term "primitive" is unnecessary. The kind of behavior he spoke of cannot scientifically be used to separate mankind into "primitive" versus "civilized." In fact, the very dichotomy of "primitive" versus "civilized" is to be questioned (Hsu, 1964). However, the idea of extension of patterns of behavior characteristic of one kinship relationship to that of another has been the basis of much valuable field research. Thus Fred Eggan, among others, has shown that the Hopi not only class mother's mother's mother and the mother's brothers as "siblings," but also extend "the sibling relationship to all the members of one's clan and phratry who are of roughly the same age or generation and also to the children of all men of the father's clan and phratry, including the clans

This hypothesis was first published in *American Anthropologist* (Hsu, 1965). It is given here with slight amplification of certain points and some changes in terminology, but no modification of the basic arguments.

and phratries of the ceremonial and doctor fathers regardless of age" (Eggan, 1950:43–44).

However, all of these works, including those aided by precise models such as those of Lévi-Strauss (1949) and White (1963), deal merely with the modification of one kind of kinship relationship by another, the degree to which kinship categories are applied to non-kins, or the bearing of these phenomena on kinship or kinship-connected behavior such as avoidance of intimacy and particularly mate selection. There have been two approaches to the relationship between what goes on in the kinship sphere and what goes on outside it. The first is the personality-and-culture one; it attempts to relate certain child-rearing practices little or not at all related to forms of kinship (such as swaddling, permissiveness, sibling rivalry, length of breast-feeding, alleged or real sudden changes in parental attitude when the child reaches a certain age), to the personality of the individual or culture of the society. The other approach, by social structure, either ignores the question or tries to explain social development without reference to kinship at all.

For example, according to Murdock (1949:226–28, 236–38), the Eskimo, the Yankees of New England, the peasant Ruthenians of Eastern Europe, the agricultural Taos Pueblo, and the Andamanese Pygmies, among others, all share one type of kinship structure, while the Fijians, the Tallensi, the Manchus, and the Chinese all share another type. The striking thing is that the diverse peoples in each of the two groups have few cultural characteristics in common despite the similarity of their respective kinship structures. This lack of correspondence between their kinship structures and their other cultural characteristics inevitably leaves us with the impression that kinship structures are of no consequence to social and cultural development in general. Is the study of kinship structure but a mathematical game?

Lévi-Strauss, whose work on kinship structure is also well known, seems to abandon kinship altogether when the going gets rough. Lévi-Strauss reports with enthusiasm the work of Sutter and Tabah, who computed the average size of isolates (groups of intermarrying people) in all French *départements*. The average size of the French isolate varies from less than 1,000 to over 2,800 individuals. Lévi-Strauss then observed:

> This numerical evaluation shows that, even in a modern society, the network of people united by kinship ties is much smaller than might be expected, *of about the same size as in primitive groups*. The inference is that, while the absolute size of the inter-marrying group remains approximately on the same scale in all human societies . . . a complex society becomes such *not so much because of an expansion of the isolate itself as on account of an expansion of other types of social links* (economic, political and intellectual); and these are used to connect a great number of isolates which, by themselves, remain relatively static [Lévi-Strauss, 1953:534–35; my italics].

The remarkable thing is that Lévi-Strauss, while looking at the clearest evidence that kinship structure studies are thus far irrelevant to the crucial problems of social and cultural development, tries to gloss over the difficulties by insisting that it is the "expansion of other . . . links (economic, political and intellectual)" that "connect" the static isolates that were presumably responsible for the complexity of French and other Western societies as contrasted to the "primitive" groups. This "inference" by Lévi-Strauss seems to be founded on nothing more than fantasy. While marriages have been contracted here and there because of economic, political, and intellectual "links," such links have also divided and united men regardless of marital and kinship bonds. We have no evidence that economic, political, and intellectual links have any significant connection with Lévi-Strauss' "inter-marrying isolates" in any society, "primitive" or "modern." Of course, if by "connected" Lévi-Strauss means "embraced," his "inference" is safe—so safe that it is meaningless. The political link alone in every modern society certainly embraces all forms of isolates, from Lévi-Strauss' intermarrying kind to communities, unions, syndicates, regions, gangster organizations, sororities, fraternities, classes, religions, and other obvious or hidden circles of inclusion or exclusion. Lévi-Strauss' conclusion regarding the importance of his intermarrying isolates to the development of complex societies is therefore scientifically as useless as the notion that the development of complex societies can be gauged from the structure and function of the sororities, or the gangster organizations, or the business syndicates.

Whichever way we look at the matter, we are compelled to admit that the study of intermarrying isolates in France or in a "primitive" society has not clarified and is not likely ever to clarify the differential development of the two types of societies.

Yet kinship plays such a basic part in the upbringing of the human individual, and has such a universal place in every human society, that it is not likely to be so irrelevant to social and cultural developments.

The hypothesis developed in the following articles is designed to do a number of things. First, going beyond Radcliffe-Brown and others, we hope to show that not only are the influences of one kinship relationship upon another a general phenomenon, but these influences can originate from one relationship and extend to all other relationships so as to shape the entire kinship system. Second, when these influences exert themselves in this way, the effector relationships do not simply change into secondary versions of the affector relationship, as Radcliffe-Brown and others have observed—and the kinship systems in question make no assumptions of such formal changes either. Instead, what occurs much more generally is that the qualities and patterns of interaction in the effector relationships assume characteristics similar to those of the affector relationship, so that the husband-wife relationship or the father-son relationship, for example, *as husband-wife or father-son relationship* in one kinship system appears drastically different from that in another. Third, we hope to show that the same influence becomes visible in the qualities and patterns of behavior among those other members of the same society who, though not related through kinship, act in non-kinship roles. In other words, we hope firmly to link interaction patterns in a kinship system with the characteristic modes of behavior in the wider society of which that kinship system forms a part. In doing so we hope to convince students of psychological anthropology that it is the broader aspects of interpersonal interaction patterns in the nuclear family and not merely certain limited child-rearing practices that are crucial to human development; and to convince students of social structure that they have unnecessarily restricted the scientific fruitfulness of their efforts by ignoring psychological anthropology.

In order to accomplish these aims, we have to scrutinize kinship relationships in terms other than their commonly accepted ones. A brief illustration will clarify this. Common sense informs us that food is necessary for body growth and health, and that lack of it causes illness and malfunction. But had scientists stuck to food names such as green pepper, beef, pork, chop suey, or crepe suzette, they would never have developed the science of nutrition. It was only when they converted foods into their component elements, such as carbohydrate and iodine or vitamins A, B, and K, that the science of nutrition truly advanced. What we propose to do is to convert kinship relationships into their attributes, to enable us to see more clearly the influences of particular relationships within and without a particular kinship system. We hope to ascertain these influences not only where human beings are structurally linked through terminological or other kinship-connected categories, but also identify their ramifications outside the kinship organization, far beyond their boundaries throughout the society.

STRUCTURE AND CONTENT

Before going into our hypothesis it is first necessary to define a number of basic terms, two of which are "structure" and "content."[1]

By "structure" we mean the express or understood table of organization of any social system. That table of organization defines the socially recognized roles of the various persons in the system with reference to each other. By "content" we mean the characteristics which govern the tenacity, intensity, and variety of interaction among individuals related through that table of organization.

To illustrate: A newborn infant may have contact only with parents or mother and mother's brothers, plus a few siblings and occasionally some others; or his early contacts may also include a vast array of other relatives and nonrelatives. These are matters of kinship structure and are part of

1. I first dealt with the importance of distinguishing between the structure and content of social organization in a paper entitled "Structure, Function, Content, and Process" (1959:790–805).

the difference between the conjugal family and a more extended larger unit. However, two infants who come into contact with an equal number of individuals may be affected differently. In one case the relatives may act as though they possess the infant and can jointly control him; in the other, they may act as though they are mere spectators, while the infant's own mother is in complete control. These are differences in kinship content. The former pattern is an expression of a kinship content that is characterized by mutual dependence, while the latter is an expression of a kinship content characterized by individualism or self-reliance. Individualism, as it is expressed in the West, prescribes that each human being is his own master, but his discipline and control are exclusively in the hands of his parents until he reaches maturity. Mutual dependence in China and Japan means that each human being is not his own master; whether he is seven or seventy, his actions and destiny are tied to his parents, ancestors, clan members, and descendants.

The difference between the two types of content may be made clearer if we scrutinize the matter of discipline more closely. The average American woman is a guest in the house of her daughter-in-law. She is not supposed to give orders to her grandchildren, much less to contradict her daughter-in-law's orders. Even if she comes into the younger woman's home during an emergency to take over the temporary care of her grandchildren, she is still supposed to follow her daughter-in-law's wishes. Not infrequently the younger woman will leave a memo indicating what her children can do, when they should go to bed, and so on. Interference is an accusation that most American mothers-in-law hope to avoid, even if in reality they do succeed in interfering to some degree by subterfuge. Conversely, before the impact of the West, the average Chinese woman in her daughter-in-law's house was a mistress over the younger woman. The average Chinese family contained no more than 5.3 members, structurally composed of parents and their unmarried children. But whether or not the mother-in-law lived under the same roof with her son and his family, she was not only accustomed to oversee the welfare of her grandchildren, but thought nothing of overruling her daughter-in-law in such matters if she preferred to do so. The younger woman might resent this, but no one would criticize the mother-in-law for it. This difference between a singular authority and multiple authorities (some of which negate others) over the children is but one of hundreds of ways in which the two differing kinship contents are expressed.

At this point some structuralists may retort that the distinction made here consists of no material foreign to them, and is in fact part of what they mean by "structural difference." My reply is that it is of course possible for the structuralist to be aware of the facts I have pointed up, but that my case does not rest on the novelty of these facts. Rather, my case is based on the need to separate facts which have been lumped together willy-nilly under the term "structure." That lumping together is an obstacle to further progress in our study of the role of kinship in social and cultural development which must be removed.

In the family organization, structure describes the size of the group, the variety of related individuals who live together, and the expected or actually practiced relationship pattern in terms of obligations, privileges, actions taken, and actions not taken. The family may be individual or joint. In one type of individual family, the father is the breadwinner, the mother does the housework, and the children have no duties; in another type of individual family, the mother may be the breadwinner while the father stays home and the children assist the mother in her work. These are matters of structure. But the father or mother may support the family willingly or reluctantly; the breadwinner may feel that he has an obligation to support the family or that he is merely being benevolent, in which case the family is indebted to him for the kindness. These are matters of content.

The structure of a university shows the usual pattern of organization with its board of trustees, administration, faculty, and students, as well as the usual chain of command, communication, and responsibilities. But by examining its content we can gain a much better idea whether the institution is academically oriented or run like a business; whether the faculty is subordinate to the administration or vice versa; or whether the institutional morale is high or low.[2]

Dominant Dyad and Dominant Attribute

The other terms central to our hypothesis are "dyad," "attribute," "dominant dyad" and "dominant attribute."[3] A dyad consists of two linked persons. In the nuclear family, eight basic dyads are apparent: husband-wife, father-son, mother-son, father-daughter, mother-daughter, brother-brother, brother-sister, and sister-sister.[4] The term "attribute" refers to the logical or typical mode of behavior and attitude intrinsic to each dyad. The words "logical," "typical," and "intrinsic" are crucial to this definition. In this sense, the attributes of each dyad are what David Schneider describes as "constants" (Schneider, 1961:5) because they are universally the potential and inherent properties of that dyad.

2. Elsewhere I have discussed how the Eskimo and New England Yankee kinship systems are similar in structure but dissimilar in content (Hsu, 1959:802–804).

3. When the hypothesis was first published (Hsu, 1965), I used the word "relationship" instead of "dyad." In the course of the symposium we decided dyad is a better term for our purposes, since only the simplest kinship relationships are dealt with here. Among physical scientists the term "property" is generally used in place of our term "attribute."

4. Besides these there are at least nine other primary kin dyads in the nuclear family: father-child, mother-child, parent-son, parent-daughter, sibling-sibling, older sister-younger brother, older brother-younger sister, older brother-younger brother, older sister-younger sister.

The most easily understood example of this is perhaps the employer-employee dyad. The intrinsic attributes of this dyad are, for example, functional considerations, calculated obligations and rewards, and specific delineations in duration. A man generally enters into such a relationship because he has work he wants done, or he desires wages or their equivalent. Furthermore, the length of time during which the relationship lasts is likely to be understood or made specific in advance. The details vary from society to society, but these intrinsic attributes can be found wherever an employer-employee dyad is said to exist. On the other hand, these attributes intrinsic to the employer-employee dyad do not obtain in the case of a romantic dyad. The intrinsic attributes of each dyad are the basic ingredients and determinants of the interactional patterns between parties of that dyad.

The validity of the use of the terms "logical" and "typical" has been questioned because we cannot "observe" them "in a pure state anywhere." Critics insist on the need for "prior demonstration from ethnography" before we can use them as intrinsic attributes (Strathern and Strathern, 1966:997–98). Such objections come from a misunderstanding of the nature of hypothesis-building. Few hypotheses in any discipline are ever built on elements all of which are exactly known and proved. And even if we use only elements that have been previously proved, the relationship between the elements must be unknown or only vaguely known; otherwise there is no need to make much ado about any hypothesis concerning them. We construct a hypothesis because we want to develop a clearer knowledge about the relationship, and in order to do so we have to make various suppositions as if the relationship were (or that it were composed of) x or y or z or whatever you wish to call it. The test of a hypothesis resides not in its origin (for example, it may come simply from the mind of one scientist), but in its fruitfulness in regard to new data.[5]

No nuclear family would seem to give equal prominence to all its basic dyads. What actually occurs is that in each type of nuclear family one (or more) takes precedence over the others. When a dyad is thus elevated above others, it tends to modify, magnify, reduce, or even eliminate other dyads in the kinship group. Such a dyad is designated in our hypothesis as the *dominant dyad* while others in the system are *non-dominant dyads.*[6]

5. The fact that our attributes cannot be observed in a pure state anywhere is no permanent stumbling block either. Our knowledge about most of the physical universe began with phenomena in their nonpure states. But each refinement in analysis or success in experimentation brings us closer to the pure state. The elements in medieval conception, such as water, fire, earth, and wind, are less pure than atoms; atoms are less pure than electrons and neutrons, just as cells, chromosomes, genes, and DNA form a sequence in which each succeeding postulate is purer than the last. But if the biologists and physicists had waited until all their postulates could be seen in a "pure state" or be empirically verified before they constructed their hypotheses, they would not have made much progress.

6. In the first version of the hypothesis (Hsu, 1965), I used here the term "recessive" instead of "non-dominant."

For example, if the father-son dyad in the nuclear family is the dominant one, it will increase the social importance of the father-son dyad at the expense of other dyads such as husband-wife, so that the father and mother will have more to say about their son's future wife than the son himself. In such an eventuality the kinship group or kinship team as defined by Naroll (1956:696, 698) tends to extend itself far beyond the nuclear family of parents and unmarried children because of its inclusion of a variety of other consanguineal relatives and their wives and children. Conversely, if the husband-wife dyad is dominant, it will alter the parent-child relationship into a temporary arrangement to be replaced or discarded when the child grows into adulthood. In such a case the kinship group tends to correspond to the nuclear family at all times because of the exclusion of all consanguineal relatives as soon as they are married.

The intrinsic attributes of the dominant dyads are designated in our hypothesis as the *dominant attributes,* while those of the non-dominant dyads in the system are designated *non-dominant attributes.* In each form of nuclear family, the dominant attributes so influence the non-dominant attributes that the latter tend to converge in the direction of the dominant attributes.

The dominant attributes prevail over and give shape to all the non-dominant attributes. The sum of all the attributes converging toward the dominant attributes in the kinship system is designated its content, just as the sum of all the dyads under the influence of one or more dominating dyads is its structure.

The interrelationship may be roughly represented in the following diagram:

Structure —————————— Content

Dominant Dyads —————————— Dominant Attributes

↑ ↑

Non-dominant Dyads —————————— Non-dominant Attributes

Figure 1.1. Kinship System

The Hypothesis

Having defined the terms, we are ready to state the hypothesis, which, in skeletal form, is: *The dominant attributes of the dominant dyad in a given kinship system tend to determine the attitudes and action patterns that the individual in such a system develops towards other dyads in this system as well as towards his relationships outside of the system.*

We shall explicate this hypothesis in three parts: first, an examination of four basic kinship dyads and their attributes (Table 1.1); second, the effect of dominant dyads on other kinship dyads in the same kinship system; third, the effect of dominant dyads on non-kin relationships.

Table 1.1. Four Dyads and Their Attributes

Dyad	*Attributes*	*Definition of Attributes*
Husband-Wife	1. Discontinuity	The condition of not being, or the attitude of desiring not to be, in a sequence or connected with others.
	2. Exclusiveness	The act of keeping others out or unwillingness to share with them.
	3. Sexuality	Preoccupation with sex.
	4. Volition*	The condition of being able to follow own inclinations, or of desiring to do so.
Father-Son	1. Continuity	The condition of being, or the attitude of desiring to be, an unbroken sequence, or connected with others.
	2. Inclusiveness	The act of incorporating or the attitude of wishing to be incorporated.
	3. Authority	Personal power that commands and enforces obedience, or the condition of being under such power.
	4. Asexuality	The condition of having no connection with sex.
Mother-Son	1. Discontinuity	(Already defined above)
	2. Inclusiveness	(Already defined above)
	3. Dependence	The condition of being or the attitude of wishing to be reliant upon others.
	4. Diffuseness	The tendency to spread out in all directions.
	5. Libidinality	Diffused or potential sexuality.
Brother-Brother	1. Discontinuity	(Already defined above)
	2. Inclusiveness	(Already defined above)
	3. Equality	The condition of being or the attitude of wishing to be of the same rank and importance as others.
	4. Rivalry	The act of striving, or the attitude of wishing to strive, for equality with or excellence over others.

*In the first version of this hypothesis I used the term "freedom."

Six points should be made clear at the outset. First, the different dyads overlap to a certain extent in their attributes. The attribute of discontinuity is common to husband-wife, mother-son, and brother-brother dyads, while inclusiveness is common to father-son, mother-son, and brother-brother dyads. It is the particular combination of attributes, not single attributes, which differentiates one dyad from another. Second, the differences between attributes are rarely if ever absolute, but as a rule used in a comparative sense. Continuity versus discontinuity, or inclusiveness versus exclusiveness are illustrative of this view. In the geometric sense of a line being a set of points, continuity is made up of a set of discontinuities. Third, when an attribute is listed for dyad A but not for dyad B it does not mean that it is entirely absent in the latter. Thus the authority attribute is not entirely absent in the mother-son dyad, but this attribute tends to be so overshadowed by one or more others, or embraced by them, that it is not independently significant. Fourth, some attributes, such as authority and sexuality, are opposed to each other, while others, such as authority and dependence, are intimately related to each other. Fifth, the list of attributes given for each dyad is not exhaustive. Further analysis may yield new ones. Finally, in this and later analyses the reader should bear in mind the contribution of Parsons in his essay "Family Structure and Socialization of the Child" (Parsons and Bales, 1955: 35–133). Some of our attributes are similar but not identical with some aspects of Parsons' "role structure" of the nuclear family and their differentiations. These will be pointed out as we progress. More pronounced differences between our analysis and Parsons' will occur in later sections of this chapter.

Let us examine the links between these dyads and their attributes. The attributes of the husband-wife dyad are discontinuity,[7] exclusiveness, volition, and sexuality. It is discontinuous because, and here I must ask leave for elaboration of the obvious, every husband is never a wife, and every wife is never a husband. Every husband-wife dyad is a unit by itself, independent of all other relationships. There is no structural necessity for any husband-wife relationship, as such, to be related to other husband-wife relationships. It is exclusive because, while marriage in every society is a public affair, every husband and wife must universally carry out by themselves alone some activities which are crucial to the conjugal relationship. This remains true regardless of the form of marriage. It is well known that in the polygynous societies of Africa each wife has her own hut where her own children live and where her husband visits her. It is also well known that the wife in the few polyandrous societies of the world receives her husbands separately and each of the several husbands usually establishes some kind of individualized ritual relationship with a particular child.

7. The term "discontinuity" in this hypothesis is not identical with the term discontinuity that Parsons regards as one of the basic discoveries of Freud in analyzing the socialization process (Parsons and Bales, 1955:40). As our analysis will show, our term discontinuity refers not to an absolute break in the child's socialization process, but to a quality of interpersonal relationships in comparative terms throughout life. This relationship is either very long, measured by decades, and therefore more continuous, or very short, measured by a few months or a few years, and therefore more discontinuous. However, sharp breaks in the socialization process are probably more likely to occur in a social system where discontinuity is one of its dominant attributes than in other systems where it is not.

Among these exclusive activities, sexuality has an obvious and central place, which is another attribute of the husband-wife dyad. The connection between sexuality and husband-wife dyad needs no elaboration. Of all the eight basic dyads in the nuclear family, the husband-wife dyad is the only one in which sexuality is universally an implicit and explicit constant.

The attribute of volition is commensurate with both exclusiveness and sexuality. Of all the eight basic dyads, that of husband-wife alone is one which, by virtue of sexuality, involves a need for individual willingness unknown or not required in the others. Even in societies where caste or other customary rules exclude individual choice, individual preferences enter into the making, continuation, and termination of the relationship. Sometimes the volition may be exercised by parents or family heads and not the man and woman entering or forming the relationship. But that is a kind of choice, nevertheless, which is not naturally true in the other basic dyads in the nuclear family. Furthermore, in this dyad the male at least has universally more room for personal maneuver no matter what the kinship system he lives in.

The basic attributes of the father-son dyad are continuity, inclusiveness, asexuality, and authority. The relationship is continuous because every father is a son, and every son, in the normal course of events, is a father. Therefore every father-son dyad is but a link in an everlasting chain of father-son dyads. It is inclusive because while every son has only one father, every father actually or potentially has many sons. Therefore the relationship between the father and the son is inherently tolerant rather than intolerant toward sharing with others. The attribute of authority comes from a basic difference between men and women in every society. The role of men as men is defined as that of having authority over women and children, as contrasted to that of women as women, which is responsibility for the care of children (Schneider, 1961:6). The attribute of asexuality simply means a quality which has nothing to do with sex.

A closer examination will reveal that the several attributes intrinsic to each of the two dyads are mutually commensurate with each other. Take the attributes of the father-son dyad first.

Continuity means relatively lengthy existence of that relationship in time. With the normal birth and marriage, more lengthy existence in time means greater chances of involvement of others who were not previously in the picture. Thus two bachelors may develop a friendship. If the friendship lasts more than a few years, there are chances of each of them being married. If their friendship ends before they are married there will be no question of inclusion in their friendship of the two women who come later. But if they continue their friendship after marriage, it is reasonable to expect that the new wives will be involved in the relationship. If their friendship continues still further, there is the likelihood of their having children who are involved in some way in the friendship of the two older men.

However, the widening of the circle of involvement as this friendship continues is not restricted to birth and marriage. One member of the friendship team may move for business or other reasons to another locality where he will meet new people and make new friends. If he discontinues his friendship with his older friend, then indeed his circle of friendship need not be more inclusive than before. But if he wants to continue the older friendship, then it becomes obvious that the circle is inevitably enlarged. Thus we may generate the following subsidiary hypothesis: The more continuous a dyad, and the longer it lasts, the more inclusive it will become of other individuals who were not previously in that relationship.

Authority can be exercised generally in one of three ways: first, by brutal power on the part of the superior over the subordinates; second, through what Max Weber would designate as charisma, which in my view should include sex appeal; third, by conviction on the part of the subordinates of the superior's right, duty, or privilege to exercise authority just as it is their right, duty, or privilege to obey it. It is obvious that the first two ways of exercising authority are likely to be less permanent than the third. In the first, resentment is likely to occur among those who are subject to the authority so that they may revolt or attempt to get out from under the authority at the first opportunity. In the second way, authority is likely to be disrupted as soon as there is a reduction of charisma or sex appeal on the part of the superior through old age or loss of capacity in some manner. At any rate, death is likely to end his position of authority once and for all. In the third way, since the subordinates are taught to respect the superior's role of authority, the latter is not so easily subject to ups and downs as in the other cases.

The lines separating these three ways of authority are relative, but the third way is more likely to characterize authority in the father-son dyad, especially since the attribute of continuity enables the sons to cooperate, because they themselves expect to exercise it in the same way when it is their turn to do so. In this situation the idea of authority permeates the dyad and is not tied to the accident of the brutal power or the special qualities of a single person. Under such circumstances authority does not disappear with the death of the person in authority; it tends to continue after his death in the form of the cult of the dead (in the kinship sphere) or worship of the past or tradition (in the society generally). Furthermore, on the basis of what we said before of the link between continuity and inclusiveness, we can say that the more continuous the worship of the ancestry of a kinship group or tradition of a society, the more inclusively that authority is likely to apply to wider circles of human beings.

In the same light we may see the attributes of the husband-wife dyad. Discontinuity is more commensurate with exclusiveness than inclusiveness. Going back to the same friendship example discussed before, it is obvious that the shorter the duration of friendship, the less the chances of involvement in friendship with others who are not originally part of that friendship. Sexuality and exclusiveness are necessary for each other, because no matter how widely distributed the sex appeal of a single individual, the core of sexuality, that is the sexual act, is universally carried out between two individuals, and experienced orgasmically by them. There are many forms of self-eroticism such as masturbation which can be restricted to one individual alone, and there are other forms of sexual practices which can involve more than two individuals, but there is no question that the universal norm of the sexual act is between one man and one woman.

Sexuality as a physiological phenomenon necessarily waxes and wanes even during that period of the individual's life when the sex drive is strong. Then as the individual grows older, the sexual drive diminishes and recedes. There are known differences between the male and the female in this regard and there are also known individual differences. But there is no question that sexuality recedes and then disappears as age advances. Furthermore, death concludes it. Unlike authority, which can be exercised many centuries after a man's death, sexuality cannot be exercised in absentia. Consequently sexuality in contrast to authority is much more commensurate with discontinuity than with continuity.

Turning now to the mother-son dyad, we find five differentiable attributes: discontinuity, inclusiveness, dependence, diffuseness, and libidinality. In common with the husband-wife dyad, it is discontinuous because no mother is a son and no son is ever a mother. But the next two attributes are more particularly its own. These are dependence and diffuseness, built on two closely related facts. First, since the mother comes into the newborn child's life at the earliest possible moment, she caters to its wants at a time when it is at its most ineffectual. For the infant, the mother is the principal agent for all satisfaction. She is his answer-all. Second, the mother's relationship with her infant involves more interaction of an unstructured nature than that of the father's, since, as some psychoanalysts would put it, the "mother normally achieves identification with her infant through libidinally charged processes which permit her to become a child with [him] again. . . . The identification with the baby permits her to enjoy her 'regression' and to repeat and satisfy her own receptive, dependent needs" (Alexander, 1952:104, 106).[8]

Therefore, though dependence is not entirely absent in some of the other kinship dyads, it is the outstanding ingredient in the mother-son dyad (as it is also naturally in the mother-daughter dyad). Dependence obviously enters into the father-son dyad. But there it is greatly modified by the fact of growth. Intensive interaction between a father and his son usually occurs some months or years after the son's birth when the latter is less ineffectual and helpless than when he first began life with his mother. In Parsons' terms (Parsons and Bales, 1955:47–55) the father-son dyad is

8. In this presentation we will resort to some specific psychoanalytic observations on parent-child relationships wherever useful, but we do not follow any particular theory of personality development.

one step farther in the process of role differentiation from that of mother-son. This means not only far less dependence, but that dependence when it occurs has changed its nature from one due to sheer inability to comprehend or perform any task to one in which the need is for guidance, channeling, wisdom of experience, or punishment. In Parsons' terms these are characteristic of "instrumentality" rather than "expressiveness" (1955:45).

In the mother-son situation, dependence is found in its pristine state, but in the father-son situation, dependence is only an element of what can better be described as authority (Parsons' "power"). The attribute authority includes a degree of dependence, but it is much higher on "instrumentality" and on "power." Conversely, though "power" and some "instrumentality" are not totally absent in the mother-child dyad, these (especially "instrumentality") tend to be overshadowed by other more characteristic attributes. This is why diffuseness is an attribute of the mother-son dyad, but not of others. Diffuseness is related to lack of differentiation and therefore of specialization. Of the basic dyads in the nuclear family, those of mother-son and mother-daughter are the least structured and differentiated in role because the younger member of the dyad is, to begin with, so completely helpless and dependent.

The last attribute, libidinality, associated with the mother-son dyad is present whenever the partners of the relationship are not of the same sex. But this attribute is likely to be stronger in the case of mother-son dyad than that of father-daughter or brother-sister because of greater physical intimacy at a time when the son is least differentiated with reference to his place in the social system. In general our libidinality is related to what Parsons designates as "expressiveness" insofar as the latter contains a sexual component, but his concept would seem to embrace two other of our attributes as well: dependence (partially) and diffuseness (entirely).

However, although we derive the term "libidinality" from the Freudian term "libido," it is not identical with the latter in significance. Freudian libido is conceived as the raw material of a sexual nature which is the fountainhead of all psychic energy and which, through socializing mechanisms such as repression or sublimation, becomes greatly modified, warped, diverted, or its sexuality driven from consciousness. It is strictly a matter of personality dynamics. Libidinality in our sense does not preclude the possibility of repression or sublimation. But these mechanisms are not presumed, certainly not to the same extent emphasized in Freudian psychology. Consequently our libidinality involves the possibility that the sexually oriented primitive psychic energy tends to express itself throughout the culture in diverse ways in its native state without significant modification, or at least with the sexual component still visible.

On the other hand, the attribute "libidinality" is very different from that of "sexuality," which is exclusive to the husband-wife dyad. Sexuality involves a specific and recognized urge and motive with relatively clearly defined objects for its satisfaction, while libidinality is more nebulous, un-

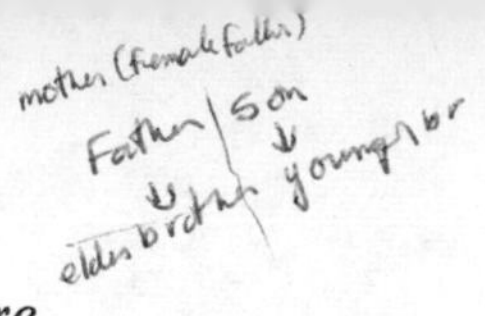

differentiated, usually without clearly defined objects for its satisfaction as sexuality. The attraction between two lovers is characterized by sexuality, but that between certain types of entertainers and their public, between the temple lingam (male phallic representation) and its worshippers, and even between certain pieces of art and their viewers, contains libidinality in our sense.

The brother-brother dyad is discontinuous because solidarity among brothers marks each generation out from the last and the next. Each set of brothers has no structural connection with the brothers of the generation above, or the brothers of the generation below. It is inclusive for the same reason that father-son and mother-son dyads are inclusive, for there are likely to be more than two brothers. It is tolerant of the inclusion of other parties.

Two attributes, equality and rivalry, are peculiar to the brother-brother dyad. Of all the dyads in the nuclear family, brothers are more likely to be equal in age and occupy more nearly equivalent positions in the social system than others. Husbands and wives may be more similar in age to each other than some brothers, but they seem to be universally complementary in function and differentiated in work. Consequently, a greater degree of general equality tends to obtain between brothers than between all other related persons in the nuclear family. With greater equality comes greater chances of rivalry. Rivalry can occur in any situation wherever there are individuals who think they ought to at least be as well situated as others. But it is between equals, within a structural arrangement where they are more equal among themselves than between themselves and others in that configuration, that rivalry becomes most intense.[9]

The link between equality and rivalry in the brother-brother dyad would seem to suggest that all the attributes intrinsic to this dyad are mutually compatible with each other. This is not the case. While the attributes of the father-son dyad are mutually supportive of each other and those of the husband-wife dyad are also mutually supportive of each other, the attributes of the mother-son dyad and again those of the brother-brother are not always harmonious. In the mother-son dyad dependence is commensurate with diffuseness and libidinality, but it is not always supportive of inclusiveness, because the dependent may be so jealous of the person on whom he depends as to be intolerant of other parties. This incompatibility may be moderated by the fact that, since it is usually the depended upon and not the dependent who provides the initiative, the dependent is necessarily tied down in his decisions by the preferences of the depended upon and therefore cannot exclude with as much ease as an independent. But

9. Rivalry embraces competition, but it is more extreme. Competitive parties all want the same objective, but rival parties may desire the "destruction" of each other. The attribute of rivalry does not, of course, preclude cooperation among the rivalrous parties either for a common objective or for the destruction of a common enemy.

dependence is highly incommensurate with discontinuity. By all psychological evidence, one who is dependent will normally seek the continuation of the relationship in time rather than its break-up. The problems of weaning and of the first few days of any nursery school are but two of the most common illustrations of this fact. Finally, discontinuity is also incommensurate with inclusiveness because the two undercut each other. Viewing all five attributes of the mother-son dyad as a whole, we find discon-
lems for the predominantly dependent.

In the case of the brother-brother dyad, the attribute of equality is compatible with inclusiveness. It is under such ideals as "all men are brothers" or "all men are created equal" that universalistic religions or political philosophies are usually based. Similarly, the attribute of rivalry reinforces discontinuity. The essence of rivalry expresses itself in the effort to excel over others or at least to show that they are not as good as we are. Therefore it is separatist in consequence no matter what rationalization is used to soft-pedal it. One of the most universal signs of status or achievement is separation from others. Yet these very links between discontinuity and rivalry on the one hand and inclusiveness and equality on the other pit these two sets of attributes against each other; for the former is centrifugal while the latter is centripetal. Not only is discontinuity incompatible with inclusiveness, but rivalry and equality are usually at odds with each other, for, as we noted before, rivalry heightens itself as greater equality is attained.

THE EFFECT OF DOMINANT KINSHIP DYADS ON OTHER KINSHIP DYADS

Our next order of business is to examine the way in which the dominant
tinuity alone to be especially discordant, which must create serious prob-
dyads in a kinship system affect the other dyads in that system. Since it is impossible in a single chapter to analyze the complicated possible effects of each dominant dyad on all the non-dominant dyads in any system, we shall confine ourselves to the effect of the dominant dyad on one non-dominant dyad in each instance. We shall begin with a system where the father-son dyad is the dominant one. Previously we noted in passing that in such an eventuality the parents will have more to say about their son's future wife than the son himself. In the light of the respective sets of attributes intrinsic to the father-son and husband-wife dyads, this means that the attribute of exclusiveness intrinsic to the husband-wife dyad is greatly modified in favor of the attribute of inclusiveness characteristic of that of father-son. Hence married partners in this system can be expected to be aloof to each other in public, for they often place their duties and obligations toward parents before those toward each other. Custom will strongly disapprove of any sign of public intimacy between spouses. Instead it enjoins them to exhibit ardent signs of devotion to their (especially his) elders. In case of a quarrel between the wife and the mother-in-law, the husband must take the side of the latter against the former, es-

pecially in public. Polygyny with the ostensible aim of begetting male heirs to continue the father-son line is a structural necessity.

Yet in spite of all this the marital bond in a father-son dominated system tends to endure. Divorce is possible but rare. The attribute of continuity and the attribute of authority militate against the dissolution of the marital bond. Continuity means that all bonds including the marital bond are likely to last once they are formed. Authority, with all that it implies toward the past and the superiors, means that the pleasures or displeasures of the married partners are less important considerations for staying together than those of their elders. Inclusiveness extends the effects of continuity and authority to the kinship group as a whole.

This form of kinship is likely to be associated with a strong cult of ancestors[10] and a maximum tendency for the development of the clan.

Where the husband-wife dyad is dominant we should expect the father-son dyad to be temporary. In all likelihood the latter relationship tends to end or nearly end upon marriage of the younger man, after which the father will no longer have strong authority over him. The cohesion between a husband and wife takes precedence over all other relationships, and mate selection is at least theoretically entirely in the hands of the prospective spouses. Not only will the father or mother have no right to initiate divorce for his daughter or son, but any over-intimacy between a son and his parents against the objections of his wife is likely to lead to serious marital disharmony. In such a situation monogamy is the only form of marriage possible to satisfy the exclusiveness of the husband-wife dyad. Discontinuity makes for lack of respect for old age, tradition, and the past in general. Therefore there will be sharp gulfs between the generations, and no true ancestor cult of any kind.

The attributes of sexuality and exclusiveness make public exhibition of marital intimacy (by such things as terms of endearment and kissing) easy and almost imperative, for in the ardency of their exclusive feelings for each other, they need to pay no attention to the rest of the world. In spite of all this, the marital bond is brittle. Divorce is likely to be far more common than in a father-son dominated system. The attribute of discontinuity and the attribute of sexuality are both conducive to this. Disconti-

10. Some sort of cult of ancestors is to be found in different parts of the world. So far, the term "ancestral cult" or "ancestor worship" has been applied in anthropological literature to such facts without precision. A research project at Northwestern University attempts to examine the existing ethnographic literature bearing on the subject according to the following gradations: (1) no concern for the dead whatsoever; (2) some attempt at tracing genealogy as a means of increasing or defending one's status; (3) offering a prayer to the dead as a means of propitiating them so that they will not harm the living; (4) propitiating the souls of the dead as a means of solicitousness toward the dead by offerings and other rituals with occasional concern for avoiding possible anger and harm by them; and (5) concern over the comfort of the dead in all the known generations with no signs of concern about ill will on the part of the dead. According to our hypothesis, ancestor cult of grade 5 is most likely to be correlated with a father-son dominated kinship system (Tatje & Hsu, 1969).

nuity means that all relationships including the marital one are not really forever, since there is little concern for the past. Sexuality adds to this impermanence since its emphasis means that marriage is likely to be precarious, as sexuality waxes and wanes during any period of time and throughout life. Therefore, while in the father-son dominated system the marital bond is not endangered by long periods of separation, in the husband-wife dominated system even separation of a moderate duration creates great marital hazards.

A dominant husband-wife dyad has other effects on the father-son dyad than making it temporary. The father-son dyad in a husband-wife dominated system is likely to be imbued with sexuality and exclusiveness. Parents insist on exclusive control of their children, are likely to be extraordinarily sensitive about their rights over them, and resent all advice from grandparents and other relatives (the inclusiveness intrinsic to parent-child dyads is lost). Furthermore there is even likely to be competition between the parents for the affection of the youngsters. Add to this the attribute of sexuality and we have then a most fertile soil for the Oedipus complex. Since the resolution of the Oedipus complex involves such mechanisms as repression or sublimation, it is not at all fantastic to suggest that modern-day emphasis on sex education on the part of parents is a devious expression of the repressed or sublimated sexuality rooted in a husband-wife dominated kinship system. By contrast, sex as a subject cannot even be touched upon casually between parents and children in a father-son dominated kinship system.

In a mother-son dominated kinship system the father-son dyad tends to exhibit discontinuity rather than continuity. For one thing the father-son tie is not eternal so that the cult of ancestors, even if it exists, tends to be minimal (according to our scale, see footnote 10). Authority of the father will be greatly reduced so that the father is less a strong, guiding, channeling, and punishing figure than a nourishing, supportive, and succoring one. Furthermore, the father image is blurred so that there tends to be the need for the son to seek other "father" figures, not to replace the real father but to assure himself of adequate sources of nourishment, support, and succor. In fact, the line of distinction between the father figure and the mother figure is often unclear.

The attribute of inclusiveness of the mother-son dominated system, like that of the father-son dominated system, is not incommensurate with polygyny, for the marital bond need not be exclusive. But lacking the attribute of continuity, the custom is not primarily for the purpose of maintenance of the patrilineal line as it would be in the father-son dominated system. Rather it seems to be strongly related to the attribute of libidinality or diffused sexuality, and therefore the mother-son dominated system is likely to be associated with more than just polygyny. If the attributes of exclusiveness and sexuality are commensurate with monogamy, and those of inclusiveness and continuity are in line with polygyny, then those of inclusiveness and libidinality or diffused sexuality favor plurality of spouses in general, including polygyny and polyandry, as well as other practices such as cicisbeism defined by Prince Peter as "an arrangement between the sexes, wherein one or more of the male partners is not related to the woman in marriage" (Prince Peter, 1963:22), or conjoint-marriage in which polygyny is combined with polyandry, enabling several males (often related) to be married to several females, or a passing connection between one woman and more than one man for several reasons, including insemination of the childless female by a male other than her husband with the latter's consent.

In a brother-brother dominated society there will be strong tensions between fathers and sons. Rivalry among brothers will spill over to the father-son dyad and the attribute of equality will seriously affect the authority of the old over the young. In fact, these attributes are conducive to sexual competition between fathers and sons. At any rate, the possibility of such emulation is real enough to produce many forms of hostility such as suspicion or witchcraft accusations against each other. Therefore the cult of ancestors is likely to be either nonexistent or minimal. Even when some form of ancestor cult may be said to exist, the central effort will be directed toward preventing the spirits of the departed from punishing or performing wrathful acts rather than showing concern for respecting the ancestors and for their comfort.

In the husband-wife dyad calculatedness tends to rise above everything else. Rivalry and equality reduce the need for protection of one sex by the other. In fact they tend to make the dichotomy of a "weaker" versus a "stronger" sex superfluous. The complementary element between the sexes is so greatly diminished that the questions of devotion, fidelity, and sentiments between married partners are less important than or subordinated to considerations such as calculated advantages and disadvantages. Their relationship may be marked by a contest of power, economic or otherwise, rather than a depth of intimacy. Polygyny, instead of being rationalized in terms of the need for continuing the family line, as in the father-son dominated systems, is practiced primarily as the man's sign of status or wealth. On the female side a sort of polyandry is practiced, not necessarily fraternal from the point of view of economy among the males, but primarily as the woman's symbol of ability and affluence. This is the only kind of kinship system in which exists the condition for true male concubinage. One feels almost compelled to term it female polygyny (as distinguished from the usual polyandry). In addition, pre-marital and extra-marital relations are likely to be common in theory and practice. The custom of surrogate fathers whereby a childless woman is inseminated by her husband's brother or someone else is not likely to be rare. For sex is apt to be used as a means for conquest or for other gains rather than as an expression of emotional or moral commitment, or social privilege and obligation. The marital bond tends to be weak. We can expect divorce to be common, especially where it is not mitigated by plurality of spouses or lovers in one form or another.

Earlier we noted the observation of Radcliffe-Brown (1952:19) that among the Bantu tribes and Nama Hottentots of South Africa the mother's brother is a male mother of a sort and the father's sister is somewhat of a female father. In the light of the effects of the dominant dyad in each system on some other dyads in that system, we may say with a good deal of justification that husbands in a father-son dominated society are younger fathers, mothers in a husband-wife dominant society tend to be older wives, fathers in a mother-son dominated society tend to be male mothers, while wives in brother-brother dominated societies are to some extent female brothers. However, such observations tend to miss the point and obscure the truly significant effects of each dominant dyad on non-dominant dyads. The fact is *not* that the husband-wife dyad under the dominance of the father-son dyad is changed, in terms of that kinship system, or in the minds of the individuals concerned, into a father-son dyad. What occurs is that *the intrinsic attributes of the husband-wife dyad are so influenced by the intrinsic attributes of the father-son dyad that the characteristic qualities and modes of interaction of the husband-wife dyad in that system, as husband-wife dyad, are very different from those in other systems where the father-son dyad is not dominant.* Furthermore, if our hypothesis is correct, the characteristic qualities and modes of interaction of the husband-wife dyad (or any other basic dyad) in any kinship system become predictable once its dominant dyad is known. Conversely, knowing something of the characteristic qualities and modes of interaction of the husband-wife dyad (or any other basic dyad) in any kinship system will guide us to its dominant dyad (or dyads).[11]

Similarly, for those in husband-wife dominated systems, the male in the father-son dominated society would seem to suffer from lack of ambition; for those in the father-son dominated society, the male and female in the husband-wife dominated system would seem to be oversexed; for those in both of these systems, the male in the mother-son dominated society would seem to be unsure of his sex identity; while for those in all three systems, the male and female in the brother-brother dominated society would seem to be too callous or calculating with reference to the matter of sexual attachments and too lacking in concern for fidelity. Sex seems to be

11. In my earlier publication distinguishing kinship content from kinship structure (Hsu, 1959), I accepted the fact, based on Murdock (1949:226–228), that the Eskimos and the Yankees of New England have a similar kinship structure. What I tried to demonstrate in that article was that the contents of their two kinship systems made their behavior patterns so different. In view of our present analysis, it should become obvious that the Eskimos and the New England Yankees do not even share a common kinship structure. In fact, the Eskimo pattern of kinship does not belong to any of the four forms analyzed in this paper. Whether the concepts of dominant kinship dyads and attributes defined here or some other factors must be resorted to in order to explain Eskimo behavior is a problem to be tackled by future intensive field research.

a commodity to be satisfied or conquered through almost commercialized means. But these "problems" from the point of view of outsiders reared in kinship systems with other dominant dyads may be no problem at all in the minds of those persons who exhibit the characteristic behavior in question.[12] Until we appreciate the role of the dominant kinship dyad of each system in shaping the other dyads in that system, our understanding of human behavior will hardly be cross-cultural.

THE EFFECT OF DOMINANT KINSHIP DYADS ON NON-KIN BEHAVIOR

Had space permitted, we would have considered the possible effect of each of the dominant dyads on other non-dominant dyads; however, we must proceed to the next task. In considering the effect of dominant kinship dyads on non-kin behavior we will once more confine ourselves to a limited exercise. We shall only comment upon one cluster of facts: the problem of authority.

Reviewing the four kinds of kinship systems dealt with above, we should expect authority to be less problematic in societies with father-son and mother-son dominated kinship systems than in those with husband-wife and brother-brother dominated kinship systems. Authority is a major attribute of the father-son dyad. Nurtured in this attribute, both the father and the son are attuned to its necessity. The superior does not have to disguise his power because he knows this is his due, and the subordinate has no need to disguise his obeisance since it is not necessary to be ashamed of it. Authority and compliance to authority are therefore carried

12. According to Whiting: "In societies with maximum conflict in sex identity, e.g., where a boy initially sleeps exclusively with his mother and where the domestic unit is patrilocal and hence controlled by men, there will be initiation rites at puberty which function to resolve this conflict in identity" (Burton and Whiting, 1961:90. See also Whiting *et al.*, 1958). The situation of Hindu India fits this picture of maximum conflict, but as far as can be ascertained, no initiation rites exist other than donning of the sacred thread at puberty or before. The initiation rites in Whiting's studies predominantly comprise hazing, genital mutilation, seclusion from women, and tests of endurance. There is nothing like them connected with puberty in Hindu India. The sacred thread rite has no trace of overt sex symbolism and is primarily restricted to Brahmin (and in some parts to those belonging to Kshatrya and Vaishya categories as well) and only occasionally extended to lower castes such as the Pancha Brahma of Shampiret, Hyderabad, Kayastha of Bengal, or (in modified form) the Lingayat of Deccan, for caste raising purposes. Yet projective materials indicate that Hindu males would seem to have uncertainty of sex identity. Presuming Whiting's hypothesis to be correct, our inference is that this seeming uncertainty is more of a problem to the outside observer than to the Hindu. The fact that a majority of Hindu males undergo no initiation rite, and that those who do regard it, primarily as a matter of caste status, is important evidence in support of our inference. Whiting's hypothesis on initiation rites has recently been challenged by Yehudi Cohen (1964), whose grounds for the challenge do not, however, eliminate the possibility that initiation rites may be at least partially related to the problem of sex identity in many societies. On the other hand, the Hindu rite connected with donning of the sacred thread obviously is commensurate with Cohen's idea of the need for the society to manipulate "the child in relation to the boundaries of his nuclear family and kin group in order to implant a social emotional identity and values consonant with the culture's articulating principles." In the Hindu case the boundary is that of caste instead of kin group and the principle is hierarchy as explained here and elsewhere (Hsu, 1963).

out openly and elaborately with no qualms on either side. Difficulties may arise if the superior becomes too oppressive, but the salvation of the oppressed lies in finding individual relief from it, not in challenging the entire social structure in which such oppression occurs. The individual reared in the father-son dominated system will have no resentment against benevolent authority; in fact, he will love it.

In a mother-son dominated kinship system, authority is a major component of dependence; therefore, its exercise and compliance to it are also undisguised. However, while in the father-son dominated system the child is already conditioned to achieve a good deal of autonomy so that he can proceed independently once the specifications are given, the child in the mother-son dominated kinship system tends to retain more of his undifferentiated outlook and therefore needs continuous guidance, supervision, and restraint in order to conduct himself within the specifications desired by the authority. In a mother-son dominated society authority must be much more elaborately implemented with heavy reliance upon minute negative barriers to make this type possible at all. There will be challenges to authority, but the challenges will be ineffective and have little real impact on the society and culture. The central problem for the leader is not merely to urge his followers to action, but to get them to sustain their efforts toward specific, positive goals without being sidetracked by diverse or unrelated issues.

It is in societies with husband-wife and brother-brother dominated kinship systems that the problem of authority is most acute. In neither system is authority a dominant attribute, or a major element of a dominant attribute. The individual who is a product of such a system tends to resent authority or regard it as an obstacle to be overcome by all means. However, in this regard, the difference between these two types of societies is considerable. In the husband-wife dominated system the complementary nature of sex, pregnancy, and the care of the young provides the basis for two related developments. On the one hand there exists a certain amount of inevitable authority of the male over the female which came from man's primitive past and which, as far as we can see, will last indefinitely into the future. This is a kind of authority to which the female has to submit by voluntary cooperation *for her own satisfaction.* On the other hand, there is the idea of protection of the weak and the helpless which is at the root of chivalry or noblesse oblige. Therefore the authority can be exercised and maintained, in spite of the waxing and waning of its basis, as long as there exists functional interdependence between superiors and subordinates, or between leaders and followers. But in exercising and maintaining their authority, the superiors or leaders must disguise their position by minimizing external signs of authority in their interaction with their subordinates or followers, buttressing their own decisions with public opinion, or resorting to other devices which tend to make them appear to be at most authority-transmitters but not authority-originators. Since chivalry is so obviously linked with women and children, adult males welcome the status of being protectors of the weak but resent that of being protected.

In the brother-brother dominated society authority is not an element of any of the attributes. It is true that the older brother can physically coerce his younger brothers, but there is no need on the part of the latter that must be satisfied through some inevitable cooperation with the authority-attempting older brother. Consequently the exercise and maintenance of authority is inclined to be brutal (for there is no idea of chivalry to encourage protecting the weak) and easily subject to rebellion and opposition (for the desire for power is widespread). The divisive tendency is extremely apparent. Superiors or leaders will be constantly in fear of harm from their followers and subordinates by assassination or, more diffusedly, by witchcraft. The problem of succession will be most difficult to solve in these societies, for rival claims are not silenced except by force. Yet, in contrast to husband-wife dominated societies, superiors or leaders in such societies do not have to disguise their power to originate decision, since being dependent or under protection is a matter of expediency rather than of admission of basic weaknesses as in the other system.

Our analyses of authority in the four systems enable us to question the cross-cultural validity of certain sociological findings concerning the incompatability of "task" and "emotional" functions. A number of sociologists have dealt with this problem (Marcus, 1960; Kahn and Katz, 1960; and Blau and Scott, 1962). Bales has presented evidence from small group experiments to support the position that differentiation between task (our attribute, authority) and emotional functions of groups gives stability. Taking five-men groups, Bales gives subjects problem-solving tasks requiring cooperation. The researchers, behind a one-way mirror, observed and recorded interaction (*see* Bales, 1950, for methodology). Some of the findings are as follows: (1) the task leader (best idea and guidance man) was less liked by other members than the emotional leader; (2) the emotional leader was least likely to be a task leader; and (3) through a series of problem-solving sessions, the emotional leader was less likely to be chosen as task leader (over time). In contrast, the task leader was less likely to be chosen as emotional leader through successive trials (Bales, 1953:111–161). Our analyses above give us reason to suspect that these findings are probably characteristic of the husband-wife dominated society, where authority is resented and where the attribute of exclusiveness makes it additionally necessary to have sharp differentiation and separation of roles as well as everything else, but will not hold true for the father-son, mother-son, and even brother-brother dominated societies. In father-son and mother-son dominated societies, submission to and dependence upon authority are not resented and therefore present no conflict with affective relationships between the superior and the subordinate. Furthermore, in both of these and in brother-brother dominated societies, the attribute of inclusiveness will make separation of roles far less mandatory.

Our hypothesis concerning the effect of dominant kinship dyads on nonkin behavior can equally well be applied to illuminate many clusters of facts from the nature of friendship, sexuality, and free associations, to forms of economy and patterns of social development, but these exercises cannot be attempted here.

THE QUESTION OF PERSONALITY DYNAMICS

To the extent that our hypothesis is built on the basic premise that early experiences of the individual, especially those associated with members of his nuclear family, are extremely important in shaping the way he relates to the wider world, it is Freudian in orientation. There is no doubt, from what we now know about the dynamics of individual personality, that every person as he goes through life resorts to past experiences to deal with present and future problems that confront him. Since the nuclear family in which he grows up provides him with the structure and content for social action to begin with, the experiences in his early years cannot but serve as the basis for action in the wider human area.

But here our hypothesis and Freudian psychology part. Freudian psychology puts overwhelming emphasis on the parent-child triad; our hypothesis stresses the fact that, depending upon the kinship system, the relationship of central importance may be one other than that triad. Furthermore, the dominant dyad in the nuclear family, whether it be that of father-son or brother-brother, may seriously alter the very nature of that triad, as our analyses show, so that no universal Oedipus situation such as Freud and his followers conceived can be assumed. Exclusiveness and sexuality are indispensable attributes inducing the Oedipal problem; this combination is characteristic only of the husband-wife dyad. The father-son and the brother-brother dyads have neither attribute, while the mother-son dyad has diffused sexuality but not exclusiveness. In the brother-brother dominated system, with its frequent and obvious rivalry between father and son even over sex, there will be many sentiments and expressions that, to observers familiar with the Freudian theory and reared in a husband-wife dominated society, easily suggest the Oedipal situation. According to our hypothesis, on the other hand, there is a distinct possibility that the latter type of observation will, on closer inspection, prove to be wide of the mark. For sexual rivalry between fathers and sons in a brother-brother dominated society is likely to occur when the sons are already adults; it is not likely to be resolved in the Freudian fashion if resolved at all; and it is merely one of many forms of rivalry in a kinship system where rivalry is a dominant attribute.

There are other differences between our hypothesis and the Freudian position. These bear particularly on the manner in which the individuals in different kinship systems tend to make use of their early experiences. In the husband-wife dominated society the individual makes use of them by their rejection, suppression, or repression because the dictates of his kinship system encourage him to depart from his parents as quickly as possible and to reject their authority as he grows up. When he chooses a wife because he needs his succoring mother, or cannot tolerate his boss because the latter reminds him of his authoritarian father, he is indeed being affected by his early experiences. But the operation of these early experiences, whether he wants to go back to them or get away from them, is likely to be denied because they are resented or unconscious.

In the father-son dominated society the individual makes use of early experiences by their deliberate maintenance, application, or extension, because the dictates of his kinship system encourage him to remember and cultivate his roots—his parents and his forebears. When he enters into ritual brotherhood with his business partners, or addresses his teachers as fathers, he is also affected by his early experiences. But the operation of these early experiences is likely to be spoken of openly because they are desired and conscious.

In yet another aspect, our hypothesis is different from both the relatively orthodox and certain revised Freudian positions. The relatively orthodox Freudians focus their attention on the influences which come to the individual by way of the erogenic zones. Others primarily deal with developmental problems connected with dependence and aggression (Whiting and Child, 1953, Chapter 4; Erickson, 1950, Chapters I and II; and Whiting *et al.*, 1958). Our hypothesis, though it is not unconcerned with sexuality, dependence, and aggression, addresses itself far less to individual personality dynamics or its genesis than to that intricate but broad area of social and cultural life where different individuals meet and interact, the patterns of that interaction, which can be scrutinized independently of the actors involved, at least in analytic terms (Chapple and Arensberg, 1940:24–25), and the genesis of those patterns. To do so is not to deny the existence of unconscious motives on the part of the individual in any system.

Finally, the reader who has come this far probably realizes that our hypothesis is also very different from that of Parsons (Parsons and Bales, 1955:35–187). Our hypothesis and that of Parsons begin with the universal elements of the nuclear family. We have seen how some of our attributes and Parsons' differentiated roles are identical or related to each other. But our hypothesis becomes very dissimilar to that of Parsons when we go beyond the universal elements of the nuclear family and see the circumstances under which the same universal elements can help to give rise to *different* intra-kinship and extra-kinship patterns of interaction. For example, Parsons observes that although power (our attribute, authority) is a basic element in both father-son and mother-son relationships, a "critical change" in the evolution of the personality organization of the child occurs later when "the instrumental-expressive distinction comes to be differentiated out from the power axis" (1955:135). Our hypothesis leads us to suspect that the extent of the differentiation of parental roles may vary greatly from one kinship system to another depending upon its dominant dyad and attributes. In a father-son dominated society the power or authority role of the father is likely to be greatly accentuated at all stages of personality development. His authority role is accentuated not merely because he wishes to exercise power but also because his sons and others subordinate to him tend voluntarily to concede it to him. Furthermore, while according to Parsons the mother's role is "disassociated" at the stage of "second fission" from power authority (Parsons and Bales, 1955:135), our hypothesis suggests that the mother's role in a father-son dominated society is not likely to be easily separated from the power or authority element. In fact, as she grows older she is invested with more power or authority rather than less. Consequently the kind of binary differentiation that Parsons discusses as occurring between the roles of the father and of the mother, respectively "instrumental" and "expressive" varieties, tends neither to be so clear nor so final. In such a society both the father and the mother tend to lean toward "instrumentality" rather than "expressiveness." Following the same line of reasoning, our hypothesis will lead us to believe that in a mother-son dominated society where dependence (rather than authority as such) and libidinality are dominant attributes, both the father and the mother tend to lean toward "expressiveness" rather than toward "instrumentality," while in the brother-brother dominated society both parents tend to be less "instrumental" and "expressive" than in either the father-son or the mother-son dominated societies, because of the greater impact of the sibling relationship. Parsons' analysis fits well with a husband-wife dominated society, where, according to our hypothesis, differentiation of parental roles tends to be most pronounced.

THE ROLE OF FACTORS OTHER THAN KINSHIP

This hypothesis does not attempt to deal with the roles of geography (e.g., isolation or topography), diffusion through historical contact, size of population, political or military conquest, human or natural catastrophe, or hereditary endowment in human affairs. It aims at probing primarily the role of human beings in shaping each other, and within that scope kinship occupies a uniquely central place.

Our hypothesis does not, of course, say that, for example, any form of marriage or sexual connection will *definitely* occur under the dominance of a certain kinship dyad. What it does say is that certain dominant dyads are compatible with certain forms of marriage or sexual practices, and that, if such a form of marriage or sexual practice is already in existence in a given geographical region for any reason whatever, it has a better chance of continuation with one dominant dyad rather than another.

ANTECEDENTAL EVIDENCE FOR THE HYPOTHESIS

The bulk of the data in support of this hypothesis from the qualitative point of view is to be found in *Clan, Caste and Club* (a comparative study of Chinese, Hindu, and American ways of life [Hsu, 1963]). In this work my main effort was directed toward the link between the forces in the kinship organization and the development of what I term "secondary groupings" in the larger society outside of the kinship organization. The present hypothesis identifies the principal of these forces in the kinship organization as dominant dyads and dominant attributes. This hypothesis leads us to expect that these forces affect the behavior patterns within and without the kinship organization in diverse ways including the development of secondary groupings. The American, Chinese, and Hindu kinship systems fit the picture well if we assume the first to be dominated by the husband-wife dyad, the second by the father-son dyad, and the third by the mother-son dyad.

Some antecedent evidence for our postulation for the brother-brother dyad is to be found in the African portion of "Kinship and Ways of Life: An Exploration" (Hsu, 1961:400–56). It is also to be found in a very interesting article by Melville and Frances Herskovits entitled "Sibling Rivalry, the Oedipus Complex and Myth" 1959:1–15). If we assume many African societies of the patrilocal type to be dominated by brother-brother dyad, we shall find many central features of African life understandable.

In addition, unexpected support for our hypothesis on the mother-son dominated society is found in a recent book by Prince Peter of Greece and Denmark entitled *A Study of Polyandry* (1963). It will be recalled that, according to our hypothesis, the mother-son dominated kinship system structurally favors plurality of spouses in different combinations, in contrast to the father-son dominated kinship system which structurally favors polygyny, and the husband-wife dominated kinship system which structurally favors monogamy. Our hypothesis also leads us to believe that the brother-brother dominated kinship system tends to be similar in this regard to the mother-son dominated kinship system, except to a lesser extent.

According to Prince Peter's survey, of a total of eighteen societies practicing true polyandry, eleven are to be found in India or nearby such as among the Kandayns of Ceylon and the Tibetans, while three are found in Africa. Of a total of twenty-seven societies practicing some form of cicisbeism,[13] fifteen are found in India or nearby, while five are found in Africa. Of a total of four societies where the rule is passing connection between one woman and more than one man, three are found in or near India. Of a total of four societies practicing a combination of polyandry and polygyny, three are found in or near India (Prince Peter, 1963:506–11).

Prince Peter's survey does not, obviously, cover the Eskimo and the Chukchee custom of wife-lending as a matter of hospitality. But his figures are highly suggestive for at least one portion of our hypothesis.

13. "So-called boarders in the U.S.A." (quoted by Linton) is listed as one case in Prince Peter's compilation of cicisbeism. This case is dropped from our count.

PART I

Theoretical Explorations

TWO MARION J. LEVY, JR.

Notes on the Hsu Hypotheses

The moralists, the sentimentalists, the theologians, and the politicians were, and are, all correct. The family is certainly fundamental in human life. It is to the analysis of this universal organizational element of human history—not from a moral, not from a sentimental, not from a theological, and not from a political point of view, but from the scientific point of view—that Professor Hsu has again turned his attention. His most fruitful work, whether on China or at large, has never lost sight of this point. For all of the criticisms and contumely one may visit on the social sciences, there are very general propositions possible in the field—applying not just to a single type of society as a single isolated part of it, as most of the work under the heading of social sciences does. There are such generalizations which apply to all societies at all times, if those societies have been at all stable over any considerable period of time. Furthermore, there is, of course, an even greater wealth of such propositions at lower levels of generality. Most of those at the most general level involve the concept of family or kinship in general, either directly or by inference. Despite this—which I take to be a fact, though anyone reading this should regard this and all subsequent such propositions as hypotheses about the facts—we know little indeed about the origins of such organizations. We do not know if the family was explicitly and self-consciously invented after the fashion of the creation myths of China, or from what or how it evolved. It seems to me absolutely clear that if one does not try to replace the soul as a dividing line between man and other animals by similar dividing lines, the probability is for evolution inexplicit and unplanned by the actors involved rather than for explicit invention. This, however, is pure speculation and based on nothing more than an inability to conceive of what life for representatives of this species could have been like in the absence of such an organizational device.

Let me count some of these generalizations:

1. There is no known case of a society lacking families as sub-systems thereof.
2. There is no known society in terms of which initial placement of individuals fails to be in family terms—and almost certainly overwhelmingly, if not exclusively, in family terms.
3. There is no known society in terms of which not only initial but a substantial part of the basic learning—that is the learning institutionally expected to be shared by all or virtually all of the members of the given society—is not learned in a family context for the vast majority of the members of the society. As a minimum, this learning covers the following:
   a. bodily movement, including especially walking, but also all forms of gesture and applications of energy not biologically explicable
   b. talking
   c. control of bodily functions in some ordered fashion
   d. response to other human beings in general, and especially in affective terms (see S. S. Tomkins, *Affect, Imagery, and Consciousness*, Vols. I & II, Springer, 1963)
   e. role differentiation—initially especially on the bases of age, generation, and sex
   f. solidarity, initially with other kin, with the high probability that the biological mother or some feminine substitute for her be most prominently involved
   g. allocations of goods and services
   h. allocations of power and responsibility
   i. structures of integration and expression
4. For the general membership of any society, an incest taboo is always part of the ideal structures, and that taboo as a minimum extends to father-daughter, mother-son and sister-brother relationships.
5. The best current anthropological research seems to hold that, despite emphases on matrilineality, all known societies and kinship organizations are, ideally speaking, patriarchal rather than matriarchal.
6. Regardless of how many different types of family units, whether of orientation or procreation or whatever (see Fallers-Levy, 1959), are distinguished for a given society, the overwhelming majority of all individuals of all known societies are expected to have membership(s) in some sort of family unit(s) at all periods of the life cycle.
7. All non-family organizations, in terms of which people behave in the context of all known societies, may be divided into one of two categories. They are either organizations in terms of which, ideally

and actually, family (and perhaps kinship in general) considerations enter prominently if one wishes to understand the behavior of the individual, or they are organizations in terms of which family (and perhaps kinship in general) considerations do not enter ideally, but do enter actually. The family is the only organizational context of which this statement can be made for all known societies.

If one leaves the level of any society and goes to the level of any of the relatively non-modernized societies—and that level certainly covers the great majority of all societies, past and present—additional generalizations can be set up:

1. Regardless of whether family orientations are expected to take precedence over others, the vast majority of all individuals, in fact, orient most of their behavior to family contexts most of the time—that is to say, they are more likely to operate in family terms than in any other terms.
2. The vast majority of all education for all individuals takes place in a family context—not just infant and childhood socialization, but practically all socialization is in a family context.
3. Family units, while never predominantly economically or politically oriented, ideally speaking, are the most important foci of economic and political allocation for most individuals most of the time.
4. Rarely are general structures of control highly independent of family considerations in relatively non-modernized contexts.
5. Regardless of variations in the ideal structures of family organization (for example, preferences for nuclear as opposed to extended families), well upward of 50 per cent and probably upward of 80 per cent of all family units have, in fact, been units which have varied little in terms of the numbers of individuals present, the numbers of generations represented, the number of marital spouse pairs present, the age distribution, the sex distribution, sets of siblings, etc. Maximum variation on these respects has been with regard to the average numbers of individual members per family, and that has probably never exceeded 75 per cent for extended periods of time (Coale *et al.*, 1965).
6. The overwhelming probability of identification for the vast majority of individuals in such contexts is always a family identification specifically and a kinship one in general.
7. Anything interfering with one set of ideal structures for selection, regardless of how particularistic those may be, is most likely to be some other kinship consideration not generally considered proper under the circumstances. Breakdowns of institutionalized nepotism are likely to be a function of other forms of nepotism.
8. Ideally speaking, family organizations are rarely vulnerable to other priorities, and ideally speaking, most other organizational contexts are vulnerable to family considerations—if conflict appears.

In the most highly modernized of societies, many of these immediately previous generalizations no longer hold, but even in those cases the first set of generalizations hold, and all of the subsequent ideal priorities of other spheres for the vast majority of all individuals, must be superimposed upon the early socialization that takes place in a family context. In a social context like our own, for example, children learn so much outside the family context, that we have fallen out of the habit of thinking of any education as taking place in family terms. We are currently undergoing a rude awakening in these respects, as witness the problems posed for people who place increasing emphasis on advanced education for any sort of a satisfactory career, and the difficulty posed in those terms by children, who by the age of six, because of lack of response as reinforcements of learning—by others in their family environment—are already apathetic or positively disinterested in any of the line of achievement that makes secondary, let alone advanced, education possible.

This is the setting in which Professor Hsu has developed his hypotheses. As I understand Professor Hsu's hypotheses, he maintains:

1. In terms of any kinship arrangement (Professor Hsu uses the term "kinship" much as I would use the term "family"), dominant relationships can be distinguished.
2. Those dominant relationships have dominant attributes.
3. Other relationships in the kinship system will be affected by the dominant relationship and, more importantly, by the dominant attributes of the dominant relationship.
4. Finally, relationships of a non-kinship sort will also be affected by the dominant relationship and the dominant attributes of the dominant relationship.

Although I happen to agree with most of the argument insofar as I understand it, the most questionable part of it has to do with what one is most likely to take for granted, namely the argument to the affect that there are dominant relationships as far as the kinship structures are concerned. I would like to return to this somewhat later. A main part of the argument in Professor Hsu's paper cannot be denied unless one is prepared to deny the very structure of science itself. This has to do with the effect of what goes on within the kinship context for action in other social contexts—regardless of whether the argument is in terms of dominant attributes and dominant relationships. In terms of any society, whether highly modernized or not, it is well-nigh inconceivable that what happens to individuals subsequent to the early socialization they undergo in family contexts be totally unrelated to their family experiences. For the vast majority of all people who carry out most of their behavior in family contexts most of the time, it would be even more bizarre to assume or imply that what happens in those contexts has little or no relevance for the way in which they behave in other contexts. I suspect that the whole argument on this point would be taken for granted were it not for the fact that most of the people who have been concerned with such questions have been reared in terms of a society like that of the modern United States. United States society is one in terms of which many contexts are such that we are quite likely to assume that the family has nothing to do with the case, though that is as unlikely for us as for others.

Insofar as family influence is so pervasive, and insofar as the members of all societies use some family structures in terms of relationships of the sort referred to by Professor Hsu, again nothing is more likely than that action in terms of family relationships affect other relationships, whether as direct crude models or in some other respect. Here again, it is the inverse hypothesis that is exceedingly unlikely. The probability of there being no relationships outside the kinship sphere affected by the structures of kinship relationships is the least likely of hypotheses.

This brings us to the question of dominant relationships. All of us take this so much for granted that I have become uneasy. It seems to me quite clear that in terms of the ideal structures of Chinese society, at least during most of its history, the father-son relationship takes precedence over all the others, and it seems to me that, ideally speaking in terms of our own society, the husband-wife relationship is what Professor Hsu would call the dominant one. It is the ready agreement on this sort of proposition in a field in which so much else is suspect that bothers me. In the first place, the ideal-actual distinction is essential here. In the second place, the mother-child (especially mother-son) relationship is in some senses dominant for both traditional China and modern United States society, though how and why take quite some specifying.

Certain questions about the concept of the dominant relationship may be put somewhat more clearly. If one distinguishes a given number of relationships in terms of a given family organization, there is one sense in which the argument, the hypothesis about a dominant relationship, is banal. Nothing is less likely than that all eight of the relationships mentioned by Professor Hsu—or even the four he distinguishes for special treatment—have exactly the same evaluation, affective import, or whatever. What makes me uneasy, however, is the old question of comparing utilities. I suspect that the avenue along which we tend to identify a given relationship as the dominant one is primarily the avenue of political aspects or strength of solidarity—it is the relationship that takes precedence over the others if a conflict arises. I take it that in some sense in arguing the line of effect through the dominant attributes, Professor Hsu is seeking not just a development of implications, but an explanation of this state of affairs.

Of the various relationships possible, Professor Hsu assumes that only four can be dominant ones. These are father-son, mother-son, husband-wife, and brother-brother. This assumption rests on some prior assumption about the universality of the nuclear family as an ideal. I think that is a fundamentally wrong and misleading assumption, but I doubt that it affects the current set of hypotheses to any substantial degree. I think all such possibilities in some sense must focus around questions of authority and possible succession to authority. If the modern anthropologists are correct and there are no truly matriarchal societies, the dominant relationship in kinship contexts must involve a male. Since, under these circumstances, a female could not ideally succeed to authority, although she may actually do so, the younger person, presumably being prepared for authority, could not very well be a daughter. Thus it is possible to have father-son relationships as dominant, but not father-daughter ones. It is possible to have mother-son relationships as dominant ones, but not mother-daughter ones. I leave out the question of first and third generation mixtures, since those are left out of the original set of hypotheses. The sister-sister (similarly for brother-sister) relationship is also ruled out by this question of authority and succession, but I would reduce Professor Hsu's list of four to three and the three to one for the vast majority of cases in world history.

We know or suspect that in all of the highly modernized societies, if there is a single dominant relationship in the kinship sphere it is the husband-wife relationship, for which there are speculative explanations aplenty among the members of a group like the one that meets in this seminar. Therefore, the major line of variance for the other three of Professor Hsu's possibilities or the other two of mine must crop up overwhelmingly in examples from relatively non-modernized contexts. For all such societies as those, I would drop the category of brother-brother for two reasons. One is strictly demographic. The other is that it ignores the problem of the relevance of succession to authority (and vice versa) and socialization in terms of those relevances. In the last analysis this explanation is in part related to demography too.

For all of the societies of relatively non-modernized people in world history prior to the development of modern medical technology, the probability of more than two siblings surviving into maturity is relatively quite small. Of these two siblings per marital pair, the distribution of probabilities is roughly of the following order: 50 per cent will consist of one brother and one sister; 25 per cent will consist of two sisters; and 25 per cent will consist of two brothers. Since it is unlikely that the dominant relationship can be a relationship between immature individuals explicitly, there will not be more than 25 per cent of families in terms of which the biological possibilities of the brother-brother relationship being the dominant one will be present. For this to be present in the other 75 per cent of families, there must be a continual policy of collapsing units lacking two mature male siblings, so that those are present. This seems to me a much more improbable assumption than the hypothesis that the brother-brother relationship is not actually likely to be the dominant one.

Even for those families for which the brother-brother relationship could be the dominant one, the probability of there being a sufficient gap in ages as between the two surviving male siblings to account reliably for the socialization of the younger in matters relevant to succession by the older seems to me highly improbable.

There is a sense in which brother-brother relationships seem to me to assume a special importance. When brothers do exist in a given family context, the relation between them is likely to persist at a stage in life when the relationship between father and son or mother and son is no longer possible because of the death of the representative of the older generation. This being the case, the solidarity as between brothers is likely to have a role in non-kinship contexts that may appear to give it precedence over the father-son relationship, but this sort of consideration represents the kind of qualification about dominant relationships raised earlier in these speculations on Professor Hsu's hypotheses.

One may now extend the argument somewhat further. The mother-son relationship clearly cannot be the dominant one in any save matrilineal situations, and even that can only be the case if one sticks to a strict nuclear family context, since the mother is not likely to be the ruling member of the family and this would imply that the son's solidarity with her took precedence over his relationship with the family head. On the other hand, the father-son relationship could conceivably be the dominant one for any kind of a society—even a matrilineal one, if one extends the notion of father to include the possibility of an uncle of some sort.

It is exceedingly unlikely that the husband-wife relationship can be the dominant one for any society save one in terms of which the nuclear family is the ideal family. It is exceedingly unlikely for any society with extended or stem family ideals, because of the well-known vulnerability that this emphasis gives to the relationships emphasizing continuity. Even when the nuclear family is the ideal structure for a society, the period during which it is absolutely essential that the husband-wife relationship be the dominant one need not extend beyond the duration of a marriage prior to pregnancy. In the contexts of all of the relatively non-modernized societies, stress on the husband-wife relationship is likely to be at the expense of emphasis on continuity, as indicated by Professor Hsu, and the members of all of these societies are very much concerned with continuity. Therefore, it seems to me that the dominant relationship, even in cases with the nuclear family as the ideal—apart from the relatively highly modernized societies—is very likely to be an inter-generational relationship. Of these two possibilities, as set forth by Professor Hsu, the lack of matriarchy is extremely likely to result in the emphasis being on father-son relationships. Thus, while the argument is not nearly as tight as I would like to see it, I think that for the general membership of most societies in world history, exclusive of highly modernized ones, the dominant relationship for the vast majority of the population is overwhelmingly likely to be the father-son relationship or some analogue to it, such as an uncle-nephew relationship in matrilineal contexts.

It may be added as an aside that if failure to emphasize the father-son relationship is as rare as this line of argument would hold, one of the aspects of relatively modernized and relatively modernizing contexts becomes somewhat less mysterious. This has to do with the phenomenon of juvenile delinquency, alienated youth, hooliganism, "teddy boys," taiyozoku, call it what you like. These are societies for which a nuclear family is institutionalized, and these are societies for which it seems to me the husband-wife relationship is certainly dominant, by contrast with the father-son relationship, and the father-son relationship would certainly seem also to take a back seat by contrast with the mother-child relationship, regardless of whether the child be son or daughter. The problem of female juvenile delinquency in general seems to follow by a fair time lag that of the development of the male phenomena, and to be on the whole less highly developed. One might argue that this could be related to the fact that the mother-daughter relationship is more likely to be the main one emphasized in the socialization of daughters for all societies in world history. While this does not in one sense challenge the statement that a father-son relationship is the dominant one, it states vis-à-vis females a different kind of limitation on the effects of the dominant relationship than would presumably hold true for males.

Three additional points need making. All three are relatively easy to take care of. First, the use of the term "dominant attributes" seems to me to cause no problem, but the residual category—non-dominant—is wildly preferable to the category of "recessives" in this case. Given general usage in the scientific field, the "dominant-recessive" pair are going to be linked to genetics. It is essential to Professor Hsu's hypotheses that one be able to talk about the dominant attributes giving shape to all the non-dominant ones, or as he says "the recessive attributes." [1] This is exactly what does not happen in genetics. The probability is that the dominant traits will emerge rather than the recessive traits as far as the particular organism is concerned, but on the other hand, given the relevant genetic possibilities, there is a probability of the recessives emerging *in place of* the dominant one. This sort of legitimate binary implication is exactly contrary to Professor Hsu's hypotheses. This confusion can easily be eliminated by using the terms "dominant" and "non-dominant"—or many others.

Second, the caution with which Professor Hsu presents his six points on page 641 and following (Hsu 1965), and his great concern for empirical accuracy, make the argument more difficult to pin down than might otherwise be the case. It may be true that the differences, for example as between attributes, are rarely if ever absolute; but it is essential not to leave this as a sort of vague matter of overlapping degrees. The object is to find out precisely what type of circumstances contradict strong formulations of

1. The term "recessive attribute" was used in Hsu's first article stating the hypothesis (Hsu 1965), but has been changed to "non-dominant attribute" since. See Hsu, "A Hypothesis on Kinship & Culture," Chapter 1 in this book, p. 10.

the hypotheses. On every one of the six points one would be better off phrasing the hypotheses strongly so that confrontation of the ideas with the material would be far more fruitful for further qualification in the light of the assembled data. Given the various qualifications, it is quite difficult to tell whether the data contradict or support the propositions.

Third, Professor Hsu's discussion of relationship structures and attributes requires some qualification for purposes of clarity, but again the problems are largely technical and simple. For example, if:

S_j = a structure
a_i = an attribute
$A_j = \sigma\, a_i$
B_j = a relationship
C_j = a content

then, following page 10 in this book, S is not equal to a_i; $S_j = B_j + C_j = A_j$. But on the same page S appears as $= \Sigma B_j$ and as different both analytically and concretely from C_j. It would seem to be easier to reformulate this whole discussion in terms of Figure 1.1 than otherwise. Although that would certainly do violence to the term "structure" as I would ordinarily employ it, I see no reason why that should deter others.

THREE PAUL BOHANNAN

Dyad Dominance and Household Maintenance

As I read the "Hsu hypothesis" about which this symposium centers, one kinship dyad may, because of the importance attached to it within some specific cultural tradition, provide the image and metaphor for ethical solutions that dominate the larger society. In this paper I propose to examine four types of kinship relationships that derive from the biological nature of man, and then to examine some of the ways in which these four type-relationships can be culturally handled in terms of kinship terminologies and household institutionalization.

Because of the animal nature of the human species, there are at least four specific types of psychosocial problems that must be solved in every surviving community. It is impossible for any human society or very many human individuals to escape these problems. They center around (1) perpetual sexuality; (2) the matricentric family, which is the outcome of viviparity and what Earl Count (1967) has called the lactation complex; (3) the so-called Oedipal struggle, some form of which is discernible whenever cultural solutions to the above two points are brought into juxtarelation within a single social arena (as they are in every human society) (LeBarre, 1954); and (4) the sibling rivalry that derives from the long period required for maturation and mothering of the young (parents are usually shared by several children, usually of different ages and degrees of maturation; thus important considerations of power and learning are always present in the sibling relationship).

It seems to me that these distinctions are logically prior to the Hsu hypothesis. The fact that all of these givens must be handled successfully by all surviving societies means that what Hsu calls dominance may be classified in terms of the patterns that are created by different priorities and means of solution.

In other words, we must examine mating problems, nutritional and learning problems (including learning of affect), Oedipal problems, and sibling problems in several societies to see the ways in which they are culturally solved and the solutions patterned.

There are also some necessary subordinate inquiries: If there are dominant dyads following on dominant solutions, then there must be secondary or even submerged dyads. For example, in households formed on the basis of husband-wife relationships, the secondary dyads of parent-child are present and undoubtedly vastly affect the qualities of the primary dyad. Moreover, the submerged dyads of siblings are present. They affect it less—but they affect it, and the institutionalization of the syndrome is important. Does the ethical content work "up" from the dyad to the institution to the whole society, or "down," or both—that is, from the dominant through the secondary to the submerged, or vice versa? We might then ask whether a Gutmann scale can tell us anything about the ways in which qualities or "attributes" are correlated in any given structural situation.

Another subordinate query: Is the Hsu hypothesis reversible? That is to say, may the ethical system of the entire culture determine the content of any specific role dyads to the same extent or even to a greater extent than the role dyad can be said in the original hypothesis to determine the ethical system? This quickly leads us to the difficult frontier of cultural metaphor.

With these problems in mind, if not clearly "formulated," I shall present data and interpretations of material on household structure and divorce among middle-class Americans, the Tiv of Nigeria, and the eighteenth and early nineteenth century Seneca Iroquois. On the basis of these materials, I shall at the end of the paper draw up some summaries and further hypotheses about the nature of household structure, morality, and dominance of kinship dyads.

The American Household

THE OPTIMAL HOUSEHOLD STRUCTURE OF MIDDLE-CLASS AMERICANS

Kinship terms in English distinguish people along three axes: differences in generation, differences in sex, and differences between lineal descent and collaterality (shared descent). Differences in generation are always reflected in English terminology: differences between fathers and sons, uncles and cousins, grandfathers and grandsons. Differences of sex are made in all English kinship terms except "cousin." Differences between lineality and collaterality are always drawn: Fathers are never called by the same name as uncles, cousins by the same term as brothers. Not only are all of these qualities found in all the terms (with the one exception noted), but there are no others to be found in any of them.

Moreover, American marriages are ideally neolocal—the American way of putting this is that a couple will "set up their own home." Americans go so far as to think that any household except a neolocal household is unfortunate for the newly married pair. Most Americans frown on all three-generational households, even when as individuals they have had pleasant experiences growing up in them.

The "optimal" household, as I use the term here, is the household containing the minimal number of people that will allow the analyst to use all of the kinship terms within a household, each term in dyadic pairings with all the other terms it can be paired with. The optimal household for middle class Americans is shown in Figure 3.1.

Figure 3.1. Optimal American Household (Middle-class)

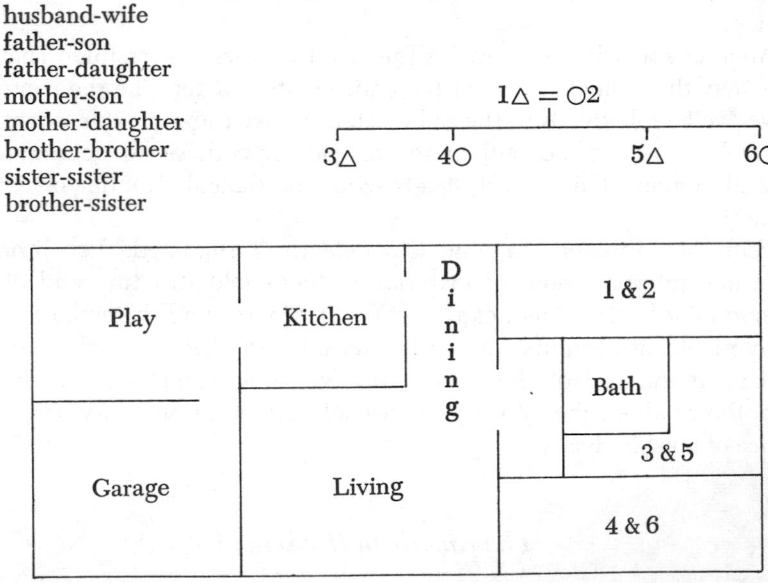

husband-wife
father-son
father-daughter
mother-son
mother-daughter
brother-brother
sister-sister
brother-sister

1△ = ○2
3△ 4○ 5△ 6○

Play
Kitchen
Dining
1 & 2
Bath
3 & 5
Garage
Living
4 & 6

This household cannot be expanded (other than addition through the birth of more children) without increasing the number of terminological dyads.

There are eight kinship terms in English for members of the nuclear family household: husband, wife, father, mother, son, daughter, brother, sister.

These terms and the roles they signify do not exist in a vacuum; rather, the words must be given meaning in terms of the behavior and the expectations on the part of persons who are called by them, and the roles thus established must be understood by all the various players as well as by the community as a whole. Each role, in order to be acted out, requires first a reciprocal. A wife is not a wife without a husband. Just so, there is no father without a son or daughter—neither is there a mother without a son or daughter. And, significantly, the mothering or fathering of sons makes somewhat different demands on the mother and father than does the parenting of daughters. Thus, the role is affected by the nature and the expectations of the reciprocal.

The family-household of middle-class America can thus be seen as a collection of individuals who are given kinship terms—a man and his wife and their sons and daughters. But, since each of these kinship terms must be validated by reciprocals, it can also be seen as a structure of dyadic relationships: Each relationship is formed between two people who stand in one of the reciprocal kinship relationships to the other. Ultimately, therefore, everybody in the family calls everybody else in it by one of these eight terms, and each stands in one of the dyadic relationships with every other person in the nuclear family household.

The most important characteristic of the household based on the neolocal nuclear family is that it depends for its existence on the husband-wife relationship. It is formed at the same time, or soon after, a marriage is formed, and it ceases to exist (for all that some or all of the people do not) when the marriage is broken, either by death or divorce, or at "separation," when the marriage is preserved by what might be called a legal or religious fiction in spite of the fact that any meaningful husband-wife relationship is broken. When something goes wrong in the neolocal nuclear family, it is likely either to be a difficulty in the husband-wife relationship or to depend for its repair on that relationship. The burden of marriage in societies with this type of household is very great. Parentage depends on successful marriage—and the usual obverse is that successful marriage depends on successful parenting. A weak link in the parenting chain can cause damage for generations to come.

INSTITUTIONALIZED MATING

This particular kind of household is an institutional answer primarily to the problem of perpetual sexuality. I mean to imply that the other problems are more overtly moralized and less densely organized or institutionalized than is the marital or mating relationship. The relationship of mates is assumed rather than repressed or moralized. The priority given to this particular need, by household structure, means that the institution which results is not as readily questioned in that society as are all the other relationships and needs. It is hidden not by repression but by axiomization.

In the American example institutionalization of the mating relationship is axiomatic. Parenting is very much less axiomatic; indeed, mothering is moralized, and fathering is partly moralized and partly repressed. The way in which siblings behave through life to one another is not subject to axioms, and scarcely even to moralizing, because it is so largely personalized.

The Tiv Household

THE OPTIMAL HOUSEHOLD STRUCTURE OF THE TIV

Kinship terms in the Tiv language distinguish people along different axes than do English kinship terms. Instead of generational differences, pure and simple, Tiv first distinguish by lineal and collateral distinctions. Then they distinguish by a simple tripartition of the generations: all those in senior generations, all those in ego's generation, and all those in younger generations. In the younger generations, indeed, the lineal-collateral distinction disappears. And only a part of the terms are distinguished by sex.

The word *ter* means "father" and all male ascendants, in whatever lines. The word *ngô* means "mother" and all female ascendants. The word *wan* means all one's own children plus all one's kinsmen younger than one's self. The word *wanngô*, literally "child of mother," is applied to all persons with whom one shares an ancestress; the term *wanter,* literally "child of father," to all persons with whom one shares a male ancestor. If a kinsman is both your *wanngô* and your *wanter,* then he is your *wangban,* but this term is one that is used more as a sign of affection than of social role.

The word *nom* means "male" or "husband;" the word *kwase* "female" or "wife," but the meanings are not precisely parallel to those in English because each of these terms has reciprocals in addition to the other. That is to say, the husband and wife refer to one another as *nom* and *kwase,* but a woman may refer to her husband's father, or anyone else whom her husband calls *ter* (and some of those whom he calls *wangô*) as her *nom;* the reciprocal is usually *kwase* or wife, but the form is "our wife" (*kwase wase)* and seldom "my wife;" they may also call her *wan* or "child," as a sort of diminutive term indicating approval or affection. Similarly, the woman may be called "our wife" by a child, whom she in turn calls "child." A woman calls her husband's mother *ngô* and is in turn called "my wife."

Tiv marriages are virilocal. In my entire twenty-eight months in Tivland, I found only three uxorilocal marriages—and one of those was in the official record of a murder that resulted when a man was taunted for living with his wife's kinsmen. Most Tiv males live patrilocally, and hence most Tiv marriages are patrilocal as well as virilocal—83 per cent of Tiv adult males lived in the households of their fathers (including, of course, deceased fathers) during our work among them in five widely separated communities, in 1949–53. The remainder lived with their mothers' fathers or, in 2 per cent or fewer cases, with other kinsmen.

Thus, whereas in America the domestic situation at marriage is seen as a "new couple" establishing a "new home," in Tivland the analogous situation is seen as the people of an established—indeed, permanent—compound "acquiring a wife." If the husband's mother is alive, the bride is her "wife" and goes directly into her hut. After a few months of marriage, and certainly after the birth of her first child, the new wife is entitled to a hut of her own, close to that of her husband's mother. Tiv consider it unfortunate for a young bride to be deprived of a mother-in-law. Tiv households contain three or four generations, and those that do not are considered to be incomplete.

Tiv are also polygynous. Although it is recognized that having several wives at once may be difficult for a man because of the added burden of maintaining equality among them and of intervening if they quarrel, most men desire polygyny. Women accept it, and can cite the advantages of it. Given the brittle marriage bonds that exist among them, almost all Tiv men are polygynous from time to time, and most women live from time to time with husbands who have other wives simultaneously. Polygyny creates the relationship among co-wives (*wuhe*).

Given these basic factors, the sort and number of dyadic relationships that make up a Tiv compound are different from those that make up an American household. They are (a) relationships of marriage—*nom-kwase*. Several such relationships will exist in any single household, and the terms are not limited to the actual spouses, as they are with us, but may be used by others without implying the full range of the marital relationship. There are in addition (b) affinal relationships that are not marriage: *nom-kwase wase, nom-wan, kwase-wan, ter-kwase, ngô-kwase*. None of these relationships exists in a Western household based on the nuclear family, although something like them may turn up occasionally in a three-generation household—the son-in-law mother-in-law relationship probably the most common of these nowadays uncommon relationships.

There is a further affinal relationship that turns up in Tiv polygynous households that is specifically illegal in America, where monogamous marriage is the only form. That is the relationship between co-wives. Only when that relationship is as secure in its expectations as are the others is it possible to work out satisfactory relationships among co-wives in a polygynous household.

The other relationships among Tiv are terminologically simpler than those of Americans, because they do not make distinctions by sex. They are (c) two relationships of parentage: *ter-wan*, and *ngô-wan*, which include the grandparent relationships as they would not in middle-class America, where the relationships of alternate generational parentage become extremely complex (reflecting and adding to the complexity of the power relationships between generations in such a situation). Finally there are (d) two fairly simple sibling relationships: *wanter-wanter* and *wangô-wangô*. The sibling relationships among the Tiv would also include the relationships of uncle-niece, uncle-nephew, aunt-niece and aunt-nephew, and cousin-cousin in the English system. The Tiv have, in short, a simple system of kinship terminology which keeps their role obligations and role expectations simple, even as the number of persons in the household may become very large.

The Tiv household (Figure 3.2) simplifies the types of parentage and sibling relationships and proliferates the affinal relationships that are not marriage relationships. There are, in the household, two relationships of parentage (as against four in America); one relationship of marriage (as in America); one relationship of co-marriage (as forbidden in America); five relationships of affinity that exclude marriage and co-marriage (also forbidden); and two relationships of siblingship (as against three in America), based on the sex of the ascendant linking kinsman rather than on the sex of the persons themselves.

If we assume, as I think we can, that a role is simpler if it has fewer reciprocal terms rather than more, we can see that the Tiv role of *kwase*, woman/wife, is the most complex in the entire household—it has four reciprocals, whereas no other term has more than two, and the sibling roles have only one. A woman must be a *kwase* to her husband (*nom*), to

Figure 3.2. Optimal TIV Compound

nom-kwase (2–3; 7–8)
nom-kwase wase (5–6; 5–1; 1–3; 4–5; 4–8; 5–7; 6–8; 1–8)
nom-wan (1–8; 1–5; 2–5; 2–8)
kwase-ter (2–8; 2–5)
kwase-wan (8–9; 3–4)
kwase-ngô (3–8; 3–5)
wuhe-wuhe (5–8)
ter-wan (1–4; 2–6; 2–7; 2–9; 6–9)
ngô-wan (3–6; 3–7; 3–9; 5–9)
wanter-wanter (1–2; 1–6; 1–7; 2–4; 4–7; 4–9; 4–6; 1–9)
wangô-wangô (6–7; 7–9)

[5–1 and 5–2; 1–8 and 2–8 are repeated, with different terms.]

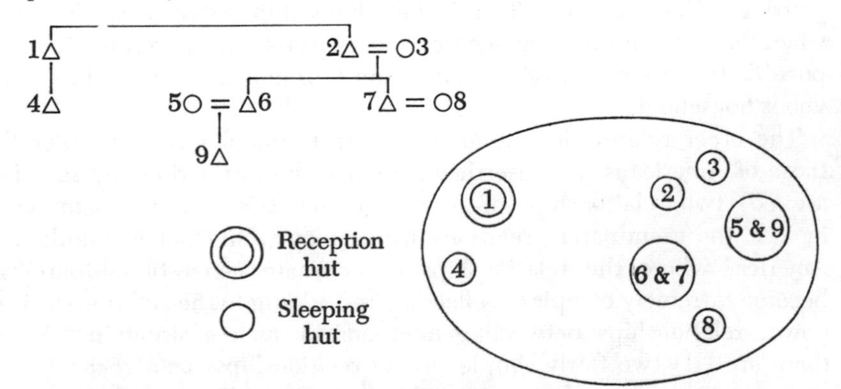

This household is infinitely expandable numerically without increasing the terminological dyads.

her husband's male kinsmen (that is, his older *wangô* who may call her "child"—*wan*), to her husband's father's father whom she will certainly call "father" (*ter*), and to her husband's own father whom she may call "father" (but may call "great husband"—*nom u tamen*), and to her husband's mother, whom she will call "mother" (*ngô*). This besides being "co-wife" to her husband's other wives and to the wives of his kinsmen, and mother (*ngô*) to the children she bears and to some of the children in the compound (although all these children except for her own may call her "our wife," and her husband's children by his other wives will certainly call her that unless they are the children of wives that the husband has specifically linked with her).

No other role syndrome in the Tiv household and none at all in the American household is as complex as this one that must be played out by every Tiv woman once she marries.

INSTITUTIONALIZED OEDIPAL SOLUTIONS

The most important characteristic of the Tiv household is that it is based on the father-son relationship. Since its ultimate existence depends on relationships of parentage, Tiv households do not "come and go" with marriages as do American households. They divide, as we shall see, in given circumstances—but the operation is analogous to cellular division, whereas the neolocal American household propagates itself and dies rather than dividing and continuing in multiple versions of the same old components.

The Tiv base their households on an institutionalized Oedipal solution, just as the Americans base households on an institutionalized mating solution. The father-son relationship is socially simple and "given," for all that it is psychically complex—just as the husband-wife relationship is socially simple and given, but psychically most complex among Americans. Among the Tiv, the roles of wife/mother are extremely diffuse, and this point shows up in the sanctioning procedure. If a wife cannot fit into her husband's patrilineal family and patrilocal household, maintaining a host of "new" relationships, she either leaves of her own accord or (in very rare cases among Tiv) is sent away.

The "interfering wife" is as deadly in a Tiv household as an "interfering mother-in-law" in American middle-class household. The cause is the same—in both cases the interloper is causing difficulty in the "cornerstone relationship" on which that society builds its households. A Tiv woman acquires a firm place in a household only as a mother of sons.

Marriage does not significantly alter a father-son household, for all that it provides its growing point. As we shall see, neither does divorce. Marriage adds a member, and ultimately several members, through birth. But the authority structure of the household, and its continuity, are to be found in the father-son relationship.

Just as divorce is a dire threat to the American household, so strife between father and son is a dire threat to the Tiv household. A Tiv household subdivides with the growing apart of siblings after the death of their common father—it is a process that may take several generations. However, it strikes at the foundations of Tiv society—the entire witchcraft system is there to buttress and express the danger when fathers and sons break their relationships.

In Tivland, the only thing that can reasonably be called a "broken home" occurs when sons move out and leave their "wicked" father "sitting alone"—he is by definition "wicked" and probably an evil "witch" (*ormbatsav*) or they would not have been "driven out."

The power situation in a father-son based household like that of the Tiv is the balance of power between fathers and adult sons, and thus secondarily among brothers. The power situation in a marriage-based household like the American is a balance of rights and duties between husband and wife, and subordinately between parents and children. In the husband-wife household, the sibling relationship is of minimal importance; in the father-son household, the marital relationship is of minimal importance. To repeat: The Tiv household structure takes solution of the Oedipal problem as primary, and all the other problems depend from that solution.

The Iroquois Longhouse

THE OPTIMAL HOUSEHOLD STRUCTURE

Iroquois kinship terminology recognizes more kin types than do the other two terminologies that we have encountered, and the dyadic structure within the household is more complicated. This is so in spite of the fact that the fundamental principles of Iroquois household formation are extremely simple. The women, linked into a uterine descent group, own the longhouse, and their husbands come to join them there.

Mother-daughter dyads form chains of even more effective and permanent strength than do father-son dyads. A "chain" of lactational relationships is simply stronger than a chain of Oedipal relationships. Both are, of course, what Hsu calls continuous, because the same individual is likely to play each role in such a relationship at different stages of his life (whereas husband-wife dyads are obviously discontinuous, as are mother-son or father-daughter dyads).

The basic kinship group of the Iroquois was not the family in the household—rather it was a segment of the matrilineal clan. Therefore marriages were structurally irrelevant to the household—in the same way that Tiv marriages are more or less structurally irrelevant to the basic household. This does not mean, of course, that marriages are emotionally or personally unimportant—but only that the household structure is not either created or undone on the basis of them.

The dyads in the matrilineal clan are fairly simple (see Figure 3.3)—

Figure 3.3. Optimal Iroquois Household

Morgan's spellings are retained, without the diacritics; I have not followed Lounsbury because he does not provide affinal terms in the transcriptions he uses.

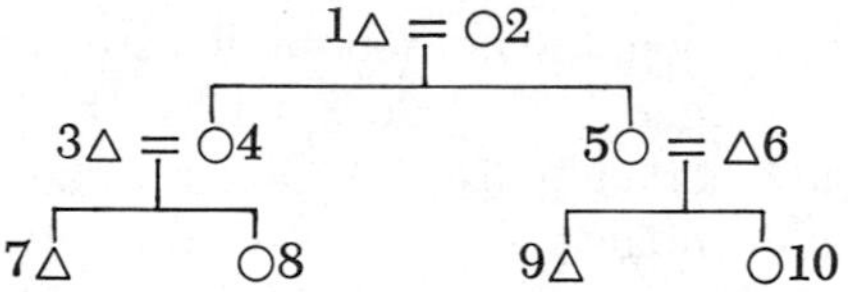

1△ = ○2

3△ = ○4 5○ = △6

7△ ○8 9△ ○10

Dayakene-Dayakane	*(Hu-Wi)*
Nohyeh-Haahwuk	*(Mo-So)*
Nohyeh-Kaahwuk	*(Mo-Da)*
Ocsote-Hayada	*(MoMo-DaSo)*
Ocsote-Kayada	*(MoMo-DaDa)*
Hocsote-Hayada	*(MoFa-DaSo)*
Hocsote-Kayada	*(MoFa-DaDa)*
Hanih-Haahwuk	*(Fa-So)*
Hanih-Kaahwuk	*(Fa-Da)*
ahje-kage	*(eSi-ySi)*
haje-haga	*(eBr-yBr)*
haje-kage	*(eBr-ySi)*
haga-ahje	*(eSi-yBr)*
kayao-ageahneo	*(WiSi-SiHu)*
Ocnahose-ocnahose	*(Wi parents-DaHu)*

1–2; 3–4; 5–6
4–7; 5–9; 4–9; 5–7
2–4; 2–5; 4–8; 5–10; 4–10; 5–8
2–7; 2–9
2–8; 2–10
1–7; 1–9
1–8; 1–10
3–7; 6–9
3–8; 6–10; 1–4; 1–5
4–5; 8–10
7–9
7–8; 8–9
9–10; 7–10
3–5; 4–6
2–3; 2–6; 1–3; 1–6

1–2	3 & 4 7 & 8	5 & 6 9 & 10	others . . . . ?

The Morgan kinship terms do not supply the terms for "wife's sister's son," so numbers 3-9, 2-6, 3-10, and 6-8 cannot be put down here.
Morgan states specifically that 3-6 are not related–i.e., there is no word for "co-husband" or men married to sisters.

This household is infinitely expandable numerically without increasing the number of dyads.

they are those corresponding to *mo-da, mo-so, br-br, si-si, momo-dada,* and *momo-daso.* Beyond the alternate generations, the terms are merely repeated, and the principle of equivalence of siblings is utilized, so that *mosi-sida* is the same relationship, terminologically, as *mo-da.* These relationships form the basis of the household.

When the husbands join the household, we are not on such sure ground. In the first place, Morgan (1871) does not list the term for "wife's sister's son" in spite of the fact that he lists 268 possible categories of relationships. Lounsbury's componential analysis (1964) does not deal with the affinal terms. But Morgan does say specifically (1871) that men who are married to sisters do not have a kinship term for one another—or, to be precise, in the space provided for the term he says "No kin" (and he does give such terms in other languages).

It is my inclination to see in all this a terminological reflection of the fact that husbands are considered peripheral to the household. We know from Wallace's work (see especially his paper in this volume) that the Iroquois husband/father is lightly attached to the household, and that these men form hunting and war parties that were gone from the household for months at a time.

The household is, in this society, a chain of women to which is accreted their young sons and their husbands.

INSTITUTIONALIZED MATRICENTRIC SOLUTION

It appears to me that when households are based on the mother-daughter relationship, the chained matricentric families are so hard-core and so fully complete that the result leads to the problem of the peripheral male. In Wallace's view (expressed in this symposium) these men show personalities reflecting this social position. Tiv women are not peripheral to the same degree as Iroquois men—but there is a tendency in that direction.

Death, Divorce, and Compound Fission

Death disturbs social groups everywhere, of course, and every society has to be equipped to deal with it. It is especially true that death of one of the spouses puts the neolocal household into jeopardy, because the "team" of husband-wife is broken; death of an elder compound head puts a patrilineally extended household into jeopardy, because it was his very person who held together the various members of the core-group of agnates, and among the Iroquois death not only put a strain on the uterine core group, but also had vast psychic repercussions among all members of the household. Wallace tells me (private communication) that "*The* problem institutionalized in solution for the Iroquois was death rather than divorce or the father-son conflict or mother-daughter conflict, because death invoked (in Iroquois belief invariably, and often enough in actuality) a sequence of anaclitic depression and paranoid suspicions of witchcraft. Elaborate ritual was devoted to abbreviating and deflecting this process in order that it not break up the community in a series of obligatory blood feuds. These feuds were initiated by co-lineage or co-clan survivors, particularly the women in response to the death of a male clan member. Death—and more generally, separation—are universal problems. . . . This problem, via a matri-clan system, adoption, war, condolence ritual, blood feud, etc., the Iroquois system did solve, although it created many other difficulties in solving it, and it remained a point of vulnerability in the system."

A similar statement can be made for the Tiv: The death of the elder and the situation it creates is settled in Tiv culture, particularly the institutions of the lineage rights of all agnates, the mode of "going to the farm" (Bohannan and Bohannan, 1968) and the witchcraft syndrome (Bohannan and Bohannan, 1954). They leave problems as grave as they solve—the tearing apart of community trust and the political indecisiveness and weakness that comes from lineage fragmentation.

On the other hand, it is questionable if the results of the death of a spouse in the American system are solved at all—but I am not prepared to make a case for such a statement here, mainly because the problem is peripheral to the present problem, which is the situation that leads to the break-up of a household in events other than death of a member or the leader.

Break-up of households is probably considered unfortunate in most societies. Tiv and Americans consider it woefully so. However, because their households are based on different institutions, the details of their breaking up are not comparable directly and simply. An American household breaks up, in one sense, when the children leave to establish homes of their own. A Tiv household breaks up, in one sense, when the sons or grandsons of a deceased patriarch decide that the time has come for fission of the compound. Both these situations are "normal" in the society.

However, both societies show "abnormal" break-up of households as well. That time comes at divorce in the United States and in father-son estrangement among the Tiv. Whatever it is psychically, divorce is a serious *social* problem only in societies in which the household is based on the husband-wife relationship. Father-son estrangement is a serious social problem only in societies in which the household is based on father-son dominance. The reason is the same in both cases: Smashed role orbits and inadequate role sets are the reward to the people involved.

When a maritally based household splits "naturally" at the maturity of children, there is not (in the opinion of the householders) any necessary role function that is unfulfilled. However, when a maritally based household splits by death or divorce, the result is one of shattered role sets and faulty relationship orbits. In the same way, when a patrilineally based household splits naturally several years or generations after the decease of the linking ancestor, all roles and all functions are found in both new households. But when the split results from strife in the dominant relationship, there are likely to be shattered role sets and faulty relationship orbits.

These two ways in which households break up is of absolutely prime importance to the health and happiness of the people who live in them. Tiv households normally break into structurally complete households, but they may now contain three generations instead of four. Aside from that (which, as we have seen, neither reduces nor increases the complexity of the structure in terms of dyads and role orbits), the new Tiv household is just like the last. American households, on the other hand, *never* split except into structurally incomplete households—instead, they "outgrow" the role orbits and return to being the home of a couple, having spawned new households. The difference is clearly seen by comparing the Tiv situation to reproduction by cellular division, the American situation to sexual reproduction.

We have, thus, come to a significant difference between Tiv households and American households. Tiv households may split, sometimes after the death of the "father," but when they do, the new households do not contain vast gaps in the range of dyadic relationships. Tiv households do *not* split at the time of divorce, although a child's role-set may be affected.

If he is old enough that he chooses not to accompany his mother when she leaves, and so is without a "mother who bore me directly," he still has, in his father's mother and her linked co-wives, a "mother who bore me," and he still participates in relationships of *ngô-wan*. Just as important, there are a large number of other *ngô-wan* relationships for him to observe. He may be deprived in the sense that he lacks the tender attentions of his very own mother, but his needs will be provided for by people who love him, and he has models all over the place of what the relationship should entail.

If, on the other hand, the child accompanies his mother when, at her divorce, she leaves the household of his father, he nevertheless enters a complete household. His mother goes either to her father's (or brother's) household or directly to the household of what Tiv call her "new husband." In either case, the household is complete and all roles and dyads are present. Step relationships are not as complex and certainly not as difficult as they are with Americans. Tiv have no special kinship terms for step-relatives, not even anything analogous to the modifier "step" of English.

In summary, then, much of the difficulty that arises from divorce in the United States is a function of American household organization. "Broken homes" are necessarily a result of "breakable homes." So long as we have breakable homes, *some* will be broken. There are, on the other hand, some societies that have households that are not breakable on divorce. It is, obviously, true that they may be breakable in some context or another—among Tiv it is father-son conflict—and it will be *that* condition rather than husband-wife conflict that is dreaded by those people. One of the many reasons that Tiv surround the death of elders with involved funeral moots, and with witchcraft accusations and counter-accusations, is the maximal fragility of the household (and of the Oedipal solution) in the days and weeks following death of an elder.

It should not be assumed that any one form of household has only disadvantages. Americans know, and value, the many advantages that their household structure allows them. Most of all, perhaps, it allows the husband-wife relationship the freedom and the privacy that are required to allow "love" to "work." Moreover, such households make a minimal requirement of all kinship relationships save those of marriage and of parenting during the children's dependent years. American households allow Americans to "be themselves." Its disadvantages are borne by children who lack a sufficiently large range of role models and by old people who have become "obsolete" for householding purposes. Tiv households, on the other hand, provide maximum security by "spreading the personal regard" (I hesitate to say love because Tiv have no word for it). They allow not for individualism but rather for assurance of membership and support. Americans get lonely. Tiv get bewitched.

The American type of neolocal household has another special danger: Children do not see intimately any marriage save that of their own parents. If their own parents' marriage is strained or feeble, it makes little difference that the marriages of their parents' siblings may be good ones. The child is usually not in a position to use these "once removed" marriages as models, because he is not sufficiently acquainted with the intricacies and intimacies of the workings of any household save his own—the one founded on the marriage of his parents. The neolocal household so narrows the range of role models and relationship models that the difficulties in a marriage in one generation are apt to be visited on the next generation, whereas in an extended and more open household, the lack of success of one's own parents does not become the only model that one has for family relationships. The middle-class American household, based as it is on the nuclear family, is not merely private ("a man's home is his castle"); it is also a monad in a collection of monads. American houses have big windows—but they are to look out of, not to be looked into. Everything inside any house that is not one's own (or to which one does not have the limited and temporary right as guest) is "none of your business."

Given American houses, not only marriage but also parentage takes on a high degree of individuality. Children cannot look into the next monad to expand their knowledge of marriage. Neither parents nor children are encouraged to look into the next house to expand their awareness of parental models. The result is the rise of a group of "specialists;" Dr. Spock and his cohorts have introduced a great deal of "uniformity" by providing a sort of aseptic "norm" as a model, in the absence of more direct experience and observation. Americans worry about such uniformity. It seems to me, however, that they worry less about actually being alike than about their own emotional and intellectual ignorance of the life processes and vital relationships in their communities, and fear that there is nothing more in it than the mere superficial "uniformity" that would appear to be shared.

The American type of household has created the culture of American cities and suburbs, as well as the primary problem of loneliness in American life. But privacy has been maintained—few Americans would change it.

Tiv and Iroquois households create very different problems for the people who live in them. These peoples do not value privacy—instead, they have raised the fulfillment of certain kinship obligations to both an art and a heavy moral obligation. However, they differ vastly; in one case it is the women who bear the psychic brunt of the parent-child household, and in the other it is the men. And the two are not merely the obverse. When women move at marriage, as among the Tiv, they reintegrate themselves as mothers into the household—women are, in all societies, closely allied to household tasks. When men move, as among the Iroquois, they tend to reintegrate themselves *not* in households, but in non-kinship social groups (in the case of the Iroquois, war parties, hunting parties, and the like). However, the rewards that people get in either sort of extended household were considered by them to be the major ones: complete security in a family and household system that "spread the wealth" of concern, moral obligation, and love over a very wide range. Somebody always wants something from you—but somebody is also always there to give you the something you want, if it is deemed a reasonable thing to have and it is available.

In short, the most telling characteristics of marriage and parenting, of divorce and failure-of-parenting, are characteristics of the household structure. The kind of houses people build reflects their social training and inclinations—and in turn also forms and restricts the social relationships they engage in and the experiences they undergo. Ultimately, therefore, practice reaffirms training and values underscore values.

The Emotional Structure of the Household

In this essay we have discussed households based on the marital relationship, those that are based on the institutionalization of the Oedipal conflict of father-child, and those based on the institutionalization of the mother-daughter link. The first is concerned primarily with spousing, the other two with parenting. The first "dies" after propagating itself, the other two form corporations that extend fully into time, well beyond a single life span, and they propagate by cellular fission.

Each of these household forms, with its institutionalized solutions, produces what might be called "side effects." That is, there are results that are not intended, some of which may cause as much trouble as the original "symptom" that the institution is designed to cure (and may even be successful in curing).

Both spousing and parenting are, of course, vital in all family-based households. These words—spousing and parenting—are ugly, but they are useful. The "adequate" American household is built on successful spousing. When spousing ceases or becomes unsuccessful, the household either breaks up or becomes deranged. Obviously, parenting is one of the primary activities of every household, including those based on spousing. But in the American middle-class household, parenting is limited in time: It occurs, in some form, from the birth of the eldest child until the departure of the youngest. Significantly, there is no concept in such a household—or, indeed, in the society that includes it—of parenting between adults. The very concept "adult" precludes receiving parenting—and if it occurs, it must take place between equals or it must be bootlegged in.

The Tiv household, on the other hand, is built on successful parenting. When parenting ceases or becomes unsuccessful, the result is either the derangement or the breaking up of the household. Spousing in such a household is of limited duration, even when the spouses stay together. Men almost always marry younger women, and their old wives stay on more importantly as their sons' mothers than as their husbands' wives.

Such cultural emphases as these, which coincide with and thereby "cause" and are "caused by" the household structure, lead to differences in what can be called the "emotional structure" of the household. Spousing households demand one set of emotional attitudes and values; parenting households demand quite a different set. The kind of personal adjustments that are demanded by each household type are different in many significant regions. Different demands are made on people at different ages and among different *dramatis personae*. Differences in attitude and in personality structure can be expected to follow as a result.

PARENTING IN TIV AND MIDDLE-CLASS AMERICAN CULTURES

There is, in every culture, a set of more or less overt beliefs and a body of more or less factual knowledge about the way in which human beings are created and procreated, how they grow and mature, how they age, and what their nature is at various stages of the life cycle. Everywhere, there are provided a number of patterns along which a life can be allowed to develop. Basically, the primary division into patterns is by sex. There is one over-all role for males, another for females. There is a greater or lesser variety of ways for being male or female; but sex roles are differentiated early in life and, although influenced by age-roles, are constant through life. Few cultures wait even as much as a few hours after birth to begin, albeit unconsciously, the habituation of the newborn to being either male or female. There are comparatively few roles that are not affected by the sex of the player, either in the eligibility for the role, the suitability in the form of cast-assignments, or the style in which the role is played. Sex roles are, obviously, the most pervasive of all roles. Except for some race roles (particularly "Negro") in the United States and perhaps such status roles as royalty or pariah in a few cultures, no others have anywhere near the range of applicability as have the sex roles.

Intermingled with ideas about sex roles and the nature and development of human beings is a set of ideas about the kind of parenting that is required to create individuals that exhibit the desired characteristics. Children everywhere need effective parenting. Every culture must deal with the dependency of children's first few years. The type of dependency changes constantly from infancy until the point at which the culture claims dependency should cease. In American middle-class families, there is a norm—achieved in a surprisingly high number of instances—that parenting should be finished well before the child reaches the "age of majority." There, parenting is confounded with authority, and it is postulated that the authority aspect of the relationship should gradually disappear as the child becomes an adult. The relationship between parent and child must, concurrently, be rebuilt without the element of authority—a new kind of relationship that Satir (1964) has called "making colleagues of the parents."

Americans tend, therefore, to see as desirable the withering away of parenting as the child approaches and reaches majority. Parenting is associated with authority; it is non-egalitarian. Such withering away of parenting coincides with and indeed hides another assumption: that as the need for parenting diminishes, the need for spousing grows. Middle-class Americans establish a sort of antithesis between parenting and spousing: Continuation of parenting can interfere with the capacities of a spouse, either to give or to receive attention and love from the other spouse. Thus, an axiom develops—and is sometimes overtly stated—that spousing depends on successful completion of parenting.

Tiv, on the other hand, make no such neat separation of ideas about spousing and parenting, and certainly they have no notion that the one (parenting) must be successfully "completed" *in order that* the other (spousing) can properly begin, and certainly none that being an attentive son or daughter detracts from spousing.

As I understand the Tiv view of the matter (put into terms that they might find difficult, but with adequate explanation would, I think, agree with) a person never ceases to need parenting. In response, the roles of son and daughter, of father and mother, are a steady claim on one's time, activity, and emotions. Being a child is not antithetical to being a spouse—and spousing is rather less wide-ranging than it is with Americans. Moreover, one is a parent not only to one's own children, but to one's children's children; and one is a "child" to all of one's ascendants.

There is no point in the psychic or social development of Tiv at which parenting "should" be complete. There are persons playing parental roles to all Tiv save the very most aged. The range of parenting is reduced to little after middle age, but it never disappears completely, and it almost never masquerades as a part of spousing. The authority and "power" structures of the society are such that parenting activity forms the idiom for all other types of authority, while the range of power of the actual parent who may be in authority is vastly reduced. Thus, there is no "revolution" against parent figures—there does not have to be, because adult status and the capacity (let alone the right) for spousing is not considered in any way dependent on the completion of such a "revolution." The maturation of the relationship does not demand a sharp, revolutionary break in order for the power structure within it to be changed from a child-rearing to an adult-cooperating one.

Thus, among Tiv, a spouse is a spouse, and a parent is a parent. One demands different things of them throughout life, whereas in American culture, one demands and gets some of the same things from each at different periods of life. The Tiv spouse is the *last* person from whom parenting is to be expected. When it is found—and in a few cases of "romantic love" it *is* found—it is considered evil and dangerous.

There is, in such a situation, obviously never any need for a Tiv to get covert parenting from his spouse. The concomitant problem is, of course, that the definition of a fully adult personality, one that has achieved what psychoanalysts call "maturity," must be different. One psychoanalyst with whom I had long and careful discussions on some of these points found it difficult to see how it was possible to achieve maturity if Tiv never got out from "under the shadows" of their parents—even after the death of parents, there are likely to be parental substitutes. We agreed that we might as sensibly ask how middle-class Americans can be expected to achieve adult maturity when their spouses have to take on so many aspects of adult parenting—or else it has to be overcome. Ultimately, we might even ask whether both societies do not have poorly conceived ideas of maturation, dependency, and the nature of the human personality.

The answer is to be found, first of all, in the fact that both parenting and spousing are highly diffuse in Tiv society, and just as astoundingly concentrated in American society. An American child has one "mother," and Americans have not made any really satisfactory adjustment to situations in which mothering is done by persons other than the biological mother. Adoptions have accompanying problems (Kirk, 1964); step-mothers notoriously find problems in "mothering" that extend far beyond the relationship of step-mother and child (Smith, 1953; Simon, 1964). A Tiv child has several "mothers." His father's mother and her linked co-wives, if she has any, are his mothers when he is in his own compound. His mother's mother and her linked co-wives are his mothers when he is with his non-agnatic close kinsmen. Moreover, there is a whole household full of people to whom one is a "child;" all the adult women married into the compound call one "my child"—the reciprocal term is "our wife," and is the only place in which spouse terms are used in parenting relationships.

The whole of "brothering" contains elements of parenting, because no two people are precisely equal in rank among Tiv, and parenting is part of the task of every elder *wango*.

"Brothering" and its relationship to parenting in a Tiv compound is best observed in the activities of child nurses and their infant charges. Tiv babies are handed over to nurses when they are about six months old—children five or six years older than themselves, who take charge of much of the parenting, particularly the habituating and educating. Tiv children learn more of Tiv culture from other children than they do from adults. That may be true of all children, but among Tiv it is noticeably greater to Western observers than it is in their own societies, and gives them the impression that children are more responsible there than in America for the enculturation of younger children. The nurse comforts a child when he is being weaned; the nurse is in charge of toilet training.

Thus the parenting functions are, among Tiv, spread out to include, in a very real sense, all the senior kinsmen. Parenting is not limited to the parents in the Anglo-Saxon sense, but is rather the task of the parents in the Gallic sense of "kinsmen."

Typically, moreover, parenting is a life-long relationship for Tiv. Not only are they parented from the time they are born; they begin the process of being "parents" by the time they are six or so—when they are handed a young charge to nurse. This particular relationship is reflected in the terms *orvesen* and *wayne*—elder and younger. These ideas (usually translated as senior and junior) are the prototype of the parenting relationship, and extend throughout Tiv culture.

Thus, Tiv do not have to perform the *volte face* that Americans must perform to be "adult." They do not go through the period of "freedom and choice" that middle-class Americans of both sexes experience in late adolescence and early adulthood; of leaving home and going to college (most of the Americans we are talking about here do go to college); of being put into the position of "free individuals" when parenting is minimal and spousing is one's own responsibility. It is probably trite to repeat the insight here that one of the main reasons why age at first marriage is being lowered in the United States is that marriage, for young people, vastly reduces the social and psychic tensions that his culture thrusts upon him, at the same time that it solves the problem of sexual expression. Parenting has stopped, more or less abruptly. Most college students and other young unmarried persons are in a position of very great independence, not to say *anomie*, with choices to be made that will reverberate through their futures. Having a spouse is the first step in creating a group in which one begins to validate oneself as a person who can make the choices in a worthy way; it also makes the subsequent choices less independent, lonely affairs. Erich Fromm has, with justice, called this a part of a "flight from freedom," but there is also something to be said for the Tiv point of view that freedom is something that one achieves more slowly, and with greater security. An old Tiv, who had had dozens of wives and scores of children, once told me that the way to secure a group of followers who were fully trustworthy was to beget them. It might be as truly said of Americans that the only way to find a relationship in which one can fully be oneself is to marry.

Discussion

It seems to me that Hsu's concept of the "dominant" relationship should be reconsidered in the light of the patterns in which these universal human problems are solved institutionally, morally, or not at all. The institutionalized solution dominates everything, for the very reason that it is institutionalized—it is part of what Durkheim and Freud, each in his own way, called the collective unconscious. The principles are more compelling for being unstated and the sanctions more powerful for being collective. Dominance, seen so, means that the attributes of the dominant relationship are diffuse in the system of social axioms of that society, brought to awareness and "theorized" about in many small areas of life. It is no accident that Westerners have created an ethic of love, the Chinese an ethic of filial piety, the Indians a mother goddess and a lingam cult (Hsu, 1963; 1968), or that the Tiv have an oedipally based witchcraft syndrome. All of these "dominant" areas of life are, in their particular societies, set out as ethical principles—insofar as they are set out at all—which are thought to underlie all behavior in human relationships.

The dominant, institutionalized area of life, of course, influences all the others, especially those that are solved morally, with less institutional basis. "Honor thy father and thy mother," as that commandment is understood in twentieth century America, is oceans removed from an ethic of filial piety. It is a moral precept. "Brotherly love" is so diffuse in America that it means a regard of humanity, not a directive for the relationship of actual kinsmen.

Among the Tiv, the dominant institutionalized area of life is summed up in their concept of "one man" (or *môm*). Fathers and sons, agnatic brothers—all agnates—are "one man." Brothers are separated by their wives and mothers; they are united through their fathers. Marriage is the growing point of the group described as "one man," but is subordinate as a concept.

In an analogous way, the Chinese would seem to handle marriage as a set of moral precepts within the overwhelming ethical terms of institutionalized filial piety. Chinese culture could never have discovered the Oedipus complex—not because they do not have it or because some of their members may not suffer from it, but because it constitutes the milieu of the society, and therefore Oedipal problems show up as sin or disgrace rather than as neurosis. In much the same way, the West is not likely to discover the "complexes" that are immured behind the ethic of love, because "love" is axiomized as a solution to problems.

Americans assume that filial relationships can be ended—in fact, their successful end comes when the child is "ready" for marriage. And marriage lasts forever (it says here). The Chinese make precisely the opposite assumption. Marriage must be rendered "successful" so that filial piety can persevere and bloom. To Tiv, marriage is relatively unimportant; considerations of spouses must always give way before the "one man."

In every society, the greatest difficulty comes, apparently, in dealing with the institutionally solved set of interpersonal problems, when those solutions become outmoded or when they prove destructive or when they bog down. Every social institution would seem to have more or fewer "side effects." An institution (in Malinowski's classic sense) is a group of people organized for a purpose; no matter how brilliantly it achieves the purpose, there is always the possibility that the "side effects" make the victory a Pyrrhic one.

We can now restate the hypothesis: The American household is "based on" the husband-wife relationship; that is, the marital bond is the institutionalized relationship. Therefore, divorce strikes at the basis of the institutional solution of the family problems. The Tiv household is, in the same sense, based on the father-son relationship. "Splitting the compound," especially one constituting the descendants of a living man, strikes at the institutional Tiv solution of the panhuman family problems.

Americans "expect" their children to "leave home" and "set up homes of their own." The main educational or training problem is to create the kind of people who can do this and who can come back to their parents as social equals and colleagues. Tiv "expect" their children to go through a number of marriages, and not to be "hurt" by that experience.

On the other hand, Tiv "expect" their children to come to terms with the adult son-parent relationship and settle down as efficient and orderly compound members, not given to witchcraft, but exhibiting power nevertheless. Americans, conversely, expect their children to outgrow the Oedipal struggle, rather than to come to terms with it institutionally, and to settle down as "mature individuals."

Among the Tiv, it is onto women that the bulk of the pressure is displaced; among Iroquois, it is on the men. In America in the 1960's, the load would seem to be about equally shared between the sexes but to be heaviest for all in youth and age.

Among Americans, the greatest concern about inadequacy is inadequacy in the marital relationship. Among Tiv, the gravest inadequacy is in the filial relationship, especially father-son. Among Iroquois, the gravest inadequacy would seem also to have been a filial one, especially the mother-daughter. Americans assume that the marital relationship demands an adequate educational and moral solution to the Oedipal struggle. Tiv assume that adequacy in the filial relationships demands adequate moral solution of sibling relationships. For Americans, the sibling relationship is "left over"—more or less unsolved, because lack of an institutionalized solution does not destroy households. Similarly, for Tiv the marital relationship is left over—because marital break-up does not destroy households. A high but comparatively harmless, divorce rate results for the Tiv. A high but comparatively harmless rate of rupture between siblings is found in the United States. If social science had been invented in Tiv culture instead of Western culture, we might not be interested in divorce rates at all, but rather in rates of compound fracture or paternal disinheritance. The key concept would not be "divorce" at all, but rather some word that would mean rupture of the father-son relationship. "Broken homes" would mean something very different.

The moral of this essay is simple: If you break the relationship around which the household is institutionalized, "disorganization" results—not just because the household is shattered, but also because the keystone relationship is removed. There seem never to be parallel institutions for the dominant ones. Thus, divorce in the United States is a catastrophe. Among Tiv it is not, and among the Iroquois it would seem (structurally, at least) scarcely noticeable (see Table 3.1).

Conclusions

In summary form, the argument of this essay runs:

Major Premise: All human societies must find solutions for
(a) perennial sexuality,
(b) lactation and learning,
(c) the Oedipal conflict.
a solution is to be found in one of three forms:
(1) institutionalized,
(2) moralized,
(3) deemed irrelevant.

Minor Premise: Each human society must give priority to solving one of the problems, over the others, when it establishes and maintains households.

Conclusion: A classification can be created on the basis of the juxtarelationship and priorities among problems and solutions.

Table 3.1 summarizes the material for the three societies on which the body of this essay is based. Figure 3.5 summarizes the three patterns that we have discovered and shows the basis on which other comparable patterns might be discerned.

Table 3.1. Summary

	American middle-class household	Tiv compound	Iroquois longhouse
Solved institutionally	Marital problem	Oedipal problem	Electra problem
Solved morally	Oedipal problem	Sibling problem	Sibling problem
Unsolved	Sibling problem	Marital problem	Marital problem
Basic relationship in household	*Hu Wi*	*Fa-So*	*Mo Da*
Congruent personality problems	Oedipus complex	Orphans; wives (become attached as mothers—especially barren women and bastards)	Unattached males

COROLLARIES:

1. When the Hu-Wi relationship is institutionalized in the household, the parent-child relationship may be moralized. The sibling relationship may be deemed unimportant (American). Psychic problem: Oedipus complex.

2. When the Fa-So relationship is institutionalized, the sibling relationship may be moralized. The marital relationship may be deemed unimportant (Tiv). Psychic problems: fear of agnatic witchcraft by males; peripheral attachment and diffuse personality of females.

3. When the Mo-Da relationship is institutionalized, the sibling relationship may be moralized. The marital relationship may be deemed unimportant (Iroquois). Psychic problems: witchcraft; the unattached and diffuse male personality.

HYPOTHESES:

1. If a dyadic relationship in the nuclear family is deemed irrelevant, there is minimal content, and nothing happens if it is broken.

2. If a dyadic relationship is moralized and is broken, then more or less grave social concern is taken, but there is no institutional result.

Figure 3.5. Patterns of Residence Dominance

SECONDARY \ PRIMARY	a Perennial sexuality	b Lactation & learning	c Oedipal conflict	d Sibling rivalry
1 Institu-tionalized	U.S.	Iroquois	Tiv	
2 Moralized		U.S. Tiv	U.S.	Iroquois Tiv
3 Deemed irrelevant	Tiv Iroquois		Iroquois	U.S.

So we have three patterns:

U.S.	=	1a	2b	2c	3d
Tiv	=	1c	2b	2d	3a
Iroquois	=	1b	2d	3a	3c

3. If a dyadic relationship is institutionalized and is broken, then the social structure is affected in such a way as to create serious "social disorganization" or fear of it.

4. It would seem (but this observation needs serious investigation) that institutionalized solutions to household problems are seldom or never backed up by parallel institutions that can take over the function of the household when that household fails because of the breakdown in the dominant relationship. There is no adequate institution to take over the unfinished tasks of the "broken home" that results from divorce in America; the Tiv who has split from his brothers is permanently "crippled" socially. Although it is recognized that family life is threatened by decomposition when the basic institutionalized dyadic relationship is broken, there is reluctance to foster parallel institutions for fear the dominant solution will be undermined. Yet, most peoples would seem to realize that "morals" are inadequate to such a situation.

PART II

Ethnographic Explorations

FOUR

IGOR KOPYTOFF

The Suku of the Congo: An Ethnographic Test of Hsu's Hypotheses

This paper will examine Hsu's hypotheses (Hsu, 1965) by way of a specific ethnographic case: the Suku of the southwest of the Republic of the Congo (Kinshasa), whom I studied in the field. I shall describe and analyze Suku kinship relations in terms of structure and content (cf. Hsu, 1959). I shall then compare the results of my analysis with Hsu's hypotheses about systems of which the Suku should be an instance. Finally, Hsu's formulations will be reexamined in the light of the discrepancies that emerge.

The Suku number about 80,000. They live in open rolling savanna of low population density (15–20 persons per square mile), in villages ranging in size from a score to two hundred persons and located at intervals of a couple of miles. Their subsistence rests on horticulture, done exclusively by women, and on hunting and fishing, done mainly by men. Traditionally, they were organized into a kingdom of typical Central African pattern, with the king standing at the apex of a pyramid of regional chiefs and sub-chiefs. Complementing this formal organization was another system in which conflicts were often resolved through self-help, hostage-taking, armed fighting, and the use of mediators.

THE LINEAGE

The basic social grouping is the very strongly corporate matrilineage. Typically, it numbers some two score persons; less than ten of these would be mature male adults, and lineage authority is vested in them. The oldest among them is automatically the formal lineage head.

The lineage principle permeates almost all economic, political, jural, and religious activities. The lineage, as corporation, holds title to all property. The larger fixed resources, such as hunting territories and palm groves, are held outright as corporate property. Fluid property, such as utensils, money, and domestic animals, is controlled by individuals only in their roles as lineage members. There is always considerable free circulation of goods within the lineage. When a person dies, his or her property reverts to the lineage as a corporation, to be redistributed within it. In times of collective need (for example, legal fines, political tribute, marriage payments), the elders, in their capacity of corporation managers, pool their resources and demand contributions from the younger members. Almost all legal interpersonal relations between members of different lineages are fused with the system of interlineage relations, and these are rigidly reciprocal. It is the lineage, not the individual, who is the debtor or the creditor, the claimant or the defendant. Debts never lapse and no past loss may remain uncompensated. When legal settlement fails, theft is balanced by counter-theft, homicide by counter-homicide.

There are no other widely multi-functional institutions competing with the lineage. The lineage is unique not only in the range of its functions but also in that it is the only Suku institution in which membership is ascribed for life and which constitutes a self-perpetuating corporate group. The strongest formal social tie in Suku society is the one binding the individual to his matrilineage. The bond here is between the person and the institution—a symbolic entity uniting living and dead by the tie of common "blood." The lineage is as concrete a part of Suku social ecology as are individuals, as concrete as are corporations qua legal persons in our society. The relation between a person and his or her matrilineage must, therefore, be viewed separately from the relations between the individual members of the lineage.

Authority in the Lineage. Within the lineage, authority varies with age, generation, and sex. Other things being equal, males are superior to females. As to age and generation, these principles partly intertwine under the concept of "eldership." The term "elder" must be understood in its relative form. Strictly speaking, any elder of mine is anyone in the lineage (male or female) who is older than I. This person has authority over me because he or she represents to me the legal and (to us) "mystical" power of the corporation, a power without which success in life is thought impossible. A curse by an elder is a fearsome thing: It removes from the accursed the supernatural (and sometimes the physical) protection of the lineage.

Since eldership is always relative, as one gets older more and more junior members come under one's authority. Dead members of past generations are the oldest of all, and their authority is further reinforced by the power and knowledge that only the dead possess.

But relative authority is not tied entirely to the continuum of age; authority also clusters around generational positions. Each generation in the lineage is a kind of corporate subgroup within it, set off from the other generations by the solidarity of siblingship. It is presumptious for the young to inquire into the activities and decisions of the old. Consequently, a curse or a bewitchment by a generational senior is seen, in the absence of more information, as representing the action of the entire body of senior generations. Similarly, the welfare of the entire lineage is also seen as the collective responsibility of the senior generations; misfortunes are blamed on them as a group. The elders in turn can and do blame the elders above them—who are dead and have to be upbraided and beseeched at the graves in the same way that the living elders are themselves upbraided and beseeched in the village. Thus, what anthropologists may be tempted to call here (wrongly) an "ancestor cult" is, in fact, part of the wider "eldership cult." (There is, significantly, no Suku equivalent for our term "ancestor"—a matter no less important to the analysis of Suku kinship than to understanding Suku religion.)

The Lineage in Space. It is clear that the Suku matrilineage is so organized that it can operate only when its members are able to communicate frequently and to get together when necessary with relative ease. This leads to the question of residence rules.

Suku marriage residence is virilocal: The husband is the sponsor of the couple's residence. As to inter-generational residence, sons live with their father at least until the father's death; they move with him when he moves (for example, upon *his* father's death). When the father dies, a son has several choices open to him. He may remain with his father's living brothers (and perhaps move with them when they move), or he may join one of his lineage elders (who himself lives, and moves, in terms of his particular choices within the same system of residential decisions). Space forbids going into the details of this system of choices (cf. Kopytoff, 1964). Suffice it to say here that while the individual system is relatively simple and predictable for any given set of specific conditions, the actual place where an adult male lives with his wife and children is always the end result of a chain of previous decisions by others.

It is thus impossible to speak of a "typical" residential life cycle for a Suku or of a "typical" cluster of co-residing nuclear families. One finds structures ranging from what anthropologists would call "three-generational extended patrilocal families" all the way to "three-generational avunculocal families," with various other combinations of linked patrilocal and avunculocal families in between. But what matters for the Suku is the localization of the matrilineage sufficient for its corporate existence. The matrilineage is indeed dispersed among several villages, in an area some ten to fifteen miles in diameter. Within the area (which can contain as many as 5,000 members of other matrilineages equally scattered, and over a hundred villages), the lineage is anchored on the village that it "owns"—the one it founded and that bears its name and contains the lineage-head, some elders, widows, divorced women, and a few younger members. The rest of the members live in surrounding villages and may shift their residence among them. But "their" village is always the one the lineage "owns"—this is the "home office" of the corporation, where all important matters are referred, decided, and ritualized.

In terms of the focus of this paper, how do these residential arrangements impinge upon the growing child and the young adult? Assuming for the moment longevity and no divorce for the parents, the child and his siblings grow up where the father lives; they will grow up with the children of his father's brothers (uterine brothers tend to live and move as a group), and they are likely to move to a not-too-distant village at least once before adulthood. Upon adulthood, the females will move away and join their husbands, but the sons will continue living with the father. By adulthood, however, they frequently visit their own lineage-village and other villages where their elders (mostly real and classificatory mother's brothers) live, as they become increasingly involved in lineage affairs, making demands upon their elders, resisting in turn the elders' demands, assembling money for bridewealth, profiting from the exploitation of lineage property. At this time, residence with the father is a welcome thing, for exactions by lineage elders can be better avoided when one does not live with them. There is no great advantage for a young man to live at the center of lineage affairs. As he approaches middle age, and as he accumulates property, the demands on him of both the old men and the young grow. His father may by then be dead, and he can formally move to join his elders at the lineage-village or elsewhere; but it is still often to his advantage to reside at the periphery. It is only when he is himself in the oldest living generation that both the advantage and the obligation of actively managing lineage affairs become unambiguous. The male adult's patrilocal residence is thus something of a refuge from the pressures of lineage membership—pressures that can be mitigated but never really escaped, given the on-going social system. It is, of course, precisely this corporate unity of the lineage that makes it possible for patrilocality to be a refuge, since the son is excluded from the affairs of his father's lineage and therefore its pressures. He is treated as a resident guest, and he has the rights and obligations of a guest. But the security of patrilocal residence is this: Unlike ordinary guests, he has the *right to be* a guest.

It should be emphasized that the above is the ideal situation. In specific cases, various factors may intervene. If one's mother dies early, the child will be taken on by the mother's real or classificatory sister. If the father dies early, the mother may or may not remarry in the same lineage;

usually she does not, and the child will follow her wherever she goes, to one of her mother's brothers and then to a new husband. Finally, divorce here is frequent, and pre-adolescent children always stay with the mother. Upon adulthood, however, a man must return to live with his father; if the father is dead, he may return to live with the father's brothers and lineage.

MARRIAGE

Marriage is a contract between lineages, in which reciprocity prevails. Bridewealth is given by the groom's lineage to the bride's (which in turn, and as a matter of its own contractual relation with the bride's father, hands over to the groom a large portion of the bridewealth). The husband acquires over the wife the rights to exclusive cohabitation, to her domestic labor, to a portion of his daughters' future bridewealth, and to having his sons live with him until he dies. Upon divorce, if the entire bridewealth is returned, the husband loses all of these rights. If he wishes to retain his rights over his children, the reimbursement is diminished by a quarter for every son and by half for every daughter.

In marriage, the wife continues to be an active full-fledged member of her own lineage. The couple's property is strictly separate. The corporate nature of the respective matrilineages divides the family, economically and legally, into two parts, each affiliated to separate solidary groups: the husband-father on one side, and, on the other, the wife-mother with her children.

THE NATURE OF INTERPERSONAL RELATIONS

I have emphasized until now the jural framework which is formally cast in terms of relations between an individual and the following corporate groups: 1) the person's own lineage (containing his uterine siblings and parallel cousins, his mother and her sisters, his mother's brothers—real and classificatory); 2) the father's lineage (containing father and his uterine siblings); and 3) the wife's lineage (containing the wife, her uterine siblings, and her mother and mother's brothers). These lineages are indicated in Diagram 4.1, together with the principal individuals with whom Ego's relations will be discussed. To simplify matters, Ego is male.

I shall now describe the following principal relationships with an emphasis on what Hsu calls their "content":

Man/Own Lineage:	1. Man/Mother's Brother
	2. Man/Brother
	3. Man/Mother
	4. Man/Sister
Man/Father's Lineage:	1. Man/Father
	2. Man/Father's Siblings
Man/Wife's Lineage:	1. Man/Wife
	2. Man/Wife's Mother's Brothers

Man/Own Lineage. The relationship to one's own lineage as corporation is the overriding fact of Suku social life. Jurally, it involves considerable constraints and these are concentrated in a person's relationship with his lineage elders and specificallly with his "mother's brothers" (that is, males in the generation above him) who are the active representatives of lineage authority unmitigated by intra-generational (as with brothers) or alternate-generational (as with mother's mother's brothers) solidarity, or by sexual inferiority (as with mother and classificatory mothers). It is the mother's brothers who, in the name of the lineage, exact contributions for its corporate needs, define these needs, and resist counter-claims to its wealth. A mother's brother can legitimately curse a junior in the name of

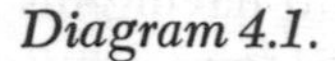
Diagram 4.1.

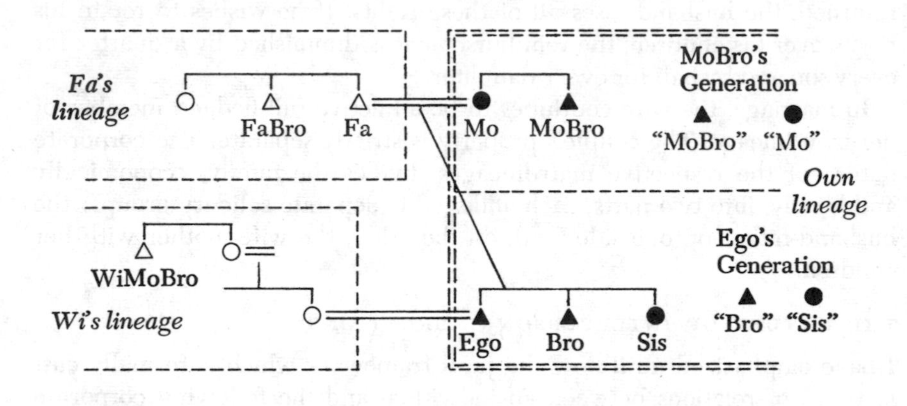

the lineage, exposing him to misfortunes; also the mother's brother is often suspected by the junior of being a witch. The death of his mother's brother brings a junior closer to controlling lineage affairs and wealth. The relationship is filled with ambivalence, with mutual legal dependence and mutual mistrust. It is authoritarian, legally constraining, tense, and inescapable, and it pervades most adult activities. The legal framework here is such that it is difficult for personal liking to overcome the structurally induced hostility. Culturally, it is well stereotyped by the proverb: "A sister's son is like a dog you own; you think he is sitting obediently at your feet while in fact he is about to gnaw at your leg-bone."

In dealing with a man's relationship with his brothers, we are concerned with uterine brothers, as opposed to brothers by the same father in a polygynous household. In general, there is considerable solidarity among uterine brothers. They live together and they tend to change their residence together. Their entire generation in the lineage (their classificatory lineage "brothers," i.e., matrilateral parallel cousins) represents a group in common tension with their mothers' brothers and, later, with their sisters' sons. However, the relationship among brothers is not entirely one between equals. An older brother is an "elder," with an elder's formal authority over a younger brother; if the difference in age is considerable, his authority approaches that of a mother's brother. The relationship is thus not without possible conflicts, and generational equality gives it a competitive flavor. (In the case of the mother's brothers, their clear, unambiguous authority precludes competition.) The relationship between brothers can thus be defined as only mildly authoritarian and constraining; on the whole, it tends to be solidary, pervasive of many adult activities, and potentially competitive.

A man's relationship with his mother and sisters stands in greatest contrast to that with his mother's brothers. It is generally warm and even sentimental, allowing full play to affect. Though the mother is and the sister may be a lineage elder, their jural inferiority as women and their very separate areas of activity preclude effective authoritarianism on their part. As to the man, his authority over his sisters increases with age, as he becomes a lineage elder, but this authority is generally suffused with protectiveness; before middle age, the relationship is characterized by "shyness," formal avoidance, and great warmth. The potential strain in later years lies in the nature of the brother/sister/sister's son triangle, in which the woman is caught in the middle of the tension between her brother and her son. The relationship of a man with his mother and sister can be summarized as legally unconstraining, non-authoritarian, contextually diffuse rather than specific, and tinged with sentiment.

Man/Father's Lineage. His father's entire lineage are a man's collective "fathers," and the already rather minor obligations to the father are extended in attenuated form to the father's uterine brothers and, in still more attenuated form, to the father's lineage as a whole. The son must live with the father, but he only *may* live with the father's lineage. He must give his father portions of game and gifts; after his father's death, and especially if he moves away, these gifts to the father's lineage diminish in frequency. The relationship with the father himself allows full play for affect: The son cannot inherit anything of value and the father cannot interfere with the son's primary obligation to his own lineage. The relationship need not be warm, but it can be and usually is, just as the relationship with the mother's brother does not exclude warmth but does discourage it. The relationship may be summarized as mildly authoritarian, legally unconstraining, contextually diffuse rather than specific, and suffused with mutual respect. It is close in feeling-tone to the relationship with the mother, but because it involves males, the area of common activities is large and the authority of age does come in actively.

Though formally a projection of the relationship with the father, that with the fathers' lineage lacks direct personal attachment, is more exposed to the vagaries of personal likes and dislikes, and consequently varies considerably. There is a potential for strain here: The father's brothers have an emotional investment in their own sons, each may try secretly to pass on property to their sons, and each tries to make sure that the others do not do the same. Thus, unless personal attachment is strong, a man may consider moving away once his father dies; but there are some who remain with their father's lineage to the end of their lives.

Man/Wife's Lineage. The relationship with the wife's lineage is heavily contractual in tone, and this affects the relationship with the wife herself. The insistence by the lineages of both husband and wife upon their respective rights puts a constraint on purely personal feelings in the husband-wife tie. The economic separation between the partners involves the domestic sphere. Structurally, the marital tie is weak and easily broken; when there is discord, it is easily exacerbated by mutual accusations of failure to live up to the rigidly defined formal obligations. Unlike stressful lineage relations, this one can be escaped from and often is. Within its preceisely defined and limited contexts, the husband-wife relationship is legally constraining, involving potential conflict that is easily aroused. As a female, the wife formally has an inferior status, but the relationship is mutually respectful and independent rather than authoritarian and unequal: The wife's inferiority is monopolized by her lineage and not by her husband.

Formally, the relationship of a man with his wife's lineage is that of mutual "respect," mixed with some avoidance. It is focused on the wife's elders (usually her mother's brothers) in the early years and, later, on her brothers. It is with them that the marriage is initially negotiated and that arguments will arise in the not unlikely event of a divorce; it is they who try to exact additional gifts from the husband, sometimes by using their legal right to recall the wife temporarily or to impose a tabu on sexual relations with her; finally, it is they who hold the legal rights over the man's children while at the same time being the witches who "kill" them and try to blame the death on the father. The jural configuration results in one-sided exploitation and considerable tension. The relationship may be summed up as formally reciprocal but in fact unequal and tense; formally again, it is contextually restricted and specific but in fact it can constrict the husband in a variety of contexts chosen by the wife's lineage. While the relationship is easily escapable in the jural sense, it impinges on very basic socio-biological drives, and this adds to the ambivalence and tension.

THE SYSTEM OF INTERPERSONAL RELATIONSHIPS

It is clear that the relationships described are not independent configurations but are intertwined within a system. The primary unifying feature is the jural importance of lineage membership; the distribution of rights and duties, of power, authority, and dependence connected with it is the skeleton on which the system hangs. The lineage so monopolizes the individual that relationships between members of different lineages are overwhelmingly cast in a contractual mold. Here, the rights, duties, and relevant social realms are very specifically defined. When such inter-lineage relations are, by their nature, strongly personal (as with father and wife), a potential conflict arises. But the time when the conflict comes to the fore is an important variable. With the father, the son's lineage membership does not impinge on the relationship until early adulthood, while in the early years it, in fact, leaves room for developing a personal tie in a non-authoritarian atmosphere. By the time the relationship is affected by the separate lineage obligations of each, it can well withstand the strain; furthermore, it becomes simultaneously advantageous to both, as a kind of refuge from the legal rigidities of lineage affiliation. The personal tie is weaker between the son and the father's brothers, and weaker still with others in the father's lineage. Consequently, it is not surprising that after the father's death these relations sometimes attenuate to the point of a merely formalistic fulfillment of the minimal jural obligations required.

In the husband-wife relationship, such a withdrawal from interaction with the wife's lineage is not possible. The relationship is "voluntary" and can only be broken off through divorce (as the "involuntary," ascribed relationship with the father's lineage cannot be). As long as marriage lasts, the relationship continues in full force and the control of the wife by her lineage puts them in a position of power vis-à-vis the husband. In contrast with the father, the strains of separate lineage membership impinge on the husband-wife relationship from the very beginning and, in fact, before any strong personal ties can be established. The brittleness of marriage is thus understandable. As with the father's lineage, the solution to the strains of separate lineage membership is in withdrawal—in this case, however, withdrawal from a contractual and breakable relationship.

The overwhelming structural dominance of lineage membership clearly undermines relationships outside of it, unless these are formed early enough and are strong enough to withstand the strain; paradoxically, they then become a refuge from the very dominance of lineage obligations. Psychologically, one's relation to one's lineage is an ambivalent one: Existence outside of it is culturally inconceivable—it is the source of well-being in the profoundest sense of the term—but it is also the source of overwhelming constraints. The elements of this ambivalence are, however, parceled out among one's lineage relations. One's identity is with the lineage as corporate group; the source of constraint and of authority—the mother's brothers' generation—is also the target for potential hostility; the non-authoritarian mothers and sisters are the emotional refuge in which sentiment can be given full play. The relationship with the brothers—that is, one's own generation—remains ambivalent, however. It is both a constraint and a refuge from the elders, somewhat competitive but also solidary.

Application of Hsu's Formulations to the Suku

In trying to apply Hsu's hypothesis to the Suku, an immediate difficulty arises. Hsu's model is concerned with relationships within the nuclear family, precisely the group that among the Suku is so clearly subordinate to the lineage. Hsu deals with the family as an autonomous, quasi-closed system—something one clearly cannot do in the Suku case. One solution is to see as dominant within the nuclear family those relationships that are also part of the lineage system. This means man/mother, man/sister, and man/brother relationships. But which of these is the dominant one? In the absence of a precise method for determining this, we must rely on knowledgeable intuition, but even here another problem arises: dominance in the sphere of sentiments, as opposed to dominance in the jural sphere. On the jural side, the man/brother relationship stands out. But if the jural sphere is to be chosen, then the man/mother's brother relationship stands out even more. Hsu (1965:657–58) has indeed suggested that the man/brother relationship may be the dominant one in African societies, but the selection of this relationship here would seem to be merely an artifact of Hsu's restriction of the model to the nuclear family.

Yet, the Suku resemble Hsu's model of a man/brother dominated system, though only symptomatically. The Suku do have a somewhat manipulative relationship with the ancestors—but not because rivalry and equality in the man/brother relationship spill over into the world of ancestors. Rather, the lineage structure leads *both* to the mild rivalry with brothers and to the manipulative relationship with elders—and ancestors are elders. Again, as in Hsu's model, Suku polygyny is indeed not for perpetuation of the kin-group but for prestige and gain in rights over children (and, it must be added, partly for sexual reasons); but then how could it be otherwise in a matrilineal society? Similarly, the marriage bond is weak, but not because of "rivalry" transferred from the man/brother relationship. Both the rivalry in the latter and the weakness of the marriage bond are traceable to the lineage organization. Women may be seen as having a kind of "polyandrous" attitude: Suku women do have passing affairs rather easily. But the Suku sex *code* (as opposed to occasional tumbles in the bush) is not at all loose, but very rigid legally, and attitudes to sex are, ethnocentrically speaking, prudish. Contrary to Hsu's model, the male-female dichotomy is strong; the wife is certainly not a kind of "female brother," but rather a female outsider. The independence of each partner also derives not from "equality" and "rivalry" in the man/brother relationship but from their deep dependence on their respective lineages; the Suku family cannot be analyzed without reference to the larger system.

When we compare the Suku to Hsu's "father-son" dominated system, which the Suku are clearly not, there are also impressive similarities.

There is great "continuity" (structural) in the matrilineage; there is a large amount of "sharing" within the kin-group; there is a great durability of relationships (they are, in fact, unbreakable) and an "inclusiveness" of lineage members that goes beyond the grave; there is very strong "authority" whose continuity also extends beyond the grave. But, in contrast to Hsu's father-son system, the Suku marriage bond is unstable.

The application of Hsu's hypotheses to the Suku shows obvious empirical and theoretical difficulties. A glaring one is the confinement of the model to the nuclear family, which excludes from consideration the large ethnographic sample of matrilineal-avuncular societies. One can partly deal with this problem by treating the mother's brother as surrogate father; some of the structural traits in the father-son relationship that Hsu postulates do occur in the sister's son-mother's brother relationship (a point we shall return to later), and this may account for the considerable convergence of the Suku with Hsu's father-son dominated system. But the substitution of mother's brother for father refers primarily to the jural realm; it is this fact, after all, that has always struck anthropologists about avuncular societies—their redistribution of the father's "normal" (so it seemed) role among two people, with father retaining some of its elements. This also brings up the question of the division between the jural and the affective, sentimental, expressive—call it what you will—realms. The division is absolutely essential for analyzing African societies, which are so strikingly legalistic as a matter of overt cultural orientation. "Dominances" in these two realms may distribute themselves quite differently; indeed, among the Suku, they seem to be distributed in complementary fashion.

Finally, there is a problem about the manner in which relationships influence each other. Hsu's theory postulates a kind of diffusion of content from the dominant to the other relationships. This may well be true in the psychological realm: The content of the dominant relationship may be important in personality-formation and the relevant personality traits may show up in the handling of other relationships. In this case, dominance is best reserved for the affective sphere and, probably, that of the earlier years of life. But such diffusion of content cannot be postulated for the structure of jural relations, where content is of necessity differentially distributed. Lineage solidarity can exist precisely because, in given contexts, there is no solidarity with outsiders. Diffusion of content is conceivable but never as random. Thus, jural authority, as an attribute of the father-son relationship in Hsu's model, can perhaps be tacked on to a patrilineal chain, upwards to the male ancestors, in a way that the content of the husband-wife relationship cannot be. With the Suku, the structural equivalence of brothers seems to allow a diffusion of content from father to father's brother, but there is a tautology in this statement; after all, we say that Suku brothers are "structuarlly equivalent" precisely because they are treated somewhat in the same way. There is also an unwarranted assumption about the direction of diffusion and even of causality. It is cultural definition that makes for what we abstract into structural equivalence—otherwise, American brothers would also be similarly equivalent.

Does this mean, however, that the cultural elaboration of kinship or any other interpersonal relationship is entirely arbitrary? And if structures—as cultural artifacts—are also arbitrary, is extension or diffusion or equation of content also cross-culturally arbitrary, though systemic in any given social structure? These questions seem to be at the heart of Hsu's theory, which claims that certain structural features are inherent in certain kin relationships, regardless of cultural differences. The cultural position adopted in this paper is not irreconcilable with this claim, but the reconciliation requires a restatement of Hsu's model. This is presented in Diagram 4.2. Hsu's "attributes" are in italics and sometimes preceded by a modifier necessary to the present restatement. I have restricted the diagram to the four relationships that Hsu emphasizes. I have also added a fifth—the sister's son-mother's brother relationship.

The diagram first isolates certain "bio-social givens" of the relationship. The term "bio-social" frankly avoids the thorny problem of the extent to which purely biological traits, such as sex or age, must inherently have a sociological relevance. The traits we have selected seem to have it universally; some of them have it in primate societies in general. Whether they must of necessity have it in human, that is, cultural societies, is another question. From the cultural-evolutionary perspective of the broadest kind (involving the transcendance of biology through culture from the Australopithecines to the present and into the unknown future), these biological traits *need not* possess social significance. In a more limited perspective, however, suffice it to say that it is highly unlikely that these traits can be cognitively missed and ignored and therefore not used in some way as raw material for symbolic, cultural elaboration.

Once these traits are recognized culturally, they shape to some extent the relationships that are built around them. For example, the age difference usually accompanying a difference in generations tends to make the relationship a dominant-subordinate one. But it only *tends* to do so. In this sense, "authority" may be seen as an attribute of content that tends to inhere in the structure that itself rests on biological givens. Finally, with reference to the fourth column in the diagram, there may similarly be a tendency for the content of relationships to be projected more easily along structural pathways that are congruent with the appropriate biological givens. To continue the example just mentioned, the authority inherent in the relationship with a male in the generation above me is more easily diffused to another male, especially if he is also in the generation above me, and to still higher generations, and it is less easily diffused to younger females.

It may be noted that the content features in the diagram are more numerous than those in Hsu's model. One of his encompasses several in

Relationship	*Bio-Social Givens of Relationship*	*Structural Features of Relationship*	*Tendencies In Content*	*Structural Possibilities for Projection of Content*
FATHER-SON	Inter-generational (Senior/junior) →	Dominant/subordinate →	*(Authority)*	Projectable lineally onto an *inter-generational chain* of similar links and/or to structurally equivalent individuals of equal sex and/or generation
		Differential roles →	*(Authority)*	
		Roles can be arranged in chain over time →	*(Continuity)*	
		with junior taking senior alter's role later →	*(Continuity)*	
	Same sex →	Reproductively asexual →	*(Social asexuality)*	*(Continuity)*
	Primary consanguinal →	Relationship can be durable and part of a durable chain →	*(Continuity as Durability)*	
		Relationship can be part of a set of similar relationships (other sons/brothers) →	*(Inclusiveness)*	
MOTHER-SON	Early biological dependency →		*(Emotional dependence)*	Projectable inter-generationally onto *groups rather than along a chain;* also onto structurally equivalent individuals of equal sex and/or generation
	Different sex →		*(Libidinality)*	
	Inter-generational (Senior/junior) →	Differential roles that cannot be arranged lineally in a chain of similar links, since alter's role unavailable to son →	*(Discontinuity)*	
			(Diffuseness)	*(Discontinuity)*
	Primary consanguinal →	Relationship can be durable →	*(Durability)*	
		Relationship can be part of a set of similar but contemporary relationships (other sons) →	*(Inclusiveness)*	

BROTHER-BROTHER

Intra-generational (seniority minimized) → Not a link in potential inter-generational chain → *(Discontinuity)*

Intra-generational (seniority minimized); Same sex → Structural equivalence and potential role similarity → *(Equality)* → *(Rivalry, separation)*

Secondary Consanguinal → Can be durable

Secondary Consanguinal → Can be part of a set of similar but contemporary relationships (other brothers) → *(Inclusiveness)* → *(Rivalry, separation)*

Projectable *intra-generationally*, in a "horizontal" chain of contemporary links; onto groups or onto structurally equivalent individuals of equal sex and/or generation

(Discontinuity)

HUSBAND-WIFE

Different sex → Alter's role unavailable; relationship cannot easily be a link in a chain of similar relationships (though can be part of a set of linked, similar contemporary relationships, as in polygyny) → *(Discontinuity)*; *(Exclusiveness)*

Different sex; Sexuality an integral part of relationship → Differential roles → *(Exclusiveness* as privacy*)*

Sexuality an integral part of relationship → Reproductive sexuality → *(Exclusiveness* as privacy*)*; *(Freedom*, with much role-playing in private*)*; *(Emotional sexuality)*

Affinal ("achieved") → *(Freedom*—potentially breakable*)*

Affinal ("achieved") → Inception of relationship not necessarily linked to existing relationships; need not be durable → *(Discontinuity)*

Not projectable *inter-generationally*

(Discontinuity)

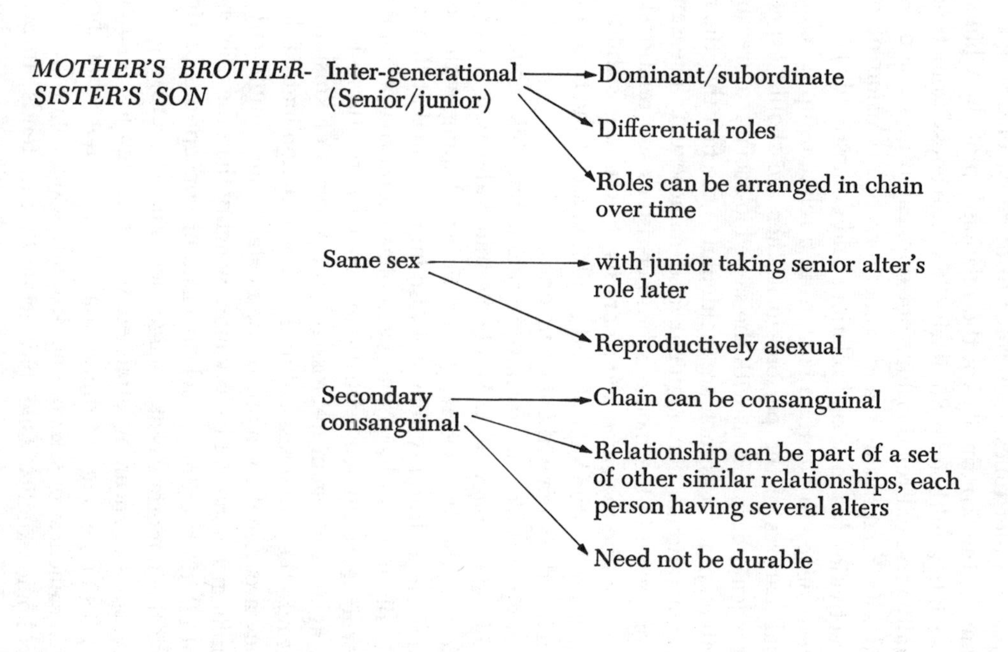
MOTHER'S BROTHER-
SISTER'S SON
Inter-generational
(Senior/junior)
Dominant/subordinate
Differential roles
Roles can be arranged in chain over time
Same sex
with junior taking senior alter's role later
Reproductively asexual
Secondary consanguinal
Chain can be consanguinal
Relationship can be part of a set of other similar relationships, each person having several alters
Need not be durable

the diagram. This is necessary because Hsu's attributes combine phenomena which, in terms of this analysis, are of different orders. "Continuity" and "Discontinuity" are particularly striking in this respect. Sometimes they refer to *structural continuity* between a series of relationships over time (such as the continuing, chain-like duplication of father/son-father/son links); at other times, they refer to *duration* of a single relationship (for example, the "continuity" of the relationship of the Chinese son with the father into adulthood). Similarly, "Exclusiveness" sometimes refers to structurally terminal relationships not duplicated in a chain (such as the husband-wife relationship) and sometimes to exclusion of others from private activities (as in sexual relations and domestic life).

If the tendency to a certain content in a relationship is relatable to the bio-social features of the persons in it, then we should expect a similar content when other persons with the same bio-social features are involved. Thus, father and son as such are incidental to the fact that the relationship is inter-generational, consanguinal, and monosexual. The same features appear of course in the mother's brother-sister's son relationship; its content, then, can be the same and so are its structural possibilities. It is thus not surprising that the Suku should exhibit many of the traits of the father-son dominated system without being one.

We may now ask the crucial question about this model: What is the degree of determinacy in it? While, as stated above, it is well-nigh inconceivable that the "bio-social" givens we are dealing with will be totally ignored in any cultural system, it is also improbable that they alone will be symbolically used; rather, other symbolic criteria that are not biologically given will be combined with them. To be sure, these biological traits appear again and again in cross-cultural surveys of kinship systems. But just because they are cross-cultural common denominators does not mean that they are somehow more fundamental to any single cultural system. Their influence need not be any more weighty than the influence of purely cultural arbitrary criteria, such as caste or conceptions of rights in marriage or the importance of lineage ties. Furthermore, they provide categories, but the meaning attached to the categories is another matter. Differences of sex suggest differential roles, but not what these roles will be. Even sameness of sex does not exclude sexuality in the relationship, as witness homosexuality. One may argue that it "tends" to exclude it, but one may also argue (as some homosexuals indeed have done) that the tendency is systemic only in certain sociological configurations (e.g., when the socioeconomic system requires the nuclear family to be the primary socializing institution, binding sexuality to reproduction). Such configurations dominate our cross-cultural samples, which are biased toward small-scale societies and ignore the culture-historical emergence of recent "modern" configurations favoring the increasing autonomy of sexuality and its functional separation from reproduction and socialization.

The biological fact of inter-generational differences may similarly lead to indeterminate results. It is highly probable that in institutionally simple societies with a relatively limited range of criteria for role differentiation, inter-generational age-seniority leads to a dominant/subordinate relationship. But what this string of derivations assumes is that the older man knows something that the younger man has to know before he can play the older man's role and that this is indeed the role that he will have to play. This need not be the case in complex industrial societies. (I don't mean that this cannot be the case—hereditary occupations need not be incompatible, theoretically, with industrialization; in fact, one can argue that they are quite compatible with the later stages of automation.) The multiplicity of roles in an industrial society and a rapid change in required roles may create a generational lag in knowledge that will weaken inter-generational authority.

The same factors may also minimize the importance of sexual differences. The culture of a complex society need take less notice of age and sex in its allocation of roles. This in turn makes the possible content of relationships involving sex or age differences more open to variation. This would account for the "modern" Western family organization (or at least for its sociological stereotype). What we seem to find is neglect of generational and sexual differences, weakness of inter-generational authority, and relative equality of married partners. Hsu sees these features not as flowing together out of the larger social and economic organization, but rather as the result of the dominance of the husband-wife relationship. His argument is convincing on the level of personality dynamics and personality formation, but not on the historical-sociological level. For example, Hsu sees the mother, in the husband-wife dominated system, as becoming analogous to an "older wife." From the point of view of this paper, one would merely say that both wife and mother in Western societies are treated as belonging to the category of "close women relatives"—a category with rather smudged criteria, given the increasing proliferation of other criteria for roles. From this perspective, the conflict between these two relatives in modern Western societies flows out of the indefiniteness of their jural roles vis-à-vis the husband-son—this in contrast to other societies (such as peasant Eastern European and Mediterranean) where the same conflict arises because the roles are jurally well defined but mutually unadjusted.

We should expect, then, the influence of bio-social features to be greatest in societies where other criteria interfere least with them in role allocation. In such societies, the possible "inherent" content of these relationships would provide some of the bearings around which kinship relationships may be mapped out—but even here one should expect to find other bearings, equally crucial to each specific system, that are purely cultural and arbitrary. Such societies are most likely to have relatively simple institutional structures or, at least, relatively autonomous kinship institutions (as in the great non-industrial "civilizations"). The import of

Hsu's theory is thus not universal, and its applicability depends on variables that should be possible to isolate. The contribution of the theory is precisely in that its explicitness makes it testable in a way that allows other variables to emerge, for the central problem here hinges on traditional anthropological concerns: How far can culture transcend biology? Is cultural cognition entirely arbitrary, or are there universal cultural tendencies related to certain objective features in the world that no cognitive system can ignore? We have, for example, always found it easy to accept the idea that sex and generation (or age) should always be culturally "noticed," but we hesitate to go much beyond this. Hsu's theory demands, for its verification, a comparative social psychology of kinship behavior in the same way that the newer "componential" methods of analyzing kinship terminologies demand a comparative psychology of cognition (cf. Wallace, 1965). It is in the eventual linkage between the two that the old problem of the relationship between kinship terminology and kinship behavior may begin to be resolved.

One final query: Are there cultural systems that demand greater integration among relationships, and others that minimize the need for consistency? And even when there is a consistency in the structure, how does it affect the actors in it? As a system, Suku kinship structure is rigidly integrated, but the people occupying the various slots in it can be shifted around. For example, a person can shift from the slot of patrilateral cross-cousin (with whom one jokes, and whom, if female, one can marry) to the slot of "father" or "father's sister" (whereupon one stops joking and starts respecting and marriage becomes forbidden). Such shifts reverberate throughout the system. Whole groups of relatives get reclassified terminologically and behavior toward them shifts accordingly, but the system itself remains rigidly consistent. It would seem that the culture here allows a kind of discontinuity of roles in specific persons that another culture would not (for example, from sexual joking to avoidance or *vice versa*). Do relationships in such systems influence each other in the same way as in systems emphasizing a different kind of integration? What happens in systems where relationships are essentially dyadic and treated atomistically? The questions concern something anthropologists have yet to tackle, namely the effect of the cultural conceptions of how it should work on the way an existing system works—in short, the influence of a people's own ethno-sociology on their "objective" sociology.

FIVE

FREDRIK BARTH

Role Dilemmas and Father-Son Dominance in Middle Eastern Kinship Systems

This paper attempts to show the way in which behavioral characteristics in one kinship relationship are in part constrained and determined by the existence of another, dominant kinship relationship. It seeks to explore the mechanism whereby this dominance is effected, through an analysis of role dilemmas. The main factors that are given explanatory precedence are the general values prevalent in the population concerned and the external circumstances that shape the situations in which kinship behavior takes place. In the latter part of the paper I illustrate and to some extent try to test my assertions with data from my own field work among Pathans—an agricultural people with a patrilineal and patriarchal family system—and from the literature on Cyrenaica Bedouins.

The paper thus takes up for discussion one of the many problems that arise from Hsu's stimulating development of the concept of a dominant kinship relationship. There can be no denying that this concept enables us to bring out certain regular patterns in the empirical material, and thus has great descriptive utility. But the concept of dominance entails no analytical framework for understanding and explaining these patterns. It would obviously be unsatisfactory to interpret dominance literally—that is, to give concrete behavior in one institutionalized relationship causal priority over concrete behavior in another such relationship. Hsu himself looks for sources of dominance variously in the value emphases of each culture, in the requirements for maintenance of the social and cultural system, and especially in the developmental history of socialization that is common to the members of the society. I shall take a more limited and synchronic view, and concentrate on the question of the possible interactional mechanisms whereby characteristics of one social relationship can determine behavior in another social relationship. Since we are dealing with social behavior in stable institutionalized relationships, it further seems legitimate to require any explanation to be consistent with a general theory of social behavior, in this case the analysis of roles. The mechanisms we look for should thus be found among the general mechanisms of role formation.

Once this synchronic and structural framework is adopted, rather than the developmental one, there is no a priori basis for restricting the analysis to the kinship domain, and I shall need to consider the connections between kinship and extra-kinship behavior. More concretely, I shall try to show how general values regarding descent, masculinity, and sexuality are made relevant to the behavior of males in a variety of situations in Middle Eastern societies. Furthermore, I shall argue that these values are such as to give a prominence to the father-son relationship that may legitimately be characterized as dominance, while other relationships, such as that between husband and wife, become recessive so that behavior in them is strongly modified and in part suppressed. I find the mechanisms effecting this in the process whereby actors are led to select predominantly only a small range of behavioral elements within their present repertoire when shaping a social role.

To argue that behavior in a relationship is being modified or suppressed, one needs some canon by which to characterize its *un*modified form and judge that some distortion has taken place. Hsu's development of the concept of "intrinsic attributes" of relationships, most simply exemplified in the employer-employee relationship (Hsu, 1965: 640), serves him in this necessary purpose: "The intrinsic attributes of each relationship," he writes, "are the basic ingredients and determinants of the interactional patterns between parties to that relationship." As I understand them, then, these "intrinsic attributes" are the basic specifications of the relationship which no party to that relationship can deny in his behavior without repudiating the relationship as a whole; that is, they are the minimum specifications of the *statuses* involved in the relationship. Hsu's view of dominant kinship relationships depends on the view that some of these attributes are naturally determined, and thereby provide a primitive, cross-cultural canon for judging the extent of modification of behavior in kinship relationships.

However, the connection between such minimum specifications of statuses in dyads or larger sets, and empirical behavior, is more complex than this model indicates. Not only is actual behavior a great deal richer and more varied than these minimum specifications; the standardized institutionalized behavior that emerges in the roles that an observer may record reflects these specifications only partially and imperfectly because, though it is constrained by them, it is simultaneously constrained and formed by other determinants. The following analysis depends on the recognition that a role is also constrained by the setting where behavior takes place: Some forms of behavior require physical props, others become necessary only as a response to characteristics or changes in the environment, including the presence of other persons. In other words, regularities of behavior—in the present case, kinship roles—can be understood in part from the constraints that status specification impose, in part from external or "ecological" constraints in the contexts where the behavior takes place and the role thus has to be consummated.

This view of the complex transformation from status to role derives mainly from Goffman (1959), and I have made use of it elsewhere (Barth, 1966). I wish to show here how some features of the phenomenon that Hsu describes as "dominance" between kinship relations may be understood by means of it. Most important, it implies that when seeking to understand how behavior in one relationship affects or is affected by the actor's relationships to third parties, we need to separate two different levels on which the interconnections may be found: the level of statuses, as a distribution of rights and resources on social positions, and the level of actual behavior in role play.

One type of consistency and interdependence between the forms of behavior in different kinship relations is clear: Where exclusive rights, *jus in rem* (Radcliffe-Brown, 1952) are vested in the encumbents of kinship statuses, behavior relative to these rights becomes systematized throughout the kinship system. Indeed, it follows from the very definition of such rights that they affect the behavior of third parties: They are rights as against the world to certain services from certain persons. Some of the features of "dominance" referred to by Hsu might therefore be interpreted as the expression of such rights.

Most kinship behavior, however, derives from *in personam* rights which do not entail the same degree of systematization on the level of statuses. However, I shall argue that the domestic setting in which these rights are consummated is one that produces some degree of consistency in role playing, even where *in personam* rights are involved. This follows from the intimacy and comprehensiveness of interaction within households: Alter in one relationship is audience and spectator to ego's interaction with others in other relationships. In shaping one's behavior towards one alter, one is constrained by the need to avoid repudiating that which is important in one's relationship to another, who is present though the relationship may be latent at the moment. Especially when several kinsfolk are interacting simultaneously, each person involved needs to find a pattern of behavior, and an adjustment of the various kinship roles that allows them to be pursued simultaneously.

This I feel is the main sense in which certain kin relations can become "dominant": They are important and clear enough to take precedence over other relations and to block the use of certain idioms and the expression of certain qualities in those relations which would challenge or repudiate the "intrinsic attributes," or status-defining characteristics, of the "dominant" relationship. I would argue that persons, in shaping their kinship roles, in many kinship systems do act in terms of some such priorities and avoid the behavioral forms and the embarrassing situations in which key relationships and obligations might seem to be challenged or repudiated, and that the patterning of behavior that Hsu notes and describes in terms of dominance and recessivity is generated by this fact.

One advantage of this view is that it distinguishes "strata" of determinants of behavior, and enables us to identify functional equivalents in related systems of kinship behavior. To illustrate the whole argument, including this last feature, let me discuss some material on the father-son relationship, and other kinship behavior, among tribal peoples in the Middle East.

If the criteria were clarified, I believe one could make a very good case for the father-son relationship as the dominant relationship in most Middle Eastern kinship systems. Especially in tribal areas, where political life is structured by patrilineal descent groups and productive resources are held collectively by patrilineal groups, the importance of the father-son relationship is overwhelming; and throughout the area the family system can be characterized as patrilocal and patriarchal. The attributes which Hsu lists as intrinsic to this relationship are descriptive of its form in these Middle Eastern societies. The attributes of continuity, inclusiveness, authority, and asexuality have institutional correlates in patrilineality, joint property and responsibility, paternal authority, and incest taboos embracing the spouses of close agnates. They are furthermore continually expressed and confirmed in etiquette summarized under the heading of respect behavior by the son towards the father.

This behavior is somewhat at variance with the general ideals of male behavior. Masculinity and virility are very highly valued, and are recognized and asserted in behavior that exhibits independence, aggressive courage, dominance, and the repudiation of superordinate authority in others. But in the case of father and son, this repudiation is not necessary—as agnates their masculinity and virility, their honor, is joint. The honor of the father is transmitted to the son, and the son's feats of courage and strength sustain the honor of the father, of the joint patriline.

The husband-wife relationship, on the other hand, has attributes that are discordant with those of the father-son relationship. Not only is it characterized by discontinuity and exclusiveness, creating a small realm into which a father's rights and authority do not reach; the Middle Eastern view of what is intrinsic in the relationship goes further, and particularly emphasizes sexuality in the form of male aggressiveness, dominance, enjoyment, and privilege. The husband's honor also demands that he should fully monopolize the woman; no one else should be allowed a share of the pleasures she gives by seeing her beauty or interacting with her as a woman. This aggressive monopolization of male rights over a woman is a virtue in a man; it epitomizes masculine dominance and autonomy, and no husband should repudiate it in his behavior towards his wife. Yet such behavior in its very essence is a repudiation of the virtues of obedience, discipline, and respect that are demanded from a son in the father-son relationship, and it goes against the sharing of honor, and particularly of the masculinitiy and aggressiveness that characterize their relationship. The "intrinsic attributes" of these two relations, in the form which they will take within a general Middle Eastern value system, are thus highly incompatible, and provide a convenient case for the analysis of dominance between kinship relations.

The incompatibility poses behavioral dilemmas in all Middle Eastern societies. Indeed, the highly unequal and complementary view of what is intrinsically male, or virile, and female, or feminine, makes for difficulties in all public interaction between male and female. There is hardly any adequate way of shaping roles so that they allow diversified interaction between a man and a woman without highly compromising the public image of both. This impasse has been created, or is resolved, by the seclusion of women: the systematic separation of two spheres of activity—one where men interact with each other and observe each other, in public; and the other the private sphere were interaction in the husband-wife relationship is consummated, and a role can be constructed between the two which may be at variance with the public image of themselves that they each individually wish to project. But to the extent that the "continuity" of the father-son relationship is realized, fathers and sons will be found inside the same compound walls, as potential observers of each others' interactions across the sex boundary. Thus the dilemma of the kinship roles remains.

Two forms of solution may be compared: that of sedentary, village dwelling Swat Pathans (Barth, 1959) and that of nomadic, tent dwelling Cyrenaica Bedouin (Peters, 1965).

The Swat Pathan solution depends in part on the men's house—an institution with a number of political and economic functions. Almost all men spend most of their free time in the men's house, and the man who spends much time at home is ridiculed. The institution thus provides a way of affirming publicly the priority of male life and one's relations to men over one's relations to women, no matter what the emotional realities may be. In some areas of Swat, all men sleep in the men's house; and in all of Swat, young unmarried men sleep in the men's house.

As marriage approaches, the prospective groom tries to avoid situations or behavior that confirm the impending event, but his juniors and equals try to discomfit him and he rarely avoids giving expression to his embarrassment. The father plays the active role and represents the groom in the preliminary negotiations and the legal marriage ceremony. When the marriage takes place, the groom plays no part in it at all and runs away and hides for days on end during the celebration, while heartless friends spend quite a bit of time looking for him. Consummation takes place in great secrecy, aided by female agnates. As soon as possible, the new couple establish an independent household, within the walls of which they can have privacy. Until such time, the son-and-husband spends an emphatically great deal of his time away from the home, and the newly wed spouses do not speak to each other and have no interaction when others are present. They especially avoid being simultaneously in the presence of his father (her father-in-law). In the powerful landowning families, where patrilineal extended households are the rule, rooms are allocated to the new couple into which the father would never conceive of entering, and the husband-wife relationship is in relative latency outside of these rooms, when others are present.

The later phases of a man's life cycle give an opportunity to judge relative dominance of kinship relations more concretely than by the canon of intrinsic attributes. Especially in patrilineal extended families, it is instructive to compare behavior in the husband-wife relationship where the husband is senior male in his line and has no relationship to a living father, with that of husbands who are simultaneously involved as sons in a father-son relationship. The absence of the superordinate party in the father-son relationship gives opportunity for more assertive and more public behavior in the husband-wife relationship.[1]

One major difference is a freer dominance in the senior male's behavior, contrasted with the junior male's reluctance to assert authority over his wife in front of his father. A senior male will occasionally engage in loud, demonstrative assertion of such authority, both in the presence of kinsmen and within earshot of others. He also more freely interacts with his wife as an object of sexuality and affection. Senior males are far more indulgent in pampering a young attractive wife, in favoring her and protecting her as against other women in the household, while a junior undercommunicates his interest in his wife as a sexual object and supports general household views of "fairness" that are usually discriminatory against a young wife.

Finally, the senior male is freer to enjoy his wife at will. Though all areas of the house are open to a son, it is his responsibility not to disturb the father, and unmarried sons sleep in the men's house to avoid the shame of witnessing the intimate life of the parents. Where a married son

1. Inevitably, there are other variables that may be responsible for some of the contrasts. The husband's physiological age differs in the two situations; but I assume the "social age" of seniority to be the more significant variable. The wife's age need not differ, as the husband's behavior is frequently directed at younger, sexually more attractive later wives as well as at an original first wife. The existence of sons should have little effect in suppressing most aspects of the husband-wife relationship, since there is a harmonious authority regime of father and husband over both son and wife.

lives in the extended household of his father, the young couple are reserved private space, as noted above; but the son cannot withdraw at will to his wife, and his obligations to give his time to his father always prevail over his obligations or enjoyment in the husband-wife relationship.

The same privilege of the superordinate male, to enjoy sex himself but monopolize the subordinate males' time and the time available to them for cross-sex interaction, is seen in public life. In areas of Swat where all men sleep in the men's house, only the chief goes publicly to enjoy his wife, while other married men wait and slip off discreetly to visit their wives unnoticed, after the chief has left and the men's house has quieted down for the night.

Compare this to the situation in an entirely different technical-ecological regime, among the Bedouin pastoral nomads of Cyrenaica. Without the paraphernalia of houses and compound walls, and engaged in tasks that require women to move in public among the men, the Bedouin cannot achieve the same degree of privacy and segregation as the Swat Pathans. Peters (1965) gives a detailed and intriguing account of father-son and husband-wife roles in this system, and of their expression at ceremonial occasions. The pattern can be summarized as one of ritualized avoidance and fiction. At the wedding the groom tries to escape but is "caught" by the young men and brought to the nuptial tent, whereas his father is completely inactive and feigns ignorance of the whole affair. Having established his own tent, adjoining that of his father, the son continues to play-act the role of an unmarried boy, returning to his father's tent in the morning to "wake up" in his usual place there, eating with his father out of his father's bowl, etc. In the presence of the father, no statement or action is made that would force him to acknowledge the change in the son's position.

In other words, in the Bedouin setting where husband-wife interaction cannot be as effectively contained within a secluded, private sphere, the role dilemma is resolved by the relative latency of the husband-wife relationship, and by symbolic behavior which confirms the father-son relationship. The fictions and stereotypes of Bedouin kinship behavior provide a shelter for discrepant roles that is functionally equivalent to the compound walls of the Swat Pathans. But they do not have precisely the same effects. The complete dichotomization of secluded private life and public life that is possible in the village protects the senior male very adequately and allows him to play his different roles at the appropriate occasions; the dilemmas are concentrated in the son-and-husband combination. In the Bedouin ecology, on the other hand, the father-son dominant relationship needs to be protected by special behavior on the part both of father and son. There is no way for the senior party to prevent the intrusion of information that is discrepant with his own pose and interests; as a result he must develop a role solution that actively both over and undercommunicates aspects of the situation and asserts the dominance of the father-son relationship.

My point of view could be summarized as follows: I believe that the empirical substance of Hsu's thesis of dominance in some kinship systems is valid and can be demonstrated. But I think that the pattern he has observed does not need to be cast in the descriptive and analytical mold that he has chosen. For the kind of data I have at my disposal, an explanatory model based on role theory appears to be both adequate and economical. It starts with the view that the distribution of rights on different statuses is never entirely integrated and harmonious. Where status sets and relevant social situations are clearly differentiated, this disharmony matters little to the actors, who can then pursue discrepant roles and project variant social personalities in different social situations. Routinized social life will in part be shaped by these considerations: Persons will seek the situations where successful role play can be consummated and avoid the situations where serious dilemmas keep arising—to the extent of grooms in Swat avoiding their own weddings. In general, difficulties can be resolved by avoiding simultaneous encounters with the parties toward whom one has discrepant relations—by patterns such as the seclusion of women, for example.

Where, as in the domestic unit, practically all role playing in one relationship takes place with the parties to other relationships present, problems arise for the actor in composing his behavior, his role, in such a way that activity in one relationship does not repudiate obligations or qualities important in the relationship to the others who are present. Here, one relationship may emerge as dominant over others; it takes precedence and is relatively little modified, whereas other relationships become latent and/or behavior in them is strongly modified, because tactical considerations of possible gains and losses are such as to make one relationship by far the most critical. In these cases it becomes important for the actor in shaping his role to avoid all idioms that are discrepant with his obligations in the dominant relationship. Thus, substantial sectors of the interaction appropriate between parties in non-dominant relationships may become suppressed, as between husband and wife in the presence of husband's father in Middle Eastern society. I would suggest that behavioral solutions to such dilemmas may go to the extent of imposing latency on the whole relationship—so that formal avoidance behavior may be analyzed from this perspective.

Which dilemmas will arise will depend not only on where the main discrepancies of status obligations occur, but also on the structure of co-resident groups, and the other institutional forms that channelize and segment social life. Which solutions will be adopted, furthermore, depend on the "ecology" of the behavior in question: the setting, the technology, and the tasks required.

The perspective provided by Hsu, in conjunction with such a view of how role-patterned behavior is generated, thus seems to bear promise of refinement in our analysis of kinship behavior. It allows us to relate more closely the different patterns of behavior between descriptively separable but functionally connected kinship dyads, especially within domestic units and other high-commitment living units, and may also give an improved perspective on such institutionalized forms of behavior as avoidance and joking relationships.

Some Implications of Dominant Kinship Relationships in Fiji and Rotuma

The purpose of this paper is to explore the implications of "dominant kinship relations" as defined by Professor Hsu (1965:640), in the two Oceanic societies of Fiji and Rotuma. Before getting into the ethnographic material, however, I would like to consider briefly some of the difficulties inherent in Hsu's framework.

Perhaps the most fundamental problem in operationalizing Hsu's scheme lies in the very concept of "dominant kinship relationship." Is there an unequivocal way of defining dominance so that it satisfies the demands placed upon it by the scope of Hsu's hypothesis? Even a precursory examination of the papers contained in this symposium should convince the reader that the answer is no. Dominance cannot be determined in the abstract, but only in relation to well-defined contexts and specific hypothetical variables. Thc difficulty in applying Hsu's concept is that it fails to take into account some important analytical distinctions. For example, a fundamental distinction can be made between defining a dominant relationship on the basis of importance for the social system and defining it on the basis of importance for the psycho-social development of individuals growing up within the society. If one takes the systemic view, stress is likely to be laid upon such matters as the control and transmission of property, integration of the domestic group and larger social units, marriage and residence choices, and the like. From this vantage point the possibility must be allowed that a triadic or even larger set of relationships can more appropriately be selected as the unit of analysis than any of the dyadic sets that compose it. In this regard Lévi-Strauss's argument for the inclusion of a pair of spouses, their children, and the wife's brother in the fundamental kinship set for most societies certainly cannot be summarily dismissed. If one takes the developmental approach, stress is more likely to be laid on such matters as the importance of particular classes of people as role models, as dispensers of reward and punishment, and as objects of hostility or affection. This point of view involves complications also. For example, developing children engage in a sequence of relationships, and the one that is dominant at one stage in development may not be at a later stage. Thus, during infancy the mother is apt to be most important in any society, but as the child matures, his father, siblings, and perhaps others may become more central to his development. Furthermore, males may go through a different sequence than females. At a particular point a boy's mother's brother may provide his most important role model, while his sister may look to her mother. We must also acknowledge the possibility that non-kin may assume socialization roles of primary significance, as peers or nursemaids do in some societies. Another problem, one that is relevant to either view, has to do with the dimensions of interpersonal relations. For example, if we take the systemic view, do we rely solely on formal qualities of interaction or do we take into account informal, or sub-institutional, qualities? Or, if we take the developmental approach, do we concentrate on cognitive or affective learning? It is quite possible that the most important person for shaping cognition is not the same person that is most important for shaping emotion.

While it is conceivable that in a given society the strength of one dyadic bond is so great that it is dominant no matter how one approaches the problem, as may be the case for China where Hsu makes a strong case for father-son dominance, a review of the ethnographic literature suggests that this is rare. Furthermore, there are good logical and empirical reasons to assume that, with the possible exception of the father-son bond, a single dominant relationship is highly unlikely, if not impossible, in the sense that Hsu uses it (cf. Marion Levy's paper in this volume). Comparable difficulties could be detailed for Hsu's concept of "intrinsic attribute," but since it is not germane to my analysis of the ethnographic data, I will not discuss them here.

Even though the grandiosity of Hsu's scheme may render it impracticable, the central idea underlying it—that the strength of particular kinship ties within the domestic group exerts pressure toward certain cultural possibilities and places constraint on others—is credible and deserves attention. In my opinion the best way to explore this proposition is to look for specific correspondences between kinship relations and cultural patterns or institutions. Where correlations are found, the mechanisms that produce them must then be designated if we are to develop any measure of theoretical sophistication. The lack of postulated mechanisms constitutes one of the most serious weaknesses in Hsu's original formulation.

In the analysis that follows I take the developmental view. Within this framework I explicitly consider only the cognitive development of males. My thesis can be summarized as follows: In Fiji a boy's father is his chief socializer and provides him with his most significant role model, while in Rotuma, primary-group relations are more diffuse, with peers playing a much greater part in the socialization process. These differences produce different cognitive styles that are in turn reflected in social organization and in political behavior.

The Fiji Islands consist of approximately 300 islands in the southern Pacific Ocean, of which about 100 are inhabited. In 1874 the group was ceded to Great Britain and has been administered as a colony since then. The island of Rotuma lies some 300 miles north of Fiji and is not considered part of the group. Nevertheless, it was included in the colony in 1881 and has been politically and economically integrated with Fiji since then. Racially, linguistically, and culturally the Rotumans are distinct, having more in common with such Western Polynesian peoples as the Samoans, Tongans, and Futunans than with the more Melanesian Fijians.

For data on Fiji I shall rely mainly on Marshall Sahlins' excellent ethnography of Moala, an island in the Fiji archipelago with a population of slightly more than one thousand. Sahlins offers the following general description of social relations within the Moalan family:

> The distinctive characteristic of the Moalan family is its organization by seniority. This organization functions, as shall be seen, to effect a co-operative domestic economy. But the rigor and principles of family ranking transcend the requirements of domestic co-operation, and they reflect more than adaptation to nature. In its system of internal ranking, the family is the microcosm of larger kin groups and communities. The principles of rank within the family, and even of the terminology of rank, are identical to those which politically organize higher levels of social integration. Thus the family seniority system at once reflects the larger organization of society and supplies, in the activities of daily life, a set of principles of social behavior consistent with effective political action at higher levels.
>
> Thus "every man is chief in his own house," Moalans say. The head of each dwelling unit—be it only an element in an extended family, the leading house of such a family, or an independent house—is its *turaga*, "chief." His wife is the *marama*, the "lady" of the house. These are polite terms of reference for married men and women so long as the reference is to their position in the home. Yet they are the very terms applied to people of high status in supradomestic groups: in large kin groups, villages, or in the island as a whole.
>
> The children of the house are, of course, subordinate to their parents, but they are also ranked relative to each other by birth order. In aboriginal polygymous families children were first ranked by order of marriage of their

> mothers, and then, between full siblings, by birth order. The first child of the family has a special status and title of reference, *ulumatua*, and the oldest male child is the successor of the father. An older brother is politely and euphemistically the "chief" (*turaga*), relative to a younger brother, while the latter is "common," "of low rank," *kaisi* relative to his older siblings. The term *kaisi* also has the more general denotation of "peer (or group) of low status" in a local kin group, village, or island. (Daughters enter the rank hierarchy in the same way as sons and are treated respectfully by both younger brothers and sisters, but normally a girl marries out, and she does not succeed to the headship of the family.) [1962:105–106]

It is evident that within this context a boy's father is his main socializer and primary role model:

> Obedience and respect are demanded of the child by the father. After infancy the child is constantly taking orders, doing tasks delegated by his parents, from whose command there is no recourse save fleeing from the house.
>
> Punishment by the father is the outstanding disciplinary mechanism in the family. The father's anger is proverbial; younger children he whips, older children he lectures harshly (*vunauci*). The child should accept either punishment stoically.
>
> A boy of sufficient strength is enlisted by his father to work in the family gardens, and receives his life training here. [1962:113]

If a boy has an older male sibling the latter may substitute for the father in teaching necessary skills, but in such cases he is quite clearly a father substitute and assumes an authoritative posture. Relations between elder and younger brothers, in other words, replicate to a marked extent the relations between father and son.

> Social relations between brothers are very much affected by seniority. The older brother is to be implicitly obeyed by the younger. The duty of the younger is to serve: "If I see my older brother pick up his knife to go to the bush," observed one man, "I follow."
>
> A definite atmosphere of reserve seems to grow between brothers after childhood. As one man put it: "The custom of brothers is mutual embarrassment." [1962:112]

All this is in marked contrast to social relations within the Rotuman family. Rank and seniority are relevant principles, but their jural force is mitigated by a strong concern for the feelings and opinions of others. According to jural rules the head man of a household is in charge of all male activity, and he has the authority to give orders to his sons and other male residents in his household; but in fact he rarely does so. Only if there is a special job to be done that he is unable to do alone will he request assistance, and even then it is apt to be done apologetically. One almost never hears commands being given.

Compared to Moala, the relationship between fathers and sons in

Rotuma is unauthoritarian and congenial. Mothers are the main disciplinarians; fathers are indulgent and discipline their children only in unusual circumstances. A young boy may learn something about farming or fishing by accompanying his father, but he is not obliged to do any serious work until he has finished school, usually at about the age of sixteen. Until that time there is little serious instruction as to adult role performance. Upon leaving school he assumes the status of "youth" (*haharagi*) and begins to hang around with the other unmarried young men in his locality. Boys generally leave their homes at this age to sleep in a young men's house, although they eat at home and contribute to their family's economy. They spend most of their time in each other's company and work together in the bush. They usually obtain a plot of land from one of the large landholders in their district and work it together, often sharing the produce communally. The younger boys learn from the older ones, and they avoid working under the direction of their fathers except under special circumstances. It is significant in this regard that in the district of Itumuta, in which I systematically collected information on farming patterns, there were no instances in which an adolescent son was working on the same land as his father. This may be interpreted as an attempt on the part of both to avoid turning their relationship into an authoritarian one. The older boys informally instruct their juniors in a wide variety of matters pertaining to adult roles, whereas their fathers rarely do. When adults do participate with such groups, they do so as quasi-elder siblings, just as elder siblings in Fiji interact with their juniors as quasi-fathers.

What are the implications of these different relational modes for socialization? In attempting to answer this question let us consider two dimensions of role models that contrast in Fiji and Rotuma. One is the specificity versus diffuseness of available role models. In Fiji a boy's father constitutes a specific focus for socialization. His elder brothers may also help "train" him, but they in turn have modeled their behavior after their father's. The relationship between a boy and his father is intense and specific, although not ordinarily affectively positive. In Rotuma, on the other hand, the socialization role of the father is minimized. A boy's role models are diffuse and include his siblings, more distant relatives, and peers. The second dimension is the extent to which the burden of education falls upon completely socialized persons versus incompletely socialized persons. The former can be considered more characteristic in Fiji, since the father of an adolescent boy is a mature adult, while the latter is more characteristic in Rotuma, where peers play an important role in the socialization process.

In this instance these two factors are mutually reinforcing and lead to different cognitive styles. The Fijian father has fully learned and used for some time the skills and techniques that he passes on to his son. As a result he can teach whole solutions to whole problems, often down to the finest details. The son is only exposed to one mode of operation, since he has restricted exposure to alternative models. He is not very likely to be able to suggest innovations that will be accepted, and the difference in status tends to make his learning role one of acquiescing imitation. Under such circumstances there is a strong tendency for learning to be a rote process. Problems are specifically defined and their solutions specifically prescribed. Where this is the dominant mode, one would expect to find a society in which the rules governing behavior are prescriptive, leaving little room for innovation or reorganization. Authority is relied upon to resolve new issues and there are massive restrictions upon the expression of individuality. The learning of behavior patterns by rote not only produces these overt patterns, but also an alloplastic cognitive mode; that is, a cognitive style resistant to reorganization when events demand that problems or their solutions be seen in a new light.[1] Such circumstances favor continuity—the direct replacement of sons in their fathers' status positions. The whole learning process is geared toward such an eventuality.

In contrast to the Fijian case, in Rotuma there is greater flexibility built into the learning situation. A developing child learns from a number of different role models, each with a somewhat different way of doing things. Problems and their solutions are less likely to be prescribed, and innovations on the part of the person being socialized are more likely to get a hearing. Since the difference in status is not great, there is likely to be a tolerance for individual variations in style, and learning is apt to involve an active exploration of possibilities, if not a competition to do things better. Under such circumstances, learning is less likely to occur by rote. Instead, the younger men learn a set of general problem-solving, or decision-making, principles, which they can apply to both recurrent and new situations. There is, in short, less prescription either with regard to the definition of problems or their solutions than where rote learning predominates. Where this is the primary socialization mode, one would expect to find a society in which the rules governing behavior were generalized and unrestrictive. Instead of authority being relied upon to solve new problems, there is a tendency to experiment, either collectively or after a thorough discussion among peers. The learning of generalized, instead of rote, problem-solving principles favors an autoplastic cognitive mode—that is, one that permits relearning or reorganization when new problems arise. It follows, also, that in such societies there is less emphasis on continuity, or the direct replacement of the socializer with the socialized. Correspondingly, and in accordance with Professor Hsu's postulation, there is more room for the expression of status competition, or rivalry.

The social and political implications of these contrasting modes of socialization are multiple. To begin with, we may have an important key

1. I have attempted to point out elsewhere the implications of this for adaptation to a developing economy. See Howard, 1966.

to a controversy that has plagued students of Polynesian social organization: whether or not most Polynesian societies are best considered as unilineal or non-unilineal in structure. Those scholars who insist on treating them as unilineal place their emphasis on ideology, which in most societies concerned has a definite patrilineal bias. Those who favor the non-unilineal interpretation generally place their emphasis on actual choices of group membership or succession patterns.

Now let us assume for a moment that the basic "plan" of Polynesian social organization, the underlying structure if you like, is patrilineal, but that in some societies for various reasons the father-son relationship comes to be emphasized (or continues to be emphasized) while in others it has been de-emphasized. What is likely to happen? First of all, we would expect a son's allegiance to his father's kin to be stronger in the former case, and for patrilocal residence choices to be made far more often than not, with the resulting effects on social structure postulated by Murdock (1949). Succession to chieftainship is likely to be governed by the principle of primogeniture, in which mature sons ordinarily replace their fathers as headmen. Where the father-son link has been de-emphasized, however, we would expect to find a weakening of all of these principles. Allegiance to the father's kin and patrilocal residence would no longer be as significant, since sons would no longer be thought of as direct replacements for their fathers. Correspondingly, there likely would be an increase in the significance of uterine links in tracing ancestry. This would not only occur because allegiance to the father's kin is lessened per se, but also because there would be a lesser emphasis on following the ideal rules; that is, there would be a greater degree of freedom in choosing either residence or successors. In short, where the father-son link is weakened, the culture may be opened up for manipulation and negotiation, with a corresponding increase in the degree to which choices contrary to ideal patterns are made.

At this point let us compare, very briefly, the character of Fijian and Rotuman social structure and the implications of our preceding speculations on the institution of chieftainship.

The Fijian social structure is basically of the ramage type, as defined by Sahlins (1958:139–51). In its ideal form it consists of a series of three agnatic descent groups. In order of their inclusiveness these are known as *vavusa, mataqali*, and *itokatoka*. The *mataqali* that compose a *vavusa* are ranked according to seniority of the founding ancestors, who are presumed to be related, usually as brothers. According to Geddes, "The *mataqali* regarded as being founded by the eldest son is the *mataqali turaga*, that is to say the chiefly *mataqali*. It provided the *vavusa chiefs*" (Geddes, 1959:206). Within this *mataqali*, as well as the others, the chiefs come from the senior line "and thus are supplied constantly from the same *itokatoka*, but there are usually otherwise no significant distinctions of rank among the component *itokatoka*" (*loc. cit.*). Within this organization, therefore, the *vavusa* chief held authority over each *vavusa* member by virtue of his real or putative kinship seniority over them.

The traditional Rotuman social structure corresponds more closely to Sahlins' descent line type (Sahlins, 1958:139–51). It was divided into seven districts which in turn were divided into kin-based units known as *ho'aga*, each of which was headed by a titled male. These titles were ranked, and indications are that district chiefs were chosen exclusively from the *ho'aga* owning the highest ranking title. Titled men from other *ho'aga* acted as sub-chiefs. They exercised primary authority over their own units, including the allocation of land and women. Choosing the successor to a title was the right of the cognatic group tracing ancestry to the *ho'aga* which possessed the name. Although kinship seniority based upon agnatic descent was ideologically significant, just as it was in Fiji, any adult male in the cognatic group was eligible to succeed to the position, and strong consideration was given to personal character and other pragmatics. The important point is that lineal linkages, based upon father-son bonds, were not given as much weight as ideology would suggest, and that lateral links, based upon sibling bonds and uterine ties, were given prominence in actual decision-making procedures.

The differential emphasis on the father-son link also affects the nature of chieftainship in the two societies. Viewed superficially, the roles of the Fijian *vavusa* chief and Rotuman district chief were nearly identical. Like his Rotuman equivalent, the *vavusa* chief orgainized activities in his locality, was arbitrator of disputes, and was ceremonially honored through precedence in *kava* drinking. He did not exercise primary allocative rights in the land—this was left to the *mataqali* chiefs—but he received a portion of the first fruits, just as the Rotuman district chief did. But despite these similarities, there were some significant contrasts. For example, the *vavusa* chief was a ritual leader by virtue of his direct descent from the deified founding ancestors. His political power was therefore backed up by supernatural sanction, while the authority of the Rotuman district chief was almost entirely secular in conception. Also, since there was closer adherence to the rule of primogeniture, the likely successors to chiefly titles were limited. As a result, the few potential titleholders were treated with considerable respect from birth, and were socialized with an eye toward the chiefly role. From childhood they were trained toward superordination, and their peers learned to be subordinate to their wishes. The Rotuman pattern of succession, as we have pointed out, was much more fluid. The contenders for a title were often numerous, with any ancestral link to a previous chief making a man eligible for consideration. Consequently the number of male children who might eventually succeed to chieftainship was at any one time extensive, and no one was apt to receive the special privileges normally given the Fijian chiefs' elder sons.

These two differences lent to the character of chieftainship in Fiji and Rotuma a distinctly different flavor. Ideologically, both leaders held similar kind of authority, but while the Fijian chief exercised a genuine dominance, in the psychological sense, over his subjects, the Rotuman chief did not. To put this another way, in Fiji the powers of the office were conceived as being embodied in the proper individual. They were personalized. In Rotuma, the powers belonged to the office alone.

As a result of these differences in culture "content," the nature of political behavior in Fiji and Rotuma displays some definite differences in style. In Fiji, group decision-making places a greater emphasis on chiefly opinion, and the weight of customary rules and ritual is heavy. The chiefs tend to be political leaders in a very real sense. Their opinions are sought after and are usually offered freely, and they carry considerable authority by virtue of the fact that they are chiefly opinions. Only when chiefs clearly violate customary rules or act flagrantly in their own interests are they likely to be taken to task. Essentially then, Fijian society is "apolitical" in the sense that there is a tendency for individuals to rely on established authority for taking care of their interests. The game of culture is played according to traditional rules, and people are required to swallow most of their grievances rather than to press for their interests against the "system." This does not mean, of course, that chiefs do not play politics among themselves, or strive for power and influence. They most certainly do, but this kind of activity primarily involves the chiefs and excludes non-chiefs. In Rotuma the situation is quite different—nearly everyone is an amateur politician. Chiefs in Rotuma cannot readily inflict their will on their subjects. Instead of acting as authorities, and offering their opinions as to courses of action, they tend to stay out of discussions until a consensus has been reached. At district meetings their role is to sum up arguments and put into action decisions arrived at by others. It is not that they do not have a right to express their views; they do have such a right, and some chiefs make use of it. But they are risking insubordination, for Rotumans do not hesitate to resist demands they consider unfair, particularly if they sense that public opinion is on their side. In contrast to Fiji, Rotumans express rather than swallow their grievances. They argue their cases in public as well as in private in an attempt to gain support for collective actions that are to their advantage. In short, Rotuma is a political society to a much greater extent than Fiji.

To summarize: It is not difficult to conceive of both Fijian and Rotuman societies as constituting variations on a single structural plan, one in which the father-son link was emphasized, the other in which it was de-emphasized. In Fiji, father-son dominance can be hypothesized to have led to continuity in social units (Sahlins' "ramages"), reliance upon authority in decision-making, and a generally apolitical society. In Rotuma, a de-emphasized father-son relationship can hypothesized to have led to discontinuity in social units (Sahlins' "descent-lines"), rivalry for power and influence, and a generally political social orientation. The difference, if our presumptions are correct, is the cumulative result of day-to-day decisions rather than of fundamental differences in structural plans.

In general, I regard the evidence from these two societies as favorable to Professor Hsu's hypothesis. It should be emphasized, however, that the differences described in this paper are better thought of as differences in degree rather than kind. Within Fiji, in particular, there are variations by regions and no doubt even between adjacent villages in the extent to which the generalizations made in this paper apply. Finer tests of the covariances suggested by Professor Hsu and this study can only be properly done on the basis of well-planned field investigation.

Components of Relationships in the Family: A Mexican Village

It is our purpose in this paper to apply Hsu's general hypothesis to materials from a rural Mexican village[1] in order to both evaluate the framework of analysis upon which the hypothesis rests and to organize our Mexican data from this point of view.

In 1965, Hsu stated the proposition thusly:

> . . . the dominant attributes of the dominant relationship in a given kinship system tend to determine the attitudes and action patterns which the individual in such a system develops towards other relationships in this system as well as towards his relationships outside of the system. [1965:641]

It is apparent both from this statement and from the analysis presented in Hsu's empirical works, that an analytic framework of considerable complexity is involved. From the point of view of our own work, there are at least eight propositions found in or deduced from Hsu's work which are

1. The field work in Mexico that supplied the data for this paper was generously supported by NSF, Grant GS-87 to my wife and myself, and for which we wish to express our gratitude. I also wish to thank Francis Hsu and the Wenner-Gren Foundation for the opportunity to present and discuss this paper at Burg Wartenstein. Lilo Stern read an earlier version of the paper, and I have profited greatly from her comments. I wish especially to thank my wife, Eva Hunt, for her extensive editorial labors, and for the many hours of discussion we have had concerning the material presented here.

important for a consideration of the usefulness of his hypothesis. These eight propositions may be briefly stated as follows:

1. Relationships (by which he means primarily dyadic relationships) can be seen as composed of components, such as authority. Hsu calls these "attributes."

2. These components are defined in such a way as to be universal.

3. These attributes are given specific definitions (cf. Hsu, 1965:642, for brief definitions of his ten attributes).

4. Kinship relationships can be defined in universal terms using English role-names (for example, father-son, husband-wife), and the attributes of these relationships occur universally (*op. cit.*, p. 640).

5. In any kinship system, one relationship is dominant over all the others, and the attributes of that relationship dominate the attributes of the other relationships (*op. cit.*, pp. 640–41).

6. The dominant relationship determines the structure and content of all other relationships in the same system (the kinship system) (*op. cit.*, p. 640).

7. The dominant relationship determines the structure and content of many relationships outside the kinship group (*op. cit.*, p. 641).

8. Four different models of kinship and extra-kinship dominance have to date been postulated: the father-son, husband-wife, mother-son, and brother-brother. Hsu has intimated that these are universal models, in the sense that if any cultures are father-son dominated, then all such cultures are similar because the father-son dominance model is meant to be a universal model, not specific to particular societies.

In this paper we will discuss propositions 3 through 8. We agree with propositions 1 and 2, but since they are not crucial to the level of argument attempted here, they are being developed elsewhere (Hunt, 1967b). In general, we disagree with proposition 5, revise propositions 3 and 4, and reformulate the matter of the extension of components outside the kinship group (propositions 6–8) so that it is not dependent upon the assumption of dominance.

The Attributes in Hsu's Models

In the summary chart in Chapter 1 of this book, Hsu presents ten attributes, which he defines in the surrounding text. They are continuity, discontinuity, inclusiveness-exclusiveness, authority, freedom, equality, rivalry, sexuality-asexuality, libidinality, dependence, and diffuseness. Another variable which is not included there, but which receives some prominence in his analysis of the structure (content, in Hsu's terms) of the marital relationship in different cultures is intimacy.

Inclusiveness-exclusiveness is defined in terms of structural combinations of role properties. Fa-So, Mo-So, and Br-Br are said to be inclusive, whereas Hu-Wi is exclusive. Hsu defines these in strictly structural terms, and it would seem to indicate that for some roles, some relationships are not confined to two people. For example, a father can have more than one son, and therefore the social "field" is not limited to two people, but by definition may contain others. If this is indeed the case and our analysis is correct, then one is at a loss to understand why the marital relationship is not included, for in polygynous cultures it also is not restricted to only two people. In any case, Hsu has not given behavioral or affective dimensions of this attribute, but seems to distribute them among the other attributes in non-specific ways. We have not found it useful in our analysis of the Mexican family.

Continuity-discontinuity is structured in terms of lineality and sexual symmetry. For Hsu, of the four only the Fa-So relationship is continuous, whereas Mo-So, Br-Br, and Hu-Wi are discontinuous. It is structured therefore so that where continuity holds, every person involved in one of these dyads can, at least potentially, play both roles (although not with the same particular alter). Presumably this is important due to the kinds of learnings (and projections) that are consequent upon this kind of relationship, but they have not been spelled out by Hsu. Diffuseness is the least clearly defined of the variables, and is utilized by Hsu only in terms of the Indian Mo-So dominance materials. For our purposes we are unable to apply either one to the Mexican materials.

For the other eight variables, we discuss the Mexican materials in terms of dependence, which has been redefined in terms of *responsibility-dependence; intimacy;* authority, which has been merged with freedom, equality, and rivalry, under the label *dominance-compliance;* and sexuality-asexuality which has been merged with libidinality, under *sexuality.* The Mexican family shall here be analyzed in terms of these four components.

We have, due to limitations of both space and data, limited our discussion to only four of the relationships in the nuclear family. These are also the relationships which dominate the four models which Hsu has presented, and are Fa-So, Hu-Wi, Mo-So, Br-Br. Mexico is an essentially male-dominated culture, and these four relationships seem to be the most important from the male point of view. As a man, it was impossible to get adequate information on intimate aspects of the mother-daughter and Si-Si relationships. The Fa-Da and Br-Si relationships have been excluded, for they do not appear to seriously complicate the four main relationships. Our analysis is therefore incomplete. We hope to be able to fill these gaps in the future.

Rural Mexican Family Structure

Mexico is a civilization with a long tradition of self-examination and study, and the production of its students is impressive both for its quality and for its quantity. In addition, many perceptive foreigners have added to the argument concerning Mexico and Mexican character.[2] To date, two reviews of the literature on Mexican national character have been done in English, by Hewes (1954) and Batt (1965). There are, as Batt pointed out, important arguments involved concerning which model best applies to Mexican character, and further work is necessary to refine, define, and settle them. This task is not attempted here.

Rather, we shall concentrate on the town of San Juan (without necessarily implicating the larger society, unless so stated). Our San Juan materials concern primarily the elite. This is useful for an examination of the Hsu hypothesis, for the elite clearly dominate extra-familial activities and institutions. But it also means that the relationship of these people to those who have served as subjects for the other literature is indeterminate. Much more work is needed comparing the elite patterns with those of the lower classes.

However, it is one of our purposes in this article to include material on extra-familial relationships. We primarily concentrate upon the San Juan data. But San Juaneros are *mestizos* and are integrated into the wider society, which is thereby relevant for our concerns. As pointed out above, the literature on the topic is extremely heterogeneous, and it is difficult to imagine how this part of our study might be done systematically.[3] In-

2. There are several bodies of argument and/or data that are at least potentially relevant to this kind of study: the Mexicans' arguments about Mexican national character (Paz, 1959; Ramos, 1934; cf. Hewes, 1954; Batt, 1965); technical psychological studies of Mexican nationals (cf. Aramoni, 1961, Diaz-Guerrero, 1961; Maccoby, 1964, 1967; Maccoby *et al.*, 1964; Ramirez, 1966; Ramirez and Parres, 1957); the various studies of Mexican culture, society, and individuals (e.g., Iturriaga, 1951; Bermudez, 1955; Wolf, 1959, Lewis, 1951, 1959, 1961); and our own field data from towns in the northern part of the Mexican state of Oaxaca.

3. The literature on Mexico is vast, to say the least. In many fields of endeavor, such as poetry, theatre, the novel, movies, criticism, philosophy, history, etc., the productivity of Mexicans and of foreigners resident in Mexico has been enormous for at least the last 150 years. We doubt that a single scholar could read all of it in a working lifetime. One dimension of the Mexican projective system that is interesting from the point of view of presentation of family dynamics is the theatre plays. We have spent scores of hours coding the themes found in the abstracts of these plays, and have not as yet tackled the plays themselves. But in addition to these, one ideally should also consider the translations into Spanish of plays from other traditions, in terms of which plays of all these extant are selected for presentation in Mexico, and in terms of the language style used in the translation. One should be well versed on the performance history (what kinds of groups put a play on, for what kinds of audience, and with what success) and the reactions of the critics. Thus, for only one dimension a complete survey turns out to be a very considerable task. This is true not only for the projective systems but for the economic and political systems as well.

Obviously, it is impossible for a single person to cover all this ground. It is equally

stead, we have utilized diagnostic illustrations or examples from historical and contemporary studies, newspaper articles, and our own field work experience outside San Juan. The methodology is considerably less tight than for San Juan itself, but under the circumstances nothing better is feasible.

Our material on San Juan is derived from anthropological field work.[4] In addition, we have behavioral observations on mestizos in other areas of Mexico, including two small towns, one provincial center, and the metropolitan center, Mexico City.

San Juan is a Spanish-speaking town which depends primarily upon agriculture and commerce and contains about 2,500 people, almost all of whom are identified as mestizos or Mexicans by themselves and outsiders. As we have pointed out in other papers, the economic, political, and social

---

obvious that most of it is very relevant to our concerns here. The problem lies in sampling it adequately, and it is difficult to imagine how this could be done. Should one take a random sample of all plays, novels, regions, economic reports? But it would be very easy to miss significant variations. Should one stratify one's population? But then, on what basis is this stratification to be done? Should one take only a few manifestations, such as crimes, movies, economic development, child rearing techniques, and religion? But on what predetermined theoretical basis is one to select these aspects, when one is interested in Mexico rather than in the theory? None of these approaches seems adequate to achieve the goal of scientific knowledge.

The usual practical alternative is to follow one's inclinations, and to do as much as one can. But this is not a *systematic* way of coping with a modern (or ancient, for that matter) nation. And it is this *systematic* way of studying a nation that we are unable to imagine.

4. Much of the data were gathered by participant observation and both formal and informal interviews by my wife and myself with a sample of seven extended families (corporate kindred groups). While in the field, we lived for several months at a time with each of two elite family households, one in San Juan and another in a highland village. Each contained three generations and married couples of two of these. We took meals with the families, shared their living space, and had members of the household in and out of our "private" bedroom quarters as we were in and out of theirs. Living this way, we were able to observe, and be involved in, much more intimate behavior than would have been the case if we had lived in a dwelling of our own. Much important family interaction takes place in the evening, for during the day the household members are busy at their jobs, away at school, etc. During the day there is a higher emphasis on task-oriented (instrumental) rather than expressive aspects of interaction.

After the working day is over, however, other kinds of things begin to happen. First, the adults now can have some uninterrupted leisure activity, such as playing with children or gossiping with the anthropologist about the day's events or family problems. If these sessions go on into the wee hours, defenses fall and intimacy rises. Many of the most revealing interviews took place at 1 A.M. after several hours of playing their favorite card games, joking and exchanging confidences. Second, family crises happen at irregular intervals, and in most cases with a low frequency during the field season. If the investigator is not regularly in a household, he stands an excellent chance of missing most if not all of them. In addition, besides adult dreams, nightmares of children provided significant data, and it is very important to be there at night to get accurate ideas about the child's report of the content of the dream, the content of the previous day's (or days') events, and to observe the ethos of the family as it deals with the experience. It is our suggestion, in other words, that some events are highly significant, highly infrequent, and distributed in the day in such a fashion that most anthropological observations will miss them unless there is co-residence. Actually, living with the family seems the only efficient way to gather some of the kinds of data we did.

life of the town is dominated by a small number of elite families (Hunt, 1965b, 1968). The data presented in this paper have been derived primarily from these elite families, but we have data on most of the points for both male and female members of the middle and lower classes (cf. E. Hunt, 1969, for a description of the class structure, and kinship organization, for San Juan).

For all classes in San Juan, the primary kinship unit is the nuclear family (*la mera familia*), which occupies a house (*casa*). There are, however, two important variants on this. At one stage of the developmental cycle of the family, it is likely that a woman and her children will occupy a residence, and the man involved will only rarely be present. As soon as the conjugal relationship becomes stabilized, and begins to look successful, the middle- or upper-class man will convert it into a full nuclear family, and all will reside in the same place (cf. E. Hunt, *op. cit.*).

At a later stage, when the family among the upper two classes is stable, the parents of the major couple dead, and the man well established, the household may contain all or any of the following: spinster sisters, one or several female and male servants, for a short period of time a married son and his family, and perhaps other marginal relatives, for longer or shorter periods of time.

Another important variant on the residential patterns is the practice of a family having two or more residences. Since San Juan is rural and situated in a climate that can only be described as arduous, once one becomes wealthy enough to do so one establishes another residence in an urban center. Children will repair there for school, and the wife may spend a considerable amount of time there. This urban residence will be used for recreational purposes, and is normally located in a city where the head of the family has his most important business and political connections. Thus the family members present in the household in San Juan will vary considerably, depending upon the time of the year.

The kinship system in San Juan has been described elsewhere (E. Hunt, *op. cit.*). Briefly, it looks like a bilateral system with a patrilineal bias. Among the upper classes, it is organized so as to be specialized for economic cooperation. The *familia* among the elite is a cognatic corporate group which is homogeneous with respect to class and faction, and all members of it are discussed in kinship terms (E. Hunt, *op. cit.*).

Each nuclear family, among the upper class, is organized around what we have elsewhere called the enterprise, a large, diversified family business (Hunt, 1965b). Two aspects of this are of interest for this paper: the fact that only one son, and a legitimate one, is to inherit the major part of the family property, and the fact that managerial help is very hard to come by, and desperately needed if the desired expansion of the business is to take place. This is a major problem to the family, and will be a constant drive behind what we are discussing in the following pages (cf. Hunt, 1965b, for an extensive discussion).

DOMINANCE-COMPLIANCE

The word "authority" is fairly prominent in Hsu's analyses of family systems, and the response to authority and authority-wielding figures is a major variable in his models. Conceptually, however, the variable is not as clearly defined as it might be.

It is common in the Western world to differentiate between authority—the legitimate right to expect compliance from others—and power—the ability to force the compliance of others (cf. Easton, 1958). This differentiation is to be explained partly by a deep Western preoccupation with the legitimization of power in social relationships.

Since our materials encourage the separation of these two dimensions, we prefer a label that both keeps the distinction clear and at the same time makes it consistent with similar concepts in other disciplines (for example, ethology). We therefore propose to utilize the term dominance-compliance for the attribute. We here take dominance to mean the manipulation of others, and compliance, being manipulated by others. The term manipulate has at least two distinct and important meanings in English. Since a good part of this paper revolves around the Freudian ego-ideal of manipulation or control of the environment (including the self), and since manipulate is a strongly loaded and ambiguous word in English, it is best that our usage of it be made clear.

The first meaning that we use refers to the organization and/or directing of things and/or activities and/or people, and being so subject. In this sense, any antientropic activity is manipulation. The second meaning, a pejorative one, refers to the maneuvering of people and, secondarily, of events, in such a way that one's own profit is the only goal, and implies (a) that those manipulated are often not aware of the purposes or goals of the maneuver, (b) that the goals are often not acceptable to those involved, and (c) that this is an undesirable state of affairs (for Americans) because an agreement on the goals of action, conscious at best, but certainly widespread, is a condition for moral interaction. The analysis of this second sense of manipulation in fact takes us deep into the American value system, being concerned as it is with such things as rightful exercise of authority and power, morality, freedom, and the like. For this reason also, a different word would be desirable, for the pejorative meaning is the dominant one in American culture. However, the more general meaning is an extremely important concept, and as yet no adequate substitute for the word has been found.

It is clear that social systems have rules about the distribution of dominance. These rules indicate not only what roles are supposed to manifest dominance, but also the objects or persons which are to be manipulated, and the contexts in which they are to be manipulated. The social system has rules about compliance as well, including the roles, objects, and situations.

Dominance can be divided into a component of power and a component of authority. The second implies legitimacy. For any given social system, the relative importance of these two varies. In Mexico the power component is much more important than the authority component, and authority is in most cases a consequence of power. This is well exemplified in the political system in the rural areas, where being a *jefe* or *cacique* (important political figure) is a function of personality, wealth, and at times willingness and ability to use small-arms violence, rather than being an office holder. There is another facet of dominance which must be pointed out: the difference between the expected and actual behaviors of the persons occupying specific roles. It is the case that modern Western bureaucracies (such as the armed forces) attempt to make congruency or identity of expectation and actual behavior, a reality. In most systems, however, the dominance displayed by any particular individual is only in part explained by the role he is playing. There is always present, to a greater or lesser degree, a component of individual, idiosyncratic behavior. The degree of compliance achieved is due in part to the role system, and in part to the personal, perhaps idiosyncratic, ability of the role occupier to persuade or force others to comply. In other words, while a relationship is said to contain a certain amount of dominance-compliance, the individuals who play the roles may show more or less than is usually called for or expected. In addition, there may be an imbalance between the dominance demands of one and the compliance demands of the other.

A complete discussion of dominance, and the social distribution of dominance, in a culture should therefore include an inventory of roles, objects, and situations and degrees of freedom for idiosyncracy. Whenever our data permitted, we have attempted to provide this information.

The distribution of dominance in the Mexican family is ideally a function of sex and age. Males are said to be absolutely superior to females (cf. also Diaz-Guerrero, 1955) and elder to younger. The family forms virtually the primary social context in which it is legitimate to speak of authority. The father and husband, regardless of other considerations, is treated with fear and deference a good part of the time. Final authority is normatively ascribed to the *jefe* of the *casa*, who is the elder male, unless senile. The male head of the family is expected to have a very great deal of authority over the other members of his family—who may actually fear him and his power. Realization of the authority that is supposed to go with the role of family head is to a certain degree a function of the personalities involved and to a certain degree a function of the amount of property that is involved and who controls it. In a few cases, a female head (*jefa*) of a family who is adept at managing (and increasing) the property base will have as much power over the other members of the family as would a male in the same position, but these cases involve the absence of an adult male head of her generation, and, in fact, her taking over a male role.

To take the relationships one by one, the father-son relationship is ideally one of dominance of the father throughout their lives. Even if a son is married, living in a separate household, and financially independent, informants agree he should still obey and "respect" his father's desires. As long as the son is dependent upon the father for anything (including money, a job, a place to live, education), the son will actually do what the father orders him to do. But even though there is a strong ethic supporting this distribution of dominance (people say a son should obey a father *all* his life even when both are old), its realization is primarily a function of a) the age of the son and b) the amount of property that is involved. If there is a large estate, the inheritance of it will be in doubt, and this induces many sons to be obedient—to yield to power—at least until the heirs are apparent. Insofar as the sons of the elite are connected with the business of the family estate, then, compliance is likely to be the frequently found behavior. In other cases, the father will provide an education in a technological field (such as law, medicine, accounting, engineering), and then help set the son up in a practice which is expected to benefit the family business through its know-how and the professional, political, and business connections derived from it. As long as the son is in school, he is obedient to his father (by getting good grades in the profession chosen by the father, staying out of trouble, not spending too much money, and so on). Then, once the practice is set up, it is expected that the son will practice in such a way, and in such a place, that he will be useful to the father and family. But here the economic power of the father is less, for in the expanding Mexican economy the son with a degree can get a good job most anywhere. If there is little or no property base, as in most of the poorer San Juan families, the father is unable to do anything important to get his son launched in life, and a grown son is unlikely to respond to the attempts of his father to exercise power. Thus, normative paternal authority becomes watered-down power.

Soon after adolescence the sons rebel against the father's commanding behavior in a very open manner. It is common in San Juan that in the period between a son's coming out of childhood and his finally leaving home (between the ages of 12 and 25), the relationship between fathers and sons consists of alternating periods of avoidance, during which the mother acts as intermediary, and periods fraught with verbal and at times physical conflict between the two. In extreme cases this may lead to homicide. Since the normative pattern strongly emphasizes "that a son should never raise his hand against his father," these exchanges usually take place under the influence of alcohol. In fact, since Mexicans believe that a drunk is not responsible for his actions, drunkenness is sought as a justification of this behavior, and is achieved prior to the opening of hostilities.[5]

5. Most forms of physical aggression in this culture normally occur while the initiator is under the influence of alcohol, and the influence of alcohol is both a mitigating circumstance, and a justification for the action.

Thus, although there is a strong cultural position that the father ought to be and is an authority figure, in actual fact this is not always the case. The power does not inhere in the father-son relationship, but instead has to be achieved, is usually materially based for adolescent and adult sons (unless a very dominant personality is involved), and has constantly to be revalidated.

There is very clear evidence that many San Juan sons bitterly resent the dominance displays and posture of their father. This pattern seems to be prevalent in Mexican culture in general. The tragedy page of any Mexican newspaper frequently carries stories of patricide. In San Juan, if the family has considerable economic resources, the conflicting desires to be free of the power of another and still to be cut in on the pie is particularly disturbing.

There seem to be two main types of response to this situation, an effective and ineffective one. The effective son bears up under the authoritarian regime easily, enjoying the benefits (considerable local power over females and younger family members, over hirelings, and so on), and not suffering under the restrictions. He is often the father's favorite, and as long as he obeys he is allowed much greater freedom in his relations with others than his other siblings. The ineffective son's response to this situation is also stereotyped. His behavior is usually characterized by apparent meekness, sullenness, avoidance of face to face exchanges, and inadequate or poor performance of direct commands. The various jobs they are given will be done, but badly. For example, the performance in school will be mediocre, although their intelligence appears to be equal to or higher than many better-behaved siblings, and they will make little effort to learn things that would be useful to the family business. The weak son rarely engages in open, direct rebellion, but when older and out of school will instead resort to such activities as drinking heavily, gambling, making friends with persons in the opposite political faction as his father and/or with men of lower social status than himself. This is seen by San Juaneros themselves as attempts to challenge the father's authority when they are afraid of direct, open hostility. The extreme solution from the point of view of the father is to extrude the son from the relationship, deny him his inheritance, whereupon the son goes to live in some other place, a form of exile. The most abject of these failures often become hired help for their successful brothers after the father's death. This secondary relationship has many of the characteristics of the previous father-son interactions. In several San Juan family histories these men have ended as alcoholics.

Closely related to this picture is the *macho* complex and the concept of the *chingon*. Briefly, the *macho* complex calls for very dominant masculine behavior. To be *macho*, to be a *chingon*, is to defend one's honor, to be able to command, to be virile, to be brave and bold, to be able to push other people around, and especially never to be so pushed. Small-arms violence, so noted for Mexico, is often a response to a challenge in this area. (Exclusive possession of sexual and intimacy rights in females is an integral part of this complex, but we will discuss that under sexuality.) The *chingon* is the person who is *macho*, who organizes and manipulates others. The *chingado* is the person who is manipulated, and in the Mexican male conception (as analyzed by Paz in the *Labyrinth of Solitude* [*op. cit.*]) anyone who is not a *chingon* is by definition a *chingado*. Men in general do not like to be subjected to the actions of *chingones* and try to avoid it where possible.

The typical American picture of *machismo* is essentially a negative one: of a poseur, a man with a gigantic inferiority complex who is obvious about being tough and violent, about drinking a lot, being sexually "potent," but who at heart is insecure, unsure, and weak. A great deal of the bragging in San Juan men is just that, although the threat of violence is certainly real enough. But this is a one-sided picture.

The other dimension of this complex concerns the man who is really tough and in command. Successful San Juan men (real *machos*) have an assurance of command that is truly impressive. Many of them are highly puritanical, and often deeply committed to what they call progress, honesty, and justice. They are the pluperfect example of what by their culture norms the perfect father ought to be: tolerant, wise, just, honest, and very effective in coping with all aspects of the world. These men are also usually hard-driving organizers and manipulators (cf. Paz, 1959). It is our supposition that these men realize the best parts of the ideal male identity. We do not as yet, unfortunately, understand how this image is communicated to the young in families and under what circumstances it is adopted. But that it occurs cannot be doubted. Hopefully, future research will solve this problem. The father-son model is carried over, in terms of ideal dominance, to the older brother-younger brother relationship.

Brother-Brother. Given the realities of Mexican life, with the scarcity of resources and the tendency to centralized, monopolistic control in both the family and in the society as a whole, it is painfully necessary to be subject to the decisions (and power) of others.

Younger brothers are supposed to obey elder brothers, but they generally do not. Open rebellion flares among children, and it is recognized as normal and inevitable by parents, who often warn the elders to ease up and the younger to be more "respectful." By the time a group of brothers of the San Juan elite is at the point of maneuvering around each other to secure the inheritance of the family estate, the stage of open rebellion will usually be over, and the winner eventually establishes himself as the head of the household. He will then immediately begin to treat his brothers as if they were his children. They in turn either cannot stand this and move away, or stay in the family and accept the subservient role of children. The succession problems usually manage to sort themselves out without open conflict between the brothers (where more distant relatives are involved in inheritance fights, severe conflict including small vendetta wars is relatively common). In the arrangement finally arrived at in almost all cases, there is no direct question of dominance in the interaction system, but constant re-testing of mutual strength. Siblings avoid direct confrontation whenever possible, and later family structure is designed so as to reduce contact later on between adult brothers who are unequal in wealth or power. Should a younger brother happen to become powerful and wealthy on his own, then he can treat the elder as an equal. But in general, except for brief periods in the developmental cycles of families in the elite class when brothers are forced to live together, they avoid any intimation of authority amongst themselves by physical as well as social and psychological distance. The culture says dominance ought to be there, but it is avoided if at all possible.

Husband-Wife. The husband-wife relationship is not quite so complex in terms of dominance. The husband, by virtue of being a male, is ideally expected to be dominant over the spouse and often in extreme fashion. This is frequently the case. The man orders and the woman obeys. In a formal interview context, the only justifiable reason for a wife's disobedience that appeared was if the husband asked the wife to murder or steal. The man controls the amount of money the woman has to spend, and tries and often succeeds in controlling her activities, her circle of friendships, her entertainment. Many Mexican men are said to be real tyrants, and we have seen enough households in San Juan at firsthand to realize that this is often the case. There is a saying in San Juan that suffering is the daily share of the married woman. In fact, the women develop what has been called a martyr complex in response to their position, expecting the worst and having to accept it when it occurs (cf. Diaz-Guerrero, 1955). The worst includes knowledge that the husband has one or several other women that he is supporting (with their children), a low and often intermittent amount of support for her household (at times forcing her onto her own resources for income), abandonment, infrequent visits to the house, beatings. He often invokes a good deal of fear. In our experience it is rare that there is any open rebellion on the part of the women, but small bickering and verbal complaining to others (including female relatives and their own children) is expected as an expression of their lot. We have heard of very few fights over authority. Rather the wife's activities will include some subtle non-performance of duties (for example, not having his food warm when he comes to eat at home) and manipulating the relationships between a man and his children so that the children become wedges between them. Women of the lower class will often prefer that they not be married and not have a man in attendance so that the mother-children group can exist in and of itself without adult male interference. Children are seen by women as a form of property, and lower-class women quite openly regard especially their sons as a form of old-age insurance. If the father is of a higher class, he may take the child away by recognizing it (a common legal procedure), and the child will sever the relationship with the mother in order to move up the class hierarchy under his father's aegis, thus becoming lost as a source of support for the mother.

Among the elite, children, especially legitimate sons, are seen by women as a form of social insurance. The men of the San Juan elite have a pattern of not marrying legally before the woman has produced several children, primarily sons. The legitimization of status has the effect of considerably raising the status of the women in the household and *familia*, and legitimate sons are highly desired. San Juaneros agree that children are the primary object of dominance for women, and one of our informants said that the more children and servants a woman has in her household, the better off she is, since she has more people to order around (these are the only people she can order around, except for the occasional daughter-in-law living in a compound household).

Mother-Son. The mother-son dyad is perhaps the most difficult for an American to understand. If the reciprocal of dominance is obedience, the Mexican conceives of this obedience in terms of respect (cf. E. Hunt, *op. cit.*). Respect for San Juaneros means social distance, but tempered with positive feelings of affection. One is supposed to respect one's mother and to obey her is implied; obedience, they say, is the sign of respect and love. However, the ultimate dominance in this culture is supposed to reside in the hands of males, and if there is a male head of the family, that male head will be *the* source of authority. Thus, the mother's power is tempered by being only a secondary executive. One is supposed to give deference to one's mother, but punishment of non-performance comes not from her but her male partner. But the San Juan mother is not only the expressive leader; she is an instrumental leader with restricted realms of authority and action, primarily because the sanctions against those who deviate are not in her hands, but in the hands of the male head of the household.

The reality is more complex. As in all cultures, there occur families in which a woman with a very powerful personality effectively dominates all within the group. (A cross-cultural count of the relative frequencies of such families might be very interesting.) Since it often happens that the woman acts as a broker between a man and his sons with respect to the dominance-compliance dimension, she is able to maneuver herself into a position of power behind the scenes by manipulating information between them. She will plead a child's case with the father, try to prevent rebellion and open breaks, and if these occur, will promote their reconciliation. This is especially the case if the father is the one who initiated the break. Even though the son may still be at home, the mother will, in many cases, be the only parent who sees the son frequently (due to the pattern of male spouses spending little time at home). This latter can occur for several reasons. Among the rich elite members who have several residences, the father and some of the elder sons may, for business reasons, spend much of the year in different parts of Mexico (overseeing operations of their ranches, their stores, or whatever) while the wife and daughters and smaller sons will spend the time in a more civilized place (a large Mexican city). The two groups will visit each other, the family perhaps spending part of the pleasant time of the year at the provincial seat in San Juan, and the males coming to the town centers for business or recreational purposes. In these cases, then, the wife-mother stands *in loco autoritas* for the husband-father with the children, and she has, if she agrees with what her husband wants, a very great deal of power. With poor women, there is another reason for the separation: the *casa chica* pattern, whereby a man more or less supports two or more households and is seldom present in any of them. His word is law when he is present, but his infrequent presence tends to make the mother the effective head of the household, with correspondingly greater dominance over the sons.

We have here a developmental cycle. The mother never has complete independent authority over the son, except for the cases in which there is no man in the family. Her secondary authority grows less with time, as the sons grow up and come more and more under the direct tutelage and supervision of the father and then move out on their own. Because of a complex emotional field surrounding the mother-son relationship (due to Oedipal tensions, of which more below), and the presence of a legitimate higher source of authority, the dominance that a mother has over a son is highly subdued, but persistent and very much subject to manipulation on the part of all parties.

A further complication arises from the fact that mothers and fathers usually have favorite sons. This is virtually institutionalized, and usually the mother's favorite is not the father's. The basis for the distinction between the mother's and the father's favorite son can be found in the strikingly different values that males and females in this society have. San Juaneros agree that women are the only "moral" people in this culture. Women value truthfulness, non-aggression, and passivity. For a woman a good child is one who does not engage in fighting, is asexual, warm and affectionate in the family and with others, polite, gentle, well-mannered, and quiet. Women in general complain bitterly about the sinfulness of men, and this is clearly the case in terms of formal religion, where church attendance and confession are expected only of females. But a son who behaves in agreement with these "high moral standards" is considered by other men, including his father, a weakling. A *macho* by definition cannot afford to be pacific, gentle, or quiet because he has to be authoritarian and untruthful in a cutthroat world of business competition, *mordidas* (bribing), and commercial treason. Since a *macho* is expected to be sexually promiscuous, he is by definition sexually sinful. In the mother's view he is promoting the disgrace of other women and defiling her own honor.

Thus, women in this culture prefer sons who behave in a way other men do not accept. San Juaneros agree that women prefer the children (including sons) who are like themselves (or who fit their expectations), while the fathers prefer the children who are closer in behavior to the male ideal. This ideal includes being strong-willed and self-reliant, traits preferred by men in their daughters also (even though it is not the norm for female ideal behavior and although they want their daughters to be feminine and affectionate with them). Women prefer their daughters to be obedient, well behaved, and domestic. Since young unmarried females are seldom allowed to leave the enclosure of the home without direct supervision, their public behavior conforms much closer to general cultural expectations than that of male offspring, and in general there is much less open conflict than with their male siblings. San Juaneros believe that this difference of behavior is inborn and point out that girls are much easier to handle than boys from their very first month of life.

The mother will be fairly vigorous in promoting the interests of her favorite son if she is powerful enough of personality to be able to push. But some women are so weakly endowed with family power that they are little more than servants whose job it is to organize the logistics of the household, and their favorite children suffer the consequences of their "protection." In this latter case the mother will have considerable power over her son and acquire some authority over him, but this authority will be the subject of constant disputes with the male head of the household, who may in fact despise the weak child. Another complication is that the mother will not be above utilizing her favorite son as her "avenger" against her husband, thus dividing the son and father, who are already estranged by differences in character. It seems likely that the mother has a secondary gain from promoting a son whose character is a blemish on the good public image of her husband, in addition to all the other dimensions of this situation, to be explored more fully in the sexuality section.

In addition to the above sketch, there is a strong ethic concerning a proper filial relationship in San Juan culture, which pertains to the wider society as well. According to this ethic, which refers to all hierarchical relationships, a proper son (or subordinate) will love and respect his superior, will be obedient to direct commands, and will look out for the interests of his superior (will not embezzle from him, undermine his authority, be a traitor, and so on). The superior and "father," conversely, will take care of each of his dependents in case of need, will protect them from the depredations of others, will be completely loyal to them regardless of the facts of the case, will provide for their material well-being to the best of his ability, will settle intra-group disputes with a fair hand, and will love those in his charge (Tannenbaum, 1950:96–98). This ethic applies equally to a father and to the President of the country and to all in between who are in a relatively permanent relationship with others that is hierarchical in nature.

But the ethic of obedience to superiors is tempered, if not contradicted, by the Mexican ideal of intense individual freedom and the right to "do one's wish" (*gusto*) in life. In the end, since men are more likely to love sons who show one pattern of behavior, while women usually favor those who show a different pattern, males are presented with two male identities, and the two typical responses imply considerable about the individual's posture in the outside, adult world.

DEPENDENCE

Dependence, like manipulation, is a red herring of considerable stench to Americans. Like manipulation, it is a bad sort of thing to be or do. Like manipulation, it is a complex word, highly ambiguous. The prime, and neutral, meaning of dependence refers to the fact that no person can completely satisfy all of his or her own needs by himself. For the satisfaction of some needs, therefore, every person needs the help of some others, and this is what is meant, in general and neutral terms, by dependence.

The other meaning of dependence, a pejorative one, is linked with the perception that some members of the group do not sufficiently abandon certain kinds of dependency. The kinds of dependency which have to be abandoned vary from culture to culture. An American, for instance, is not supposed to live with his parents after he is married and is reluctant to accept monetary help from them. A Tzeltal Indian, on the other hand, is expected to live with his parents after marriage and is dependent upon his father for his sustenance. When an adult American says of another adult American that he is dependent, he generally means that that person is dependent in a way that he should have outgrown and is thereupon judged to be neurotic.

We know distressingly little about the distribution of normal and "neurotic" dependencies for any given culture. For example, it seems likely that the husband-wife relationship in the American family (and perhaps in all domestic groups) can usefully be looked at as institutionally legitimized prolongations of dependencies, many carried over from childhood more or less intact. For instance, for American males the wife takes over the mother's job of providing food, clean clothes, and ordering the household. For American females, the husband takes over the father's function of making many decisions, supporting the household, and providing many of the social characteristics (for example, social and economic class) for the women of the household. On the other hand, the man will have to shift from having no authority over members of the household to having and exercising that authority, and the woman will have to shift from a role where food and clothing and order are provided (by her mother) to providing them for herself and the rest of the household. The neurotic forms of adjustment are often those in which the person is unwilling to give up behavior appropriate only to the natal household and is also perhaps unwilling to provide equivalent services for the conjugal household.

The reciprocal of dependence is responsibility. Independence is *not* the opposite of dependence, for this is part of a different axis. If one person in a relationship is dependent upon another, then it is, often, incumbent upon the alter to satisfy the needs of ego, and this is responsibility, not independence. In a society such as the Mexican, especially in San Juan where there is a consistent and unavoidable hierarchicalization of social relationships, one is either subordinate or superordinate, dependent or responsible, according to the ideal outline of the culture.

The degree of difference of dependence and authority as principles or attributes deserves much more attention than it has received. One can separate them on this basis: Dominance involves actions designed to benefit those who exercise it, while in dependence the actions are designed to benefit those who receive it. If I read Hsu correctly, he argues that in the Chinese nuclear family these two attributes co-occur in the father-son relationship. It is imaginable, however, that the two need not co-occur in any one relationship, and Diaz has argued that this separation applies to Tonala, in Mexico (1965). It thus becomes necessary to separate the two.

If, however, there is a separation of dominance and responsibility, then there is no way for the dependent to enforce the carrying out of the duties which attach to the responsible end of the relationship, and this often is the cause for the disengagement and alienation so commonly remarked in Mexican culture. It has been pointed out by many people that for at least several decades the dominant motif of Mexican interpersonal relationships has been lack of trust. To be *desconfiado* (distrusting) is in fact seen by many San Juaneros as a virtue.[6] San Juaneros expect or suspect anybody to try to cheat them, kill them, betray them, steal their money (even the closest family members, as is often the case in fact). Nobody is to be trusted, and it may be this which lends the definite flavor of alienation and inward direction common to the larger Mexican scene. This value can be seen as an attempt to gain independence (Batt, *op. cit.*).

Since neither dependence nor responsibility are sufficiently rewarding, withdrawal to alienation appears more satisfactory to the San Juanero. Dependence does not work for them, for the alter may take advantage of his position, and perhaps abandon the dependent. Responsibility does not reward one's efforts either, for people cannot always be trusted to do what they are told to do, and they may have a constant desire to betray those whom they depend upon. This attitude is pervasive in the family, in business, and in other aspects of San Juan life, such as politics. There is much work, therefore, cut out for the person who would be responsible.

There are, of course, realms where it is easier to achieve control and predictability than others. Politics is one of these, and one of the major aims of the PRI (the official, government political party which controls the economic and political life of Mexico) is to achieve just this degree of control and predictability by creating an extensive patron-client system

6. At a busy intersection on Mexico City's largest freeway, there is (1966) a large black and white sign that states *sea desconfiado*, "distrust," and in small letters, "this advertising is a public service."

within the local political structure. The PRI structure has worked out a system of positive and negative sanctions which not only works locally, but has raised Mexico to a degree of peace and calm and economic growth unknown for at least a century and a half (cf. Tannenbaum, *op. cit.*). But the system in San Juan is based on a tenuous maintenance of the status quo, and flares of rebellion and political unrest between factions are a permanent feature of the local political landscape.

Father-Son. Turning first to the father-son relationship, it is immediately obvious that the son is supposed to be totally dependent upon the father for support as a child and adolescent. His spending money and his social characteristics are in the largest part derived from his father. This dependency is not ideally expected to drop when the son gets married, but to change in kind. If the son has broken away and has a job of his own, he can successfully cease being economically dependent upon the father. But he is ideally expected to ask for advice on any important actions he may take. If he is working his way into the family business and competing with his brothers for the inheritance, as occurs in some of the San Juan elite, then the dependence does not cease, but may go on for years. But the strong sons will, in addition to participating in the family business, be busily building up a similar business of their own. They will be investing the money they get in land or businesses, taking on managerial jobs for others at the same time, etc. These sons seem to wear the burden of dependency rather easily, as they do submission, and willingly accept advice and receive help in the form of money, or connections, from the father although they seldom ask for it.

The weaker sons, more closely allied with the mother, remain in many ways paradoxically much more and much less dependent upon the father. They have much more trouble establishing an independent household and job, live with the parents after marriage, and often appear to be wastrels. They are continually in need of more money and things from parents; getting them is a difficult job which only meets with success through the mother. These sons appear to identify strongly with the father, in the sense of ego-ideal, and yet cannot produce the behavior which is like the father's. Several of them whom we interviewed have strong fantasy lives in which they move away from home, become successful and rich, and return to San Juan to show their father his mistake.

Husband-Wife. In the case of the Hu-Wi relationship, the San Juan elite wife is far more dependent upon the husband than is the reverse. Ideally she gets her household money from him on a daily basis (this is called the *gasto*) [the expenditure]; cf. Lewis, 1959:196), and is largely dependent upon him for housing, support, social standing, and sex. Among the lower classes she may, however, prefer, or be forced, to rely upon her own resources, for it is standard practice for the poorer husbands to be unable or unwilling to completely support the household. In this case she will go to work herself, or rely upon her own family (which seldom, for these purposes, includes consanguines of her consort). Outside the elite families, the support of the women by the men is uncertain, and thus they attempt to establish economic independence on their own.

The man, on the other hand, is far less dependent upon his wife, in any class. In the ideal case, the wife supplies his needs for laundry, meals, sleeping quarters, socialization of his children, and sex. A man, in distinction to a woman, can turn elsewhere for these services, to consanguines, secondary spouses, or they can even be contracted for on a short term basis. Normally his laundry, meals, and sleeping quarters would be taken care of by the spouse, but as long as his mother or sisters are alive, he can always rely upon them. It is a common pattern in this culture for male friends to eat together in the market place or local eating places. The *palomilla* or close friendship of men of the same age is an institution, and in most Mexican restaurants the typical parties during the day consist of men (or unisexual groups) of about the same age (cf. Rubel, 1965, for a Mexican-American case). Many men will also attend parties at night with their friends, and without their wives, and spend their nights in the local whorehouse as a group (see later discussion of prostitution and homosexuality). Mothers and sisters and schools will take over the socialization of the children.

Sexual dependency also fits this pattern. A man may with impunity have as many steady mistresses with children (*casas chicas*) as his income and greed allow, and sometimes more. He also has the outlet of prostitution, and neither behavior is seen as illegitimate by him or the culture. His wife, however, seldom has the outlet of a lover, and if adultery is her choice, she must keep it secret, since her life would be endangered if the husband found out. A San Juan man would seldom be jailed for killing an adulterous wife.[7] As we shall see in the discussion of sexuality, this is often no solution for the woman, who may find herself in a marital situation that is highly unrewarding sexually.

The woman, then, is more dependent upon her spouse than the man. Most women adapt to this condition with a martyr complex, resigning themselves to the "bestiality" and irresponsibility of their men (husbands or consorts). In only a very few cases does this relatively unsuccessful dependency (which often forces them into playing more active, instrumental roles) lead to rebellion and abandonment of woman's typical lot in life.

Brother-Brother. In the brother-brother relationship, aside from meeting needs for sociability and companionship in early childhood, the only time dependency and responsibility are significant is in the rare case when one of the brothers becomes the head of the family, and the other subject to him. As in the case of dominance-submission, this situation implies a Fa-

7. The most common pattern in murder cases is for him to leave the village for a few years, until "the tongues stop chatting about it," whereupon he may return with impunity.

So relationship, and is avoided if at all possible. Indeed, for most of the strata of society, it rarely occurs that there is any economic muscle in this situation. If the family is poor, the elder will be able to do little for the younger that the younger cannot do for himself. It is in the case of the rich that this relationship becomes problematic, for here the elder is in a position to do considerable for his younger siblings, and indeed is expected to do as much as he can. But this relationship cannot endure unless the authoritarian aspects of it are mitigated considerably. If the elder takes his role as head of the family seriously and tries to enforce strong compliance with dependence, the stronger siblings rebel and leave (or kill him), while the weaker siblings meekly give in. But in most of these cases, family surplus will go to the children of the elder, rather than to his younger siblings.

Mother-Son. Dependency in the mother-son relationship is very complex. This is the only relationship in which a man can rely upon the responsibility of alter, and in which women can, relatively speaking, rely upon the dependency of alter. A man can count on his mother for affective comfort, room and board, advice, intimacy, for as long as she lives. If a woman has a "good" son, she can rely upon him to give her the pleasures of having a grown man dependent upon her as long as they live. This is the only relationship in the whole culture where this is the case, both ideally and in fact. Many Mexican popular songs illustrate this point.

As pointed out above, a man can well remain dependent upon his mother for food and clothing and housing for much of his life, and certainly more so than upon his wife. (We will discuss the intimacy and sexuality aspects of this dependency in later sections.)

We have already pointed out that in San Juan, females are considered inherently inferior. But they are also the dispensers of much of the comfort of life. It is the right and duty of women to provide these comforts for the men associated with the families with which they are at the moment residing. In the lower classes of San Juan the women do it themselves, while in the higher ones these women are responsible for supervising other women (maids) who provide these services.

Feelings of being "neurotically" dependent upon a woman are not significant for these particular aspects of interaction, because the women can be relied upon to be responsible and the culture dictates this as their duty and privilege. Men can, of course, take care of themselves, and sometimes have to. But doing so seems to evoke none of the feelings of independence from mother which is a characteristic of American middle-class males. On the contrary, a man who is not able to find a woman to care for him is seen as effeminate and a failure as a man. In this rather restricted sense of the word dependency, then, no special problem is posed for the mother-son relationship. Intimacy, authority, and especially sexuality, are far more important in the mother-son relationship than is dependency.

INTIMACY

By intimacy we mean roughly that there is a relatively great degree of exchange of privileged, private information, usually of an emotional nature, although more objective information such as plans and goals may also be involved. The attribute would seem to revolve around revelation of self and freedom to reveal information and states that are potentially damaging if the other person should use the information as a weapon. In America this is conceived as a relationship between equals of a symmetrical sort, and the relationship is not one which is subject to treason (that is, the information is privileged).

Father-Son. In the Mexican family, the Fa-So relationship is definitely an anti-intimacy one. It is part of the nature of dominance that it is distant (Parsons and Bales, 1955), but this is especially the case in the San Juan family. Whereas in other cultures the exercise of dominance might be tempered with persuasion, explanation, and a considerable amount of information permitting the smoother manipulation (in our general sense) of human relations, in Mexico there is no such softening. The father is not only expected to be distant, aloof, unbending, and commanding, but unlikely to regard the suggesting of alternative plans of action as anything but a sign of mutiny. Only rarely is the confidence or advice of the son sought. The typical son in San Juan is not at all close to his father.

Brother-Brother. In their early years, brothers are apt to develop a fair amount of intimacy, providing that they are roughly similar in interests and temperament. Later, as property and winning the competition for inheritance with the other siblings become more important, intimacy and cooperation between siblings drop to their lowest point. Later still, when two or more brothers have definitely established independent careers and property bases, then intimacy and cooperation again become possible, although the intimacy is likely to be restricted to business and family affairs. Other affairs are not so likely to be discussed. An adult man is more likely to have a non-kin friend with whom he is very intimate, while a woman is more likely to confide in a married sister.

Husband-Wife. The husband-wife relationship is in most cases not remarkable for its intimacy. If the pattern of partial abandonment and of maintaining several houses at once is adopted, there is little intense contact between spouses. In addition, there is a strong psychological dynamic which drives husbands and wives apart. The relationship can probably best be described in terms of strong latent (and often manifest) hostility, distance, and little sharing of information.

Mother-Son. The mother-son relationship often attains a considerable degree of intimacy, in our judgment the most intimacy afforded in the four relationships discussed here. Again, there is a powerful psychological structure which draws these two persons together, and which we shall discuss in some detail later, under sexuality. Information is likely to flow in both directions. A man is likely to regard his mother as his most loyal friend (again, many Mexican songs are dedicated to this theme). She certainly is the female with whom he has the most intense emotional relationship. Each tends to resent the other's establishing an intense cross-sex relationship with a third person. This is in part the source of hostility of the son toward the father, and of the mother toward her daughter-in-law (the two most standard axes of open conflict in San Juan families), and each will either try to break up a developing relationship between alter and a third, or, if defeated in this, will withdraw as gracelessly as possible.

The mother also gains intimacy by serving as mediator between the sons and the father. An opposite of intimacy, secretive behavior, is characteristic of daughters toward both mother and father. With the mother they have a high rate of interaction in the household, but although they share the house work, daily responsibilities (shopping, cleaning, ordering servants), and gossiping, they seldom if ever share private information about each other. This is especially so during the period when adolescent girls are constantly watched to stop them from seeing young men. The young daughters develop standard ways of lying to the parents to get out of the house for secret rendezvous, and have very few legitimate occasions in which they are permitted to leave the home alone. Since the mother is the principal sentry, the Mo-Da relationship is in no way improved by this activity. The father, moreover, is likely to be highly punitive if he suspects that the daughter's virginity is threatened (a not very unlikely possibility), and any show of social independence on the daughter's part is seen as threatening the father's honor. This, of course, is directly related to the fact that most marriages in San Juan are initiated through seduction and elopement (*robo* or *huida*). There are very few young men indeed who are willing to risk the wrath of a father by asking for the daughter in marriage.

SEXUALITY

The primary variable to be discussed in this section is the developing organization of sexuality. Of secondary interest is the development of sexual identity. Hsu would seem to include only the first of these in his attributes of sexuality and libidinality, but where information makes reasonable speculation possible, it seems more informative to include the second, as it illuminates and expands the whole subject.

In dealing with organization of sexuality, we are fully in the middle of the Oedipal situation. Anthropologists have for several generations clung to the idea that the Oedipal conflict as described by Freud and his followers for Vienna is not a universal situation for mankind, as claimed by some Freudians (for example, Roheim, 1932), but instead was the working out of emotional conflicts in only one kind of nuclear family structure. Malinowski, analyzing data ex post facto, claimed that the Trobriand core triangle was brother, sister, sister's son, which made sense in a culture with matrilineal clans, avuncular residence, and avuncular inheritance of goods and titles. The father was not an authority figure, while the mother's brother was. The libidinality between brother and sister was very strong, and the incest strongly suppressed (1927, 1929). In Vienna the triangle involved the father, mother, and male child, and the authority and libidinality involved the father-mother relationship. In each case, it is assumed that there is a strong libidinal attachment between the son and his mother (and daughter and father) and the conflict is engendered because the child feels jealous of the libidinal (and often sexual) attachment of the loved parent to some other adult, hates him (or her), and then feels afraid and guilty by reason of that hate. In the Viennese situation, the ideal solution to the conflict is for the boy to identify with, and be closely attached to, his father, and the girl to her mother. The cross-sex libidinal attachment to a parent or sibling is supposed to be repressed if not obliterated in the normal process of growth. Failure to achieve this is grounds both for the label of unresolved Oedipal fixation and, among middle-class Westerners, for psychotherapy.

More recently, Anne Parsons has delineated what she called the South Italian nuclear complex, which is in turn different from both the Viennese and Trobriand complexes. In this cultural solution to the conflict engendered in the young, the major attachment continues to be between two consanguines of different sex and different generation without giving rise to neurotic patterns of behavior. Looked at from the point of view of the young, a boy remains attached to his mother, and a girl to her father, throughout life, and the culture takes this as a model (1964).

We intend to show that the Mexican family structure engenders a cultural solution similar to the South Italian one; but before we do so, two points must be made concerning most discussions of the Oedipal conflict. Psychoanalysts' and social scientists' discussions typically ignore the fact that in the conflict engendered, the adults may play a very vigorous role. Usually discussions of this conflict start from the position that it is the biology or the ecology of the family that is responsible for engendering the conflict. The child is caught in a natural, and biological, bind, from which he must extricate himself. There is little or no discussion of the role that the parents have in fostering the conflict, guiding it, prolonging it, or resolving it (although it was noted by Freud [1952:217–18]). And yet it is the case that each culture has typical ways in which adults handle children, and further, these adults have needs, not only with respect to the behavior of the children, but also with respect to other adults (cf. Ackerman, 1958:170). From the infant point of view, the triangle typically includes ego, mother, and father. But this is a triangle to the other two members as well, and as we shall see, the Mexican material clearly indicates that a full understanding of the playing out (or the playing) of the strains of the conflict cannot be had without a clear idea of the stakes, and the strategies, of all members of the triangle. A knowledge of only the supposed biological drives of the infant is not sufficient for an understanding of the long or short term interaction process.

The second point, increasingly discussed by social scientists, is that from one point of view the sexual conflict inherent in the Oedipal conflict is beside the point. But this includes the extremely crucial point that a major accomplishment of this process is the establishment of the ego ideal of the young male of the species.

The crucial leap for the male is from identification with the mother, engendered by the early helplessness and close contact, to complete and successful identification with the male role.[8] An unresolved Oedipal conflict refers primarily to the fact that this transfer has not adequately taken place, and the male is still to a degree tied to his mother's *persona*. This is the part of the argument that was virtually ignored in the early discussions of the topic. Malinowski, for example, confined himself to the sexual fantasies and strivings associated with individuals or roles involved, as did Roheim (1932). Talcott Parsons has been notable for paying close attention to the ego-ideal formation aspects of the conflict, and from the middle 1950's on, this topic, under his leadership, has assumed a more and more important part in the discussions. Anne Parsons' discussion of the South Italian nuclear complex is very nicely balanced in this regard (1964).

The ego ideal dimension may be far more important, in terms of the structure of the wider society, than the sexual dimension of the Oedipal conflict. First of all, it is the direct origin of the kind of manipulative activity which is commonly expected from the males, or types of males, in the society. This then implies a very great deal about the economic and political dynamic of the society involved. Hsu has often pointed out that Western Europe has been much more dynamic in economic terms than has China (1954). Surely more knowledge of ego ideal formations would give us a more complete understanding of this marked difference.

With this background, we may proceed to a discussion of sexuality in the San Juan family. To the American or northwestern European eye, the male in San Juan culture has never been able to fully transfer his libidinal energies from his mother to an outsider. (A discussion of female identification follows a different route.) There is abundant material, in Oscar Lewis's publications and elsewhere (Lewis, 1959, 1961; Diaz-Guerrero, 1955), that shows this typical Mediterranean pattern.

The most obvious parts of this complex are the following: the mother, sister, and wife are regarded as sacrosanct in a sexual sense. The wife is supposed to be a virgin at marriage, pure in heart and body, and is not supposed to be lascivious. This is extended to all females in the family from mother and wife to daughters and sisters. Sexual intercourse with the

8. Bettelheim has pointed out that Oedipus not only had an attachment to the mother, but he grew up without an affectionate father model in his crucial years (1966). One of Oedipus' problems was the lack of a positive father figure to facilitate the transfer from female to male identity.

wife should be primarily for the purpose of having children, not pleasure. For pleasure, a man turns to pornography and to prostitutes and mistresses. Physical contact in San Juan (often of an intimate sort) in public is most often seen between people of the same sex and age. (To the American, the male-male interaction [especially when drunk] smacks of homosexuality.) Occasionally a heterosexual couple will be seen publically exchanging physically intimate contact, but in these cases it is rarely a husband and wife, but a couple who are courting. Husband and wife do not act in an intimate way in public.

A word should be said concerning marriage, and our designation of the husband-wife relationship. This has been discussed in great detail elsewhere, and a short summary will suffice here (cf. E. Hunt, *op. cit.*). There are several kinds of more or less permanent relationships recognized between a man and a woman which involve sexuality. They vary in terms of permanence and in terms of legitimacy. Starting with the most impermanent, young men in San Juan initiate their sex life with brief associations with an older lower-class woman, the object of which is sexual pleasure (and practice) for the man, and to a certain degree sexual pleasure, but more importantly, economic aid for the woman. The relationship between the man and the woman will not be publicly acknowledged by the man's family, and seldom publicly by the man himself.

A more permanent relation, which may last several years, is the case where a man establishes a woman (again of lower class than himself) in a house, supports the house and the illegitimately born children. He may also recognize the children legally. He does not in any sense permanently reside in this house, but will visit there from time to time, and irregularly sleep there. San Juaneros call this *amasiato* or *union libre*, and is the first which we can call marriage. A private ceremony called the *pedida de perdon* often ritualizes the "marriage contract" of this type. *Amasiatos* when a man is already legally married are called *la casa chica* (the small home).

Following the initial affairs are a group of alliances which, while legally different, all amount to what a native speaker of English would call marriage. The association of *amasiato* or *union libre* can be by what in Anglo-Saxon law is called common-law marriage (long-term cohabitation). Two other forms of marriage may follow: civil marriage and religious marriage. In many cases both of these last two are performed together. These three types of marriage differ in prestige and class connotation, but for the purposes of this discussion these differences are not significant. (For example, a marriage between two upper-class people of the same rank and prestige is almost always a religious marriage, in addition to the legally necessary civil ceremony.)

A man may be simultaneously involved in at least one of each of these types of marital association. (For example, Jesus Sanchez [O. Lewis, 1961] was involved in a legal marriage and had two *casas chicas* at the same time.) It is therefore tempting to call this an optional polygyny, but the women involved do not normally acknowledge the others' existence, and when they do, do not relate to them as co-wives, but rather as jealous suitors of the same man, at times fighting each other over him. They deeply resent the drain on time and income (and estate, if any) that other alliances mean for the man.

Under the circumstances, then, there is a rather wide variety of relationships that might be called husband-wife. Common to them all is the fact of non-incestuous relationship, sexual cohabitation, and the desire to produce children. As we come up the scale we add first recognition of children, then support of children, then support of the woman (and the house, which is implied), then co-residence, and then designation of woman and children as legal heirs of the estate (although this may mean little; cf. Hunt, 1965b). If we were to accept this as a form of polygyny, then we would call the *casa chica* a form of marriage. And as the *casa chica* becomes stabilized, the interaction between the man and the woman takes on many of the properties of the more complete marital relationships. So we shall mean by the husband-wife relationship, the interaction of a man and woman who have at least established a stable *amasiato* or *casa chica.* (Before this stabilization, the relationship has the characteristics of that of a mistress-lover or a prostitute-customer.)

The married women of San Juan often complain of male impotence, and that the sexual life of the married woman is rarely pleasurable. Many males feel that sex is not and should not be very important in marriage. Any public display of an intimate sort by the wife is likely to deeply embarrass and intimidate the man. This is usually phrased in terms of the children; a woman of respect, whom one considers a spouse (rather than a mistress) is usually referred to as "the mother of my children," and expected to act constrained and demure in all public settings. Moreover she is expected to be passive and non-demanding in private.

The cultural ideal of the *macho*, the *chingon*, is one of great sexuality. It is in this realm, perhaps more than in any other, that there is a vast gulf between what the cultural ideal expects of a man and what the man is psychologically prepared to do. The man is supposed to be tireless, and potent for many many years. A large sexual organ is greatly admired and often desperately wanted. Men fear impotence, while women fear sterility (and *not* frigidity).

At the same time, excessive sexual activity, especially on the part of a male, is despised by other males. Two terms for this sort of person are *cojete*, a pejorative which means a male who has intercourse very excessively, and *cabron*, the term for the male goat, which also means a despised male who has only sex on his mind. There is very deep ambivalence on this subject, with the negative feelings usually stronger than the positive ones. For the San Juan male, there is a constant association between threatening sexuality and the animal kingdom (especially the goat and dog symbols). An overly sexy female is said to have "dog." Little boys are threatened with the statement that if they do not behave, a dog will eat their genitals. And there are many local stories about the dangers for a man who urinates in the open at night (after having had sexual intercourse), for there is always the chance that a supernatural magic dog would come flying in the sky and snap at his penis. Hence, even though sex and sexuality is a strongly pushed male goal, the males are afraid and at times disgusted by the prospect.

This deep ambivalence suggests that the males have never adequately learned to channel their sexual energy into self-approved activities and away from their mothers. In the first place, it is unlikely that they would learn by example what a properly sexed man is, for their father had the same difficulties with their mother as they do with their wives. Secondly, a woman will strive, insofar as possible, to keep her sons firmly attached to her in an emotional sense. Once a woman came to my wife to ask if it was abnormal for a woman to want sexual intercourse, as she did, but her husband did not. Her husband's mother had reportedly told him, just before marriage, that the only reason for sexual intercourse with a wife was to produce children, and that it was a dirty, disagreeable form of behavior which should be confined to "professionals." The son took her word for it, and in several years of marriage had approached his wife only three or four times after they had had the number of children he desired.

A common occurrence in San Juan is that a woman of relatively high social class will maneuver an ineffective son into a civil or religious marriage with a woman of little wealth and social standing whom she feels she can easily dominate. After several children are produced, she will then do her utmost to break up the marriage, and will try to take the children into her own household. When the son's household finally breaks up, he is as likely as not to move in with his mother for at least part of the time.

It is also a characteristic of this culture that all women want children, especially sons. While the men have fantasies about losing potency, women's nightmares involve the loss of the capacity to have children. A typical woman's dream is that she lost her purse with all her money in it; and one of our informants reflected that her daughter "could not have any more children probably because she had such a dream." The vagina and uterus are called euphemistically the "doll's box" or "the little jewel box" (by women; men usually call it "the shell") and woman's fertility is proudly displayed. Women spend a great deal of time gossiping about others' pregnancies, exchanging information about medicines or herbs to increase or produce fertility, to prolong the ability to bear offspring, or to augment milk output. Asked about aphrodisiacs, they indignantly said that "only men are preoccupied with such things." In fact, men in San Juan do have quite a large store of spurious knowledge on local herbs, magical potions, and drugstore pills to increase sexual strength. Children are not only a form of old-age insurance; equally important, they provide the primary relationship in which the woman can control others, and in which others are willingly dependent upon her. With the earlier unions often taking place in the middle teens for the girls, their mothers may be in their thirties and forties, and still very energetic. It often happens then that the young wives are totally dominated by the mother or mother-in-law and have only minor privileges as married women, while the older woman takes the responsibility of caring for the household. A young mother will often find that her mother or mother-in-law is running roughshod over her in the successful attempt to gain control over the infants and small children. A strong-willed daughter will react to this by virtually severing contact with her mother. A weaker one will allow herself to be maneuvered and bullied, and will wind up a womb at the mother's or husband's mother's disposal. But it is much more difficult to sever relations with a mother-in-law, since the spouse is very unlikely to allow her to do so.

Given that most women want to control as many children as possible, and that there is a strong attachment to the sons, in San Juan there is an added Oedipal fillip to a woman's taking over her son's children (the children often call *her* "mother," especially if they live in the household). She becomes, we would speculate, a surrogate mother to her son's children, and therefore as close to a wife to him as the incest rules allow. The major libidinal attachment for males, we would argue then, remains the mother throughout their lives, and for a woman it is her sons.

A woman facilitates this state of affairs by manipulating her children, and by giving them advice that tends to prevent their shifting to the outside world. There is some incentive for this, for the husband has typically proved to be an inadequate and unsatisfying source of sexuality and intimacy; it is sublimated, and gets redirected to the son(s). It is interesting to note in this regard that most women have no difficulty in coming to terms with the ideal of marital love, but readily agree that after a few months of marriage it is very difficult to preserve—especially, San Juan female informants agree, after children arrive. "Then only your children would love you," one said. Given a marriage to what a Western European would call a sexually inadequate male, the women do not rebel. Rather, their usual reaction to the realities of married life is the martyr complex, which involves passiveness, surrender, regard of males as brutes who do what the men want (not what the women want), plus unconscious and sometimes conscious sexual frustration. They then often use this martyr posture to further capture the libidinal drives of their sons, who find an emotional vacuum created by the failure of their father to satisfy their mother emotionally. It is symptomatic that a spouse being affectionate would call the other *mamacita* or *papacito* (little mother or little father), while when being possessive or authoritarian would call the other "child" (*hija* or *hijo*).

In summary, the husband-wife relationship is a deeply ambivalent one.

It starts out with the expectation on both sides that a fully intimate and sexual relationship will be established. The man has trouble with it, however, for he has never transferred his libidinal instincts fully away from his mother, and he comes to identify his wife with his mother. (This could be easy to do in most cultures, for, as we have been at some pains to point out above, the wife takes over many of the functions of the mother with respect to intimacy, household management, care while sick, and so on.) The result is interference with sexuality, to the point of abstention, and often to impotence. Males, caught in this bind between the ideal and their unconscious, may resort to alcohol, prostitutes, violence against wives, homosexuality, and escapism in a variety of forms. A very common one is spending a great deal of time with male friends, eating, drinking, and being intimate. Two patterns are quite repetitive and suggest homosexual overlays: men friends in San Juan go to prostitution houses and share the same prostitute (cf. Blanchard, 1959), and they take baths together, in which a great deal of horse-play and physical contact take place.

Father-Son. Of the other two relationships being discussed in this paper, the father-son and the brother-brother, there is little to be said about the brother-brother relationship in the matter of sexuality. The father is of course involved in the triangle (although perhaps a case could be made out for the chief Oedipal triangle of adults as involving mother-son-son's wife). The son in part despises the father for "violating" his mother. On the other hand, he tries to identify with the male role in society. He is to a degree frustrated in this, for the father is distant, authoritarian, and not inclined to be rewarding to a man who has such a close (and libidinal) relationship with a woman whom he thinks of as his exclusive property and of whom he is likely to be jealous. An important feature of this culture is that once a male comes to regard a woman as his, any hint of her attentions being attracted elsewhere is likely to mean a violent death for all concerned.[9] A man is therefore the more likely to withdraw rewards from the son. At the same time, the father is the *macho* model, and the son wants to be like him. Some sons are more successful than others in identifying with the male role. In a sense, some men are healthier than others, and can be better husbands or sons than others, irrelevant of the general cultural pattern.

In this respect as well as in many others it is necessary for us to differentiate between effective and ineffective children. The strong ones dissociate themselves from the parents, sometimes in open, violent struggle, and adapt very successfully to a life of manipulation of the environment. These often achieve satisfying, stable monogamous marriages as well.

9. We arrived at a party one night and remarked that we had seen the charred remains of a bus rammed against a wall. It turned out that the girl whom the bus driver regarded as his *novia* (sweetheart, close to fiancée in sharing with others connotation) was walking along the street with a young man whom the *novio* did not know. He got mad and rammed his bus into the couple, killing a dozen people with flaming gasoline in the process. The males at the party regarded this as a roaring success.

They may run away from home, steal (elope with) a local girl and take her away from the village, and cut off almost all contact with parents. Apparently their libidinal drives have been detached from the parents and transferred to a stranger, and they have successfully assimilated a manipulative ego ideal as well. This is as true for the male as for the female. Many San Juan girls end adolescence by running away from town with a local man or a visiting outsider.

The far more numerous ineffective sons, however, remain strongly attached to the mother, although often ambivalently so, and seldom manifest an ability to successfully manipulate the environment. Sexually and emotionally they are not able to adjust to a spouse, and are soon back with mother. They are relatively ineffective in the business of earning a living as well, and become appendices of "dependent relatives" in a joint household run by their parents, or take minor bureaucratic jobs in remote areas.

If our analysis is correct, then a major problem to be worked on in the future is the explanation of this dichotomy between the psychologically obviously successful and the obviously unsuccessful children of a Mexican family.

The South Italian nuclear complex, as outlined by Anne Parsons, has therefore many of the same elements as the Mexican. In both cases, the male's sexual energy typically does not get transferred to an outsider, and the father is, especially among those families where there is a very low level of material control of the environment, not a highly cathected ego ideal for the young male.

The differences are just as interesting, however. Women appear to cathect only to sons, after marital failure, and not to carry this from an earlier father cathection. This is sensible enough, once you consider that the fathers are, many of them, rarely around the house, distant and authoritarian when present, and the source of much negative affect. Many women expand this to hatred of men in general, and wish to have little to do with them. The exception to this is the males that a woman suckled, and they are the subjects of a strong cathection. A major source of bodily pleasure for women comes from nursing, which in San Juan involves an enormous amount of time, leisurely relaxation, extensive skin-to-skin contact, and much warmth and lolling about. Men in San Juan resent this closeness. Ramirez and Parres (1957) point out that this is the period in which many lower-class men abandon their spouses. They attribute it, however, to projected sibling rivalry with the newborn.

On the subject of cross-sex sibling attraction, we have as yet reached no conclusion. It appears as if there is little to it, but the prevalence of spinster sisters living in and caring for a man's home, at times to the exclusion of the wife, and the sibling incest fears (which in part can be explained by the parenthood and illegitimacy patterns, but which in part may also be generated by a strong libidinal attraction) suggest the need for more research. Diaz-Guerrero mentions the mother-wife identity of the sisters to their brothers, and this is also suspicious. Ramirez and Parres (1957) stress the importance of sibling rivalry, but do not discuss cross-sex attitudes. Further detailed research hopefully will resolve this important question.

The successful male ego identity would seem to be more easily achieved, at least by some, in Mexico than in southern Italy. This is at least in part a function of our having sampled higher classes. The higher a person's class, the more likely it is that a) he has a father who is effective in wresting a living from the environment, and therefore is a more effective model, and b) he will be successful in wresting a living from the environment himself. In cultures that build male identities at least in part around their finding and keeping economically good occupations, it must surely be the case that the greater the probability of achieving such an occupation, the greater the probability of maintaining satisfactory male identity.

We have seen, in the previous pages, how a family in San Juan may prevent, by various strategems and manipulations (in the negative sense) a son's realizing the male ideal. It is not certain in San Juan that a son of a wealthy family is going to be a successful man. Mobility both upwards and down has high rates within a generation. Many other factors are at work. But it seems highly probable to us that one of the factors at work is the probability of achieving status through wealth. In this respect, a developing economy, especially one with a high rate of growth like Mexico, ought to have a considerable effect upon the character structure of at least the males. As more and more jobs become available, as there is greater differentiation of skills useful to the economy, then more and more people ought to be able to realize the male ideal, given that a useful one exists in the culture, as it does in Mexico.

MAJOR AXES

In summary, there are two relationships of great importance in the Mexican family and society, the father-son, and the mother-son. The father-son relationship is marked both by the ambivalence toward dominance and by reverberation of the ambivalences inherent in the husband-wife-son triangle (one original Oedipal triangle). The mother-son relationship is also a dense one, and for many people in San Juan it is actually the core of the family and household. This is as true of mothers who are frustrated by their husbands as it is of sons who are frustrated by their fathers and wives. Furthermore, there are two distinct modes of adaptation to the culture on the part of children, and two distinct modes of adaptation on the part of the parents to these modes. It is difficult to make any judgment of frequency of these different types, but it is our clear impression that the weaker of the two is much more common than the stronger. On this basis, therefore, we will proceed as if this weaker (to an American, unresolved, Oedipal conflict) mode is the standard Mexican pattern. (The questions which a bimodal distribution raises are complex, crucial, and fascinating. We cannot attack them here.)

The father-son relationship, insofar as it can be separated from the Oedipal triangle, is organized around the principle of dominance, and the ambivalence regarding dominance so widespread in Mexican culture. There is both a desire to be a dutiful son, by which one gains the approval of the father, and to avoid any semblance of subjection and inferiority, by which one escapes the unpleasant and often unrewarding relationship involving dominance.

On the other hand, the son's relationship to his mother is equally complex and dense, emotionally speaking. The mother is the representation of morality. She is the intermediary between the son and the husband. She is often the only parental figure who is with the children continuously and is available to them, not being a distant, authoritarian, cold, or feared person. But the mother will often share the burden of early child-raising with her mother or mother-in-law, and may even be pushed completely out of the picture by the other woman.

The mother-son relationship contains the most satisfactions in the family or outside it. There is in it little of the dominance about which San Juaneros are so ambivalent. Both can trust in the fulfillment of responsibility of the other (a responsibility which reverses as the two grow older). This is the relationship with the greatest intimacy. Overt sexuality is excluded because of the incest taboo, but covert sexuality is an important component of the relationship. Unconsciously, a man has not made a full transference of his ego energy away from his mother, and due to the confusion of the dependency distribution, regards his wife as a poor substitute for his mother. His overt sexuality is directed away from the family (for he has never learned that it is acceptable to express sexuality in the family), toward prostitutes and short-term mistresses. His conjugal family is in effect a substitute for his natal family, and he will remain close to his mother, emotionally, throughout life.

The husband-wife relationship is a resultant of the other two. A man looks forward to a satisfactory sexual romance with a woman, but is typically disappointed by his wife, for his personality is not equipped to cope with a steady, legitimate sexual relation. His wife is supposed to fear him, and usually does; she is also supposed to respect him, which is more problematical. She is sexually frustrated, and usually undersupported, and turns to her sons for emotional and often, later, financial support, thereby increasing the density of the relationship between mother and son, and increasing the difficulties of the son's identification with the father.

DOMINANT RELATIONSHIPS

To a certain extent it is useful to analyze the Mexican family in terms of three dyadic relationships. But, as we have seen, these three dyads also form the classical Oedipal triangle. Choosing the dominant relationship out of this welter is our next task, and it is not an easy one.

It is obvious that, at least from a male's point of view, the central relationship, if there is one, is not the brother-brother. It seems that we can rule out the husband-wife relationship, for this is too subordinate to the mother-son relationship. We are left, then, within the framework we have somewhat arbitrarily established for this paper, with the choice between the father-son dyad and the mother-son dyad as the dominant relationship in this essentially patrilateral, patriarchical society.

It appears that there are *two* dominant relationships in this family structure. From the male point of view, the father-son and the mother-son relationships are each extremely important, and in one way or another ramify throughout the society. Each of these relationships ramifies more, we would judge, than any of the other relationships. But they are constructed differently, of different materials. The society as a whole is very interested in the proper filial relationships, makes a great deal out of hierarchical authority and dependence relationships, and in general, in terms of its ideals and ideas about how it operates, looks patriarchical. The ideal father-son relationship is the model for the employer-employee relationship, the relationships between the governors and the governed, and so on. Most of the material for this relationship is out in the open, stated as ideal or idea, or as precept for action. There are pretty clear ideas in the culture about what a good son and a good father are. The only bit of unconscious material that was important in the discussion of this relationship concerned the ambivalence toward dominance, which is formed in the family and found ramified throughout the culture. The rest of the analysis is derived from pretty straightforward conscious data.

But the mother-son relationship is equally important, although the main characteristics of the material for this relationship are mostly unconscious, and hidden from the members of the culture in any clear-cut, verbally stated ideal, the ideal being one of respect and asexual affection, of protecting the family women's honor on the one hand, and of effective sexuality in the abstract on the other. The particular kind of resolution of the infantile dependency which is the lot of all humans means a particular kind of emotional and personality structure for the adult. Many kinds of data point to this condition, including the attitudes toward wife and conjugal family, attitudes toward sons, and postures toward productive work. One kind of typical male in San Juan society exhibits the classic inferiority complex, and this conglomeration of behavioral characteristics summarizes one dimension of this particular resolution of the dependency problem. For this male, then, attitudes toward his wife, his job, his children, his conjugal family, his honor, and much else, are conditioned by the structure of the mother-son relationship in this particular culture. Part of the tension for the males in this culture then derives from the fact that there is a gap between the personality as set up by the mother-son relationship and that set up by the father-son relationship. The father-son produces a model to manipulate the environment masterfully, easily, manfully. The mother-son generates a model of dependency and stunted emotional growth, and does not usually generate the ability to produce masterful, independent, adult behavior. Which model a man follows shapes most of his future interactions, inside or outside the family.

The typical posture toward the world, toward fellow human beings, and toward family members, is derived from both the father-son and the mother-son relationships in different degrees for each man. From the aspect of the cultural ideals and cultural ideas, the father-son is the dominant relationship, and much can be found in the extra-familial social organization to support this view. From the aspect of psychological processes, the mother-son is the dominant relationship, and much can be found in the extra-familial social organization to support this view. Under these circumstances, I find it impossible to choose which is the dominant relationship.

This conclusion opens up other problems. Benedict, in *Patterns of Culture,* suggested it was quite probable that not all cultures were organized in terms of a single configuration (1934). Some were. Some others, she suggested, like the United States, had not been able to integrate. This is perhaps the situation to be found with respect to dominant kinship relationships.

EXTRA-FAMILIAL RELATIONSHIPS

One problem with which the symposium wrestled was the exact meaning of our proposition 7, that the dominant kinship relationship determines relationships outside the kinship group. Several different ways of approaching this proposition are possible. The one which we prefer is one which was utilized extensively by Bateson and Mead in their writings on national character in the early 1940's (Bateson and Mead, 1947; Bateson, 1943; Mead, 1942; cf. Hunt, 1965a, for an extended discussion of these materials). In their analyses of Balinese, German, American, and English familial and other behavior they utilized a mode of analysis that is highly relevant to our concerns here.

First they analyzed the components of the important relationships in the nuclear family, with special reference to variables such as authority and aggression, which are analogous to Hsu's attitudes. They isolated particular patterns in this limited social field. Then they discussed relationships that occurred outside this field (such as in relationships of citizens with leaders, employees with employers). These extra-familial relationships were again analyzed in terms of the same variables as the familial relationships. Some variables occurred in much the same fashion in both environments, especially with respect to authority and aggression. Mead and Bateson did not propose any specific learning process, nor did they claim that there was a one-way causality between the familial and extra-familial environments. In this they were consistent with, and perhaps following the lead of, Erich Fromm, whose position on the causality chain was very clearly set out in *Escape from Freedom* (1941; cf. Hunt, *op. cit.*, for a discussion of the development of this position).

This is the position we adopt here. The component of dominance-submission in the familial relationships, and especially in the father-son relationship, occurs in much the same way (in a homologous way?) in extra-familial relationships. Responsibility-dependency are also to be found outside in highly similar form. We do not agree with Hsu's position that there is a simple determinacy involved here. Rather, we agree with the Bateson-Mead-Fromm viewpoint—that while for any individual the attitudes occur in and are first learned in the family, the wider society is at least in part determining the structure of action in the family, and therefore in this wider sense the extra-familial structure is determining the familial and subsequently the individual one. It has become increasingly popular to argue the kind of hypothesis that Hsu presents; it is to be found for example in McClelland's arguments for the role of achievement in economic development (1961).

It is immediately apparent that for the individual, things start in the family. But the more important question is the causal factors. To do this we must determine if the society is causing the family to treat its children in these ways, or if the chain starts with the family itself. The crux of the causality proposition is to be found in the social milieu, we believe, and not in the developmental cycle of the individual. This will rarely be an easy matter to determine, and we find ourselves unable to demonstrate it at the moment for most of the Mexican materials. We agree with Hsu that there is often an obvious correlation between the pattern of relationships in the family and the structure of extra-familial relationships, but we wish to dissociate this correlation both from the idea of dominance and from the idea that the familial environment is the independent and the extra-familial environment the dependent variable.

With the variable of sexuality we have another kind of problem, for here it seems that the typical organization of sexuality inside the family is the reverse of the organization outside the family. In the Western psychiatric ideal, the successful transfer of sexual energy to an outsider means that little such energy is put into those who are tabooed sexually after approximately the age of five. Conversely, in the South Italian, Mexican, and northern European unresolved, Oedipal configurations, there is much libido focused on tabooed individuals and little left for outsiders. This kind of thinking is based upon an assumption of a zero-sum game (the "conservation of energy" hypothesis of Freud) where only so much of this energy is available, and must be distributed in only a few possible ways to maintain itself within the ranges of "normality." How a culture defines what is normal, however, may be far removed from Viennese ideals.

With respect to the family/non-family distinction, then, we have a basically different kind of distribution to contend with. Whereas the attitudes toward dominance can be easily transferred from the father to the president or king without conflict, the libidinal attachment of mother and child cannot be directly transferred to the outside without disruption of adult marital life. Rather, in this latter situation some sort of complementary distribution is required to meet the standards of normality presented by psychiatric theory. In this view, the extension of the libidinal attachment of mother and child rather than relocation to the outside environment (as in the Italian or Mexican case) is not without conflict, even though it may be culturally accepted.

Summary

At the beginning of this paper we stated eight propositions that in our opinion formed the core of Hsu's argument. We have found six of these to be extremely useful in the analysis of our field materials. More specifically, the propositions and our conclusions regarding them are as follows:

1. "Relationships are composed of components, such as authority, etc." We completely agree with this, and find it a powerful tool for the analysis of social interaction.

2. "These components are defined in such a way as to be universal." We agree with this, and think that the effort of defining them in a universal way well worth the effort. In this way, our science of the behavior of some humans may become general enough to be a science of animal behavior (cf. Hunt, 1967a, 1967b).

3. "The components are given specific definitions." We have attempted in this paper to refine and expand the definitions of the components, in the attempt to find a maximally useful set of them.

4. "Kinship relationships can be defined in universal terms using English role-names, and the attributes or components of these relationships occur universally." We have seen no reason to stop using English role-names for these relationships, although in some cases the definition of a relationship is likely to be very different from the American folk definition (for example, our difficulties in the analysis of marriage, above). There seems to be no reason why any particular relationship, as defined in this way, should contain more than a minimal few of components, and perhaps not even this is necessary. One is reminded of the distinction between mater and genetrix, which usually are the same individual, but needn't be. Normally, one of the two is necessary for the relationship to exist. In general, we doubt that any significant number of components will universally inhere in a relationship named by English kin role names.

5. "In any kinship system, one relationship is dominant over all the others, and the attributes of that relationship dominate over the attributes of the other relationships." Our Mexican data fail to support the universality of dominance.

6. "The dominant relationship determines the structure and content of all other kinship relationships." Putting aside the matter of dominance, we can heartily support the idea that strong relationships affect the other relationships in the system. In the Mexican case discussed here, these reverberations are fruitfully organized around the Oedipal conflict. But the general proposition is supported.

7. "The dominant relationship determines the structure and content of many relationships outside the kinship group." Again leaving aside the idea of a single dominant relationship, which does not apply in our material, we find definite evidence that there is often intimate connection between the familial and extra-familial relationships. We doubt, however, that the family is the independent variable.

8. "There are universal models of dominance, four of which have been postulated (father-son, etc.)." We have not been able to examine this proposition because we found no single dominant relationship in our Mexican materials.

Hsu's hypothesis combines several ideas. It states that cultures have styles, that these are describable, that relationships in the family can be described in terms of components, that one relationship dominates all others in the family, that extra-familial relationships are a product of the dominant familial relationships, and that the cultural style is a product of the structure of familial relationships. All of these ideas are old, and many of them have been combined in the past. One of the values of the hypothesis is that it does combine this large number of ideas in an interesting way.

In most respects the hypothesis has been supported. There are two very powerful relationships in the San Juan family; the structure of these two greatly affects the other relationships, and the properties of these two affect the extra-familial relationships which in turn are closely integrated with the structure of extra-familial institutions. In addition, we have found two different responses to the family system on the part of males, and these two "styles" are each important to, and well integrated into, the economic and political systems of the town (and the nation). Two parts of this hypothesis seem to us of doubtful value. The first is the notion of dominance. It apparently is the case that in some societies dominance occurs. But it is by no means universal. Secondly, we think it unlikely that any small number of types or styles of dominance will be found. With these adjustments, however, we find the hypothesis to be interesting and fruitful.

In this paper we have concentrated primarily on expansion and refinement of the componential frame. Many of the other ideas are relatively easy to apply and utilize. A major methodological problem remains, however, and that is the determination of the "style" of the culture. It seems likely that a few diagnostic items would adequately characterize a culture, and for modern nations the class structure or the rate of economic development, for example, might well be the ones. But as yet we have no clear rules for the selection of these characteristics. Such rules must be produced if this sort of hypothesis is to be useful, for, as we have pointed out, for modern literate nations it is impossible to cover the whole of the cultural product. A system for selection must be developed. Intuition is valuable, but it is not easily replicated. Once a clearer notion is developed of how this can be done, an extensive testing of this hypothesis would be relatively easily accomplished and, in our opinion, well worth the effort.

Father-Son Dominance: Tikopia and China

In this paper I will review the ethnographic material for Tikopia in relation to the following four propositions contained in Hsu's 1965 article and compare my findings with his interpretation of traditional (pre-communist) Chinese kinship and culture. I shall stay as close as possible to the intent of the Hsu hypothesis as I understand it.

The four propositions are:

1. A dominant relationship can be distinguished in any kinship arrangement.
2. Each relationship has certain universal attributes.
3. The attributes of the dominant relationship will affect the qualities and patterns of the non-dominant or "recessive" relationships.
4. The dominant relationship and its attributes will also affect the qualities and patterns of non-kinship relations.

Tikopia was not selected at random, but rather because it appeared to have a number of striking similarities with China. Like China, Tikopia has a strong emphasis on the father-son relationship. It also has a well-developed ancestor cult and a patrilineal clan organization.[1] On the other

1. Use of the term clan for both the Chinese and Tikopia patrilineal extended kinship groups is convenient for several reasons. It is the term commonly applied to the Chinese group, and Firth (1959) also proposes the term for Tikopia. It serves to show the basic similarities between the two, but several points need clarification. Murdock (1949:67–69) proposes residential unity as one criteria of a clan. In neither China nor Tikopia is residential unity a characteristic of the clan system. Several differences between the two clan systems should also be noted. The Chinese clan is exogamous, the Tikopia is not. In China women join their husband's clan, whereas in Tikopia they remain in their father's clan for some purposes while joining their husband's for others.

hand, in contrast to China, Tikopia is non-literate, it shares many cultural traits with other Polynesian cultures, it is an isolated island society with a small population, and its economy is relatively simple.

I shall examine how well Hsu's predictions for father-son dominant societies apply to Tikopia. If what Hsu proposes to be the effect of father-son dominance on Chinese culture also applies to Tikopia, we will have some confirmation of the value of the hypothesis to studies of ethnographically quite distinct situations.

The expectation is not held, by either Hsu or myself, that two cultures characterized by the same dominant relationship will be identical in culture content. If the two cultures have similar orientations, and if these orientations coincide with what Hsu has predicted, the hypothesis will find support.

My interest, however, is not restricted to simply testing Hsu's propositions about father-son dominance. I will offer an explanation for significant variations in relationships and cultural orientations between Tikopia and China in terms of Hsu's hypothesis. To do this I will depart from his approach by also considering the way non-dominant relationships influence dominant ones. This will allow my analysis to include secondary influences, and seems more consistent with a conceptualization of kinship as a psycho-social system.

I. Specific Relationships

I propose to distinguish between jural and affective ties. Jural ties will be defined as those rights and duties between specific kinship roles expressed as rules of *behavior*, whereas affective ties are those *attitudes* and *feelings* toward kin which are socially prescribed. A jural tie is exemplified for the father-eldest son relationship by the rule of primogeniture. An affective tie between husband and wife would be the prescription "love thy wife." All relationships may, of course, embody both kinds of ties. Cultures may put greater emphasis, however, on one or the other kind of tie in the construction of their ideologies of human relations. Differential emphases would to some extent parallel the distinctions between what have often been termed the expressive and instrumental qualities of social interaction. The two kinds of ties must be distinguished, because they form two partially independent systems, an affective system and a jural one, which, it would seem, have separate characteristics and may have different dominant relationships. Two men may behave toward their wives in precisely the same fashion but have very different feelings about them. The difference between the two will in all likelihood be most apparent in their behavior toward others who fill a category that substitutes for the affective ties with wives (mistresses, mothers, homosexual partners, and the like). Partial independence of this sort seems to have relevance at the cross-cultural level in the same manner as it has at the individual level.

It should be made clear that affective ties as defined here are not identical with individual, ontologically determined emotional ties in the usual sense that psychologists and psychiatrists conceive them. Affective ties in the sense used here are social prescriptions. They form part of the social system, the part that tells individuals how they "should" feel and think about specific alters.

THE BASIC RELATIONSHIPS

Father-Son. On Tikopia the ties between father and son are primarily of the jural type. Descent is traced patrilineally for purposes of transmission of family or house name, land, special religious knowledge, status, and authority. Furthermore, it is through his father that the son is connected to his *paito*, or lineage. Firth observes that, "The position of an individual as a member of a *paito* is one of the most crucial factors in his social status. From it, through his father, he receives guardianship from others of the group in his young days, rights to the product of lands and later a share in them and other property, a house site and an associated name when he marries, economic and ritual assistance on the necessary occasions, and privileges in the use of religious formulae and in appeal to the principle ancestral deities. Wealth, rank and clan membership are all primarily determined by the *paito* into which he may be born" (1957:299). Through the father the son is also tied to his clan, *kainage*. The clan has important religious functions, and its chief has considerable authority over the activities of its members. Finally, the son's relationship to his ancestors is traced patrilineally. On Tikopia this is of extreme importance, for the ancestors control the productivity of clan and lineage lands. Only those of direct descent may perform the rituals designed to obtain the ancestors' beneficence. No other jural tie in the Tikopia kinship system supersedes the father-son tie.

The jural ties between father and eldest son are, however, different from those between father and younger sons. Rules of land inheritance prescribe that the eldest son receive more than other sons. The eldest son succeeds to the status of his father, whereas younger sons, because they will form families removed from the main line of descent, have slightly less status. On the question of authority, the difference between sons is not a matter of degree. The eldest son receives his father's authority and this applies to his predominant position in relation to his brothers. The eldest also assumes the position of family representative to its ancestors. As the eldest matures, his mother and siblings come to defer to him, but he remains subordinant to his father until the latter dies (Firth, 1957:153). It is interesting to note that Firth in 1929 observed that younger sons were often urged to remain unmarried in order that family land not be further divided. This practice was being abandoned in 1952.

With the exception of younger sons being encouraged to remain bachelors, the jural ties between father and sons in China are the same as on Tikopia.

The affective ties between father and son present a very different situation. "In this land the man favors his female children, the mother favors her male children. The woman, great is her affection for her male children, the man, great is his affection for his female children; it is done from affection" (Firth, 1957:154), as Pa Fenuatara explained to Firth.

Thus we have chains of cross-sex, cross-generational affective ties that run counter to the patrilineal system founded on the father-son relationship. Another of Firth's informants illustrates the consequences of this set of affective ties. Said Pa Vainunu, "Now, I who am sitting here, I have desire only for my female child, to give her my goods. I do not desire for my male child. As for my male children, I do not say to leave my property for them because their own wives come hither from other families. They go to their fathers and speak for something for themselves to be given hither by their fathers. Thereupon these give it, because they have affection for their daughters" (1957:154). This contradiction will become more apparent as we discuss the other relevant relationships.

The passing of goods from father to daughter in contradiction to the rule of patrilineal inheritance is most often a covert maneuver, because the sons may object, basing their arguments on the fact that the goods are part of their legitimate inheritance (Firth, 1957:154). A son, it would seem, is not expected to be affectionate toward his father, but is to regard him with respect and fear.

A distinction in terms of affective ties is also made between eldest and younger sons. "The married pair who have many children, great is their affection for their youngest, and for the girls, but as for the eldest, there is not affection" (Firth, 1959a:152).

In situations where the jural and affective ties conflict, the jural ties usually are of greater importance. The example of a father giving goods to his daughter is an exception to this, but in the crucial case of land inheritance the patrilineal rule remains dominant.

The Chinese affective system does not emphasize the feelings of a father for his daughter as against his feelings for his son. In contrast to China we might expect the Tikopia father-son relationship to be more involved with resentment, suspicion, and fear on the part of the son, and irritation and lack of tolerance on the father's side.

Husband-Wife. This axis does not seem to be of primary importance in either the Chinese or Tikopia systems. In China, where marriage is arranged by the parents, affection between husband and wife is subordinate to filial duties to parents. The Tikopia situation is different, since the wish to marry is recognized as being a matter of affection, especially since premarital liaison is common. However, affection is not prescribed between Tikopia spouses. "There are no open signs of affection between them, no public caresses, no use of terms corresponding to 'dear,' or of those diminutive suffixes which so delight the heart of Teuton or Slav" (Firth, 1959a: 121–22). Because the wife brings with her at marriage the right to the produce of certain of her father's land, she has a degree of leverage vis-à-vis her husband that the Chinese wife does not have. The affective ties between father and daughter and the importance of cross-lineage relationships after marriage (such as wife with her father and brothers) serve to raise the wife's status in Tikopia.

The wife's relationship to her husband's clan is described by Firth: "on the one hand for formal privileges she remains a member of her own clan, but on the other for economic and social cooperation she is included in the group of relatives of her husband" (1959a:317). It would be interesting to know with which clan she is buried, but there is no information on this point.

Also in contrast to China, the husband-wife relationship is apparently not viewed as being primarily important as a source of sons. At least Firth does not mention this point. Nor are the few cases of Tikopia polygyny rationalized as serving to provide sons, a common rationale in China.

In Tikopia the husband-wife relationship does not appear to influence the father-son relationship to any notable extent, since neither inheritance nor affection create problems between the two. Firth makes no mention of fathers and sons competing for the wife/mother's affection. Divorce is similarly rare on Tikopia and in China.

Father-Daughter. I have already noted the affection prescribed between father and daughter. Unlike the Chinese, the Tikopia (perhaps only fathers) desire daughters. In one case a man with six daughters and a son was disappointed when his eighth child was male. Girls are adopted more often than boys. It is significant that sons are not adopted expressly to maintain lineages, several of which have been allowed to end.

Affective ties reach across lineage lines through married daughters. The maternal grandfather has a special place in his heart for his daughter's children. The failure of the lineage to dominate the lives of its sons' children is reflected in the Tikopian idea that both sets of grandparents have equal interest in their grandchildren (Firth, 1957:194).

The affective tie between father and daughter and the degree of bilaterality found in the Tikopia system appear to be related and serve to reinforce each other. All relationships are affected by this situation, just as they are by the dominance of the jural ties between father and son. We have seen, for example, how the wife's status is raised by powers derived from her father and his lineage.

Mother-Son. The mother has great affection for her son, just as her husband has great affection for his daughter. Reinforcing the affective tie between mother and son are the ties, also primarily affective, between the son and his maternal uncles and grandparents. Firth reports that, "A person usually speaks of the family group of his father as '*toku paito*,' 'my house,' and that of his mother as '*te paito kuou ne afu mai i es*,' 'the house from which I spring' " (Firth, 1957:218).

The land the mother has in trust from her father is of some importance to this relationship, since the son depends primarily on his mother's land until he marries (Firth, 1957:350). She also encourages her father to pass some of his goods to her for her sons' benefit. Disputes over the return of land given in trust to married daughters and their sons are not uncommon (Firth, 1957:351).

Although married women retain membership in their fathers' clans for many activities, they are enjoined to raise sons for their husbands' clans. The mother's kinsmen do, however, play an important role in the ceremonials marking the stages in her son's life cycle.

The Chinese mother, by comparison, has different ties with her son. As in Tikopia, her role is to provide and raise sons for her husband's clan, but she is not a source of land or goods for her sons, nor do her relatives figure importantly in their lives. In China the mother-son and father-son axes appear to reinforce each other, whereas in Tikopia they do not. Because the Tikopia son seeks affection and some material support from his mother and her relatives, he is less dependent on his father and his father's clan.

Brother-Brother. This relationship is characterized by intimacy and cooperation. There is little evidence of brother-brother rivalry. Brothers often live together, particularly bachelors with their married brothers. They cooperate in utilizing the same land, assist each other in finding wives, and they unite to oppose the drain of land and goods from their lineage resulting from the father-daughter relationship.

Solidarity results from their shared position of submission to their father's authority. They are also allied through lineage and clan membership. Importantly, they have orderly relations as a result of the clear authority of the eldest. The greater degree of affection fathers have for younger sons does not appear to create fraternal disharmony.

Sister-Sister. This relationship is of little significance, since the most important ties for women are with males. Before marriage sisters may be intimate, but on marrying they separate and may come into competition over their father's favors.

Brother-Sister. Brothers and sisters are said to be mutually supportive, and ties of affection are prescribed between them. The exception is, of course, the situation where they conflict over the disposition of their father's land and goods. Brothers are said to oppose their sisters' marriages, for it creates a new and stronger set of interests for her which are in opposition to their common lineage interests.

In contrast to the friction over property, brothers, in the capacity of maternal uncles, have affective and systemic ties with their sisters' sons.

The affective and supportive ties between brothers and sisters appear to moderate the potential conflict resulting from their competitive relationship to their father.

Mother's Brother-Sister's Son. This relationship replicates the brother-sister relationship. Ties of affection and support are prescribed, but conflict over property is possible.

It is more informal and intimate in contrast to the father-son relationship. It appears to weaken the father-son relationship by providing the son with an alternative source of male support.

The mother's brothers are responsible to see that her sons are properly buried. They are also prominent attendants at other ceremonial occasions involving their sister's sons.

Father's Sister-Brother's Son. This relationship follows the pattern of the father-son relationship. It is not one of affection, but a matter of authority and respect. Many of the taboos that apply to the father also are prescribed for his sister.

In conclusion, we can say Tikopia is characterized by the dominance of the father-son relationship, but we must also note that this relationship is based on jural ties and conflicts with the dominant affective bond which exists between father and daughter. The result is ambivalence between father and son, who are jurally united but emotionally divided. One result is that affective ties tend to overreach and weaken clan boundaries while jural ties support the unilineal principle.

II. Hsu's Predictions for Father-Son Dominant Societies

The basic attributes of this relationship according to Hsu (1965) are continuity, inclusiveness, authority, and asexuality. Dominance by the father-son relationship means, in terms of the Hsu hypothesis, that these attributes also characterize (to a lesser degree perhaps) the other relationships within the kinship system. Further, they should be characteristic of relationships outside the kinship system, and finally, they should typify the dominant orientations of the culture.

Except for the fact that China appears to manifest these characteristics to a greater degree, Tikopia bears out most of Hsu's predictions. I will discuss each attribute in turn.

Authority. We have already described the Tikopian father-son relationship as one of authority and respect. Similarly, the elder brother-younger brother tie is clearly based on the authority of the senior. Lineage and clan relationships are also organized hierarchically, with authority being related to considerations of directness of descent and generation. The head of the lineage and the chief of the clan have the same relationship to their adherents as the father has to his sons. Within the patrilineage, then, relationships are characterized by authority and are similar to those in China.

However, the cross-sex relationships in Tikopia are not replications of the male-male relationships. The ties between husband-wife, father-daughter, mother-son and mother's brother-sister's son (which, since it is founded on two cross-sex ties, I have put in this category) are more characteristically affective; authority does not seem to be an important consideration in them. These relationships are certainly not between equals, but neither are they based primarily on superordination and subordination. Familiarity, rather than respect, characterize them.

In China the mother's position in relation to her children is said to derive from her relationship to her husband. Similarly, a Chinese daughter shares with her brother the position of subordinance to their father. This is in sharp contrast to Tikopia, where the mother's position depends less on her husband's because she maintains significant connections with her natal family and kinsmen. Her relationship with her sons is therefore somewhat independent of her relationship to her husband. The Tikopia husband-wife connection is also less one of authority and respect than it is in China.

Tikopia politics is primarily a matter of lineage and clan authority. Within the clan political authority, like the authority of a father over his sons, is unquestioned. Succession is strictly governed by the rule that the eldest son takes his father's place. Even with the decline of the ancestor cult, the authority of the chiefs has remained stable (Firth, 1959a:296–98). Commoners with leadership potential exercise their ability by working as executors for the chiefs. This system of coordination between ascribed authority and men of talent is similar to the Chinese combination of the emperor and scholar-official systems.

A further similarity between the Chinese and Tikopia political philosophies is that both conceive of the ruler as the chief representative of the people to the spirit world. Prosperity results when the ruler performs this task well. In both instances the moral qualities of the ruler are considered basic to his success.

The ancestors in Tikopia also have considerable authority. They sit in judgment of their descendants' behavior and punish transgressors with bad crops or illness. In fact, the chiefs often refrain from taking strong action to punish offenders because they expect the ancestors to do it for them. There is no emphasis on equality in the spirit world. Ancestors and deities may have different spheres of influence, but there is still a hierarchy among them.

Continuity. This quality is certainly a characteristic of the patrilineally organized relationships. To a lesser degree, it is also important in the cross-sex, cross-lineage ties.

Traditional relationships between separate clans usually established through marriage are maintained and play an important role in many religious ceremonies. Brothers and sisters continue relationships with each other's children. On Tikopia patrilineal genealogies are often traced for eight or more generations, but relationships with uterine and marital links are seldom significant beyond three generations.

The ancestor cult, which will be described later, clearly reflects the importance of continuity to the Tikopia.

The principle of patrilineal succession imbues land holding, housing, and politics with this orientation.

In a less specific sense, the value of connections with the past is expressed in such things as the preservation of sacred adzes and other relics said to have once been used by Tikopia's ancient ancestors, and the interest in maintaining the religious rituals in the same form from year to year. Even without a literate tradition the past is a prominent dimension of Tikopia thought.

Inclusiveness. I understand Hsu to mean by this term the readiness with which a group incorporates others. The distinction I think Hsu is making relates primarily to a characteristic of non-kin groups. When he says China is inclusive, he means not only that the clan is ready, even anxious, to include all related members, but that Chinese non-kin groups are characteristically ready to admit any who wish to join. This willingness to disregard such things as status considerations in secondary groupings is, it would appear, a function of the degree social needs are satisfied by the kin group. According to this argument, in China where social needs are relatively well satisfied by kinship membership, there is less motivation to make secondary groups exclusive. The exclusiveness of secondary groupings increases as their importance to the satisfaction of individual social needs increases.

On Tikopia, where uterine as well as agnatic kin are widely recognized, there are few functionally significant non-kin groupings by which to measure this attribute. There are no men's houses or secret societies that are expressions of exclusiveness.

Tikopia society is, however, unquestionably inclusive in the kinship sphere. Wherever a kinship tie can be demonstrated, it is accepted, and relationships which cannot be traced exactly are often accepted.

Village and the locality create the main non-kin groups on Tikopia. In each case there seem to be no exclusive arrangements. People of one clan may live in the village or locality of the chief of another clan. The multitude of kin ties crossing clan lines is more relevant than in the Chinese case.

A more revealing situation occurs when someone from another island migrates to Tikopia. Not only is he or she allowed to stay, they are adopted by lineages so that the men may have land and ancestors and the women may have relatives.

Asexuality. This is the most difficult attribute to deal with for Tikopia. Similar to China, (1) wives are expected to be faithful while husbands may attempt extra-marital conquests, (2) sex is not a matter of overt display of affection, (3) polygyny is possible but infrequent, and (4) divorce is rare. In contrast to China, (1) pre-marital sex is not forbidden, (2) marriage is primarily a matter of sexual attraction, and (3) incest is not defined in clan or lineage terms. Firth reports no sexually oriented rituals in Tikopia except the brief circumcision ceremony in which an "obscene" song is sung. There are curses which refer to sex, but they are not the most common.

The father-daughter and mother-son relationships may contain a degree of libidinality, but this is impossible to judge. In general we find a lesser degree of suppression of sex than in China. This may be related to the fact that cross-sex relationships are not subordinated to the father-son relationship, but one cannot conclude that the attribute of asexuality is or is not characteristic of Tikopia behavior.

In conclusion, authority, continuity, and inclusiveness are characteristic attributes of Tikopia culture. Whether asexuality describes Tikopia or not is impossible to judge. Thus Hsu's predictions are on the whole confirmed, but we should ask whether attributes Hsu does not predict for father-son societies are or are not also significant. Lengthy consideration of all the attributes Hsu lists is impossible, but one, diffuseness, illustrates the problems of definition and comparative methodology involved in applying the Hsu hypothesis. Briefly, Tikopia would seem to have more diffuseness than China as a result of the importance of cross-sex, cross-generational ties. Each kinship position faces one way in terms of the jural system and another in terms of the affective system.

Firth also notes that a variety of kin on both sides encourage the young child to consider them its parents, thus extending the diffusion of cross-generational affect. This kind of diffuseness is different from that described by Hsu for India, where the mother plays many roles for her sons. In Tikopia many people play parental roles for each child. We have here several different meanings for the attribute diffuseness which are not mutually exclusive and depend on comparative, relative judgments in their application. Even if we accept only one meaning for the attribute, our conclusions are on the whole products of the comparative framework we select.

SPECIFIC CULTURAL FOCI

Filial Piety. As in China, the ethical system in Tikopia emphasizes proper behavior of children to their parents. "In Tikopia the father is termed the 'head' of the son, indicating his superiority of relationship. The respect shown by child to father is a matter of social injunction, not mere personal choice, and is backed by the moral sanction of strong disapproval in cases of breach, and even, it is believed, in extreme cases by the intervention of the gods. A man who lifts his hand against his father would be worse than a criminal, he would be committing sacrilege and a parricide would be looked upon with greatest horror" (Firth, 1957:165). Firth goes on to describe the father-eldest son relationship: "The native theory is a situation of mutual respect and deference between father and eldest son, each supporting the other in the family interest" (1957:166). These descriptions agree very well with the orientation of filial piety in China. The conception of the parent-child relationship as reciprocal is also common to both societies. "No amount of evident sentiment can excuse the neglect of a parent to provide food for his child, no plea of silent affection can extenuate the failure of a child to mourn audibly for its parent" (Firth, 1957: 160).

Certain taboos related to parents, particularly to fathers, serve to emphasize the respect they are due.

The duties of children to care for their elderly parents and to mourn them properly are stressed in both societies. The responsibility to provide for aged parents is "referred to in a formula recited over the infant a few hours after birth, ensuring that this obligation is inculcated as early as possible" (Firth, 1957:172–73). Children are also expected to make preparations in advance for their parents' funerals by accumulating the necessary mats and cloth. Failure to do these things is strongly disapproved by others.

In relation to agriculture, particularly cooperative landholding and labor, Firth notes that there is a moral bond between father and son transcending economic individualism (1957:163).

Ancestor Cults and Religion. The supernatural worlds of both cultures have a strong resemblance. Both have spirit worlds comprised of ancestors and deities. The distinction between the two appears to rest, in both cases, primarily on the fact that ancestors are directly related to their worshippers, whereas deities derive their importance for other reasons and have a general significance. In Tikopia the boundaries between deities and ancestors and between ancestors of the different clans are notably hazy and often unimportant, whereas in China the distinction between ancestors and deities is quite sharp.

Chinese ancestors are not feared, for they never punish or bring harm to their descendants. Unrelated spirits, on the other hand, are capable of many different kinds of behavior. They may be beneficial, capricious, or harmful. Deities are feared, petitioned, and even bribed, but ancestors are never treated in these ways. The Chinese worship their ancestors for reasons of filial piety, clan unity, and social approval. They do not worship ancestors to avoid their wrath or gain their favor.

In Tikopia the situation is significantly different. Ancestors and deities are credited with similar behavior. The favors of both are sought by the living, and both are quite capable of punishing those who displease them. Tikopia ancestors are feared for the harm they may cause their own descendants.

Another aspect of Tikopia's ancestor cult distinct from the Chinese is the degree of self-abasement on the part of the worshippers. A common phrase used in many rituals is "I eat ten times your (the ancestors') excrement." But this self-depreciation is essentially hypocritical, for in the same ritual a deity may be chided about his love life in order to encourage him to deliver more quickly the worshippers' requests.

We have seen that the son's respect for his father and the father's authority over the son are not supported by affective ties on Tikopia as in China. Underneath the façade of strict filial piety may lie a degree of hostility not found in China. It seems reasonable to interpret the differences between the two ancestor cults in terms of this difference in the father-son relationships.

Tikopia ancestors have to be petitioned for assistance, a reflection of the fact that they are not totally inclined to aid their descendants, just as the father is not inclined to aid his sons. The self-abasement of the Tikopia in addressing their ancestors is related to the submissiveness required of sons, and their occasional jests at the expense of the deities coincides with the fact that the sons' respect for their father is more the result of his authority rather than of affection for him.

Further evidence of the difference between the Chinese and Tikopia attitudes concerning their ancestors is provided by their response to Christianity. The Tikopia have embraced Christianity, and many have abandoned their ancestral cult to a large degree. The primary reason for this change appears to be their readiness to believe that the Christian god has greater powers than their own ancestors and deities. Conversion was essentially a matter of switching their respect and submission to a foreign god believed to punish and reward with more effectiveness. Protected by their new god, they felt few qualms about ignoring their ancestors. This is very consistent with the kind of attitude toward ancestors we have been describing for the Tikopia. The Chinese, on the other hand, have never been as susceptible to Christianity. Their deep entrenchment in their ancestor cult is one of the effective blocks to the latter. Giving up their ancestors constitutes a greater loss for them.

Conclusion

We have found that the Hsu hypothesis about father-son dominant societies deals rather successfully with Tikopia. When compared to China, differences, primarily of degree, appeared between the two societies. I have attempted to explain these differences as the result of a dominant affective tie between father and daughter, which in turn is the keystone of a system of affective ties between other cross-sex, cross-generational kin relationships.

Theoretically, I have proposed that the analysis of any kinship system along the lines of the Hsu hypothesis requires that a distinction be made between jural and socially prescribed affective ties.

Methodologically, it is suggested that comparisons be made between similar kinds of kinship systems (in which the dominant relationships are the same). Such studies should provide a better understanding of the kinds of variations possible in similar systems and allow the study of how one form of dominance produces or fails to produce its predicted attributes.

It is suggested that certain affective tie systems may correlate with certain formal kinship principles. For example, the coincidence of father-daughter and mother-son affective ties and bilateral tendencies in what are essentially patrilineal systems may be common phenomenon. We may also find other regularities in the articulation of jural and affective systems. This distinction might also serve to clarify cross-cultural studies of socialization, for it provides a perspective by which the *goals* of a society's socialization process (the learning of the ideal set of attitudes, emotional and behavioral prescriptions) can be distinguished both from the stages of that process and from the ever apparent failures to reach the goals. The stages of socialization would be defined in terms of the major shifts required to reach the ideal system of relationships in somewhat the way Parsons and Bales (1955) have proposed.

This paper may serve to illustrate some of the possibilities for cross-cultural comparison using the Hsu hypothesis, but it has not provided answers for a long series of fundamental questions which must be answered before the hypothesis assumes a satisfactory form. One of particular relevance here is whether the concept of father-son dominance is adequate to explain the similarities between Tikopia and China. We might ask whether patrilineality is not equally sufficient. This would in turn lead us to ascertain the nature of the relationship between father-son dominance and patrilineality. Such questions are only symptomatic of the problems yet unsolved in filling in the causal chains between dominance and its assumed effects. In making these observations I have in mind the materials on Manus presented by Mead (1930) and Fortune (1935), both of which seem to indicate that the Manus father-son relationship (which appears from Mead's analysis to be the dominant one) is of a very different nature than its Tikopia and Chinese counterparts. The Manus father, instead of being a stern authority figure for his son, is excessively indulgent. Manus boys, through the agency of instant temper tantrums, apparently maintain a tyranny of influence over their parents, by which they receive what they desire at their own initiative and without the subsequent development of a sense of obligation to their parents. Manus sons dominate their fathers; the reverse is true of Tikopia and China. If contrasts of this magnitude exist between Tikopia and Manus, one wonders just how great the variation might be among other father-son dominant societies and what factors would serve to differentiate them.

In making this study it became apparent that another difficulty with the present formulation of Hsu's hypothesis is the manner of defining attributes. While the terms he employs have the implication that the qualities are absolute, they actually refer to qualities which have meaning in relation to the particular comparative framework being employed. In this paper the comparison has explicitly been between China and Tikopia, but implicitly the meaning of the attributes derives from our understanding of our own societies. It was impossible to make a determination about sexuality, asexuality, or libidinality in reference to Tikopia because these attributes and the comparative framework used provide no clear distinctions.

Obviously, all cultures express to some degree all of the qualities listed as attributes in the hypothesis. Hsu is actually attempting to underline emphases and de-emphases in particular cultures; but if attributes are actually emphases (and therefore matters of degree) then we can only judge them according to some comparative scale. The choice of what is compared will influence decisions about the presence or absence of attributes in given cultures.

Furthermore, the terminology used in the hypothesis is not consistent; in some cases attributes are presented as pairs of opposites, in others a single term without an opposite is used, and in still other cases three or more attributes having some sort of interrelationship are introduced. This creates a situation in which the meaning of each attribute cannot be understood in terms of the other attributes.

It would seem that a great deal can still be done to clarify and formalize the definitions of attributes so that discussions and applications of the hypothesis would be more meaningful. We might also ask what other attributes might be added to the present list.

These criticisms do not invalidate the hypothesis, but they do indicate that much of its logic has yet to be specified and many of its concepts need to be restated in a more precise, consistent, and limited manner.

Social Relationships Among Two Australian Aboriginal Societies of Arnhem Land: Gunwinggu and "Murngin"

My purpose in this Chapter is to discuss some aspects of Hsu's (1965) hypothesis in relation to two Australian Aboriginal societies: *Gunwinggu,* which is primarily matrilineal, and "*Murngin,*" which is primarily patrilineal: the first is located on the western side of Arnhem Land, the second on the east. I shall not discuss the socio-cultural situation in either case, but references appear throughout. Published material is available on the Gunwinggu by my wife and myself and on the "Murngin" by Lloyd Warner and ourselves: we have carried out fieldwork over several years in both regions.

My focus in each case is on the relevant kinship system, and on the behavioral patterns associated with the range of acknowledged kin relationships. I shall examine these empirically, indicating what may be regarded as dominant and influenced relationships. In the course of this examination I shall also discuss Hsu's main contentions.

I should like to make clear what is being attempted here. There is a question of socio-cultural context, and also a question of methodology.

In the first case, I am deliberately not giving a summarized account of the socio-cultural picture. The reader should consult the published material to see the present contribution in perspective. I am concerned primarily with Hsu's hypothesis on kinship relationship dominance. To explore this satisfactorily here, it is necessary to look at the structure of kinship and the organization and content of the relevant behavioral patterns. There is a constant interplay between these two features and, in fact, what is revealed appears to be a fairly reliable reflection of the *total* picture. Showing this is possible because, among other things, Aboriginal society was kin-oriented.

In actual life there is, as one would expect, considerable variation. To some extent such variation is allowed for, or indicated, in the conventional systems themselves. To discuss this fully would require an analysis of actual examples against the background presented here, showing persons interpreting the "rules" (or the patterns) in terms of personal interests—the exigencies of day-by-day living, the interplay of loyalties, family and local group ties against others, interpersonal friction and its resolution, as well as personal idiosyncrasies. While I have indicated what I consider to be the most important of these, I have not really dealt with this broader aspect; that would constitute a different study. The problem is that of kinship relationship dominance within a social system, and its implications for the total system.

One point must be made about kin-oriented Aboriginal societies. A different quality is involved in all forms of interaction from that in societies not organized predominantly along those lines. Living with people regarded as kin, even though many of them may be only classificatory kin, establishes a different sense of the intimate and the personal. In such circumstances, within the structure of one's society or community there are virtually no strangers, no one toward whom one has no responsibilities and no obligations. The emotional connotations relevant to actual kin relationships are diffused as genealogical distance increases, declining in intensity but nevertheless retaining their essential substance. Behavioral variations are not obtrusive. Even in the case of variation in marriage type, ideally marriageable spouses are already linked in kin terms and in terms of marital preferences so that social behavioral patterns are simply shifted and have no further structural ramifications.

The second case concerns Hsu's hypothesis in relation to the broader socio-cultural context. Hsu's discussion (1965) really deals with dominant kinship relationships within the nuclear family [1]—in other words, with those eight relationships that are built up in the course of a marital unit being established and offspring being produced. The focus therefore is on the family and on the socialization of children into adulthood. This kind of focus, in relation to Hsu's problem, is not adequate insofar as Aboriginal Australia is concerned. The Aboriginal family cannot advantageously be conceptually isolated in that way: many other kin are relevant to it. These

1. See P. Bohannan's reference, in Chapter 3, to the nuclear family concept. Among the Tiv four relationships are categorized in what can be called the nuclear family. Among the Gunwinggu and Murngin six relationships are distinguished, if one excludes terms for elder and younger siblings. As in the Tiv case, such terms are not solely the prerogative of the nuclear family and are found outside that unit.

others and the total range of *recognized* kin relationships available in any one Australian Aboriginal society must be considered. This is what I am attempting to do. I have not concerned myself here with the broader issues of socialization, although a brief statement (an Appendix) is included at the end of this Chapter, because I do not think that this particular problem is made clearer by examining those processes in detail.

The Gunwinggu

Basic to the Gunwinggu system are two exogamous matrilineal moieties, *nangaraidjgu* (feminine form *ngalngaraidjgu*) and *namadgu* (feminine form, *ngalmadgu*). Associated with each moiety are two phratries (or semi-moieties),[2] also exogamous and matrilineal in descent; a couple of others have been added from neighboring groups, but are regarded as peripheral up to the present time. (See R. and C. Berndt, 1964: 60–61.) A person may marry into either of the two semi-moieties in the opposite moiety. Thus:

Nangaraidjgu		*Namadgu*
jariwurig *jarijaning*	=	*jarigarngulg* *jariwurlga*

A man and his mother are always of the same semi-moiety; and, depending on his son's marriage choice, a man and his son's son may be.

The subsection system is comprised of eight named categories, four in each matrilineal moiety; descent is "indirectly matrilineal" in two fixed cycles, and a person's subsection is not the same as his mother's but depends on hers. There are four sets of intermarrying subsections. The Gunwinggu system in its simplest form is as follows. Only male subsection names are shown.[3]

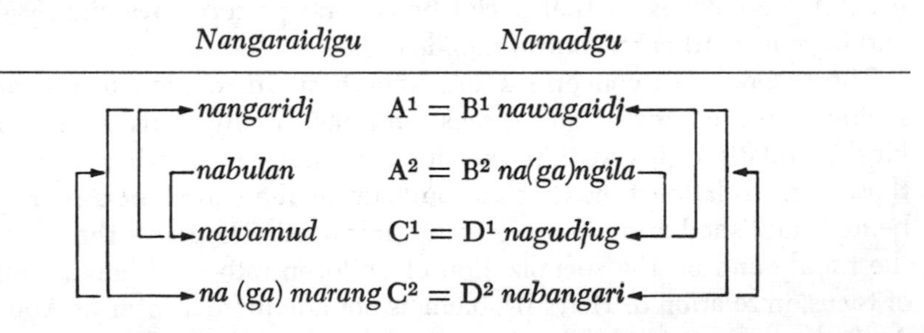

A^1 and A^2, C^1 and C^2, make up one matrilineal moiety; B^1 and B^2, D^1 and D^2, the other. Each pair, A^1–A^2, B^1–B^2, C^1–C^2, and D^1–D^2, is viewed as belonging together, related as grandparents and grandchildren, so that, for example, a child and his mother's mother belong to one pair, but not to the same subsection. Each of the two pairs in one moiety stands in an

2. Initially I labelled these units *phratries*. I prefer now to call them *semi-moieties*.
3. = signifies marriage; arrows point to offspring.

intermarrying relationship to the corresponding pair in the opposite moiety. The system is arranged also on the basis of alternating generation levels, with parents and children in succeeding (i.e., adjoining) generation levels, the first two alternating with the second two. That is, $A^1 = B^1$, $A^2 = B^2$ alternate with $C^1 = D^1$ and $C^2 = D^2$.

Kin distribution is as follows, assuming a male EGO in subsection A^1: see Table 9.1 for the key to kin terms.

gogog, dada, jabog	$A^1 = B^1$	*gagali, ganjulg*
gagag, mawa	$A^2 = B^2$	*maga, mamam*
garang, ngadjadj	$C^1 = D^1$	*ngabad, belu, ngalgurng, nagurng*
ganggin, wulubulu	$C^2 = D^2$	*gulun*

Because each pair of subsections is considered to belong together, marriages may take place between the relevant intermarrying pairs of one's own, one's grandchildren's and one's grandparents' generation levels: one should not marry into succeeding generation levels. In the case of an alternative marriage, subsection affiliation of offspring is determined by the mother's subsection.

The alternative marriage system is as follows:

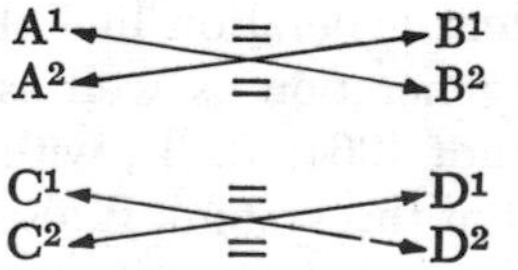

$$\begin{array}{ccc} A^1 & = & B^1 \\ A^2 & = & B^2 \end{array}$$

$$\begin{array}{ccc} C^1 & = & D^1 \\ C^2 & = & D^2 \end{array}$$

As in the above examples, equal signs represent ideal marriage type (i.e., $A^1 = B^1$, etc.), while diagonal two-headed arrows represent alternative marriages. This diagram points up certain features of the kinship system: that junior and senior kin terms are distributed in one generation level, and that a man and his GAGAG (mother's mother's brother) may marry a *gagali* (conventionally, a mother's mother's brother's daughter's daughter): for certain purposes, grandchildren and grandparents are equated.

THE KINSHIP SYSTEM

The Gunwinggu use several sets of kin terms. One is the ordinary system of address, and it is largely this that I shall draw upon here. Another is the ordinary system of reference, which brings in a number of alternative terms. In the more "polite" system of reference, *gundebi*, a speaker needs to be aware of other people's relationships as well as of his own; some of the terms are the same as in the ordinary reference system, but others are not. The special vocabulary used between a man and his "mother-in-law" (see under *ngalgurng* relationship) also includes a set of kin terms. Moreover, what I am giving here is a simplified picture, bringing in only a few items of content.

It is Hsu's contention that kinship systems reflect the influence of dominant relationships on others of a secondary ("recessive") nature, and that these tend "to shape the entire kinship system" (1965: 639). With this in mind, and without yet considering the question of dominant and secondary relationships among the Gunwinggu, I shall examine briefly the ideal construct of their kinship system: the question, as far as I am concerned, is, what does the system itself reflect?[4]

The Gunwinggu system, schematically arranged in Tables 9.1 and 9.2, may be categorized in conventional Australian kinship typology as primarily of Nyul-Nyul or Aranda type (Elkin, 1954: 70), since the pattern is constructed upon the basis of a man's marriage with a *gagali* who is a m.m.b.d.d. or a f.f.sr.s.d.[5] This is not dissimilar to what Meggitt (1962: diagrams between 84–5) has set out for the Walbiri (Wailbri) and Hiatt (1965: 48) for the Gidjingali system. However, in discussions with the people themselves, bilaterality is not emphasized and the assumption is that a man's wife is a m.m.b.d.d. "from the GAGAG line." Only rarely would a *ngalgurng's* (w.m.) husband be also the son of a *mawa* and a MAGA.

Additionally, marriage is preferred with a *gagali* who is a f.sr.d.d.d. or m.b.d.d.d., in the descendent generation line of a man's S.S. Selection of wives from a man's own generation as well as from his grandchildren's generation (R. and C. Berndt 1964: 72–4), within this framework, underlines the matrilineal aspect of this system. It also explains the use of junior and senior kin terms in the grandparents' generation, as is the case too in the granchildren's generation. It underlines the identification between a man and his GAGAG (M.M.B.) who may, in fact, often marry a woman

4. Granted the disadvantages of using an Ego as a point of reference within a kinship system there are, nevertheless, two telling arguments for its retention.

The first is that people see their relationships as person-centered, and that no kin term stands by itself. All terms of address are conceptualized as reciprocal pairs, indicating a direct dyadic relationship from the perspective of specific persons. Gunwinggu terms of address number 20, deployed in 17 "terminological dyads," Murngin, 24 terms in 16 "terminological dyads." A couple of terms have male and female forms but the same basic stem. (Inclusion of the various reference categories would add considerably to the list of terms.)

The second argument rests on the question of what one expects to have revealed in a diagrammatic representation of a kinship system. Briefly, we expect to see at a glance *a.* the main recognized kin categories, lineal and collateral, consanguineal and affinal; *b.* conventional marriage patterning and the structural implications of this, as far as kinship is concerned; *c.* descent; and *d.* generation levels, succeeding and alternate. Bohannan's simplified "componential analysis" is no more abstract and yet no closer to empirical reality than the conventional systems treated in this Chapter, nor is it any closer to the way in which the people themselves view their kinship.

5. English kin terms are abbreviated: f = father; m = mother; sr = sister; b = brother; s = son; d = daughter; h = husband; w = wife: males are shown in capitals, females in lower case.

Ego called *gagali*. Further, husband and wife use different kin terms for their own children, the wife taking the same perspective as her brother. And the system reflects the general opinion that men prefer young women, especially adolescent girls, as wives or sweethearts.

While the preference for a *gagali* as spouse can be called first choice, a second choice is matri- or patri-cross-cousin (*ganjulg*) marriage. In this respect the Gunwinggu system has a submerged Kariera-type pattern (Elkin, 1954: 61), with certain major differences. Only a few instances have been recorded of a man marrying his actual *ganjulg*; the relationship is usually more distant, derived from junior descent as noted in Table 9.2. Cross-cousin marriage is structurally consistent with m.m.b.d.d./f.f.sr.s.d. marriage, but the use of different terms clarifies the demarcation between the two. The practice of including junior along with senior kin terms in one generation level indicates that this is a permissible alternative. The system *in toto* differs radically from the Kariera-type in that it provides for *gagali*-marriage in the grandparents' and grandchildren's generations.

In Tables 9.1 and 9.2, the numbers 1 and 2 attached to each kin term represent the matrilineal moieties: I have made no attempt to correlate the semi-moieties and subsections. Against these three structural features based on matrilineality is one centering exclusively on patrilineal descent —the *gunmugugur*, named units with specific territorial referents. These are significant in social identification and in religious ritual, but they do not vitally affect discussion of kin terminology and behavioral patterns. More broadly, the use of junior and senior kin terms in *all* generation levels is structurally important, but it does not appreciably alter the basic emphasis on matrilineality (see Tables 9.1 and 9.2, where Table 9.2 is an extension of Table 9.1).

This is positively expressed, as noted, in reference to the GAGAG line: the M.M.B. line, reinforced through the use at the great-grandparents' generation level of a term for GAGAG's mother and M.B.—i.e., *wulubulu* (m.m.m. and m.m.m.b.): no other great-grandparent is singled out by a special term.[6] One might, therefore, expect to find dominant relationships located in that line. However, the Ego-*wulubulu* relationship has been, in practice, virtually ineffective, and the same has been true to a lesser extent for an actual GAGAG; but increased life-expectancy appears to be altering

6. It is unusual in Australian Aboriginal kinship systems for great-grandparents to be terminologically separated out in this way. The Maung, who adjoin the Gunwinggu on the north, use the term MAIAMAIA for a M.F.F./S.D.S.; their system, too, is of Aranda type but differs in certain respects from the Gunwinggu. (See Elkin, R. and C. Berndt, 1951: 281.) The Maung also emphasize matriliny, but the mother's father's line is particularly important in defining marriage patterns.

I do not propose to get involved in such issues as terminological lag, or functional connection between terminology and behavior; but the singling out of relationships like this by means of special terms does suggest that they need to be looked at more closely—that they point to some area of significance, whether this concerns kin relationships specifically, or one descent line rather than another, or provision for certain co-residence arrangements, and so on.

Table 9.1. *Gunwinggu*

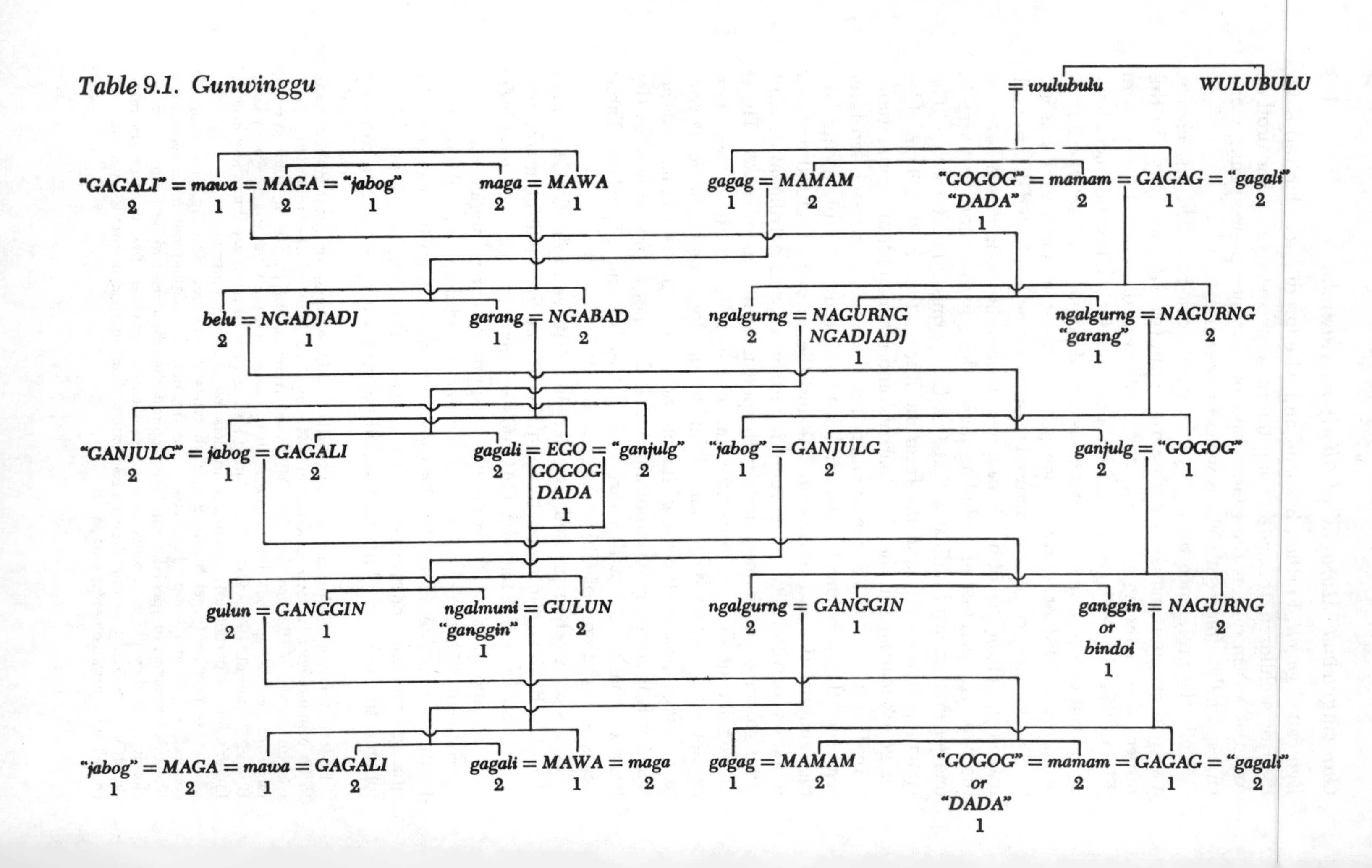

Table 9.2. Gunwinggu

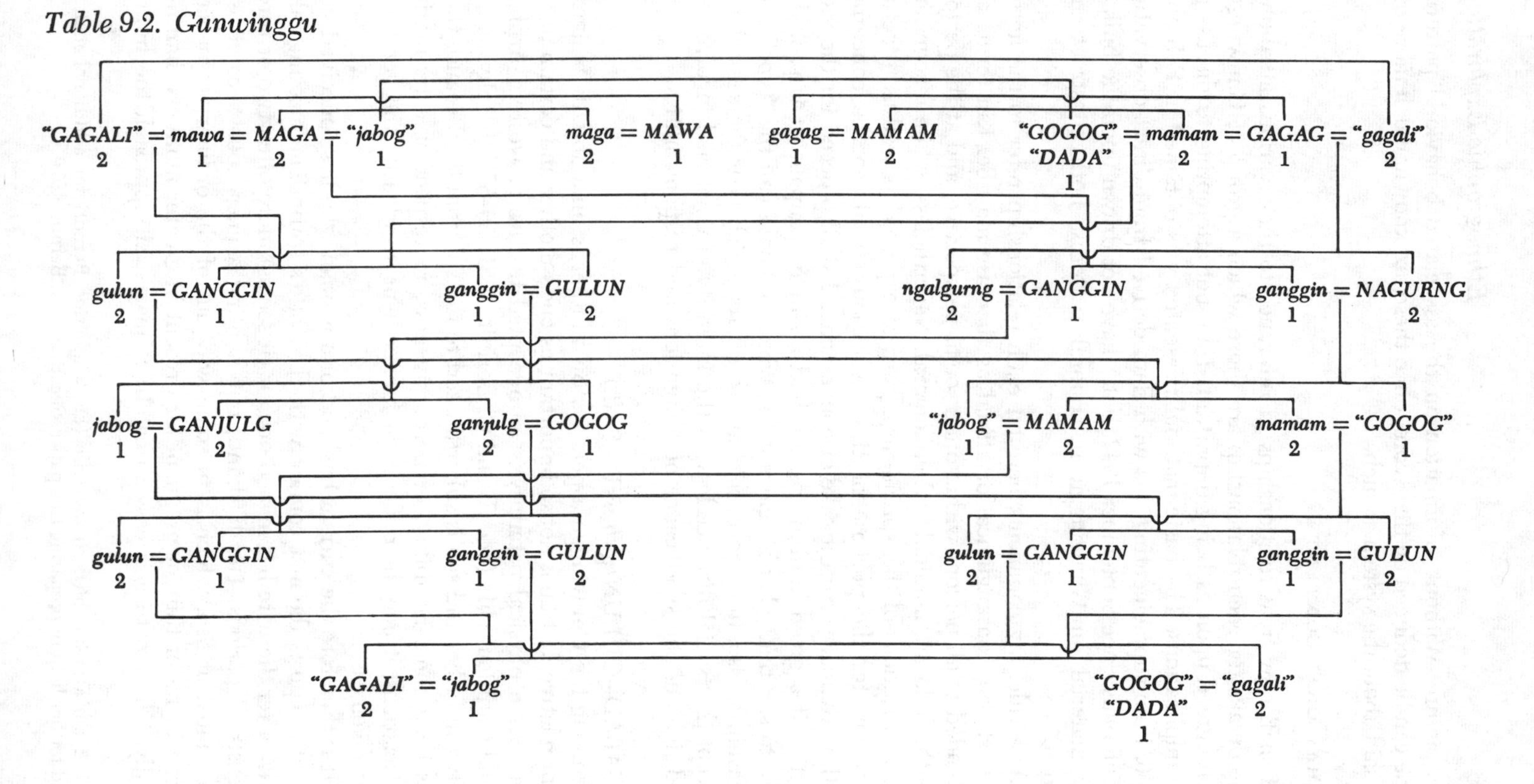

this picture. Without information on the associated behavioral patterns, little can be deduced on that score; once these are known, much more can be said about the system as such.

BEHAVIORAL CONTENT

I shall now treat relationships in reference to their various attributes. The details for each relationship are those which a group of Gunwinggu men agreed upon as being important. I am not attempting to discuss all the implications. The basic material presented was obtained in Febraury 1966. I am supplementing this with data derived from direct observation at intervals since September 1947, but I have not drawn upon the bulk of my material on Gunwinggu behavioral patterns, both construct and actual.[7]

As a rule, my comments here on each relationship refer to the actual (closest) tie, consanguineal or affinal as the case may be. Kin terms are extended to all persons within one's social perspective, and at the periphery the links are nominal and ephemeral. Nevertheless, while recognizing the implications of this spread, in regard to expected as well as to actual behavior, for the purpose of this discussion I shall not be concerned with it. Similarly, for the sake of convenience I shall proceed for the most part as if a given kinship position had a single occupant. It is probably safe to say that what is relevant for what we could call the "type" relationship is also, in essence, relevant to others which bear the same label, except that social distance lessens the intensity of emotional involvement and lightens the significance of obligations and responsibilities.

NGABAD–GULUN/*gulun* (F.–S./d.):

Among the Gunwinggu a person's own father is undoubtedly a significant relative, but he is not so important as one's mother and certain of her kin. While physical paternity is an accepted feature of western Arnhem Land traditional life (See R. and C. Berndt, 1951: 80–83), the physical tie between father and son is subordinated to the spiritual tie. Because there has been some flexibility, or permissiveness, in respect of extra-marital associations, it may be difficult, or inexpedient, to identify the genitor in any given case.

It is therefore the current husband of a woman who has conceived who usually reports the first contact with the child's spirit. The meeting takes place after the wife has missed one, or (it seems) more often two or three, menstrual periods. Her husband, out hunting, comes upon a catch, say an animal or fish, which is in some way out of the ordinary—especially large, or fat or thin, or pregnant, or present in greater numbers than normally. The creature is easy to catch: it may even approach the hunter.

7. I am also indebted to my wife (Dr. Catherine Berndt) for additional material and for her help in preparing this paper. See R. and C. Berndt, 1970.

When he spears it the spirit may jump on to his shoulder, addressing him as "father;" he carries it back to his camp, and it passes to his wife during intercourse. The term *NGABAD* is said to indicate "shoulder," but the allusion is clearer in the ordinary term of reference for father—*gongomu*; in everyday speech, the stem *gom* means "neck" (or throat). Another reference term for father, inflected to show person and number, is made up of *bo* (an infix indicating water or liquid) and *nang*, "saw." Thus, *bibonang*, "his father," *nganbonang*, "my father," and so on. (The term for the creature which serves as the agent, or vehicle, is *gain-gen*, "flesh-concerning." At least one, often more, is associated with the pre-natal experience of every person. This is a personal association, not inherited, and it entails no special ritual attitudes or food tabus.) Although a man spends a fair amount of time with his children and there is the assumption of strong affection between them, the relationship is marked by some constraint. A person must be careful what he says to his own pater, his own acknowledged social father. Freedom of speech between father and son is qualified by choice of topic; for instance, men say that to raise matters of sex in this context would provoke a father to anger. But they say, too, that a man should insist on his son's marrying the daughter of an actual *ngalgurng*, and should firmly oppose any alliance with a daughter of an "ordinary" (classificatory) *ngalgurng* if the consanguineally closest one is available.

The early spiritual association between father and son (or daughter) is expected to continue throughout life. A structural medium for the expression of this—and, ideally, for the handing on of personal names—is the *gunmugugur*. (The Maung term is *namanamaidj*; see Elkin, R. and C. Berndt, 1951: 294–98: R. and C. Berndt, 1964: 62.) This is the named unit of patrilineal descent associated with a defined and named stretch of territory, including various mythological sites. With this identification, and often confused with it by younger people, comes the *igurumu* or *ngwoia* —its specific form of address or reference, exclamation or benediction. (For instance, a mother or M.B. whose child or sister's child sneezes may call out the child's father's *igurumu*, "to wish him luck.") In a few instances, step-children or adopted children have assumed the *gunmugugur* of their new father. Also, there are examples of marriage within the same *gunmugugur*. I was told that if a child were born in such circumstances the father should discard his wife, the child's mother, and marry again. I have recorded no examples of this, but Gunwinggu say that intra-*gunmugugur* marriage creates a condition of "spitting (or dribbling spittle) at the breast"—that is, bringing it into disrepute. In a few other cases, for example in an intra-moiety marriage, a child may take its *gunmugugur* not from its actual father but from its mother's preferential spouse, or promised husband.

Moreover, a man is not in a position to grant his own son permission to attend sacred *maraiin* rituals (see R. and C. Berndt, 1964: 233–34). A young man should wait to be invited and should not make direct enquiries on his own account; he should certainly not approach his father with the request, "I would like to go in to the *maraiin*"—a step which would not only annoy his father but would also delay his ritual acceptance, perhaps for some years. He may, however, go about this indirectly, obtaining the services of an intermediary (e.g., a GANJULG or a genealogically remote father) to approach his father with the same request. The father cannot respond immediately. He must first consult his wife's brother, his son's NGADJADJ, to whom he must defer in ritual matters, as in many others. The NGADJADJ has the final say; if he replies negatively, the boy must bide his time. This is sometimes phrased as, "NGADJADJ has power for me"—not "over," but "for;" he can withhold or provide ritual power.

The relationship between a father and a daughter has much the same overtones, except as regards entry into men's secret-sacred rites. In summary, these overtones are spiritual and thus, indirectly, of ritual significance. The undertones of constraint are not crystallized into specific tabus; and although the relationship is asymmetrical, in terms of superordination, and subordination, this is not so clear-cut as in some other relationships. Structurally, its most important feature is that of establishing an agnatic descent link, focusing specifically on "ownership" of a specified stretch of country, and to a lesser extent on a specific language (Gunwinggu, in contrast to others) or dialect (of one area, in contrast to others), as a counterbalance to the heavy stress on matrilineality.

garang—DJEDJE/*djedje* (m.—S./d.):

The importance of the mother-child relationship lies in the image of the mother as nurturing and giving. This, it is said, is established from the first cry of a child —"ga!"—as it demands its mother's breasts—hence the term, *ga-rang*. (*dang*, "mouth"). A mother's sisters, in general, are also *garang*, except that a distinction is drawn between elder and younger sisters, *mula* and *garang*. The term *garang* in this case implies that "she's carrying a big load," in the sense of having young children to provide for; *mula* implies that she is not carrying a load, that her own children are grown up and that in these circumstances she is an ideal mother surrogate. In one view, a *mula* is conventionally responsible for severing a *djedje*'s umbilical cord at its birth.

The emotional bond between mother and child persists from childhood into adult life, partly because of this initial dependence, but also because her brother (her child's NGADJADJ) is extremely important to her son and because she is a primary link in the GAGAG line, which provides first choice wives and husbands for her children. In fact, that dependence continues in somewhat different forms. A woman is expected to be an advocate and champion of her children, to give them food, and to help them where she can, irrespective of their age. They can talk to her more freely and with less constraint than they can to their father—even about sexual matters, providing these concern persons in correct intermarrying relationships. She is in a position to take the initiative in arranging, or opposing, her children's betrothal and marriage; she is expected to show both anger and shame should one of them become involved in an irregular liaison, or, especially, in a "wrong" marriage. Fear of the consequence is put forward as a major reason: such a union could lead to quarreling, and so to injury or death for her child. Marriage is a critical sphere, particularly in relation to extra-marital affairs, because a very high proportion of ordinary dissension and fighting can be directly traced to it. It is this point, a mother's concern for the *physical* welfare and protection of her child, and especially of a son, which is stressed.

In structural terms, mother and child belong to the same moiety and semi-moiety, and their subsection affiliation is mutually interdependent. There is a strong preference for the mother's language or dialect, where this differs from the father's; and a woman likes to camp near her married son or daughter when that is possible, helping to mind their children, until eventually the roles are reversed and she herself is the one to be nurtured and helped.

belu–GULUN/*gulun* (f.sr.–B.S. and b.d.):

This is not dissimilar to the father-child relationship. A *belu* is said to be "like a father," and the ordinary term of reference (*ngalgongomu*) indicates this equivalence (*ngal* being the feminine prefix, attached to the "father" term). A *belu* may pre-natally meet the spirit of her brother's child in much the same way as he does. (Again, the same reference term may be used as for the father himself, *bibonang*, in her case with a female-indicator such as *ngalbu*.) Foraging with a group of women she may find, for example, a "fat" tortoise or a large yam: the women talk to one another, saying "this must be a child;" later, when she sits or dives for lilies or sleeps near the child's mother, the *belu* "passes the spirit" to her. Should the child approach its father first, people say, it will have a face like his; should it choose the *belu*, it will resemble her.

A *belu* "stands for" an actual father in some circumstances and can, to some extent, take over his responsibilities toward his children. The main exception rests on her exclusion from men's secret-sacred ritual. At the same time, if her brother is absent or dead she can speak on his own son's behalf, for instance, regarding the boy's access to certain *maraiin* rites. Following marriage, a couple are expected to set up their own camp (windbreak or hut); however, it is said that traditionally they would often stay close to the husband's *belu*, and that conventionally the wife would be expected to "work" for her–i.e., performing domestic tasks. Should a man's mother and *belu* be in different places at the time of his marriage and both send messages expressing a wish to greet the new wife, it would be to the *belu* that she was taken first. A new baby, however, would be taken first to see its father's mother, its own *maga*/MAGA, and only after that to its father's *belu*. In either case the *gagag* takes precedence over the *garang* and *belu*.

Briefly, then, the *belu*-GULUN/*gulun* relationship is that of a "female-father"—son/daughter with undertones of the responsibilities and obligations inherent in the mother-child relationship. There are virtually no speech restrictions, and much less constraint than in the father-child relationship.

NGADJADJ—GANGGIN/*ganggin* (M.B.-Sr.S. and sr.d.):

Just as a father's sister "stands for" a father, so the NGADJADJ acts as a "male-mother." It is said that they (the *garang* and NGADJADJ) come from the "same womb," *gunwalilgudji*, and that the ordinary terms of reference for them mean the same: for example, *baidjan*, male, and *ngalbaidjan*, female (literally, *baidjan* ="big"). They are brother and sister, with mutual obligations and commitments reflected in the attitudes of their children toward them and to one another. It is a pivotal relationship in the GAGAG line. A NGADJADJ has more authority over his sister's sons than over her daughters. If he wants to arrange a marriage for his sister's son, he must speak to her first; if it does not have her approval she can delay negotiations or actively block them. It is said that he must defer to his sister, that she has authority over him. The ordinary reference term for a woman's brother is (*na*)*rangem*. A mother, for example, uses it in teaching her daughter the proper sister-brother behavior and attitudes. It is sometimes attached to the "M.B." reference term, *baidjan*, to point up the two facets of the relationship, particularly when this is consanguineally very close. A *baidjan* is an "uncle," and for most practical purposes this is treated as a direct personal tie; but the primary "brother-sister" link underlying it is not forgotten, and is made explicit in the double-barrelled label of *baidjan-rangem*.

A man should insist, where possible, that his son marry the daughter of an actual *ngalgurng*. Gunwinggu say, nevertheless, that if a man has a son and his sister a daughter, the two may marry; but in practice this does not apply to a genealogically close relationship. (See Table 9.1. Also, see below under B.-sr. and GANJULG-*ganjulg* relationships.)

Ganggin are children of a man's sister, whether her husband is a GAGALI (first choice) or a GANJULG (second choice). The term *ganggin* is said to refer to scratch marks on the breasts and belly of a pregnant woman, made by the baby inside her as a sign that it wants to be born. The scratches are "very close" to the woman's brother, and it is for this reason that he calls her children *ganggin*. A male *ganggin* should not talk freely with a NGADJADJ, although this is relaxed as the relationship becomes increasingly "long-way." A NGADJADJ should not speak directly to his close female *ganggin*. He appears to have more authority over his *ganggin* than their actual father has. He can order his male GANGGIN to carry out tasks for him and to supply him with gifts. These days, if he wants money he may demand it from his GANGGIN on Mission "pay days"—"I want a £1 each from you;" and it is said that he always receives it, that "one cannot refuse a NGADJADJ." Conversely, a NGADJADJ is expected to see that a GANGGIN receives his due rights. For instance, when a man's promised wife is declared to be ready for marriage it is customary for him to travel to where she is living (if necessary) to collect her. However, he may strike some resistance to taking her away with him. Should he return without her, his NGADJADJ is likely to accompany him on his next visit and insist that the girl join him.

Despite this role as man's principal male protector and sponsor, he is not always appreciated; and in fact some men stated, as a general proposition, "we hate our NGADJADJ." This is mainly because of his personal demands, but also because he can block their association with girls promised to other men. There are numerous examples. If a man shows liking for such a girl, his NGADJADJ can put a stop to it, even to the extent of forcing him to leave the area. If he "walks around" with a sweetheart, his NGADJADJ may call out, "Get off that girl." The basis of his concern is ascribed to self-interest on the grounds that the girl's betrothed husband can come after him as an "enemy" and cause trouble. In other words, a man is held responsible for his close GANGGIN's behavior. To use one expression "he scolds him (his GANGGIN) so that he doesn't break the law." If the NGADJADJ is unable to stop a love-match, he may even come to blows with his GANGGIN. From a GANGGIN's point of view, "He (the NGADJADJ) is strong, he won't listen to me. We can't stop him; we let him have his own way." If a GANGGIN persists with the love-match and eventually elopes, against his NGADJADJ's advice, he cannot expect any help from that direction—although he may call on others.

The NGADJADJ, then, is a major figure of authority, critical and demanding, ideally insistent on his GANGGIN maintaining the conventional patterns of law and order, with the power to bring his GANGGIN back into line, or at least to attempt as much. This authority in mundane affairs is supported in the ritual sphere. A close NGADJADJ not only gives permission for his GANGGIN's entry into the *maraiin*, but also instructs him in the symbolic significance of the ritual. In brief, he is both a general advisor, and a teacher in the field of sacred affairs (although the GAGAG is ritually more important), and helps his GANGGIN to observe the tabus relevant to the ritual stages in his life.

GOGOG-DADA (elder B.-younger B.):

Uterine brothers, elder or younger, are said to be from the "same womb;" but the youngest (in contrast to younger, brothers, DADA) or "last" is sometimes referred to by an expression meaning "he goes between the legs" of the elder brothers.

Between actual brothers there is a degree of formality, and they should not speak freely to one another—as more "distant" brothers may do. Ideally, there should not be competition between them for wives or for sweethearts, although in actual practice this occasionally happens. One man put it, "My brother has his own wife, I have mine. Our wives come from different *ngalgurng*." It is also said that actual brothers, younger or older, should not have access to one another's wives ("it is not good to mix a man's sweat with that of his actual brother's wife"), and that a symbolic stick lies between them, blocking their access. However, it is acceptable and quite common for a man not only to joke but also to have intercourse with the wife of a step-brother or genealogically more distant brother–provided her husband is agreeable. (This applies also to a man's GAGAG —not his actual M.M.B., the "old" GAGAG, but his grandson GAGAG, who may sleep with and look after a man's wife in his absence.)

Normally, close siblings of the same sex, whether brothers or sisters, and whether they have one or both parents in common, should present a solid front. One ordinary term of reference puts this literally–e.g., where two are concerned, *benedangin*, "they two stand (together)." But it is recognized that some brothers do habitually quarrel or bicker. In ordinary camp life, brothers may live in close proximity and so be in relatively constant association. If one asks another for something, he does not normally get it himself but tells his wife to do so–underlining the assumption of relative equality between them.

It sometimes happens that a wife's parents want to take her away from her husband, ostensibly because he is not looking after her properly, although the real reason may be a desire to negotiate a new marriage for her with another man. In such circumstances, brothers should act in concert: "if one fights, we come in and help him." If a man is involved in a quarrel or fight, even some distance away, his close brothers are expected to go to his aid. A man has more authority over his younger brother's sons than the actual father himself has, and can even contradict the father's decisions without, ideally, causing an argument. He also has some say in his younger brother's son's marriage, but less than the young man's NGADJADJ. Where gifts (*bulg*) are to be distributed, a special procedure is involved between close brothers. If an elder brother receives something, it should be handed to each brother in turn, and it is eventually the youngest who divides it on a kinship basis; if a younger brother receives gifts, it is the eldest who should distribute them. (The brothers' wives, sons, and daughters have no part in this. Distribution is to GAGALI, to wives' parents, and to the wives' NGADJADJ; these would be regarded, for example, as betrothal-sustaining or marriage-sustaining gifts.)

Brothers are expected to aid one another in the ritual sphere, too. For instance, in a Kunapipi (Gunabibi) sequence (see R. Berndt, 1951), one man receives the *dudji* gift, a wrapped bundle of sacred bullroarers. His acceptance automatically involves certain responsibilities devolving not only on himself but also on his close brothers. This means that there must be unanimous agreement among them beforehand; should one, even a younger brother, refuse to accept all the others can withdraw. But it is only one brother, not always the eldest, who accepts the *dudji* on behalf of all of them.

jabog-dada (elder sister-younger sister):
This is seen as a close and mutually sustaining relationship. Like brothers, sisters are expected to "stand together:" and the same word is used for this (e.g., for two, *benedangin*). They are "mothers" to each other's children, and for close sisters this is more than a nominal label. The fact that full sisters do not normally share the same husband (although there are isolated cases) is said to reduce the risk of jealousy between them. There are no tabus or restraints between them, simply straightforward expectation of mutual aid.

jabog-jabog or *dada* (h.b.w.-h.b.w.: i.e., sisters married to two brothers):
If a woman's sister is married to her husband's brother, the two women should not speak freely to each other.

DADA-*jabog* (elder or younger B.-sr.): Siblings of opposite sex:
This is a key relationship.
A female calls all her brothers, irrespective of age, by the kin term DADA (younger brother), never GOGOG. However, men, when they use a kin term at all, may refer to sisters in general (never to their own or close sister, or the sister of a man they are addressing) as *jabog* without distinguishing between younger and older. A more general term for sister is *je'jeng*, "thing"; another is *ngalwari* (*ngal*, the feminine prefix: *wari*, a stem meaning "bad," "weak," "wrong," etc.), sometimes translated into English as "rubbish"; other terms mean "old woman" or "corpse." The overtones of disparagement provide a "front" for a relationship which is quite the opposite of that: one which is highly charged emotionally, involving dependence and obligation, as well as constraint in the shape of the strongest of all Gunwinggu interpersonal kin and affinal tabus. (See also discussion of B.-sr. relationship for the "Murngin.") In discussing the term *ngalwari*, men said it was used because "a sister is under us." A mother, they said, takes greater care of a male baby than of a female. Because of this imbalance in babyhood and the fact that a sister looks after, nurses, and attends to her younger brothers, she serves as a mother surrogate, even for a brother a little older than herself, and therefore classifies all her brothers as "younger."

In keeping with this, the constraints and prohibitions fall more heavily upon a man (or boy) than on his close sisters. They should not talk together freely, and if they do speak they must stand some distance apart. Ideally, siblings of opposite sex should not go near one another, and certainly not touch one another, even accidentally; a man should not enter a house if he knows or even suspects his sister to be there. Being in the same house or in the immediate vicinity of a sister is said to make a brother "feel strange" or uncomfortable. No teasing should take place before a sister. Nor should a sister's name be uttered in the hearing of her brother. His response would be, at the least, embarrassment, at the most, anger. (Nevertheless, brothers conventionally choose their sisters' nicknames—but not vice versa.)

A man is particularly upset to see or hear a sister in a compromising or intimate or conflict-charged situation, including a camp quarrel in which she may be only a victim or bystander, not an aggressor. He is taught to react to these by attacking anyone in the vicinity whom he calls sister with spear or stick or some other weapon, but never his bare hands. ("Our brothers mustn't touch our skin," women explained.) The threat of such an attack is used by other people in attempts to stop domestic fights. On several occasions in my experience, noisy arguments were quite effectively silenced, or almost so, by warnings to the combatants themselves or others near them. (For example, "Can't you see that her brother is over there?" or "You can't stay there to fight, so-and-so is in the next camp," or simply "Don't you think about your *brothers*?") The appeal is never, or rarely, to what a father might say or do; it is the brother's authority that is invoked. Even a distant "brother" can apply sanctions that an actual father can not.

A man should not hold his close sister's child, his *ganggin*. Nor should he sleep in the same room or shelter as his sister's daughter; in fact, his attitude toward that daughter is said to be much the same as toward her mother. There is a partial tabu on speech between them. (See NGADJADJ relationship.) However, he has a major say in arranging the girl's marriage. A young man who wants to marry a girl not already betrothed may persuade his mother, mother's sister, and father to approach the girl's NGADJADJ; in other words, a woman's brother has, with her, the final say in deciding betrothal arrangements for her daughter.

A woman has no comparable restrictions in relation to her brother's children—except that should she see him kiss one of them, she will refrain from doing the same, at the same spot, to avoid spittle-contamination. A man, or boy, should not touch water or food obtained or handled by his sister; if she should inadvertently drink from her brother's cup, his wife will give the cup away. And she is warned from childhood not to share directly in any food he catches himself. In describing this situation, one man said: "If a man has a disease, the doctor tells others not to touch anything associated with that person. It is the same with a sister. If we drink from a cup she has used, or if we hear bad language used in relation to her, we brothers might have an accident—something dangerous might happen."

In structural terms a sister is, generally speaking, socially equivalent to a brother. Two men may exchange sisters in marriage. This provides one theme in formalized joking between GAGALI—"You didn't give me your sister," using the term *ngaldalug* (feminine prefix plus the ordinary word for "woman") which in ordinary polite speech refers to a man or boy's close sister; a woman employs it, for instance, in teaching her small son the rules of this relationship.

Further, in the kinship system itself, with its alternate generation levels, the balancing of junior and senior terms in the same generation level leaves the way open for sr.s.d. marriage. (See Tables 9.1 and 9.2.) That is, a sr.s.d. is *gagali*; her mother is *ngalgurng*, although she might otherwise be classified as *gulun* ("daughter"). Alternatively, a Sr.D.S. is called GAGAG and may marry a woman ego called *gagali*—a man and his GAGAG are equated structurally in this sense. The balancing effect of the exchange of wives between a man's side and the side of his *ngalgurng* is important, and a sister is seen as reciprocating for her brother's marriage. (See Table 9.3.)

Table 9.3.

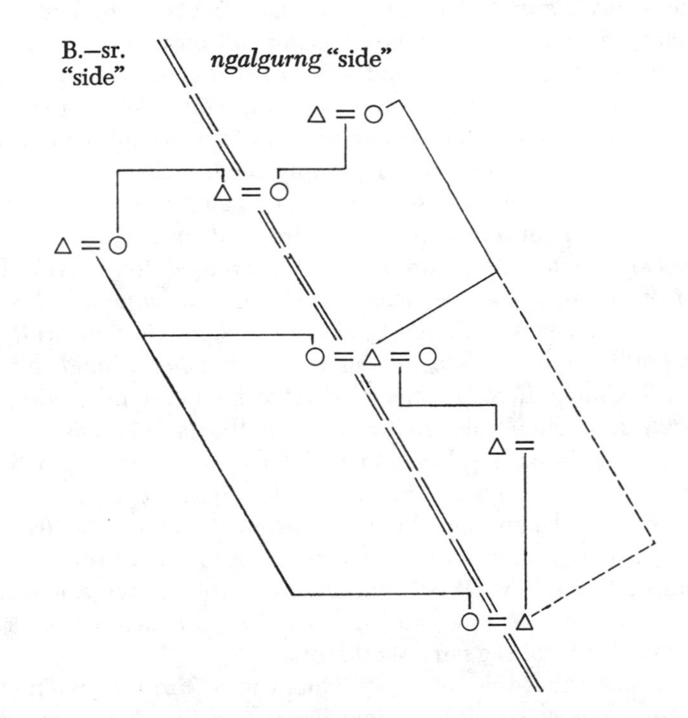

Supposing a man's *ngalgurng* has a daughter, whom he marries; this is said to mean that "a fire is burning on his side." If a man's sister has no daughter, it is said that "no fire is burning on the *ngalgurng* side;" or, "Only he (the brother) has a fire, for nothing;" or "We've got nothing for them (the *ngalgurng* side)." Should his full sister not be able to provide a return, an approach is made to a half-sister whose mother and his mother share the same father; her daughter may go in exchange to the *ngalgurng* side. In teaching her son, as a child, the tabus he must observe in relation to his *ngalgurng*, his mother may relate them positively to this central theme: "she will make a baby for us, for our side." And women declared, "If we don't look after our children, if they get sick or die, then our brothers make trouble for us."

In terms of emotional content, the B.-sr. relationship is equal in significance of that of the m.-child and M.M.B.-Sr.D.S. relationships.

DADA-*jabog* (Sr.H.-w.sr.):

This is an extension of the brother-sister relationship, but modified because it is only rarely a close consanguineal tie.

MAWA-MAWA/*mawa*, *mawa*-MAWA/*mawa* (F.F.-S.S. and s.d.; f.f.sr.-B.S.S. and b.s.d.):

A man's relationship with his *mawa*/MAWA is sometimes referred to as *bigebmawa'meng*, "(s)he takes the *mawa*'s nose;" that is, "makes the same face;" *Mawa* are said to be the same not only in cast of features but also in physical stature. F.F. and S.S. are said to be the same in another sense, too, referring not only to the structural equivalence of grandparents' and grandchildren's generation levels but also to subsection affiliation. The same in this context means simply having the same subsection or belonging to the companion subsection in a pair (see subsection table). For instance, say, a man is *nangaridj*, his wife *ngalwagaidj*, his son *nabangari*, his son's son *nabulan*; or, with diagonal-marriage (alternative), if a man is *nangaridj*, his wife may be *ngalgangila*, his son *nagudjug*, his son's son *nangaridj*; or, again with diagonal-marriage, he is *nangaridj*, his wife *ngalwagaidj*, his son *nabangari*, his son's wife *ngalwamud*, his son's son *nangaridj*. Unless there are special reasons for doing otherwise, a man of *nangaridj* subsection calls all the men of that subsection "brother;" his son's son of this same subsection is "of the same skin" and therefore a "brother." Those in the paired subsections, because they can marry the same women and stand together, are "brothers"—hence the distribution of junior and senior kin terms in one generation level. However, Gunwinggu say that, "Although MAWA, F.F., are like brothers we cannot call them brother, and use *mawa* instead;" nevertheless, a *mawa* is "like a brother." They may also be of the same semi-moiety.

It is obvious that this is not equivalent to a "brother" relationship, but it certainly has some of the same characteristics. There is, ideally, no rivalry between MAWA; they speak to each other more freely than brothers do; the relationship is seen as, up to a point, a symmetrical one; and while MAWA may take wives from the same category of women, as close brothers do, they may not have access to each other's wives. The difference lies primarily in the disparity in age between them: one

MAWA is usually much older than the other, and consequently senior in status and in a position to offer advice and guidance to the younger. A close MAWA symbolizes the linkage with the patrilineal *gunmugugur*, much more than does a father. A MAWA's ritual knowledge will eventually go to his S.S. (they are both of the same matrilineal moiety). A man is shown, for instance, the secret-sacred *maraiin* (ritual objects and dancing, etc.) of his father. On such an occasion, should his own sons be old enough they will be present, and they will "have more say" in this than their father, who is of the opposite matrilineal moiety, because they will expect to take over the ritual privileges eventually from their MAWA.

With close female *mawa* the relationship is a neutral one, again marked by distance in age. Although it is also regarded as resembling to some degree a sibling relationship, it lacks the constraint and emotional involvement so obtrusive between brother and sister.

maga-MAGA/*maga*, MAGA-MAGA/*maga* (f.m.-S.S. and s.d.; F.M.B.-Sr.S.S. and sr.s.d.):

This is similar to the MAWA/*mawa* relationship, but the female *maga* receives most attention. It is explained that a man's mother calls his son MAGA, while a man's father calls his son MAMAM. Because she does so much "work" for him when he is a small boy, he must call his father's mother (his *maga*) "daughter"—she is "like a daughter." This implies protection on his part, and the obligation to give food. The symbolic relationship is interesting in the light of the fact that a man may call his MAWA (F.F.) "brother."

There is relative freedom of speech between *maga*, but, as between father and daughter, this must be circumspect and a man should defer to his f.m. A person who angers his MAGA/*maga* angers his father also, and the *maga* relationship is conventionally one of mutual kindness: "one should never hurt a female *maga*." While this is true for male MAGA too, it is not emphasized; male MAGA do help a little in ritual, but this does not receive much attention because it is assumed that a MAGA has obligations in this direction to his own sister's sons.

gagag-GAGAG/gagag, GAGAG-GAGAG/gagag (m.m.-D.S. and d.d.; M.M.B.-Sr.D.S. and sr.d.d.):

The GAGAG "line" is of major significance, for reasons already mentioned. It is said of the GAGAG, *bidjumdoi dunin* ([s]he struck his [her]-forehead; *dunin* means fully or truly). This refers to his threat to hit on the forehead the unborn baby who is causing his daughter pain at childbirth so that the baby, hearing the warning, will emerge quickly. This direct interest in his daughter's welfare and in the child she bears continues throughout the lifetime of those concerned. A woman can, ideally, leave her children with their GAGAG/*gagag*, confident they will be well looked after.

After a young man has grown to adulthood he and his GAGAG are not likely to spend much time together. Recognition of the closeness of the kin bond is mutual, but the disparity in age is seen as a handicap to regular association. And although an elder GAGAG undoubtedly helps a younger in the ritual sphere, it is the NGADJADJ who really shoulders this responsibility. Female *gagag* do have much say in the control of a man's life, but this is largely channelized through his mother and NGADJADJ. In many respects women appear to loom more significantly in a man's kin patterning than do men, and this is not entirely an outsider's impression. For instance, when comparing the relevant obligations of male and female *gagag*/GAGAG men affirmed that female *gagag* are more important to a man than male GAGAG, "because his actual female *gagag* bore his mother."

Further, the part played by an elder male GAGAG in marriage supports the contention that the GAGAG relationship is of major significance: "we call a M.M.B. GAGAG (and his sister *gagag*) because his daughter (a *ngalgurng*) gives her daughter (*gagali*) to a man as wife."

MAMAM-MAMAM/*mamam*, *mamam*-MAMAM/*mamam* (M.F.-D.S. and d.d.; m.f.sr.-B.D.S. and b.d.d.):

A MAMAM has a special part to play in regard to children born to his own daughter. It is said that the spirit of a child comes first to its MAWA and *mawa*, secondly to its father, thirdly to its MAMAM, who "holds the MAMAM's beard" (*bidjawurgarmeng*), and finally enters its mother.

Apart from this association, the relationship does not differ radically from that between MAGA, except that a MAMAM is not considered to be a "brother," or a female *mamam* a "daughter." However, as in the case of a *maga* the relationship should be one of kindness and consideration. One should not consciously hurt a female *mamam*—the female, not the male, is singled out in this context. To do so would be to court the anger of one's mother and of one's NGADJADJ, who would feel obliged to help his father's sisters. There is also the point, although this is not emphasized as much as one might expect, that MAMAM is the husband of *gagag*, and, as such, and as the father of a man's own mother and mother's brother, is of more than peripheral importance.

wulubulu-*DJEDJE*/*djedje*, *WULUBULU*-*DJEDJE*/*djedje* (m.m.m.-D.D.S. and d.d.d.; M.M.M.B.-Sr.D.D.S. and sr.d.d.d.):

Although the term *wulubulu* is now commonly used by Gunwinggu it is said to be a Maung (Gunmarung) term. (See Elkin, R. and C. Berndt, 1951: 285, where *wulubulu* is used for the mother of a m.m. and M.M.B., as in the Gunwinggu system.) The fact that the only kin term used in the great grandparents' generation level refers to the m.m.m. and M.M.M.B. underlines the significance of the GAGAG line. Apart from this, the relationship is hardly active because difference in age precludes any real association. "We have respect for a *wulubulu*," it is said, "because (s)he will soon die." But it is also said that "a *wulubulu* can be a nuisance"—always calling out for something, and sometimes without reason.

Women, talking about *wulubulu* in general and their own in particular, almost invariably looked back to "*gagag*'s mother," and they restricted the term to that specific person and her close siblings without extending it to more distant kin.

In a construct example given by men to demonstrate this relationship, however, the situation was looked at (see Table 9.4) in descending generation levels and in relation to subsections, thus:

Table 9.4.

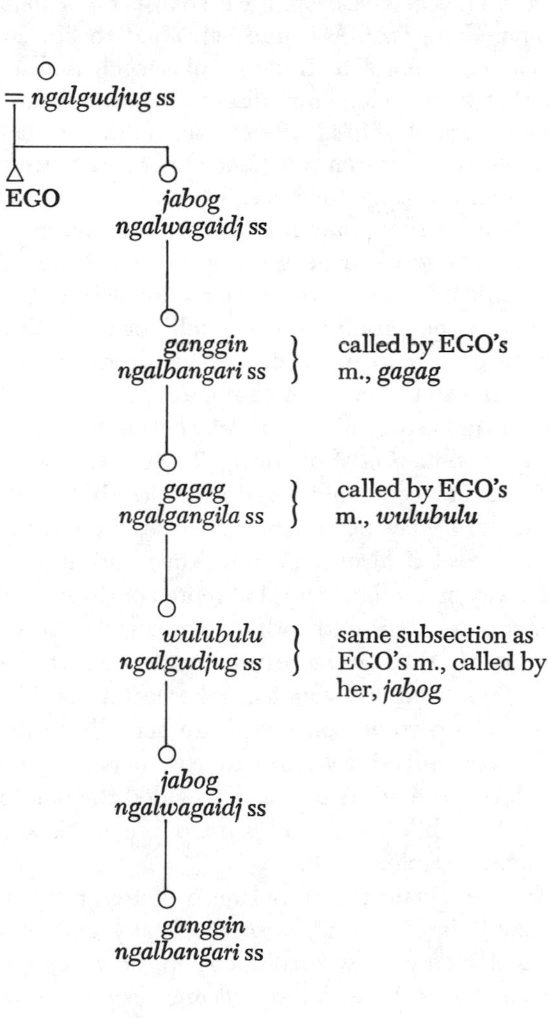

ss = subsection

GAGALI-*gagali* (Husband-wife, first choice: M.F.Sr.D.S., F.M.B.S.S., M.M.M.B.S., M.M.F.Sr.S-m.m.b.d.d., f.f.sr.s.d., f.sr.d.d.d., m.b.d.d.d.):

The connotation of the term *gagali*, referring to *gagali* of opposite sex, is that "they sleep together," (*gurabu gabenedi*, "they-two-stand"). After marriage a husband normally no longer uses the term *gagali* but the term for wife, whereas she may continue to refer to him as a *gagali*. This is the freest, and frankest, joking relationship, with the content of the exchanges mainly sexual in flavor. All *gagali*/GAGALI are potential spouses or sweethearts—except as already noted, for the husband or wife of a sister or brother. In practice, care must be taken to avoid jealousy on the part of an actual wife or husband.

Gagali are first choice wives; an ideal spouse for a man is an actual *gagali* of his immediate GAGAG line, betrothed to him at the moment of her birth. There is complete freedom of speech and action between *gagali*, except that a man does not discuss his sweetheart liaisons with his wife, and vice versa. A wife's M.B. and her father have a direct interest in her, and if she wants children but none appear they can take her away and arrange another marriage for her: "That fire (referring to the female *gagali* and her child-bearing potentiality) is there for nothing: we will take her back and pay where we have got a fire." (See under *jabog* relationship.) A man should not have two or more full sisters as wives simultaneously, but there is no prohibition on "half" or more distant sisters. If his own wife's sister is married to one of his brothers, he does not talk freely with her and may not visit her camp.

Although the sexual aspect of marriage is not underestimated, the main emphasis is on the production of offspring. The union is seen as binding in terms of children, and economic responsibilities, but not necessarily of sexual relations; these may be satisfied fairly easily outside marriage. It does seem that a great deal of a person's time and attention is devoted to *gagali*, in one way or another, and that more consistent interaction takes place between spouses than with other relatives. At the same time, this is the only relationship that can be severed, with the curtailment of obligations, excepting the sexual one which is inherent in the relationship itself —whether or not the persons concerned are actually husband and wife. Conventionally, more affection is said to exist between *gagali* who have been affianced during the wife's infancy, provided the bond is not allowed to lapse during her childhood; and a marriage made on this basis is thought to be more durable.

It is difficult to evaluate the importance of this relationship. No one would deny that it is important *both* personally and socially, because structurally it is not an exclusive relationship, however much it may be so in interpersonal terms. Its wider significance lies in the way it is linked socially with others—with other *gagali* and with the GAGAG line itself, in the provision of offspring who may be used in betrothal arrangements "to keep the fires burning" (see above, and under *jabog*). Continuity rather than discontinuity is stressed in this context (Hsu, 1965; 642).

gagali-gagali (b.w.-h.sr.):

The behaviour of these two women emphasizes mutual aid; because of strong brother-sister avoidance, the wife serves as an intermediary between her husband and his sister.

GAGALI-GAGALI (Sr.H.-W.B.):

An actual sister's husband is *nanwudgami*, as distinct from other ordinary *gagali*; the word means that he is considered to be "the same" as the sister, that he "counts for her." There is also a restriction on speech between a man and his actual sister's husband: in his presence the wife's brother should only whisper, and in matters of communication generally must use an intermediary. This restriction is partially lifted in relation to husbands of "half" or more distant sisters—a man may speak to them but, in doing so, must not stand too close. In either case, personal names are not used.

A significant feature of the relationship between close GAGALI is a speech tabu. This is imposed ritually, and not necessarily when one marries or is betrothed to the other's sister—although it takes place when a man is fairly young, and the assumption is that he is eligible to marry her. Young men are taken to the sacred ground by an older GAGALI: there they witness fully initiated GAGALI, decorated with feathers, dancing for them. From that time, those who have been danced for may say only "*si si!*" to their GAGALI. The tabu may, however, be lifted after a number of years by a ritual exchange of sweat: the GAGALI concerned smear sweat from one another between their cheeks and mouths and exchange goods, and can then speak freely. In special circumstances the tabu may be broken, but usually in a sacred context. For instance, in the Kunapipi, *maraiin*, and *ubar* rituals a man looks after his GAGALI. This is also the case in the *lorgun* mortuary rites in which GAGALI participate. In everyday situations, the exception could be if GAGALI quarrel, which is relatively rare, or when they are singing together, or if they are engaged in fighting a common enemy.

This tabu expresses a deep emotional bond between male GAGALI. Its significance is colored by the brother-sister relationship (see above). Also, men should take the part of their close GAGALI in fighting or quarrelling before even brothers do, or anyone else. This is done, so it is said, because a GAGALI considers his own children; they would say, "What kind of father is this, who doesn't help our NGADJADJ?"

Once the speech tabu is lifted, this is, conventionally, a joking relationship. Men bandy accusations such as "I'll spear you because you didn't give me your sister" or *gagag*; "you've got my *gagag* lighting a fire for you and I have nothing, no woman." But this licensed joking about sisters does not seem to take place between full GAGALI.

gagali-GAGALI (b.w.-H.B.):

An attitude of constraint is expected between persons related in this way. Terminologically it is still a spouse or sweetheart relationship, but a man's marriage to a previously eligible *gagali* alters it in practice for his close brother(s); the circumspection in behavior now imposed extends to the wife's full sisters. This relationship is considered to be a "husband-wife" one, but in reverse; that is, the assumption is that one cannot be a sweetheart of one's own wife or husband. At the same time, the sexual relations which usually take place between a husband and wife are in this case denied, because it is the brother's wife who becomes a "husband" and the husband's brother a "wife."

gagali-gagali (f.m.b.s.d.-m.f.sr.d.d., etc.):

In summary, this is a relationship involving mutual aid: "if a *gagali* asks for something, we can't refuse." It involves also some formalized joking.

ngalgurng-NAGURNG (w.m.-D.H.; m.m.b.d.-F.Sr.D.S.; sr.s.w.-H.M.B.):

The term *ngalgurng* is usually, for some reason, translated into English as "cousin." Alternatively the terms, from the special *gungurng* vocabulary, are *nabulgdjamu* (male) and *ngalbulgdjamu* (female). This is a crucial relationship in the GAGAG line. The GAGAG is important because he has a man's *ngalgurng* as daughter, and the *ngalgurng* is important because she has *gagali* daughters. Ideally, all infant betrothal arrangements involve daughters of a man's *ngalgurng*, preferably his own full *ngalgurng*, and such promises are graded chronologically; the first goes to the eldest brother, the second to the next in age, and so forth.

The significance of this relationship has already been discussed. Here it is sufficient to say that the element of avoidance is most marked. It is associated with a partial tabu on speech, and a prohibition on a man's use of anything which has been in contact with his wife's mother. This masks, however, both dependence and obligation on his part, as well as a strong emotional attachment to his *ngalgurng*. He is, ideally, dependent on her for a wife; and throughout his life, whether or not he is actually living with her daughter, he should provide her with gifts and with food (which she does not handle freely, but in accordance with certain rules). He should look after her, and see that others do the same. This emotional bond is reinforced by her position in the GAGAG line; through this line his life takes shape, and, again ideally, through it he has children. Both men and women claim that a man will "do anything he can to help his *ngalgurng*," that he should not offend her, and that in any trouble or fighting he should take her part. However, close as this relationship is, it is fraught with conflict. Women do interfere in the domestic life of their daughters and through them seek to influence their sons-in-law; and before marriage, if a choice has to be made between potential sons-in-law, a *ngalgurng* can withhold or withdraw betrothal confirmation by playing one against the other, and assessing the amount of assistance and gifts to be expected from either. She can also insist that her daughter leave her husband if the girl seems to be unhappy. But this is more likely in the early years of marriage, and in any case, if her own full NAGURNG is involved she should, ideally, try to patch up the situation and not exacerbate it.

Although ordinary speech should not be used between *ngalgurng* and NAGURNG, a special feature of their relationship is the *gunmigmi* (*gunmimigan*) or *gungurng* (see R. and C. Berndt, 1964: 75), similar in structure to ordinary Gunwinggu but with a substantially different vocabulary. Ideally, this is used between all *ngalgurng* and NAGURNG, whether or not the formal tie has been activated through a specific marriage link, but it is especially associated with this more personal relationship.

NAGURNG-NAGURNG (Ego's W.F.-D.H.):

These are brothers or husbands (W.F.) of a man's female *ngalgurng*, or the husband of his *ganggin* (sr.d.); a sister's son's wife is also a *ngalgurng*. There is much the same attitude of dependence as in the case of a *ngalgurng*, and prohibition on the use of anything, except food, which has been in personal contact with him. The *gungurng* vocabulary is usually relevant only as far as a man and his *ngalgurng* are concerned; however, speech between NAGURNG should be extremely circumspect. Gifts are expected, and it is obvious that a NAGURNG does play an important part in the marriage of his daughter and sister's daughter. A *ngalgurng*'s husband is either a GANGGIN or NGADJADJ, classified as a NAGURNG; her brother marries a woman whom ego calls *garang* or *ngalgurng*, and their children (unlike those of an actual or classificatory daughter of a *gagag*) are as brother and sister to him.

As in the case of a *ngalgurng*, a man is expected to defend and support his NAGURNG in arguments or fights.

ganjulg-GANJULG (F.Sr.S./M.B.S.-m.b.d/f.sr.d.: cross-cousins of opposite sex: second choice husband-wife):

Ganjulg/GANJULG are children of a man's M.B. (NGADJADJ) and f.sr. or a woman called by the term (*belu*) used for her. Although a *ganjulg* is a man's second choice wife, it is said that the term implies "wife" and is "on the right side." If none but distant *gagali* are available, then, we are told, a man's NGADJADJ says, "I will give you my daughter" because she is "the same as" a *gagali*. However, it is not usual to marry an actual m.b.d. "If you come from a long way" (both spatially and genealogically), Gunwinggu say, "then you can sleep with her." It is also a joking relationship, with much the same content as between *gagali*/GAGALI.

However, the *ganjulg* relationship is not as straightforward as it seems. An actual m.b.d. may be called "daughter," reciprocating with the term NGABAD "father." Similarly, if a man's NGADJADJ dies he himself can assume that role, taking over the dead man's responsibilities in relation to his children. This identification of a man with his NGADJADJ may obliquely reflect the authority pattern between them, and the significant position of a M.B. who is of the same moiety and has ritual obligations in relation to his nephew. However, if a man is not married to his actual *ganjulg* her children are *ngalgurng* and NAGURNG to him, with the daughter (*ngalgurng*) a potential mother-in-law. But, *ganjulg* who are not consanguineally related, and who are classified as distant or "long-way," are accessible and can simply be called *ganjulg* or, if they are sweethearts, *gagali*. One term of reference for an actual m.b.d. is *mudjalgdoi-jiburg*, (*jiburg*, somewhat like *dunin*, means "fully" or "wholly"). If a man walks with his *mudjalgdoi-jiburg*, it is said, "people know she is not his sweetheart, she is like a daughter; only long-way *ganjulg* are sweethearts."

This terminological and behavioral change between actual *ganjulg* is reflected elsewhere. For instance, a man calls his GANJULG's son and daughter by the special term *gugudji* (a modified form of GOGOG), which is said to mean "brother and sister." A man's son and daughter call his NGADJADJ, not "F." (although they call his NGADJADJ's son *gugudji*, "brother"), but "MAMAM." This, although in the grandparents' generation, is said to have the connotation of "son," and its reciprocal MAMAM, in this instance, to mean "father." This is because they regard the female *ganjulg* as a "mother" and her father (their father's NGADJADJ) as a M.F. (i.e. MAMAM). The fact that a man may call the female *ganjulg* "daughter" is not taken into account by his children in this context, but it is in the context of the *gugudji* relationship.

Except for the special father-child relationship between *ganjulg*, those who may be classified as ordinary *ganjulg* are treated virtually as *gagali*.

GANJULG-GANJULG (M.B.S.-F.Sr.S.: cross-cousins of the same sex, male):

The behavioral pattern between male GANJULG is not dissimilar to that between cross-cousins of opposite sex. Again, actual M.B.S./F.Sr.S. are classified as "son." However, the relationship between ordinary male GANJULG is reversed to some extent; it is said, "they are like fathers" rather than "like sons." There is no speech tabu between them, but GANJULG should be circumspect in each other's presence; they should not display anger or use violent language or talk about sweethearts, except that there is evidence of joking behavior between them. A man should aid his GANJULG and for general purposes treat him as a father; in turn, a GANJULG can offer advice and help in obtaining a wife; conventionally, he is a son's wife's father. A GANJULG has no ritual associations with his counterpart.

ganjulg-ganjulg (m.b.d.-f.sr.d.: cross-cousins of same sex, female):
In summary, this is a cooperative relationship, without the same constraint as between males, and with some formalized joking.

ngalmuni or *ganggin*-NAGURNG or NGADJADJ (s.w.-H.F.):
We have already discussed the relationship between NGADJADJ and *ganggin.* When children of a man's male GANJULG marry, a daughter's husband remains a GANGGIN, but a son's wife becomes a *ngalmuni* or *ngalbinmuni*, the content of the relationship closely resembling that of *ngalgurng*, but without avoidance. The reciprocal of *ngalbinmuni* (also used by a woman for her son's wife) is its masculine form, *nabinmuni* (used in reference to her husband's father). This term is said to mean "relating to the shoulder" because the spirit of the woman's husband jumped first on to her *nabinmuni*'s shoulder (see F.-S. relationship), and because he "grew up that boy for her."

GANGGIN-NGADJADJ (D.H.-W.F.):
The same relationship as between a M.B. and his Sr.S.

The *bindoi* relationship:
A *bindoi* is like a *ganggin* (see above), if he or she marries a man's *ngalgurng* or NAGURNG. For instance, if a man's sister's son marries a *ngalgurng*, their daughter is a *gagali*, a potential spouse. This is a *bindoi* relationship, a marriage made possible through a *ganggin.* Or again, a man's GAGAG (M.M.B.) has a daughter, *ngalgurng*, who normally marries a man's classificatory NGADJADJ, or NAGURNG, and their daughter is a *gagali*, a potential wife; if the *ngalgurng* marries a man's GANGGIN, the daughter is still a *gagali* to him but the relationship is a *bindoi* one. There are cases of a man's *belu* (f.sr.) marrying a GANGGIN (actually an alternative marriage in subsection terms), their children being *ganjulg* to him. However, this female *ganjulg* is not marriageable, "she is at the same time both *ganjulg* and daughter." (See under *ganjulg* of opposite sex.) She can marry a man who could be a NGADJADJ to her GANJULG. This is rationalized on the basis of the *ganjulg* in question being classified as his "daughter;" a man's real daughter would marry a GANGGIN, reciprocal NGADJADJ. Being in the ascendant generation level it is NGADJADJ rather than GANGGIN who marries a man's *ganjulg*; even though this is not correct when subsection intermarrying pairs are taken into account, it is still in conformity with moiety exogamy. But this is not a *bindoi* relationship.

Just as a *ganjulg*-daughter can marry a man's NGADJADJ, so a man's actual daughter, who normally marries a GANGGIN, can marry a NGADJADJ; this is a *bindoi* relationship. In these circumstances, the daughter of a *gulun* and a NGADJADJ is a *mamam*, and her children are *ganggin* or NGADJADJ. They are known as *maiamaia*, "like grandparents," and it is said that this now "comes back to the marriage line," strengthening it after the *bindoi.*

A *bindoi* relationship therefore exists between a man and his actual or classificatory NGADJADJ (reciprocal GANGGIN) if the NGADJADJ marries the other's daughter (the NGADJADJ's sister's son's daughter: see Table 9.1). See Table 9.5 (below).

Table 9.5.

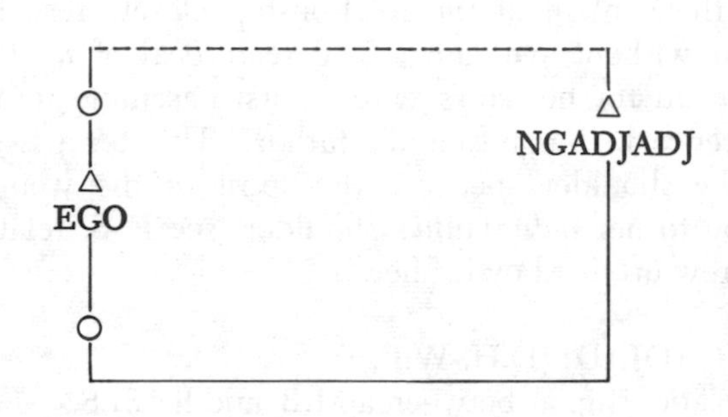

However, if a man arranges the betrothal of a "close" but not actual m.b.d., *ganjulg*, whom he calls "daughter," and who receives gifts, but the "promise" (betrothal arrangement) is broken; then, because of the initial *ganjulg* relationship between them, he will now call her *gagali.* This, where a daughter is now called "wife," is a *bindoi* relationship.

From GANGGIN's point of view the *bindoi* relationship is expressed as *ngandoibun* (an inflected form, the prefix *ngan* indicating first person singular object). From NGADJADJ's it is *ngadoibun* (the prefix *nga* indicating first person singular agent).

ANALYSIS

I have now examined briefly the behavioral content of Gunwinggu relationships. As would have been expected, the attributes of the relationships noted by Hsu (1965: e.g., 642) differ considerably. Where similarities exist they are mostly based on biological elements inherent in the relationships themselves. The Gunwinggu system is predominantly matrilineal, and this should serve as a guide to what relationships are considered dominant, what recessive. The actual content of the behavioral patterns and attributes makes relatively clear which are considered most important against those of lesser significance. However, this is not necessarily revealed in an examination of the structure of the system itself, nor in the preferential forms of marriage which serve as the core of the system and about which conventional structures are built. We are unable to evaluate dominant and recessive kinship elements simply on the basis of kin terminology. It is the content of the social relationship itself, in terms of behavior patterns, that offers the key. This is one reason why it is essential that the empirical material be considered first.

While it seems fairly clear that among the Gunwinggu the brother-sister relationship is predominantly significant, it should not be taken as an isolated relationship—it is enmeshed with others, especially the NGADJADJ and *garang* and the GAGAG line generally. From one point of view the *gagag-wulubulu* line is pivotal, because from it are derived three relationships of major significance: brother-sister, M.B.-m., and *ngalgurng-gagali*. All of these set a person in his family of orientation and provide him with the nucleus of his family of procreation. However, we cannot overlook the patrilineal emphases manifested in the *gunmugugur*, and the spiritual associations of the father and his "line." But these do appear to be less important than those which cluster around the GAGAG "line," especially in terms of ritual privileges, although there is increasing use of the patrilineal moiety concept and labels, from eastern Arnhem Land, as a means of ensuring ritual continuity in the paternal line. (See R. and C. Berndt, 1964: 62.)

Still, in considering the relative importance of social relationships one inevitably asks such questions as "Important to, or for, whom? Under what conditions? In connection with, or in the context of, what other relationships?" In any actual situation one relationship is likely to be highlighted; and because situations vary, as does interaction within them, there is a continual shifting of emphases. Under such conditions, the importance of any one term (or pair of terms) and its content will vary in accordance with the roles assumed in the ordinary process of social interaction with kin and non-kin.

Each relationship, especially those grouped under A, B, and C in the following table (9.6), is important—each supplies or fulfils certain needs which another does not, or does only partially. In these circumstances, how may they be graded in order of their relative importance to any one person? Any process of grading in such terms must inevitably be somewhat arbitrary. However, I have attempted to do this, and my criteria are not simply the individual attributes associated with the relationships themselves. Obviously these are duplicated throughout this listing of behavioural kin patterns, but in many cases, they also vary quite considerably in their combination. I have considered primarily how Gunwinggu themselves have evaluated them and the implications of one relationship for others.

RELATIONSHIPS

In the following table (9.6), Groups A and B comprise dominant relationships, graded in terms of what is considered to be their importance to any one person. They are subdivided into primary and secondary. A primary-dominant relationship has implications over and above simple interpersonal connotations; it affects other relationships and is, itself, likewise affected. Secondary-dominant relationships are important in interpersonal terms, but are also directly influenced by primary ones, with which they are linked. (For example, the GAGAG and *ngalgurng* relationships are significant in the light of the brother-sister relationship.) Yet, the NGABAD relationship has been placed under B because of the importance accorded to the *gunmugugur*.

In Group C are what can be called "uninfluenced" relationships or relationships of equality for all intents and purposes uninfluenced by those in A and B. More correctly, I suppose, we could call them contingent relationships—contingent on A and B. Under D are so-called "recessive," or, as I prefer to call them, subordinate or derivative relationships. The attributes and behavioral patterns associated with them are influenced by or reflective of those listed under A, B, and C: they are relationships which do not provide a distinctive action pattern in their own right, although their attributes are not always directly framed and a one-to-one relationship between them and those under A, B, and C is not always discernible. For instance, 8, *belu*, is influenced by 1, but is reflective of 3, while 3 is influenced by 1. But subordinate or derivative relationships as noted here (D, 8-23) are not graded in terms of their importance; such grading could not be made in this context. In any case, many of the relationships listed under D are, in fact, important in interpersonal terms; this is especially the case with 8, 9, and 10.

Relations may be grouped as follows:

Table 9.6.

Group A
Dominant relationships (primary):

1. *jabog*-DADA (sr.-B.)
2. *a.* NGADJADJ-*ganggin*/GANGGIN (M.B.-sr. child)
   b. *garang-djedje*/DJEDJE (m.-child)

} Content of these two relationships is reflective of the B.-sr. relationship

Group B
Dominant relationships (secondary):

	Content influenced by or influencing
3. NGABAD-*gulun*/GULUN (F.-child)	1
4. GAGAG-*gagag*/GAGAG (M.M.B.-d. child)	1
5. *ngalgurng*-NAGURNG (w.m.-D.H.)	1

Group C
Uninfluenced relationships (of equality):

6. GOGOG-DADA (siblings of same sex, males)
7. GAGALI-*gagali* (H.-W.)

Group D
Subordinate or derivative relationships:

	CONTENT OF RELATIONSHIP	
	Influenced by	*Reflective of*
8. *belu-gulun*/GULUN (f. sr.-B. child)	1	3
9. *gagali* of same sex	1	–
10. *ganjulg* of opposite sex	3	7
11. *ganjulg* of same sex	3	3
12. MAWA (F.F.-S. child)	–	6
13. *maga* (f.m.-s. child)	–	3
14. MAMAM (M.F.-d. child)	6	–
15. *wulubulu* (m.m.m. and M.M.M.B.)	1	4
16. NAGURNG-NAGURNG	1	5
17. *bindoi*	–	–
18. b.w.-H.B.	–	7
19. b.w.-h.sr.	–	7
20. h.b.w.-h.b.w.	1	–
21. Sr.H.-w.sr.	1	–
22. s.w.-H.F.	–	5
23. D.H.-W.F.	–	3

ATTRIBUTES

The attributes I have singled out for correlation emerge from an examination of the content of each social relationship. They do not coincide with those noted by Hsu (1965). I have, rather, chosen a short series of what I would call significant elements which may or may not be present in all social relationships. I am interested in how Gunwinggu themselves explicitly categorize these attributes, not in what may be merely inferred. As regards the attributes of "continuity-discontinuity" and "inclusiveness-exclusiveness" (Hsu), I see these as abstract statements; they concern the way the empirical material is interpreted and are *not* necessarily statements of fact.

While certain relationships of a consanguineal and affinal kind (e.g., F.-child, m.-child, siblings, H.-w., w.m., and so on) do have inherent properties, the various socio-cultural patterns in which they are activated give rise to additional attributes which often overshadow those derived from the "nature of the relationship;" and these, in combination, are more significant to the persons involved in that relationship. I do not think we can assume that intrinsic elements continue to influence *other* relationships. It is more likely that these inherent issues remain personal, being categorized as the state of a particular relationship rather than being confused with its content.

The nature or state of a husband-wife relationship, for example, consists of the union of two persons of opposite sex who live together in a recognized and regular fashion, acknowledging that each has rights of some kind over the other. In its basic form this is sexual association, with or without the production of children, with the death of one member destroying the relationship as such. These features are non-communicable to other relationships. Yet, attributes concern the way in which the union is perceived, the recognition of obligations between the pair, decisions on the division of labor between them, emphasis on childbearing or otherwise, the impinging influence of affines, attitudes toward sexuality, and so forth. These features are communicable to other linked relationships and represent the cultural "skin" of the relationship itself. I shall confine myself to the cultural content of the relationships.

Each relationship has associated with it several attributes which must be considered in combination. And each relationship, too, even those categorized as dominant, is influenced by others. The degree of such influence cannot always be decided. What appears to be an influence may not necessarily be so. While I have categorized primary and secondary dominant relationships, and suggested that some of these are influenced by the brother-sister relationship, each could in fact be seen as a separate relationship with its own attributes. It simply *seems* that those (for instance) in Group B (Table 9.7) have certain attributes which are derived from the brother-sister relationship, while those in Group C (Table 9.8) have no obvious association with that relationship. I shall note below the reasons why I have selected the brother-sister relationship as dominant among the Gunwinggu.

The attributes I set out are intended to be straightforward ones.[8] For instance, if brothers are expected to provide aid in fighting, entries appear under "Obligation and responsibility" and "Cooperation and aid." If a father encounters the spirit of his child before its birth, an entry appears under "Dependence: spiritual." If a brother may not drink from the cup used by his sister, "Avoidance" is indicated. If a man is dependent on his M.B.'s decision for his advancement in the ritual sphere, and this help can be withheld, then "Authority: in ritual sphere" is referred to, and so on. The following tables reveal the spread of attributes relevant to Gunwinggu relationships. Attributes are listed vertically and kin horizontally. The attributes of kin are to be taken as being relevant to a man and his sr. (1), NGADJADJ (2 *a*), *garang* (2 *b*), NGABAD (3), GAGAG (4), and *ngalgurng* (5), etc.

Undoubtedly, the six relationships in Group A and B (Table 9.7) are the most significant to a man. Each of these is oriented by the relationship between siblings of the opposite sex. The NGADJADJ's authority over his GANGGIN is derived from his tie with his sister and from his position in the GAGAG line. The *garang*'s position is, of course, unique,

8. In the course of the Symposium at which this paper was presented in its original form, much was said concerning the importance of seeing dominant kinship relationships in perspective and within the wider system. We must look in the direction of the "attributes" to achieve this broader view in general terms.

Table 9.7. Groups A and B: Dominant Relationships

Attributes	Sister 1	NGADJADJ 2 a	garang 2 b	NGABAD 3	GAGAG gagag 4	ngalgurng 5
Obligation and responsibility	mutual	mutual	mutual	mutual but not strong	indirect[xx]	on part of D.H.
Emotional bond	mutual	some hostility on part of GANGGIN	mutual	constraint	mutual	mutual
Cooperation and aid	mutual	on part of GANGGIN	mutual	mutual but not strong	indirect[xx]	on part of D.H.
Dependence: spiritual	–	–	–	on part of child	toward male GAGAG	–
physical	on part of B.	–	in childhood on part of child, later vice versa	in childhood on part of child, later vice versa	–	on part of D.H.
emotional	mutual	on part of GANGGIN	mutual	–	–	–
Sexual association	–	–	–	–	–	–
Neutral-passive	–	–	–	–	–	–
Avoidance	mutual	partial constraint	–	–	–	mutual
Authority: in secular sphere	sr. over B.; B. disciplining sr.	over GANGGIN[x]	–	indirect	–	over D.H.[xxx]
in ritual sphere	–	over GANGGIN	–	indirect only	indirect	–
in relation to marriage	B. over sr.'s children	over GANGGIN	active role	indirect	through GAGAG line	through GAGAG line
Inheritance	–	direct	indirect	in *gunmugugur*	indirect	–

Notes:
x Authority derived from B.–sr. relationship and NGADJADJ's position in GAGAG line
xx Channelized through a man's m. and M.B.
xxx Because of her d., who is a man's potential or actual wife

but the brother-sister linkage enters to establish the NGADJADJ-GANGGIN relationship between her brother and her children. In the case of the NGABAD, there is his linkage with the *gunmugugur*; but conventionally NGABAD's sister, actual or more distant, is an actual or potential wife of his children's NGADJADJ, and he should help this man, his own GAGALI, before his own brothers. The GAGAG line is relevant to the brother-sister relationship, as it is to that between a man and his *ngalgurng*.

In Group C (Table 9.8) are relationships which are relatively uninfluenced by the dominant ones. Nevertheless, it is obvious that the husband-

Table 9.8. Group C: Uninfluenced Relationships of Equality

Attributes	*GOGOG DADA* 6	*gagali* 7
Obligation and responsibility	mutual	mutual[x]
Emotional bond	mutual plus constraint and formality	ideally, between betrothed pair; diffused to sweetheart relationships, not necessarily present in husband-wife relationship
Cooperation and aid	mutual	mutual
Dependence: spiritual	–	–
physical	–	on part of spouse, especially wife.
emotional	equality	–
Sexual association	–	mutual: relationship not exclusive: production of children
Neutral-passive	rivalry at minimum	–
Avoidance	–	–
Authority: in secular sphere	–	on part of H.
in ritual sphere	aid on equal basis	–
in relation to marriage	–	–
Inheritance (general)	indirect only	–

Note:
x Significance of relationship lies in its linkage with others: e.g., GAGAG-*ngalgurng* relationships

wife relationship is colored by, although not necessarily dependent on, the brother-sister relationship and the GAGAG line.

In Group D (Table 9.9) a wide range of relationships is represented, all more or less influenced by the above. Some, however, retain a distinctive character in relation to the combination of attributes relevant to them.

Apart from discussion of the brother-sister relationship in the context of behavior patterns, and data on it obtained more obliquely in case material and through observation, direct questions were asked of several Gunwinggu men. Because this was a tentative enquiry I made no attempt at sampling, but the men ranged from young to elderly, and I knew them all personally from my earlier visits to the area. In no case was it possible to persuade a man to give a direct answer concerning the ranking of relationships in order of importance; that is, apart from remarks made during discussion of the content of the various relationships (as above). The men were then asked to imagine a storm at sea, in which all their relatives, both consanguineal and affinal, were in a canoe about to sink: if they could rescue only one, whom would they choose?[9] This gave rise to much discussion and some resistance. A few refused to answer. Of those who did, some chose their own youngest son, others their father, and in one case a younger brother. Other categories of kin were not mentioned. It seemed that each person looked at the situation in relation to his own relatives living in the local environment. Because these informants were adult men, those in their grandparents' generation were excluded because they were mostly dead, and in most cases their mothers were dead too. All had brothers and sisters, wives, etc. Despite the deep emotional attachment between actual brothers and sisters, because of the avoidance aspect of their relationship one would not expect a sister to be mentioned in this context. A man would not be in a position to save his sister in such circumstances; she would not, or should not, be in the same small canoe. Thus, the fact that sisters were not mentioned in this context is itself significant.

As a second experiment, informants were asked to imagine being at sea in a storm with only their mother, wife, and mother-in-law and able to save only one. Many avoided this question on the grounds that, should one choose a mother or mother-in-law instead of a wife, one's wife would get to hear of this and make trouble. Those who did answer, and who had wives (and, as far as could be seen, were reasonably attached to them) wanted to save both mother and mother-in-law rather than wife. Several took a long time to decide, and eventually settled on the mother. This

9. Dr. J. W. Fernandez in his Chapter on "Bantu Brotherhood" reports more or less the same procedure, which he calls the "ultimate circumstance situation," and suggests that it represents one way in which the Hsu hypothesis could be tested. However, in dealing with Australian Aboriginal material some difficulties were encountered, and are noted here.

Table 9.9. Group D: "Recessive" or Subordinate Relationships

Attributes	belu 8	GAGALI 9	ganjulg 10	GANJULG 11	MAWA mawa 12	MAGA maga 13	MAMAM mamam 14	WULUBULU wulubulu 15
Obligation and responsibility	mutual but not strong	mutual[x]	mutual	mutual	on part of younger	mutual	dependent on age	respect for
Emotional bond	mutual but not strong; some constraint	deep	varying, depending on "distance"	not emphasized	mutual	mutual	not strong	–
Cooperation and aid	mutual but not strong	first call	depending on "distance"	mutual	mutual	mutual, especially female	especially in reference to female *mamam*	age intervenes
Dependence: spiritual	on part of GULUN/*gulun*	–	–	–	through *gunmugugur*	–	on part of younger	ultimate relationship in GAGAG line
physical	–	–	–	–	on part of younger	–	–	–
emotional	–	–	–	–	equality	–	–	–
Sexual association	–	–	depending on "distance"	–	–	–	oblique with female	–
Neutral-passive	–	–	–	–	age neutralizes	–	–	age neutralizes
Avoidance	some constraint	varying degrees	–	–	–	–	–	–
Authority: in secular sphere	not marked	–	depending on "distance"	–	–	if female young	–	–
in ritual sphere	–	on part of either	–	–	–	–	–	–
in relation to marriage	–	–	–	–	–	–	–	–
Inheritance (general)	–	–	–	–	relevant to *gunmugugur*	–	–	–

Attributes	*NAGURNG* 16	*bindoi* 17	*b.w.-H.B.* 18	*b.w.-h.sr.* 19	*h.b.w.-h.b.w.* 20	*Sr.H.-w.sr.* 21	*s.w.-H.F.* 22	*D.H.-W.F.* 23
Obligation and responsibility	if W.F.	relevant to relationship between *bindoi*	mutual	–	–	similar to B.-sr. relationship	similar to *ngalgurng* relationship	similar to NGADJADJ relationship
Emotional bond	–	–	–	–	–	–	–	–
Cooperation and aid	if W.F.	ordinarily	mutual	intermediary between brothers	on occasions	–	–	–
Dependence: spiritual	–	–	–	–	–	–	–	–
physical	if W.F.	–	–	–	–	–	–	–
emotional	–	–	–	–	–	–	–	–
Sexual association	–	–	–	–	–	–	–	–
Neutral-passive	–	on occasions	–	neutral	–	–	–	–
Avoidance	partial constraint: varies	dependent on relationship between *bindoi*	reversal of H.w. situation	–	constraint	–	no avoidance	no constraint
Authority: in secular sphere	–	–	–	–	–	–	–	–
in ritual sphere	–	–	–	–	–	–	–	–
in relation to marriage	xx	xxx	–	–	–	–	–	–
Inheritance (general)	–	–	–	–	–	–	–	–

Notes:
x Reflection of B.–sr. relationship
xx Significance in relation to B.–sr. relationship, and as W.F.
xxx Involving form of marriage between *bindoi* partners

was explained first in economic terms. A man and his brothers give food to his wife's parents, and a man's wife and her brothers give food to his parents and, because of this both mother and mother-in-law are important in terms of production of spouses for their respective children. In other statements, the mother's position as a sister was stressed, "My mother did a lot for me; she is the sister of NGADJADJ; I would save her first." Again, it was said that even a wife "would save her mother-in-law first, because that woman gave her son to her as a husband," but this appears to represent only male opinion. It was, however, generally conceded that one would not save a wife at the expense of a mother or mother-in-law, "She gave me nothing. I gave her a child, she gave me a child; this balances it out." Other comments were, in summary: "We worry about a father and a mother first. If a man goes out hunting they (the parents) get meat first before a portion of it is passed on to his wife."

This procedure for obtaining opinions on the importance of specific kin did not work out satisfactorily. Despite some more general comments, the responses suggest that choice was made on the basis of personal inclination at the time rather than on weighing and assessment of the totality of kin relationships.

The "Murngin"

The people of north-eastern Arnhem Land have been called "Murngin." In social organization they differ from the Gunwinggu. The whole region is divided among named eogamous "clan" (*mala*) and dialectal units (*mada*), and the people have no overall name to cover all of these; "Murngin," or Murungun, refers to one small clan. In earlier writing I used the name Wulamba, and more recently Malag. Their kinship has been the subject of some controversy. Warner (1937/58) initially discussed it, followed by Lawrence and Murdock (1949), Leach (1951), Elkin (1950), Radcliffe-Brown (1951) and Berndt (1955), among others. I shall not go into the problems raised by these writers. It is sufficient for my present purpose to indicate the general structure of the kinship system itself, to locate the range of relationships available and to note how the system itself works. The major emphasis throughout this eastern Arnhem Land region is on patriliny. The basic social categories are two patrilineal exogamous moieties, named *jiridja* and *dua*.

SUBSECTIONS

In the local subsection system, the same basic principles are involved as in the the Gunwinggu example, but the matrilineal moieties are in this case unnamed. Again, a child's subsection label is dependent on its mother's. The patrilineal moieties are integrated with the subsection categories.

The normal system is as follows (only male terms are given):[10]

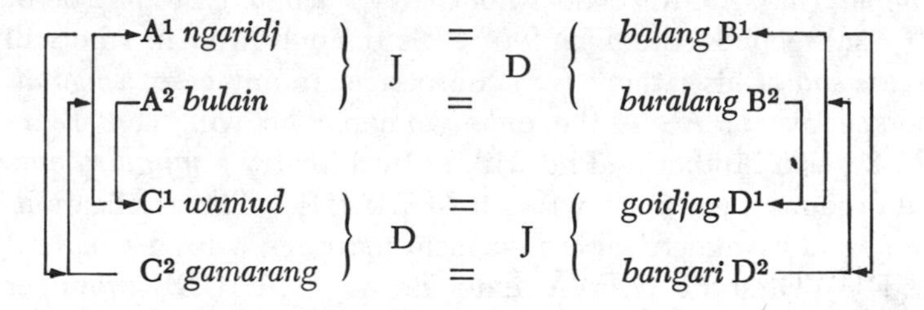

The patrilineal moieties cut the system diagonally: A^1, A^2, D^1 and D^2, *jiridja*; B^1, B^2, C^1, C^2, *dua*. Descent follows the same pattern as among the Gunwinggu and the terms used stand in the same relation to one another.

The following shows the formal distribution of kin among the subsections (see Table 9.11 for the key to kin terms).

mari, gudara	*wawa, jugujugu, jaba, maraidja*	$A^1 = B^1$	*galei duwei*	*ngatiwalgur, mumalgur, dumungur*
	marimo	$A^2 = B^2$	*momo, ngati, gominjar*	
wogu	*ngandi ngabibi*	$C^1 = D^1$	*baba mugulbaba maralgur mugulrumurung*	*gurung*
	—	$C^2 = D^2$	*gadu*	

The two main central columns list terms relevant to a single subsection; that is, if A^1 is a man's or woman's subsection, other persons having the same label will be his/her brothers, sisters, and son's sons; ideally, marriageable partners are to be found in B^1, in which *galei* and *duwei* of both sexes are located. In the alternate generation level A^2 persons marry those in B^2. However, alternate generations are classified together; a man's or woman's *mari* and *gudara* are of subsections A^1 and/or A^2, and NGATIWALGUR, *mumalgur* and *dumungur* B^1 and/or B^2. The same is the case with succeeding generation levels.

From this it is seen that a man and his son's son are of the same subsection, and *galei* are eligible partners for both (see Table 9.11). For this to be practicable a GADU (S.) must marry a woman of the alternative

10. The same symbols are used as in the Gunwinggu system; however, in this case J. = *jiridja* and D. = *dua*.

marriageable subsection, in the alternate generation above him, who is his father's *ngandi* (m.). A GADU does not marry a *wogu*, who may be of either C^1 or C^2 subsections; the *ngandi* of C^1 is the only woman who will definitely have a son of his father's (A^1) subsection. In any case, a *ngandi* (from the perspective of A^1) is the only woman who will have Ego's NGABIBI (M.B.) as a brother and he will, in turn, marry a *mugulrumurung*, who will produce a *galei* as a wife for MARAIDJA. The implications of this pattern lie in asymmetrical cross-cousin marriage, with a *jaba* (sr.) marrying her DUWEI and a WAWA (elder B.) or JUGUJUGU (younger B.) marrying his *galei*. A *galei*'s brother is GALEI, and the only woman conventionally available to him is Ego's *mari*, who will produce terminologically suitable d. and s.d. for a man's S. and S.S. to marry, if matrilateral cross-cousin marriage is to take place.

The following correlation of subsection labels with the kinship terminology is interesting. Reference should be made also to Table 9.11.

Table 9.10. "Murngin" Kinship System correlated with Subsections

L3	L2	L1	O	R1	R2	R3	
△ ○	△ ○	△ ○	△ ○	△ ○	△ ○	△ ○	
$B^2 = A^2$	$A^2 = B^2$	$B^2 = A^2$	$A^2 = B^2$	$B^2 = A^2$	$A^2 = B^2$	$B^2 = A^2$	
$C^1 = D^1$	$D^1 = C^1$	$C^1 = D^1$	$D^1 = C^1$	$C^1 = D^1$	$D^1 = C^1$	$C^1 = D^1$	
$B^1 = A^1$	$A^1 = B^1$	$B^1 = A^1$	$A^1 = B^1$	$B^1 = A^2$	$\left\{\begin{matrix} A^1 \\ A^2 \end{matrix}\right. = B^2$	$\left\{\begin{matrix} B^2 \\ B^1 \end{matrix}\right. = A^2$	AREA OF
$C^2 = D^2$	$D^2 = C^2$	$C^2 = D^2$	$D^2 = C^1$	$C^1 = D^1$	$D^1 = C^1$	$C^1 = D^1$	ADJUSTMENT
$B^2 = A^2$	$A^2 = B^2$	$B^2 = A^1$	$A^1 = B^1$	$B^1 = A^2$	$\left\{\begin{matrix} A^2 \\ A^1 \end{matrix}\right. = B^2$	$\left\{\begin{matrix} B^2 \\ B^1 \end{matrix}\right. = A^2$	

The subsection system is not systematically correlated with the kinship system. Alternative subsection marriages are prevalent, but only in the area outlined as an "area of adjustment." The reasons for this are straightforward; marriages are "adjusted" to enable a S.S. to marry a *galei*, and a S. to marry a *ngandi*, and to maintain the ideal of matrilateral cross-cousin marriage. The bracketed subsection labels refer to equivalents. For example, a C^1 woman should have an A^1 child, but in this position the child is A^2; a D^1 woman should have a B^1 child, but for this position the child is B^2.

The two major points revealed in this subsection system are (*a*) that intermarriage should take place between members of opposite patrilineal and matrilineal moieties, and that offspring belong to the (unnamed) matrilineal moiety of their mother and the (named) patrilineal moiety of their father; and (*b*) that marriageable partners belong to the same or alternate generation levels, and their parents and children to succeeding generation levels.

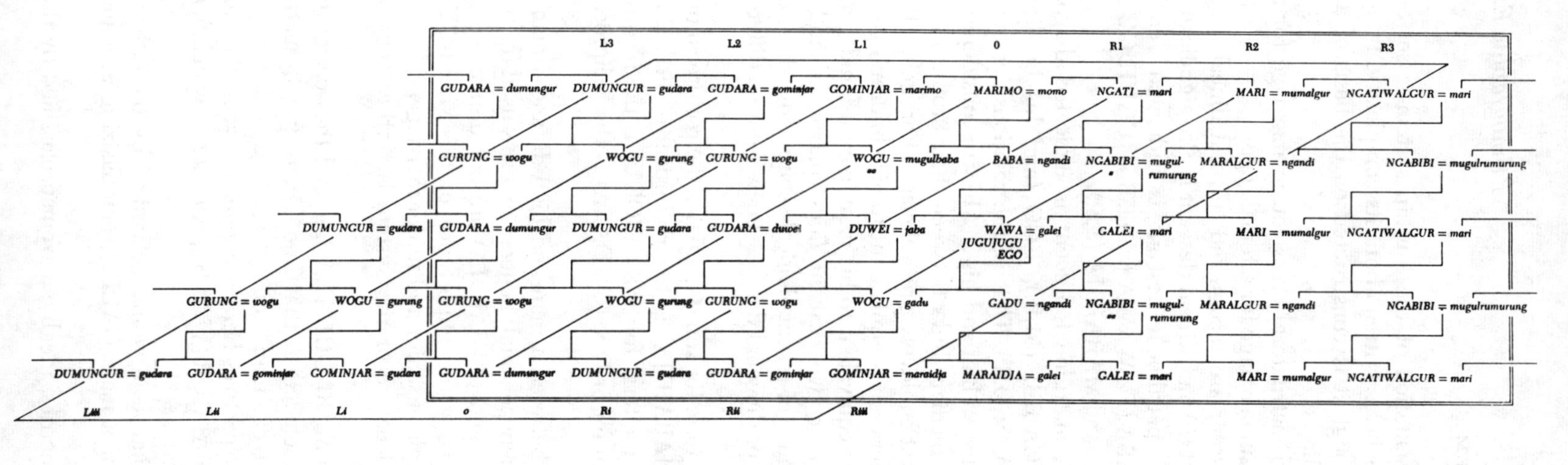

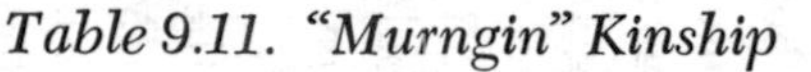

Table 9.11. "Murngin" Kinship

THE KINSHIP SYSTEM

A construct representation of the kinship system is set out in Table 9.11. A great deal has been written about its complexity. In actual fact, it is quite simple, although it is constructed on the basis of a number of rules. These are as follows:

1. There is preferred matrilateral cross-cousin marriage for a male ego, patrilateral cross-cousin marriage for a female ego.
2. Two forms of descent are recognized: (*a*) patrilineal descent is considered dominant, but (*b*) matrilineal descent is also significant.
3. (a) Schematically, patrilineal descent is indicated vertically: thus, MARIMO (F.F.), BABA (F), WAWA (elder B.), JUGUJUGU (younger B) and EGO, GADU (S.) and MARAIDJA (S.S.)

(*b*) Schematically, matrilineal descent is indicated diagonally: thus, MARI (M.M.B.), NGABIBI (M.B.), EGO (and his brothers), WOGU (Sr.S.) and GUDARA (Sr.D.S.). That is, the relationships between a man and his M.B. and between him and his MARI are considered pivotal, and women serve as intermediary links between their brothers and their sons.

4. Alternating generation levels are relevant. For general purposes, a person's parents' generation is equivalent to his children's generation, and his generation level is equivalent to his grandparents' and grandchildren's generation levels. These two *descent lines* (patrilineal and matrilineal) demonstrate the balance of terminological reciprocals which do not occur in any other vertical or diagonal descent lines, where a different principle is involved.

In the first (*a*), the term for son (GADU) is the reciprocal of BABA (F.); the term for S.S. (MARAIDJA) is the reciprocal of F.F. (MARIMO).

In the second (*b*), the term for Sr.S. (WOGU) is the reciprocal of M.B. (NGABIBI); the term for Sr.D.S. (GUDÁRA) is the reciprocal of M.M.B. (MARI).

The relationships between a man and his F.F. and a man and his S.S. are considered uniquely personal; hence, the terms used for these relationships (i.e., MARIMO and MARAIDJA) are not duplicated elsewhere in the system. Emphasizing the importance of the MARI-GUDARA relationship is the principle of senior and junior marriage.

5. The asymmetrical nature of the system is further suggested by four features:

(*a*) A man's wife's MARI-GUDARA line and the special terms used to designate relatives included in that line. Or, to put it another way, the MARI-GUDARA line of a man's son.

From a man's perspective, here are persons whom he calls *mugulrumurung* (w.m.), MARALGUR (W.M.B.), *mumalgur* (w.m.m.), and NGATIWALGUR (W.M.M.B.).

(*b*) A man's son marries a woman classified by the father as a *ngandi* (i.e., the daughter of a male GALEI), emphasizing asymmetrical cross-cousin marriage.

(*c*) A man's S.S. marries, ideally, a woman classified by the F.F. as his *galei* (or "wife"), suggesting that a man and his S.S. are structurally equivalent.

(*d*) But, although a man and his S.S. are structurally equivalent for certain purposes, they cannot compete for women in the F.F.'s generation, only in the S.S.'s generation. While the terms MARAIDJA and MARIMO are unique, and not duplicated, the term MARIMO is often equated with MARI, and a man and his MARI do not compete for women classified as wives of a GUDARA.

6. In the vertical system (double outline), terms in the first ascendent generation level and those in the first descendent generation level are the same—except for BABA and *mugulbaba* in the former and *GADU* in the latter. (The terms for F., F.B. and classificatory F. and for Ego's children are not duplicated at other points within the system as such.) In all other cases, the relevant patriline shows an equivalence of kin terms in the generation level immediately below and above the level of a male ego.

Grandparents' and grandchildren's generation levels differ insofar as they show, not senior-junior reciprocals (as in the case of a man's patriline), but equivalents.

7. Horizontally, patrilines to the left of a man's patriline (0: see Table 9.11) contain reciprocals of those to the right: that is, in the grandparents' generation, L1 are reciprocals of R1; L2 reciprocals of R2; L3 reciprocals of R3.

In the generation level above an Ego, L1 are reciprocals of R1, L2 are reciprocals of R2, and L3 are reciprocals of R3.

In an Ego's own generation the same is the case, as in the generation level below him (his son's generation).

In a Ego's S.S. generation level, the pattern is altered because of the MARAIDJA who marries a *galei*. L3 are reciprocals of R3, L2 reciprocals of R2. L1 and R1 *can* be regarded as reciprocals *if* a man can marry the potential wife of his S.S.; if he does so, the MARAIDJA would regard the woman previously called *galei* as his *momo* and her brother as NGATI, thus providing reciprocals between L2 and R2.

8. Diagonally, except for the NGATIWALGUR, the MARI-GUDARA and the NGATI lines, terms in alternate generations are equivalent—except in small o (see Table 9.11) with *marimo*/MARIMO (as a special case, noted above), and Li where *gudara* marry DUMUNGUR and GOMINJAR.

9. (*a*) Males in a man's own patriline marry women of their own or senior alternate generation level.

(*b*) Females in a man's own patriline marry men of their own or junior alternate generation levels.

Or, to put it another way:

(*a*) Males in ascendent generation levels from an Ego's point of view marry women of their own generation level; males in descendent generation levels marry women in the alternate generation level senior to them.

(*b*) Females in ascendent generation levels from an Ego's point of view marry men in the alternate generation level junior to them; females in

generation levels descendent from Ego marry men of their own generation level.
10. Patrilines headed by male NGATI (R1), MARI (R2), and NGATI-WALGUR (R3) take their marriage patterning from males in Ego's patriline; that is, all marry men or women in their own or senior alternate generation levels. These are regarded as the senior patrilines, as senior terms predominate.
11. Patrilines headed by L1, L2, and L3, take their marriage patterning from females in Ego's patriline: that is, all marry men or women in their own or junior alternate generation levels. These are regarded as the junior patrilines, because all terms are junior to those found in R1, R2 and R3, except for DUWEI, which is the reciprocal of *galei*/GALEI.

BEHAVIORAL PATTERNS[11]

BABA-*gadu*/GADU (F.-child):

Warner (1937/58: 67) notes five varieties of the father-child relationship, and adds that the same is true for many other relationships. I shall not, here, demarcate these differences because in actual practice they are difficult to distinguish—except in the case of an actual consanguineal linkage. What I shall say about each relationship refers primarily to the actual relationship itself: genealogical closeness is significant, but what is relevant for an actual father (for instance) is also relevant in large measure to his brothers, whether or not they have both parents in common. However, the binding ties of obligation, responsibility, avoidance, and so on (in the case of any specific actual relationship) are weakened with genealogical distance, according to whether a genealogical connection can be established or is acknowledged. There are one or two exceptions to this, mainly associated with avoidance between a woman and her daughter's husband; that is, *any* woman classified as a wife's mother. But the extension is also relevant to *any* woman classified as a sister; and to *all* women a man calls *galei* ("wife," actual, potential, or implied). In these circumstances, emotional intensity certainly differs, but the outward conventions of the relationship are mostly observed.

In this patrilineally-oriented society, the F.-S., F.-d. relationships are especially significant. A strong emotional bond exists between children and their father and his brothers, and in fact is extended to all men belonging to their own dialectal unit (and clan) who are classified as "F." But a distinction may be drawn between "fathers" who merely belong to the same dialectal unit and those who are directly linked genealogically to

11. As in the case of the Gunwinggu material, I am relying here mainly on data collected in February 1966. However, this is supplemented by other information gathered in north-eastern Arnhem Land since 1946, when my wife and I first carried out research in that region. My comments here will be briefer than for the Gunwinggu, since Lloyd Warner's study (1937/58) is substantially correct; it provides a good coverage of this topic (e.g., on pp. 60-104). Additionally, there is my earlier paper (R. Berndt, 1955) and my chapter in Nimkoff (1965: 77-104).

one's actual F.; these latter belong to one's *babaru*. The *babaru* is often vaguely conceived and the word is used loosely. However, for general purposes, it refers to those persons counted as being within the male descent line (see R. Berndt, 1955: 85, 96-7). Warner (1937/58: 69) has emphasized the importance of the actual F., and shown that physiological paternity is acknowledged.

A child is "found by," or makes itself known to, its father or father's sister. This is called in English the "spirit-landing." The unborn child's spirit appears in a dream, having come from a sacred site associated with its father's dialectal unit territory; this in turn has mythological implications for the child after his birth, and when he is accepted as a participant in the great religious rituals. Initially, the spirit-child is seen in the context of a specific incident. It takes the form of some creature which allows itself to be caught or escapes in a peculiar way. Soon afterward the prospective father or his sister sees the child in a dream; in this context it is in human shape and its sex may be distinguished. It speaks to its father, asking where its mother is, telling him it is ready to be born. The father points out his wife and the child enters her. There are variations on this theme; and there are instances of men having spirit landings outside their own dialectal unit territory, or of their mothers eloping with other men before they were born, and so on. However, patrilineal descent is of the utmost significance.

As Warner has pointed out, a man's social position is enhanced on producing children and his marriage is ratified by the birth of his first child. Parents observe food tabus before the birth of a child; and there are varying periods of sexual abstinence, but this is not so important for the husband. More significant are the social relationships reaffirmed and created through the birth of a son (for instance)—the new sets of relationships centering on matrilateral cross-cousin marriage, with a man's wife's brother now being NGABIBI to his son. A man's own relationship with his wife's mother and her brother, and her father, are strengthened; his son will, in adulthood, have a strong bond of mutual aid with his own NGABIBI, and a man's *mugulrumurung* becomes his son's *mari*. This latter relationship—that between a man and his *mari*, especially his male MARI (his M.M.B.)—is, along with the F.-child relationship, one of the most important, if not the most important.

Father and son are relatively close to each other; cooperation and mutual aid are expected, and there is freedom of speech and action between them. It is a father who arranges for his son to be initiated and makes gifts to those who paint and circumcise him. Further, it is through his father and father's brothers (and MARIMO) that a boy achieves full membership in the sacred ritual in the possession of the elders of his patriline. Inheritance is patrilineal, and the right to use special emblems, designs, songs, dances, invocations, and so forth is handed down through the *babaru*.

In the course of establishing this close personal bond, in his early youth a son is frequently in the company of his father. Two major elements affect this relationship. Over and above its positive qualities, there is the question of a father's authority. Lip-service is paid to the importance of a father's position in this respect *vis-à-vis* his son. Structurally, he is in a position of seniority and control; yet a father does not consistently discipline his son, any more than a mother does. A man's real authority over his son lies in the ritual sphere—in his power to provide or withhold this kind of knowledge and to favour one son as against another. Conventionally, preference rests simply on relative age: the eldest first, the youngest, last. In everyday life, once a son is accepted into the ritual sequence this is a fairly free and easy relationship; but rivalry may enter, in the shape of dissension over women.

In general, men compete for women, and actual betrothal arrangements demonstrate this feature quite clearly. Specifically, in what I have called the patriate (in Nimkoff, 1965: 89-90) a son inherits his deceased father's widows, except his own mother and her close sisters. Alternatively, a man whose son is too young to marry may take over the boy's betrothed wife (the boy's *galei*, normally a *ngandi* to his father), who becomes the father's *galei* and the son's *ngandi*. The father should hand her back to his son when the boy reaches maturity, but this does not always happen. Additionally, the system is so structured that a man and his son's son may compete for *galei*. Strained relations are not uncommon in this context. When actual father and son are involved, these tensions are not usually openly expressed; but in the case of "distant" fathers and sons, in the past fighting was one means of resolving them.

ngandi-wogu/WOGU (m.-child; s.w.-H.F.; w.m.b.w.-H.Sr.W.H.):

This is a basic relationship, between a man and his own mother and her sisters, who may be married to his father or father's brothers. If his mother's sisters are his mother's co-wives, his bond with them is very close indeed. In contrast to the Gunwinggu example, full sisters may marry the same man.

The term *ngandi* is said to connote breasts: a mother is regarded as being like the fertile earth, a father like rain. (This theme permeates the major religious rituals of this area.) A mother's intake of food nourishes her unborn child, and whether a person is physically strong depends, men say, on the food he received before his birth. Obviously, there is a strong sense of dependence on the part of a child toward its mother (see Warner, 1937/58: 96–98; R. Berndt, in Nimkoff, 1965: 97–98, 100–102), because a child's physical welfare rests on her and not on the father. In addition, a child usually learns his mother's dialect first.

At quite an early age, in contrast to his sisters, a boy ceases to accompany his mother on food-collecting trips, but it is not until after circumcision that he spends most of his time with his father, closely related "fathers," and older youths. Before the boy's circumcision his mother puts up a show of resistance—sometimes more than a show—to the men who take him away from her. During the proceedings she makes gifts to the initiators, and wails for her son's ritual death and his change in status. Throughout life, the general emphasis is on a mother as looking after her children, always being kind to them, and helping them where she can. The emotional quality of the relationship between actual mother and child is especially strong, but this is extended to mother surrogates. There are no restrictions on speech between them. And while a mother is reluctant to discipline her child, except for occasional blows, the converse does not apply: a child, especially a boy (mostly before puberty, and not as an adult), freely criticizes and sometimes violently attacks his mother. Sibling rivalry is one reason for such behavior; another is a supposed slight or supposed neglect on her part.

A man calls his son's wife "little *ngandi*," and the normal relationship is much the same as in the case of an actual *ngandi*. Structurally, however, the *ngandi* a man's father marries is derived from his NGATI and *mari;* she differs from the *ngandi* his son marries, who comes from his GALEI and *mari*. Yet, as mentioned, a father has rights over his little *ngandi* while his son is young, and this possibility does color the relationship and lead to jokes about sexual relations with a "mother." The third type of *ngandi* is the kind who marries a MARALGUR, the brother of one's wife's mother. Again, the behavioral content of the relationship is, in general, as for an actual mother, but without any strong emotional tie.

mugulbaba-gadu/GADU (f.sr.-B. children):

This relationship is straightforward. The term *mugul* seems to imply control or arrangement of marriages. One kind of *mugul* produces a daughter whom a man may marry; the other kind of *mugul* produces a son whom that man's sister may marry. One kind of *mugul* has a husband upon whom a man is dependent; the other kind has a husband who is dependent on his wife's brother's son. One kind of *mugul* marries into the senior grade, the other into the junior grade; one belongs to a man's own *babaru*, the other to the important MARI descent line. The father of one is a MARIMO, the father of the other a MARI; it is interesting that the term *mari* is often substituted for *marimo* (see R. Berndt, 1955: 87). To distinguish between these *muguls* the terms *baba* and *rumurung* are added; but in ordinary conversation they are not always used, and, unless one specifically inquires, the distinction is not always indicated.

The *mugulbaba* is a female "father," and the same kind of association exists between her and her brother's children as between a father and his children, without the competition and rivalry. She is a person's protector, from whom food may always be obtained. Moreover, the closeness of this tie may be reinforced if her son is a man's brother's daughter's husband; her children are a man's DUWEI/*duwei*, and this is an important relationship. She is also the only female who may be present when her *gadu*'s bones are collected and cleaned after his death.

NGABIBI or GAWAL-*wogu*/WOGU (M.B.-sr. children; W.F.-D.H.): There are several kinds of NGABIBI-*wogu*/WOGU relationship; the model is that existing between a man and his M.B., his NGABIBI, who is also a man's wife's father and/or the husband of a man's *mugulrumurung*. This NGABIBI's father is a NGATI and his mother a *mari*, who belongs to the MARI line. The other kind of NGABIBI has as his father a NGATIWALGUR, and a *mari* as his mother; but this *mari* is not related to the other, not closely. Conventionally, the NGATIWALGUR signifies a man's wife's mother's mother's brother's line (a man's wife's MARI line). Ideally, this NGATIWALGUR's son, a NGABIBI, marries a woman also classified as a *mugulrumurung* but does not have an eligible daughter from the viewpoint of male Ego; instead, her children belong to the MARI line of Ego's S.S. wife. However, in view of what has already been said about a man's probable identification with his S.S., his MARI line could be identified in turn with his wife's MARI's line.

In part, the emotional bond between a man and his sister's children is dependent on the brother-sister relationship (between a man's mother and her brother); but, more specifically, it rests on the NGABIBI's position in being able to give or withhold a wife for his sister's son. Warner (1937/58: 94) notes that a NGABIBI is obliged by custom to give his daughter to his WOGU.[12]

Generally speaking, a WOGU is in his NGABIBI's debt. Obviously it is an asymmetrical relationship, because a NGABIBI has more to give than a WOGU can return. Yet, in discussions it was considered to be a reciprocal relationship in which a man receives from his NGABIBI a wife (or wives) and food, and returns food (a man "feeds his NGABIBI because of his wife"). It is also said that during a NGABIBI's lifetime his WOGU looks after him, and that after his death this duty is "turned" (redirected) toward his wife's brothers, as a man's GALEI. The feeling toward an actual NGABIBI is ambivalent. He is like one's mother and one should ideally be "free and easy" in his presence; yet one is shy (*gura*), and although one can joke with him this is not done frequently. Gifts of a ritual nature are also made to a NGABIBI, and these strengthen the bond. A man gives aid to his M.B. to the same extent as to his F., and if there is an argument or fight between a M.B. and a F. it is a WOGU's duty to stop it. The NGABIBI and his sons (a man's GALEI) help their WOGU and DUWEI. These relatives constitute, in fact, a small in-group focused

12. Although "withhold" is not strictly correct in this context, I have used it here because a great deal depends on whom a NGABIBI selects; it is not usually on an impersonal basis—for example, the daughter of the eldest NGABIBI going to the eldest sister's son—especially in consideration of economic advantages of a betrothal (see R. Berndt in Nimkoff, 1965: 84).

on mutual aid, on whom a man may depend—much more than on his own brothers (actual or otherwise).

It is also said that WOGU are "like DUWEI," they come from one's DUWEI (a sister's potential husband). If one does not marry an actual m.b.d., and a sister does not marry her F.Sr.S., mutual aid between WOGU and NGABIBI is not weakened except that gift giving is not so frequent or sustained. If a NGABIBI is looked after by his WOGU, "he listens to their requests;" but, if not, the NGABIBI looks sideways when talking to them and "talks to the ground." The WOGU who is the husband of a f.sr., although probably older than his wife's brother's son, is classified within the junior kinship grade; nevertheless, the tenor of their relationship does not appreciably differ.

A NGABIBI also disciplines his WOGU's wife if necessary, and if she elopes he should set out after her with her brothers. He is responsible for her to her husband. The NGABIBI-WOGU relationship is extensively used for trade exchanges between those who are not genealogically linked relatives and live a considerable distance apart. A man's relationship with his female *wogu* receives much less attention.

WAWA-JUGUJUGU or GUDA (elder brother-younger brother):

Several varieties of this have as a basic model the full B.-B. relationship: sons of the same father from the same or different mothers, whether these are full sisters; or sons of different fathers who are brothers, from the same or different mothers—that is, brothers belonging to the same *babaru*. Or they may share the same mother (or their mothers may be close sisters) while belonging through their fathers to different linguistic units within the same moiety. The intensity of the bond between brothers depends on whether a genealogical tie is acknowledged, and how close this is. Actual brothers from one father are *babamanggal* (father blood), the first born being *bugurangul* and the "lowest" (or youngest) JUGU-JUGU. The relationship is ambivalent, primarily because in practice brothers do compete for wives. Rivalry is stimulated by the junior levirate through which, after a man's death, his younger brother next in age and consanguinity should, ideally, become the husband of the widows (R. Berndt, in Nimkoff, 1965: 89). Furthermore, a man has access to the wives of younger brothers, but this is not reciprocal at the formal level. Also, an elder brother who has more women promised to him than he wants may distribute one or more of them to younger brothers; or he may formally hand over one of his own wives, especially one who is blind or lame or otherwise unsatisfactory. Conventionally, younger brothers must wait their turn in the distribution of *galei*; and if elder brothers are "selfish" and intent on accumulating wives, the younger may have to wait for quite a long time. Sororal polygyny reinforces the position of the elder in this respect. In the full Kunapipi ritual, coitus takes place between a man and his brother's wife, usually the wife of a "long-way" brother but not excluding actual consanguineal brothers (see R. Berndt, 1951: 48-9).

While brothers formally stand with brothers and there is normally freedom in speech between them, then, dissension is expected. When there is no quarrel, it is said, brothers "look each other directly in the face"—they have nothing to hide. But when there is a disagreement, "brothers do not look at each other," nor speak freely. Even if their quarrel extends over a long period their personal differences should, ideally, be submerged in the common interests of their family. However, a JUGUJUGU is in a subordinate position, and an elder brother may take the place of a father who is senile or dead. A younger brother is also at a disadvantage in sacred ritual. The elder has prior rights, and the younger must wait to be invited by him to participate. Elder brothers are always put through sections of the sacred ritual before younger ones.

All in all, the relationship between brothers of different ages is not one of equality. However, balancing this is the junior levirate and mutual aid between them. Brothers conventionally help one another in providing gifts for their NGABIBI and share generally in one another's property. And, in terms of inheritance, all of a dead man's belongings should, ideally, go to a close younger brother—his wife or wives, children, canoes, some sacred objects, and so on (see R. Berndt, in Nimkoff, 1965: 96).

jaba-jugujugu or *guda* (elder sister-younger sister):

As in the case of brothers, there are several varieties of this relationship. A strong emotional bond links full sisters, especially if they are also co-wives. No actual tabus exist between them, but the elder is the younger's protector and guide and there are ties of mutual aid. Sisters do not talk together freely before their brothers.

jaba-WAWA or JUGUJUGU (siblings of opposite sex):

The sister-brother relationship is one of partial avoidance and is viewed as resembling to some extent the *mugulrumurung* relationship. A brother does not speak freely or directly to his sister. She is not supposed to hear him, and when brothers and sisters speak in one another's presence they usually do so softly. They should not use one another's personal names. Obscene words should not be uttered in a sister's hearing by a brother, or by anyone else in her vicinity if a brother can overhear them. Sisters should be circumspect when brothers are nearby. This is associated with the *miriri*, a powerful sanction against irregular behavior on the part of a sister. (See Warner, 1937/58: 109–113; R. Berndt, in Nimkoff, 1965: 96.) A brother is expected to guard his sister's honor. If he hears or sees his sister behaving indiscreetly or quarreling, or hears someone swear at her, a man is ashamed—it is *miriri*—it is distasteful and humiliating for a brother to hear this in relation to a sister. He is therefore obliged to make a show of attacking her and all his sisters (actual and classificatory) present in the camp by throwing spears at them. This, men say, is because his attachment to his sister—to all sisters—is so strong. A sister's husband (a DUWEI) should watch what he says about his wife in the presence of her brother. In fact, a man does not wish even to hear anything about a sister; if he does, it makes him angry. Should a sister give birth to a child, a brother is not told of this directly; he must find out about it in a roundabout way. To hear of the birth of a sister's child is offensive or shaming; it would be "like hearing about a sister and her husband copulating." Sisters must not let their brothers know when they urinate or defecate. And when a girl's betrothal arrangements are being made her brother should not conventionally hear of them.

A man refers to his sister (or any sister) as *wakinngu* (see Warner, 1937/58: 66, 110), which means "without kin" or "worthless" or "rubbish." The words I have usually heard are *mirigu*, referring to "rubbish" or *munggoiba*, translated as a malignant spirit of a dead person or bones. This was explained as being not words of disparagement but words that are used to underline the need to keep away from the affairs of a sister. "You do not put your nose into rubbish—so you do not put your nose into your sister's business." Likewise, "behave yourself as you would with a *mogwoi* (spirit); you don't go with a *mogwoi*, so you don't go with your sister." The words express the state of partial avoidance and of social distance between siblings of opposite sex.

A brother may eat "dry" food (such as flour or damper, cycad nut bread, ground-seed flour) given to him by a sister, but not fish, oysters, wild honey, and so on, and not water which has been directly handled by her. However, if the fish or honey is wrapped up by someone else (like a *galei*, MARALGUR, *dumungur* or *gominjar*) a brother may eat it. The reason is said to be that one must not eat the spittle or sweat of a sister; in the preparation of fish, for instance, a sister uses her hands which also touch her body. But it was not explained why it was all right to eat dry food, because this involves the same if not more handling.

It has been said that a brother is "like a father" to his sister and is her protector; he should see that her husband does not ill-treat her. Men also expect their sisters to supply husbands for their daughters, and gifts are made to a sister with this in mind, just as they are made to her husband (a man's DUWEI).

marimo/MARIMO-*maraidja*/MARAIDJA (F.F.-S.S./s.d.; f.f.sr.-b.s.children):

Marimo/MARIMO are at the apex of the patrilineal descent line and are important symbolically and ritually rather than in regard to everyday obligations and responsibilities. Men say that a MARIMO is "like a F."—he looks after his S.S. "He's important, I (the MARAIDJA) am nothing; my father and MARIMO are above me." It is generally a relationship of respect as far as both male and female MARIMO/*marimo* are concerned, and one is expected to "look after" them. The female *marimo*, it is said, "comes from a man's big GADU (S.)," referring to the generation level above the *marimo*, which is equated with one's son's. Again, in reference to MARAIDJA, it is said that "a man's son and his MARAIDJA's son are the same;" they regard their MARIMO as a *bunggawa*, leader.

As already mentioned, a man's identification with his MARAIDJA is close, and a S.S.'s wife is a *galei,* while his mother is a *ngandi*. Additionally, a MARIMO is a kind of MARI, and in some cases a F.F. is called MARI too.

It is principally within the areas of ritual knowledge and spiritual affinity that a male MARIMO assumes major importance. When the title *bunggawa* is used for him, it usually refers to these spheres. He helps his S.S. in ritual, and some men say, "we get everything from our MARIMO." But even so, it is mainly an emotional attitude, and in ritual activity the boy's father normally takes the older man's place. The spirit child mentioned in relation to a father or father's sister comes directly from a sacred waterhole or site from which the MARIMO himself came, and this site is located in the patrilineal clan and dialectal unit territory. A MARAIDJA assumes some of his MARIMO's personal names and all of his totemic associations; female *maraidja* take some of the names of their female *marimo* and their female *mari.*

momo-gominjar/GOMINJAR (f.m.-S. children):

This is not such an emotionally charged relationship from a man's point of view, and its significance lies in the NGATI-*gominjar*/GOMINJAR relationship rather than in itself. Respect is due to a *momo*, but there is no special obligation or responsibility.

NGATI-*gominjar*/GOMINJAR (F.M.B.-sr.s.children; or M.F.-d.children):

There are several varieties of NGATI and of *gominjar*/GOMINJAR. A NGATI always marries a woman whom his sr.s. children or d. children call *mari*, while female *gominjar* marry Ego's GUDARA (reciprocal of *mari*) and male GOMINJAR marry Ego's female *maraidja* and *marimo*, as well as *gudara*. Reciprocal aid is usual between NGATI and GOMINJAR, but less in the case of female *gominjar*. Also, NGATI, with MARI, may discipline their *gominjar*/GOMINJAR when these are small more than do the actual parents. The relationship is said to be "not far from that of a *ngandi*;" NGATI and GOMINJAR help each other with food and there is no obvious restraint between them. The importance of the relationship lies in the fact that a NGATI is or could have been the father of a man's *ngandi* and NGABIBI, and this is reflected in all dealings between them. Also, in ritual life they exchange *rangga* (secret-sacred emblems). A NGATI may circumcise his GOMINJAR in the *djunggawon* rituals and later give him a wife. And a NGATI also helps his daughter's sons to establish their position in secret-sacred affairs.

mari/MARI-*gudara*/GUDARA (m.m.-d. children; M.M.B.-sr.d. children): This relationship is pivotal in reference to both males and females. The MARI is at the head of the MARI line, the patriline of a man's m.m. and his M.M.B. A female *mari* has, primarily, Ego's *ngandi* and NGABIBI as children; a male MARI, Ego's *mugulrumurung* and MARALGUR. The actual relationship is the model for all other varieties of *mari*/MARI and *gudara*/GUDARA. It is a relationship of strong emotional quality.

The connotation of the term *mari*, not its literal meaning, was described as follows: "I (*mari*/MARI) am your tree, so that you may sit under me." Other men have said, "we get everything from a MARI." Obviously, "everything" is an exaggeration, but it does underline the significance of kin designated in this way. Freedom of speech is usual between them, as well as dependence and mutual aid. But, even though a GUDARA helps his immediate *mari* (both male and female) on nearly all occasions, *mari*/MARI are viewed more as givers than as receivers. The structural significance of the MARI-GUDARA line has been noted in Berndt (1955: 89-91), where I called it the *maribula*. Warner (1937/58: 99-101, 113-16) also emphasizes its importance, both organizationally and personally.

Personal names come from the *mari*/MARI (as well as from the MARIMO); these have both spiritual and sacred mythological associations. MARI-GUDARA should stand as one in camp quarreling and fighting; a MARI takes over the responsibility of avenging the death of an actual or close *gudara*/GUDARA, and vice versa. A *mari*/MARI too has authority to discipline and to teach his *gudara*/GUDARA; as far as a boy is concerned, he spends a considerable amount of time in his MARI's company, and this is especially the case after his circumcision. After a death, the spirits of deceased *mari* and *marimo* (male and female) aid the ghost in facing the trials it must overcome to travel to the Land of the Dead. Warner (*ibid.*, 101) notes cases of *gudara*/GUDARA having greater affection for their *mari*/MARI than for their *ngandi*, and my own material includes some evidence of this too.

There is a close identification in certain respects between MARI and GUDARA, partly because of the handing on of names; but not, probably, as much as between MARAIDJA and MARIMO with conventional access to the same women. As far as a MARI is concerned (even with MARI-MARIMO identification), there is no hint of competition for women; and because women are responsible for most conflict between men in this situation, that contentious issue is absent from their relationship. MARI marry women whom their GUDARA call *mumalgur*; female *mari* marry men whom their GUDARA call either NGATI, NGATIWALGUR, or GALEI. The identification of the first two is demonstrated by the terms used by GUDARA in relation to their children (*ngandi* and NGABIBI), while a *mari* marrying a GALEI has children whom a GUDARA addresses quite differently. The importance of *mari* (male and female) is enhanced in the part they play in arranging marriages for GUDARA/*gudara* and *gudara*/GUDARA's father. The MARI is NGABIBI of Ego's NGABIBI, and this alone places him in a position of some authority; moreover, he is the father of Ego's wife's mother, the *mugulrumurung*. Warner (1937/58: 113-4, Chart VI), by means of a diagram, demonstrates the positive aspect of the MARI relationship. MARI occupy a highly important position in the north-eastern Arnhem Land system of social relationships, especially in their power to influence decisions in the marriage arena. But also, they are significant in ritual and sacred matters. Over and above inheritance in the patriline, the MARI's line, diagonally conceived (see Table 9.11), implies the handing down of rights and privileges from MARI to GUDARA, through the NGABIBI as an intermediary, or more correctly through the *ngandi*. The MARI line, the *maribula*, reinforces patriliny. (See R. Berndt, 1955: 89-90.)

In the sacred sphere, the MARI gives emblems, teaches, and hands on songs and song cycles, invocations, designs, dances, and so on for which a GUDARA must pay. The matter of compensation is well developed in sacred activity; benefits, privileges, and sacred knowledge must be paid for, and this is true even when they are given by a father. However, the sacred objects given by a MARI to his GUDARA are the "biggest," the most important.

A MARI stands as a man's father. If a man's father dies without revealing the sacred knowledge which it is incumbent on him to pass on to his sons, his MARI should come forward and take over that responsibility. In this capacity a man's MARI is serving as the father's MARALGUR; it is common practice for a father to show and tell all associated sacred matters relating to his own line to his MARALGUR, so that if he were to die the son's MARI would be able to pass this on to his GUDARA. This is one of the major obligations of a MARI, as a father's MARALGUR. Also, a MARI, on the death of his GUDARA's father, should ensure that his GUDARA is betrothed. For young female *gudara*, too, a MARI is a father figure, who can aid them in betrothal arrangements.

mumalgur-dumungur/DUMUNGUR (m.m.b.w.-h.sr.d. children; w.m.m.-D.D.H.; m.m.m.b.d.-f.sr.d.d. children):

The *mumalgur* is in a tabued position in relation to her male DUMUNGUR; the avoidance is just as strong as for the *mugulrumurung*. The two may not speak to each other, and there is no freedom of action between them. This avoidance is not relevant to a female *dumungur*. There are several varieties of *mumalgur* and *dumungur*/DUMUNGUR, which I shall not delineate. A *mumalgur* is tabu because male MARI and GUDARA, although closely identified, do not compete for women. She is tabu also because the term used for her is broadly described as "referring to the marriage ground;" that is, she is a man's NGABIBI's *mugulrumurung* and his own relationship to her is an extension of that. Strong emotional ties bind *mumalgur* and *dumungur*/DUMUNGUR, and there is an obligation of mutual aid and cooperation. A *mumalgur* defends the good name of her *dumungur*/DUMUNGUR, and in turn the latter must "work for" her, supply her with food and so forth. She is also important in a man's betrothal and marriage. If a man's NGABIBI and *mugulrumurung* seek betrothal arrangements for their daughters outside what are regarded as preferential or first-choice partners (and this often occurs; see R. Berndt, in Nimkoff, 1965: 85-6), it is the *mumalgur* who attemps "to bring one's *mugul* back to the right choice." She "won't let anyone from outside take the woman" in question; ideally, she "settles things smoothly." If the DUMUNGUR "goes outside the marriage ground" (that is, the permissible area in which any one person may choose a wife), his *mumalgur* and *mugulrumurung* "bring the DUMUNGUR back for *their* daughter." She "saves the DUMUNGUR from getting into trouble." It was emphasized that it is "old" *mumalgur* and not young ones who have this responsibility.

Moreover, the novice's old *mumalgur* is the only kinswoman who may accompany the party of fully initiated men to the edge of the sacred *nara* ground (the *nara* rituals being held for, e.g., the Djanggawul; see R. Berndt, 1952); it is at such a time that men bring up their sons from their own *babaru* for *rangga* (sacred emblem) instruction. The *mumalgur* walks around the outside of the *nara* ground to watch over the interests of her DUMUNGUR.

NGATIWALGUR-*dumungur*/DUMUNGUR (W.M.M.B.-Sr.D.D.H.; M.M.M.B.S.-f.sr.d.d. children):

The NGATIWALGUR relationship is close to that of the *mumalgur* because they are brother and sister; but in this case it has no element of avoidance, except that personal names are not used between them. To some extent, too, it resembles the NGATI-*gominjar*/GOMINJAR relationship, and some evidence suggests that a NGATIWALGUR can in certain circumstances be identified with a NGATI. Obligation and mutual aid are relevant to this relationship and so is a strong emotional quality, but not as great as in the case of a MARI. The real force of the relationship appears in the ritual sphere. When a *mumalgur* considers that her DUMUNGUR is ready to have revealed to him the sacred *rangga* objects used in the *nara,* she lets her brother know that his DUMUNGUR is ready: "You should give him training in the *rangga* now; you should teach him about the *mareiin* (that which is sacred)." When the NGATIWALGUR is in the *mareiin* (that is, on the *nara* ground or going to it), he tells his sister (through her son, Ego's MARALGUR) to bring up his DUMUNGUR.

This is especially the case with the making of a man's spirit bag or *badi,* with feathered tassels. As a young man, the DUMUNGUR notifies his *mumalgur* (through his MARALGUR) that he wishes to have this. The bag is woven by the *mumalgur*; she passes it on to his NGATIWALGUR, who also works on it. Then it goes to his WOGU (reciprocal of NGA-BIBI). This WOGU is conventionally the father of his NGATIWALGUR and *mumalgur*. The bag is then handed over to the DUMUNGUR himself in a special ritual dance. At this time the bag still has its fringe. Later the WOGU gives permission to cut the fringe, and that also is done ritually. At this time, "a man says farewell to his *badi*," and as soon as it is cut he no longer takes an active part in the associated *mareiin* ritual; it is given to his son. (For the significance of this bag and the cutting of the fringe, see R. Berndt, 1952.) At every point in the rituals associated with the *badi*, gifts are made to his NGATIWALGUR, and to his WOGU. Other bags can now be obtained in this way by a man, but the first from a NGATIWALGUR may not be passed on to his son unless permission is obtained from the *bunggawa* (ritual leader of the appropriate *mareiin*).

Should a man quarrel with his NGATIWALGUR or not give him sufficient gifts, the NGATIWALGUR can "pass over" his DUMUNGUR and give the sacred spirit bag directly to the DUMUNGUR's son—which is ritually humiliating. In certain respects, a NGATIWALGUR stands for his DUMUNGUR and his son. Should all of a man's close NGATIWAL-GUR and WOGU die, the DUMUNGUR must assume responsibility for their ritual objects and privileges, not as a ritual leader, but as a guardian only—he may act for them in ritual.

DUWEI-*galei* (H.-w.; F.Sr.S.-m.b.d.):

There are several varieties of this relationship, ranging from close or "promised" *galei*-DUWEI to those with no acknowledged genealogical connection. Again, the basic relationship serves as a model for others and variation is in terms of commitment and affection; all DUWEI are, conventionally, potential husbands or lovers to all *galei*, unless they are married to elder brothers. The DUWEI-*galei* relationship is the ideal sexual one. Its implications in terms of the junior levirate and polygyny have been noted elsewhere. (See, for example, Warner, 1937/58: 74-92; R. Berndt, in Nimkoff, 1965: 82-6.) No tabus are associated with it, except at menstruation and childbirth. A *galei* is conceptualized as "the bag in which you may put your belongings: it carries everything belonging to the DUWEI; it is the bag from which your children come."

Ideally, a man should marry his own m.b.d. If she is not available, he attempts to obtain a female who is as near to her as possible in terms of consanguinity. Male DUWEI and male GALEI often come to an understanding that their sons and daughters will marry. Generally speaking, mutual cooperation is expected between husbands and wives, and between co-wives. They comprise an economic unit, as well as one that regularizes sexual relations and the production of children. The claims of each in respect of the other are conventionally acknowledged, and substantiated through gift giving and through mutual services. Two sets of kin are brought together by such a marriage, which, ideally, culminates in the birth of children; the marriage, as such, is structurally "held together"—apart from personal ties between spouses—by the strength of the MARI, *mumalgur*, NGABIBI and *mugulrumurung* bonds. Interaction between these kin and affines, in relation to the marital unit itself with their responsibilities and obligations, defines the stability of marriage more precisely than anything else. Although a husband has, formally, more rights over his wife than she has over him, it is really his wife's brothers, his GALEI, who are primarily concerned with ensuring that good relations continue to exist between the spouses. The wife's parents, too, are vitally interested in this situation and are in a position to exert pressures if need be. (For a general discussion of marriage and the family, see R. Berndt, in Nimkoff, 1965: 77-103.)

DUWEI-GALEI (Sr.H.-W.B.; F.Sr.S.-M.B.S.):

There are several varieties of this relationship also, but in all of them the bond is regarded as especially strong. The closest ties are between children of a f.sr. on one hand and a M.B. on the other; it is said that "GALEI's blood comes back to DUWEI's son" and, presumably, to his daughter. Ideally, a male GALEI's daughter marries Ego's son and a male DUWEI's son marries Ego's daughter. This relationship also involves some constraint: male GALEI and DUWEI should not look directly at each other's faces, or talk a great deal together; the use of obscenity between them is conventionally forbidden; reciprocal gift-giving is frequent, especially in food. The real strength of the DUWEI-GALEI link depends on impinging relationships—on the DUWEI as a sister's husband, on the brother-sister relationship itself, and on a man's relations with his wife. Also, it is influenced by a man's relations with his male GALEI's father and mother, and his son's relations with his GALEI. Although this relationship has, potentially, plenty of avenues through which DUWEI-GALEI conflict can arise, conventionally one does not actively fight a DUWEI or a GALEI; but there are occasions when "fighting with words" (or quarreling) does take place.

DUWEI and GALEI engage in various cooperative enterprises. For instance, they fish and hunt together, build a hut or house, or make a canoe which either may use in the other's absence. A man watches over his male GALEI's property when he is not present; GALEI should not go on long trips without informing their DUWEI. On a GALEI's death, his ordinary non-traditional songs and dances are taken over by his DUWEI, but not his rights and privileges in secret-sacred *mareiin*. In an extreme situation, for example, on the death of all of a man's wife's close kin, including her brothers, their property is taken over by that man's son or by himself as a DUWEI.

The DUWEI-GALEI relationship is significant also in a ritual sense. A man can obtain his spirit bag (*badi*) from his GALEI, in the same way as the NGATIWALGUR. Although he does not paint his DUWEI's chest and body with his sacred clan and dialect-unit emblems, a DUWEI can do so for him. This happens when a man invites his GALEI to see his sacred *rangga*. The GALEI must reciprocate by making gifts of stone spears, food, and meat; these days, he must pay money (£4 to £5 or so, Australian). It is the DUWEI who indicates the probable price; and it is said that "if the GALEI loves you next to his own sister [the DUWEI's wife], then he will give you much more than what is asked for."

duwei-GALEI (f.sr.d.-M.B.S.):

A man should not joke with his female *duwei*, and should give her food. He may talk directly to her, but sexual association was traditionally forbidden. However, there are cases of it these days. A man may arrange the betrothal of his female *duwei*'s son with his sister's daughter (or male DUWEI's daughter). A female *duwei* also looks after her GALEI's children. Otherwise, this relationship is a reflection of the male DUWEI-GALEI relationship, without the overtones of ritual association or inheritance.

galei-galei (m.b.d., or b.w.-f.sr.d., or h.sr.):

Normally a cooperative relationship; degree of strain depending on whether or not it is also an affinal relationship.

mugulrumurung-gurung/GURUNG (w.m.-D.H.; m.m.b.d.-f.sr.d. children; m.b.w.-h.sr. children):

There are several varieties of this relationship, all modeled on the w.m.-D.H. one. I have already discussed the significance of this tie in the context of other relationships. The term *mugul* is held in common by a man's f.sr. and w.m. (or a male MARI's daughter); she is within the influence of the MARI line, and the addition of *rumurung* to *mugul* implies tabuness. It is said that this word is like *nara*—that is, the sacred ritual ground: uninitiated persons, including younger men, may not enter the *nara* without first obtaining permission from the ritual leaders—"and this is the same state as far as the *mugulrumurung* is concerned." There is avoidance between this *mugulrumurung* and her male GURUNG; but the relationship is not significant, nor are any tabus associated with it, in respect of the female *gurung*. A male GURUNG should not act foolishly before her; he should be circumspect in her presence and sit at a distance from her. There is a strong emotional content to this relationship, involving not only mutual avoidance but also indirect obligations. For instance, there is mutual gift-giving, and presents of food are made through the GURUNG's wife, who serves as an intermediary. Furthermore, the *mugulrumurung* is strategically placed and has, as noted, authority over her GURUNG because her daughter is a potential wife to him. She is also in a position to discipline a man's wife for misbehaving. There are cases of *mugulrumurung* sharing the same house as their GURUNG, but only when a barrier is placed down the middle of the house or room; or, if they sleep outside in the open, another person always sleeps between them.

The strict rule of sexual avoidance on the part of a *mugul* and GURUNG appears to have been broken, in the past, only on ritual occasions, most notably at the Kunapipi (see R. Berndt, 1951: 48-50, 68-9 and Plate XVII). In ordinary everyday life, the avoidance between them is lifted only when the *mugul* is old.

MARALGUR-*gurung*/GURUNG (M.M.B.S.- f.sr.d. children; W.M.B.-Sr.D.H.):

Again, there are several varieties of this relationship. A man's MARALGUR is his wife's NGABIBI; but, in contrast to the relationship with MARALGUR's sister, Ego's *mugulrumurung*, there is no avoidance or constraint. To some extent this MARALGUR relationship reflects the closeness of the male MARI and NGATIWALGUR relationships—since a man's M.M.B. and his NGATIWALGUR are his MARALGUR's father and M.B. respectively. Under the MARI heading it was noted that a man may reveal sacred matters concerning his own patriline to his close MARALGUR so that, should he die, this knowledge will be passed on to his son.

A man may talk freely to his MARALGUR and joke with him. It is said that this is the "right" relative to "have fun with." They are often companions, and the only tabu is that they should not use each other's personal names. The relationship itself is like that with a *mugul* or NGABIBI, but without the element of constraint; the emotional quality is the same. Throughout his life a male GURUNG gives food to his MARALGUR, and in return he can help his GURUNG in many ways. It was emphasized on many occasions that "the MARALGUR is a MARI's son" and a GURUNG should defend him and prevent others from quarreling with him.

A GURUNG makes arrangements for the revealing of certain *mareiin* rites to his MARALGUR; and an older MARALGUR has ritual authority and takes a direct part in helping his GURUNG, for example, in the *djunggawon* and in various *mareiin* rites. A MARALGUR may also make a special sacred *rangga* emblem for his male GURUNG, who passes it on to his son (whom the MARALGUR calls GUDARA). (See MARI relationship.)

The relations between MARALGUR and his female *gurung* differ from those between himself and male GURUNG. In this case, there is a relationship of partial avoidance. With a *gurung* one "runs sideways," it is said: one looks at the ground. One may joke with her, but one "jokes for fun;" sexual relations are debarred. A MARALGUR gives food to his *gurung*, and she reciprocates.

ANALYSIS

Much of what I said in relation to the Gunwinggu system is relevant here too. In trying to decide what could be called a dominant relationship in north-eastern Arnhem Land, I narrowed the field to three terms: *mari-gudara, marimo-maraidja,* and *baba-gadu*. Beyond that point, there were some difficulties. The last two, combined, represent all major linkages in the patriline of any one person, and in personal terms they are the most significant relationships. This is especially the case if one takes into account the sisters of each such relative, in whom the basic male patri-tie is reflected; and also the wives of each, whose behaviour is formally subordinate to that of their husbands. However, my major criterion of dominance, in terms of the content of the relevant social relationships, is based on how one relationship either directly or indirectly influences a relatively wide range of others—not necessarily in the way its content is reflected in others, but in the ramification of relationships stemming from it, in the implications arising from these, and in the importance of these derivative relationships (derivative in the sense of their presence in a system being directly traceable to the dominant relationship) to any one person. The MARI-GUDARA relationship fits these conditions.

RELATIONSHIPS

In the following list (Table 9.12) I have used the same divisions as in the Gunwinggu case. In Group A are dominant relationships of a primary kind. In Group B are those which may still be considered dominant but are regarded as of secondary importance. Again, the label "secondary" does not concern their importance to any one person, but points to their reflective or derivative qualities. However, I have not placed them under Group D because all of them have implications in relation to marriage, and because they ensure the continuation of the conventional system as such. To divide them from those in Group D is arbitrary and not particularly satisfactory. The division is made, nevertheless, because those in Group B possess qualities which are more obviously linked with those in Group A (more obviously than with Group D). Group C contains what I have called "uninfluenced" relationships; or, to put it another way, each in this Group contains elements relevant to all relationships irrespective of category, or of dominance or derivation; they are, in a manner of speaking, "hinge" relationships—that is, a man or woman as husband or wife, as brother or sister.

Dominance or derivation in this context is not measured in terms of the emotional intensity of a specific relationship or in the degree of interaction between the partners involved, or in dependence, reliance and so forth. In actual fact, although ordinary conversations among the north-eastern Arnhem Landers do give the impression that MARI are of major significance in many areas of social living, much more interaction takes place between other kin—brothers, sisters, MARALGUR, actual DUWEI, *galei* and so on, and certainly much more between a woman and her young children. In this area too there is a high density of avoidance, either total or partial; and when a relationship involves this element it is usually of special importance, at the personal level, to those involved.

Again, as in the Gunwinggu section, I have noted the reflective or influencing aspects of each relationship in terms of its content. In the majority of cases, there is not a one-to-one correlation—often it is a combination of elements. Also, not all relationships outside Group A (primary) are ranked in order of importance; I found this impossible to do.

Relationships may be grouped as follows:

Table 9.12.

Group A Dominant relationships (primary):	*Content reflective of*
1. *mari-gudara* (MARI line)	2
2. MARIMO-MARAIDJA (F.F.-S.S.) }	3 and 1
3. BABA-GADU (F.-S.) }	2

Group B Dominant relationships (secondary):	*Content*	
	Influenced by	*Reflective of*
4. NGABIBI-WOGU/*wogu* (M.B.-sr. children)	1	3, 9
5. *mumalgur*-DUMUNGUR (w.m.m.-d.d.H.)	1	7
6. NGATIWALGUR-DUMUNGUR/*dumungur* (M.M.M.B.S.-f.sr.d.d. children)	1, 16	5, 7
7. *mugulrumurung-GURUNG* (w.m.-D.H.)	1	4
8. MARALGUR-GURUNG/*gurung* (M.M.B.S.-f.sr.d. children)	1, 6	–

Group C Uninfluenced relationships:	*Content reflective of*
9. WAWA-*jaba* (B.-sr.)	3
10. WAWA-JUGUJUGU (B.-B.)	2
11. DUWEI-*galei* (H.-w.)	–
12. DUWEI-GALEI (Sr.H.-W.B.)	–
13. *duwei*-GALEI (f.sr.d.-M.B.S.)	–

Group D Subordinate or derivative relationships:	*Content influenced by or reflecting*
14. *ngandi*-WOGU/*wogu* (m.-child)	1
15. *mugulbaba*-GADU/*gadu* (f.sr.-b. children)	3, 9
16. NGATI-GOMINJAR/*gominjar* (M.F.-d. children)	4
17. *momo*-GOMINJAR/*gominjar* (f.m.-s. children)	16

Table 9.13. Groups A and B. Dominant Relationships

Attributes	*MARI* *mari* 1	*MARIMO* *marimo* 2	*BABA* 3
Obligation and responsibility	mutual, strong [a]	mutual [a]	at formal level
Emotional bond	mutual, strong [a]	mutual [a]	mutual and diffused
Cooperation and aid	mutual, strong [a]	mutual [a]	mutual
Dependence:			
spiritual	indirect [a]	direct	on part of child
physical	direct	—	on part of child
emotional	on part of GUDARA/*gudara*	on part of S.S.	on part of child
Sexual association	—	—	some rivalry in sexual sphere
Neutral-passive	—	—	—
Avoidance	—	—	—
Authority:			
in secular sphere	virtual leader [b]	conventionally	as a F.
in ritual sphere	direct, over GUDARA	as leader	as representative of 2 [c]
in relation to marriage	indirect; influencing decisions	—	—
Mutual aid in ritual sphere	strong	as leader	general and direct
Inheritance	of ritual knowledge (paramount)	of ritual knowledge	direct: property ritual knowledge etc.; patriate

ATTRIBUTES

I am considering here the same set of attributes as used in the case of the Gunwinggu. As before, each relationship is associated with several attributes which must be seen in combination. Again, too, each relationship cannot be seen in isolation, but exists because it is linked with others or has implications for others. The following lists set out the attributes relevant to each of the relationships: in combination, and in reference to any one relationship, they form what can be regarded as a summary statement of the behavioral content of that relationship.

In Groups A and B (Table 9.13) are found what can be called domi-

NGABIBI 4	*mumalgur* 5	*NGATIWALGUR* 6	*mugulrumurung* 7	*MARALGUR* 8
formally	mutual	not strong	indirect	mutual, direct
mutual[d]	mutual	not strong	mutual, strong	mutual, strong
mutual[e]	mutual	not strong	mutual	mutual
–	–	–	–	–
on part of WOGU/*wogu*	–	–	–	–
–	on part of DUMUNGUR	in part	on part of GURUNG/*gurung*[f]	–
–	–	–		–
–	–	–	–	apparent equality[g]
constraint	mutual, strong	–	mutual, strong	
partial	–	–	–	–
–	indirect[h]	direct	–	direct
direct	direct	indirect	direct	indirect
general	–	direct and indirect	–	general; can stand for MARI
–	–	as guardian of ritual knowledge; not as owner	–	intermediary for F. as far as sacred knowledge is concerned

Notes:

a Also on part of female *marimo* and *mari*
b Stands for MARIMO and BABA
c Depending on age of sons
d Dependent on B.–sr. relationship
e Dependent on wife-giving
f Traditionally in certain sacred rituals
g Partial avoidance on part of female *gurung*
h Only female who has

nant relationships, the first three of which are ranged in terms of priority, but not the following five. All have positive attributes or qualities, while the females, except for the *mumalgur*, have no direct significance in the ritual sphere: the executive control of Aboriginal religion is in the hands of men. Although the actual content of these relationships differs, there is a striking similarity in their attributes, differences being accounted for in terms of sex, and of avoidance affecting both males and females. Constraint between men, where this occurs, is directly traceable to one of the male-female avoidance relationships, especially as regards *mugulrumurung* and *jaba*.

In Group C (Table 9.14) are relationships relevant to one's own generation level. Again, they extend the attributes noted under Groups A and B, with avoidance in relation to sisters and constraint in two other relationships arising from the brother-sister relationship. The brother-brother relationship is the most beset with conflict, both direct and indirect. A man competes with an older brother for wives, sweethearts, and ritual privileges, and for paternal favors; and apart from fathers, brothers are the only persons with whom a man does so compete. Competition with fathers is only indirect and mostly located in the sexual sphere. The patriate and junior levirate provide a delayed remedy in both cases; so does inheritance, when property of an older brother goes to a younger. Inheritance, it will be noted, although broadly patrilineal, is diffused. Primarily it comes from father, father's father, and brother; but ritual knowledge, especially, comes through MARI and MARIMO. Inheritance from a male GALEI is of a special character, and that from NGATIWALGUR and MARALGUR concerns custodianship, and being an intermediary.

In Group D, (Table 9.15) there is no avoidance or constraint, some ritual aid, but no inheritance.

As in the case of the Gunwinggu, tentative attempts were made to obtain specific statements, over and above the discussion of behavior patterns, on the relative importance of certain relationships. This procedure turned out to be unsatisfactory. When relatives were graded, this was done (*a*) in terms of the subsections; (*b*) as distributed between the two patrilineal moieties; and (*c*) as listed under patrilines, the father and father's father's line first, followed by the MARI's, and then the listing of affines.

In replies to my question concerning whom a man would save if involved in a situation where he would have to choose between his actual mother and his wife, most would not give a direct answer. Some insisted on saving both. Others chose a wife, mainly because their actual mothers were dead. Those who chose a mother said they could always obtain another wife, but not another actual mother.

When it came to a broader range of relatives, the NGABIBI was chosen because he would make a daughter who could become a man's wife; this was the choice mainly of unmarried men, or those desiring another wife. The *mugulrumurung* was not mentioned because of the avoidance tabu, although she would have been more relevant. Married men chose a father or a mother, in some cases a son. In no case was a MARI/*mari* noted; this may well be because of his undisputed im-

Table 9.14. Group C: Uninfluenced Relationships

Attributes	*jaba* (9)	WAWA *JUGUJUGU* (10)	*galei* (11)	DUWEI *GALEI* (12)	*duwei* (13)
Obligation and responsibility	strong, mutual	formally	mutual	mutual	indirect only
Emotional bond	strong, mutual	mutual	mutual (varies)	especially strong	–
Cooperation and aid	strong, mutual	at formal level	ideally mutual	[b]	on part of M.B.S.
Dependence: spiritual	–	–	–	–	–
physical	on part of sr.	on part of younger brothers	on part of wife	–	–
emotional	on part of both	on part of younger brothers	mutual	–	–
Sexual association	–	rivalry in sexual sphere; rights over wives of younger brothers[a]	mutual (not exclusive)	–	–
Neutral-passive	–	ambivalent; unequal	–	equality	neutral
Avoidance	mutual, partial through *miriri*	–	–	constraint	constraint
Authority: in secular sphere		on part of elder brothers	on part of H.	–	–
in ritual sphere	–	on part of elder brothers	–	[c]	–
in relation to marriage	indirect	on part of elder brothers	–	indirect	–
Mutual aid in ritual sphere	–	unequal, depending on age	–	in certain circumstances	–
Inheritance (general)	–	wives in junior levirate; all belongings to younger brothers	–	property rights (use only); of GALEI's ordinary songs, dances	–

Notes:
a Over brothers' wives in ritual
b Dependent on surrounding relationships, but always present
c In special circumstances, on part of GALEI or DUWEI

Table 9.15. Group D. Subordinate Relationships

Attributes	*ngandi* 14	*mugulbaba* 15	*NGATI* 16	*momo* 17
Obligation and responsibility	mutual	mutual	irregular	indirect
Emotional bond	mutual and diffused	dependent on F.'s B.-sr. bond	reflective of 14	–
Cooperation and aid	mutual	mutual	mutual	indirect only, not strong
Dependence: spiritual	–	on part of B.'s child	–	–
physical	on part of child	on part of B.'s child	on part of Sr.'s S.'s children[a]	–
emotional	on part of child	–	–	–
Sexual association	–	–	–	–
Neutral-passive	–	–	–	virtually
Avoidance	–	–	–	–
Authority: in secular sphere	–	–	–	–
in ritual sphere	–	–	in circumcision	–
in relation to marriage	indirect	indirect	indirect	–
Mutual aid in ritual sphere	–	–	exchange of *rangga*	–
Inheritance	–	–	–	–

Note:
a In terms of discipline

portance, which is reflected in other relationships but is probably less obtrusive in day-to-day living.

Conclusions

Empirical exploration of two kin-behavioral systems, one predominantly matrilineal and the other predominantly patrilineal, relevant to two adjacent socio-cultural blocs, makes several points quite clear. 1. Isolating a dominant relationship is not a simple matter. What may appear at first as an important relationship may come to seem less so, when considered more broadly within the perspective of the total system. Evidently, we cannot separate one as dominant without stating clearly that it is, in turn, set firmly within a network of influences. If, for instance, this is the brother-sister relationship, as among the Gunwinggu, it is not to be defined or described only by its associated attributes, but also *a* by its position in the structure of recognized relationships, and *b* by the way in which it is influenced by and itself influences other "dependent" or subordinate relationships. The term *dependent* is relevant only when we focus on, for example, the brother-sister relationship —which, in turn, is "dependent" on others, when we focus on those others. The brother-sister relationship among the Gunwinggu or the MARI-GUDARA relationship in north-eastern Arnhem Land derives its strength from such considerations and not from any inherent qualities of its own, in isolation.

2. In both socio-cultural contexts, I have separated, analytically, what may be regarded as dominant relationships. While according priority to one in each system, I have found it impossible to relegate other closely associated and obliquely dominating relationships to a subordinate position. It seems highly likely that those regarded as dominant do have many ingredients in common, but not all. Nor is it easy to distinguish subordinate kin relationships, and it is virtually impossible to order them in terms of importance. Their content can quite easily be categorized, but from comparison on this score alone it does not seem possible to say definitely that one or more reflect dominant aspects. In many cases, they apparently do; at the same time, what appear to be dominant traits may be inherent in that particular relationship. One key undoubtedly lies in how the people themselves conceptualize the relationship—such statements as "this is like a father (etc.) relationship" are significant in evaluating.

It should be emphasized that I have been looking at these two systems from a dual perspective, assessing what relationships are important from the point of view of individual persons, and also what are important structurally in regard to the systems themselves. It is obvious that two kinds of enquiry are involved here, and they could result in two different sets of answers—although one would hope there would be common ground. But in both cases I have been concerned largely with male egos, and with the total system in relation to the interests and preoccupations of men. I therefore add this cautionary note: it is possible that by taking female egos, and paying more attention to the patterning of women's behavior among themselves, I might have come up with a somewhat different picture.

3. Granted this, in both systems certain relationships stand out. In the Gunwinggu, one is quite definitely the brother-sister relationship and those which stem from or make up the GAGAG line. These are seen as

complementary. The same is the case in the north-eastern Arnhem Land system. There it is the MARI-GUDARA line—that is, those relatives strategically placed within that perspective, seen from the viewpoint of any one person, male or female. But almost as significant, and perhaps just as much so, are those in the MARIMO-MARAIDJA line. As far as both these systems are concerned, I have selected what *seem* to be the most significant relationships; and the criteria for such selection are already noted.

4. In other words, although I have said that the structure does not reveal what might be regarded as a dominant relationship, it does indicate in what direction this, or these, may be found. In the Gunwinggu system, the relationship of siblings of opposite sex is relevant to the patterning of the system itself, but especially significant in respect of the GAGAG line. In fact, as I have tried to demonstrate, the system rests on this and on those relationships directly dependent on it. Furthermore, this supports the major emphasis on matriliny.

In the north-eastern Arnhem Land system, similarly, the structural aspect is underlined—in the separation of brothers and sisters, in the significance of the MARI line, and indirectly in the MARIMO line. All reinforce the principle of patriliny.

5. The structural patterning depends on two primary aspects: (*a*) on descent, and all that this involves in ordinary and sacred terms, including inheritance; and (*b*) on marriage. Dominant relationships must depend on these two factors, and indeed they must figure centrally in any hypothesis bearing on this question. In both societies, whom one marries determines a person's relationships even more clearly than from whom one is descended. In this sense, a dominant relationship is one on which a person depends and is depended upon. I don't want to be thought facetious; but one could say, at least for these Australian Aboriginal societies, that the two most significant acquisitions for a man are women and ritual acceptance; and for women, men. One should probably add, for both, children as well, in view of the tremendous local emphasis on fertility and reproduction. For men, women are possibly more important even than ritual knowledge and privilege, although there is no doubt at all that religion is extremely important in all aspects of social living.

Among the Gunwinggu, as far as the brother-sister relationship is concerned, women are important to their brothers through their children and through the GAGAG line; ritual acceptance, too, comes through the M.B. and the GAGAG. Among the north-eastern Arnhem Landers, marriage is indirectly through the MARI line, and through the M.B. and *mumalgur* and *mugulrumurung*, and ritual through the MARI, especially. It is also highly likely that the content of relationships of this nature will influence many others; but the degree of influence is not clear, and not readily demonstrable.

6. It is obvious also that kinship systems are not to be understood only

in terms of their structure. Although structure is undoubtedly a shorthand or abstract statement of how kin relationships are ordered in respect of status and equivalence, among other things, the content of social relationships (that is, the cultural dimension) is the only medium through which meaning in a broader empirical sense can be obtained. Structure itself provides only half an explanation. All this is well recognized, and does not need laboring here. However, it is fairly clear that, if we talk about dominance or subordination in kin relationships, the actual behavioral patterns must be examined closely. I shall mention this matter of attributes below.

7. It seems fairly clear, too, that the content of each relationship consists of at least two aspects. (*a*) That which depends on the relationship *per se*, on what is ordinarily expected between the persons so related—for example, a MARI-GUDARA or a brother-sister. These expectations are a matter of cultural convenience and congeniality, part of the patterning of traditional culture dependent on broader behavioral issues. Examples of this would be the sister as a mother surrogate to her brother among the Gunwinggu, or the actual content of the avoidance tabu; or, in north-eastern Arnhem Land, the custom of *miriri*—that is to say, attributes which are peculiar to the relationship itself, *as* that relationship, in "distant" as well as in actual terms. (*b*) Those attributes or aspects which stem from the relationship of the persons related, in a personal sense, because each of them has links with others and these influence their own responses and interactions. All social relationships are *cumulative*; that is, they take on the overtones and undertones of affecting relationships. In the case of the Gunwinggu, a woman's brother is NGADJADJ to her children (his *ganggin*), and this NGADJADJ-*ganggin* relationship colors his relationship to his sister. The fact that she is expected to produce daughters to keep "a fire burning on his (the brother's) side" is another factor directly influencing their relationship. The same is the case in north-eastern Arnhem Land. In the MARI-GUDARA relationship a female *mari* has as children a man's *ngandi* and NGABIBI, while a male MARI has, as children, his *mugulrumurung* and MARALGUR.

8. Three further contributory factors in influencing behavioral patterns relevant to specific relationships are: (*a*) Terms which have classificatory or duplicating extensions. This is common throughout Aboriginal Australia. The "cloak" of the genealogically linked relationship, in terms of actual or "close" or "quite close" (still genealogically demonstrable) relationships, is assumed by all similar classificatory relationships—but in varying degrees of intensity, depending on distance, genealogical and spatial. In some cases, such relationships as woman-daughter's husband, or brother-sister (in both regions, for example in the north-eastern Arnhem Land *miriri*), retain their quality of constraint and emotional charge whether or not the relationship can be demonstrated genealogically.

But a great number do not. (*b*) In both systems, there is provision for "junior marriages" and alternative marriages (see, especially, the subsection systems). In the first case, in reference to the Gunwinggu, this phenomenon is observable at the grandparents' and grandchildren's generation levels, but has ramifications throughout the system in its extended form. In the north-eastern Arnhem Land system, the junior marriage patterns are structurally significant in relation to all women in their own or a man's patriline, and this situation ramifies in contrast to the situation in the case of males in their own patriline. In these examples, the alternate generation level is significant in that persons in alternate generations are classfied together. This has implications in defining behavioral patterns relevant to specific relationships. In the second case, excluding the question of preferential and alternative choices in marriage, certain relatives (consanguineal or affinal) of a person marry spouses who may be called by either one term or another. In north-eastern Arnhem Land, a female *mari* who marries a NGATI has as children *ngandi* and NGABIBI; she has terminologically the same children, from Ego's point of view, if she marries a GALEI or a NGATIWALGUR. However, a *ngandi* who marries a MARALGUR has children who are terminologically different from the offspring of a NGATI and a BABA. There are other examples in both systems. This means that the content of the relationship between (for example) a man and his female *mari* differs, depending on her generation level and on whom she marries. (*c*) Furthermore, the content of a relationship varies, as in the above instance, according to the marriages contracted between the pair involved in that relationship and the marriages of their children and parents, etc. The *bindoi* relationship among the Gunwinggu is a case in point; or the choice between *gagali* and *ganjulg*. Or there is the question, as in north-eastern Arnhem Land, of *how* one has obtained a wife —through direct betrothal, through the junior levirate or the patriate, as a gift from a still-living elder brother, through elopement, etc. There is also the issue raised by the fact that, from a man's point of view, in north-eastern Arnhem Land, the terms for his mother and for his son's wife are the same—as they are in the case of his own wife and the wife of his son's son, for whom he can, conventionally, compete. Additionally, there are "submerged" relationships. For example, a man's *galei*, who should marry his MARAIDJA, may instead marry the MARAIDJA's father's father; in these circumstances, she is marrying her GOMINJAR, as if she were equivalent to a *marimo*, and the MARAIDJA now calls her no longer *galei*, but *momo*. However, where actual genealogical linkage is demonstrated, kin terminology and the consequent behavioral patterns are more or less uniform. Where subsection considerations are paramount in defining relationships as well as marriages, the range of behavioral variation is much wider.

9. I have already noted that I found the lists of attributes given by Hsu

inadequate for my purpose, or not sufficiently broad to include all the main elements associated with behavioral patterns; even then, I have covered only a small range. While admitting that the nuclear family, whatever form it may take, is a fundamental unit—and from this it could be argued that the dyadic relationships within it are themselves of basic importance—I do not think it is empirically demonstrated in the above examples that these relationships *alone* are of basic significance. If we consider dominance in terms of relationships, these "basic" dyads, or any one of them, do not necessarily influence all others. It is more likely in traditionally-oriented societies—where any marriage is a union of two or more families, where children usually have parent-substitutes, and where a mother's brother and certain other relatives play an important part in a child's life—that relationships impinging on those within the nuclear family will be more significant. The Gunwinggu brother-sister and the north-eastern Arnhem Land MARI-GUDARA relationships are important for this reason and not primarily because those involved are also members of a family, whether nuclear or extended. The co-resident group, and not simply the nuclear family, is important in this context.

I cannot agree that all the attributes of each dyadic relationship noted by Hsu (1965: 642-48) are intrinsic to the relationships referred to—that "they are universally the potential and inherent properties of that relationship" (*ibid.*, 640). Women do, in certain circumstances, have authority over men. Or take the continuation of friendship between two bachelors, communicated to their wives and then to their children (*ibid.*, 644). In north-eastern Arnhem Land, friends are those who do not compete for the same women, and are related to each other as DUWEI-GALEI; the wife of one DUWEI is the sister of the other (GALEI); but because there is matrilateral cross-cousin marriage, the wife of one GALEI is not the sister of the other DUWEI. The two women would not necessarily be friends; while a daughter of a GALEI marries, ideally, a son of a DUWEI, the son of a GALEI marries a woman regarded by the DUWEI as a wife's mother. Friendship is determined largely by kin affiliation, in the case of males as for females. The tremendous reliance of a child on its mother is without question, and the Gunwinggu have numbers of stories in which the central figure is a weeping "orphan," or motherless child, neglected by everyone except perhaps his elder brother. However, it is necessary to make allowance for mother-surrogates, whether these are mother's sisters or co-wives, or father's sisters or brother's daughters and so on, or (among the Gunwinggu) an own sister. There is also the question of the extent and nature of a child's association with parents, actual or otherwise, or, as in north-eastern Arnhem Land, with its MARI. Libidinality between an Australian Aboriginal boy and his mother may be suspected (for example, a highly provocative Gunwinggu expression of abuse is "copulate with your mother!"—*not* sister); but it is yet to be demonstrated in a situation where a child's consistent interaction, even at an early age, is not confined to its actual mother.

Again, regarding brothers, the two attributes of "equality and rivalry" are not straightforward in the examples we have from our two societies. Among the Gunwinggu there is equality with minimum rivalry; among the north-eastern Arnhem Landers, inequality with rivalry. Equality is more likely to be present in other relationships, within the same or alternate generation levels, than between actual or classificatory brothers.

10. Regarding the effect of dominant on other relationships, I have already indicated the difficulties which faced me in separating these other relationships. I am not happy with the use of the word *recessive* for relationships and attributes, nor with *subordinate* or *derivative* or *secondary* ones. I believe we are dealing simply with a range of relationships which serve different purposes in different situations, and that these need not be subordinated to any others, not even to the dominant relationship. As I have tried to show, various attributes relevant to the dominant relationship are relevant also to many others. But just because these attributes can be identified in others, I do not think this necessarily demonstrates that the relationship under consideration has been influenced by the dominant one. It seems to me more likely that the patterning of relationship-attributes reflects major cultural emphases which are not inherently identifiable in the kinship system of a particular society, but are in fact reflective of the broader emphases.

Briefly, in relation to our two societies, we shall consider generally the effect of the dominant relationship on other kin relationships. Among the Gunwinggu I have suggested that the brother-sister relationship is dominant. In relation to his sister's children a man, as a mother's brother, has more to say about their marriage than their own parents. This authority is derived, not only from his relationship to his sister, but because he, like his sister, is a strategic member of the GAGAG line (through his M.M.B.). Additionally, a sister's child inherits from his NGADJADJ (M.B.) and only indirectly from his father. The husband-wife relationship is not defined exclusively in terms of sexuality, and the production of children is important. It is influenced considerably by the brother-sister relationship—with the first choice wife coming through the GAGAG line, and the second choice wife pointing to the importance of the NGADJADJ himself. Demonstrations of affection between husband and wife are more likely to occur between close *gagali* than between *ganjulg*: their duties and obligations to their own and their respective spouses' relatives are counterbalanced by mutual aid and protection, and jealousy. Public demonstrations of affection between husband and wife are not customary, but permissible between correctly related partners *before* marriage or between sweethearts *after* marriage. Extra-marital liaisons are fairly general, but with due regard for the proprieties; divorce appears to have been less common than elopement. This system is heavily matrilineal, despite recognition of patrilineal descent through the *gunmugugur*.

In north-eastern Arnhem Land the importance of the MARI-GUDARA relationship rests on the influence of the MARI line; the *mari*/MARI has a decisive say in his sister's daughter's children's marriages and in the ritual acceptance of his sister's daughter's son. The system is heavily patrilineal, and the MARI line is the patriline of a man's mother's mother and her brother, which is also the patriline of his wife's mother. The husband-wife relationship is relatively stable, and is held together by the strength of the MARI bonds; but in this system there is some opportunity for marital mobility (see R. Berndt, in Nimkoff, 1965). A wife's brother is, apparently, more concerned about the continuity and stability of his sister's marriage than she and her husband are. Affection between spouses is not publicly demonstrated; polygyny is generally permitted, but monogamy is at least as frequent. Inheritance of ritual knowledge is directly from a MARI and from a man's father's patriline; and younger brothers inherit from elder brothers both wives and material objects, as they may inherit wives from their father. Rivalry between brothers exacerbates marital dissension, and the incidence of elopement.

In both societies affines play a significant part.

Finally, the foregoing material seems to suggest that Hsu's hypothesis (1965: 641) is relevant only so far. Dominant attributes of a dominant relationship in a particular system tend to influence or to be reflected in those attributes or behavioral patterns relevant to other relationships within that system. The intrinsic attributes of a specific relationship so influenced are not necessarily submerged by that influence but retain their essential quality. Nevertheless, it is probable that this relationship and its attributes will vary in different societies depending on what relationship is in fact considered to be dominant.

Appendix

In the Conclusions I have focused, as I have throughout this Chapter, on kinship and on its wider social context, bearing in mind the problem of isolating paired relationships which may be categorized as dominant. Additionally, I have examined the relevant behavioural content of Gunwinggu and Murngin kin relationships to see each in perspective and in relation to those which appear to be dominant. Although I have looked quite closely at the range of attributes relevant to specific relationships, I have not been able to extend this to cover all or even most of their associated activities. This would have been impossible in the space available. It would entail a full ethnographic coverage, including reference to ideal and actual behavior on such occasions as birth, betrothal, sickness, death, and rites of various kinds.

Among the Gunwinggu, the brother-sister relationship has been isolated as dominant; among the Murngin, the M.M.B-Sr.D.S. relationship. It should be kept in mind that I had to have two categories of dominant relationship—primary and secondary. Leaving this aside, two aspects can be noted, one referring to residence and the other to socialization.

Residence in Aboriginal Australia in general, and these two regions in particular, traditionally reflects an intimate relationship with the land in terms of land-holding and land-using rights (see R. Berndt, 1964).

Both of these peoples live in a tropical coastal and near-coastal zone, with broadly similar climate and vegetation. The land-holding unit in both areas is patrilineally defined, and significant in religious terms. The Gunwinggu *gunmugugur* is really a local descent group of a kind well known in Aboriginal Australia (see R. Berndt, 1959). The *babaru,* or more broadly the *mada* (language unit) and *mala* ("clan"), of the Murngin, comprises one (that is, the *babaru*) or several closely affiliated local groups. In both cases territorial affiliation, mythologically substantiated, is defined through descent, although adoption is allowed for. There is no obligation for men to remain in the territory of their local group. Traditionally, however, they could possibly have been found there more often than not as far as eastern Arnhem Land was concerned—although this situation was disrupted through early Indonesian trade which attracted Aborigines to the coast. Among the Gunwinggu the local territory was more of a focus than a residential reality. In both cases, custodianship of sacred sites necessitated, in the past as often today, relatively frequent visits to local territories. The ordinary socio-economic unit among both Gunwinggu and Murngin is most conveniently called by the term which has been associated with it in the literature—the horde. It had no fixed membership but quite often it represented a nuclear or extended family, *plus*—making up a cooperative unit for the purposes of hunting and food collecting. Seasonal fluctuation and the local supply of food-stuffs determined its size. Only when food was fairly plentiful were the largest sacred rituals and ceremonies held.

Although Gunwinggu and Murngin present contrasts in their kinship systems, as well as in matrilineality versus patrilineality, their camping arrangements do not differ greatly.

It is not possible to speak of the "family" (in the minimal sense) in western Arnhem Land as matri-centred, in north-eastern Arnhem Land as patri-centred. In both instances the small scale family unit made up of husband, wife/wives and small children is the norm—although, occasionally, the parents of either spouse or the husband's brothers are present for certain periods. The small camp and its fires are part of a wider constellation. The head of this small camp is the husband. However important the relationship between brother and sister (as among the Gunwinggu) or M.M.B.-Sr.D.S. (among the Murngin), in adult life these relatives do not combine with the basic conjugal unit as a co-resident group. It should be emphasized, nevertheless, that consanguineal kin are more likely to be found within the larger camp, made up of smaller camp units, than outside of it. In other words, in these particular cases, the idea of a dominant dyad is *not* necessarily linked with residence. Residential patterning in Aboriginal Australia, although it has its structural form, is subsumed under the broader network of social relations; that is, relatives outside the conjugal unit are directly significant.

The larger camp, made up of a number of small huts, shelters, or windbreaks, contains persons with whom one is on familiar terms; one interacts more consistently with them than with people outside it. In western Arnhem Land, this wider unit, which is relatively unstable (being added to and depleted with the coming and going of people, in the interests of economic and religious mobility), is more likely to include a man's actual mother-in-law, if not father-in-law. There are numerous other differences, in terms of kin-composition, in such larger camps in each region. Even so, this does not affect the significance of kin located outside the immediate "family" unit, because virtually all major responsibilities and obligations lie outside that unit and in relation to specific categories of persons.

Hsu suggests that dominance can be determined by the way in which a specific kin relationship takes precedence over others in the value emphasis of a society, in the way it upholds the socio-cultural system, and the importance it has in the socialization of the young.

As far as the second condition is concerned, I have shown that, from a structural point of view, dominant kinship relationships (in their primary and secondary guise) are basic elements in the Gunwinggu and Murngin systems and do in fact help to maintain them. I am not prepared to comment on the first in any detail. To do so would involve consideration of attitudes and beliefs, secular and religious, including analysis of myths, stories, and songs. One can say, however, that among the Gunwinggu the very strong emotional bond existing between brother and sister is not a major theme in the oral literature—just as it was not articulated in the "ultimate circumstance situation" responses. But, as I have said, this does not rule out the importance of the relationship. In some myths, men are angered by the behavior of their sisters and express this anger through direct physical action. A few stories involve brother-sister incest; but there are examples also of incest between own father and daughter, and mother's father and granddaughter. Relationships that are highly charged emotionally, especially those hedged about with prohibitions and avoidance tabus, often find release in opposite-behavior through mythology. In north-eastern Arnhem Land mythology, for instance, women and their actual sons-in-law, as well as MARALGUR-*gurung*, engage in sexual adventures which in everyday life would be strongly condemned. However, in this region the MARI-

GUDARA relationship is also the subject of many myths, and its importance is emphasized on all counts.

The content of the brother-sister relationship in these two areas shows a striking resemblance. In both, sisters are conventionally disparaged by their brothers. Obligations and tabus are very similar. Yet there are differences, too. Among the Gunwinggu, this particular relationship impinges on (or influences) many others, and the spouses of brothers and sisters may themselves be siblings. In north-eastern Arnhem Land, the spouses of a brother and a sister are not usually so closely related in genealogical terms. In both examples, however, a man depends in a number of ways on his sister's husband, as a child does on his or her father's sister or mother's brother. It is true that much more attention needs to be placed on values within the framework of kin relationship dominance. Conflicting values are important. But equally so are the values manifested in a series of situations in which the same or different relatives play different parts or roles. In other words, certain kin may play a major part in one situation, a less active part in another, and no part (or a passive one) in a third; or the importance of the part they play may depend on *which* others are present. Frequency of reference to certain relationships is not necessarily a key to dominance, but intensity of feeling associated with them could be. However, from what I have said in the main body of this Chapter, the overtones or undertones of emotional feeling in relation to specific kin may not be structurally relevant. It does seem to be so with the Gunwinggu brother-sister and the Murngin MARI-GUDARA relationships; but there are others which approximate the emotional and value-loaded significance of these "dominant" relationships. In any case, affect alone may not be a safe guide in this respect. In Gunwinggu society much of this, in terms of sexuality, finds expression in sweetheart relationships which are only obliquely significant structurally (although more so than among the Murngin).

The third condition is interesting. Hsu's main concern is with the effect of dominant kinship relationships on processes relevant to socialization, or vice versa. (See Hsu, 1965, and in this volume, although his Symposium paper examines the problem much more broadly.)

There is little question that among the Gunwinggu a sister has an important part to play in the informal contacts of a growing brother, even to the extent of serving in a sense as a mother-surrogate when her brother is small. Moreover, constraints and prohibitions are not seriously imposed between siblings of opposite sex until a boy is, say, about five to six years old; gradually, they are enforced (adopted, would be a better word in this context) through constant reminders, through example, and through more diffusely expressed social opinion—on the part of the boy's peer group and older "brothers" as well as by adults. In contrast, a Murngin boy even at an early age has less sustained contact with his full sister, who only rarely nurses or attends to him as an infant. All the relevant sanctions are designed to keep them apart, to compartmentalize this relationship by capitalizing on the intensity of the emotional bond between them. Among the Gunwinggu, prohibitions between siblings of opposite sex dwell on differences in status and expectations between them, and the sister's pivotal position in the structure *vis-à-vis* her brother(s), without the lessening of emotional and affective attitudes. The Gunwinggu emphasis is on dependence, the Murngin on independence.

The MARI-GUDARA relationship is significant structurally in the Murngin system in more or less the same way as the brother-sister relationship is among the Gunwinggu; even more tellingly, it has a rough parallel in the Gunwinggu GAGAG (M.M.B.) line. The MARI is, in fact, broadly equivalent to the Gunwinggu GAGAG. The positioning is the same. The GAGAG line is especially significant for the Gunwinggu, as the MARI line is for the Murngin; the difference lies in the GAGAG line being structurally more important than it is in personal terms. A GAGAG does play a large part in the informal training of his grandchild, but as he grows older they spend little time together. The personal bond is more obvious in the case of a female *gagag*, but even then her influence is likely to be channelized through the child's mother. It is, therefore, the significance of the descent line with its propensity to influence other relationships which is really important, rather than the GAGAG himself (or themselves). Among the Murngin, the MARI line is certainly significant, but to that can be added the importance of the actual MARI-GUDARA relationship *per se*; and it is this dual significance which makes the relationship so vital. Furthermore, MARI/*mari* (of either sex) have a continuing influence in the socialization of their GUDARA/*gudara*, in both sacred and mundane affairs. If a sister stands symbolically as a mother among the Gunwinggu, while from a woman's point of view a brother is in a sense a symbolic father, a MARI/*mari* stands as a "father" *vis-à-vis* his or her GUDARA/*gudara*.

At the same time, let us not overemphasize the socializing powers and influences of these two roles. In both areas, limitations are imposed. A Gunwinggu sister never breast-feeds her brother (she is not usually physically in a position to do so). A Murngin MARI is more often than not an old man in his *gudara*'s infancy and is not able to play an active part in rearing him, although a female *mari* is less likely to be handicapped in that way. Of course, other MARI are usually available, both close and in a classificatory sense. Neither relationship is in fact a substitute for parental care and guidance.

Two aspects of Aboriginal socialization, in general terms, need to be kept in mind. One concerns the small camp in which the child's parents live, the other the wider framework of social relations. In the Aboriginal "family," whether polygynous or monogamous, the conjugal unit is actually more prominent than many reports have suggested. However, because of the proximity of other kinsfolk, sporadic or prolonged, it is probably more appropriate to speak of the extended family in such contexts. Children growing up rely very much indeed on their *own* (actual or adoptive) parents. A Gunwinggu father, for instance, normally spends a reasonable amount of time with his children, although his attachment to them is much more noticeable in some cases than in others; the constraint between them is more apparent as the children become adolescent. At the same time, the structural aspect of the relationship is most significant in terms of *gunmugugur* linkage. Among the Murngin the bond is much more sharply defined, both structurally and emotionally. A man's status is enhanced by the production of children. This applies to women, too, but not to the same degree. Among the Gunwinggu it is the other way round: the status of both parents is enhanced, but the mother's more obviously so. A Murngin father spends much time with his son, especially, in childhood and adolescence and later more consistently in the ritual sphere. In both regions the mother-child relationship is very close, and particularly in the first few weeks of the child's life it is virtually an exclusive one. A mother has the principal responsibility for the physical welfare of her young children, and, despite some exceptions, most appear to be, if anything, over-indulgent. Subsections aside, in north-eastern Arnhem Land the "clan" songs underline the place of women as intermediaries in ensuring moiety continuity; a woman (in the songs, symbolically a female shark, kangaroo, or other appropriate figure) must bear offspring of the opposite moiety to herself, whereas a man's offspring have the same moiety affiliation as he does. In western Arnhem Land the issue is, on the whole, presented more simply; children follow their father in *gunmugugur* membership, their mother in moiety and phratry affiliation; cross-identification is acknowledged, but not dwelt upon.

Within the conjugal unit, two elements are significant. The first is the presence in many cases of co-wives, who are all "mothers" to children who share a father in common just as the women themselves share a husband; consequently, there is diffusion of affection and collective responsibility for child care on the part of these women, at least nominally, and often more than that. The second is interaction between siblings who have one or both parents in common.

In both regions, parental discipline is at a minimum and somewhat erratic, even when children are small. Also, for a woman to discipline or attempt to discipline a co-wife's child is to invite not only censure but open quarreling. A man leaves such matters to his wife or wives; but often he does not hesitate to take a child's part against its mother, or to condemn her if the child becomes ill, especially if he suspects she has been engaging in extra-marital affairs. As the child grows, however, the father emerges as a figure of authority and to some extent becomes socially distant. Among the Gunwinggu, as far as a boy is concerned, real disciplinary action rests with the mother's brother, especially in adolescence and afterward. Among the Murngin, discipline of more than a trivial kind is the prerogative of the MARI and the NGATI (M.F.).

In both areas, the small family unit is never cut off from the wider and more ephemeral unit. Little distinction is drawn between private and public living. Children interact with other kin probably, on the whole, as much as they do with actual parents. The larger camp serves as the wider socializing environment in childhood, and the processes involved are primarily informal. As the child grows, and begins to understand the content of social relations in terms of specific persons within his range of interaction, these processes become formalized along the lines of particular kin relationships. Socialization involves, initially, a concerted—although informal, and often largely unselfconscious—effort on the part of all adults and older children within a child's interactory perspective. Emerging from this interactory "pool," specific kin begin to stand out, and become more crucial to a boy as he nears initiation. In childhood, too, his peer group, his age-mates, provide him with significant keys to adult activity. At the onset of his first initiation rites, the whole situation changes for him. Special relatives loom larger, in terms of withholding or giving, enforcing or teaching; and both they, and the relationships to which they give concrete shape, are likely to retain their importance for the novice as he moves into the world of adults. But the emergence of persons who have a controlling say in the adult life of a youth is dependent, either directly or indirectly, on the dominant kinship relationships, in their primary or secondary forms, relevant to the society as a whole. This seems to be true for both regions.

Hsu speaks of the Nuer as illustrating brother-cousin (paternal cousin?) dominance, and notes that small boys are driven from their mothers' huts but in later life retain sentimental and social alignments with them and that this is correlated with severe initiation rites. It is not clear how this is associated with brother-cousin dominance. There seem to me to be two sorts of question in this. If one kind of kin relationship dominance is apparent in a particular society, what do we find in the relevant social institutions? This question is not designed to reveal how the dominant kin relationship influences or is associated with those social institutions. It simply enquires what is likely to be found in a society with that particular dominance; it does not examine the problem of connection. For example, among both Gunwinggu and Murngin, male children leave their mothers' camps at first initiation; often they are seized forcibly by older men, and, while women wail, they are taken to or near the ritual ground. From that point onward they are introduced to a long series of rituals, and spend long periods away from the influence of women, their mothers included; this is separation from *all* women, not specifically from their mothers. After the first rites, because they are still fairly young, they may return to their parents' camp; but initiatory rites continue for some years, so the periods of residence in their parents' camp become less frequent, and just before adolescence these are terminated in preference to sleeping in a special camp with age-mates and guardians. Among the Murngin, removal from parents is earlier and more consistent than among the Gunwinngu. However, the Gunwinggu have no "severe" initiatory rites, simply instruction; the Murngin have circumcision—but this cannot be called really severe.

The second question leads on from the first: *If* this [relevant to a specific dominant kin relationship], then what? A definite connection is sought between the relevance of kin relationship dominance and some aspect of the culture or social institution. Or, to put it in another way: without the one we would not have the other, or that other would not be in the form stipulated. This is not easily demonstrated in either of our two Australian Aboriginal examples. Although I am unable to say that a particular institutional factor or cultural item is dependent on, or is causally connected with, the dominant kin relationship, it is possible to demonstrate that dominant kin relationships can and do influence quite markedly the kinds of relatives participating in particular institutions.

It may be useful here to consider, of necessity rather sketchily, what Hsu calls "kinship constellations in socialization" in relation to our two Aboriginal societies. He is concerned with the processes leading toward a particular kind of kin relationship dominance. The words *leading to* are not relevant in my examples, which are merely summaries in terms of the first question noted above; correlations are not necessarily demonstrated between the items listed. I also restrict my coverage to Hsu's. Some recapitulation is, however, unavoidable.

Brother-Sister Dominance: Gunwinggu (male bias).

General. Matrilineally oriented society, with the recognition of one important patrilineal local descent group (the *gunmugugur*). The monogamous or polygynous conjugal unit is spatially separated, but its kinship network includes the "extended" families of both spouses. Members of either are likely to be present in larger camp constellation, at least some of the significant relatives. Residence is traditionally impermanent, because Aborigines are semi-nomadic; the small marital camp is often constructed near the wife's parents, or vice versa, but not exclusively so. Husband and wife both collect food; children are more dependent on the mother than on the father for basic food. Male economic responsibilities are diffused over a much wider social range, in connection with specific relatives and within the sacred sphere. A wife's everyday responsibilities, that is, apart from food collecting for ritual gatherings, and from some involvement in trade-exchange, are mostly confined to her children and her parents. Inheritance is primarily through the M.B., *gunmugugur* inheritance through F. and F.F. There is a fairly strict sex dichotomy in sacred ritual.

Childhood. A child is exposed to a wide social interactory field from early infancy. Competition for parental affection is present, but in most cases not especially marked; the same applies to sibling rivalry in other spheres. There appears to be greater and more intimate dependence on the mother than on the father, whose relations with his children are somewhat more formal. He has a number of extra-familial obligations and responsibilities, and a F.B. has more authority over his B.S. than has the actual father, just as a brother has, in effect, more authority over his sister. Affection is not linked with sexuality, but, beyond a certain point, diffused over a range of "mother surrogates" (for example, sister, *gagag* or m.m., father's co-wives, mothers' sisters). This is a supplement to actual parental affection, not, normally, a substitute for it. A father's sister, or "female father," is a significant figure; M.B. is characterized as a "male mother," but primarily in a disciplinary sense. Strong constraint and prohibitions on part of a brother in relation to his sisters, plus some disciplinary sanctions, are expected to be in force by late childhood and before his first initiation rite. Affectionate and emotional bonds link parents and children, siblings of opposite sex, *gagag*/GAGAG, mother-in-law–son-in-law, and GAGALI. Before marriage affection is focused on a betrothed wife or, less often, husband, but later is likely to be diffused over sweetheart relationships. Authority, in both secular and sacred spheres, is mainly, directly or indirectly, through M.B. and the GAGAG line: but a man has authority over his wife (wives). Children spend much of their time with age-mates—often mixed-sex groups in early childhood, which become one-sex groups well before the boys' first initiation and before the girls reach puberty.

Initiation and Adolescence. Kinship remains important throughout life; so do the crucial relationships already noted, apart from the diminishing "exclusiveness" of the mother-child relationship from early childhood onward. No social ties are possible outside the kinship network, which extends far beyond the immediate environment and includes persons not ordinarily regarded as kin—for example, trading partners, and transients from other areas. A boy's first initiation rite occurs at approximately 10 to 12 years of age; after that he is gradually removed from the sphere of predominantly feminine activities and influence. Initiation involves four major stages, covering a period of several years, which must be completed before marriage can take place. No physical operation is involved, but numerous tabus are enforced, especially in reference to food (and these apply also to certain close relatives, especially a boy's own mother). Formal learning processes are channeled through religious ritual; special aid comes from a M.B., with a father's aid indirect. A boy's GAGALI and brothers are often regarded as equivalent in a ritual sense. All ritual is focused on obtaining sacred knowledge and on preparing the novice for social adulthood, leading to marriage and to the prestige derived from active religious participation.

Adolescence is not regarded as a period of stress, although it is one of obedience and of deferring to seniors and (for a boy) to those undergoing higher initiatory rites. For a girl, it is traditionally a time of adjustment to married life and domestic responsibilities. Ideally, a boy should not engage in sexual activity while formally a novice. Hunting and other relevant skills are taught and learnt from early childhood onward. Adolescence is the time to perfect these techniques, and to become more directly involved in economic obligations which, until then, were largely shouldered by parents on the child's behalf. Special skills in dancing, singing, and sacred decoration are usually taught to boys in adolescence, although most have already had some preliminary informal experience. Learning continues, however, well into adulthood, at least until middle age and even, to a diminishing extent, afterward.

Social Adulthood. Marriage through formal betrothal may take place when a youth reaches the age of, say, 18 to 20 years. A man's sister is important to him in both betrothal and marriage arrangements. Two men may exchange sisters, and a man has a major stake in the marriage of his sister's children. Brothers assist one another in accumulating betrothal-sustaining gifts. Extra-marital relations are to some extent expected on the part of both spouses, but they should be managed discreetly and, especially in the case of wives, surreptitiously. Elopement has been moderately frequent, especially as a feature of transient sweetheart affairs, although the number of people who have *never* eloped is increasing. Traditionally, much fighting took place over women. Sexual relations are not usual between a man and his actual brother's wife, but not uncommon between those genealogically more distant. A man's grandson GAGAG may look after his wife in his absence and have sexual associations with her. The GAGALI bond appears to be more significant to a man in some ways than the brother bond because of the brother-sister relationship, and in any quarrels or fighting he should take a GAGALI's part. Nevertheless, actual and close brothers have very strong ties indeed, and in practice it is difficult to gauge the weighting accorded these two relationships in the (rare) event of a serious clash of interest between them.

Old Age. Men have an important role to play as they become older, especially in the handing on of religious knowledge. Like older women, they are rarely neglected by their children, children's spouses, and grandchildren, and by other kin with continuing responsibilities toward them. They are deferred to in sacred matters and consulted on a variety of problems because of their experience. Very old women, "ready to die," are admitted in certain circumstances to the men's secret ground, if sponsored by, for example, a son. At an ordinary mundane level they usually have children around them; even if they are unable to walk far or to collect much in the way of food, unless they are blind or otherwise incapacitated they are expected to act as baby sitters, to help and advise their older grandchildren, and to help with small domestic tasks like cooking and keeping the fires alight.

M.M.B.-Sr.D.S. Dominance: Murngin (male bias).

General. The society is patrilineally oriented, with indirect matrilineal descent, and matrilateral cross-cousin marriage for males. The semi-nomadic camping pattern is much the same as for the Gunwinggu. The conjugal unit is monogamous or polygynous, but large polygynous "households" were traditionally more prevalent than they are now. Small camps of husband and wife/wives, and children, are part of the larger and more transient camp constellation. A wife's parents and brothers are more likely to be spatially distant. If they are present in the same large camping unit, they will rarely be nearby; the usual neighbors are the husband's brothers, father, and father's brothers. As in the Gunwinggu case, the kinship obligations of husband and wife are not equally distributed. The nuclear family relies most consistently on food obtained by a wife (and mother), while a man's economic responsibilities are more widely diffused, especially in the sacred sphere. Secular, as well as sacred, items (objects and knowledge) are inherited through the male descent line of MARIMO and BABA—but *especially* through the M.M.B., the MARI (who may be identified with MARIMO). In sacred ritual the same sex dichotomy applies as for the Gunwinggu, except that no provision is made for old women to enter the secret-sacred ground. (The Kunapipi is a special case, in both regions.)

Childhood. Here, too, a child is exposed from an early age to a wide social field. Much more obviously than among the Gunwinggu, children compete for the affection of either or both parents; and temper tantrums are quite common from early infancy to adolescence, especially for girls. Brother-sister tabus are taught quite early, and as soon as they can run about independently they are discouraged from playing together; but the brother's response in the *miriri* has not the same disciplinary connotation as its Gunwinggu counterpart. Brothers are in potential or open rivalry for women; but between close sisters friction is normally counterbalanced by affection and mutual aid even when they are co-wives. The father is regarded as an authority figure, but not to the same extent as the MARI and MARIMO; dependence on him and respect for him are weakened by rivalry for women, and by the shadow of the patriate which may lead a son to look forward hopefully to his father's death. However, a man identifies fairly closely and less guardedly with his MARIMO and with his MARI.

Here, too, affection is diffused among mother-surrogates (mother's co-wives, for example, and female *mari*), but not at the expense of actual parents. The *mugulbaba* (f.sr.) is a "female father," but without the connotation of strain and rivalry. Affection linked with sexuality is not a feature of relations with own mother or actual or distant father's sisters; the patriate encourages this combination insofar as a father's co-wives (not actual mother) are concerned, but seems to be only latent until after adolescence.

Children spend a considerable amount of time with their age-mates; mixed-sex groups are not so obvious in this area, if only because a boy may go through his first initiation rite (circumcision) at five or six years old, although occasionally not until eight or nine.

Initiation and Adolescence. Kinship remains important throughout life, and the main patterns established in childhood continue and are reinforced. Here, too, kinship provides the framework for all social relationships, not only between genealogically recognized kin. The first initiation rite is the initial move in a long series of sacred rituals which gradually bring the novice first to social adulthood and later to active participation in religious affairs; both of these involve partial removal from the influence of women. Traditionally, special camps were constructed for novices, set apart from parents and under the direction of guardians. They are subjected to no severe physical ordeals (apart from circumcision), but to a variety of prohibitions. A boy's father plays an important part in the circumcision ritual, but MARI and MARIMO more so in succeeding rituals. While these first initiation rites can be regarded as traumatic for a young novice, his subsequent adolescence is not obviously a time of stress. Sexual activity of a more serious kind begins for a boy in early adolescence. By that point he should have acquired all the main hunting and fighting skills, as well as some competence in dancing, singing, or playing the didjeridu (drone trumpet), and so on. Formal learning processes begin with initiation; and, particularly in regard to ritual and myth, revelations in this sphere of the sacred are graded, and extend over a long period of a man's lifetime.

Social Adulthood. Traditionally, youths remained unmarried until they reached the age of 18 to 20, in some cases 25 or even older. Warner reported monopolization of young girls by older men, although in actual practice constant feuding led to a numerical "surplus" of women. Sexual activity is greater with partners classified as potential spouses. The M.B. and his wife are the most important figures in attending to a man's betrothal negotiations. Elopement (through consent) was not as common as in western Arnhem Land, but abduction by force appears to have taken place traditionally. Extra-marital affairs were more dangerous in their outcome and apparently embarked on less lightly than among the Gunwinggu. Rivalry between brothers is exacerbated by the levirate and by an elder brother's right of access to his younger brothers' wives. Elder brothers can monopolize wives, and sororal polygyny reinforces this situation. Father-son relations are under similar pressure.

Murngin society, including the religious dimension, is more hierarchically organized than Gunwinggu. Leaders are consequently more significant, and of two types: religious; and "political"—entrepreneurial, emphasizing fighting or trading. Domestic issues (sex, children) aside, the foci of adult life are on religion or politics, sometimes both. Embryonic craft specialization is more apparent than in western Arnhem Land. MARI and MARIMO are extremely significant in aiding their grandsons, especially elder ones, to attain full social status—which means having one or more wives and children, being a good fighter and hunter, and, particularly, an unimpeded progress through the various religious stages. Esoteric knowledge of myth and ritual is highly valued.

Old Age. Old men play an important role in religious ritual, and some may still monopolize younger women. They rely on their sons for aid as they become older; they may either retain their own separate camp, or live close to older sons. Prestige increases with age, for men and to some extent for women; there are instances of elderly decrepit women being treated both casually and neglectfully, but not by their own sons and daughters.

Summary

These two sketches are very much in summary. I must emphasize that they should not be viewed as representative of the whole of Aboriginal Australia; they simply refer to *two* Aboriginal societies, the Gunwinggu and the Murngin. There were reputedly about 500 different Aboriginal societies on the Australian continent at the onset of European occupation —more, or fewer, depending on how we define this term "society." If all were available for analysis, it is highly likely that they would reveal evidence of *other* dominant kinship relationships. I have not attempted any comparative analysis here of other Aboriginal material.

Concerning Hsu's (1965) four relationships and their attributes: using the material I have already presented and discussed, the following comments may be made on these, with Gunwinggu and Murngin in mind. In the following lists, M. stands for Murngin, G. for Gunwinggu.

Relationships	*Attributes*	*Comments*
Husband-wife	1 Discontinuity	Provided we recognize that the conjugal unit is not structurally separable from impinging kin relationships. Every marriage is a "union" between two or more sets of kin, and this is underlined by betrothal and post-marital gifts to wife's parents and kin. M., G.
	2 Exclusiveness	Provisions for access to wife by certain relatives: M., G. Expected extra-marital relations: G. Access to wife by elder brother anticipating levirate and patriate: M.

	3 Sexuality	Regular sexual association between spouses: M., G. Real focus of sexuality on sweethearts: G.
	4 Freedom	Individual choice in betrothal (excluding child betrothal) plays some part: individual choice in pre- and in extra-marital sexual partner. Husband can divorce wife, but not vice versa; and only means open to wife is elopement. Freedom relative. M., G.
	5 Symbiotic Cooperation	In part played in production of children. Kin, however, participate in nearly all situations; no need to fall back on themselves. M., G. Unequal in care of children (G.); relatively equal (M.).
Father-son	1 Continuity	Through *gunmugugur* (G.). Through MARIMO and (indirectly) through MARI: especially important (M).
	2 Inclusiveness	Multiple fathers and sons recognized, although actual always distinguished: M., G. Interfered with by competition with father: M.
	3 Authority	Other authority figures more important than father: M., G.
	4 Asexuality	Repatriate and competition with father over women: M.
Mother-son	1 Discontinuity	Provided we remember forms of direct and indirect matrilineal descent: M., G.
	2 Inclusiveness	Multiple mothers and sons recognized, although actual always distinguished: M., G.
	3 Dependence	Primarily on part of child and later on part of mother. Dependence diffused: more interaction with mother than with father. M., G.
	4 Diffuseness	Relationship undifferentiated: M., G.
	5 Libidinality	Not obviously present: no firm evidence, except in terms of mother-surrogates

		(M.), but not in case of sister as mother-surrogate (G.).
Brother-brother	1 Discontinuity	Formal solidarity. Ties in terms of continuity just as important as in father-son relationship, especially in ritual sphere: M., G.
	2 Inclusiveness	Multiple brothers; actual brothers have stronger ties: M., G. Male GAGALI bond stronger (G.); DUWEI-GALEI bond stronger (M.).
	3 Equality	Relative equality only: G. Inequality in rights and duties, balanced by levirate: M.
	4 Rivalry	No rivalry (G.); rivalry (M.).

In my view, Hsu's attribute categorizations are not sufficiently broad or precise to cover all likely attributes associated with any paired relationship. Selection of four basic terms, even for analytic and limited purposes, is not enough; it is necessary to cover the full range of recognized kin relationships within a specific society and to think in terms of clusters of specific relationships and of how one relationship influences others.

TEN

ERIC DE DAMPIERRE

Elders and Youngers in the Nzakara Kingdom

Francis Hsu's research and hypothesis have the great virtue of grappling with large and difficult problems that too often frighten the sociologist. One must congratulate him on his endeavor which, if it is pursued, will not fail to reap a harvest of interesting hypotheses; but these quite probably will lead their author to modify his approach. Can he, in fact, confine himself to the amiable conclusions of "common sense?" Will not the conceptual tools on which he draws rapidly show themselves to be insufficient? [1] One does not wish to pour into algebraic formulae such a large number of unknowns that final results are impossible to obtain; likewise, is it not preferable to attempt to understand the logical universe by the property of the real (i.e., those things which permit one to apprehend it) rather than relying upon one or another "attribute" of a kinship relationship or even the sum of attributes of these relationships? Francis Hsu seems to be at least half convinced of this himself, since in researching the compatibility of roles he in fact singles out the incompatibilities: a more modest ambition, surely, but the only one in the social sciences capable of offering a certain degree of prediction.

I propose to submit to the critique of Francis Hsu and my colleagues a concrete case that will perhaps permit one to judge the foundation of his

* Translated from the French by Renate Fernandez.

1. I especially acknowledge sharing the objections of Andrew and Marilyn Strathern, "Dominant kin relationships and dominant ideas," *American Anthropologist* 67:997–99.

hypothesis concerning the characteristics of brother-brother relations (Hsu 1965:654) in a society where the relationships between the younger and the older seem to me to be privileged, if not predominant, and which in some measure command other sectors of the social life. This case concerns the Zandé society, which has been so magnificently studied since 1927 by E. E. Evans-Pritchard, whom I could not sufficiently praise for his scrupulous exactitude. The following analysis will deal with the system of kinship in force in the western sector of this society, the Nzakara kingdom. It supposes as known the analysis of the lineage system and anticipates the analysis of the system of the circulation of women. It explores the extensions of this privileged relationship between elder and younger, and more particularly—and it is here that it recalls the hypothesis of Francis Hsu—its metastases in the domain of authority. The stakes are not small.

Evans-Pritchard has shown us the refinement and also the fragility of the political organization of the Zandé; he has described for us the fratricidal rivalries, their difficult successions, the perpetual *remise en question* of the position of the prince in respect to that of the brother or the uncle. But what is the law of these Florentine struggles?

First some words on Zandé and Nzakara society. Filiation is patrilineal and land is unowned. A royal clan—Bandia in the west, Vungara in the east—forms a noble class which is dominant and constitutes the framework of the state. Kingdoms make and unmake themselves. The ancient, egalitarian lineage system has given way to a differentiated system where one lineage is no longer equal to another, and where one clan is no longer equal to another. The kinship system manifests, in itself, a greater permanence. This interests us chiefly because of what the Bandia have been able to make of it. The fact is that they have reworked the ancient lineage system to their personal advantage and in the same act have destroyed it. At the same time that they accepted the language of their mothers, they accepted their patterns of alliances; in Nzakara country the rules of kinship and rules of alliance hold for all, dominant and dominated. But the Bandia knew how to take advantage of these rules.

We will first set forth the kinship terminology along with some norms of behavior. We will then go on to study the significant characteristics of this terminology. The following study was written in 1958.

I. Terminology and Norms of Behavior

Nzakara terminology expresses, if we are to accept a standard distinction, a "complex" system of kinship which restricts itself to defining the circle of kin, reserves to dotted lines the determination of who are to be allies, and abandons to other mechanisms the determination of spouses. Hence we find no positive rules of marriage, no prescribed unions: only unions that are prohibited. We will treat successively the kin group, the consanguines, and those affines who are partners in marriage exchange, and then those related through matrimonial alliance. The terminology will be presented in diagrams, each diagram exploring one term or a group of terms. Terms of possible substitution are included in the scheme.

THE PARENTS *(à-gumi)*

First we will examine a fundamental opposition between elder and younger.

Diagram 10.1.

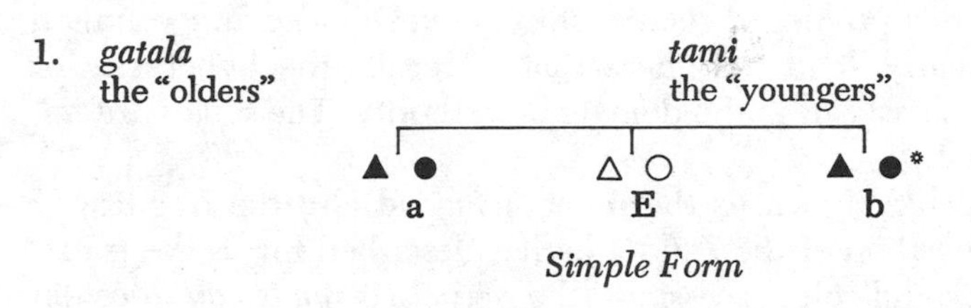

Simple Form

a = older brother, older sister
b = younger brother, younger sister

* *dịⁿlạ̀* if it concerns a last born, a youngest in *stricto sensu.*

The opposition does not establish itself except between individuals of the same sex (cf. Diagram 10.16 below).

Diagram 10.2.

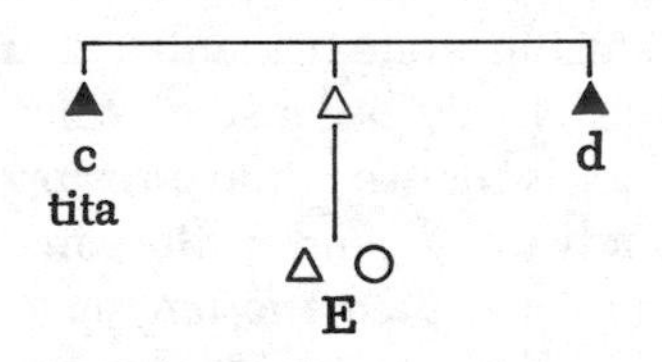

Complex Form

c = older brother of father; *gatalabe-bùba*
d = younger brother of father; *tami-bùba*

Diagram 10.3.

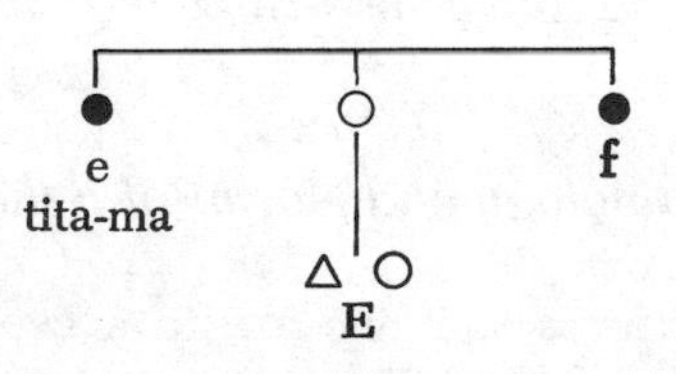

Complex Form

e = older sister of the mother (mother's older sister); *gatalabe-ma*
f = younger sister of mother (mother's younger sister); *tami-ma*

The older ones are the "pride," the "forehead" of the lineage; the younger ones form the "substance," the "body."

Diagram 10.4.

2. *ba* (for Ego: *bùba*)
the "fathers"

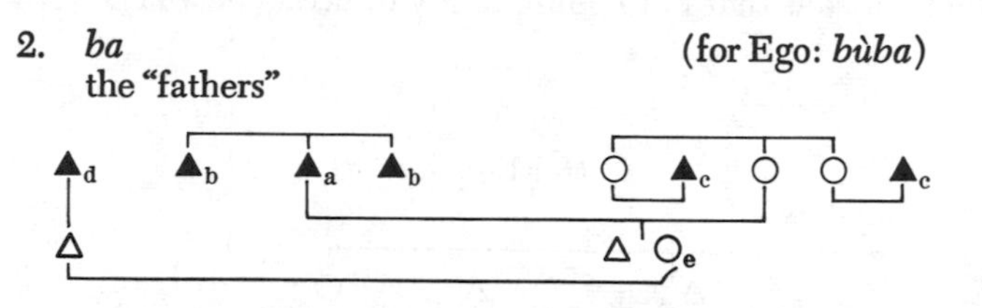

a = father (the more precise term: *ba-vùngù-è*)
b = brother of father
c = husband of the mother's sister, and by extension if Ego is female
d = the father of the husband (cf. 3e)

The father/son relationship involves reserve and respect down to open hostility when the son attains adult age. To a certain extent it can be assimilated into the elder/younger relationship.

Diagram 10.5.

3. *na* (for Ego: *ma*)
the "mothers"

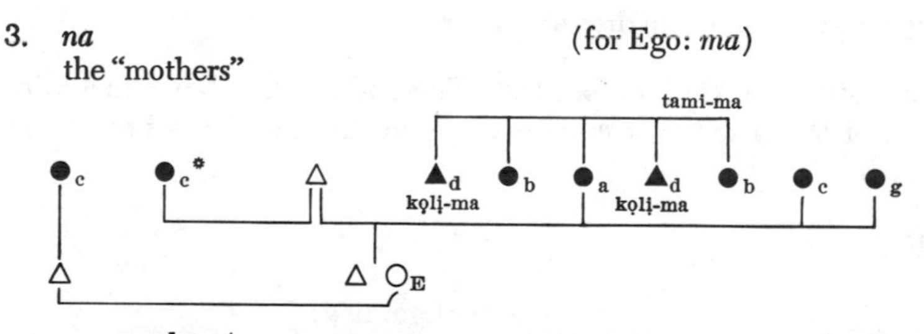

a = mother (more precise term: *na-vùngù-è*)
b = sister of the mother (Diagram 10.2)
c = wife of the father (other term: *da-bùba*), no matter what her rank and until the day that Ego inherits her (only then will he be able to call her *da-mì* on the condition that he will take her as his wife in his turn)
d = brother of the mother (cf. 7B)

By Extension:
e = the mother of the husband (cf. 2d), if Ego is female
f = all the married women of Ego's lineage, on the condition that they are not old enough to have engendered his mother (*contra*, cf. 5)
g = by courtesy, the father's wife, younger than the mother of Ego but older than himself

* When Ego is still a child or, if he has become adult, on condition of being older than the mother of Ego.

Marriage is prohibited between Ego and his mothers, except in case of inheritance. The adulterer of the father's wife is the classic adulterer in a good number of Nzakara tales; a Zandé proverb says: "He who says 'it's delicious' has already tasted of the dessert [of the wife] of his father" (Bervoets 1952: prov. 74).

Ma refers in fact to all the maternal kin: *Mī nà no k̀á s'a-ma zò,* I am going to my "mother," means that I am going to my in-laws (cf. 14a).

Diagram 10.6.

4. *bạsị* (for Ego: *bạsị-e*)
   The "sons" and "daughters"

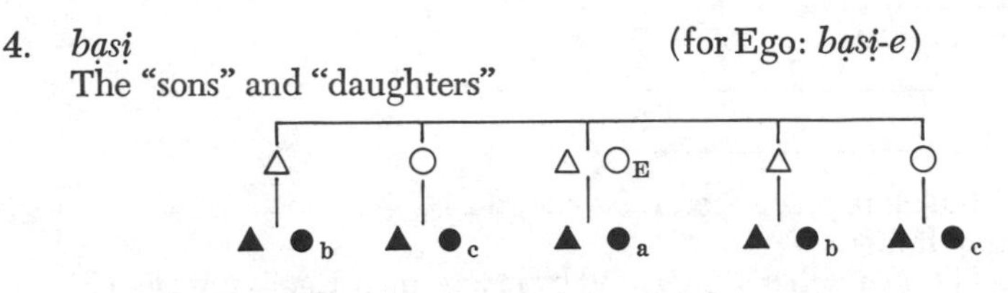

a = son, daughter
b = son, daughter of the brother (if Ego is female, she will call them more precisely *bạsị kọwị́-é*)
c = son, daughter of the sister (if Ego is male he will call them more precisely *bạsị kọwị́-é*)

By compounding one will say:
da-bạsi-e: spouse of the son of the sister
kumbâ-bạsi-e: spouse of the daughter of the sister
à-bạsị-gụ̀de b'e or *a-tìté*: children of a, b, or c

Marriage is strictly forbidden between Ego and all the above, including the daughter of the sister (if Ego is male) and the son of the brother (if Ego is female).

Diagram 10.7.

5. *tita* (for Ego: *tìt'é*)
   the "grand"
   the "little"

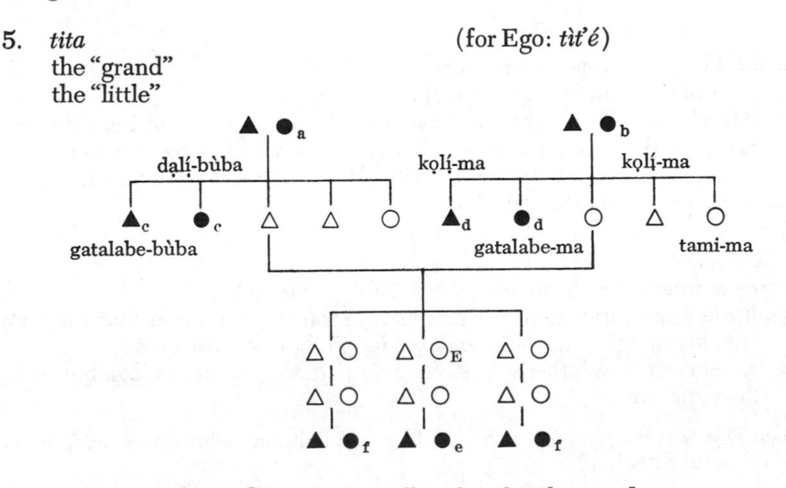

a = paternal grandparents, as well as their brothers and sisters
b = maternal grandparents, as well as their brothers and sisters (more precise term: *titá-da-mì* vocative)

c = older brother (and sister) of the father (*tìta* is rarely used in reference to the older sister of the father; it is preferred to call her dạlị́-bùba, *infra* 7Bb)
d = older sister (and older brother) of the mother
e = grand-children
f = grand-children of the brother or of the sister

By extension:
g = all the married women of the lineage of Ego which are old enough to have engendered his mother (*contra* cf. 3)

Diagram 10.8.

6. *bạsị-na* (for Ego: *bạsị-ma*)
the "brothers" and "sisters"
the "cousins"

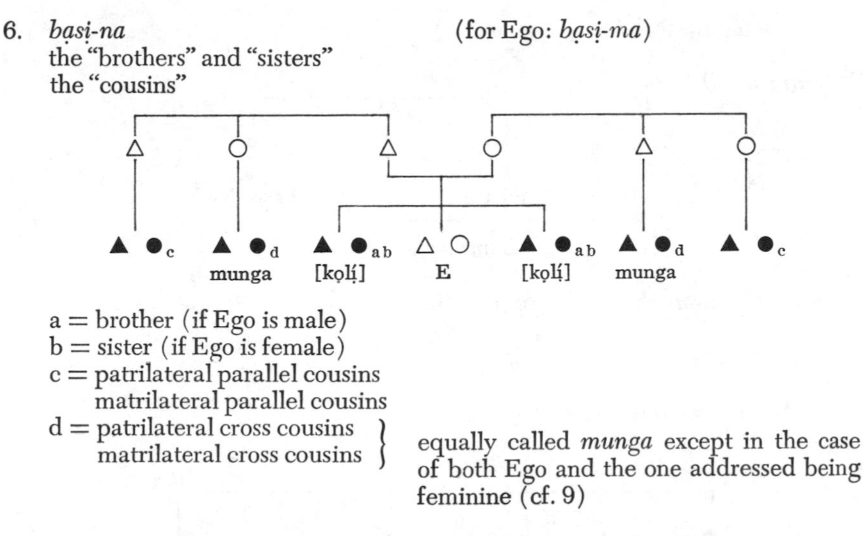

a = brother (if Ego is male)
b = sister (if Ego is female)
c = patrilateral parallel cousins
matrilateral parallel cousins
d = patrilateral cross cousins
matrilateral cross cousins } equally called *munga* except in the case of both Ego and the one addressed being feminine (cf. 9)

Marriage is prohibited between *all* the *bạsị-na*. Familiarity and joking are permitted among *certain* of these, the *munga*.

THE PARTNERS IN THE EXCHANGE OF WOMEN

We will bring together under this rubric, with a purely analytical intent, the kinship terms by which kinsmen and those allied to them through the exchange of women mutually refer to each other. We propose to analyze this series of terms, beginning with the primary consanguineal relationship between opposite sexes (the brother-sister relationship) to which the Nzakara nomenclature gives a particular distinction. This relationship thrusts us immediately into the heart of the exchange—first into the exchange of sisters, the model of which every Nzakara carries in his head and the inconveniences of which he will try continually to escape. The only veritable alliance (*kòbè*) is one that escapes the strict conditions as well as the easements of this sister exchange: one, in other words, that does not create debtors who become creditors by the very fact of their debt. We therefore enumerate the following:

Diagram 10.9.

7. The reciprocal sexes: the brother/sister relationship

kọlí (for Ego: *kọwị́-é*)
dạlị́
the "reciprocals"

A. *To the generation of Ego:*

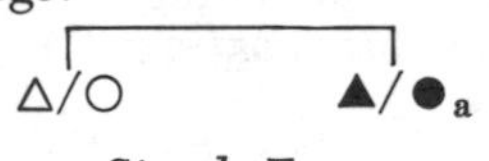

Simple Form

a = sister, brother (reciprocal terms)

Diagram 10.10.

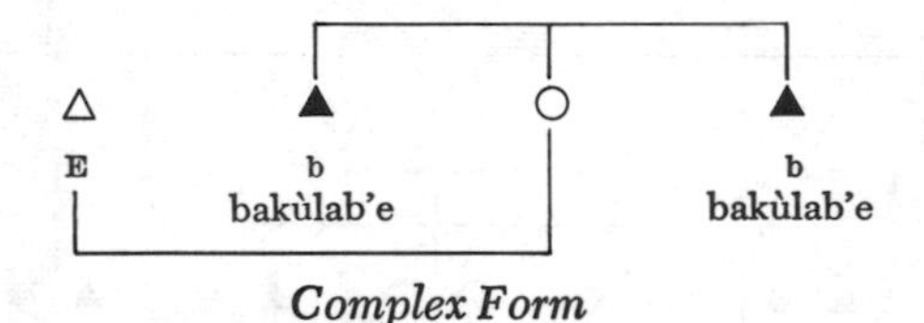

Complex Form

b = *kolị́-da-mì*, the brother of my wife

Diagram 11.11.

B. *To the previous generation:*

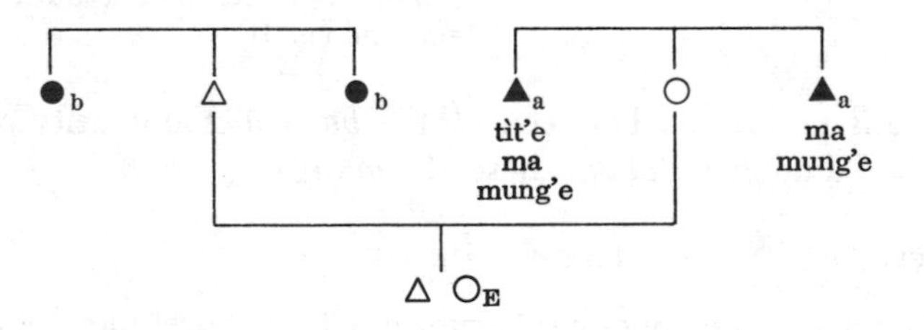

a = brother of my mother: *kọlí-ma*
b = sister of my father: *dạlị́-bùba*

Kọlị́ is essentially the object, the "reason for the exchange." It is my sister that I give in order to acquire for myself a wife, the sister which my father has given in order to acquire a wife; *kọlí-ma* is he who has given his sister to my father, who thereby made it possible for me to be born.

The brother of the mother enjoys three, or even four, different terms. *Kọlị́-ma* is the most frequent; then *ma*, literally "my mother," especially when Ego wishes to stress the consanguinity between this uncle and his mother; *mung'e* (cf. 10), even though this term is "incorrect"; and lastly, *tìt'é* if the maternal uncle is older than Ego's mother or if, without being older, he is nevertheless an older son. This last and "incorrect" term is frequent in common usage to the point of supplanting that of *kọlị́-ma.* It tends to assimilate the brother of the mother to the paternal relatives and, paradoxically, this tendency appears strong due to the fact that such an assimilation is clearly impossible from anyone's point of view—as if the language were such that any risk of confusion is, in the last analysis, excluded. In the same manner the maternal uncle will often call Ego *bạsị-e* or *bạsị kọwị́-é.* Even here the order of birth is not indifferently treated.

In contrast, the sister of the father is the object of only one kinship term, *dạlị́-bù̀ba,* the term *tìta,* in the case where she is older (*supra* 1c), being little used for her. *Dạlị́-bù̀ba* is literally "the woman who sleeps at the head of the bed of my father" (*lị* = head, head of bed) (cf. *infra* 12).

Sexual relations between brother and sister of noble rank do not seem to have been absolutely prohibited. We must be satisfied with this imprecise formulation which does not even distinguish and settle shares between legal right and fact. Many authors writing on the Zandé have mentioned the absence of such a prohibition among the Vungara.

Diagram 10.12.

8. The brothers-in-law: the husband of the sister/brother of the wife relationship

bakù̀la (vocative: *bakù̀lab'e*)
the "in-laws"–between two men; Ego is, therefore, male.

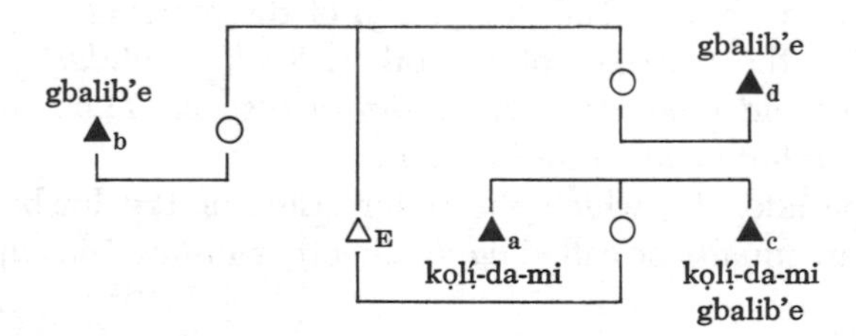

a and c = brother of the wife
b and d = husband of the sister

These two men are linked by the alliance (*kòbè*): he who gives and he who receives. The "in-law" is essentially the man who has given me his sister, *the man whom I fear.* He himself may, if he so wills, refuse the exchange or ruin the marriage. *One owes him the respect that one gives to the powerful.*

The term *bakù̀la,* in its daily usage, designates mostly the brother of the wife (a, c) as well as the husband of the younger sister (d); more rarely it designates the husband of the older sister (b).

This relationship will be inverted in Diagram 10.13, then reworked and generalized in Diagram 10.21.

The paradox must be noted in which all except the older brother of the wife may be called *gbali* (cf. *infra* 13c and d). The complement of the paradoxical terms will be found under 9a.

Diagram 10.13.

9. The mutually responsible (*les solidaires**)
waⁿlí† (for Ego: *waⁿlíb'e*)
the "in-laws"—between two women; Ego is, therefore, female.

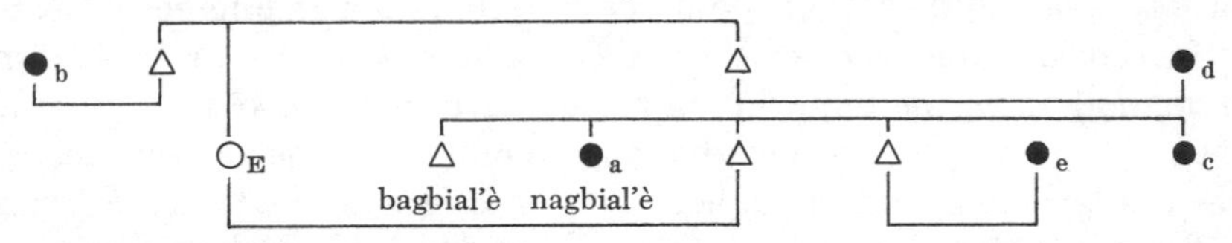

a and c = sister of the husband
b and d = wife of the brother
e = wife of the younger brother of the husband

* This term has no English equivalent. It signifies something like "reciprocally," "dependent," "answerable for one another."
†These relationships are classified by the Nzakara in the category *doobá* (cf. *infra* 13). The basis of this assimilation will become apparent in Diagram 10.24. In classifying it here, for the sake of analysis, we wish to emphasize the complementarity between the relationships under headings 8 and 9.

Diagram 10.13 is the same as Diagram 10.12, but made up of the opposite elements. The relationships are therefore inverted (cf. 14). The terms of this relationship are the two given women who are linked by the marriage alliance (*kòbè*). The dissolution of the marriage of the one can put in question the marriage of the other. *Such a solidarity permits all kinds of joking and removes all necessity of respect. Their mutual affection cannot help but be of mutual benefit.*

Note the paradox by which the older sister of the husband (Ego is female, 9a) can equally be called *nagbia*, mother-in-law (cf. *supra* 8b, c, d).

Diagram 10.14.

10. The cross-cousins: the son of the father's sister/son of the mother's brother relationship (mungate) *munga* (for Ego: *mung'e*)
cross-cousins

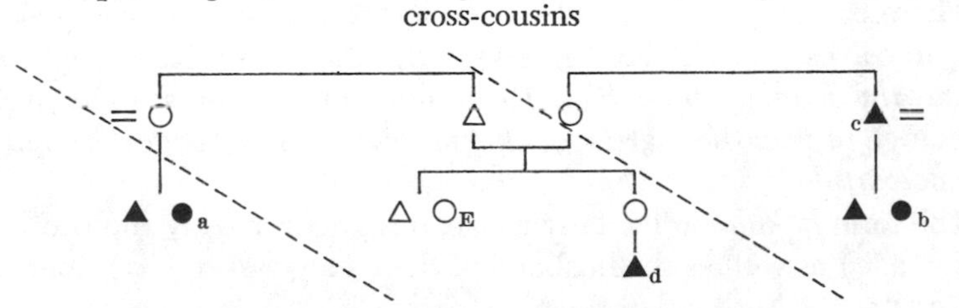

a = son, daughter of the mother's brother (matrilateral cross cousin; cf. 6d)
b = son, daughter of the father's sister (patrilineal cross cousin; cf. 6d)
c = brother of the mother (maternal uncle; cf. 7B)
d = son of the sister (uterine nephew)

The cross-cousin is the offspring of the sister exchange. He is the person with whom one banters, with whom joking is permitted, but with whom marriage is prohibited.

Moreover, it does not suffice to say that joking or insulting is permitted between cross-cousins. In fact, it is positively expected, and to refrain from it is a sign of ill will or evil intent. In meeting, one begins to converse in this manner:

Mo ã lě? Bạsị kusá! Bạsị nikè na nyã!

"Are you there? Son of a beast! A son born out of the vulva of the mother of a wild beast!" Only then does one begin the conversation.

The same "insults" can be extended by the *munga* to the members of his mother's clan, and reciprocally so, on the condition that the *munga* is known as such.

The same characteristics are attached to certain relationships with other clans, to the extent that ancestors of these clans were themselves *mungate*. But time has worked here in such a way that only some of the historical relationships have been retained in the collective memory. It is thus that the vou-Kpata lineages are the *munga* of Nguèzo because Koudou had taken a wife Nguèzo; and that the vou-Siolo are the *munga* of the Digo because the mother of the Siolo was Digo; and the vou-Ngbanda are the *munga* of vou-Mbon, the Bodengué the *munga* of the Ligui, and so on. It is not impossible that a certain form of preferential marriage formerly existed between clans or lineages *munga*.

The *mungate* does not prevail between women; Ego, a woman, calls her cross-cousin *bạsị-ma* and not *mung'e*. As do the two preceding kinship terms, the *mungate* clearly expresses a rule of matrimonial alliance.

THE ALLIES (*à-bakùla,* literally the Like-Which-Are-Different)

From here on the system of kinship terminology overlaps with that of the system of behavior. A remarkable fact is that there is no term for sister-in-law, the sisters of one's wife; they are either mothers-in-law or accomplices (*à-dòòbá*). We will see why below.

Diagram 10.15.

1. *kumba* and *da*
   "husband" and "wife"

   A. Simple form (for Ego):

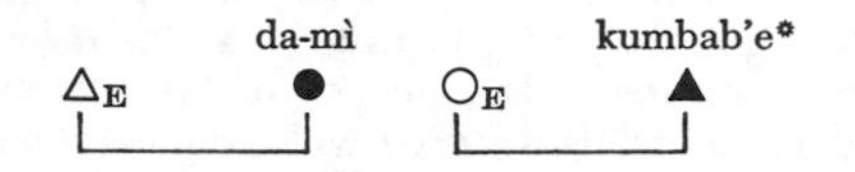

* Term of reference only, except in cases of great intimacy. Formerly the wife addressed her husband as "my lord" or "my father."

Among wives, one finds the opposition between the first and the last arrived: *gatala-da-mì*, my first wife, chronologically the first; *mvògó-da-mí*, my new wife, she who has just arrived. But if one cannot change the order in which brothers and sisters are born, it is permissible, on the other hand, for each husband to establish a rank among his wives. The distinction will be important, therefore, between *na-lá-te*, the mistress of the household, she who commands the house, and the *dwèkaná*, the preferred wife.

The first wife enjoys a privileged status. She alone is chosen not by her husband but by his father, and acquired by him in order to establish his son. She seems to have exercised certain particular functions[2] and benefited from the privilege of never being able to be repudiated or sent away.[3] In a household of two or three wives, it is the first wife who is mistress of the house, even though it is not inconceivable that these functions may have devolved onto the second or third wife. Among chiefs and those with many wives the nomenclature is more complicated and the role of mistress of the household, *na-lá-te*, is entirely autonomous. It is in her that the husband confides, it is often in her house that he maintains his most precious possessions: money, medical remedies, etc.[4] Co-wives mutually call themselves *iwàb'e*.

Diagram 10.16.

B. By compounding, for Ego:

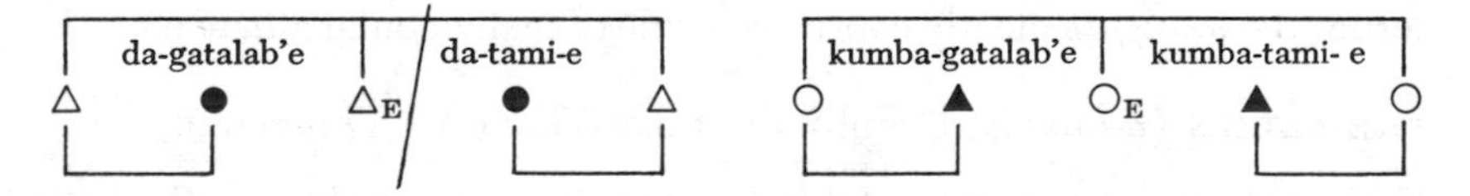

Remember that the son regularly calls the young wives of his father *da-bùda* (cf. 3c).

2. Lotar mentions, in regard to the Zandé, her permanent service to the ancestors and her lighting of the first fire in a newly founded village, "Polygamie et mariage Zandé," *Congo* 1925 (1):576.

3. *Ibid.* "If she fails to perform her duties she must be killed." Actually she is exiled to some distant village.

4. By way of comparison we recall Lotar's description (*ibid:* 574 and "Le Mariage Zandé," *Congo* 1926 (1): 730-36). He distinguishes between wives and women of the harem. Among the wives: (1) *Na-gbiya* (for the wife of the chief), *na-irá-kpwolo* (for any other), the first wife, mistress of the household; (2) *Na-gbindi,* the cook, the trustworthy wife; (3) the *à-gili,* the young favorites; (4) the *ti-be-na-gbiya,* also expressed as *de-guḍe,* those who are under the direction of the mistress, occupied in domestic tasks; (5) the daughters of chiefs, married with political intent, of equal rank to that of the mistress. Among the women of the "harem": (1) the *à-degbere,* the dancers; (2) the *à-kàngà,* the captives. See Evans-Pritchard, 1957: 701+ for the court of Gbudwe, a thousand kilometers away from the court of King Bangassou.

Diagram 10.17.

12. *gbia* (for Ego: *bagbial'è, nagbial'è*)
the "fathers-in-law" and
the "mothers-in-law"

I. Ego is male

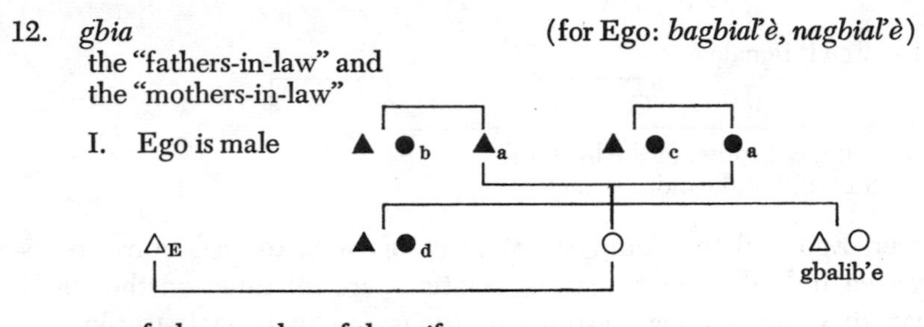

a = father, mother of the wife
b = brother (sister) of the wife's father
c = brother (sister) of the wife's mother
d = *older* brother (sister) of the wife

Diagram 10.18.

I. Ego is female

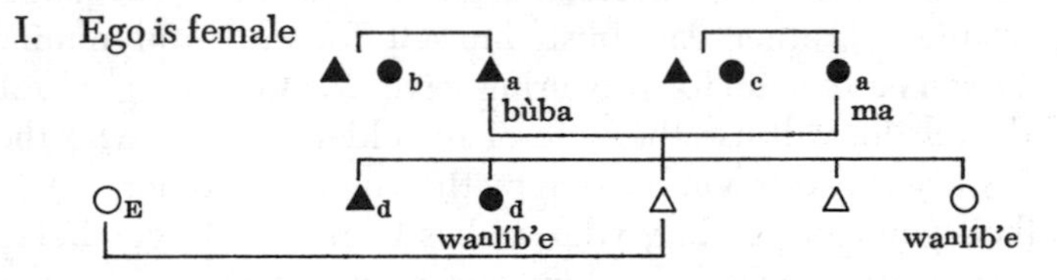

a = father, mother of the husband
b = brother (sister) of the husband's father
c = brother (sister) of the husband's mother
d = *older* brother (sister) of the husband

Once again we see here the reintroduction of the rank ordering of birth. Only the older brothers and sisters of the spouse have the right to be called "mother-in-law" or "father-in-law." To each and every one is due the greatest respect. Sexual relations are prohibited with all of them. One says of Ego and his mother-in-law *ko pì ná taka lị ko*, "she sleeps at the head of his bed." There is a Zandé proverb: "One does not fart into the eyes of one's mother-in-law" (Bervoets 1954: prov. 80). To show disrespect to your mother-in-law in 1958 would still cost you, before the king's court, a heavy fine.

Diagram 10.19.

13. *gbali* (for Ego: *gbalib'e*)
the equals or accomplices

I. Ego is male

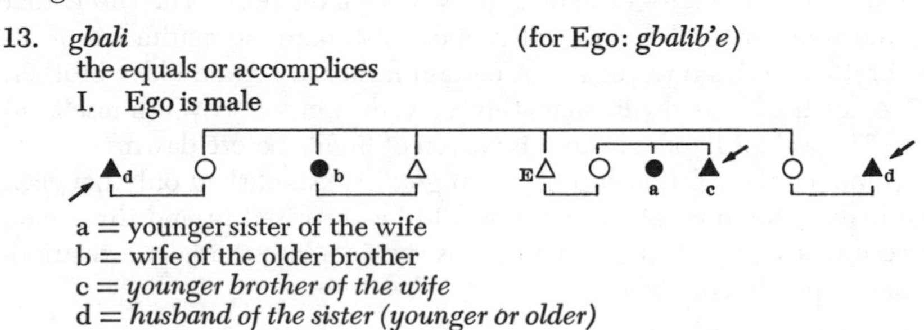

a = younger sister of the wife
b = wife of the older brother
c = *younger brother of the wife*
d = *husband of the sister (younger or older)*

Diagram 10.20.

II. Ego is female

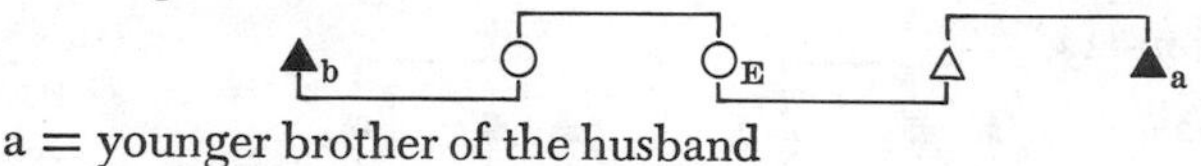

a = younger brother of the husband
b = husband of the older sister

Between Ego and the younger sisters of his wife the relations are especially free and affectionate. Sexual relations are tolerated on the condition that they remain clandestine, in the same way as between Ego woman and the younger brothers of her husband. They are obliging personages as well, accomplices of Ego, one might say. Of Ego and his *gbali* one will say *ko pì tí moⁿló ndo-ko*, "she sleeps at the end of his foot."

Let us take some concrete situations.

a. When a wife of an older brother has been gained in exchange of a sister, the younger brother can push himself forward and remind his brother that sisters are made for procuring wives for the younger brothers. In case of default he will use the wife of his elder brother, who thereby eliminates any urgency of revindication by the younger brother.

b. A well-off younger brother, who wishes to remain in good standing with his older brother, may offer him one of his most beautiful wives, sometimes even a pregnant wife. He is not, for all that, cut off from her, on the condition that their relationships are no longer public. The woman thus recognizes two brothers as husband.

c. A father or an older brother may fall sick. His wife, far from abandoning him, will take care of him, but will pass her nights with the younger brother and will manage the household for all.

It is important to note that such practices prevail only among brothers who get along well. If that is not the case, these relations are then pure and simple adultery. Nowadays the younger must pay compensation; formerly his older brother would have had the right to kill him—for if it is not suitable to hate one's brother, it is not prohibited to kill him under certain circumstances. If he is only irritated, the elder will never again share a chicken or a goat with his younger brother. If he is gravely offended, the father or the elder brother can legitimately decide for his life, and only a voluntary exile or flight will save his head. The rub is that often the younger brother does not properly estimate the sentiments of his older brothers in his own regard. A certain father, a certain elder brother, who today holds goodwill, may this very evening discover himself insulted. The web of Bandia history is woven of flights before dawn.

In principle the relationship between *gbali* is established only between individuals of the opposite sex; one would be surprised to find three men figured under I (Ego being a male). It is considered essentially a relationship of complicity (*doobá*).

14. Recapitulation of allies ("in-laws") of the same generation as Ego

Let us remember that the term *bakùla* (a) writ large, designates *all allies*, whether it be of Ego's generation or of the previous generation; "fathers-in-law" and "mothers-in-law" are also *bakùla*. *Mí ná nò ka s'à-bakùla-b'e zò*, "I am going off to my family-in-law"; (b) taken in its more restricted sense, is used frequently only for three relationships of this diagram (Ego being male): older brother of the wife (1), younger brother of the wife (6), and the husband of the younger sister (5).

Let us translate, following common usage, the opposition between elder and younger by a progression from left to right. Let us first examine the relationships of the same sex, then of the opposite sex. After a certain number of permutations we obtain the following schemes. (All of the individuals written in black are mutually *bakùla*, allies, of the same generation as Ego; substitution terms have been carefully inserted.)

We will not study here the consequences resulting from the rupture of a marital taboo. It suffices to say that the immediate sanction is the wrath of the ancestors, who will not delay in chastising the delinquents; sickness, deformity, paralysis, and stillbirth are the most frequent examples.

II. The Principal Characteristics of the System

It is now up to us to reassemble the separate threads of the analysis and sketch out the principal characteristics of the kinship system. That there is a system, a well knit one, must have already become apparent to the careful reader.

We shall analyze the system from the base of the couples of relationship 1 and 2 to find therein the law of the principles that regulate these two simple relationships and the combination of these principles. This combination is not without restriction: an independent variable is the survival and the growth of the lineage. These elements are a conscious objective in thoughts and acts. On the other hand, the mechanism of lineage fission seems itself to be governed by the principles of kinship. It would be a much greater error, therefore, to try to understand one without understanding the other.

The relationships we propose to stress are, above all, modes of consanguinity. Our interpretation shall be even more justified if it can demonstrate that the same principle which controls these consanguineal relations is also effectively at work regulating affinal relations. Affinal relations will thus furnish us the substance of our argument, particularly the relationships between *bakùla*, of which we have already seen the variety and which we have already tried to bring together in Diagram 10.21.

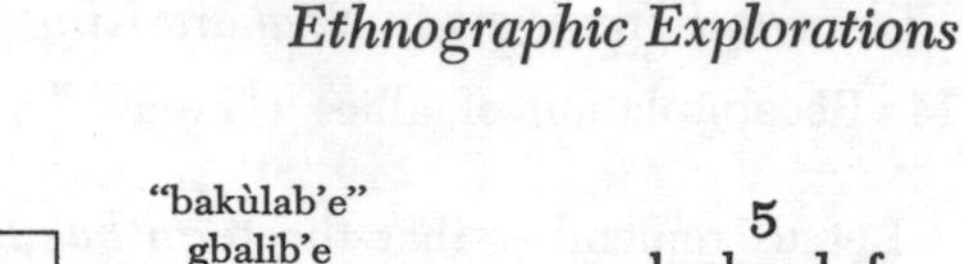

Diagram 10.21.

Left relative	Term (left)	Term (right)	Right relative
1 older brother of the woman	"bakùlab'e" bagbial'è	"bakùlab'e" gbalib'e	5 husband of the younger sister
2 husband of the older sister	["bakùlab'e"] gbalib'e	"bakùlab'e" gbalib'e	6 younger brother of the wife
3 older brother of the husband	bagbial'è gatala-kumbab'e	da-tami-e	7 wife of the younger brother
4 older sister of the wife	nagbial'è gatala-da-mì	kumba-tami-e	8 husband of the younger sister
9 wife of the older brother	wanlíb'e	wanlíb'e	13 younger sister of the husband
10 older sister of the husband	wanlíb'e nagbial'è	wanlíb'e	14 wife of the younger brother
11 wife of the older brother	gbalib'e da-gatalab'e	gbalib'e tami-kumbab'e	15 younger brother of the husband
12 husband of the older sister	gbalib'e kumba-gatalab'e	gbalib'e tami-da-mì	16 younger sister of the wife

The distinction between older and younger leads us to the first of these principles: The distinction founded on precedence (which is entirely relative) endlessly opposes "he who was born before" to "he who was born after," which in a certain manner subordinates the second to the first. This is a natural enough distinction when opposing brothers and sisters among themselves, but which invests the relationship of cousins with an abstract, and in a certain manner "civil," quality; precedence is then based on genealogy and is no longer chronological.

The terminology sufficiently indicates its importance. The best and simplest illustration is that one cannot have simply a sister or a brother among the Nzakara, but only "an older brother" or a "younger brother," an "older sister" or a "younger sister." In respect to this need for precision, for certitude concerning the rank of birth itself, I would be tempted to report a fact, apparently of another order, that has never received satisfactory explanation and that touches on the fate of twins. The birth of twins is not seen as an omen by Nzakara eyes; nevertheless, and almost as if by chance, one of the two almost always dies in the first fifteen days, without doubt the less robust, whether he be born first or second. It appears that nothing is done to prevent him from dying.[5] Is this an awareness of the difficulties to come for his posterity, which the society, informing the unconscious comportment of the mother, prefers to avoid? Meager is the testimony of the small number able to attest precedence in such a case later on. That precedence by a fraction of an hour can always be contested is a matter that certain Nzakara interpretations of Genesis clearly demonstrate.[6] It is precisely the same flimsy precedence that the white man claims in respect to the black man in order to justify his domination of the world.

How is this opposition translated within the Nzakara society? Within consanguinity, by the creation of a degree of supplementary kinship, it creates a distance which commands respect. The alternate term *tìt'é* (cf. 5) for the older brothers and sisters of one's father and mother clearly illustrates the logic of this principle. On first appearance a supplementary term does not seem necessary, particularly since the brother of the mother can already be called by three different terms (cf. 7B): *kọlị́-ma*, *ma*, and *mung'e*. If he is the eldest, the term *tìt'é* is added to it and it is often used. It has the effect of transferring the brother of the mother into the class of the "old ones" (*aïeux*), while the younger brother remains in the class of "mothers." The same mechanism transforms the brother of the father, called *bùba*, my "father," into "old one" (*aïeul*, *tìt'é*, if he is older). Moreover, these two terms pertain less to the position of Ego in respect to these personages than to those of his father and mother. The Nzakara will tell you, in fact, that all younger brothers consider their older siblings as "fathers and mothers." In the first degree of consanguinity the terminology admittedly does not express this important nuance except in a relaxed usage. But at the second degree the principle finds its full expression by transferring to the third degree the elder brother of the father. If the younger brother must consider his older brother his father, there is nothing more normal than that his son should consider this same elder brother as his *grandfather*.

At the heart of consanguinity this principle of subordination exercises its specific action, transforming into significant distinctions the contrast of

5. Zandé parallels may be found in Lagae 1926:173; *ngbandi* parallels in Tanghe 1926 and 1930.

6. Genesis XXV:20-28; XXVII:1, 4, 21-29 (Esau and Jacob).

relative precedence between individuals. When we consider the affinal relations we will find it once again at work. The consequence of its action is curious: it quite simply eliminates the sisters-in-law.

Let us examine Diagrams 10.17 and 10.18. We see individuals in the role of "mothers-in-law" if they are the older, but sweethearts in the literal sense of the word if they are the younger. In the same way, brothers-in-law become comrades in pleasure, scorning the conventions. Clearly, we find ourselves with a conflict of norms. Does this mean a conflict of roles? Let us take up the analysis step by step.

1. GENERAL NORMS

Generally custom disapproves of any diversion with another man's wife: "Husbands of young wives do not enjoy young fellows" (*à dì à-ma^{n}lò ví nga n'a-pàlàngá du*). But which husbands and which young fellows?

2. SUBSTITUTE NORMS

The general norm is broken by a usage which finds its force in the actual kinship structure. "Everybody knows that it is fitting for anyone to enjoy the wealth of the chief which he serves." The oldest brother is always considered chief, the "forehead," the "pride" of his younger brother, who is nothing but the "substance" or "body." The elder has particular obligations in regard to his younger brother, who is also his subject. There is thus a risk of conflict between the two norms. A study of the following cases will indicate that there is, in effect, a risk of conflict. In a similar case, *custom gives precedence to the substitute code.*

3. FIRST APPLICATION

a. How does a woman behave in respect to the older brothers of her husband, those whom she calls *bagbial'e*, "my father-in-law" (relation 12 IId, 3 of Diagram 10.21)? She owes them the most obedient respect. The elders become the "fathers" of her husband, hence "fathers" to herself.

b. How does a wife behave in respect to the younger brothers of her husband, those whom she calls *gbalib'e*, "my obliging friend," and again *taka bàngó*, "end of the branch" (relation 13 IIa, 15 of Diagram 10.21)? First they are subjects of her husband; by identification (with her husband), she considers them as her subjects. Therefore she may take her pleasure with them. Second, they are the possessions of her husband, just as she is their possession; *ẽ b'o sú ò*, it is a thing which belongs to you, which is in your "hand." Thirdly they are in line to inherit her, to finally acquire her by line of succession; she considers them as her future husbands. Therefore she can permit herself to have sexual relations with them as a matter of "future right." They do no more than use their lineage right in making use of the wealth of their "chief."

Such a situation does not generally present itself except under certain circumstances, which have been discussed under No. 13 above. How is such permissiveness described and justified by the interested parties and by others? The wife will say: The younger brother is young, he is attractive. The younger will assert the fact of consanguinity that joins him to his elder brother. The older brother will assert that his kin must be rewarded. And as to the others, they will from now on refrain from mentioning the names of the two "husbands" of the wife; they will be content to refer to her simply by the name of their clan, they will say—and it is a mark of respect—it is a vou-Kpata wife, or the wife of a vou-Loumani, just as the French say "X, an Untel wife" (femme Untel). Lineage consciousness concords with the modesty involved in the plural use of names.

4. SECOND APPLICATION

a. How does a man behave in regard to the older sisters of his wife (relationship 12 Id, 4 of Diagram 10.21)? The man owes respect to the elders of his wife, whom he calls "mothers-in-law (*nagbia*).

b. How does a man behave in regard to the younger sisters of his wife (relationship 13 Ia, 16 of Diagram 10.21)? The behavior is the same as in the first application above. The man may joke, even have sexual relations, with his wife's younger sisters, whom he will call "comrades," his "obliging friends" (*gbali*) or yet, by a more expressive formula, his "ends of the branch" (*taka bàngó*).

This expression bears analysis. *Bàngó* is the tree whose fibrous bark, beaten and softened, is used to fabricate the traditional men's loin cloth among the Nzakara. *Taka* are the high branches, the crown of the tree. When the tree is beautiful and vigorous one may remove the bark, not only of the trunk, but also from the large branches, "which come after." Such is the string of sisters of a wife who comes from a large family. He who acquires the trunk can eventually enjoy the branches. If certain wives are angry about it, others are indifferent. Custom prohibits it, but doesn't take offense.

All that which lies "above" the wife demands respect. All that which lies "below" the wife permits (and demands) "accommodation." But, as has been seen, this accommodation is never so by formal right. As the Nzakara say, "One has seen two brothers get along with one wife, one has seen two sisters marry the same man. That's the business of people who get along well with each other."

5. EXCEPTION

"When a child has acquired a large share, the adult shares it with him" (*ligà sú nâ du ná be gụde ni yágbà, ba-kumbá yá kiti lìli*). Nevertheless, it happens that an older *brother* takes liberties with the wife of one of his younger brothers (*da-tami-e*, 7 of Diagram 10.21) and even impregnates her. "Chieftain's rights" (*ti gbenge*) prevail in this case. Here a *third norm* comes into question which overrules the preceding norms. In a similar case, *always exceptional*, it is always the older one who takes the initiative and the tacit agreement of the younger brother is always acquired.

6. COMPARISON OF THE PRECEDING APPLICATIONS

The meaning becomes clear if we compare couples 3/4 and 15/16 in Diagram 10.21. We are confronting "the Nzakara way," which omits the brother-in-law and sister-in-law. The terminology gives each Nzakara a clear choice: either a "father-in-law" or a "comrade"; either a "mother-in-law" or a "comrade." It finds its expression in two social attitudes, one of *extreme respect* or one of *extreme liberty*. The result is that the fault of the younger brother who takes the wife of his "elder" (his father, the elder brother of his father, his older brother) is much less serious than that of the elder who takes the wife of a "younger." [7] It is for having committed the latter that the Nzakara people and poets murmured against Bangassou the Small, who had culpable relations with the wife of his father's younger brother. Because he was the son of the older brother, he had thereby inherited those prerogatives and obligations. The respect that this uncle owed him had its counterpart in the respect he owed this uncle.

7. GENERALIZATIONS

"The blood of the calf never runs in the thigh" (*Kule mvụlụgbá fú nga kă mbósò du*). The fathers do not revere the son and do not succeed him. It is up to the elders to provide for the needs of the younger, but not the inverse. The corollary is evident; it is unsuitable for the fathers or elders to commit faults against the sons or the younger brothers. It is up to the former to speak to and counsel the latter; it would be scandalous for them to enjoy their wealth or their women.

These one-way privileges remind us of other ones. We know from a previous study the mechanism by which new lineages appear. We have seen that there are no true fissions, but slow growths of a new body, the minimal lineage, in the bosom of a father lineage, the maximal lineage. Just as all the members of the minimal lineage belong to the maximal lineage without the members of the second holding any rights over the first, the relationship between the older and the younger presents the same characteristics. A relationship of inclusion between consanguines constitutes the framework and the mainspring of the lineage system, as it does in the kinship system, so one can look for the model of the first in the second. This relationship socially expresses, by means of subordination, the structural conflict between consanguines. This appears to be one of the permanent traits of Nzakara society.

The distinction between brother and sister leads us to the second generalization: absolute distinction by sex—a natural division but once again

7. Cf. Zandé: "The wife of your subject is the wife of a powerful leopard" (Bervoets 1955: prov. 81).

one anchored in consanguinity. There is a single kinship term assigned to it, designating the consanguine of the opposite sex; reciprocity is included in the term itself.

This second distinction is complementary to the first. If addressing an individual of the same sex, the terminology will indicate if he is older or younger in respect to Ego, and only that. If addressing an individual of the opposite sex, the terminology will as immediately indicate this opposition, but to the exclusion of any indication of precedence.

The force of this distinction is clearly apparent in the field of affinal relations. Take for example the wife (Z) of the brother (Secundus) of the wife (Secunda) of Ego.

Diagram 10.22.

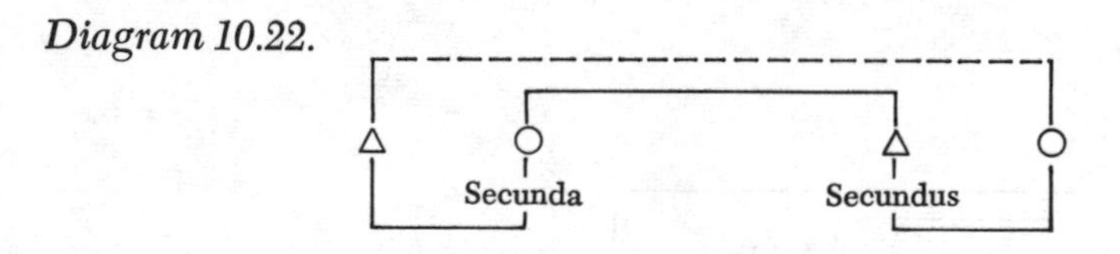

She will never become the wife of Ego, not even at the death of her husband. For one thing, Ego, being of another line, must not receive any benefits from the line of his wife's brother. But above all, say the Nzakara, "the blood, the genitalia, of a brother and a sister must not meet." But this concerns only the wife of a brother-in-law. The second restriction is of little significance, however, since the tie between Secundus and Secunda, which is the base of their relationship, separates them irrevocably.

The reason for the horror that overtakes the Nzakara in the face of any kind of commerce between Ego and the wife of his brother-in-law is illuminating: "Ego must behave vis-à-vis this woman as he would with his own sister." In other words, behind this opposition between sexes is revealed a matrimonial mode and a first principle—the exchange of sisters and the principle of reciprocity. In the above scheme, the dotted line is always "understood." It is the sister exchange that makes the distinction, in itself banal, between brother and sister; it is the principle of reciprocity that establishes the opposition of sexes in consanguineal relations.

We may well ask if and to what measure the Nzakara do practice or have practiced sister exchange. Their formation myth shows that it is a mental model and an ideal of justice constantly in their minds. The analysis of the kinship system and the system of alliances leads us to the same conclusion and, once again, presents a context of subordination at which certain members of the society seem to balk. Is it youngers or elders? It is to this same model of sister exchange that subjects refer to judge the conduct of their masters.

Numerous witnesses have reported that the Bandia, as well as the Vungara, are commonly suspected of having culpable relations with their sisters. What is there in such a suspicion but the expression of a people's covetousness, a resentment well suppressed, applied both to those princes who so rarely give away their sisters (cf. de Dampierre, *Poètes Nzakara* II: 34b, Vol. 11), preferring rather to give away female slaves, and to these same sisters who, if by chance are given away to a commoner, persist nevertheless in considering themselves free, free to take and not to be taken.

The same mental model of sister exchange explains the precautions the Nzakara society takes in that respect: precautions taken not because of principle but because of consequences for the survival of lineage. Indeed, in this particular case the female patrilateral cross-cousin and the female matrilateral cross-cousin become indistinguishable, in that the same woman bears both qualities.

Let us examine the following scheme, in which two men exchange their sisters:

Diagram 10.23.

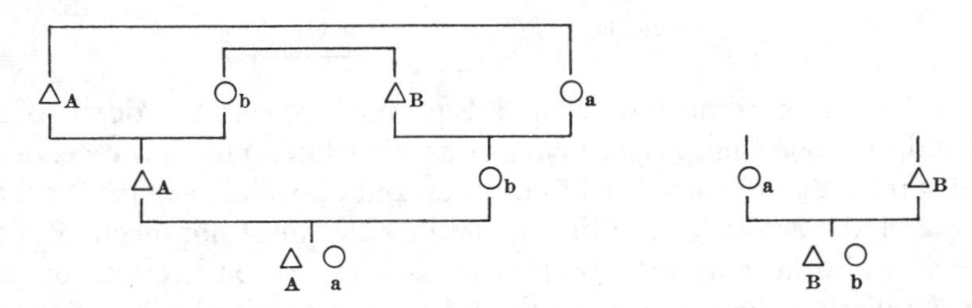

The children arising from this marriage, cross-cousins, may not contract marriage, either among the Nzakara or among the Zandé. Why do we have this interdiction when, in contrast to parallel cousins, they belong to two different lineages? It is because the equality of the transaction, so responsibly undertaken in the first generation, which was able to exclude all speculation over the future by making the one marriage the cause of the other (and reciprocally so), can no longer be respected at the third generation. The marriage of cross-cousins destroys, in the third generation, the equilibrium created by the principle of reciprocity. It is readily seen that the children born of a cross-cousin marriage belong to a single lineage A, that of the father. Lineage B in the exchange would find itself forever deprived of descendants as long as the system did not prescribe the alternating of sexes and did not make a second matrimonial couple, the inverse of the first couple, appear in each generation. In our scheme this is shown at the second generation. Only simultaneous alternation of cross-cousins would re-establish equilibrium.

The Nzakara society has not "chosen" this solution, and it refused the reiteration of the two inverse exchanges in each generation for the following reasons: first, it would have necessitated a positive prescription or injunction by which the society would have established the choice of the spouses, surely an incompatible condition for the mores of a hunting and warrior people who were in full expansion. Then a parallel restraint implies the repeating of the alliance with a single lineage of a single clan.

This is an appalling vision in a world where one needs to obtain as many allies as possible. The rules of alliance, as much politically oriented as kinship oriented, eliminate any risk of this kind. In a society in which the play of kinship is a delicate affair, where uncles and brothers, by the very structure of the system, bring you nothing but annoyances, the rules of alliance assure above all the maximization of allies. The prohibition of marriage between cross-cousins obviates forever the catastrophe represented by the repetition, among the same, of the exchange of sisters. It forces the lineages to conclude, in each union, a new alliance.

This prohibition of marriage between cross-cousins (that between male parallel cousins is taken as a matter of course) had escaped European observers. It is general, however, not only among the Nzakara and the Zandé but also, it appears, among the peoples conquered by them. Better yet, if one accepts the assimilation of not only the Kreich but also of the whole of the northern populations on the same meridians with the "Fertyt," it was long ago attested to by the remarkable observer and moralist El-Tounsy, who lived about 1808 in the court of the Sultan of Darfour. He wrote:

> These people have a remarkable custom in regards to matrimonial alliances. . . . Marriages among them never take place between close relatives; thus no one marries his daughter, nor his cousin, nor his maternal or paternal aunt, nor even a cousin. Nevertheless, in Islam, these last mentioned degrees of relationship are legitimate. Among the idolatrous populations of the southern Sudan, marriage is accepted only with those further removed in degree of relationship than the cousin. This custom, among a people so ignorant and deprived of all definite law, of all religious revelation, is a characteristic trait which merits attention, especially if one considers their daily life. For all go nearly nude, with almost no precautions taken for modesty's sake.
>
> . . . The Fertyt have no (in respect to the degree of legitimacy of unions) obligatory religious base, no legislative rules which direct them. By what manner of inspiration have they then established among themselves these conditions of legitimacy of marriages, in spite of all the suggestiveness of a carnal nature that they must encounter from their women whose charms are constantly exposed to view? There is something there of a surprising, extraordinary quality. It is neither ease nor well being which has led these people to impose an obligation of such a nature, which has led them to hold themselves to this social law, for they have nothing which renders life easy and sweet to other people.

El-Tounsy, in his wisdom, did not attribute this interdiction, which he did not understand, to any legislative act nor to economic necessity. But he did understand that it touched on the essence of this society.

The preceding considerations allow us to understand this characteristic of daily comportment by which one interdiction, in contrast with another, appears surprising: No Nzakara, Bandia or not, considers himself justified in marrying or having sexual relations with any woman considered "his mother" or with any woman belonging to the lineage of his mother. This interdiction, in so far as we have been able to ascertain, is strictly observed, while the interdiction concerning the women of the same clan as oneself, or even of the same lineage, is broken every time the material bond of kinship emerges out of the communal consciousness.

Sister exchange is an ancient model that has been actualized only when linked to a prohibition of cross-cousin marriage. In this manner not only the physical survival but also the political expansion of the lineage was assured. The substitution of modes of alliance other than sister exchange will permit certain lineages to add to this panoply the drive of a demographic expansion.

It now remains to examine how these two principles—that of subordination, which expresses itself in an opposition between older and younger, and that of reciprocity, which expresses itself in an opposition of sexes between brother and sister—combine or exclude each other. Let us consider these principles at work in the crucial domain of affinal relations.

If we accept the hypothesis of the model of sister exchange, we can abstract from Diagram 10.21 the fundamental ideas to which they refer. This diagram recapitulates the "in-laws,"—that is, the allies of the same generation as Ego. There we can readily discern four groups: givers of women, women given, parents-in-law, and "accomplices" (petit(e)s ami(e)s). Disposing of these groups according to their respective axies, we obtain the following:

Diagram 10.24.

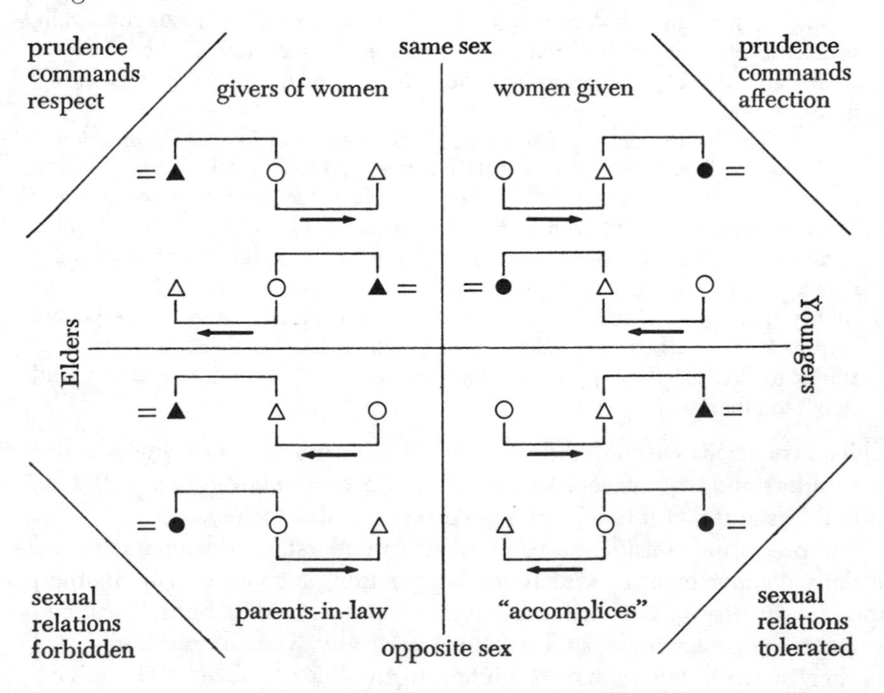

The upper part of the diagram recapitulates the relationships between individuals of the same sex. These relationships pass entirely by way of a brother/sister couple who clearly appear as the expression of affinity in the midst of consanguinity. Between givers of women prudence commands respect; they are the personages who owe each other too much (*se doivent trop*). Between women who have been given away, the same prudence calls for affection; who knows if the defection of the one won't endanger the marriage of the other?

The lower part recapitulates the relationships between individuals of the opposite sex. None of these relationships passes by way of a brother/sister couple. The principle of reciprocity is neutralized; it cedes its ground, in a manner of speaking, to the principle of subordination which gives to the opposition (between the party on the left and the party on the right of the diagram) much more assertiveness than in the preceding. Between people of the opposite sex, sexual practice constitutes the most severe test; it will be prohibited in respect to "parents-in-law," tolerated in respect to "accomplices." Nothing is more clear. In its own manner the diagram of brother-in-law resumes and symbolizes Nzakara kinship.

Diagram 10.24 is nevertheless only an abstraction, in the case of sister exchange, of Diagram 10.21. If we return to 10.21, we observe that in respect to 10.24 there are five anomalies, grouped as follows:

a. 1/5: *bagbia/gbali,* older brother of the wife, husband of the younger sister;
b. 2/6: *gbali/gbali,* husband of the older sister, younger brother of the wife;
c. 10/14: *nagbia,* older sister of the husband, for the wife of the younger brother.

These five terms are the terms of good usage, which are added to the usual terms. In themselves they do not weaken our schematization in 10.24. Nevertheless, we must take account of them; otherwise there is always the possibility of leaving the better part in obscurity. Let us try to sort out these anomalies.

First, we note that here *gbali* (5, 2, and 6) designate the relationships between man and man, while in the kinship terminology they apply to individuals of the opposite sex. This fact is not banal. Would they belong to the original system? It is a pregnant question which perhaps may lead us to the solution. It is a fact that sister exchange has hardly been practiced for a century. Let us suppose that these terms are the legacy of a later era. Diagram 10.24 would then express the situation as it was in the era t_1. The anomalies discussed under 14 (page 259) would express a situation, dated t_2, when the mutual exchange of sisters was becoming rare in order to make way for the simple reciprocal provision of women or the lending and furnishing of women against compensation. Let us examine this hypothesis.

Through such provision the relationship of couple 1/5 formally becomes a relationship of equals, though the participants are unequal by status; instead of two partners, both in turn givers and receivers of women, we now have only a giver and a receiver. The equality of the ancient pair of roles expressed itself in the reciprocal terms *bakùlab'e*. The inequality of the new pair expresses itself from here on by two non-reciprocal terms, *bagbial'e* and *gbalib'e*. These are the very terms by which the Nzakara indicate subordination (those of the *lower* part of Diagram 10.21). It would seem that to express this new inequality, the terminology found nothing better than to return to the ancient formula for indicating subordination, the opposition of precedence. He who lords it over another—the giver (donor) or "brother-in-law"—becomes "father-in-law," the term which connotes the maximum of superiority. In contrast, he who contracts an obligation, the beneficiary, sees himself assimilated from now on to "small friend," "accomplice," "the end of the branch," the term which connotes the minimum of inferiority.

The same solution does not work for the couple 2/6, because this relationship of elder/younger is the inverse of 1/5. The brother is younger than the sister. The donor is not the younger brother of the woman, but probably his father or another older brother. The bridewealth received from 2 probably will be given to the younger, so that he can in his turn procure himself a wife. But this time 2 has nothing to do with this. The decision is up to the chief of the younger. Husband of the older sister and younger brother of the wife maintain statuses passably equal. The opposition of precedence has no play here, there being no subordination by which to mark these two roles.

It remains only to explain why the older sister of the husband finds herself called mother-in-law. In t_1 a "solidarity" binds her to the wife of her younger brother. But in t_2, with the disappearance of the sister exchange, the older sister of the husband becomes the woman handed over whose dowery will perhaps serve to obtain a wife for the younger brother. In any case, the transaction remains the affair of the father or of the older brother, and it is to this latter that the older sister of the husband sees herself assimilated. The status becomes unequal between the two women, the first one shifting over to the category of mother-in-law; the couple 10/14 reminds one of couple 3/7, but for the sex of the older man.

If our hypotheses are exact, we can distinguish an ancient era, in which sister exchange constituted the primordial mode of exchange, from a condition less ancient, in which sister exchange gave way to a series of reciprocal provisions. The five anomalies for which our scheme 10.24 could not account refer to later tendencies, testimonies to a recent epoch in which the circulation of women had attained its maximum flexibility and diversity.

ELEVEN

WILLIAM H. NEWELL

Hsu and the External System

The general thesis of this paper is: Under what conditions does behavior content derived from relationships within a certain social group continue in a group of a different size or order? Does such behavior continue in the form of a psychological pattern, or does it continue in the form of external symbolic behavior, the "meaning" or justification of which has already been experienced in some form of action?

As an attempted answer to the first question, I should like to put forward a theory of levels of behavior. As an attempted answer to the second, I should like to show that Hsu's extreme characterization of Indian and Chinese society as being to some extent conflicting in content while being similar in structure (Hsu, 1963:47) is too extreme and really leaves unexplained more than it explains. Finally I would like to suggest a possible way of procedure using the idea of symbolic content.

First I wish to take three different forms of association in groups—pair groups, the elementary family, and larger social groups. The latter may be divided into those in which everyone may have face-to-face relationships and those which are bureaucratically organized, mostly units of over 800 people living or working together. In Professor Hsu's argument the kinship relations derived from the elementary family have certain attributes that may be extended to determine certain patterns of behavior in systems that are not primarily or necessarily familially oriented. These family attributes are apparently dyadic in the examples given in the *American Anthropologist* (Vol. 67, No. 3, June 1965, p. 638)—husband/wife, and so on—but even where one has a relationship like parents/son, the system can nevertheless be regarded as dyadic, for both parents, from an attributional point of view, have authority. Talcott Parsons *et al.* also shows that a unit even as small as a family can be regarded as having smaller subsystems consisting of pairs. Parsons shows that the attributes of the American family at least are partly derived from "the basic uniformity of the lines of structural differentiation" (1956:106). Hsu and Parsons are thus in fairly close agreement about the nature of the elementary family, except that Hsu goes much further in respect (a) to claiming that there is *one* dominant relationship (structure) which will have one group of dominant attributes (culture), (b) that the attributes from this dominant relationship will affect the attitudes and action patterns of attributes normally inherent to other relationships (in the elementary family) and (c) that these will in turn affect other relationships and action patterns outside of the system.

In this connection it perhaps should be mentioned that some attributes given by Hsu are essentially biological, such as sex, and others purely "structural," such as continuity; since continuity depends on some formal procedure having been taken previously, like marriage to the child's mother, or recognition of the son's status by being chief mourner at the father's funeral. In both cases some ceremony or action is required to reinforce the attribute outside the family. (There is a distinction between a legal family and an illicit family.)

I will here submit a chart to show the variability in content between the three groups in respect to size of unit, time of each separate group's life with the same members, and the number of relationships which can be handled at the same time. By "pair group" I mean the relationships between a mother and child as described by Parsons as a structural and not psychological group.

I think it is clear that there are quite fundamental differences in nature between these three groups, although the "larger social groups" possibly should be split into two, the very largest groups being bureaucratically organized. There seems a limit to the number of people one can know directly.[1]

There are three points I wish to make about this table:

1. Professor Hsu argues that in families with father/son, mother/son, and brother/cousin dominance the matricentric family (that is, the mother/child tie) is the basic unit, whereas in husband/wife dominated family there is "no real matricentric family as a start, since both parents come in at the beginning of the child's life." [2] Assuming this may be true (although in some husband/wife dominated families such as the English

1. It appears that in South China, when as a result of population increase villages increase in size to more than 600, that new villages tend to develop rather than the established villages tending to enlarge themselves (subject of course to the land being sufficient for subsistence). The same thing seems to be true also of the Punjab in India.

2. Modified report circulated by Hsu after Wenner-Gren symposium.

Table 11.1.

	Pair Groups	Elementary Family	Larger Social Groups
Number of relationships	Only 3 main types—Superior-inferior (parents/children); Sex (brother/sister; husband/wife); Instrumental or expressive	8 "basic" relationships, although more if older or younger brother/sister included	Extremely numerous
Time	Very short period before pair relationships become included in family system because of relative speed of physical growth	Cycle roughly between the birth of a female till she bears first child; After that the family deliberately self-destructive by virtue of incest taboo*	Continuous as long as "need" or "function," etc., keeps on
Size of unit	2 persons	Usually about 5 persons	Any size, but it appears that some change in formal structure takes place between about 300 and 800; Over this size some bureaucratic system apparently necessary

* Using Lévi-Strauss' argument on the family in Shapiro *Man, Culture and Society* (New York: Galaxy Press, 1960).

Bethnal Green group studied by Wilmott and others it seems fathers are not so important), it still does not follow that a pair relationship of mother/child can necessarily act as a model where more than two people are involved. In a pair relationship, the child has only the alternative of obeying or not obeying the mother, whereas in a threesome the child has the additional alternative of playing off one parent or one family member against the other. This is a different sort of technique, and the greater the number of members of the family living together, the more complicated the game that may be played.

2. Both the pair group and the elementary family have a limited and comparatively short life with the same members. Both these groups are basically self-destructive. But the rules used at each level have only a limited use at the higher level. Therefore the basic question is not so much to identify the dominant characteristics at each level, but to try to find what are the limiting features of each level that inhibit or prevent dominant characteristics becoming explicit. Hsu recognizes that at the family level some characteristics are dominant over others, but the identification of such dominance is made by cultural behavior at the wider level than the family rather than by an examination of actual behavior at each level. There are certain "model rules" at each level. An example of such a rule would be that one could not equally and with the same content obey two authorities (say, mother and father) if they should conflict on the same issue.

3. All known societies have groups with some continuity larger than the elementary family, although in many societies such larger groups use kinship-oriented behavior in order to conform. Anthropologists have tended to explain such behavior in terms of jural or behavioristic patterns. Yet the fact that kinship terms are used need not imply that in practice the actual model we should use should not rather be a bureaucratic corporation. I do not see any reason why Imperial Chemical Industries should not use entirely kinship terms between members in its operations if it wished to do so. I presume one reason why I.C.I. does not do so is because it feels it would not add to its efficiency in making profits, whereas perhaps some Japanese firms do believe the use of family terminology would do so. But the basic problem is rather the nature of profit-making bureaucracies in different societies than in the extension of family terminology and behavior to larger social groups. (I wish to modify this statement later in respect to the symbolic content of behavior.)

Our argument therefore is that the nature of the problem of the *form* of social behavior varies with the size of the group, the number of relationships, and the likelihood of the group continuing with the same membership units and perhaps with other factors. Since culture (in which I include Hsu's dominant attributes) is continuous, the particular continuity of the cultural pattern is limited by the form of social behavior at each level.

The next question with which I wish to deal is by what means are cultural forms continuous at each level? There seem to be two main ways of answering this question. The first way is by arguing that it is the same person who is at a different or the same stage of his life, a member of a matricentric group, a family, and a larger association. It is only natural therefore that behavior learned as a child should carry over into other forms of behavior. One psychologically tends to identify one's mother with all women or one's father with the head of a company. Even where family behavior is not explicit, it nevertheless lays down a primary pattern of relationships. This is what I would call the psychological explanation.

The second type of explanation would be to argue that immediately a particular way of behavior is observed by a human, the symbol of the thing perceived becomes an object in itself and the original stimulus, whatever it was, becomes of no importance in the new situation unless it continues. Thus in a pair situation at the birth of the baby, the mother/child becomes only a symbol in the mind of the actor once the two become physically separated from each other. The use of identical words cannot alter the fact that the situation is different. In the Hawaiian generational kinship system, for example, the fact that you call your mother's sister "mother" does not imply that you cannot distinguish your mother from her sister. It only implies that for reasons not yet fully understood, within a group larger than the elementary family it is necessary for an individual to identify together more than one person as mother in certain contexts. But this identification has nothing to do with the type of psychological explanation mentioned earlier, because it is the symbolic identification that induces the behavior, not the natural extension of feelings within the family welling up to include non-elementary family members.

In the case of the first approach one will look at the problem of cultural conformity by means of behavior patterns of various sorts that will keep on reappearing in different contexts. In the case of the second approach one will look at the actual symbolic content at each level, paying special attention to the behavior that is communicated between persons. It is the second approach that I wish to deal with in the remainder of this paper.

In Hsu (1963:61) a definition of clan is given based on the possession of fifteen characteristics. Murdock's specifications that a clan (1) be based on a unilineal rule of descent which unites its central core of members, (2) must have residential unity, and (3) must exhibit social integration, are quoted with approval as showing China has a clan-oriented system. This does not mean, however, that Chinese all actually live in clans, but rather that clans are representative models of pre-Communist Chinese society. It seems that no more than one-eighth of Chinese in South China actually have connections with clans directly, although according to Hsu if they could they would. The elementary family or the extended family (in the sense of more members than the elementary family living in the household) are much more well known. Among the Teochiu farmers whom I interviewed in Malaya (all formerly landless or very poor), not one could actually claim to have attended a clan ancestral service outside the household group in China.

It is the same way in India, although caste is a basic feature of the society; in fact, most Indians have only a theoretical belief in the all-Indian features of caste and acquire their instruction in caste behavior from their membership of the subcaste, a political and endogamous unit with known boundaries. A person cannot belong to two subcastes at the same time, just as in China one cannot belong to two clans. (There seem to be some exceptions to this in China. In parts of Fukien the marriage of a widow seems to be arranged by her father's family rather than her husband's.) In many parts of India the *gotra* (in some respects similar to a Chinese clan) has an exogamous characteristic within the endogamous subcaste. Subcaste membership is also acquired by unilinear descent through the father (see Newell, 1963:55–6), has residential unity, and exhibits actual social integration by the existence of caste *panchayats* or a dominant position in a village, a particular business, or an occupation. Where splits occur, they occur as groups based on increasing economic or other forms of differentiation. It is not a matter of individuals quarreling, but of groups splitting. The distinction between clan and subcaste depends on certain additional criteria peculiar to the Chinese or Indian system.

However the *number* of clans and the *number* of subcastes seem to vary at different historical periods. About 1370 there seem to have been about 1,900 surnames (clans). At the present time only about 500 seem to be used. The number of clans seems to be becoming fewer. On the other hand Hsu claims that the fissiparous nature of the Indian subcaste has resulted in the number of subcastes increasing in Indian society. However, in the latter case we do not have sufficient information as to the isogamous uniting tendencies in Indian society, so I am inclined merely to state it non-proven. However, we do know of the existence of some subcastes which have become larger in modern times, especially as a result of increased transportation. Moreover, certain subcastes seem to have disappeared in rural areas. It may well be that the situation differs in different parts of India.

This variation in size seems to depend in part at least on economic or other non-familial circumstances. Freedman points out that it is possible that the dominant lineages (what Hsu calls clans) in Southeast China result from the nature of rice cultivation.

> Intensively irrigated and worked rice paddies have initially required a great investment of labour but the rewards to this investment are extremely high and it allows the system of cultivation to be intensified in response to growth in the number of people living off it. To produce such a system, groups of men have had to co-operate. . . . It is perhaps in the productivity and co-operative nature of the enterprise that we can see a key to common estates. In some cases a joint investment of labour may have led to the establishment as an undivided estate of the land on which the labour had been expended. [Freedman, 1966:160]

Thus the reduction in the number of clans may be a feature of increased land utilization. Those people excluded from the clan emigrated to the boundaries of the developed land, so that the continued development of the clan in central China rested on surplus land being available where excluded members could settle. Fukien and Kwangtung were not fully settled till the end of the eighteenth century.

Undivided estates have been the standard pattern of land development in North India, at least in the Punjab and the Indian hill states. The basic ownership of the land remained in the control of the State (or rajah) who received taxation (or more accurately, ground rent). Those working the land retained shares of the usufruct in determined proportions but could not alienate their rights by sale, although relatives could inherit the right to receive usufruct. Thus the right to work the land was determined by membership of the clan (*gotra*) but the relationship between members of the undivided estate was determined by subcaste relationships (*jajmani*). Where the land was poor and there were no wealthy persons (since land could be the only store of wealth and disposal lay with the State), the majority of villagers were farmers; there was little caste differentiation, and the *gotra* was the basic unit by which the rights of the members to land was determined. The British introduced private ownership of land, thus destroying the basic principle of undivided rights of village members. This has been described by Ibbetson about the 1860's for the Patiala states and by Berreman for a village near Dehra Dun, about 1870, and in the Upper Ravi in Chamba State about 1951. The introduction of private land ownership automatically destroyed the *gotra* importance and strengthened the subcaste as the basic unit, which formerly had only ritual and endogamous functions. In fact, among the Gaddi people of Himachel Pradesh the subcaste covers a wide area of two or three days' journey with over a 100,000 members. The agent of the subcaste even now is in fact the *gotra* both in enforcing caste rules and in settling inheritance disputes. Formerly only male members of the *gotra* could inherit, but with the right of disposal of land increasing, quarrelsomeness is developing where fathers tend to dispose of their land to only daughters in preference to more distant *gotra* members. This fissiparous tendency is, however, not due to the mother/son dominant kinship relationships, but directly to examinable economic and social factors. (For further details of this cf. article by Newell in *Social Change in India,* Ishwaran [ed.], Leiden: in press.)

In the same way among the Teochiu vegetable farmers I studied in North Malaya in 1962, the absence of any clan relations even among those with the same surname (other than formal visiting at death) can be ascribed directly to the conflict between the ideal Chinese clan pattern as described by Hsu and the actual required behavior pattern and absence of land holding in a foreign country. Freedman (*op. cit.,* 166) describes a similar situation in urban Singapore.

Thus the attempt to directly connect the dominant kinship attributes of the elementary family with the larger society by means of generalized cultural or psychological behavior seems foredoomed to failure. However, this is not to say that the generalized hypothesis of Hsu cannot be used: Whereas the organization of units larger than the elementary family requires some economic base and some degree of continuity, the organization of the elementary family's dominant kinship terms must be consistent with the aim of the wider society. The increasing weakness of the clan in both Chinese and Indian society may result in a different form of family pattern in which father/son dominance may be replaced by other dominant relationships. Can one detect a dominant relationship among the Gaddis other than mother/son and among the Teochiu Chinese in Northern Malaya other than father/son?

A. CHINESE VILLAGE OF TEOCHIU VEGETABLE FARMERS IN NORTHERN MALAYA

The basic information about this village can be given very briefly. The Chinese population of the village is 502, of whom 401 were involved in agriculture, mostly growing vegetables for the Penang market. Of these 502 people, 152 were males, 121 females (over 12 years of age), 112 boys and 103 girls, and 14 were of ages and sex unknown. All the actual farmers were Teochiu. The total Chinese population lived in 91 households. Nineteen per cent of the village had the surname Daŋ (鄭) and 14 per cent had the surname Dang (陳), and another 14 per cent Ling (林). Of the 91 households, however, no fewer than 13 consisted of an elderly man living alone. Including these households, the average size was 5.5 persons per house; excluding these households the remaining 78 houses gave an average of 6.3 persons. These figures are within the figures of Buck for medium households in the double rice cropping area (in which the home area of Teochiuland is located).

The whole village was settled gradually, beginning about 1926, in three stages roughly comparable to the older and newer parts of the village. The three parts of the village are called the Old Garden, Betel Nut Bridge, and Over the River respectively; the latter area has mostly been settled only since the war.

The basis of introduction to the village was one's belonging to the same dialect group and coming from the same part of Chao Chou province *south* of the River Han, namely Puling, Dion Yon, and Dion Yang. However, clanship was *not* a basis of introduction. Of the 91 households, 12 bore the name Daŋ, of which two are connected father and son (living separately) and two are brothers. The remaining ones were all separate from each other and lived in different parts of the village. In the same way there were 11 households of Dang, but they were all totally unconnected except that two were father and son (living separately, with the mother living with the son). There were 10 Lim households, of which two houses were brothers. But the clans were unrelated by known blood connections.

The Dang, Dan, and Lims do not regard the mere fact that they happen to have the same surname as the basis of any familial relationship, except that at funerals a custom has either developed or been adopted from China of inviting other people of the same name to contribute money and to be present at the funeral. But with this one exception, the idea of a wider unit than the family seems to be of no practical importance. It is, of course, of theoretical importance to the members of the village, who certainly have in their minds a picture of a three generation Chinese family with a happy grandfather and grandmother doing no work and playing with their grandchildren and supported by a dutiful son and daughter-in-law. And I think it would be true to say that those families who are powerful in Chinese Malaysian society are respected for the large families they have created. Yet, in spite of the pattern, the Teochiu Chinese families in the community are not successful in building up this type of family.

There are several reasons for this: (1) sons because of their strength in cultivating vegetables exercise the dominant economic power within the family; (2) whereas the values of the senior generation are determined by the pattern of the Chinese homeland from which they came, sons are influenced by other patterns which they see around them in Malaya and European society; (3) father/son and mother/son relationship are in competition with each other. In the father/son relationship the question of authority is rather ambiguous. Even in cases where the family appears to be of traditional pattern, with the grandfather as head of the household, actual authority is usually exercised by the son with the greatest strength. Thus the eldest male ascendant may be accorded respect, but it derives rather from his skill in relinquishing actual control to the son than in asserting his political authority, a situation similar to a Western family where the oldest male has no independent source of income. His wife shares some of the attributes of her husband, especially that of being a senior ascendant, and she has the advantage of emotional ties from bringing up the children. In the case of divorce, children almost invariably go with the mother. Thus it is possible for the powerful son to choose to regard his duty to the extended family as being performed by supporting his mother if his mother supports him against his father. But this is conditional on his mother and his wife coming to an understanding, as only a wife can give birth to descendants. Thus the emphasis between mother and son is rather one of dependence than on the father/son principle of continuity. Although I did not deal with this in my book, it would be possible to account for the fact that in this village there are twelve elderly married men living alone but no elderly women by some explanation such as that the dominant relationship in the village is that of mother/son. But such an explanation would also need to rest on other relationships within the family not being opposed to mother/son dominance—namely mother/son's wife.

I thus think that when Hsu argues that the large family in China is a "tendency" (Hsu, 1943:555), even if in fact such investigators as Freedman or Buck do not find a great number of excessively large families, we are only dealing with a "model," the connection with the actual situation requiring to be proved in every instance. Such a "father/son model" for Malayan Teochiu farmers seems to be so remote as to be useless as an analytical tool, whereas among important wealthy pre-Communist families in China, it may be close. But such closeness cannot be deduced from the family itself; it needs to be worked out in the particular group to which it is applied. It seems likely that this mother/son oriented society may need to be explained in terms of the economic and landholding rules of the Malayan society. The application of family relationships occurs within the economic and political relationship.

B. GADDI PEOPLE OF HIMACHEL PRADESH

The Gaddi caste in historical times emigrated from the Punjab plains as probably four separate castes that joined together into one large caste group (caste isogamy) more than 100 years ago. The smallest unit of political control is the village *panchayat*, consisting for the most part of members of one agnatic kinship group. In the course of time more local residential units developed (villages), but consciousness of common *gotra* membership existed within the largest unit of the Gaddi caste and this consciousness rested mainly on the fact that the *gotra* was the intermediate landholding group between the rajah (representing Chamba State) and the domestic household. From 1951 agricultural land could be bought and sold without restriction, and almost immediately, conflicts developed between daughters' children and patrilineally connected cousins (representing the agnatic clan principle) over inheritance. The functional aspect of the *gotra* is disappearing with emphasis on caste solidarity and conflict. The differences between castes and within the caste are now being emphasized at the expense of common clan and kin solidarity. (A parallel example of the effect of this change in China would be if the State were to compel daughter's children to inherit land in the absence of sons.)

It also appears that among the Gaddis the dominant relationship in the past was that of brother/sister (namely discontinuity, inclusiveness, dependence, inequality, separation of material interests, and libidinality) rather than of Hsu's mother/son relationship. It is the relationship[3] between those of different sex that extends to a great distance traced horizontally, which is of importance.

If I can put this in the form of one of Evans-Pritchard's style paradoxes, it is the loyalty of sisters to the agnatic principle that enables brothers to extend their influence over such a wide area. But since every two or three generations the relationships become weak (on the discontinuous attribute), the *gotra* based on land becomes the permanent woof on which the

3. I am here provisionally accepting Hsu's argument about mother/son orientation although my own experience in the Punjab and Himalayas leads me to feel strongly that the main orientation is closer to father/son at least among the peasant families with whom I have lived.

warp of brother/sister ties are woven. (Cross-cousin marriage is forbidden in North India.)

But after the form of land ownership was changed in 1951 the *gotra* ties became weaker and caste increasingly is becoming the criterion of organization, with the disadvantages outlined by Hsu.

Among both the Jats and Gaddis the caste boundaries (judged by criterion of intermarriage) are very extensive and among the Gaddis seem to have actually become larger up to about the 1870's. It is the one clan village principle that is operative within this wide group. The strength of the clan rests largely on the principle of land ownership; among the Gaddis, since land was the only fundamental form of wealth and since it could not be alienated, the principles of influence extend horizontally by manipulating the brother/sister tie.

Yet because neither mother/son nor brother/sister relations have any continuity in Hsu's sense, the social units larger than the family do not depend on kinship terms to induce behavior. In north Malaya the more important external groups are based on dialect, trading, or territorial groups. Within the village, the cult of the Good Brothers is based on one representative per household. In Gaddiland the main ties outside the one *gotra* village are informal ties through one's sister, mother, or wife. The *gotra* heads in one village act as the village *panchayat,* enforcing caste and inheritance rules. In the case of north Malaya the mother/son is the dominant relationship; in the case of Gaddiland it is the brother/sister.

Can we now see what is the real basis and value of Hsu's theory of dominant relationship? It is not so much a cultural theory as a structural one. There are only a limited number of attributes within the elementary family. Hsu cites inclusiveness, continuity, asexuality, and authority. He then associates each of these attributes with certain pairs of family statuses. The content of these attributes may, however, be separated from the actual relationships. Sofue, among others, has shown how in Japanese society the elder son on his father's death may step into his shoes and can control his sister's marriage. He points out that in the case of the so-called Great Family the eldest son's power rested on "the excessive scarcity of land, [where] the equality principle and father-son tension hypothesis do not seem to be applicable" (p. 4, circulated paper, Wenner-Gren symposium). We have a situation in which the father/son relationship is inherited by the eldest son, so we have father/son → oldest brother/younger brother + sons → father/son. Yet the basic question here is rather one of vertical versus horizontal relationships. It seems impossible in Japanese society for any two people to be exactly equal to each other except in respect to a third party. Even in a Japanese university the exact, formal position of each professor is determined by various criteria, age, department, and date of founding of the department. In the Tokyo University council meeting the heads of the Law and Medical faculties always sit next to the President, with the Education department at the bottom. There is no informal relationship possible. Chie Nakane in an interesting article in *Economic Weekly* compares the nature of relationships in an English and a Japanese university. She argues that Japan is *situation*-oriented rather than *qualification*-oriented. A qualification is something one has personally, like membership of a family or a skill or something similar. A situation refers to membership in a social group. Thus in the example of the Great Family, the important thing is that the head of the Great Family must be *one person*, and the question of whether it is the father or eldest son is only of secondary importance.

As a result of modernizing changes in Japanese society, a number of authorities, notably Koyama, have argued that the *ie* (traditional family household) is disappearing and that the Japanese family is approaching a Western pattern. Although such a statement must be substantially qualified, it appears that larger social groups such as the Japanese National Railways continue to be based very strongly on this principle of *ie seido* (*ichizoku roto*). The alleged collapse of the Japanese *ie* does not appear to have had the slightest effect on the organization of larger groups in the society. This is because the principle of organization is more general than the *ie seido* system and a group larger than the elementary family, although often using elementary family terms is not dependent on the family for the use to which these terms are put.

Now if I can generalize from this background, Hsu is ascribing cultural content (attributes) to what is essentially a structural problem. The actual behavior in the family becomes a symbol at the higher level. The greater number of alternative ways of behavior in a company become stereotyped into relationship between groups depending on the nature by which continuity is maintained in the larger group. The clan in both China and among the Gaddis of North India rests fundamentally on the economic base, just as the Japanese National Railways depends ultimately on its efficiency. The question of which form and which family symbols it will adopt to organize itself depends not on the family but on its ability to use the symbols.

I have tried to deal basically with Hsu's argument in this paper because in many ways I am in sympathy with his main argument of a relationship within the family dominating others. Moreover, it is logical to assume that just as the original pair structure at birth affects the elementary family, so will the elementary family affect the joint family or clan. But at each level it becomes more dangerous to assume a general pattern from the previous one, first because of the increasing complexity of the units and their interrelations and second because the greater the size of the unit, the more a larger civilization tends to try to standardize the pattern by cultural, moral, or political means. Politics or religion are of importance in larger social units in controlling members totally unrelated by kinship. In the family, according to Hsu, kinship relations actually determine who politically controls whom. The significance of the Malayan Teochius and the Gaddis is that they are clearly Chinese or Indian within any definition, yet they do not fit into the standard relationships prescribed by Hsu for these societies. The reason the Malayan Teochius do not conform is that the economic pattern of this part of Malaya is different from China, and the concept of what a Chinese clan should be is just too remote from practice to be used as a model. The reason the Gaddis do not conform to the "Indian pattern" of Hsu is that because of remoteness from the plains the land system up to 1951 was of a North India traditional type instead of individual absolute ownership.

The family system of any area cannot be directly connected with cultural phenomenon because all families are self-destructive, whereas culture is continuous. The code language of the family (as shown by behavior, kin terms, relationships, and so on) can be adopted by permanent social institutions, but this is because it is convenient for the society, not because of any inherent quality within the family itself. The process of understanding this code depends on the situation in which they are used and, in my opinion, cannot yet be understood clearly because we have insufficient situation analyses of the type used by Turner (1957) or Nakane. Hsu's argument gives us one source from which the code arises, but does not enable us to understand why the code is applied in actual extra-familial situations.

The usefulness of Hsu's theory is that it has tried to isolate the attributes which must form the basis of one code in extra-familial contexts. This has still to be done and will probably be most successfully accomplished in the "fringe" areas of a culture.

Some Questions about Hsu's Hypothesis: Seen Through Japanese Data

As a specialist of Japanese culture and as a psychological anthropologist, I have some questions about Dr. Hsu's interpretations of Japanese culture. The first point on which I cannot agree with Dr. Hsu is his conclusion that Japan is a father-son dominated society.* Indeed it is true that in Japan the father has strong authority and patrilineal lines are emphasized; but at the same time, in the affective aspect, the mother-son relationship is very important. The traditional pattern of interpersonal relationship among family members in Japan is that the father is autocratic and aloof, and children (especially sons) try to avoid their father or are even hostile toward him. As a reaction to this resentment against the father, they have a sympathy with the mother; hence the mother-son relationship tends to be tinged with sentimental and emotional color.

This pattern is most commonly found in rural families in the northeastern part of Japan, where the patrilineal tie and father's high status are most strongly stressed, and among urban families of the lower-middle class (merchants, owners of small shops or factories, taxi-drivers, etc.) or of the lower class (laborers, carpenters and other craftsmen, etc.). In some

* Sofue is commenting here on interpretations Hsu delivered at the symposium. Hsu's analysis of Japanese society, which was subsequently revised to incorporate Sofue's comments, will appear in a book entitled *Japanese Kinship and Iemoto* (in preparation). Sofue's remarks here show great insights on Japanese society in light of Hsu's kinship hypothesis.

extreme cases (mostly urban families) the father spends much money on gambling or women, and is violent to his wife and children. In such cases the wife's status itself is quite insecure and, as a result, her relationship with the son, particularly with the eldest son, becomes excessively close. She feels that the eldest son is her only sympathizer, and that he will be her only supporter in the future. As a result, the eldest son receives emotional overprotection from his mother, and their relationship is characterized by mutual dependency. Among the urban families of the upper-middle class (or new middle class which consists of mostly white collar workers) the wife is rarely in such an unhappy and miserable situation, for their status has gradually become higher since World War II, mostly as a result of Western influence. However, the mother-son tie is still intense, as indicated by Vogel (1962:229–52).

This close relationship between the mother and the son, and the weak ego of the Japanese which may have resulted from it, are very often discussed from the psychoanalytic point of view. Takeo Doi, a senior psychiatrist at the Tokyo St. Luke's Hospital, pointed out that the Japanese word *amae* is a special term meaning the psychological state "to depend and presume upon another's benevolence," and this is "generally used to describe a child's attitude or behavior toward his parents, particularly his mother." He speculates that this *amae* exists in the Japanese continually, even in the period of adulthood, and should be a key concept for understanding Japanese personality structure (Doi, 1956, 1960, 1962, 1963). William Caudill, a psychoanalytically oriented anthropologist at the National Institute of Mental Health, discovered the over-representation of eldest sons among Japanese psychotic patients, which should be related to the eldest son's dependent relationship with the mother (Caudill, 1963). He also points to the fact that Japanese male schizophrenic patients show physical assaults most often against their mother, and he interprets this as being caused by their strong desire for *amae* with the mother (Schooler and Caudill, 1964). He stresses that one of the factors strengthening this desire may be the traditional sleeping arrangement whereby parents continue to sleep in the same room as their children, frequently until the children leave home (Caudill and Plath, 1966). My own data from the Sentence Completion Test collected from several hundred urban and rural junior high school students in various parts of Japan (Sofue, 1965) and my study of neurotic students at a university in Tokyo (Sofue, 1964) suggest the same general features as mentioned above, which tend to create a "mother complex" and a "dependent personality," causing in extreme cases maladjustment to college life. Today this "mother complex" is a very popular topic in Japanese newspapers and journals. I conclude that although in Japan the father-son relationship is explicitly dominant—or borrowing Dr. Hsu's own word, legally (jurally) dominant—the mother-son relationship is implicitly (covertly) dominant, or more exactly, affectively dominant. This may be in some sense similar to the case of Mexico discussed by Mr. Hunt. There, both the father-son and mother-son relationships are equally dominant, and he concludes that it is hard to state which of the two should be more important. There must be many other similar cases in the world, and I would say that it is not always necessary to find only one dominant relationship; in Japan the father-son and mother-son relationships should be closely related to each other and must be regarded as two sides of the same shield. To theoretically separate overt (explicit) dominance and covert (implicit) or affective dominance, as already mentioned, would be one method needed to explore the problem.

My second question refers to the brother-brother relationship. According to Dr. Hsu, equality is its basic characteristic, and in the brother-brother dominated society there will be strong tensions between father and sons. Can we generalize this as a universal phenomenon in any society? In the case of Japan, for instance, the status and authority of the eldest son are much higher than those of younger sons. This has been a traditional pattern, especially among agricultural communities in the northeastern part of Japan. Among them the distinction between the eldest son and the younger sons has been considerable until only recently. In some extreme cases, which must have existed until about forty years ago, only the eldest son was permitted to marry, while all younger ones were compelled to work for him as unmarried servants throughout their lives. A conspicuous example is the case of a mountain village called Shirakawa, in central Japan. Here, a traditional custom which persisted until the end of the last century was that only the eldest son be permitted to live with his wife, while younger sons were supposed to live duolocally. The eldest son and his wife, their children, his parents, his younger brothers, as well as his sisters (excepting those who married eldest sons of other families) and the children of these married sisters, and so on, lived in the same house. The resulting household consisted of from forty to seventy members. These members had to be absolutely obedient to the almighty power of the eldest son (Ema, 1940; Koyama, 1954; Befu, 1966). In these cases, which apparently resulted from excessive scarcity of land, the equality principle and father-son tension hypothesis do not seem applicable.

My final question about this hypothesis concerns the effect of dominant kinship relationships on non-kin behavior. I admit that there are many examples that support this hypothesis, but I would like to emphasize that the effect of general patterns of non-kin behavior on kinship relationship are also relevant. For example, the brother-brother relationship in Japan is largely influenced by the general pattern of Japanese friendship among men, which is somewhat different from that among women, because a hierarchy of age and status distinctions are much more stressed among men. Therefore a dyadic and mutual friendship among men is only possible between two equals of the same age, whereas this is never the case among women. Such a sex difference is reflected in the terms of address among friends. In the case of men it takes a long time to move from the formal to the informal, and even longer from the informal to the intimate type of address. Each transition represents a certain psychological step similar to *duzen* in Germany and *tutoyer* in France. In the case of friends of different ages the transition is much easier for the senior than the junior; the latter must retain formal terms of address accompanied with formal grammatical forms. This is hardly the case among women; each level fades easily into the next, and the transition from the formal to the informal and from the informal to the intimate level takes place quite easily and freely. This applies equally to female friends of the same or different ages.

These characteristic cultural patterns seem to be an influential factor in both the brother-brother and the sister-sister relationships. While younger brothers should be obedient to their elders, younger sisters are not supposed to obey their elders, including the eldest sister; they are usually more intimate and sentimental with each other. The above factor plays a role in the relationship between brothers-in-law and between sisters-in-law; the former is much more formal and compartmentalized than the latter, which tends to be quite informal and intimate.

PART III

Methodological Explorations

THIRTEEN

FRED L. STRODTBECK

Sex-Role Identity and Dominant Kinship Relationships

The concern of this paper is narrower than Hsu's hypothesis. We treat the possible effects of a heavy emphasis on the mother-son relation, of the type found in Hindu culture, on problem-solving strategies of sons—and eventually societies. Our expectation is that mother-son dominance produces unconscious feminine identification in males, and our task is to show that certain of the emphases of Hindu culture are similar to the behavior which, under controlled conditions, is associated with such identification.

Unlike other participants in this symposium, we do not draw our illustrations from different cultures, but from the experimental behavior of members of our own culture who have been observed in a social psychological experiment. We will describe the types of measures of sex-role identity we employ and report the nature of the relationships between sex-role identity and parental behavior that have been found in our culture. We shall speak of "unconscious femininity," as it is measured in our studies, as if it were an equivalent to a "strong identification with a Hindu mother" construct, even though the equivalence is a matter that must be established. Our analysis rests upon the assumption that, if an empirical

*This research was supported principally by a grant from the Resources for the Future Foundation and by grants from the United States Public Health Service (MH 05572) and the Office of the Surgeon General, U.S. Army Medical Research and Development Command (DA-49-193-MD 2790).

study were undertaken, males from North Central India would, in fact, be more feminine on our tests than Chinese or United States males.[1]

The structure of our argument is quite simple. We write as if we believe the laboratory behavior of subjects of a given personality characteristic is analogous to the elaboration of a culture that results when a society has many members of a given personality type. We are aware that this formulation when stripped to this form will offend by its simplicity. We have no intention of evoking memories of "long shot" studies that related very early child training to cultural beliefs by means of very generally defined mechanisms. It is our hope that through the development of cross-cultural experimental social psychology—this includes cross-cultural testing, observation, and experimentation—methods can be evolved that will more clearly explicate the linkages through which regularities like those involved in Hsu's hypotheses are being affected. Hence, the analogizing between laboratory and culture is not set forth as an appropriate empirical method, but presented as a way of thinking, a gambit for describing what is believed to be a very fundamental mechanism for relating sex-role identity and strategy as it may operate in a cultural context. It is hoped that even those who have reservations in this instance may find the possibility of a laboratory approach stimulating to the study of other culture and personality problems.

MOTHER-SON DOMINANCE

In the absence of firsthand knowledge of Hindu culture, the writer did not appreciate the pervasive and long-continuing mother-son relationship until he read the Hitchcock-Minturn description of the Rajputs of Khalapur. The following passage indicates the degree to which this culture supports the role of the mother as an agent of nurturance and control (Hitchcock and Minturn, 1963:202–362, esp. 240–41):

> The symbols of woman's status inferiority are easy to perceive. The ameliorating factor in the status inequality of such a social organization, however, is the strength of the bonds which exist between mothers and sons and between sisters and brothers. Adult males are taught that they should be respectful and considerate to their mothers and because of their early, prolonged intimate contact with her are influenced by her wishes. The mother feeds her son even after he is married and even has strong influence on his marital life. She runs the family as long as she wishes to assume the responsibility.
>
> . . . women crouch on the floor and pull their saris over their faces when in the presence of their husband or any man older than their husband. This is a sign of respect for the man's status. Covering the face in the presence of

1. Richard W. Moody, as part of a Ph.D. dissertation at the University of Chicago, has collected responses from more than 800 subjects in North Central India. It will be possible to check the directional prediction between Hindu and United States males with his data.

one's husband is also a sign of respect for his mother, another of the customs designed to protect the mother-son relationship from being threatened by the son's attachment to his wife. When a man has entered the house for his meal, he will quickly retire into a room behind the wall of his hearth. The women are then free to move about their business quietly. His meal will usually be served to him by his mother, if she is living, or by an adult sister. Only if some woman of his own family is not present or does not wish to assert her prerogative will his wife be allowed to serve his meal.

Ideally, a man and his wife are not allowed to talk to each other in front of the older members of the family. Since the mother-in-law is virtually always present in the courtyard and the young wife cannot leave the courtyard, this means in effect that the young couple may converse only surreptitiously at night.

A husband is not supposed to show any open concern for his wife's welfare; this is the responsibility of his parents. If the wife is sick, the mother-in-law and father-in-law see that she goes to a doctor; if they do not, neither she nor her husband should complain. The villagers report one or two cases where a woman has remained childless for years and, despite the great importance of having children, has not seen a doctor because the husband was too shy to ask his negligent parents to take her.

After the death of the mother-in-law, a woman can talk to her husband in the presence of her sisters-in-law. When her sons marry, she assumes a new and prestigeful role. She is now in charge of the young women and is released by virtue of her relative age from many of the restrictions of purdah.

The Hitchcock-Minturn description is consistent with the description in Hsu's article. The fathers clearly have a negligible role in the care of infants. To an unusual degree, by virtue of the childless woman's very low status, the birth of a child is status-conferring. The mothers are continuously responsible for infants, nurse for as many as five years if no other child intervenes. Khalapur mothers, like other mothers who live with little privacy, train for "control" rather than "expressiveness" in child behavior.

The Rajput mothers do not emphasize self-reliance and are willing to help their children bathe, dress, etc., even when the children could do these tasks themselves; but they are notably unresponsive to the emotional needs of their children. They frequently scold children for crying, even when they have been physically hurt. Demands for attention, fussiness, and whining meet with similar impatience. . . .

Training in emotional unresponsiveness begins at birth. Babies are put to sleep on cots and completely covered with thick cotton quilts. Unless they are hungry or fussing they are allowed to stay there undisturbed. With rare exceptions, neither adults nor children play with babies. They are fed and picked up and held when crying, but they are not encouraged to respond. It is interesting to note that most Rajput children are not upset by weaning. . . . This disruption of affection does not accompany the weaning of the Rajput child, since it was never lavished on him as an infant.

The absence of praise is the result of a deliberate policy, designed to train the compliant personality required in an extended family. The parents believe that if children are praised they will become spoiled because they will think that the parents "love them too much." The concern here seems to be that the child who is "loved too much" will be not only grudging in obedience, which, like minor bickering, is tolerable but will also be openly rebellious and recalcitrant. This policy was emphasized so strongly that, although we almost never heard a woman praise a child, the men complained that women lost control of children because of too much praise. [Minturn and Lambert, 1964:230–31]

The Rajput mothers establish their power superiority more clearly over boys than over girls:

> They also tend to use frequent and intense physical punishment with boys rather than girls. This hostility to boys is particularly interesting in view of the fact that these Rajputs, like most Indians, want to have sons rather than daughters.
>
> Since a good wife is never hostile to her husband these resentments cannot be expressed directly to the men. It may be that they are expressed in the coldness with which these women treat their sons.

The fact that the Rajputs are 2,000 persons of high status in a community of 5,000 means that they use servants for many of the duties that otherwise would be done by children. Boys help in the field during the short period of the harvest and sometimes play in the men's quarters where they are supervised by older men, but this is very sporadic. Sons of rich families do not work in the fields at all. Rajputs, who were originally warriors, do not instill in their sons love of farming or pride in its accomplishments—it is considered beneath them. Since they are no longer warriors, there is little encouragement of athletic skill or development—it is almost as if it were better not to put to a test the social presumption that the Rajputs are physically superior. The teaching of boys to be brave does not necessarily mean one should fight; it is more that one should not run from a fight (*ibid.*, p. 237).

The mothers suppress aggression among children whenever it threatens the required solidarity of the courtyard, but they indulge the child's aggressive acts toward the mother. In addition—and this is most interesting—the mothers are very permissive about aggression directed by the child toward their own selves. If a child becomes angry with himself while being scolded, mothers may shift from scolding to actually consoling the child (*ibid.*). This is consistent with the hypothesis that if the mother is the primary disciplinarian, the probability of an in-turning of aggression as a response to frustration is increased.[2]

2. See Martin Gold's reconciliation of social constraint (i.e., Durkheim) and child development (Funkenstein and King) in his article "Suicide, Homicide, and the Socialization of Aggression," *American Journal of Sociology* LXIII (May, 1958), 6, 651–61; see also R. R. Sears, Eleanor E. Maccoby, and H. Levin, *Patterns of Child Rearing* (Evanston, Illinois: Row Peterson and Co., 1957).

The emphasis upon "peace at any price" in the courtyard supervised by the women results in little attention being given the justice or injustice of any complaint. Thus, the training in universalistic norms characteristic of peer group relations in many societies seems almost completely absent. While "men are usually held in more awe than women and are usually obeyed without question," in their play the children live out the "bickering, name-calling and semi-aggressive teasing" (Minturn and Lambert, *op. cit.*, p. 238) of women at their work. It is to reduce this general tension that most mothers restrict their attention exclusively to their own children —there are fewer fights that way (*ibid.*, p. 234). The absence of men from the supervision of any pre-enactment by children of institutionally constrained adult interaction is a further example of the absence of experiences which would counterbalance the mother's dominance.

From this description of the mother's role in early and later child rearing and with the knowledge of the Whiting, Kluckhohn, and Anthony hypothesis, one is sensitized to look for both the two-year (or more) post-partum sex taboo (which is present [Hitchcock and Minturn, *op. cit.*, p. 304], though not always observed by younger couples) and for a punitive initiation ceremony at adolescence (Whiting, Kluckhohn, and Anthony, 1957:359–370), which is *not* present.

According to their hypothesis, the highly exclusive relationship between the son and mother will increase the emotional dependence of the child on the mother, and this in turn will cause his relations with a father who usurps his intimacy to become hostile. The initiation ceremony is stressful; once passed it heightens identification with the male community, and the role expectations associated with the new status require solidarity with other men and preclude regression to earlier role-relations with the mother. In their article, Whiting *et al.* treat the Rajput case as only a partial exception to their hypothesis, for they call attention to the fact there is a change of residence for the son at adolescence. But unlike the Trobriand case, which is similarly an exception, there is no mother's brother involved. In none of the available sources thus far consulted is there a description of life in the men's house that would indicate that this is a sufficiently stressful experience to result in the development of a compensatingly strong masculine unconscious identity. Nor is there evidence that the boy receives the sustained nurturant interest of a competent male that would provide the opportunity for development of strong masculine conscious identity.

It may be noted that the need for "hostility control" postulated by Whiting *et al.* does not become important among the Rajputs. It may be the non-intensive mother-child relations that account for this, but there are other elements of the situation that are relevant at a later stage of the development of the child. Since the Hindu son's grandmother cares for the father, the son does not compete with him for nurturant attention. In the case of the Ganda, a transfer to father's brother's household is seen to obviate the need for harshness in suppressing hostility. We here suggest that Whiting should recognize the Rajputs as a different kind of exception. We believe that non-competition for nurturance with the father has the net effect of leaving the son with an identification with the mother which, due to the greater tolerance by Indian culture of feminine ways of behaving, there is no need to suppress.

The ethnographic facts of Hindu culture that lead to the belief that many more sons will have strong attachments to their mothers may also be drawn upon to illustrate what is not implied in feminine identification. One does not doubt that a boy can learn what boys must do without relinquishing all that he has taken on in his relation with his mother. The sense in which a son can be like his mother includes, of course, mannerisms and temperamental characteristics. There are, in addition, concepts of roles with the attendant patterns of duties and actions. These combine to create the idiosyncratic and defining elements in the social definition of mother or father, woman or man—all by a process in which specific rewards and punishment are either absent or very hard to associate with the resultant behaviors when they begin to emerge in appropriate stimulus situations (Sears, 1957). Values, expectations, and ideals come to be elaborated around role-relations in almost the same mysterious way rules of grammar come to be used to make new sentences as a child learns to speak. It is the fact of the emergence of such structuring of behavior that causes the hypothesis of identification to be formulated.

At a simple level, it may be observed that as the child moves from being a recipient of knowledge toward becoming a user, he fills in gaps in what he has been taught. It is therefore not surprising that a father who patiently teaches his son a system of agriculture, repeating the cycle each year, will create a son who does things like his father—things that his father never explicitly taught—such as his posture of contentment when the day's work is done or the wrinkle on his forehead when the success of an operation is in doubt; even perhaps, the pose of suspended emotionality as the requirements of a new situation are being studied. It is highly probable, particularly in a traditional society, that father-son teaching plus son-father identification is an efficient way to transmit culture.

But what if the responsible adult, the Hindu mother for example, is of the opposite sex. Much of what the mother does for the boy, such as dressing and feeding, is sex-specific behavior which the boy can never use in his relation with others. When we speak of identification, we are referring primarily to the motivation engendered by weakness in the presence of power (Burton and Whiting, 1961). It is an imperfect process—particularly when cross-sex relations are involved.

A sublimation of the desire to possess the mother as a love object provides a solution which both reduces the number of competing role-relations and makes the adult male's life more like that of older women who have ceased having sexual relations. It is a way of life in accordance with moral teaching received from the mother. Perhaps the degree to which being holy is equated with asexuality, or as in Yoga, with erasing the distinction between the sexes, is a possible outcome in the Hindu case. While only very few Rajputs proceed to the third stage of an idealized life cycle (that is, retiring with their wives to live as celibate hermits), the prominence of this as a social ideal, *after* one has his children married, suggests two points. There is a strange twist on the Western idea of curbing the unfolding sexuality of the young. It is almost as if non-celibacy in mid-life is a socially required interval in a span which is otherwise normally asexual. Second, renouncing worldly things is substantively similar to assuming the status of one with non-temporal power—a status like one's mother had as a young daughter-in-law in the courtyard of a paternal Hindu home. Social support for the belief that sexuality should eventually be repressed is for a culture something like intropunitiveness for an individual. We believe intropunitiveness is more characteristic of the unconsciously feminine male.

Such matters of personality style are most prominent in our conception. The unconsciously feminine male is not thought of as having had a reduced capacity to learn male sex-role requirements.[3] He knows where to stand in a procession, the requirements of his occupation, the accepted relations for overt sexual contacts, and so on. In the Rajput case, he would carry his weighted staff and he would direct his servants; he would utilize traditional ways to accomplish traditional jobs; but it is beyond these requirements—when there is a range of religious beliefs to choose between, when there is cross-pressure between alternatives of action—it is at these points that behavior measured against universal bench marks can show the feminine components.

UNCONSCIOUS FEMININITY IN MALES AND EGO DEFENSE

Shifting to our culture, unconscious femininity in males is a construct that has to be separated from a context of lay meaning like that accorded the term "sissy." If it did refer to men behaving like women, the referent would be clear even though it would still be hard to generalize cross-culturally. If it does not, what is a definition of potential usefulness in cross-cultural work? We were encouraged to seek such a new and potentially cross-culturally valid conceptualization in our own work as a result of Miller and Swanson's (1960) research investigating the relationship be-

3. For a 28-item bibliography in an article which presents the argument of this paragraph in a much expanded form, see Daniel G. Brown, "Sex-Role Preference in Young Children." *Psychological Monographs* 70, 14, No. 421, 1956—this is the primary description of the "IT" test.

tween the selection of defenses by an individual and his unconscious and conscious sex-role identity.

Miller and Swanson used the Franck Drawing Completion Test (Franck and Rosen, 1945) as their measure of unconscious femininity. The test is composed of 36 simple line drawings that are to be "completed" or added to as the subject desires. This process encourages the subject to organize stimuli in a manner that reveals his expressive style. Franck suggests criteria for scoring the completions. Some stimuli are to be scored only on content and others, quite similar, are to be scored by quite different abstract criteria. Franck permitted the use of several scoring criteria on each stimulus, and by her "multiple criteria method" a completion generally would get a unit score as feminine if it met any one of several criteria suggested as appropriate for the stimulus. This unit score would not be increased if the drawing met several of them.

In our laboratory Franck's various criteria were viewed as plausible in any given case, but it was not at all clear that any one criterion was more appropriate for one stimulus than another. For this reason all of the completions in a set of 417 protocols (obtained from a sample of boys and girls from the second, fifth, and ninth grades) were scored by all of Franck's criteria and then analyzed to determine which criteria differentiated abstract drawings by boys from those by girls at each of the three grade levels. After these steps, we chose eleven stimuli that, in terms of composite abstract and content performance, discriminated at all three grade levels. When the protocols are scored with the new, provisional scoring manual, the characterization of a completion as feminine or not corresponds relatively closely with the characterization one would make in terms of the criteria of the original Franck manual. Thus, as Franck expresses it:

> . . . men expand from the stimulus outward, tend to build it up, emphasize angles, rely upon the strength of simple lines. Women tend to leave the stimulus area open, elaborate within the area and draw round or blunt rather than angular, sharp lines. They seem to feel a need to give support to single lines.

The second test, the Gough test (1952), is a true-false, Likert-type attitude scale based upon self-reports. The shortened version used in our research consists of a set of twenty-four true-false items. The subject indicates whether statements concerning culturally sex-typed preferences, interests, and attitudes are characteristic of himself. A few of the items from this test are:

> I would like to be a nurse.
> I very much like hunting.
> I prefer a shower to a bath.

Miller and Swanson use the fact that scores on the Franck test are uncorrelated with scores on the Gough test, or with other popular tests of masculinity-femininity (Heston, 1948; Shepler, 1951), to argue that the Franck test provides a measure of "unconscious" femininity.

> If it is a test of unconscious identity, it should not correlate significantly with tests of conscious identity when administered to a large enough population. . . . It is not significantly related to any of three popular verbal tests of masculinity-femininity, the Terman-Miles Attitude Interest Analysis Test, the M-F Scale of the Strong Vocational Interest Blank, and the M-F scale of the Minnesota Multiphasic Personality Inventory. Each of these three calls for reports of attitudes and interests. We felt, therefore, that Franck's test must measure something other than conscious sex identity—something which also discriminates between males and females. [p. 93]

Our results are parallel to those of previous investigators in that the Gough Brief Femininity Scale and the Single Criterion Franck Score are uncorrelated. Empirical evidence from all sources is thus unequivocal on the point that the correlation between the Franck (when scored by the original or the revised criteria) and Gough departs from zero by only an amount which may be attributed to sampling error. However, in our work, we have taken the fact that the Franck correlated with no other test as simply anomalous and set about to design some related experiments that would provide more direct support for the assumption that an "unconscious" process was involved. These further tests (Lipsitt, 1965; Parkman, 1965), although not definitive, were congruent with such an assumption. Hence we follow Miller and Swanson and refer to the Franck test as the unconscious measure and the Gough as the conscious identity measure.

Since these two tests are uncorrelated, they generate four types: MM, MF, FM, and FF; if they are used jointly, with cuts at the median, the first letter refers to the Franck (the unconscious) classification.

Miller and Swanson discuss the development of sex-role identity as follows:

> . . . each boy initially identifies with his mother and then transfers to his father. As an infant . . . he becomes very dependent on her because she feeds and cleans him, protects him from harm. . . . Later, the father usually becomes the more significant person. . . . He has certain unique abilities which the son admires. . . . By identifying with his father, a son gradually acquires the expressive gestures, the habits, and the interests that are typical of males rather than females in our society. We thought these earlier identifications would not be conscious, since they are embedded in a large number of activities and occur before events are labeled verbally.
>
> Whether he is masculine or feminine in his underlying identity, the average male child, as he matures and develops friendships, feels an increasing social pressure to act in a masculine manner. . . . [These] later identifications are probably matters of conscious concern for every normal boy. They are part of his conscious sex identity. [p. 89]

In this passage the authors make no effort to go beyond their own culture, but they touch on the possibility of universal mechanisms with the thought that unconscious sex-role identity could arise in pre-verbal exchanges between children and their parents. They also write:

> . . . the less masculine the boy is, the earlier his developmental problems occurred. A boy with feminine identification who is relatively impervious to the meanings of his feminine traits to his peers must be fairly immature. A boy with feminine identification who wants to be masculine is more mature, since he is sensitive to the reactions of others and tries to conform. A boy with masculine identification on both levels is most mature. [p. 91]

This argument predicts a maturity sequence MM>FM>FF.

In support of their formulation of the relationship between sex-role identity and selection of defenses, Miller and Swanson reported data from experimental studies. One of these by Lansky (Miller and Swanson, 1960) demonstrated that FF males show a significantly greater tendency, after rating nude pictures in the presence of a male experimenter, to write story endings exhibiting *denial and withdrawal.*[4] The stories involve a hero who is frustrated by a well-meaning adult to whom he is very attached. FM males show a significantly greater tendency to write endings in which the hero expresses *aggression against the self,*[5] and MM males show a significantly greater tendency to write endings in which the hero engages in *realistic problem-solving.*

To summarize the Miller and Swanson (and Lansky) studies, these authors assume that in order to withstand social pressures toward masculine identity, these pressures must either be denied or treated as if they were irrelevant to self-esteem. They assume that if such a process occurs in this area it will result in a tendency to use similar mechanisms in other situations. The FF boy who denies social pressures toward masculinity will deny other social pressures. Thus, they believe decisions made by such persons will in some sense be inferior to so-called realistic decisions. Results from a subsequent experiment (Lipsitt, 1965) conducted in our laboratory has led us to reject the formulation that MM decisions are functionally superior. We do not concur, however, with their assumption that response styles developed to deal with the core issue of sex-role identity will be more generally utilized in other spheres of life. Our procedures and the basis of our conclusions are illustrated in a small-group experiment.

4. An ending was scored as indicating denial if it was obviously incompatible with one of the facts in the story beginning. Withdrawal was a physical retreat from the scene of the conflict.

5. Turning against the self was scored when the hero ignored the authority's wise counsel and suffered the consequences or if the ending described an injury to the hero.

The Experimental Design[6]

Using the format of a public affairs interview, four stimulus tapes were constructed. Each tape consisted of a discussion about problems of water pollution by four experts in the presence of a radio interviewer. The four principals were: a conservationist, a public health officer, a hydrologist, and a political scientist. Their speeches were written to be constant across our experimental design, except for one crucial section in each speech where the speaker varied his argument depending on the treatment condition desired. These differences in the speeches for each participant comprise our experimental variation. The four speeches taken together lasted 10–15 minutes depending on the version presented. Table 13.1 presents the design, with the row titles indicating the substance of the speeches made by the public health officer and the hydrologist, and the column titles indicating the content of the speeches by the other two speakers.

To simplify our discussion of predictions, we have created a measure of the subject's willingness to act and then developed our interpretation in terms of this measure. The subject's willingness to act is measured by the shift, as a result of the experimental intervention, in his response to four questions which were first presented after giving the subject the following description:

> Health Officers report that if cities and industries nearby continue to dispose of their wastes as they do now, the water in your hometown will become contaminated. However, the contamination is not yet serious and people are permitted to swim in the lake and in the river. Many continue to swim, fish, and boat there.

Each subject was asked how probable it was that he would:

> Sign a petition
> Persuade friends to change their minds
> Persuade strangers to change their minds

(and in a slightly different format), feel that it was his own personal responsibility to do something about the problem.

The mean of these four items, where each item was rated on a 7-point scale, is the Will-act score (where 7 indicates the subject was "sure" he would perform an action, and 1 indicates that he was "sure" he would *not*). After the experimental tape was played, the individual was asked the same questions again. Taking into consideration the substance of the

6. I express my thanks to William E. Bezdek and Don Goldhamer, who co-authored with me a chapter, "Personal Efficacy, Problem Severity and Willingness to Act to Reduce Water Pollution," which is to appear in the volume, *Attitudes Toward Water: An Inter-disciplinary Exploration* (in preparation) for their kindness in permitting me to use substantial portions in this article; to Margaret A. Parkman, for her assistance with the water project and the review of the identification literature; and to Meda White for preparing the experimental script.

experimental tapes, one can make three plausible predictions as to the relative willingness to act of the subjects in the four cells of the design shown in Table 13.1:

1. $(A + B)$ will be higher than $(C + D)$ assuming subjects are more willing to act when the problem is *serious* [i.e., $(A + B) > (C + D)$].
2. $(B + D)$ will be higher than $(A + C)$ assuming subjects are more willing to act when they believe their efforts will be *efficacious* [i.e., $(B + D) > (A + C)$].
3. The treatment outcomes will be ordered $B > A > D > C$ assuming 1 and 2 above are correct and *seriousness* predominates over *efficacy*; or, $B > D > A > C$ if 1 and 2 above are correct and *efficacy* predominates over *seriousness.*

The relative weight given efficacy and seriousness is, we believe, an element of the distinction between unconscious masculinity and unconscious femininity. While we believe unconsciously feminine males have identified with their mother, we use the term "identified" to refer to a process resulting in the incorporation of cognitive and affective orientations universally associated with the female role. How can one justify assuming the existence of near-universal communality in the cognitive-affective orientations of all women?

If one follows Guttman (1965) and reasons that, save for those few women who view their work as a career or profession, women are invested in domestic and maternal roles, then the domestic-maternal milieu may be

Table 13.1. Treatment Components of the Design

Arguments about the Problem's Seriousness		*Arguments about Efficacy of Interpersonal Action*	
Public Health Official argues	Hydrologist argues	*Conservationist argues* PEOPLE ARE ILL-INTENTIONED or *Political Scientist argues* THE INDIVIDUAL CAN DO NOTHING or	PEOPLE DON'T YET FULLY UNDERSTAND INDIVIDUALS CAN BE EFFECTIVE
A SERIOUS PROBLEM : : : or	PREVENTION IS THE ONLY ANSWER : : or	A	B
: A MINOR PROBLEM	: THE SERIOUSNESS OF A LITTLE POLLUTION IS CONTROVERSIAL	C	D

viewed as the generating mechanism for such orientations. The daily interactions of women occur in a home environment which "bears the imprint of the wishes, values, and techniques of the person central to its maintenance"—the adult female. "Within the tested and secure confines of the home, most possible and reasonable actions have already been performed, by oneself or by well-known others, and their effects are known." Moreover, developing children, unable to communicate their physical and emotional requirements, seem to require mothers who can respond intuitively to such needs. Such quick assessment precludes a rigidly maintained ego boundary and requires an intuitive responsiveness to the motivational states underlying overt behavior. Men, in contrast, daily depart from the home to confront a milieu structured by others and "in some sense their task is to impose on constantly fluctuating situations a more personal and predictable order." A persistent sense of self-other distinctions and an orientation toward assessing the likelihood that one's own goals may be realized is more likely to be generated in a milieu "in which personal ends can be achieved only by dealing with agents who have a direction, logic, and structure of their own."

From this comparison, it may plausibly be suggested that the tendencies to respond intuitively to needs and to abolish self-other boundaries could be regarded as a cognitive style which develops out of women's social environment. In contrast, the tendency to detach one's subjective reactions from the processes that must be understood and to maintain a persistent sense of self-other distinctions seems better coordinated to the man's environment. In the present experiment an extrapolation from Guttman's analysis leads us to postulate that the aspect of the female complex most accessible to the FF male is just that which is involved in the contrast between the home and work environments. It is our further belief that this can be described as a tendency toward "pragmatically purposeful" versus "personally sensitive" responses rather than as "defensive" versus "non-defensive" reactions.

In the present experiment this response style would dispose the FF to "personalize" assertions in the speech by the public health official when he says that the problem is a *serious* one likely to affect the welfare of others. By contrast, the self-oriented MM would be likely to defer or suppress his response to the seriousness of the situation until some recurrent and predictable structure emerges which reveals the path of effective action. A positive response to the political scientist's demonstration of personal efficacy would not, however, be withheld.

Or, stated another way, the allocentric, self-directed MM would conceive of action primarily in terms of its effects on the environment, while the autocentric, collectively-oriented FF would conceive of action primarily with regard to its effects on the people involved. Rapaport (1964) has labeled these two cognitive orientations "strategic thinking" and "conscience-driven thinking." The latter arises because concern for the interpersonal effects of action leads more inevitably to a consideration of values. Rapaport writes:

> The basic question in the strategist's mind is this: "In a conflict how can I gain an advantage over him?" The critic (conscience-driven thinker) cannot disregard the question: "If I gain an advantage over him, what sort of person will I become?" [p. 189]

To relate the theoretical analysis suggesting MM-FF differences in cognitive-affective style to the previous predictions of the willingness to act as a result of the treatments alone, the following systematization results. We have previously predicted that *serious* will predominate over *non-serious*—that is, $(A + B) > (C + D)$—and *efficacy* will predominate over *non-efficacy*—$(B + D) > (A + C)$. Predominate here means cause greater shift in the "Will-act" scores. Our further analysis and theorizing enables us to relate these two earlier predictions in different ways for our two classes of subjects.

For FF's, we predict that *seriousness* is more important than *efficacy*. In the notation of the treatment cells, this is:

$$[(A + B) - (C + D)] > [(B + D) - (A + C)]$$

which reduces to,

3 a) $A > D$ (for FF);

and for MM's, we predict that *efficacy* is more important than *seriousness*. In the notation used above,

$$[(B + D) - (A + C)] > [(A + B) - (C + D)]$$

which reduces to,

3 b) $D > A$ (for MM).

The revised forms of the Franck and Gough tests were administered to 356 sailors undergoing hospital corps training at the Great Lakes Naval Training Center. Ninety per cent of the men were between 18 and 22 years of age. For the experiment to be reported we cross-tabulated the scores from the two tests and selected the 40 most extreme feminine cases on both tests (FF subjects) and the 40 most extreme masculine cases on both tests (MM subjects). From this total experimental sample of 80 subjects, an equal number of MM and FF subjects were assigned to each of 4 cells in a 2 X 2 treatment design previously presented in Table 13.1.

ANALYSIS OF "WILL-ACT" SCORES IN THE "LOST CAUSE" EXPERIMENT

There are no differences in the "Will-Act" scores between the subjects assigned to different treatments *before* they were exposed to the arguments by the experts. This can be determined by examing each degree of freedom of the pre-experiment "Will-Act" scores in the following paradigm:

Source of Variation		Degrees of Freedom
Between Groups		7
1. A Serious Problem vs. A Minor Problem (I)	1	
2. Individual Non-efficacy vs. Individual Efficacy (J)	1	
3. Sexual Identity MM vs. FF (K)	1	
4. Problem Seriousness vs. Individual Efficacy (IxJ)	1	
5. Problem Seriousness vs. Sexual Identity (IxK)	1	
6. Individual Efficacy vs. Sexual Identity (JxK)	1	
7. Problem Seriousness vs. Individual Efficacy vs. Sexual Identity (IxJxK)	1	
Within Groups: Residual, Error		72
Total Degrees of Freedom		79 (N = 80)

The scores after the exposure to the taped arguments is given in Table 13.2. The scores there—for example, the 4.85 for the grand mean—are the average scale positions (on a 7-point scale) for all subjects. These re-

Table 13.2. Mean Post-Treatment Responses on the "Will-Act" Scale, by Version of Experiment and Sex-Role Identity

Arguments about the Problem's Seriousness by: Public Health Official	Hydrologist	Sexual Identity of Subjects	*Arguments about Efficacy of Interpersonal Action* — *Conservationist argues:* PEOPLE ARE ILL-INTENTIONED / *Political Scientist argues:* THE INDIVIDUAL CAN DO NOTHING	*or* PEOPLE DON'T YET FULLY UNDERSTAND / *or* INDIVIDUALS CAN BE EFFECTIVE	Totals
A SERIOUS PROBLEM	PREVENTION IS THE ONLY ANSWER	MM	4.07	5.20	4.64
		FF	5.59	5.02	5.31
		Combined	4.83	5.11	4.97
A MINOR PROBLEM	THE SERIOUSNESS OF A LITTLE POLLUTION IS CONTROVERSIAL	MM	4.60	5.25	4.92
		FF	4.02	5.02	4.52
		Combined	4.31	5.14	4.72
	Totals	MM	4.34	5.22	4.78
		FF	4.81	5.02	4.92
		Combined	4.57	5.13	4.85

sponses were collected after they had heard the tapes. Before hearing the tape, the average scale position was 4.52.

We proceed now to examine values in Table 13.2 for each line of the analysis of variance paradigm. For example, for the row effects,

serious	4.97
non-serious	4.72

Line 1.	The "Will-act" score for the *serious* versions were not significantly different from the *non-serious* versions.	$F = 1.23$ n.s.

Thus, our prediction that (A + B) > (C + D) is *not* confirmed. For the column effect,

efficacious	5.13
non-efficacious	4.57

Line 2.	The "Will-act" score for the *efficacious* versions is significantly higher than for the *non-efficacious* versions.	$F = 4.53$ $p < .05$

Thus, our second prediction is confirmed. This prediction is of no great scientific consequence because there is very little that is counter-intuitive in the assertion that people will work harder when they can be effective. On the other hand, the non-confirmation for *seriousness* is mildly surprising. Our data do not enable us to say whether seriousness was just not responded to, or whether the serious version raised anxiety so that subjects were disturbed and withdrew attention and commitment.

With regard to the main effect of sex-role identity, our analysis led to no prediction. Extrapolation from Miller and Swanson's assertion of lesser "relative maturity" and greater disposition to deny responsibility by FF would lead to a prediction of MM > FF. The finding is, no difference:

$$MM = 4.78$$
$$FF = 4.92$$

Line 3.	The "Will-act" scores are not significantly different for FF and MM subjects.	$F = 0.31$ n.s.

This finding is of interest in the somewhat oblique sense. It indicates that a reasonable expectation from Miller and Swanson did not materialize.

No predictions concerning the interaction between *seriousness* and *efficacy* were made; however, it may be deduced from our guess that the cells would be ordered B > A > D > C or B > D > A > C, that we would not have expected a significant difference from $(B + C) - (A + D)$. In fact, none materialized. The non-significance of this effect does not touch a theoretical issue, hence it requires no further explanation.

Line 4.	There is no interaction between *efficacy* and *seriousness*.	$F = 1.35$ n.s.

The next three contrasts are of greater importance.

Line 5.	The difference in the "Will-act" scores for *serious* less *non-seriousness* versions is greater for FF than for MM subjects.	$F = 4.24$ $p < .05$

Or, rephrasing slightly, FF subjects are more willing to act when the problem is *serious*, MM subjects are more willing to act when the problem is *non-serious*. This is an important confirmation of the theoretical analysis.

With regard to efficacy, the picture is not quite so clear.

Line 6.	The difference in "Will-act" scores for *efficacious* less *non-efficacious* versions is greater for MM than FF subjects —but not significantly so.	$F = 2.00$ n.s.

Thus, our prediction that MM's would exceed FF's when efficacy alone was considered is in the right direction but not significant. However, when we take the next step and inspect the joint effects of seriousness, efficacy, and sex-role identity, the interaction is significant. The values are as follows:

MM – FF Differences

A (–1.52)	B (0.18)
C (0.58)	D (0.23)

Line 7.	The I x J x K interaction is significant.	$F = 4.28$ $p < .05$

It is in the *serious* and *non-efficacious* version that FF's clearly exceed MM's and though in the *non-serious*, *efficacious* version MM's exceed FF's, the burden of the contribution is in Cell A. Translating this back to the hypothesis,

$$A > D \quad \text{for FF} \quad [\text{i.e., } (5.59) > (5.02)]$$
$$\text{and } D > A \quad \text{for MM} \quad [\text{i.e., } (5.25) > (4.07)]$$

it is clearly sustained. This joint hypothesis can be tested by a reallocation of the variance already considered, and when this is done, the alternate hypothesis that A = D is clearly rejected.

To consider this finding in still another light, it can be contrasted with what might be called a "relative maturity" formulation. The presence of "relative maturity" as here conceived should increase the "Will-act" score when one could be *efficacious* against a *serious* problem more than when *neither* problem *seriousness* nor personal *efficacy* were present. If MM's are more mature, one can predict that the difference between the "Will-act" scores for MM's on the B – C case would be greater than for FF's. This is patently not so.

	B	C	(B – C)
MM	5.21	4.57	0.80
FF	5.00	4.04	0.96

The effect of these interpretations is cumulative in that the rejection of the A = D hypothesis (in favor of the A > D for FF and D > A for MM) utilizes one half of the observations and supports the "differential response strategy" analysis, while the failure of the "relative maturity" formulation utilizes the other half of the data and shows that a plausible alternate formulation does not work. Taken together they give strong empirical support to the formulation which utilizes a theory of the differential identification with male and female role strategies in explaining the present data.

ON THE REPLICABILITY AND VALIDITY OF THE FINDINGS

Before taking up the question of the implications of the findings, it is to be noted that the important theoretical effect was a third order interaction. There is a possibility that the finding capitalizes on error variance. We were curious to determine if it could be replicated, and can report that Bezdek and Strodtbeck (1970) have replicated the study using high-school students and have found the predicted effect.

With regard to the relationship between "willingness to act," expressed on a questionnaire, and post-experimental, goal-directed behavior, one very modest validity study has been carried out. The subjects in the water experiment were requested to discuss with four others (of their own sex-role type) the contribution of the four specialists whom they had heard on the experimental tape. Their group task was to evolve a ranking of the speakers in terms of their relative helpfulness. After the discussion, their individual task was to rank their co-participants in terms of their contribution to the discussion. If willingness to act has validity beyond the questionnaire, then one would expect that the two (of the five) who were given the highest rank should have the higher increase in scores on the "Will-act" criterion measure. This proves to be the case:

Mean "Will-act" scores: Pre-treatment
Leaders = 4.49
Followers = 4.54
Mean "Will-act" scores: Post-treatment
Leaders = 5.28
Followers = 4.56
Difference between the last two scores significant (p 0.02).

This exercise also demonstrated that the difference between leaders and non-leaders is the same for MM as for FF groups—this rules out the possibility that there is a confounding of sex-role and the relationship of "willingness-to-act" score to demonstration of leadership.

SEX-ROLE IDENTITY

Having demonstrated that being FF and having a "willingness-to-act" on a serious problem when chance of success is low, we reconsider the evidence that pervasive, long continued, undivided contact with a mother who controls the child's environment (and makes selective use of reward and punishment), but whose status in the larger community is not high, will result in unconscious femininity. Within American society, the social psychological literature suggests that warmth of the parent is important in creating parent-child similarity on a variety of measures, but as our ethnographic data indicated, the Hindu mother's tolerance of creating a fuss with other children in the courtyard is low. She does, however, tolerate aggression toward herself, and will quickly console the child when he is intropunitive. In addition to so-called "anaclitic" identification, there is some evidence indicating that a dominant parent creates more identification (Hetherington and Brackbill, 1963; Mussen and Distler, 1959) and in general, both girls and boys identify more with a male than a female (Bandura, 1962; McDavid, 1959). There are also small-group studies that suggest that the smaller the power difference between two persons, the more positive the attitude of the weaker person to the more powerful (Mulder, 1959, 1960, and 1965). And finally, when the weaker person acknowledges the right of the other to exert power over him, this so-called legitimate power relation will result in positive attitudes toward the powerful other (Kelman, 1961; Raven and French, 1958).

We cite these heterogeneous sources for their possible relevance to the case of the Hindu mother. Since her status in the larger social system is very low, her so-called power-distance from her son is low. Since she largely controls the moral teaching, her efforts at control are in all probability perceived as completely legitimate. One would therefore guess that the Hindu mother's influence could be exercised—even in the absence of frequent displays of great warmth—without the son's ever experiencing the sharp reduction in positive affect which would motivate him to "break free." As long as a son has reason to believe that what he wants for himself, his mother also wants for him, and as long as the two of them constitute a sub-unit in the household, then the motivation for clear self-other distinctions between son and mother is greatly reduced. If the mother moved through the sequential marital relations, the boy would sense more clearly the boundaries of his claims, but he continues his almost exclusive claims on his mother who continues to feed him. Between a father and son, there are almost certainly competitive concerns about amount of work done, ownership claimed, ideas originated—discounting entirely the Oedipal competition. These would work changes if the son were in effective contact. But not only is there little effective early contact with the father; the later contact is shielded by the tradition for filial deference.

To contrast with the Hindu situation, one can cite experience with mother-son identification in American cities. The data from a study of 47 apparently normal, reasonably well-adjusted families indicate that when the father participates more actively in the family problem-solving interaction than the mother, and exercises greater power over the son, the adolescent boy earns a more masculine score on the Franck test. These data thus suggest that the development of masculine expressive orientations may possibly be the result of the boy's internalizing the characteristics of the more powerful parent in an effort to predict that parent's behavior and hence gain more control over his own environment (Parkman, *loc. cit.*). Or to take another example, in the Hetherington study, the investigator used family decision-making over revealed differences to find 36 mother-dominant and 36 father-dominant families (Hetherington, 1965). Another 254 families were tested, found less extreme, and not used. The investigator then obtained measures of sex-role preference using the "IT" scale; judgments by others of parent-child similarity; and an experimental measure of imitation on a picture-preference test. There are many conclusions from the study, but crucially at point is the statement: "Boys from mother-dominant homes acquired non-sex typed *traits like the mother* and also *more feminine sex-role preferences* than boys from father-dominant homes" (p. 193; author's italics). Since this result was consistently found for children age 4–5, 6–8, and 9–11, it shows that mother-dominance effects are present over a broad age period. This study is not explicit on how the motivation for the identification was created, nor how long the effects may last. Also, it does not clearly answer whether a mother's dominating the father in what Hsu would call a culture with husband-wife dominance is the same as a mother who controls essential resources (Whiting, 1960) in a Hindu courtyard. But for now, it seems wise to assume these are equivalent for the child involved.[7]

7. To check this we have arranged for Richard W. Moodey to collect 100 male and 100 female Franck and Gough expanded protocols in the vicinity of Jaipur, Delhi, and Patna—along with other observations in Nepal. His travel is jointly supported by the Committee on Far Eastern Studies at the University of Chicago and the Council for Intersocietal Studies at Northwestern. Our operation will be to score both tests to de-

Discussion

On July 1, 1966, *Time* used the terms "impractical, theoretical, and vaguely religious" to characterize India and "practical, pragmatic, and irreligious" to characterize China. Thus, even at the level of popular journalism, the distinction between "conscious-driven" and "strategic" is made in just the way Hsu's hypothesis would require. In the face of such consensus it seems almost unnecessary to analyze further the way in which the outcome behavior of the experiment is similar to the Hindu cultural emphasis. As an alternate, recourse may be taken to aspects of Professor Parsons' theory that can serve as a meta-language for relating the cultural and experimental materials. He would describe the distinctions at issue as Universalism and Ascription:

> . . . the primary relevance of universalistic standards shifts to the validation of the quality-ideal. The focus is in the attainment of an ideal state of affairs, which once attained is considered to be permanently valid. But the universalistic element introduces a factor of strain since, in its main line, it is scarcely possible to maintain that any status quo of a social system conforms with any sharply defined ideal state. Hence a tendency to a dualism of ideal and real. . . . Broadly, the philosophy of "idealism" . . . seems to conform with this pattern. [1952:108*ff*.]

and Universalism and Achievement:

> The Universalistic Achievement Pattern is best exemplified in the dominant American ethos. The combination of universalism and achievement puts the primary emphasis on universalistically defined goal-achievement and on the dynamic quality of continuing to achieve a particular goal. It does not emphasize the "final" goal state, which once achieved is to be maintained in perpetuity . . . [it] puts the primary universalistic accent on process, that is on means-choice . . . leaving the goal system fluid. In some sense, the philosophy of Pragmatism epitomized this orientation. . . . [*Ibid.*, pp. 107–108]

Parsons offers no general hypotheses as to how one, in contrast with the other, would be related to alternative kinship systems; his very important contribution is to stress that both are allowable variations in United States culture.

---

termine the criteria that differentiate male and female. If these prove to be the same in Hindu culture as in the United States, certain direct comparisons can be undertaken. Indian and United States scorers will be trained to use both U.S. and indigenous norms, if two sets are necessary. In short, we will generate the data by parallel means and then take from the data the indigenous norms. From that point, the tree of possibilities branches rapidly, and on only some of the routes is there a sequence of circumstances which will lead to an unequivocal interpretation. If a satisfactory test does emerge, then, on a later trip, additional appropriate validating tests can be carried out.

> . . . any one of the major pattern variable combinations can be internalized as a result of the socialization processes and presumably . . . without a primary part being played by recourse to the operation of mechanisms other than the learning mechanisms, that is, without "neurotic" deviations from it; for example, (without deviations from) some pattern of "mature personality *in general*." [*Ibid.*, p. 227]

We find Parsons' formulation consistent with our rejection of the "elaborated defensiveness" argument of Miller and Swanson. We are in debt to Parsons for the clarity with which he directs attention to the linkages between the development of sex-role identity and cultural value systems. For the situation to be as he (*and* we) suggest, there must be a wide tolerance (in occupations, work-groups, social networks, and so forth) for variations in sex-role identity of the magnitude here at issue.[8]

While we believe that there is a wide tolerance for different sex-role identities, we do not believe that the total composition is a matter of little significance to the operation of the system. To join squarely the argument of the conference, one can represent this perspective by formulating the counter-hypothesis to Hsu's. Instead of assuming as a point of departure that societies are differentiated by the four classes of dominant relations, assume that *all societies elaborate sequential developmental experiences to counterbalance any "dominance" in earlier socialization.* The Whiting, Kluckhohn, and Anthony hypothesis would be a special case of this hypothesis. If the hypothesis were treated as true, one would seek historical and ecological explanations for the reason why the current dominance of mother-son relationships has persisted in Hindu culture. In an even stronger form, one might be disposed to believe that a society that alternated intensive home and universalistic non-primary dominance environments during socialization would hedge against the threat of too much concentration in personalities of one type and the possibility that all males were MM and all females FF—a situation that would provide too little variation in personality for the spectrum of occupational specialties of the society.

Under either Hsu's hypothesis or the counter-hypothesis, there is a role for the social psychologist in the continuing inquiry. Whenever it is asserted that a particular, persistent role relationship has a given outcome, the social psychologist can be asked to create a personality measure, and in terms of some experimental intervention, look for concomitants of the relationship as it exists at different intensities between and within cultures. If what Herskovits (1948:239) has called the "rounded study of a

8. Heberlein from our laboratory has demonstrated in a summer camp that FF boys are just as likely to be chosen as sociometric leaders and friends as are MM boys, and they are no more likely to be sociometric rejects. In intimate friendships and work relations, boys disregard the sex-role identity here under analysis as a basis for social preference. In support of our general argument, Heberlein also finds MM boys are more frequently seen by their friends as "least emotional" and FF boys as "most responsible."

culture" is to develop, attention must be given to activities that allow for clearer manifestation of personality than the drawing of water or the hewing of wood. One must give attention to those aspects which, "in giving meaning to the universe, sanction every day living, and in their aesthetic manifestations afford men some of the deepest satisfactions they experience." Micro-cultural experimental settings can be created that allow latitude for the expression of choice and the displays of evaluative criteria. When the parameters of such situations are identified, both the cognitive and affective determinants of choice can be postulated to have roots in earlier social psychological group experiences.

Just as Hsu recognizes "content differences" within kinship structures, so a social psychologist would look for structural concomitants that enhance or suppress the content of given dominant relationships. For example, a Japanese mother who acts as a go-between for the father and son fills within the family a role that the son must play outside the family if he is to play it at all. We would conceive of his desire to play such a role as having arisen through identification with his mother, but as is always the case with "positional" identification, what is learned in one context must be acted upon in another (Slater, 1961). Positional identification implies an actor and at least one alter who participate in a protracted role-relation. One learns his own, and the others', part, as in a play. In the Japanese case, the go-between skills, the alter's role in the home, becomes ego's role in the community. But in the Hindu case, an even more elaborate transformation is required. The mother, the alter in this case, behaves toward her son in a particularistic way, which cannot be replicated in kind in the manifold, extra-familial, work and religious world. Hsu's criterion behaviors—the attitude of incorporating (or the wish to be incorporated), preference for the condition of not being in a sequence (or a rational bureaucratic hierarchy), the desire to be reliant on others, diffused potential sexuality—and the tendency to spread out in all directions, are all examples that must be examined. How can it be that they are products of transformed traits learned through identification with one's mother?

Our experimental results suggested only that men who made woman-like completions (FF men) seemed quicker to "spread out" and accept responsibility when "seriousness" was asserted, while the other subjects (MM men) were concerned about efficacy. The original experiment clearly does not cover a wide enough range of behavior to be fully relevant. To treat more squarely the manifestations in action of feminine ideologies, it is helpful to consider a part of a report on a whole community.

THE SEXUAL DILEMMA IN CRESTWOOD HEIGHTS

In a widely read, recent book (Seeley, Sim, and Loosely, 1964) the authors describe basic differences in the beliefs of males and females, then suggest that *in matters of social action, each sex moves as if it held the ideology of the other.* For those who find the fusion of elements of action in Professor Parsons' theory somewhat perplexing to work with, it might appear that the Seeley, Sim, and Loosely formulation were a substitute. Since we feel that Rajput males will be guided by an ideology that is in fundamental ways the *same* as their mothers', we feel that it is necessary to reconcile ideology and action. We believe it is possible to clarify our own position while giving a more fundamental view of behaviors that the authors have described well but, in our thinking, explained poorly.

For example, the authors describe a moral difference between males and females that we would tentatively treat as universal (*ibid.*, p. 453 *ff.*).

> For the man (say, a father), a given act (say, his child's) is one of a series of acts classified, according to its formal quasi-legal properties, with other acts having similar external consequences—particularly, naturally, for government, authority, and the maintenance of norms and practices. For the woman (say, a mother), the same act is seen chiefly as embedded in its immediate context of meaning and emotion, with roots reaching back to previous, perhaps formally dissimilar acts, in that particular child's emotional history. The man's first step in the analysis of a problem is analytic and categorical; the woman's is synthetic and contextual. The man has the "play" as the frame of reference for the act; the woman has the "actor." The "universe of acts" of which the given act is a sample is, for the man, the universe of acts (regardless of agent) that have similar effects; for the woman, the universe of acts of which this is a sample is the universe of that particular actor's acts. For the man, effect and achievement are the paramount dimensions of classification; for the woman, motive, intent, and feeling.

They then err by describing the woman's behavior as if it were something like the convictions of Rousseau or Thoreau:

> For the women (and their allies among the experts, male and female), the supreme value is the happiness and well-being of the individual, which taken in its immediacy determines day-to-day policy. Does a general rule press heavily on a given child? Then the child ought to have special support, or an exception to the rule should be made, or the rule should be amended or abolished. The particular, the unique, the special, the case, the individual is both the focus of concern and the touchstone of policy. The institutional regularities are seen rather as obstacles than as aids to the achievement of the good life. Mores, folkways, laws, norms are considered to function as obstructions to the development of those unique characteristics, configurations, and activities which are the height of value, if not its very meaning. Individuals so reared and freed will, it is felt, produce the minimum of order which may be required—if any is—for concerted action where that is necessary.

It is our belief that women come to view their socialization task as the transmission to children of a system of values with which to regulate life. They therefore attempt to act with moral superiority and to see themselves as charged with the punishment of value deviations. In their day-today relations in the family, the rigidity of this pose is mitigated by their mercy and particularistic concern for their child. Hence, the authors err in assuming that the particularistic disposition toward one's own child is generalized to all mankind. Through this error, they are led to conclude that though ideological individualists, women

> notably act in groups to persuade or coerce individuals into making changes in the conditions of group life, for example, a change in a norm system or activity. It is they who, instead of taking direct individual-to-individual action, organize, work in concert, know and use the techniques of group pressure, and so secure alteration in the circumstances of the group.

They suggest that while women in action are collectivists,

> men, who allege the supremacy of the organization, the collective, are the practitioners of skills which rest, consciously or not, upon contrary beliefs. They bring to rare perfection and are secretly (within or between themselves) proud of those arts of interpersonal manipulation that are intended to make the organization work to the benefit of a particular individual. They have the "know-how"; they know "who's who" and "what's what." Business is thus chiefly an interpersonal operation in which the ostensibly worshipped collective and its norms are *felt* to function (as the women *say* they do) as obstacles to be dealt with or circumvented as far as prudence will permit. The appeal is taken by the individual to the individual for the sake of the individual, although the best cover for action is reference back to the welfare of the organization as the apparent ground.

To reconcile their observations, the authors feel that the male collectivist ideology reverses to individualism in action, while the process is the reverse for women.

We would approach the same distinctions more straightforwardly by assuming that women do not ordinarily have an opportunity to develop that special class of value relativity required for business dealings. Men are not ordinarily confined in their attention to the socialization of children; they are less apt to develop the implicit faith in their value position that comes when one deals with a co-participant as plastic as a child. It is assumed to be somewhat disabling to males socialized in a mother-son dominance situation if the son comes to act as if he expected the rules to be suspended because he fuses identities that are factually distinct or is over-rigid and moralistic about distinctions that are non-essential.

In the matter of beliefs concerning the power of the individual to modify external affairs, we see no ideology-versus-action interchange between the sexes. We see the universal disposition of women to incline toward the recognition of and adaptation to external circumstances. Similarly, we see the disposition to place rationality at the service of the emotions as a woman's disposition which is congruent with accessibility to a child rather than service to a boss. The Crestwood Heights authors speak of the disposition to

> "philosophize," to integrate experience in an intellectually consistent, comprehensive fashion . . . [as] markedly a female characteristic; the urge to leave experience as an enjoyable muddle, or, at most, to organize small areas of it intellectually *ad hoc* by crude rule of thumb, is quite definitely male.

We see the woman's search for closure in systems of belief as the equivalent of a search for motive in a relationship with a loved person. Things have to be closed and understood so that the proper expressive feeling will be present for the next interaction.

Seeley, Sim, and Loosely hold, and we agree, that women's thinking

> attaches less to the immediacies of time and place, and tends to take into imaginative consideration not only the here and now, but the new generation, the "children yet unborn," altered circumstance, and perhaps even a new society as yet only vaguely envisioned. The men, on the contrary, much more earthbound and datum-driven, take into consideration an evanescent present or, at most, a very short-run future, in which things will be much as they are now and have always been. It is perhaps not a contradiction—on the assumption of changelessness—that the men, in action, are the makers of long-term plans and the builders of persistent material and social edifices. They, predominantly, are the authors of enduring building, indestructible dams, business and social organizations that are intended to and do have an immortality transcending their own lives.

This is a subtle matter; it suggests that "future-thinking" does not lead to "future" consequences. The substantive emphases of Hindu culture are scarcely touched by their phrase "children yet unborn," but it still evokes an image of a concern with the cycle of transmigrating souls.

Summary

In barest form, the argument of this paper is that mother-son dominance produces men who think in typically feminine ways. It is suggested that both Hindu ideology and strategies of action are "conscience-driven" rather than "strategic" and may have come about in interaction with aesthetic dispositions and action orientations of unconsciously feminine men. The presence of a concern about the moral implications of action in the construct "conscience-driven" differentiates this polarity from the well-known "instrumental" and "socio-emotional" distinction of Parsons and the Bales and Slater paper (1955). The present distinction, and particularly the implementation in the "lost cause—seriousness" versus "pragmatic efficacious" versions of the experiment, turns the focus of analysis toward what the actor attends to in the situation. The generating mechanism suggested for development of sex-typed strategic orientations relates to the differences in typical male and female adaptation environments: the person-oriented, familiar home versus the object-oriented changing world of work. The transmission of the strategic orientations is held to be like the transmission of other micro-cultural distinctions; that is, through identifications—usually in reciprocal role-relations. Being low-powered in the presence of the legitimate power exercised by and nurturance provided by the mother is believed to be the crucial requirement. Correlates of mother-son dominance suggested in Hsu's hypothesis, such as emphasis upon intent more than effect, the attitude of incorporating, reliance on single authorities, and diffused potential sexuality, are quite consistent with our argument.

As a matter of caution, these suggestions concerning the Rajputs of Khalapur should not be generalized to other Rajputs, to other Hindus, and, most particularly, to other forms of mother-son relations such as those prevailing in the matrifocal families of Caribbean culture without a careful check of ethnographic facts. But where present, we believe the process is quite general; mother-son dominance creates unconscious feminine identification which carries with it a reduction (on the part of the men so affected) of the concern with "strategic" emphases (roughly equivalent to "getting the job done") and an expansion of "conscience-driven" thinking —a concern for the spirit and moral implications of action. Both in the argument and in the example of the small-group experiment, the question of the inherent superiority of being moved by "efficacy" or "seriousness" is played down. It is assumed that at one point it is one—at another, the other. Optimal functioning of a society probably requires leadership dedicated to both. This leads to the thought that strong mother-son dominance of the type experienced by the Rajputs of Khalapur would eliminate itself if it were not for the condition of caste stratification which prevents the Rajputs from experiencing the full consequence of their narrowing of the representation of conventional MM sex-role types. On the other hand, it is just such narrowing as it operates over protracted periods that is believed to have created a broader tolerance for departures from Western masculine roles in Indian culture.

In summary, this social psychological analysis of the possible effects of a dominant mother-son dyad in a primary family unit is not inconsistent with Hsu's hypothesis.

FOURTEEN

ROBERT B. EDGERTON

An Examination of Hsu's "Brother-Brother" Postulate in Four East African Societies

Introduction

The Hsu thesis concerning the "dominance" of basic kin relationships is certain to generate controversy. For one thing, Hsu's general formulation offers a provocative view of the causal influence of specific dyadic kin relationships upon much of the content of culture. No less provocative are his postulates concerning the influence of particular "dominant relationships" within particular cultural systems. It is no exaggeration to conclude that a serious examination of the Hsu thesis calls forth a bewildering variety of problems, many of which are fundamental to an understanding of the structure, process, and content of social systems.

This paper concerns one of these problems—Hsu's "brother-brother" postulate for African societies. It begins by examining this postulate, and some of its derived theorums or hypotheses, in four East African societies. It then considers whether an alternative explanation might better account for the content found in these four societies. Finally, it offers some general observations on the theoretical implications of the Hsu thesis.

THE NATURE OF THE DATA

The data I shall discuss here were collected in 1961–62, during participation in the "Culture and Ecology in East Africa Project" under the direction of Walter Goldschmidt.[1] This project was an examination of possible covariation between "culture" and "ecology." The design of this research called for the controlled comparison of the farming mode of life with the pastoral mode in four tribal societies, each of which contained both of these economic modes. Thus, a highland farming community and a lowland pastoral community within each of the four tribes was chosen for intensive study. In each of these four tribes, an ethnographer divided his time between the two communities, and a cultural geographer collected comparable data in all eight communities. In addition, I collected data on values, attitudes, and personality characteristics in all of the communities. As a result, although the investigation was not explicitly directed toward the concerns of the Hsu thesis, it did nonetheless cover many of the areas that are of relevance to his "brother-brother" postulate. Moreover, it examined these areas within a comparative design that permitted unusual standardization, both in data collection and in the units of analysis. The four societies involved were the Sebei of Uganda, the Pokot and Kamba of Kenya, and the Hehe of Tanzania. The Pokot and Sebei speak closely related Kalenjin languages of the Eastern Sudanic grouping within the Nilo-Saharan stock. The Kamba and Hehe speak more distantly related Bantu languages.

Because the force of the data I present here rests upon questions of methodological validity, a discussion of some of the data collection procedures is essential. The tactics of eliciting information and the actual forms of the questions and stimulus materials were worked out during a pretest among several East African tribes, including the Sebei and the Kamba. Following pretesting and staff conferences, the final interview was constituted as follows: 85 questions covering varied subject areas, 10 Rorschach plates, 9 values-pictures, and 22 color slides.

For each tribe, the ethnographer and the geographer collaborated (often using air photos) in selecting the most appropriate pastoral and farming communities for study. Within each of these eight selected communities, a probability sample of at least 60 persons (30 married men and 30 married women) was drawn. All told, 505 persons were interviewed. The interviews were conducted in the native language through a carefully trained and frequently cross-checked interpreter who was a member of the tribe. Each of the 505 respondents was interviewed in private and the circumstances and format of the interview were carefully standardized. The degree of standardization was equal to that commonly achieved in Western survey research, and the degree of privacy exceeded that usually attained in Western household interview surveys.

1. The research was supported by a Research Grant from the National Science Foundation, and P.H.S. Research Grant M-4097 from the National Institute of Mental Health. I would like to express my indebtedness to my colleagues in the "Culture and Ecology Project": Francis Conant, Chad Oliver, Philip Porter, Edgar Winans, and Walter Goldschmidt, the director.

At the close of the interview, which averaged approximately 75 minutes in length, each respondent was offered a gift (either native beer or something of equivalent value and appeal). Although tribulations occurred as expected, both men and women in all communities cooperated well; the overall refusal rate was less than 5 per cent of the sample and the highest refusal rate in any single community was slightly under 8 per cent.

The interview itself was carried out without notable difficulty or disruption, and the "face" validity of the responses was excellent. The respondents typically neither evaded questions nor obviously withheld information. However, in an effort to confirm the apparent validity of the response patterns, follow-up verification sessions were conducted with key informants to ascertain any possible areas of misunderstanding, lying, or withholding of information. Through such sessions, through discussion with the resident ethnographer, and by subsequent analyses of the internal consistency of the data, it would appear that the responses given were thoughtful, basically accurate, and surprisingly frank.[2]

As critics of interview data are inclined to point out, these responses are verbal; they are not inferences from actually observed behavior. Consequently, they are subject to the limitations of any survey data. But they also have the advantages of such data in that they are quantifiable and comparable to a degree rarely possible with ethnographic observations. Yet, undeniably, ethnographic data are of value, so where it is appropriate and possible to do so, I will buttress interview data with ethnographic observations—from my colleagues, from the literature, and from my own very limited ethnographic experiences in these four tribes. In the main, however, the discussion will be confined to the interview data. Unless specifically stated to the contrary, these data have been controlled for the influences of age, sex, and acculturation.

AN EXAMINATION OF SOME "BROTHER-BROTHER" HYPOTHESES

Hsu (1961:437) suggests that the relationship between brothers is dominant in the majority of African societies south of the Sahara; more specifically, he adds that it is dominant in "African societies of the patrilocal type" (1965:658). If "patrilocal type" can be taken to refer to the common pattern of residence that is initially patrilocal, tending subsequently to be neolocal, then these four societies would qualify as the "brother-brother" type.

On the basis of my data, it is possible to examine five general hypotheses (some of which contain derivative or contingent hypotheses) about the content of cultures within which the brother-brother relationship is said to be dominant. In addition to these five hypotheses, Hsu suggests several others that are untestable from my data, either because the rele-

2. Additional details are available in Robert B. Edgerton, " 'Cultural' vs. 'Ecological' Factors in the Expression of Values, Attitudes, and Personality Characteristics," *American Anthropologist*, 67:442–47, 1965.

vant information is not available or because the hypotheses involved are based upon contrast with other, non-African societies. A consideration of these hypotheses follows.

1. ". . . wives in brother-brother dominated societies are to some extent female brothers" (Hsu, 1965:651). This relationship does not appear to be an important one for Hsu's understanding of the dominant brother-brother relationship, but it nevertheless raises some intriguing points about the husband-wife relationship and the generalization of sentiment. Hsu does not elaborate what he means by a "female brother," but I take it that he means wives who are seen by husbands as a man would see his brother—that is, as someone who is potentially equal and thus as a person with whom rivalry is likely to develop.

Let me first note that in none of these four societies is a wife typically regarded as an equal, either by her husband or by the wife herself. The degree to which a wife is regarded as being inferior to a husband varies throughout the four tribes, but in all four she is thought to be inferior. The strongest such view comes from the extremely male-dominant Kamba, one of whose men said, "A man is always superior to a woman . . . women, you see, do not have strong brains. After all, we buy them; we sell them; we give them orders; we beat them. They are not important." The following response of a Kamba wife is also typical: "We are not as good as men. We are inferior. We must obey. A woman who did not obey would be worse than a wild beast. We know we are inferior—men have stronger brains." A relatively equalitarian view is taken by this Sebei man: "A wife is a mere . . . thing. She is not equal to the husband. She can never be a man . . . that is impossible. She is a woman. [Then, incredulously, to the interviewer] Is a wife equal to a husband in your country?" In these four tribes, the husband-wife relationship is never wholly dominated by the man, especially not among the Pokot where women have considerable power (Edgerton and Conant, 1964), but it is emphatically not a relationship of equality.

Neither is there a strong sense of rivalry between husband and wife. Husband and wives are seldom rivals in the sense that they compete for the same goals or for an equivalent status. To a limited extent, they do compete for the affection or loyalty of their children, but that does not seem to be the sort of rivalry that Hsu intends when he says: "With greater equality comes greater chances of rivalry" (1965:647). Co-wives may be rivals in this sense, but the husband-wife relationship is far more clearly one of mistrust and antagonism than it is of rivalry.

2. There will be "an almost universal belief in sorcery or witchcraft among close family members, especially between parents and children, and between other individuals, who are related as seniors and juniors, but almost none between brothers and others, who are related as equals" (Hsu, 1961:439). Witchcraft was a major focus of the interview and of my ethnographic inquiries. In the following discussion, I am using the term

"witchcraft" to include both sorcery and witchcraft. Where a distinction between the two is necessary, "sorcery" will be used as a separate term. Although precise quantitative inter-tribal comparisons would be specious, I believe that it is legitimate to offer the following general comparative judgments.

(a) Witchcraft by parents against their own children is rare. Both interview responses and ethnographic investigation indicated that a father or mother very rarely employs witchcraft against his or her own children. This is true even when the parents know that a child is planning, or is taking, hostile action against them. The "father's curse" does occur (this curse is revokable and its effect can be made to vary in intensity from death to mere confusion such that the victim wanders aimlessly), but such a curse is socially sanctioned and is public in its application. It is thus by no means an act of sorcery or witchcraft. Further, the "father's curse" is only rarely inflicted in these four societies. Actual cases of witchcraft being employed by a parent against a child were found only among the Sebei.

(b) Witchcraft by children against their mother is rare. I was able to collect only one case of this sort (Sebei), and most respondents agreed that such actions were extremely unusual, if not quite unthinkable.

(c) Witchcraft by children against their father occurs but is unusual. Children, particularly sons, are often hostile to their fathers, but witchcraft is only infrequently an outgrowth of their ill-feeling. Where such witchcraft does occur, it is usually with the active collaboration of the son's mother, and it is the mother who typically takes the action. Furthermore, the action taken is much more likely to be poisoning than witchcraft. Such poisonings are feared by husbands—and they actually occur—especially among the Kamba and the Pokot. After a child has married, the likelihood that witchcraft will be used against a parent remains low.

(d) Witchcraft by grandparents against grandchildren is common. While it is unusual for juveniles or young adults to have or to use witchcraft (especially sorcery), older persons do have the power, and they employ it against the young. There is strong belief in all four societies, but most prominently among the Hehe, that elderly persons use witchcraft against their grandchildren-in-law to cause their infertility or the death of their offspring. Elderly women are particularly suspect in this regard.

(e) Witchcraft between husband and wife is common. As already stated, wives do bewitch and poison their husbands. Men also employ magic against their wives, principally in an effort to reduce their extramarital amatory adventures. It is obvious that the quality of witchcraft usage by husbands and wives is not comparable; men greatly fear the lethal witchcraft of their wives, but women are relatively unconcerned by the milder threat posed by their husbands' magic. The feelings between husbands and wives are a case in point. When asked about whom they trusted, 67 of the 252 women interviewed said they trusted their husbands; however, not one single man of the 252 interviewed stated that he would, or should, trust his wife. This mistrust reflects various things—that one's wife is of another clan, or that she is too inferior or adulterous to be trusted—but it also reflects a basic fear of her potential for malevolence.

(f) Witchcraft between siblings is relatively uncommon. Here, the Hsu hypothesis is confirmed. Witchcraft between brothers is uncommon. As mentioned before, younger persons tend not to have this power. When acts of witchcraft occur between siblings, they tend to come later in life when both persons are married adults. Even though such cases occur, cases between persons in other relationships occur far more frequently. However, as we shall now see, witchcraft between non-siblings who "are related as equals" is common.

(g) Witchcraft is most common between unrelated adults who are relatively equal in status. In these four societies, over half of the witchcraft cases mentioned were between *unrelated* adults of approximately equal status. The grievances leading to the witchcraft ranged from petty beer-pot quarrels to serious questions of property dispute. Conversely, witchcraft between brothers, age-mates, or other "related" equals is relatively uncommon.

I conclude that while there is fear of witchcraft, and the actual use of it, among close family members, and between seniors and juniors, there is still more between "unrelated" adults. And in all four of these societies it is next to impossible to discover even situationally specific criteria for equality. Hence, questions involving status equality are difficult to answer.

3. "These attributes [rivalry and equality] are conducive to sexual competition between fathers and sons. At any rate, the possibility of such emulation is real enough to produce many forms of hostility such as suspicion or witchcraft accusations against each other" (Hsu, 1965:651). Sexual hostility between fathers and sons may take the form of early Oedipal conflicts, or of later competition for women as sexual partners or as wives. Both occur. There is evidence for the existence of Oedipal feelings, and fathers and sons have sometimes been known to press their attentions upon the same unmarried girl or, for that matter, the same married woman. However, neither kind of conflict seems to generate a high degree of concern. At least, my interview data and ethnographic experiences failed to indicate that sexual competition engenders any prominent conflict between fathers and sons.

To be sure, suspicion and hostility do exist between fathers and sons. In all tribes, sons were found who admitted that they wished ill to their fathers, and it was not difficult to locate fathers who feared the intentions of their sons. But these hostilities rarely had any apparent basis in sexual competition. Rather, they typically concerned matters of *property*, especially as in matters of bride-price and inheritance. Of course, it can always be asserted that all father-son conflict has its roots in early Oedipal feelings, but such psychodynamic speculation is highly resistant to empirical scrutiny.

Sexual competition may be prominent in age-graded societies that long delay their warrior grades the right to marry, but these four societies are not so structured. In these societies, sexual competition can be severe between age-mates (Hehe excepted), but it appears to be of little concern between fathers and sons.

Hsu also derives the following sub-hypothesis from the above-stated sexual competition formulation: "Therefore the cult of the ancestors is likely to be either non-existent or minimal, and even when some form of ancestor cult may be said to exist, the central effort will be directed toward preventing the spirits of the departed from punishing or performing wrathful acts rather than showing concern for the ancestor's comfort and respect" (Hsu, 1965:651).

Among these four tribes, only the Hehe have an elaborated concern for the ancestors. And even here, there is no "cult" comparable to that existing in the Chinese family. It would also seem to be true that the Hehe involvement with their ancestors takes the form that Hsu anticipates, because while these ancestors are not exclusively wrathful, they are the custodians of morality, and most Hehe can fairly be said to be more concerned with the ancestors' unwelcome intervention in the lives of mortals than they are with the ancestors' "comfort or respect."

It need not follow, however, that this situation is a consequence of father-son sexual competition. If it is related to father-son conflict, it is much more typically and emotionally related to authority and to property than it is to sexuality.

Let us turn, then, to the first of Professor Hsu's two major hypotheses, the one that involves authority.

4. "In the brother-brother dominated society, authority is not an element of any of the attributes" (Hsu, 1965:653). This basic hypothesis is best examined by turning to the more specific sub-hypotheses that appear to be derived from it.

(a) ". . . the attribute of equality will seriously affect the authority of the old over the young" (*ibid.*, p. 650). In examination of this hypothesis, we can offer responses given by the 505 Africans to the question of when a young adult man may tell an old man that he is wrong. The results are given in Table 14.1.

Obviously, there is substantial variability here, from the marked respect of the Sebei (who are scarcely a deferential people) to the extreme disrespect of the Hehe and the Kamba. This respect is not merely an idealized remembrance of older values; it still operates. For example, young men (except for the Hehe) who are arguing or even brawling will still obey the command of an elder to stop. Furthermore, asked to indicate the kind of man they respected most, 41 persons of the 505 answered, "An old man." This is not an impressive percentage, but it is notable because it was the young as well as the old who gave this response. Finally, I would mention a comment by a Hehe man. The Hehe literally choose to trust no one. Yet,

Table 14.1.

Answers to the question, "When may a young adult man tell an old man (*mzee*) that he is wrong?"*

	HEHE		*KAMBA*		*POKOT*		*SEBEI*	
	Farm.	Past.	Farm.	Past.	Farm.	Past.	Farm.	Past.
Never	1	3	0	1	2	0	42	58
If he wastes property	0	0	1	6	29	39	6	2
If he refuses to pay bride-price	0	0	0	0	0	0	7	0
If he beats his wife too much	0	0	0	5	2	14	0	0
If he abuses people	0	0	1	32	25	5	0	0
If he commits adultery	0	9	0	2	2	1	0	0
If he lies	14	19	0	0	0	0	0	0
Whenever he is wrong	46	29	60	18	2	3	9	4
Other	0	0	0	0	3	1	0	0
Don't know	0	2	0	0	0	0	0	0

* These results, like the others to be presented here, have been controlled for the effects of age, sex, and acculturation. "Farm." stands for farmers; "Past." stands for pastoralists.

this man said: "We Hehe do not trust anyone, but if we were to trust someone, we would trust an old man." These four societies are not gerontocratic, but neither do they deprive old men of all authority and respect.

(b) ". . . there will be strong tensions between fathers and sons" (Hsu, 1965:650). Some of these tensions have been discussed earlier, and they undeniably exist. However, the father does command respect, and he is not without authority. For example, Table 14.2 presents the answers to the questions, "Should an adult man always obey his father without argument?" and, "Why?"

Again, we find variability, from the contentiousness of the ever-argumentative Hehe to the general respect of the other tribes. When it is recalled that the questions involved the obedience of grown men, not unmarried boys, the extent of the father's authority is more impressive. A Kamba man put his feelings this way: "Sons never disobey the father, it is very impossible." His statement is largely rhetorical, but it conveys an attitude nevertheless. And, while a Hehe will dispute matters with his father when the father is wrong, he will accept his father's authority completely when his father is right. For example, this statement from a married man noted for his pride and his temper: "I must respect the father. Even now that I am grown and married, he can beat me. I will not resist him. I let him beat me until he is tired. My father beats me often, when-

Table 14.2.

Answers to the questions, "Should an adult man always obey his father without an argument?" and, "Why?"

	HEHE		*KAMBA*		*POKOT*		*SEBEI*	
	Farm.	Past.	Farm.	Past.	Farm.	Past.	Farm.	Past.
Yes—it is right	6	7	17	57	26	4	30	22
Yes—should be grateful to one's father	0	0	4	1	2	0	5	3
Yes—fear curse	0	0	38	1	0	0	0	23
Yes—fear disinheritance	0	0	3	4	4	56	21	16
No—argue if he lies	9	15	0	0	0	0	0	0
No—argue if he commits adultery	0	1	0	0	0	0	0	0
No—argue if he is wrong	46	38	0	1	33	3	5	0
No—argue when he refuses to pay bride-price	0	0	0	0	0	0	3	0
Other	0	0	0	0	0	0	0	0
No answer Don't know	0	1	0	0	0	0	0	0

Table 14.3.

Answers to the question, "Whom can a person trust?"

	HEHE		*KAMBA*		*POKOT*		*SEBEI*	
	Farm.	Past.	Farm.	Past.	Farm.	Past.	Farm.	Past.
Mother	0	2	5	3	8	3	4	4
Father	3	2	28	29	31	27	14	9
Spouse	0	0	28	15	2	14	2	6
Friend	13	0	0	0	4	5	4	2
Full brother	3	5	0	1	12	6	18	16
In-laws	0	0	0	15	4	5	0	0
Son	0	0	0	1	1	0	2	5
Chief leader	6	10	0	0	0	0	0	1
No one	34	38	1	0	2	3	19	20
No answer Don't know	2	5	0	0	1	0	1	1

ever he is angry with me." I have witnessed such a beating, administered by an elderly man to his brawny and obedient son.

Again, we see inter-tribal and intra-tribal variation, but the father is often trusted.

When the question altered to read, "Is there one person you can trust beyond all others?" the response was still more impressive. "The father" is answered 139 times out of 505—more often than any other person.

This trust is not completely one-sided, as these comments by fathers indicate:

> Hehe: "I would always trust my son—he is most important to me."
> Kamba: "I can trust my son. He is mine."
> Pokot: "A father wants to trust his sons. Even if they grow up and want you to die so that they can inherit, a father still wants to trust them."
> Sebei: "I must trust my son. He will keep my name in the world."

For each such comment I could add another to the contrary, saying that a father cannot trust his own son. Indeed, there were sons who declared that they hated their fathers and wished them dead, but there were others, like this Kamba man, who said: "The father is second only to God."

Thus, while it is true that there are strong tensions between fathers and sons, there are also strong bonds.

(c) "It is true that the older brother can physically coerce his younger brothers but there is no need on the part of the latter which must be satisfied through some inevitable cooperation with the authority-attempting older brother" (Hsu, 1965:654). I may not understand what such a "need" might be, but some younger brothers in these four societies cooperate with their older brothers because they wish to maintain harmony, and others do so out of respect. It is not only the older brother's physical strength that maintains cooperation.

Even more so than was the case with other considerations of authority, the extent to which an older brother's authority over a younger brother is accepted without question varies from tribe to tribe. His authority is relatively strong among the Sebei, and quite weak among the Hehe and Kamba. Each tribe differs markedly from the others.

(d) "Consequently the exercise and maintenance of authority is inclined to be brutal" (Hsu, 1965:654). Brutality is difficult to measure, but we can probably agree that the Hehe father's beating of his son is brutal. We would probably also agree that the blows, kicks, and unkind remarks that a husband in all these tribes rather regularly inflicts upon his wife are instances of brutality. We might agree despite the fact that the recipients of these "brutal" acts do *not* necessarily regard them as brutal.

From my data, it would appear that authority in these societies is maintained and exercised not principally through acts that are physically violent, but rather through the threat or imposition of economic or supernatural sanctions. Everyone fears the fathers' or elders' curse and the loss of cattle through jural action. Few people seem much concerned with physical brutality.

(e) Authority is also "easily subject to rebellion and opposition" (Hsu, 1965:654). I have no interview data on this point. I am not certain what is intended by "easily subject," but the tendency to ritual rebellion, especially by women against men, does occur (Edgerton and Conant, 1964), although not in so ceremonial or elaborate a form as that reported by the Wilsons or Gluckman.

(f) "Superiors or leaders will be constantly in fear of harm from their followers and subordinates by assassination or, more diffusedly, by witchcraft" (Hsu, 1965:654). It is true enough that such persons are in fear of harm, but so is virtually every other person in these societies. Physical violence and witchcraft can and do strike anyone. Furthermore, there are few persons who can be considered "superiors" or "leaders" except in the general sense that men and elders are superiors. Some of those persons who have exceptional authority, such as the "laibon" or the native doctor, also have such charisma and supernatural power that they may in fact be relatively safe from harm. So are the elders, whose dominance in some of these societies is strong (Spencer, 1965). Modern political leaders are in danger, but probably no more so than any wealthy man.

(g) Many of these difficulties with authority exist because "the desire for power is widespread" (Hsu, 1965:654). If power can be inferred as the ultimate goal of the accumulation of property, then this is surely true. The desire for property is universal in these tribes, and its pursuit is unremitting. This will be dealt with in detail in the discussion of the next major hypothesis.

In summary, we find that problems regarding authority certainly do exist in these societies. In part, these difficulties are the product of European acculturation that has proscribed many traditional social sanctions, has transformed young warriors into young idlers, and has challenged the wisdom of the old. Despite these disruptive influences, authority of the old over the young and the father over his children is not lacking. Nor is authority maintained principally through physical brutality. Finally, it is obvious that attitudes toward the exercise of authority differ in these four tribes.

The second of the major hypotheses concerns equality and rivalry.

5. "Two attributes, equality and rivalry, are peculiar to the brother-brother relationship," and "rivalry heightens itself with greater equality" (Hsu, 1965:647, 648). Although brothers can be seen as relatively equal, there are some important exceptions to be noted. For one thing, as we have mentioned, the authority of the older brother over the younger can be considerable, and a younger brother in some tribes (especially the Kamba) can be markedly disadvantaged in such matters as inheritance. It is in general true that members of these tribes do not regard brothers as equals to the degree that age-mates or even sisters are equal. Further-

more, we must always distinguish between full brothers ("brothers of the same stomach") and half-brothers. Between half-brothers it is common to find rivalry reaching the point of cordial loathing and even open conflict, but between full brothers there can be trust and affection rather than rivalry.

But again there are tribal differentia. For example, attitudes between brothers appear to relate to differences between the Bantu and Kalenjin tribes. When asked, "Whom can a person trust?" the two Bantu tribes (Hehe and Kamba) mentioned "full brother" as their first choice only 9 times, but the Kalenjin tribes (Pokot and Sebei) mentioned "full brother" 52 times. The Bantu tribes not only failed to mention the brother as someone to be trusted; Bantu men sometimes voluntarily remarked that they could not trust their brothers. For example, this is a common Kamba remark: "I cannot trust my brother, he wants me to die so that he can inherit all the wealth." On the other hand, the Kalenjin men often regard their full brothers very highly. For example, a Sebei man said, "A man's best friend is his brother. No one will help you or protect you like your brother. You are like one person." Or these comments by Pokot and Sebei men: "Actually, of all people only your own brother can really be trusted"; "You do not even trust your *tilia* partner [partner in a cattle deal] as much as your own brother"; and, "I trust my father, but my brother is the only one I ever tell secrets to." I do not mean to imply that Pokot and Sebei full brothers always trust one another. Far from it. But they are more trusting than Bantu brothers. In short, while brothers may be rivals, they may also be friends. Indeed, among the Kalenjin peoples, brothers sometimes have close friendships. Rivalry is not the only, or necessarily the most distinguishing, feature of the relationship between full brothers. It *may* be the most distinguishing feature of the relationship between half-brothers.

ADDITIONAL ASPECTS OF THE CONTENT OF THE FOUR SOCIETIES

In the preceding section I reviewed data from four East African societies. Some of these data appeared to support certain of the Hsu hypotheses. However, the variability of the cultural content of the four societies, or for that matter, in the eight communities, was impressive. The four tribes were often different in their content, sometimes dramatically different.

Are there other features (attributes, if you wish) that have not yet been discussed, that are common to all four societies and that might consequently be considered characteristic of them? The discovery of such characterizing attributes is a challenge for the most intrepid analyst. I have found the task of characterizing any one of these societies to be sufficiently challenging for my taste; thus the urge to characterize all four is not one that would ordinarily attract me. However, a satisfactory analysis of the brother-brother postulate requires that just such a characterization be attempted.

After examining all the response patterns obtained in the course of the interview, I believe that a characterizing pattern—a dominant attribute—can be identified. This attribute is the ubiquitous importance of property or, more generally speaking, wealth. Although I cannot begin to present all the data from which this characterizing pattern is derived, let me illustrate it with a few significant examples.

Of the 505 persons who were asked the question, "What is the best thing that can happen to a man?" 493 gave answers. Of these 493, 466 (almost 95 per cent) answered in terms of property. Their answers specified "wealth," "land," "cattle," "wives," and "children." Subsequent interviewing indicated that, with very few exceptions, even the persons who specified "children" construed those children principally in terms of wealth or potential wealth. I should add that men and women agreed on their answers to this question.

When the question was changed to read, "What is the best thing that can happen to a woman?" the responses again pointed to property. Of 499 persons who answered the question, 463 gave property-related responses. Answers here often specified "children," in addition to more obvious kinds of wealth ("rich husband," "land," "cattle") but it was clear that in all four societies women were said to view children principally as means to future security and wealth.

The same response pattern was found when the question was altered to convey a value: "If a man could have anything he wanted, what *should* he choose?" Answers were given by 491 persons, and 481 of these said "wealth," in one or another explicit form. When the question asked what women should choose, the proportion of wealth reponses was the same. In both cases, men and women agreed in the answers they gave. When asked about the worst thing that can happen to a person, the same response pattern was found—the worst thing was a lack of wealth, or poverty.

To select but a few more examples, when asked how they felt about a poor man, only 62 of the 505 persons said that they could feel sympathetic to him; 443 were harshly critical, and many said that such a man should be openly ridiculed. Even friendship is characteristically defined in terms directly relating to property. For example, when asked, "What makes a man a good friend?" only 58 respondents gave non-property answers such as "polite," "friendly," "good company," "trustworthy," and the like; 434 persons defined a friend as a man who would give them food or drink, or help them to acquire or maintain property. Even the age at which a person is said to be happiest is most often defined as the age when he is most likely to be wealthy.

The central importance of property can be seen in the answers to many other questions. This concern is shared alike by men and women, by the young and the old. And, it is common to *all* four tribes. It is possible that the interview questions I asked would elicit similarly property-focused answers in any culture, but I strongly doubt it. I suspect that these four societies are essentially—even quintessentially—concerned with property. I do not contend that other analysts, examining these tribes from other perspectives and by other means, would necessarily agree that property is *the* essential focus of all four cultures, but I feel certain that all would agree that it is *one* of the central foci.[3]

If property, or wealth, is so important, then the effects of a universal desire for wealth must be far-reaching. Indeed, if all persons want property, then competition is inevitable, and competition can easily produce hostility and mistrust. My interview data did not provide a reliable measure of the degree of competitiveness present in these societies, but it did permit reliable measures of hostility and mistrust. For example, if one examines by means of a manifest content analysis all responses given to the interview, and compares the number of hostile and mistrusting responses with the friendly and trusting ones, a sharp contrast is apparent. Responses that were manifestly hostile, aggressive, fearful, and the like, exceeded those that were affectionate, cooperative, friendly, supporting, and the like, by a ratio of at least five to one. Indeed, were I less constrained to see positive affect and more willing to include all the recorded instances of negative affect, the ratio could be increased to over eight to one.

This predominance of hostility and mistrust over positive feelings and trust is common to both sexes in *all* of the four societies. Since the eliciting questions in the interview gave as much opportunity for positive as for negative affect to be expressed, the result cannot easily be explained away as an artifact of the method. It appears to me to be an accurate reflection of the hostile feeling that predominates in these societies. Hence, these are societies in which jural rules and processes are of primary significance.

AN EVALUATION OF THE "BROTHER-BROTHER" POSTULATE

How well does "fraternal equivalence," as the principle upon which the brother-brother postulate rests, account for the kin and extra-kin content that I have presented here? Without reviewing all the data, I would conclude that while it succeeds to some degree, to a greater degree it falls short.

Putting the minor, derivative hypotheses to one side, it does not seem to me that the brother-brother postulate fully accounts for the pattern of authority and rivalry found in these four societies. There appears to be greater respect for authority in these tribes than the postulate would anticipate, and there is clearly greater inter-tribal variability than the postulate anticipated. While rivalry exists as fully as was hypothesized, it is not clear to me that it is an outgrowth of fraternal equivalence, and thus of fraternal competition. Indeed, it is far from clear that brothers are equal. Moreover, there is often less competition and more trust between full

3. For a recent analysis of the role of property in Africa see Robert F. Gray and Philip Gulliver (eds.). "The Family Estate in Africa." Studies in the role of property in family structure and lineage continuity (Boston: Boston University Press), 1964.

brothers than there is between persons in other relationships in the nuclear, or polygynous, family.

I hasten to admit that my case against the adequacy of the brother-brother postulate is not ironclad. For one thing, the hypotheses I have attempted to examine are not in a fully operational form and for this reason alone there can be no definitive case (either positive or negative) at this time. In addition, the present paper is far too abbreviated to provide a proper arena for the data I present or for the many relationships they represent. Finally, the brother-brother postulate is complex and I have not dealt with all of its aspects.

In response to my evaluation of the brother-brother postulate, Professor Hsu might raise any of several objections: first, that I have not adequately understood his brother-brother hypotheses and thus have played them false, especially by dealing with them as though they were testable hypotheses when they have been no more than generally stated, comparative suppositions; second, that I have misread my own data and that these data do, in fact, support his hypotheses as they are presently stated; that my data are misleading because they are invalid or incomplete. I believe that the first criticism is more plausible than the second, and the second more plausible than the third. But, whether or not these objections, or still others, prove to be warranted, it is hoped that the data presented here will help clarify the brother-brother thesis.

IS THERE A RIVAL PARADIGM?

If the brother-brother formulation does not adequately explain the content of these four societies, is there a rival paradigm—perhaps another dominant relationship—that does so? Several questions arise immediately. Can we reasonably expect a single relationship, of any kind, to explain or to predict the nature of so many other relationships and so much of the content of culture? I suspect that most Africanists would throw up their hands in horror at the prospect of finding so powerful a relationship. I boggle at the prospect. For one thing, the odds against any monistic theory of this kind must be immense. For another, I have tried, and have failed, to find any single relationship that serves as the key to these African societies. Even my postulated central concern with property, if correct, is but an epiphenomenon of what I take to be sundry "causal" forces.

Might the difficulty be one of perspective? Is it possible that I (or my fictional Africanists) stand too close to the data and therefore cannot see beyond them to an underlying "dominant" relationship? Is there also a deeply ingrained reluctance to accept unicausal theories? Perhaps so. As I read the Hsu thesis concerning the father-son, husband-wife, and mother-son relationships, I am impressed by the acuity of his contrasts. From his broad comparative perspective, the ostensible accuracy of his depictions is impressive. For the tribal societies of Africa, however, I cannot ascend to a comparably Olympian perspective because I do not command a knowledge of all of Africa, and because I have here chosen to confine myself to only four East African societies. From this confined perspective, I regard the brother-brother postulate as only a partial explanation. When pressed to identify an outstanding characteristic of these four societies, I suggested the desire for property, and speculated that the high level of hostility and mistrust found in these tribes might be traced to competition over property.

If I were similarly pressed to suggest a causal explanation for the characteristic content of these four societies, I would confess to puzzlement. In the first place, I am not certain that I know what that sort of causal explanation would look like. But I do know that if I were asked to seek such a "cause" in a dyadic relationship in the nuclear (or polygynous) family, I would not necessarily turn to the brother-brother dyad. I might, for example, look with equal favor upon the "dominance" of the father-son relationship. I believe that I could argue for my four East African societies with virtually the same words employed by Fortes in his analysis of the West African Tallensi. Fortes notes that as sons grow up, their desires for independence arise, and the authority of the father becomes "irksome." The hostility between father and sons is "drained away" in ritual and in requirements for filial piety (Fortes, 1959:31). Thus, despite a substantial presence of hostility, fathers and sons do "trust and support" one another and their relationship is regulated without divisive conflict. Fortes concludes that the "pivot" of the Tale social system is the relationship between a father and his sons (*ibid.*, p. 30). If these societies are property-centered, and property passes from fathers to sons, how could the "pivot" lie elsewhere?

However, if I were pressed still further, I would abandon the father-son pivot as another partial, but only partial, explanation. The father-son and brother-brother relationships are not the only critical ones in these polygynous families. In fact, I would argue against the causal primacy of any single kin relationship or complex of relationships. I would suggest that we might do just as well by turning the causal chain around and arguing that it is the content of a culture that determines the kin relationships. In such an argument, we have the attribute of the desire for wealth as the independent variable, from which we may derive the dependent variables of hostility and competitive mistrust in *all* of the relationships of the polygynous family. As we know, for example from the earlier Kardinerian constructs, the links between "primary" and "secondary" institutions have a way of becoming circular so that the direction of the connection between them can at best be claimed, not demonstrated. As I see the kin relationships in the families of these four African societies, they *all* seem to me to display the same pattern of authority-ambivalence and rivalry over property or potential access to property. It is possible, then, to conclude that all these kin relationships are shaped by the "dominant" content—a ubiquitous desire for property.

In the last analysis, however, I would insist that the primacy of culture over kin relationships is no more demonstrated—or demonstrable—than is the primacy of kin relationship over culture content. What I would contend, and what I have been leading up to throughout this discussion, is the position that argues against the effort to discover, or to hypothesize, any causal direction at all. This position maintains that the best we can do at this stage of analysis, and perhaps at any stage, is take note of the congruence, correlation, or compatibility between kin relationships and non-kin culture content. To continue the search for relationships in the nuclear family that exert determinative force over many aspects of culture seems to me to risk a return to a personality-culture tautology that is not only unsound, but unnecessary.

Conclusion

The Hsu thesis is valuable, not only as a provocative heuristic device for theorists of kinship and psychology, but also as the basis for a series of hypotheses. The data presented here for four East African societies have questioned certain of the hypotheses within the brother-brother postulate. The most serious question raised concerns the causal nature of the basic thesis itself. As I understand this thesis, it is a causal one in which a "dominant" kin relationship determines "recessive" ones, dominant attributes determine other attributes, and the dominant kin relationship determines much in the non-kin content of the culture. Professor Hsu states his basic hypothesis as follows: "the dominant attributes of the dominant relationship in a given kinship system tend to determine the attitudes and action patterns which the individual in such a system develops towards other relationships outside of the system" (1965:641).

For reasons that require no further elaboration here, there are serious questions to be asked of any thesis that derives the content of a culture from early, "primary" relationships in the nuclear family.

I think it quite enough at this stage of the development of the thesis to set aside questions of causality, and especially of causal direction, and to concentrate upon the question of the extent to which it is possible to demonstrate interrelatedness, among and between kin relationships and non-kin culture content. Questions of causality would properly follow such a demonstration. This is not to suggest that the causal question is secondary in importance, but rather that it is the second step procedurally. Indeed, the causal question is of primary importance, for if there are dominant kin relationships that have the sovereign dominion over culture that the Hsu thesis states, then an understanding of these relationships is imperative.

That this task may be imperative does not suggest that it is feasible. Even the lesser task—of demonstrating interrelatedness—is formidable.

For example, should it be possible empirically to determine the content of a culture, how could the dominant kin relationship be inferred from this content? Or, if the dominant kin relationship is to be postulated, how is the non-kin content logically to be deduced from it as a theorem? As Professor Hsu is aware, both sorts of questions raise impressive difficulties.

Indeed, as a theory to be subjected to empirical examination, Hsu's complex thesis raises countless problems. As anthropologists have long understood, the problems of hypothesis testing on cross-cultural basis pose truly formidable hazards.[4] For all that cross-cultural comparison is the birthplace of understanding, it is also the graveyard of formal hypotheses. Even if Professor Hsu's hypotheses were to be made far more "operational" than they are now, our presently available cross-cultural methods and data give us little reason to believe that solutions to the empirical problems raised by his thesis are near at hand.

However, viewed as a metaphor, Hsu's thesis has unquestionable value. This metaphor's greatest value resides in its complex multi-variate character, pointing as it does to critical inter-connections between "kinship" and "culture." Yet, if we think of the Hsu thesis as a metaphor, we would be mistaken to consider it as merely an elegant arabesque—decorative, but solely descriptive. If it is a metaphor, it is one that serves well as a program for analysis, and it is here that it can have immediate utility.

4. For a variety of views on the difficulties of comparative method, see: Walter Goldschmidt, *Comparative Functionalism* (Berkeley, University of California Press), 1966; F.S.C. Northrup, "Toward a Deductively Formulated and Operationally Verifiable Comparative Cultural Anthropology," *in* F.S.C. Northrup and Helen Livingston (eds.), *Cross-Cultural Understanding: Epistemology in Anthropology* (New York, Harper & Row), 1964; and, Frank W. Moore (ed.), *Readings in Cross-Cultural Methodology* (New Haven, HRAF Press), 1961.

PART IV

Developmental Explorations

FIFTEEN

JAMES W. FERNANDEZ

Bantu Brotherhood: Symmetry, Socialization, and Ultimate Choice in Two Bantu Cultures

Francis Hsu has argued that other kinship relations and non-kin behavior in Africa may best be understood by reference to the dominance of the brother-brother relationship in nuclear family life (1967:437–49). I will present materials from two Bantu cultures relevant to this hypothesis. The people among whom we will search out compatabilities are the Fang of Gabon and the Zulu of Natal.[1] The discussion applies particularly to the Ntumu-Fang and the Fang-Fang of northern Gabon and the Zulu of the Durban townships and the nearby Nyuswa and Ndwedwe reserves. I want to present: (1) legendary and historical materials; (2) contemporary ethnographic materials; and (3) some materials relevant to the testing of the hypothesis.

1. The Fang are a type society of the Northwestern Bantu. They speak the neo-Bantu language, Yaounde-Fang. Guthrie uses Fang as the type language for a whole linguistic zone (Guthrie, 1953:40–44). The Zulu are the best known representatives of the Nguni-speaking peoples, all of whom are Southeastern Bantu (Doke, 1954: Chap. V).

The Shaka Complex and Asymmetrical Socialization

"Ye Children of my Father
What is the Wrong?"

Shaka's history is widely known among southern Africans. It gives us, we will argue, a "family romance" as relevant for that part of the world as the Oedipus complex in European tradition. Shaka strides grandly across the stage of Bantu history and legend. Like Oedipus, he may be that exceptional character who enables us to see how the agonies of kinship relations relate to the drama of cultures. I stress the term agonies to begin with in order to point up the difficult choices imposed on the individual in relating to various other members of his nuclear family. Hsu has suggested that there will be a dominant axis of relationship in every culture. Even if this is true, one cannot overlook the contest which goes on before that dominance is achieved. What are the outlines of this complex and these agonies? [2]

Shaka is born an unwanted child, the failure of his father, Senzasakuna, to observe the limits of customary intercrural intercourse–*ukuhlobonga*–with his mother Nandi. Nandi's mother was a Quabe whose clan intermarriage with the Zulus was taboo. Shaka thus springs from a union with incestuous implications. Marriage takes place but soon the father rejects the mother and child and they go to live at Nandi's people's kraal. When Nandi was pregnant, because of the incest involved, it was given out that she was simply harboring an intestinal beetle, *I-Shaka*. Hence his name. It can also mean–as *chaka*–a poor fellow, a menial, a servant. Shaka is bullied and mocked by the elder herd boys. Shaka vows to repay them. At 15 he is brought to his father's kraal for puberty ceremonies (*thomba*) but he is recalcitrant and refuses to fully participate. He is said to have refused the loingirdle–*umutsha*–because he wants to demonstrate he has grown to become a man. (Shaka is commonly credited with having abolished circum-

2. I should like to emphasize that my statement of the complex is my own summary of reading in Bryant and Ritter (Bryant, 1929; Ritter, 1955) and of conversations about Shaka with Zulu in Natal (summer and fall, 1965). One can make no claim to be stating historical facts any more than the Oedipus cycle can be taken at face value as history. Of course, Shaka is a historical character whose startling impact on southern Africa is a fact of history. The English traders Flynn and Isaacs give us extensive information on certain portions of his later life. But much of what was subsequently told about Shaka is hearsay passed down orally and by slow accretions assuming legendary proportions. It has, perhaps, more psychological than historical importance. In any case, we need careful work on the content of this legend among Africans, since the European accounts of Shaka's life–and he has been of particular and compelling interest to them–undoubtedly have their bias. Mofolo's vernacular novel *Shaka* (1931), though it contains much of great interest from the African perspective, is by declaration a historical romance and work of the imagination. Mofolo, moreover, was a Mosotho and not directly in the Zulu oral tradition.

cision among the Zulu though it is practiced among other members of the Nguni family.) The hostility in his father's kraal causes Shaka and Nandi once again to leave. They live with Gendeyana to whom Nandi had borne a son Ngwadi, Shaka's maternal half-brother, with whom his relations were always friendly.

But Shaka has no rightful place in this kraal. Escaping his father's emissaries who bargain for his death he finally settles with Ngomane, headman of the Dletsheni clan of the Mtetwas. This is the kraal of his mother's father's sister. The Mtetwas are ruled by King Jobe. At the time Jobe's two sons had conspired against him. One had been put to death and the other, Dingiswayo, fled. When Jobe dies, Dingiswayo returns and Shaka, because of his energy and bravery, is made an important member of his army. Here he invents the short stabbing assagai so crucial to his military successes. Its use made Nguni warfare much more bloody and devastating than the previous skirmishes carried on at a distance with throwing spears. Shaka adopts the draconian custom of accepting no prisoners. He kills all the enemy wounded and those of his own wounded incapacitated by their wounds.

Dingiswayo, whose reputation in Zulu history is one of moderation and conciliation, attempts to restrain the zeal of his chief lieutenant. Shaka is partially reconciled with his father who, however, dies shortly. Shaka sends his maternal half-brother to waylay and kill his paternal half-brothers and prevent them from taking the chieftainship. Installed as Chief he has all those who mocked him and Nandi put to death. "Now the Zulu knew what kind of a chief they had!" He does the same for those elder cousins in his mother's family.

He enforces exasperatingly long celibacy upon his warriors. He himself forms a large seraglio of women sent him in homage or from capture but visits them rarely. He is no sensualist and he vows he will never marry and cast "little bulls" to challenge the big bull of the kraal. His preferred form of dalliance seems to be "Zulu love play"—intercrural intercourse. Pregnant women of the harem are killed usually on the pretext of adultery. He refers to his wives as his "sisters"! He adopts the custom of a daily bath entirely nude before any of his people present.

Shaka's personality and draconian methods so impose their will on his councilors and advisors that they are virtually reduced to compliant adulation and obsequiousness. He is followed everywhere by his slayers who crush skulls and break necks at the slightest nod of his head. Albeit he as frequently demonstrates a spontaneous and generous sentiment as this merciless and arbitrary discipline. He is a curious and unpredictable combination. Only Nandi is completely influential with him.

Shaka's conquests have reverberations on all of southern Africa as various of the Nguni flee north, south and east to escape him. He dominates Natal. The English traders visit him. He boasts of the orderly, moral and law abiding condition of his kingdom, but inquires with great interest after European custom.

Now Nandi dies. Shaka is thrown into a profound and malevolent grief. "I have conquered the world but lost my mother." At times uncontrollably homicidal, there is great danger in his presence. In mourning, he decrees no crops should be planted for a year. In that time couples which allow pregnancy to occur will be slain. Minor reverses in his campaigns are answered by the annihilation of the truant regiments involved. To test the state of mourning among some of his long celibate troops he strips them naked and has maidens dance before them. Those who show sexual excitement are killed for their disrespect to his poor mother.

His people grow restive in his rule. His paternal half-brothers, Dingane and Mhlangane, respond to the malaise and plot his assassination. They spear him to death. Dying he turns to them and asks, "Ye children of my Father, what is the Wrong?"

From the standpoint of the Oedipus dynamic broadly construed, one may see what ensues in Shaka's life as the product of a failure to satisfactorily dissolve the attachment to the mother coupled with the failure to resolve the antagonism toward and properly identify with the father. From this point of view sexual problems seem dominant. And indeed, the sexual themes in his story have inspired frequent comment and have been identified as latent homosexuality (Gluckman, 1960). They seem at least to represent a high degree of ambivalence about his own sexuality. There is Shaka's exhibitionism, his invention of the short stabbing assagai, as symbolic male sexuality; there is the imposition of long celibacy on his warriors and his infliction of their aroused sexuality; and there is his own celibacy, his anxious relations with the women of his seraglio, and his preference for non-impregnating "Zulu love play." We note that he refers to his wives as his sisters.[3] But the sexual interpretations of this legend can only at our present state of knowledge be very cautiously attempted. Much of this sort of content may be the product of Europeanized versions of Shaka's life, the projection of typically European preoccupations. More research is needed on the content of this legend among Africans if we are to have confidence in any analysis with this bias.

I would suggest that we are much closer to important perceptions if we analyze the Shaka complex, not in terms of the problems of sexuality but in terms of the problems of power. By analyzing the Shaka legend in terms of itself and not solely in terms of the Oedipus complex, we respond to the special intention of Professor Hsu's writings—the making of comprehensible charactcrological distinctions between cultures. It is the problem of power that I feel to be more fundamental to African culture than the problem of sexuality. The Shaka complex is the drama of the working out of the impulse to power in human affairs. The tragedy arises from the

3. The sexual anxiety and the preference for love play could plausibly be explained as unresolved Oedipal attraction and the confounding of his wives with his mother—love play being the most acceptable projection on the adult level of the non-impregnating sensuality exchanged between the child and the mother in the long postpartum period. The anxiety is compounded, for Shaka himself is the product of sexual excess and incest.

failure to restrain this impulse. The seeds of this tragedy are planted in early family life. It is not tragedy in the classic sense, where the hero is destroyed in spite of his intentions by fateful events which shatter his integrity.

The Hsu hypothesis suggests the importance of the problem of power. It indicates that in the equality implicit as an attribute of the brother-brother axis in Africa, rivalry is imminent. The maintenance of authority is not an attribute of this kinship axis and is, therefore, a problem. Brutality, violence, and rebellion tend to be endemic. Hsu postulates the widespread desire for power (1965:642, 654). These portions of the Hsu hypothesis are compatible with the Shaka complex in which we see intense rivalry between brothers, an uncertain authority guaranteed by violence and brutality, and case after case of rebellion. Hsu also suggests that more than in any other society, superiors in societies where the brother-brother axis prevails will be constantly in fear of harm from their followers and subordinates through assassination and witchcraft. This too, though we have not featured it in our account here, is plentiful in the Shaka materials. There are other compatibilities which we shall examine below.

Clearly, however, the Shaka complex gives us little reason to regard the brother-brother relationship as dominant and as setting the style for other family relationships. Rather it is the mother-son relationship that is pervasive—the axis about which the agonies wheel and in which they are energized. I would tend to agree with Hsu concerning the importance of the brother-brother relationship in Africa, but I would like to argue that the mother-son relationship is at least as crucial in family life and in the dynamics of culture as a whole. In my Zulu-Fang materials dealing with what has been called the "diluted marriage complex" (Stephens, 1962), together with a tendency toward age-grading, there are two axes which have the greatest power in explanation: mother-son and brother-brother. With the Zulu, I would credit the first with greater power than the latter. Further, I would argue for a shift in emphasis in the axial relationships over time, as well as a shift in the complementarities which distinguish them.

The notion of "diluted marriage" has to do with the fact that by reasons of loyalty to lineage and because of exogamy, patrilocality, and plural marriage, the relationship between husband and wife is less intense and affection-laden than in most Western societies. Children are raised predominantly in the mother-child household (the case with both Fang and Zulu), which, ideally at least, is one of a number of households attached to the same husband. The husband has therefore diluted responsibilities to any one wife and her children. A strong mother-son bond is created, intensified by infant sleeping arrangements and by a long postpartum sex taboo that heightens the sensual satisfactions of the mother-son bond, increasing identification between them. The Fang have about a two-year postpartum sex taboo, and the Zulu have an equally long period.[4] Both societies have mother-child sleeping arrangements in infancy and early childhood. Whether it follows from such facts or not, a good many African societies evidence a feeling on the part of the men that this mother-son bond must be counterbalanced so that a mature person may be created who will be able to fulfill mature male roles and serve the society satisfactorily.

One of the most common ways of breaking this bond is through initiation ceremonies and, in fact, the Whiting thesis is well known here (Whiting, Kluckhohn, and Anthony, 1958). It identifies counterbalancing as fundamental to such ceremonies. They function to break (1) the emotional dependence of the male child upon the mother, including incestuous inclinations, and (2) the hostility and rivalry toward the male world produced in the young male by mother-son exclusivity. Burton and Whiting (1961) have significantly revised this earlier hypothesis to give greater weight to the problem of identification and status envy rather than the more vaguely drawn "disruptive emotions" of the Oedipal situation. In this rephrasing, in societies where child-training practices give the male child a strong primary identification with his mother, yet where male dominance in patrilineality and patrilocality creates secondary identification with males, initiation ceremonies will be instituted to resolve conflict in sex identity.

Now it sometimes happens that, for one reason or another, societies are unable to succeed with whatever counterbalancing may be necessary, resulting in what might be called "asymmetrical socialization." One relationship or identification—the mother-son in this case—dominates the others, providing a personality which must function compulsively rather than adaptively in adult life. This must be so because the identity which the person in question carries into adult life is inappropriate to the status that will normally be attributed to him by the values of the society—a complex, in other words: a set of interpersonal relationships in early life that linger on and create problems for effective functioning in adulthood.

With these points in mind, the Shaka complex can be stated in this way: The son raised in the mother-child household forms an attachment to her which is not successfully broken by the father and his surrogates who

4. In Murdock's Ethnographic Atlas (1962) no coding is provided for Zulu postpartum sex taboo—Item 36. The Fang are coded as between 1 and 2 years in observance of the taboo. It commonly carries into the second year with the Fang dialect groups in question here. Otherwise the Atlas or the World Ethnographic Sample (Murdock 1957) have correctly coded the Fang and Zulu with one exception. The Fang are listed as extended family households or communal households at the same time as they are registered as having mother-child households. Extended family households or communal households existed traditionally only if one ignores the partitions between sections or apartments of the long bark huts. The ideal is that every wife should have her apartment. Usually co-wives live together in different quarters of the apartment. In that sense half-brothers have greater opportunity to be socialized to each other than among the Zulu. In both cases, Zulu and Fang, the father is absent.

represent, at least in the patrilineal system, the principles of conciliation, harmony, and justice—the principles of lineage viability and interpersonal accommodation. The father, the son sees, is he who must conciliate the various self-interested households of his polygynous family. Beyond that, he must actively teach his son the various principles by which obedience to his authority as a representative of the lineage is a portion of the guarantee of lineage harmony and viability. The father must teach the supremacy of lineage solidarity over personal ambition. The mother, fundamentally alien to the lineage, cannot teach this respect and restraint. Preoccupied with the competition between her household and other households in the polygynous family for the father's attention, she breeds in her child an egocentrism and a compelling ambition. The patrilineage, through its rituals of passage, acts to break this aggrandizing maternal influence; but in Shaka's case we see that, symbolically at least, he has effectively resisted this enforced discontinuity and reincorporation into the lineage. He goes on to an adult aggrandizement and drive for power. He has internalized no principles of lineage respect or feelings of solidarity which can legitimate him on a permanent basis, and he is only legitimated by the unstable charisma of recurrent success and draconian reprisal. His half-brothers finally do him in. "Ye children of my father," he asks dying, "what is the wrong?" The wrong is that Shaka has not been, through his father, properly socialized in his lineage and is thus heir, from the lineage view, to a dangerous megalomania—the aggressive rivalry and fundamental alienation of his mother in the patrilineal social situation in which she finds herself.

Two questions arise in relation to this statement of the complex. It is implied first of all that the values and life style—the attributes in Hsu's sense—characteristic of the women's milieu, passed along to the son by the mother in the primary socialization situation, are different from the values and life style of the male milieu to be passed along to the son in his later socialization by his father or fathers. The second question concerns the failure of secondary socialization in Shaka's case and the explanation to be made for it. In respect to the values and style characteristic of the female milieu, we have suggested the alienation, the sense of competitiveness and only imperfectly suppressed aggrandizement that flourishes in the mother-child households in patrilineal, patrilocal polygynous situations. These features of the women's style of life figure prominently in the women's relationship to sons. Hsu gives us the following attributes of the mother-son dyad: discontinuity, inclusiveness, dependence, diffuseness, and libidinality (1965:642). We can accept discontinuity, diffuseness, and libidinality as characterizing the particular milieu whose values are latent in the Shaka complex, but we note exclusiveness rather than inclusiveness and a dependence which if it exists emotionally must be heavily qualified by the reality of rivalry and strivings toward mastery and dominance.[5] Inter-household rivalry, it would seem, rules out the dependence which otherwise the mother might enforce upon the son and which Hsu points out to be a characteristic of the mother-son relationship in India.

The values we are suggesting as typical of the women's milieu in which the male child obtains his first socialization—except for the emphasis on competition peculiar to the polygynous situation—are similar to the distinction between male and female values frequently made in Western culture. This distinction is made between the tendency of females to concentrate on the achievement of satisfaction for the individual and the tendency of males to more highly value the organization, the institution, the group, as the object of loyalty and valuation.[6]

On the other hand, Parsons' and Zelditch's discussion of the socialization process (1955:45–54, 313–15), in which it is argued that in the nuclear family as a social system adult males tend by specialization toward the application of instrumental values and adult females toward expressive values in relation to offspring, is not supported so simply in our materials.[7] Among the Zulu particularly, the women gain considerable respect and exert considerable instrumental type control over young people, if not over the men themselves. The Shaka complex is an expression, rueful perhaps, of the instrumental influence of the mother. The endocentric concern of the expressive orientation (*ibid.*, p. 42), while true of the mother's earliest relation with her son in the Shaka situation, is rapidly replaced by a concern that he compete successfully (and surely instrumentally) outside the mother-child household. In the Shaka complex, if we may put it this way, we see the consequences of a highly expressive instrumentalism! It falls upon the mother to give both kinds of leadership. This confounds

5. Hsu discusses the discordance between discontinuity and dependence which acts to create particular problems for the mother-son dyad (1965:648). The fact that the son can never be a mother and must become a man—something entirely different from she upon whom he was so dependent—is replete with problems. These are expressed in the Shaka complex. In either case there is a high degree of ambivalence in respect to the attribute of dependence.

6. This view of male and female values is taken in the study by Seeley, Sim, and Loosely (1956). The interesting point is made, however, that ideal declared values tend to be contradicted in behavior. As operators, men tend to be individualists and women organizationalists. We are unable to assess the degree to which this anomaly or resentment concerning it is present in our materials.

7. Zelditch, in his chapter on "Role Differentiation in the Nuclear Family" (Parsons and Bales, 1955), uses the cross-cultural method to test the expressive instrumental hypothesis against 75 societies. By choosing to replicate cases he recognizes that he sacrifices a great deal of information and more refined aspects of analysis available in close study of the best ethnographic reports (p. 315). The Zulu as described by Gluckman (1950) are rated as expressive in mother-role and instrumental in father-role. Here, as well, Zelditch recognizes how difficult it is in ethnographic descriptions of most patrilineal societies to get a clear picture of the role of the mother and of women generally. This bias makes rating difficult (p. 317) for such societies as the Fang and the Zulu. In any case, to base the rating of the Zulu on Gluckman's article (valuable as it is), in which the primary aim is comparison between the Zulu and the Lozi, is indeed to sacrifice a great deal of relevant information.

the basic postulate of the Parsons-Bales approach, which argues that differentiation by sex of instrumental and expressive roles must be made for the stability and viability of the nuclear family as a social system. Any family not making such differentiation must be "under great strain" (1955: 321). While the Zulu materials we consider here do not show the expected expressive-instrumental specialization, it does not follow that the Parsons-Bales postulate is to be called into question. In fact, the failure of secondary socialization and other facts represented in the complex are probably evidence of the "great strain" they predict as a consequence of lack of specialization.

From the point of view of Shaka's personal history, and not from the point of view of the complex which has more general application, one might speak of Nandi's mothering, by reason of her husband's rejection and the implication of incest in her marriage, as sufficiently anxious and inconsistent as to inhibit the development of basic trust in her son. This would incline him toward the lonely and suspicious adulthood he later manifested. We would prefer to emphasize the failure symbolized in the legend by Shaka's avoidance of the initiation ceremonies: the failure to develop social solidarity in the male world. Young has emphasized this consequence (1962). Male solidarity is defined by him as "the cooperation of the men in maintaining a definition of their situation as one which is not only different from that of women but which requires organized activity requiring the loyalty of all males" (1962:382). It is just this clear sense of differentiation as well as loyalty that is lacking in Shaka as portrayed in the legend. It must also be mentioned, however, that Shaka's organization of the Zulu age regiments beyond anything previously known served the functions of differentiation and strong male solidarity more fully than the former initiation. Were it not to confuse legend and actuality, one would be tempted to see his institutionalization of age regiments as compensation for lack in his own socialization in this area.

We have called the consequences of the Shaka complex asymmetrical socialization. The notion could benefit from further explanation. We have postulated in African societies a tendency for the mother-son relationship to be counterbalanced at a later date by the father-son relationship—the mother-son and the father-son relationship having complementary but opposed influence in the son's training. This postulate follows that of Parsons and Bales concerning specialization of expressive and instrumental function in the nuclear family as a small group. But our understanding of symmetry and asymmetry might also benefit from the views of Gregory Bateson, who argued that human relationships tend to be dynamically complementary (Bateson, 1936). That is, the behavior of any one category of persons tends to be in complementary opposition to that of another category of persons. The oppressive, boasting, and competitive display of the Iatmul man, in Bateson's field study, is opposed, yet in complementary fashion encouraged, by the retiring, sweet-tempered, and cooperative Iatmul woman. We are given three sets of complementary attributes (Bateson, 1952): dominance-submission, exhibitionism-spectatorship, and succoring-dependence. What is important is the symmetry or asymmetry in the disposition of these complementary modes of behavior in the socialization process. Asymmetry is likely to produce problems in the behavior of adult members of the culture and considerable instability in that culture. In traditional Zulu and Fang society the dominance and exhibitionism of men toward women was balanced by the succoring role of the women and by the dependence of the men upon them. It is also balanced by rituals of reversal (Gluckman, 1955: Chap. V) in which women take men's roles.[8]

In the Shaka complex the asymmetry that produces problems is evident in the following set of circumstances. In traditional African society, possibly for all patrilineal patrilocal societies [9] and surely for the Zulu and the Fang, we suppose the mother-son and the father-son relationships to be complementary but opposed influences in the training of the child. In terms of the complementary attributes, the mother plays a subordinate and spectator role to the son's dominance and exhibitionism. The father, on the contrary, exhibits dominance to the son who is his subordinate and his spectator. The fathers employ initiation ceremonies to assert their dominance and to offset the influence of the mother-son household. Together the mother and the father make a symmetrical impact upon the son in preparation for an even-handed adulthood in a male lineage. When the complementary role of the father is short-circuited, as it is in this complex, we have asymmetrical socialization. The problem is excessive exhibitionism and dominance in the adult—a preoccupation with matters relating to status and not solidarity.[10] The consequence is instability in the disposition of power and authority. We are thus forced to an analysis of symmetry and asymmetry, however we conceive it, in the family constellation generally. We should like to see the Hsu hypothesis deal more directly with the relationship between dominant and subordinate axes, in such terms.

Not only does any nuclear family itself go through phases in respect to male or female dominance as its members age, but one must also recognize that over the longer period of time the norms of interpersonal behavior may change. In Africa, it is well known that a good many societies give evidence of a shift from matriliny to patriliny (Murdock, 1960).

8. Among the Fang, rituals of reversal in which women took over men's roles were performed yearly in the women's cult—*mevungu*.

9. Seventy-five per cent is commonly accepted as the percentage of tribes in Africa which are patrilineal.

10. Brown (1965:85–89) discusses the status and solidarity considerations in human interrelationships. Status relationships tend to be asymmetrical and solidarity relationships symmetrical. He is concerned primarily with dyadic relationships and not with triadic relationships or complementary dyadic relationships operating in respect to a *tertium quid*, as we are here.

What the Shaka complex would seem to imply is a shift from the more traditional situation where the father-son axis was germinal.[11] While it is doubtful that this happened as early as Shaka's time, it surely happened later in Africa, in the late nineteenth–early twentieth century, and hence it is plausibly expressed in the Shaka legend as later generations gave voice to it.

The paradigm of events involved is familiar in the colonial world. Colonial domination was felt predominantly by the African male, whose competence was called into question by colonial conquest. His capacity to dominate and exhibit behavior worthy of emulation was much hampered. Relatively, the women's competence was unaffected and was even advanced by missionary evangelism directed toward the liberation of the female. That evangelism also attacked just those rites of passage, puberty ceremonies and so on, by which the fathers assured their authority over their sons, bringing them to the full responsibilities of lineage membership. The mother's response to the increased incompetence of the male was to compensate for his status deprivation [12] by exerting increased influence over her sons in favor of exhibitionism and the dominance drive—status acquisition, in other words. The Nandi-Shaka relationship is not, therefore, untypical of a continent which has undergone the particular coercions of a colonial situation.

The Shaka complex in sum shows us certain family characteristics of many African societies in transition. But its aptness may be broader. Could the matricentrism, so familiar a family pattern with the Afro-American, relate to it? And are there certain points of similarity between it and the history-legend of Dr. Nkrumah, particularly as the latter presents himself in his autobiography—his relationship to his mother, his relationship to women, his driving and, in the end, self-defeating ambitions. The very title of his autobiography, *Ghana: The Autobiography of Kwame Nkrumah,* is reminiscent of the consuming ambition of Shaka—the nation become the leader's wish, objectified. Politics, for those driven by a Shaka complex, is no longer the process of arbitration and maintenance of balance. It is the creation of a charisma and its imposition upon reality—a charisma that was first possessed by the child in his mother's eyes. In Peter

11. It is of interest that Erich Fromm (*The Forgotten Language,* 1951:196–231) interprets the Oedipus myth not in standard Freudian sexual terms, but as symbolizing some fundamental change in authority relationships; i.e. the shift from matriarchy to patriarchy. Following Bachofen, he understands this as the shift from the matriarchal principles of blood relationship, equality of men, respect for human life, and love, to the patriarchal principles of contract relationships, order, authority, obedience, and hierarchy. If anything, the Shaka complex symbolizes the shift from patriarchy to matriarchy insofar as these principles have any application to actual social situations.

12. The mother's compensatory role in child rearing as she is faced with status-deprivation in the father is crucial to the theory of social change presented by the economist Everett Hagen (*The Theory of Social Change,* 1962: Chap. 7). Nandi surely produced in Shaka the technologically creative individual. Hagen sees just such consequences of the mother's finding compensation in her son for her husband's inadequacy.

Abrahams' *A Wreath for Udomo*, the African hero prays, "Mother Africa, make me strong for the work I must do. Don't forget me in the many you nurse. I would make you great. I would have the world respect you and your children."

The Distribution of Attributes; Some Ethnographic Materials

We have been preoccupied here with the projection upon the symbolic plane of dominant family relationships in one historical-legendary account. The interpretation of events symbolically stated is always subject to many vagaries, although we have tried to tie down the interpretation to actualities in changing family structure and in historical events. Still such interpretations may be more apparent than real. There may be a consistency and aptness in the argument concerning them, but the evidence usually does not stand by itself. Among its virtues, the Hsu hypothesis is a stimulating adventure in ideas. In the preceding section, therefore, I have ventured several ideas implicit in historical-legendary materials. In this section I should like to review some ethnographic materials relevant to the hypothesis.

First, consider how the Fang in comparison to the Zulu view their own past. Common to all the Fang is the *Adzamboga* legend of origin. The essential feature of this legend involves the migration of the Fang en masse southwest through savannah Africa (Fernandez, 1962). A giant tree (*adzap*) bars their way. They hack a hole through this tree through which they pass, only to find themselves in the equatorial rain forest. This is a new and challenging environment, and they have difficulty coping with it. The help of the Pygmies is sought. Difficulties multiply and cause disputes between brothers, who disperse to become the ancestors of the various dialect groups of the Pahouin Fang—Bulu, Fang, Ewondo, Okak, Ntum, Meke. Within each dialect group, or tribe, the various clans originate in further disputes between brothers. The Fang preserve long genealogies. The historical evidence which accompanies these 10–15 name genealogies is largely given to accounts, at various levels, of brotherly disputes which led to segmentation and the founding of new lineages within the clan or even of new clans. In sum: In the present the Fang see widespread dispersal of the various segments of their social organization and in the past they know of an endless series of disputes between brothers which accounts for this dispersal. They tend, for example, to distinguish the northern Pahouin (Bulu, Ntumu, Ewondo) from the southern Pahouin (Meke, Okak, Fang) on the basis of brotherhood. The southern Pahouin are the younger brothers who split from their domineering older brothers to migrate south.

The emphasis in genealogical histories upon unending turmoil in the brother-brother relationship is clear support for the Hsu hypothesis. I should like to suggest, however, the possibility of another point of view—the importance of the mother in these historical and legendary accounts. In the first place, whenever long-separated members of the same clan meet they invariably search in the genealogy for a common stomach (*abum da*) by which to relate themselves to each other. By inspection of genealogy, they can discover brothers of the same father who split apart to form separated lineages, but they are equally anxious to discover the mother—the stomach—from which they have come and which makes them *abialebot*, "people of a common birth."

The Fang have various grouping concepts of progressively wider scale: *ndebot* (house of people), *mvogabot* (village of people), *etunabot* (people of a common segment), *abialebot* (people of a common birth), and so on. By an interesting principle of complementary filiation these various groups are traced alternatively to a common mother and a common father (*ndebot*, common mother; *mvogabot*, common father; *abialebot*, people of a common birth—hence mother). It is interesting that those groups traced to fathers are volatile and easily given to schismatic conflict, while those traced to mothers have a certain continuity and stability. We have a projection here of the strong bonds of brotherhood by the same mother over against the weak bonds of brotherhood by the same father. The reality of social life in segmentary societies is, of course, schism *and* continuity. The Fang model of that reality places these basic principles in an ascending complementary relationship.

It is well known to students of social organization that the model by which the descent group is understood is the nuclear family. In unilinear descent groups, segmentation is often conceptualized on the basis of uterine and non-uterine sibling relationships in the polygynous family. What I would suggest is that though the dynamics of Fang history, as the genealogy presents it, give plentiful evidence of brother rivalry (more exactly, half-brother rivalry) insofar as the principal concepts of social structure incorporate the content of family life, it is the father-son and mother-son relationships that are represented. Segments separated but contemporary to each other think of themselves as brothers by reason of common motherhood or fatherhood. The fact of motherhood or fatherhood is primary, in other words. The nature of brotherhood is secondary and dependent upon whether the brothers, as sons, are linked together through the father or through the mother. This is reflected in the fact that the term for brother in Fang is *mwadzang*, "child of the mother." [13] In the

13. Occasionally in Fang the term *emwan nana* (child of my mother) will be employed as a term of reference (rarely of address) to distinguish full brothers from half-brothers. Sisters call sisters *mwadzang* as well, though different terms are employed in cross-sex sibling reference and address. This usage is also present among the Zulu where, however, the terms for brother–*umfowethu*–my brother (from the root *fo* meaning man or fellow, comrade; thus *umfowethu* and shortened *umufo*–my fellow, my comrade, my brother) has status as a term which is radical and is not descriptive by reference to the mother.

kinship terminology itself, therefore, the brother-brother relationship does not exist except in relation to the mother. It is not *sui generis*.

We have argued similarly for the Zulu. There is, however, a difference in the weighting given to the mother-son relationship as between these two people. The Shaka legend contains aggrandizing and chaotic implications. In the genealogical history of the Fang, and especially in the image of their social structure given them by their various grouping concepts, the mother-son relationship is understood as having cohesive and stable implications. This may be partially a matter of focusing upon the mother-son relationship from either an inter-household or intra-household point of view, but in any case the variable weighting given to the mother-son relationship brings into question Hsu's view (1965:640) that the attributes of a particular relationship are constants, "universally inherent and potential properties" of a particular axial relationship. It would suggest that there are multivalent attributes of any particular kinship relationship and that both the general cultural context and the more immediate structural and temporal relationships serve to bring forth one or another attribute as salient.

The Zulu do not as individuals preserve long genealogies as do the Fang. They concentrate on the genealogies of their aristocratic lineages and particularly upon the Zulu clan which imposed its preeminence in the early nineteenth century through Shaka. Before the rise of the Zulu empire the Natal Nguni may have had a clan-centered, territorial-lineage organization similar to the Fang. Now the clans have virtually disappeared as functional units and are in any case widely dispersed. These aristocratic genealogies are as full of brother rivalry, however, as those of the Fang.

An hypothesis with such powerful explanatory implications as that of Professor Hsu is bound to have to confront apparently paradoxical facts. Thus we find the brother-brother relationship characterized by great rivalry and competitiveness while at the same time being a tie of great solidarity compared with the tie between generations. Hsu points to this, in fact, as an essential ambiguity characterizing this axis of relationship. In respect to solidarity we ought to mention the impact of the regimental system, which Shaka developed, upon the solidarity of "brothers" in the widest sense. The *esprit de corps* developed by age-mates in the nineteenth century military barracks is still remembered with deep nostalgia and, outside the aristocratic lineages, it created a lingering bond still evident in the homeboy dance groups and sport teams to whom such numbers cluster in contemporary South African cities. Fang brotherhood has no tradition like this to fall back upon when age-mates find themselves outside their villages. As in the case with the nineteenth century regiments however, this homeboy solidarity was largely manifested outside the local kraal. Rivalry between brothers was more the characteristic within it.

From these facts we may note the importance of distinguishing the levels and situations in which rivalry or brotherly solidarity prevail. We have seen how the Fang, at least, distribute these properties in complementary fashion in the social structure. One might suggest, therefore, that the problem is as much one of studying how properties (or attributes) are distributed in any given social system as it is of discovering those that are dominant. It may even be suggested that any social system possesses all the attributes identified by Hsu. Rather than search for dominance, the more important problem would be that of searching out the patterning of attributes—the way they are sequentially, as it were, presented to the socializing individual.

I should like to conclude this section by relating some of the other features of brother-brother societies, drawn out by Hsu, to the Zulu-Fang materials. Hsu points up, for example, the content of the brother-brother relationship in respect to witchcraft and the ancestor cult. The attributes would seem to indicate that witchcraft and sorcery beliefs will be strong particularly between parents and children and those related as juniors and seniors, and not between brothers. Because of sexual rivalry between fathers and sons induced by the attributes of rivalry and equality, a hostility is produced that gives a distinctively magical quality to the ancestor cult. The cult will be more concerned with forestalling or counteracting the wrathful acts of the ancestors than in piously guaranteeing their well-being. In fact, the cults of the dead among both the Zulu and the Fang have this protective and counteractive quality. Measures are taken against the spirits, who are believed to act very arbitrarily if not with actual hostility. Among the Zulu the spirits impose unexpected difficulties and afflictions upon their descendants. This is done to such an extent that a common synonym for ancestor is fool—*isithutha*. The Fang have more concern than the Zulu with gratuitous acts of piety (such as sacrifices) that guarantee the well-being of the spirits in the land of the dead. They have, for example, more elaborate notions about this land of the dead. Still, the Zulu usually interpret ancestral affliction as a failure on their part to properly care for the ancestors. It should be emphasized with both the Zulu and the Fang that the ancestors are known to be concerned with fruitfulness and the viability of their descendants' kinship and with the moral behavior that will secure it. Their wrathfulness may thus always have this explanation and thereby be understood as more than simple hostility.

In respect to witchcraft and sorcery, there is strong contrast to the Hsu account. The Fang evidence substantial sorcery between half-brothers (though little between full brothers). Sorcery between parents and children is relatively rare; though extra-processual anti-witchcraft movements of the 1950's revealed just such evil, to the shock of the Fang who consider the brother-brother axis to be the natural channel for these antagonisms. The Fang tend to limit the efficacy of sorcery to blood or close affinal relationships. Sorcery among the Zulu is active at a wider scale, probably in keeping with the dispersion of the social structure at the time of the rise of the Zulu empire.

Two religious movements of revitalization are of interest in respect to the projection of the brother-brother relationship into the religious realm: *Bwiti* among the Fang (Fernandez, 1962) and *Amakhehleni* (the Old Man's Cult) among the Zulu. Both of these cults explicitly deplore the hostility and sorcery that has arisen in the relationship between brothers and offer measures to counteract and suppress it. They also have as their prime aim the reestablishment of satisfactory relations between the ancestors and their descendants—a relationship, they argue, which has passed into abeyance because of missionary evangelism. In the face of brother-brother divisiveness, we might say, they offer to reestablish the bonds between the fathers and the sons by religious means.

Professor Hsu notes Radcliffe-Brown's observation that among the Southern Bantu the mother's brother is a kind of male mother and the father's sister a kind of female father.[14] This shows the effect of dominant relationships on other relationships in a system. Husbands in a father-son society tend to be younger fathers, wives in a mother-son system tend to be younger mothers. As for the brother-brother system, wives tend to be female brothers. I have difficulty finding evidence for this among the Fang, where the wife is thoroughly unequal and hardly in rivalry with the husband. However, we have Shaka's custom of referring to his wives as his sisters, which in some sense turns them into female brothers. (A Zulu man often calls his sister "my brother.") [15] Moreover, there is considerably more equality between Zulu husband and wife than among the Fang.

But Radcliffe-Brown's observations (1952:15–31) are primordial in the Hsu thesis, for they have to do with the effect of axial dominance upon the entire kinship constellation as well as with the tendency to project that dominance into other social relationships. The Fang give us some useful data here; they evidence a tendency to make the relationship between father and son more fraternal than paternal. We do not have a relationship between authoritarian and disciplinarian father and submissive or rebellious son. The authority over a young man or child is mainly in the hands of his elder brothers, and it is with them that he develops a relationship of greatest dependency and, later, greatest competition for goods. This dependent relationship is reflected in the custom by which the elder brother takes the father's kin term of address. But in any case the father-

14. The usage is actually found in the kinship terminology. Thus in Zulu the father's sister is *babakazi,* "father woman," and the mother's brother *umalume*, "male mother." This usage is not present among the Fang. The father's sister has an independent and non-reducible term—*song*—and the mother's brother is descriptively mother's brother—*nyangndum.*

15. It is said to be an honor for a sister to be so addressed by a brother. Shaka's custom of referring to his wives as his sisters is, however, quite a deviant practice in the minds of most Zulu.

son relationship is more horizontal than lineal. There is even the anomaly that the brother-brother relationship often takes, in respect of dominance and submission, the more vertical form. This would seem to be more evidence of the degree to which attributes are not constants of particular kinship relationships.

In any case, as Hsu argues, the attribute of equality among the Fang seriously affects the authority of the older generations over the younger. Fathers tend to be treated as older brothers and vice versa.[16] Authority is best guaranteed not by seniority but by a vigorous maturity. This may not be untypical of warrior societies, although my observations here have been gathered in highly transitional circumstances where elders have been preempted by rapid change. In any case the characteristic qualities and modes of interaction of the father-son relationship partake noticeably of the attributes of brother-brother dominance. This does not implicate the mother-son relationship, which is important among the Fang though not so important as among the Zulu.

A final note must be said here about divorce. The consequences of rivalry and equality working in the husband-wife relationship would tend to be associated with a high divorce rate. In fact, the Fang have a very high divorce rate [17] and the Zulu a remarkably low one. Gluckman (1950), who undertook to explain this distinction between the Zulu and the Lozi (who have a high divorce rate), credits Zulu morality in sexual relations, a general anxiety-free relation to women, ritual incorporation of the woman in the husband's line, levirate and ghost marriage, and the finality of lobolo payment and transfer of fertility in respect to children. The best explanation, however, is the fact that among the Zulu agnatic descent is traced through the mother—a son's place and his inheritance is determined by his mother's place in the compound family. This custom is associated with what Gluckman calls the "house property complex" where the Zulu husband irrevocably allots land and cattle to his wives, and their sons inherit these through them. With the Fang, this complex is vestigial. The mother does not hold lineage property, and a man's sons compete with his brothers and his father's mother's brother's family for their share. Zulu stability in marriage is occasioned, in any case, by the fact that the women's volatile loyalty to her husband is strengthened by her allegiance to the property which becomes hers and which she holds in trust for her children. Thus her competition with her co-wives is understandable, as is the strength of the mother-son bond.

16. Among the Fang there is the custom where the father and son (even a very young son) reverse roles. The father will often call his young son *ata* (the familiar form of "father"). This has a religious implication: The man's own ancestors can recreate themselves in his son. And it has a social implication, for when the father grows old the son will take care of him as a son. Correspondingly, in the ancestor cult the ancestors are treated as children.

17. In northern Gabon between 60 and 75 per cent of all married men interviewed in eight villages had been divorced at least once.

The materials presented in this section of the discussion point to the greater importance of the mother-son bond among the Zulu and the brother-brother axis among the Fang. The question of dominance, however, may not be as important as the question of patterning: the way in which these relationships and their attributes are distributed in the given culture.

The Meaning of Kinship Bonds in Ultimate Circumstances

The materials we have so far presented suggest a partial refutation of the Hsu thesis in that (1) the brother-brother relationship is not dominant in at least two African societies; (2) the attributes of specific kinship axes are not constant across cultures; and (3) the problem of patterning rather than dominance comes closer to a culturally valuable explanation in behavior. At the least, dominance shifts in the life cycle of the individual, and surely dominance shifts in the historical cycles of cultures. But these materials do not really test the thesis satisfactorily. The inability to test hypotheses except by the correlational method is, of course, a burden of the cross-cultural method which has established ethnographic materials to work with and which cannot manipulate variables in any experimental way. What we should want to test in the effort to locate dominance is the meaning of the various axes of the nuclear family to the members of a given culture. We have already produced materials relevant to the meaning of kinship axes from available ethnographic accounts, histories and legends, and the ethnographers' own field experience (which in the case of the Fang was not directed toward elicitation of materials relevant to the Hsu thesis). In this last section, though the method is still not an experimental one, we suggest a more direct means of eliciting such materials.

The problem of eliciting meaning is a major one in anthropological method. How do we get at what has been called the "psychological reality" (Wallace and Atkins, 1960) or the "folk system" of understanding (Bohannan, 1963) without imposing the analytic perspective—the structural reality—of the research worker upon the materials? There may be an equivalence for predictive purposes between the psychological and structural reality, but these are still different realities and must be separately assessed. The equivalence can clearly not be assumed. Hsu himself pointed up the distinction and urged this shift from structure to content (1959).

We presumed, structurally and analytically, a dominance of the mother-son axis. There is some evidence in our materials that this is psychologically real to the Africans we are considering. But this can only be affirmed by more direct tests. In this case we employed a series of hypothetical questions to get at dominance in kinship axis.[18] By dominance we mean difficulty of termination of bond.[19] That axial relationship is most dominant which is most difficult to break in circumstances in which a choice has to be made between various axes. It will be remembered that students of kinship are often helped to understand residence rules by reference to those relationships in the kinship system most resistant to separation in conflict situations. We have employed a hypothetical conflict situation to test dominance of kin bonds. We will discuss below just what, if anything, this measure of dominance has to do with dominance as discussed by Hsu.

The set of questions employed involves what can be called the "ultimate circumstance situation." The idea for this set of questions is African and arises from a widespread folkloric amusement. Among the Fang the favorite question is the following: "Your wife and your sister have gone down to the stream to bathe. The limb upon which they have hung their loincloths breaks and the clothes fall into the water and disappear. You are called to give aid and, combing the stream, you succeed in finding one cloth. To whom should you give it?" The situation is sufficiently provocative and the answers sufficiently non-stereotyped and challenging to provide plentiful amusement.[20]

The ultimate circumstance questionnaire devised from these and similar folkloric questions involves the choice of one family member in the face of a disaster confronting two or more. The form is the following: "If your father and your mother were drowning and you could only save one, whom would you save? Why?" Ideally, choice should have to be made between all possible axes of the nuclear family (twenty-one possible choices), but the conditions under which these hypothetical questions were administered limited inquiry to half a dozen choices. The responses were taken in Zulu culture Natal, 1965 (as a patrilineal society), in Akan culture, western Ghana, 1966 (as a matrilineal tending towards double descent society), and, for comparison, in American male collegiate cul-

18. Wallace and Atkins, discussing the aims and achievements and inadequacies of componential analysis in getting at real cognitive operations of informants, suggest the necessity of further measures (1960:78). "But the only way of achieving definite knowledge of psychological reality will be to study the semantics of individuals both before and after a formal abstract cultural-semantic analysis of the terms has been performed. Simple demands for verbal definition, the use of River's genealogical method, and analysis of the system of kinship behaviors many not be sufficient here. Additional procedures, by individual representative informants, of matching and sorting, answering hypothetical questions, and description of relationships in order to reveal methods of reckoning will probably be required."

19. Romney and D'Andrade (1964) following the point of view expressed by Wallace and Atkins, measured saliency of kin terms by requesting listing of relatives and then computing mean position of kin term in list as well as per cent of subjects who remembered term, assuming that the more salient term would be recalled more frequently.

20. The wife is the normal answer, for one must protect her respect in the village. One's sister has, as a child, already gone naked in the village. Besides, she will soon marry elsewhere. But rather ingenious reasons are sometimes put forth for giving the cloth to the sister.

ture, 1966. I will suggest the further possibilities of this form of hypothetical question below when we assess the results. In Natal these questions were included in a questionnaire on religious practices circulated randomly in the Zulu townships around Durban (*N*—85).[21] The Ghana sample (*N*—144) was collected randomly on the University of Ghana campus (Legon), in Accra, and in agricultural communities within 100 kilometers of Accra. The random sampling outside the University could not be guaranteed, though a broad age and sex spread was achieved.[22] The Dartmouth sample (*N*—70) was a portion of a class exercise. The spread of responses within the Dartmouth community was broad, but the sample was not determinedly random. The choices in percentage form are found in Table 15.1.

In Table 15.2 we rank order the various axes submitted to choice in the three cultures in respect to the percentages of the population sampled who gave dominance to the axis in question in the particular choice situation. The presumption is that the greater proportion of adherents to that axis, the greater psychological reality of dominance of that particular axis

21. A brief pretest was applied. The questionnaire was translated into Zulu and 4 field assistants attached to the Institute for Social Research, University of Natal circulated it in every Durban township–adult respondents selected randomly within randomly selected households. No follow up was possible.

22. The questionnaire was written out in English and standard Twi translations were checked through with students selected to administer the questionnaire. The actual administration of the test could not be carefully controlled.

Table 15.1.

Zulu Results:

	Total $N = 85$	%	Male $N = 48$	%	Females $N = 37$	%
Save mother	48	56.5	27	56.3	21	56.8
Save wife (husband)	25	29.1	17	35.4	8	21.6
DK-NA	12	14.1	4	8.3	8	21.6
Save father	17	20.0	14	29.2	3	8.1
Save mother	60	70.6	31	64.6	29	78.4
DK-NA	8	9.4	3	6.3	5	13.5
Save father	59	69.4	34	70.8	25	67.6
Save brother	16	18.8	12	25	4	10.8
DK-NA	10	11.8	2	4.2	8	21.6
Save brother	31	36.5	20	41.7	11	29.7
Save sister	41	48.2	26	54.2	15	40.5
DK-NA	13	15.3	2	4.2	11	29.7

Akan Results:

	Total N = 144	%	Male N = 78	%	Females N = 66	%
Save parent	100	69.4	[a]50	64.1	[c]50	75.8
Save spouse	44	30.6	[b]28	35.9	[d]16	24.2
Save father	35	24.3	16	20.5	19	28.8
Save mother	109	75.7	62	79.5	47	71.2
Save father	75	52.1	41	52.6	34	51.5
Save brother	69	47.9	37	47.4	32	48.5
Save father	97	67.4	51	65.4	46	69.7
Save mother's brother	47	32.6	27	34.6	20	30.3
Save mother	112	77.8	61	78.2	51	77.3
Save brother	30	20.8	15	19.2	15	22.7
DK-NA	2	1.4	2	2.6		
Save mother	93	64.5	47	60.3	46	69.7
Save sister	47	32.6	28	35.9	20	30.3
DK-NA	5	2.9	3	3.8		

a = savc mother
b = save wife
c = save parent
d = save husband

Dartmouth Results:

	Dartmouth male N = 70	%	Transient female N = 11	%
Save mother	8	11.4	1	9.1
Save wife	60	85.7	10	90.9
DK-NA	2	2.9		
Save father	23	32.9	3	27.3
Save mother	38	54.3	7	63.6
DK-NA	9	12.9	1	9.1
Save father	25	35.7	2	18.2
Save brother	41	58.6	8	72.7
DK-NA	4	5.7	1	9.1
Save brother	28	39.7	2	18.2
Save sister	31	44.3	1	9.1
DK-NA	12	17.1	8	72.7

Table 15.2.

Zulu (Male $\sigma\, p = 7.2\%$
Female $\sigma\, p = 8.2\%$

1.	mo-da ⩾ fa-da	78.4% significant
2.	fa-so ⩾ bro-bro	70.8% significant
3.	fa-da ⩾ bro-sis	67.6% significant
4.	mo-so ⩾ fa-so	64.6% significant
5.	mo-da ⩾ H-W	56.8% not significant
6.	mo-so ⩾ H-W	56.3% not significant
7.	bro-sis ⩾ bro-bro	54.2% not significant
8.	sis-sis ⩾ bro-sis	40.5% not significant

Akan (Male $\sigma\, p = 5.6\%$
Female $\sigma p = 6.25\%$)

1.	mo-so ⩾ fa-so	79.5% significant
2.	mo-da ⩾ H-W	75.8% significant
3.	mo-da ⩾ fa-da	71.2% significant
4.	mo-so ⩾ H-W	64.1% significant
5.	fa-so ⩾ bro-bro	52.6% not significant
6.	fa-da ⩾ bro-sis	51.5% not significant

Not comparable and non-ranked choices (Akan)

A.	fa-so ⩾ mobro-sisson	65.4% significant
B.	mo-so ⩾ bro-bro	78.2% significant
C.	mo-so ⩾ sis-bro	60.3% not significant
D.	mo-da ⩾ bro-sis	77.3% significant
E.	mo-da ⩾ sis-sis	69.7% significant

Dartmouth (Male only $\sigma\, p = 5.9\%$)

1.	H-W ⩾ mo-da	90.9% insufficient cases
2.	H-W ⩾ mo-so	85.7% significant
3.	bro-sis ⩾ fa-da	72.7% insufficient cases
4.	mo-da ⩾ fa-da	63.6% insufficient cases
5.	bro-bro ⩾ fa-so	58.6% not significant
6.	mo-so ⩾ fa-so	54.3% not significant
7.	bro-sis ⩾ bro-bro	44.3% not significant
8.	bro-sis ⩾ sis-sis	18.2% insufficient cases

in the culture. We have indicated whether the percentages are or are not significant at the .05 level.

Table 15.2 provides us with the view from within the culture. The following significantly dominant axes emerge: mo-da, fa-so, fa-da, and mo-so for the Zulu; mo-so and mo-da for the Akan. For the Dartmouth male (female is discarded for paucity of cases) the only significant dominant relationship is H-W. It will be evident that the entire set of nuclear family axes have not been submitted to rating (due to problems of diminishing returns in the field), hence the data presented here only constitute initial clarification of the Hsu hypothesis by reference to our criteria of dominance. We have employed only two-axis confrontation. More axes might have been employed! We have not matched all possible axes and, moreover, have not felt entitled by any transitive law to extend the implications of actual choices made. For example, in our data for the Zulu the following transition appears: mo-so ≫ fa-so and fa-so ≫ bro-bro, therefore mo-so ≫ bro-bro. Though this transition would refute the Hsu thesis for the Zulu, I do not feel justified in applying any law of transition in this way. It is to be regretted that circumstances prevented testing of this specific choice (mo-so against bro-bro) among the Zulu. Among the Akan the dominance of the mo-so axis over the bro-bro axis was tested and is significant and persuasive (Akan B above). In no case in Africa, in any event, is a brother-brother axis dominant, let alone significantly dominant. It may be pointed out, however, that the only significant dominance in the American sample is the H-W axis, which *is* in clear support of the Hsu thesis.

It is of interest to compare percentages (Table 15.3) between cultures—for those questions repeated from culture to culture—in order to establish significant differences in response. This will be of particular interest as regards patrilineal (Zulu) and matrilineal (Akan) cultures. Significance will be noted at the .05 level.

Between Zulu and Akan, the two significant contrasting responses show the Zulu giving dominance to a fa-so relationship in keeping with their patrilineality and the Akan giving dominance to a mo-da relationship in keeping with their matrilineality. Other choices in which the variable of matriliny-patriliny might be expected to be manifested do not show significant contrast, though differences in response are distributed in the direction that would be predicted by this variable (the mo-da/fa-da choice is an exception to this). As regards significant differences between

Table 15.3.

		Zulu	Akan	
Male ($\sigma Dp = 9.1\%$)	mo-so ≫ fa-so	64.6%	79.5%	not significant
	mo-so ≫ H-W	56.3%	64.1%	not significant
	fa-so ≫ bro-bro	70.85%	52.6%	significant
Female ($\sigma Dp = 10.1\%$)	mo-da ≫ H-W	56.8%	75.8%	significant
	mo-da ≫ fa-da	78.4%	71.29%	not significant
	fa-da ≫ bro-sis	67.67%	51.5%	not significant

		Dartmouth	Zulu		Akan	
Male Dartmouth-Zulu ($\sigma Dp = 9.3\%$)	mo-so ≫ fa-so	54.3%	64.6%	not significant	79.5%	significant
	mo-so ≫ H-W	11.4%	56.5%	significant	64.1%	significant
Dartmouth-Akan ($\sigma Dp = 8.5\%$)	fa-so ≫ bro-bro	41.4%	70.85%	signifiacnt	52.6%	not significant

Dartmouth and the two African cultures they lie in the higher value given to the mo-so relationship over the fa-so relationship among the Akan, and in the fa-so relationship over bro-bro among the Zulu—the first difference conforming to the variable of patriliny-matriliny and the second to the expectation of our argument here that bro-bro is not dominant among the Zulu. The most striking contrast—virtually a reversal—is the dominance given to the mo-so over H-W in Africa and H-W over mo-so in the American sample. Of the eight Dartmouth men who would have saved the mother against the wife, two turned out to be African students at the college. One, a Nigerian, responded with the axiom: "My mother and father are like a tree and my brother and sister are like the branches. One can cut off the branches and the tree will still live and produce, but you can't destroy the trunk." This lineage image applied to the wife as well. These results support our thesis of mo-so dominance in Africa and Hsu's thesis of H-W dominance in America.

We have supposed that some kind of psychological reality lies behind these choices—that we are getting at content. But what precisely is this reality, and can it be called dominance? The Zulu decision to preserve the fa-so bond as against the bro-bro bond, for example, may be based upon rivalry with the brother rather than upon attachment to the father. There are, obviously, many ambiguities involved in interpreting these choices and also, no doubt, in making them. We recognize, of course, that the notion of dominance put forth by Hsu is multivalent—each axis having a number of attributes any or all of which could be involved in a hypothetical decision situation. We have, for example, demonstrated that in this test with the Zulu the mo-so is dominant. But in the Zulu questionnaire an item was included: "Upon whom is the growing male most dependent in learning what he should know to become successful?" The response to this question is not so favorable to mo-so dominance: 77.6 per cent answered father and 14.5 per cent mother!

In order to get at some of the factors bound up in the decisions taken in this hypothetical inquiry, an open-ended inquiry was made after the decision in which the informant was asked to explain that decision. We do not intend to examine in detail these responses here. What seems to appear is that those who had no social or ideological value upon which to attach their responses gave evidence of considerable anxiety and resistance in the American sample. They were less willing to make a judgment on grounds of emotional attachment or solidarity alone and gave evidence of resistance and anxiety. Those who produced fairly quick responses also readily provided a rationalizing value or aphorism—youth must be served, my mother has served her function, society will benefit more this way. For these respondents culture, as a set of statements describing the normal and desirable, entered in quickly to save them from the difficulties of choice in the richly ambiguous and affect-laden web of nuclear family relationships. Though a pragmatic factor of social utility was quite evident in determining choice in the Dartmouth sample, nevertheless African respondents appeared noticeably less resistant and less anxious about responding. A number of reasons may explain this. Questions similar to this are a part of the folklore, and this may account for the readiness of the informants to produce rationalizing aphorisms and proverbs; for example, "The lucky orphan is he who is licked by the mother"—*intandane enhle omakhotwa unina* (Zulu). African family life may be conspicuously less susceptible to the overblown sentiments of togetherness and romantic love—the family perceived more as a utilitarian means to lineage and personal perpetuities, demanding hard-headed decisions and a willingness to relinquish sentimental attachments for larger goals. The family is, after all, in communal society, the chief instrument of socialization and placement. Many other institutions exist in American associational society to take over these tasks, and they leave the family freer to be sentimentalized as the arena of expressive behavior.

The African responses, it would seem, appear more instrumental and pragmatic. The American responses appear more overladen with emotion. They seem more expressive in their implications to respondents. We repeat that this may be because the kind of choice demanded in this questionnaire has status as folklore in Africa but appears entirely bizarre to many Americans.

The question still remains as to what dominance, defined as this sort of a choice, represents. Is it simply a measure of solidarity or affective bond? Or does it testify to a bond that has been the most instrumental to the individual in forming his character and providing him with the means to cope with the problems of the world? We are not able to arrive at any clear-cut conclusions about our data in this respect, and though, as we observed above, dominance in the American decisions reflect emotional bonds of solidarity and dominance decisions in Africa are based more on instrumental considerations, yet plenty of data support the opposite observation and we have no measure of significance.

I would argue in any case for a cultural definition of dominance. What we should be trying to do, it seems to me, in locating dominance is not simply to find a relationship of intense interaction or solidarity, but a relationship in which the cultural content of that interaction is crucial in forming the cognitive maps by reference to which individuals form their adult strategies. We may have strong interaction without significant change in the image of the world held by the participants in that interaction. Dominance from this point of view is understood as that relationship presenting or transferring the most significant image of the world upon which the adult will act. What are the metaphors, the representational devices, of the socialization process that pass from one pole of the dyad to the other and with which at later stages the world will be understood? In a sense the reasons given by Dartmouth students in justifying their choices may be more indicative of dominant relationships than the choices themselves. As my wife has reminded me, the son's choice of his wife over his mother in the data confirms the mother's drive in American society to have her son do better in life than his father!

Regardless of the subtlety of some of these problems, I believe the ultimate circumstance questionnaire offers an important way to test the Hsu thesis. The avoidance-avoidance conflicts of the key questions seem to be highly productive of verbal justifications which, themselves, offer important materials for analysis. The questionnaire should as we have said be elaborated for the entire eight axes of the nuclear family structure. The Hsu thesis must, in part at least, be approached in terms of role conflict, for it would seem to postulate that in various cultures, ego, himself a congeries of roles—brother, father, son, husband—characteristically resolves the incongruous demands of these various roles in terms of the requirements of one role—itself defined in an axial relationship with its opposite. Thus the youth faced with a drowning mother and wife must decide whether, fundamentally, he is a son or a husband, and as such obligated to save the person who defines him. What seems to me intriguing about this questionnaire is that its conditions are so inexorable and provocative that we gain a particularly good view of the resolution process. Surely what the Hsu thesis implies, to use the current vocabulary of social psychology, is that in the natural condition of family life, role conflict and cognitive dissonance are endemic. In an effort to achieve some peace of mind and balance in the cognitive structure, ego tends to resolve his relationships in terms of one dominant relationship. I am not saying that this resolution is general and overwhelming. I have argued that the patterned distribution of incompatible attitudes can be achieved and more often is. But insofar as this resolution tends to take place and the Hsu thesis has a basis, this questionnaire gives us some insight into that resolution—into the decision process and post-decision satisfaction, regret, or reversal.

La Voix du Devin Isanoussi

Réfléchi bien Chaka, je ne te
force pas. Je ne suis qu'un
devin–un technicien.

Le pouvoir ne s'obtient sans
sacrifice, le pouvoir absolu
exige le sang de l'être le
plus cher.

L. S. Senghor, *Chaka*

Conclusion

The Hsu thesis has been employed by this writer to great effect as one of the basic vehicles in a course on Culture and Personality. It has always proved to be, for all concerned, an adventure in ideas to which the students cannot fail to respond and into which they are inspired to dig their teeth. I have tried to dig my teeth into brother-brother dominance in Africa with the following conclusions:

1. There are legendary-historical data from the Zulu in which we can identify something called the Shaka complex where the mother-son axis is dominant and in which the emergent problem is not energy in the form of the sexual drive, but energy in the form of the power drive. This complex illustrates what can be called asymmetrical socialization. Its consequences are problems in legitimatization of power. Beyond the Zulu I have suggested the relevance of this complex to "diluted marriage" cultures in which the mother-child household is present and in which the complementary socialization of the father has been preempted by acculturation and rapid change. The problems of counterbalancing in socialization, of shifts in axes and patterning of divergent attributes over time, is presented.

2. Ethnographic materials from the Fang and Zulu cultures were introduced. Among the Fang the brother-brother axis is clearly a preoccupation in a great deal of behavior both present and past. Yet, from another perspective it is the father-son and mother-son axes which are patterned in the Fang cognitive structuring of past and present. The brother-brother relationship from this view is secondary and only reflective of these more basic relationships. It was noted that the content of the mother-son relationship among the Zulu differed from that among the Fang; hence the constancy of the attributes of particular axes across cultures was brought into question. The household property complex among the Zulu, virtually absent among the Fang, accounts for much of this difference. It was suggested that the question of the dynamic distribution of attributes within a culture was at least as profound a question as that of the presence or absence of given attributes in given cultures. This important point may be made by reference to a diagram of the various axes of the nuclear family: 1, mo-so; 2, sis-bro; 3, fa-so; 4, H-W; 5, bro-bro (Figure 15.1).

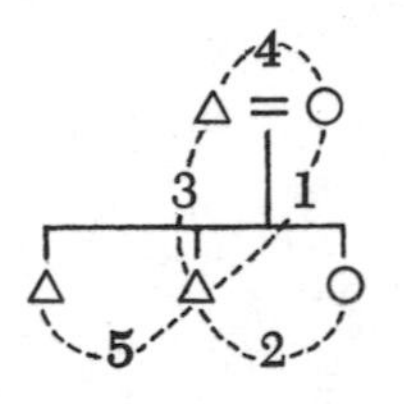

If we presume by dynamic distribution that at any given time in the socialization process one axis is more important than the other in effecting that socialization, and that there is a structural progression of succeeding axes, the normal progression for patrilineal-patrilocal societies in Africa may be stated as: 1–2–3–3/5. The mother's nurturance is appropriated by younger siblings and correspondingly the child is given over to the care of older siblings, most often sisters. The fathers, as children reach puberty, extend their influence and the male is incorporated into lineage solidarity with fathers and brothers. A progression which has appeared in the transitional period, where the fathers have not been able to successfully incorporate their sons because of failing ritual and because of status deprivation, is 1–2–3–1. The father's dominance asserts itself briefly and weakly around puberty but the very close and nurturant relationship with the mother reasserts itself shortly thereafter. We have called this social pathology the Shaka complex. The Zulu manifest it much more strongly than the Fang.

3. The materials presented in the first two sections suggested the complications involved in applying the Hsu thesis to two African cultures, but did not validate or refute it. An "ultimate circumstance questionnaire" in which drastic choices had to be made between various relatives was suggested as one method of testing the hypothesis. Results on a limited number of axes were presented from Zulu, Akan, and Dartmouth samples. Brother-brother dominance was refuted for Africa and husband-wife dominance confirmed for the American sample. An experiment was suggested based on these questions in which the content of kin relations might be examined, the strength of various bonds quantified, and dominance in axes studied as a problem of congruence achieved in the face of role conflict and incipient dissonance in the cognitive structuring of the family.

Handsome Lake and the Decline of the Iroquois Matriarchate

During the seventeenth and eighteenth centuries, Iroquois Indian men earned a reputation among the French and English colonists for being the most astute diplomatically and most dangerous militarily of all the Indians of the northeast. Yet at the same time the Iroquois were famous for the "matriarchal" nature of their economic and social institutions. After the colonial era came to an end with the victory of the United States in the Revolutionary War, the traditional diplomatic and military role of the Iroquois men was sharply limited by the circumstances of reservation life. Simultaneously, the "matriarchal" character of certain of their economic, kinship, and political institutions was drastically diminished. These changes were codified by the prophet Handsome Lake.

Handsome Lake, the Seneca prophet, founded a new religion in the early years of the nineteenth century. His religion was enthusiastically adopted by many of the Seneca and other Iroquois Indians then living on small reservations in the eastern United States and Canada. Its code emphasized sobriety, the practice of agriculture by males in the white man's style, the abandonment of witchcraft, and certain changes in kinship behavior. The changes in kinship behavior which he recommended, and which to a considerable degree were carried out by his followers, amounted in Hsu's terms (1965) to a shift in dominance in kin relationships from mother-daughter to husband-wife. Handsome Lake's reforms thus were a sentence of doom upon the traditional quasi-matriarchal system of the Iroquois. An examination of the conditions under which this event occurred may throw light on the problem of change implicit in Hsu's theory of dominant kin relationships.

THE CLASSICAL IROQUOIS PATTERN

In ethnographic tradition, the Iroquois have sometimes been regarded as a quasi-matriarchal society because of the important role women played in the formal political organization. An Iroquois tribe, of several thousand persons, was typically divided into several sibs, each of which in turn was divided into lineages. Inheritance of lineage, and therefore of sib, membership was matrilineal. A town was usually composed of members of a number of lineages, from several different sibs, each lineage owning a house (the so-called "longhouse"). The occupants of a longhouse were (theoretically) all of the living female members of the lineage in that locality, plus their unmarried sons and their husbands of the moment. Marriage was monogamous, but a woman might have a number of husbands in the course of her life. Residence after marriage was in the wife's longhouse. The women of a lineage are believed collectively to have worked their own cornfields near the village. The men of the village were responsible for hunting, for trading peltries, for warfare, and for diplomacy, all of which kept them away from their households for long periods of time, and all of which were essential to the survival of Iroquois society. An expedition of any kind was apt to take months or even years, for the 15,000 or so Iroquois in the seventeenth and eighteenth centuries ranged over an area of great size, on the order of a million square miles (literally, from the Hudson and Delaware rivers on the east to the Mississippi on the west, and from Hudson's Bay on the north to the Carolinas on the south). It is not an exaggeration to say that the full-time business of an Iroquois man was travel in order to hunt, trade, fight, or talk in council.

The women exercised political power in three main circumstances. First, whenever one of the forty-nine chiefs of the great inter-tribal League of the Iroquois died, the senior woman of the lineage he represented nominated his successor (although the nominee could in principle be rejected by the council itself). Second, when tribal or village decisions had to be made, both men and women attended at a kind of town meeting, and while men normally did the public speaking, the women caucused behind the scenes and lobbied with the spokesmen. Third, a woman was entitled to demand publicly that a murdered kinsman or kinswoman be avenged by *lex talionis* or be replaced by a captive from a non-Iroquois tribe, and her male relatives, particularly lineage kinsmen, were morally obligated to go out in a war party to secure scalps and/or captives, whom the bereaved woman might either adopt or consign to torture and death. Adoption was so frequent during the bloody decades of the beaver wars and the early colonial wars that some Iroquois villages were preponderantly composed of formally adopted war captives. Thus Iroquois women were entitled *formally* to start war, to nominate chiefs, and to participate in consensual politics.

Such a quasi-matriarchy, of course, had a certain face validity in a situation where the division of labor between the sexes required that men be geographically peripheral to the households which they helped to support and did defend. Thus, an Iroquois village over time might be regarded as a collection of infinitely long strings of successive generations of women, domiciled in their longhouses by their cornfields in a clearing while their sons and husbands traveled in the forest on supportive errands of hunting and trapping, of trade, of war, and of diplomacy. The Iroquois population was, in effect, divided into two parts: sedentary females and nomadic males. Given the technological, economic, and military circumstances of the time, such an arrangement was a practical one. But it did have an incidental consequence: It made the relationship between husband and wife an extremely precarious one, for the husband, away from the household for long periods of time, was apt in his travels to establish a liaison with an unmarried girl or a woman whose husband was also away. Since such liaisons were, in effect, in the interest of everyone in the longhouse, they readily tended to become recognized as marriages. The emotional complications introduced by these serial marriages were supposed to be resolved peacefully by the people concerned. The traveling husband who returned to find his wife living with someone else might try to recover her; if she preferred to remain with her new husband, however, he was not entitled to punish her or her new lover, but instead was encouraged to find another wife among the unmarried girls or wives with currently absent husbands. She was expected to keep the children.

THE REVISED IROQUOIS PATTERN

Handsome Lake was deeply concerned with the fragility of the classic Iroquois nuclear family. Under the quasi-matriarchal system, marriages were dependent upon the mutual satisfaction of the spouses. Couples chose one another for personal reasons; free choice was limited, in effect, only by the prohibition of intra-sib marriage. Marriages were apt to fray when a husband traveled too far, too frequently, for too long; on his return, drunken quarreling, spiteful gossip, parental irresponsibility, and infidelity led rapidly to the end of the relationship. Handsome Lake deplored this process and devoted much of his preaching to homilies on domestic tranquility. His "Great Message" contains, in Parker's published version of the Code, about 130 sections (Parker, 1913). The first four sections define the four cardinal sins: drinking whiskey, practicing lethal witchcraft, using magical charms, and using medicines to sterilize a woman. Three of these four contributed directly to the instability of the nuclear family, for drunkenness led to quarrels between husband and wife, the magical charms included love charms which facilitated promiscuity, and sterility unnaturally limited not only the number of a woman's descendants but also the number of children in the household. In the latter case, Handsome Lake singled out the mother-daughter relationship as centrally responsible for the problem:

> Now the Creator ordained that women should bear children.
> Now a certain young married woman had children and suffered much. Now she is with child again and her mother wishing to prevent further sufferings designs to administer a medicine to cut off the child and to prevent forever other children from coming. So the mother makes the medicine and gives it. Now when she does this she forever cuts away her daughter's string of children. Now it is because of such things that the Creator is sad. He created life to live and he wishes such evils to cease. He wishes those who employ such medicines to cease such practices forevermore. Now they must stop when they hear this message. Go and tell your people.

Following his discussion of the four evil words (whiskey, witchcraft, magic, and abortion), the prophet in the next twelve sections delineates his conception (attributed, of course, to the heavenly messengers of the Creator) of how the members of the nuclear family should and should not behave. He condemns the mother who urges her daughter to leave her husband:

> Tell your people that the Creator has ordered regular marriage customs. When the young people are old enough to marry, tell them so. When they marry they will live pleasantly. Now it may happen that the girl's mother discovers that she is very happy with her husband. Then she endeavors to make her daughter angry with her husband when he returns from a journey. But when the husband returns the young wife forgets the evil advice and greets him lovingly. Now the older woman, the mother, seeing this, speaks again hoping to stir up an ill feeling. Says the old woman, "My daughter, your spirits are dull, you are not bright. When I was young I was not so agreeable. I was harsh with my husband." Now the Creator is sad because of the tendency of old women to breed mischief. Such work must stop. Tell your people it must stop.

He condemns quarreling between husband and wife:

> The married often live well together for a while. Then a man becomes ugly in temper and abuses his wife. It seems to afford him pleasure. Now because of such things the Creator is very sad. So he bids us to tell you that such evils must stop. Neither man nor woman must strike each other. . . . Love one another and do not strive for another's undoing. Even as you desire good treatment so render it. Treat your wife well and she will treat you well.

He condemns scandalous gossip about the misbehavior of wives while their husbands are away hunting:

> Now some live together peaceably and keep the family as should be. Then after a time the man resolves to go off on a hunting excursion in the woods

for a certain number of days. So he goes, having agreed with his wife about it. All is well and he returns with a load of game. He feels well and thinks he is doing well in thus providing for his family. On his way homeward he meets some one who tells him that in his absence his wife has been living with another man. When he hears this report he feels sad and angry. He refuses to go to his home and turns from his path and goes to his relatives. Now whoever makes mischief of this kind does a great wrong before the Creator. So he bids his people to forever stop such evil practices.

He praises the wife who forgives her husband who strays, but condemns the erring husband:

Now this concerns both husband and wife. Now it may happen that a man and wife live together happily. At length the man thinks that he will go to another settlement to visit relatives there. His wife agrees and he goes. Now when he gets to the village he induces some agreeable woman to live with him saying he is single. Then after some time the man goes back to his own family. His wife treats him cordially as if no trouble had occurred. Now we, the messengers, say that the woman is good in the eyes of her Creator and has a place reserved for her in the heaven-world. Now the woman knew all that had been done in the other settlement but she thought it best to be peaceful and remain silent. And the Creator says that she is right and has her path toward the heaven-world, but he, the man, is on his way to the house of the Wicked One.

He condemns philandering men:

This concerns a certain thing that human creatures follow. It is concerning gakno'we'haat. Some men desire constant new experience, that is some men are always following yē'o^{n}'. Now it is a great evil for men to have such desires. This is a thing that the so sinful must confess. A man who desires to know gagwēgo^{n} yē'o^{n}'sho' will never be satisfied, for yē'o^{n}' will arise whom he can not know and he will fall flat. Now we, the messengers, say that all this is sinful and men must not follow such desires.

He condemns the punitive mother:

An old woman punished her children unjustly. The Creator is sad because of such things and bids us tell you that such practices must cease.

He urges the mother to heed her daughter's admonitions against wrongdoing:

Parents disregard the warnings of their children. When a child says, "Mother, I want you to stop wrongdoing," the child speaks straight words and the Creator says that the child speaks right and the mother must obey. Furthermore the Creator proclaims that such words from a child are wonderful and that the mother who disregards them takes the wicked part. The mother may reply, "Daughter, stop your noise. I know better than you. I am the older and you are but a child. Think not that you can influence me by your speaking." Now when you tell this message to your people say that it is wrong to speak to children in such words.

He condemns the drunken father:

> Some people live together well as man and wife and family, but the man of the family uses strong drink. Then when he comes home he lifts up his child to fondle it and he is drunk. Now we the messengers of the Creator, say that this is not right for if a man filled with strong drink touches his child he burns its blood. Tell your people to heed this warning.

He urges the childless couple to adopt children of the wife's sister (rather than separate):

> Some people live together righteously as man and wife according as the Creator ordained, but they have no child. When this is so let this be the way: If the wife's sister has children, of these let the wife without issue take from one to three and rear them and thereby fulfill her duty to the Creator. Moreover when a woman takes children she must rear them well as if born of herself. We, the messengers, say that you must tell this to your people.

He condemns gossiping women who spread rumors that a woman's husband is not the father of her child:

> Tell your people that ofttimes when a woman hears that a child is born and goes to see it, she returns and says in many houses where she stops that its mother's husband is not its father. Now we say that is exceedingly wrong to speak such evil of children. The Creator formed the children as they are; therefore, let the people stop their evil sayings.

And he urges grandchildren to care for aged and helpless grandparents.

The remainder of the code contains a number of admonitions concerning the proper social and economic roles of men and women. A woman should be a good housewife: generous, serving food to visitors and neighbor's children, never a petty thief, always helping the orphans of the community, and avoiding gossip. A man should "Harvest food for his family," build a good house, and keep horses and cattle: he should not be boastful and vain of his appearance or strength; he should be respectful of his father.

And those who disobeyed these various injunctions, the prophet said, were punished in the next world in a special house reserved for the unending torment of the wicked. Here the drunkard was compelled to swallow molten metal, the loose woman had red hot penises inserted into her vagina, quarreling spouses were forced to dispute until their eyes bulged from their heads, their tongues lolled out, and flames spurted from their genitals. Punishments of similar severity were designed to fit other crimes.

In review of Handsome Lake's moral admonitions, it is plain that he was concerned to stabilize the nuclear family by protecting the husband-wife relationship against abrasive events. A principal abrasive, in his view, was the hierarchical relationship between a mother and her daughter. Mothers, he believed, were all too prone to urge their daughters toward sin, by administering abortifacients and sterilizing medicines, by drunkenness, by practicing witchcraft, and by providing love magic. They set their daughters' minds against their husbands, condoned mothers' severity to their children, and were above accepting advice from their own offspring. Thus, in order to stabilize the nuclear family, it was necessary to loosen the tie between mother and daughter. Furthermore, men were supposed now to assume the role of heads of families, being economically responsible for their wives and children, and not frittering away their energies on strong drink, gambling, dancing, and philandering, nor in mother-in-law trouble. Although he did not directly challenge the matrilineal principle in regard to sib membership, or the customs of nominating sachems, he made it plain that the nuclear family, rather than the maternal lineage, was henceforward to be both the moral and the economic center of the behavioral universe.

Explanations: Motivational and Functional

Just why should Handsome Lake have developed and expressed such views as these at this time? And why did the Iroquois so wholeheartedly endorse and follow his injunctions?

Handsome Lake himself was, in some respects, a classic Iroquois: that is to say, he had been a hunter and warrior, had himself undertaken many times the long hunting, warring, and diplomatic journeys characteristic of the colonial period; he had become, by the nomination of a clan matron, one of the forty-nine chiefs of the great Council of the Six Nations. He and his famous brother Cornplanter were sons by different fathers, Cornplanter reputedly having been sired by a wandering Dutch peddler, and Handsome Lake by a Seneca warrior. He had seen the death of his wife and some of his children and nieces, and at the time of his visions was living as a drunken invalid in the house of his brother, along with his own daughter and her husband—unsustained, in other words, by the classic matrilineal system but dependent instead upon his brother and the remains of his own nuclear family. And his visions occurred only after the reservations had come into being and he was no longer a notable hunter, warrior, and forest diplomat, and was cooped up in a little slum in the wilderness, exposed to precept and example from various pushing white people, including Quaker missionaries then living in the same village.

But most Iroquois men found themselves in similar circumstances, no longer able, or needed, to range over thousands of miles to hunt, to fight, and to negotiate at treaties and councils. In these new circumstances, the irritations inherent in the classic matriarchal system became intolerable. The classic system, with its pattern of sedentary females and nomadic males had been workable only with a combination of belief in romantic love and easy divorce; now, with the small reservations perennially crowded with unemployed and demoralized males, the old pattern of sexual freedom simply aroused endless jealousy, bickering, quarreling, drunkenness, mayhem, and murder.

The European system of agriculture offered both a motivational and functional solution to the dilemma. By adopting the family-farm system, with private property, fenced fields, frame houses, horses and cattle, and the plow, the Iroquois male would be given a new role and, potentially, a new self-respecting identity, both intra-tribally and vis-à-vis white men. But for the family farm system to work, the continuous economic cooperation of a husband and wife was necessary; it required dispensing with the open cornfields tilled by the women of a lineage, the loosening of the tie between mother and daughter, and the stabilization of the nuclear family.

These functional prerequisites Handsome Lake undertook to define. Just how aware he was of the combination of emotional and functional advantages of the new system, it is impossible now to say. But his proposals were, by and large, accepted by most Iroquois and the reservations were parceled out into family farms owned, worked, and inherited, as long as they were in use, by men as heads of families. To be sure, the system was not, and is not, perfectly followed. Many men continued to travel, as circus entertainers, high steel workers, soldiers, and so on; but the old matriarchy was never restored.

On the Conditions of Change in Kinship Dominance

As we have seen, the Iroquois during the classic two centuries of the colonial period were a population of sedentary females and nomadic males. The men, frequently absent in small or large groups for prolonged periods of time on hunting, trading, war, and diplomatic expeditions, simultaneously protected the women from foreign attack and produced a cash crop of skins, furs, and scalps which they exchanged for hardware and dry goods. These activities, peripheral in a geographical sense, were central to the economic and political welfare of the Six Nations. The preoccupation of Iroquois men with these tasks, and the pride they took in their successful pursuit, cannot be overestimated. But the system depended on a complementary role for women, who had to be economically self-sufficient, through horticulture, during prolonged absences of men, and who maintained genealogical and political continuity in a matrilineal system in which the primary kin relationship (not necessarily the primary social relationship) was that between mother and daughter. Under these conditions, a marital system based on virtually free sexual choice, the mutual satisfaction of spouses, and easy separation was a necessity.

When the Iroquois were confined to reservations, between 1783 and

1797, the system changed. No longer were females sedentary and males nomadic; both males and females were sedentary. The system—under encouragement from whites—shifted to a family farm economy, with the man as the major farm worker, with the nuclear family replacing the matrilineage as the effective socioeconomic unit for the sedentary population, and with the husband-wife replacing the mother-daughter relationship in kinship primacy.

The Iroquois system was, to a significant degree, pre-adapted to this change. The existing marital pattern, although characterized by domestic instability, already emphasized the importance of emotional attachment between spouses and permitted virtually free mate selection, based on mutual attraction, satisfaction, and compatibility. Modifications in the social context of this marital pattern could be made so as to adapt it to the family farm system. The system that emerged was not yet a peasantry, and was neither patrilineal nor patriarchal, in any sense comparable to European, Asian, or African traditions; the sib system was unchallenged, polygyny was not endorsed, and the contracting of marriages for reasons of family alliance or economic convenience was not practiced. In a sense, the pattern that emerged was more similar to that of America of the twentieth century than that of the nineteenth.

This sequence suggests that, far from copying Europeans, the Iroquois were creatively developing potentialities inherent in their own kinship system to their new technological and political circumstances. And this in turn suggests that, in societies of sedentary females and nomadic males, one functional adaptation will be matriliny with relatively free marital choice; and that, when for any reason both sexes become sedentary, the next adaptation will involve de-emphasizing the mother-daughter relationship and developing and stabilizing the husband-wife relationship in a nuclear family system, rather than shifting to patriliny.

Indeed, one may speculate that a nice, rhythmic, unilinear evolutionary sequence exists in kinship dominance, associated with technological and economic development:

Dominant Kin Relationship	Economy
Husband-wife	Hunting and gathering requiring mobility of both sexes
Mother-daughter	Horticulture for women and hunting, war, trade, and diplomacy for men; females sedentary, males nomadic
Husband-wife	Farms managed by nuclear families; males and females sedentary

Dominant Kin Relationship, *continued*	Economy, *continued*
Father-son	Rural-urban civilization with capital accumulations managed by males and inherited patrilineally among both peasantry and urban dwellers; males and females largely sedentary
Husband-wife	Industrial urban civilization with capital accumulations managed by bureaucratic organizations; mobility of both sexes

In this scheme (and in the preceding discussion of the Iroquois) dominance in kin relationships is estimated not so much in terms of emotional closeness but in terms of legal and economic importance. It is an interesting question whether dominance in this legal-economic sense corresponds well with emotional closeness. In the case of India, as analyzed by Hsu in *Clan, Caste, and Club,* it would appear that the closest emotional relationship is mother-son even though father-son is more important in a legal and economic sense. Such discordance may not be rare and, where it occurs, may give rise to strain in social relationships and personality structure and perhaps ultimately to culture change.

Ambivalence, Social Structure, and Dominant Kinship Relationships: A Hypothesis

"It is axiomatic that science must aim at explaining more and more facts with fewer and fewer theories." This statement was made by Francis L. K. Hsu in his book *Clan, Caste, and Club* (1963:135). His hypothesis that dominant kinship relationships have an effect on kin and non-kin behavior is a step in this direction of simplification. According to this hypothesis the comparatively few and simple intrinsic attributes of such dyadic kin relationships as those between father and son, husband and wife, and brother and brother, provide the frameworks within which a variety of socio-structural and cultural aspects of whole cultures could be understood. The general content and structure of human interrelationships are reflected in the prime and most direct relationship that confronts man, the relation with his kin.

At the Kinship and Culture Conference of August, 1966, this interesting

* Translated from the Dutch by Nanette Jockin. This paper is an elaboration of the second part of my paper, prepared for the Kinship and Culture symposium, and primarily based on ethnographic data I gathered in India. Proceeding from such data contributed by the participants in the symposium, I shall now try to illustrate my hypothesis in more detail. The discussions at Burg Wartenstein, in particular the conversations with A. Howard and A. F. C. Wallace, have greatly contributed to my understanding of the problem. I also want to thank A. J. F. Köbben and N. A. Treurniet in Amsterdam for their stimulating and critical remarks with regard to the general line of ideas forwarded here.

hypothesis was the subject of detailed discussions. Most of the speakers, however, even those who expressed serious doubts concerning the hypothesis and methodological starting points as a whole, recognized the fact that the characteristic patterns of behavior in dominant kin relationships in a given culture tend to converge with those of non-kin behavior (see the summary remarks of Barth and Edgerton).

Undoubtedly Hsu has drawn attention to an important connection, the interlinkage between the interaction patterns in a kinship system, particularly in dominant kinship relationships, and the characteristic modes of behavior in a society as a whole. Several members of the symposium agreed that this was a useful starting point for an analysis of ethnographic data (see the summary remarks of Fernandez, Howard, Hunt, van der Veen).

In the following analysis the intrinsic attributes mentioned by Hsu (1965:642) will be taken in their general sense, irrespective of their validity in any specific kinship relationship. Our analysis will be based on two questions; whether Hsu attaches causal implications to the undeniable convergences, and secondly, whether these convergences can be related to a more basic system than that of kinship relationships.

Although Hsu nowhere explicitly says so, his discussion of the importance of dominant kinship relationships does suggest a causal connection. He speaks of *the effect* of dominant kinship relationships on other kinship relationships and non-kin relationships (1965:648, 652). As he further writes that his hypothesis "aims at probing primarily the role of human beings in shaping each other" (1965:657), the assumption of a sequential causal relation seems obvious. Since adults shape children so as to conform to specific cultural norms, dominant kinship relationships will give rise to a specific cultural behavior. This assumption directly leads to the second question, to what extent dominant kinship relationships may be related to a more basic system. Edgerton put forth the question to what extent "there might be an economic variable or a technological one or some kind of historical process."

In this paper we will try to outline the characteristics of such a basic system and to define some fundamental characteristics that may facilitate an understanding of the content of a culture, particularly the characteristics that explain the dominance of a specific kinship relationship in a specific culture. Dominance is here used in the sense that it "tends to modify, magnify, reduce or even eliminate other relationships in the kinship group" (Hsu, 1965:640).

SOCIAL ASPECTS OF THE AMBIVALENCE OF HUMAN NEEDS

The way in which people interrelate is determining for kin and non-kin behavior.[1] Every human relationship holds two opposing components

1. Cf. Arensberg's thesis on cultural content and the structural principles in the systematized regularity of interactive measures of relationships and roles.

which can only be defined in their most extreme forms: on the one hand there is Ego's need to interrelate, to be interdependent with or even dependent on the other person, while on the other hand Ego needs to express himself and be autonomous, he needs to render the other dependent on him or to be altogether independent of the other. This ambivalence directly springs from man's existence as a social being. The need of independence or of interrelation with others can only be actualized if there are others. This ambivalence is always manifest in some way. In each culture such ambivalent relationships are shaped according to sanctioned patterns.[2] In each culture the interaction between father and son will differ from that between brother and brother or sister and brother, since it arises from the different biologically and culturally determined positions of the interacting persons. Of essential importance for every human relationship is the way in which the inherent ambivalence of the relationship is solved. A relationship between father and son, where authority opposes dependence, includes other ways of solving this inherent ambivalence than a brother-sister relationship. And this is the cue to the convergence between dominant kinship relationships and the general content of interaction patterns in a specific society.

It should be made clear here that the inherent ambivalence in every human relationship is not always overt or consciously felt. It is in fact often denied in consequence of cultural imposed values. This denial of the ambivalence of man's social existence is an important starting point for the major theme of our theory.

The idea that the two components of human relationships both have the opportunity to be expressed in the social norms has been little emphasized in sociology. Social norms are generally seen as expressions of group interests.

> . . . everywhere man is caught between the conflicting interests of his own personal ends and a recognition of the proper and legitimate interests of his fellow-men. He is by nature drawn to living in social aggregates and must therefore have the capacity to suppress his personal desires when these are in conflict with the expectations of his society. Yet he must and does see these external, communal obligations also in terms of prevailing self-interest. It is not an enlightened one, but rather one that has been inculcated as a part of his cultural training. *Much in culture involves the delicate balance between these opposing forces: personal versus group interests.* [Goldschmidt, 1960:25; my italics]

The contrast between personal and group interests is usually taken to imply that *social norms* automatically tend to restrict opportunities for autonomous behavior and for the individual need for self-assertion in particular.

2. Within this framework the aspects of this very complex process cannot be expounded in detail. The division used is only a provisional indication of the most essential components.

> The stability of a social relation will be stronger to the extent that the gratifications each person receives are dependent on those he provides others. *Consequently arrangements that increase mutual dependence should enhance stability and that decrease mutual dependence should increase the likelihood of tension.*
>
> There is a possibility that there is a tension between the functional autonomy, or independence, of individuals and the requirements of a stable social system. *In other words, if a society or group is to remain stable some autonomy or independence of the individual must be sacrificed.* If on the other hand, individuals demand or want some degree of autonomy they must pay the price of group tension, and with this, group change. [Gouldner, 1963:555–56; my italics]

The interpretation of social norms put forward in this paper differs fundamentally from the general use, on which we will comment shortly.

In our opinion, social norms not only shape the human need to cooperate with others but they also give a culturally accepted form to the need to defy others. Sociologists have usually recognized that certain social structures and social norms offer ample opportunity to satisfy the individual need for self-assertion (by way of authority over others, prerogatives, honor by others, and so forth). However, social institutions such as status, rank, and leadership have often been interpreted as *secondary effects* of the need to cooperate.

> If we examine the motives we usually call individual self-interest, we shall find that they are, for the most part, neither individual nor selfish but that they are the product of the group life and serve the ends of a whole group, not just an individual. [Homans, 1950:95]

> Status may be defined as the position of a person vis-à-vis others. And a social system may be regarded as a set of standard positions that interrelate all members of the community. [Goldschmidt, 1960:81–82]

> *Self-assertiveness,* or the prestige drive . . . is found in the large majority of human societies, but shows marked differences. *It may be understood in large measure as an extension of the need for social approbation* which is required for the satisfaction of fundamental needs. [Klineberg, 1954:123; my italics]

Group norms are thus seen as the expression of group interests only. Following this interpretation of social-group norms, in the last instance there theoretically would be no conflicts if all individuals conformed to group norms. According to this view the conflicts and inconsistencies to be found in reality result from the clashing of personal and group interests (that is, social norms). The ambivalence, which is in our opinion fundamental, has thus been interpreted as a dichotomy—personal versus group interests. The importance attached to the realization of the need for self-assertion of all the individuals of a society has been relegated to the background. But the belief that an ideal group norm could exist has remained unimpaired.

In this sense the sociological interpretation of social reality gives ample proof of the extent to which cultural norms may be arranged to recognize one component only of the fundamental ambivalance. This interpretation resembles the earlier interpretations of individual human possibilities which were also regarded as dichotomous—the conflict between good and evil. If it was theoretically possible for man to conquer the evil tendencies, perfect human beings would be the result. The scarcity of "saints" in this world was due *only* to the difficulty of conquering evil.

If we proceed on the inherent ambivalence of human behavior we can no longer accept such an absolute valuation either of people or of social norms. The assumption that in social norms justice is also and always done to the need for self-assertion of all individuals rules out the possibility of a "perfect" society. Even if all people should conform to the social norms, the inherent ambivalence of these norms would still provoke conflict and deviance.

It may seem hardly necessary to emphasize these matters since no sociologist will nowadays deny the existence of social conflict or deviance. But the recognition of the essential ambivalence of social norms is at the same time an attack on the sociologist's unexpressed "desire to be certain" which always results from the human need for autonomy and independence. Social anthropology, too, wants to be certain, and it is therefore useful to stipulate the uncertainty of our starting point.

Our starting point may be uncertain and ambivalent, but we can distinguish some regularities in it. It is important to gain an insight into the way in which the fundamental ambivalence of each personal relationship is given space within a specific culture, and thus to get an insight into the social structure as a whole.

The conflict of impulses makes it complicated to satisfy the need for dependence and the need for autonomy at the same time. Within the framework of a social structure there is always a complex of connected norms. It is impossible to point out one norm that is directed at the realization of the one component, and one other norm directed at the other component. In a theoretical analysis, however, these norms can very well be separated from the whole. Some institutions and norms may make for the satisfaction of one of the components especially. In the social context such emphasis often signifies the absoluteness of this one component in the ideology (or norm system) connected to the institution. Ideally the divine king is really divine (that is, non-dependent) and his subject has really to fulfill all his wishes (that is, he is completely dependent).

TYPES OF SOCIAL STRUCTURING OF MAN'S AMBIVALENT NEEDS

The ambivalence of human relationships admits of an ideal-typical division into three main forms. This division is analogous to the tripartition used by Sahlins concerning "forms, material conditions, and social relations of exchange" (Sahlins, 1965:139) and to the division used by Parsons concerning the "types of action in relation to the supernatural powers" (Parsons, 1964:375–76).

The following forms will be discussed:

I. Intermittent and alternative accentuation of each of the two components of the fundamental ambivalence by all members of a social system.

II. Accentuation of one component for one group of members of a social system, and accentuation of the other component for other groups of members of the same social system.

III. Accentuation of one component for all members of a social system and ideal denial of the other component by all members of the social system.

These three types are to some extent chronological in order. The three types do not occur separately, but side by side. It is, however, possible to characterize, in a specific society, one form as dominant. There is of course a continuum, but only societies which were considered at the Kinship and Culture symposium and in Hsu's book *Clan, Caste, and Club* (1963) will come under discussion here. The way in which the ambivalence is socially structured will be related to the dominant kinship relationships that were indicated for the given societies.

I.

In societies with a simple socioeconomic structure the interdependence of all members is so great that the existence of the need for autonomy, by many sociologists, is often denied or its fulfillment thought impossible, even if such a need is felt.

> There are in each of us . . . two consciences; one which is common to our group in its entirety, which, consequently, is not ourself, but *society living and acting within us*; the other, on the contrary, represents that in us which is personal, *that which makes us an individual self*.
>
> The more primitive societies are, the more resemblances there are among individuals who compose them [that is, the more the individuals represent a collective conscience].
>
> Solidarity which comes from likenesses is at its maximum when the collective conscience completely envelops our conscience and coincides in all points with it in all points. But *at that moment, our individuality is nil. It can be born only if the community takes smaller toll of us.*[3] [Durkheim, 1960: 129*ff*.; my italics]

As a result of the limited technical and economic development of these societies, the institutionalization of interdependencies is accentuated, so

3. The denial of an actual ambivalence of the social structure of human needs was clearly demonstrated by the theories of Durkheim. Although he likewise premises the existence of two components in the human tendency, he denies an ambivalent expression

much so that the realization of the individual need for self-assertion also depends entirely on the presence of another individual. Reciprocity is the key institution in this respect.

A great number of sociologists interpret reciprocity primarily as the social structure of human dependence.

> The disruptive potential egoism is restrained by several social mechanisms. One of these is reciprocity; one is often constrained to satisfy the other's wants in order to get his own satisfied. With reciprocity indeed, *egoism becomes a social force binding two persons together* because egoism in this case, motivates one to pay attention to and satisfy the other's wants. [Gouldner, 1963:561; my italics]

The institution of reciprocity is therefore regarded as a social means to subordinate the tendency toward demonstrating the individual need for self-assertion subservient to the opposing social group interests. The possible satisfaction of the individual need for self-assertion is then seen as a secondary effect of an institution that is primarily directed toward realization of group interests.

But in our view the institutionalization of reciprocity also contains a quite independent possibility towards fulfilling the individual need for self-assertion. Reciprocity means a mutual obligation to give *as well as to receive*, and here we touch upon the aspect of reciprocity that provides the social structure for the individual need for self-assertion. "He who gives magnifies himself in the eyes of the others; he who receives is diminished in importance" (Firth, 1959b:431). By the act of giving the recipient is put under an obligation, and as long as he does not reciprocate he may be made subservient to the wishes and desires, however limited, of the donor. The obligation to be a receiver is essential. Mauss (1954) was the first to point out the emotional significance of reciprocal gift-giving. In his *Essay sur le Don*, however, he showed himself in the last resort a proper pupil of Durkheim. Mauss also viewed reciprocal gift-giving as a dichotomy and stated, "In these primitive and archaic societies there is no middle path. There is either complete trust or mistrust. . . . It is in such condition that men, despite themselves, learnt to renounce what was theirs and made contracts to give and repay" (Mauss, 1954:79).

---

of this tendency either in an individual sense or within a socially structured pattern. "There are here two contrary forces, one centripetal, and other centrifugal, which cannot flourish at the same time. *We cannot*, at one and the same time, *develop ourselves in two opposite senses*. If we have a lively desire to think and act for ourselves, we cannot be strongly inclined to think and act as others do. . . . When . . . solidarity exercises its force, our personality vanishes . . . for we are no longer ourselves, but the collective life" (Durkheim, 1969:130; my italics).

It is the notion that the *development* of these possibilities could only be uni-directional that is essential. This thought is in entire agreement with the then existing evolutionary theories on an unilineal development towards a "better mankind and a better society."

Mauss emphasized also the obligation to receive (Mauss, 1954:39–40). The intricate manipulations to avoid this obligation may be seen as indicative of the significance attached to it in primitive societies.

It will be clear that in these societies the structure of a need for self-assertion is very relative. It is first of all a need to assert one's rights with the person obliged. The idea of exchange between interacting persons is an important starting-point for our interpretation.[4] The greater the number of people that have been made dependent, the greater the opportunity to demonstrate one's need for self-assertion. An illustration of this may be found in the position of chiefs with "achieved status." But in these primitive societies the *obligation to receive* is also strongly stressed and the opportunities for a permanent accentuation of the individual need for self-assertion are few.

In societies with little socioeconomic development (for example, Australian tribes, Bushmen, Melanesian societies) direct exchange which exists between all members of such a society is the central theme. In direct exchange both partners need each other, on the one hand to express dependency, and on the other hand to assert themselves (toward the other or others). In the socially sanctioned and institutionalized process of reciprocities each component receives intermittent and alternative accentuation. The partners are equally vulnerable, which they openly admit, but they both get alternately the opportunity to accentuate their own "pride and glory." The potlatch is the extreme expression of the alternation of opportunities. Belshaw says that the Kwakiutl potlatch "contains the component of challenging one's rival to do better . . . but it also includes a strong element of denigration, of deriding the other fellow, and this carries over into a show of contemptuous and arrogant hostility" (Belshaw, 1965:25). Belshaw rightly interprets the Kwakiutl potlatch as an inflationary development in the system of exchange. In most systems of direct exchange the obligation not to give too much is of great significance. The general norm is a regular exchange of possessions of approximately the same worth. The significance of the exchange not only as an expression of dependence but also as a means to satisfy the need for self-assertion makes the question as to who should and could be the partner in such an exchange of the utmost importance. For through direct exchange other people can be made dependent (however minimally). The group of bio-

4. In his article "Social Behavior as Exchange," Homans drew attention to the interpretation of "interaction between persons . . . as an exchange of goods, material, and non-material. This is one of the oldest theories of social behavior and one that we still use every day to interpret our own behavior, as when we say 'I found so-and-so rewarding,' or 'I got a great deal out of him,' or even 'Talking with him took a great deal out of me.' But perhaps just because it is so obvious, this view has been much neglected by social scientists" (Homans, 1962:279). See also Eissenstadt, 1965:22–30; Lévi-Strauss, 1958:155–80; and Leach, 1961:101–103.

logical kin is of paramount importance in this respect, since members of this group inevitably become partners.[5] Exchange relationships have to develop between close kin, between man and wife, and between parents (at any rate, the mother) and children.

In primitive societies it is impossible to deny the fundamental ambivalence of human relationships. The members of the group depend so much on one another that only the social obligation of the one to receive (to show dependence) can balance the individual need for self-assertion of the other. This presupposes, however, an equality of all members of the group.

It will be obvious that the relationships between adults and children is not compatible with this pattern of structure. For children can only be dependent on their parents so long as they are young. They can make their parents dependent on them only when they are grown up and supporting them.

Typical in this respect is Berndt's discussion of the kinship relationships of two Australian tribes, the Gunwinggu and the Murngin. The relationships between parents and children among these tribes cannot in his view be characterized as being dominant, although the mother-child and the father-child relationships are quite important.

> The importance of the mother-child relationship lies in the image of the mother as nurturing . . . (see p. 168).
>
> . . . a mother's concern for the *physical* welfare and protection of her child, and especially of a son . . . is stressed (see p. 169).
>
> Throughout life, the general emphasis is on a mother as looking after her children, always being kind to them, and helping them where she can. The emotional quality of the relationship between actual mother and child is especially strong, but this is extended to mother surrogates (see p. 205).
>
> Among the Gunwinggu a person's own father is undoubtedly a significant relative, but he is not so important as the actual mother and certain of her kin (see p. 116).
>
> In this [Murngin] patrilineally-oriented society, the [father-son, father-daughter] relationships are especially significant. A strong emotional bond exists between children and their father and his brothers, and in fact is extended to all men . . . who are classified as ["father"] (see p. 202).

Despite the significance which these kinship relationships perforce have, Berndt concludes that, if there is any question of dominant kinship-relationships at all

> in both systems certain relationships stand out. In the Gunwinggu, one is quite definitely the brother-sister relationship and those which stem from or

5. A distinction should always be made between biological and social kin. The restriction to unilineal groups is indicative for a more dichotomous structure of the fundamental ambivalence. However, this is outside the scope of this paper.

make up the [MoMoBr] line. These are seen as complementary. The same is true in the [Murngin] system. There it is the [MoMoBr/SiDa-children] line—that is, those relatives strategically placed within this perspective, seen from the viewpoint of any one person, male or female. But almost as significant, and perhaps just as much so, are those in the [FaFa-SoSo] line (see p. 225–26).

Characteristic of all these relationships is their direct significance for the regulation of marriages and the selection of a marriage partner. According to Berndt:

> The structural patterning depends on two primary aspects: (*a*) on descent, and all that this involves in ordinary and sacred terms, including inheritance; and (*b*) on marriage. Dominant relationships must depend on these two factors, and indeed they must figure centrally in any hypothesis bearing on this question. In both societies, whom one marries determines a person's relationships even more clearly than from whom one is descended (see p. 226).

In these Australian societies the marriage regulation is very complex, and it certainly cannot be explained by means of so general a principle of organization as the structure of the ambivalence of man's social actions.

In these societies, which are based on a very simple economic structure, direct exchange is, however, found to be the most important social structure of social and economic human interrelations. In such a system marriage constitutes a central link. Marriage involves the individual in a system of exchange more extended than that of his own family group. In addition, only marriage can give a man an established position in the system as a whole. He must be able to dispose of goods suitable for exchange. The material contributions made by a wife are important, for a man can only meet his obligations by the combined activities of man and wife.

> . . . one could say, at least for these Australian Aboriginal societies, that the two most significant acquisitions for a man are women and ritual acceptance and for women, men. . . . For men, women are possibly more important than ritual knowledge and privilege (see p. 226).

To realize his need for self-assertion a man must be able to participate in the system of reciprocities. This applies also to women.

In these societies the ambivalence of interhuman relationships is very overtly and directly acknowledged. Therefore it is the kinship relationship, which allows the acquisition of a wife, that is the most important. It is not a specific spouse who is important, but the kinsman or kinswoman through whom one has a title to a spouse.

Lévi-Strauss pointed out the importance of marriage as an exchange between groups and, as such, as a principle of structure in each society (Lévi-Strauss, 1949). Among the Australian Aborigines the form of direct exchange—i.e., by exchange marriage—is not in general use, but the thought of such an exchange is most certainly felt and pronounced. Berndt has the following statement on the Gunwinggu, where a man may marry his sister's son's daughter:

> Supposing a man's *ngalgurng* [wife of sister's son] has a daughter, whom he marries; this is said to mean that "a fire is burning on his side." If a man's sister has no daughter, it is said that "no fire is burning on the *ngalgurng* side." . . . In teaching her son, as a child, the tabus he must observe in relation to his *ngalgurng*, his mother may relate them positively to this central theme: "she will make a baby for us, for our side" (see p. 175–76).

The idea of such an exchange between two groups makes it unnecessary to accentuate a specific partner, "She will make a baby for us, for our side." The interchangeability among individuals in the system is an (ideological) absolute condition in a system of direct exchange. Thus it is not the husband-wife relationship that is dominant, but the kin relationship determining the possibility of a marriage. The interchangeability of the partners is necessary to give all members of the group the alternating opportunity of accentuating one component of the ambivalence. There does not exist any social structure of one component. There are no people to whom dependence always has to be shown, nor people who always have to show dependence. Everyone in turn gets an opportunity to assert himself.[6]

> Fighting men, ritual experts, medicine men, [and] elders [do] not furnish extensive or permanent leadership in the [Australian] tribe. [Then] who did organize large-scale activities that involve the whole of the local community or even several neighboring communities? The answer is that *at some time or other these tasks fell to every man of mature age in the group.* The man [or men] who took the lead in arranging matters for a particular revenge expedition, or a betrothal, or a circumcision ceremony did so because of his [or their] putative *kinship connection* with the central figure, be it the deceased, the groom, or the novice. . . . On the next occasion, however, a different individual would be central character [living or dead] in the drama. The people who had previously occupied the significant statuses would be related now in other ways to the new figure and consequently would now play different and perhaps unimportant roles. There was, therefore, no simple correlation in these societies between prestige and authority. [Meggit, 1964:178: my italics].

Kinship relationships are a primary organizational principle in assigning the opportunity for self-assertion as well as interdependence. A system of direct exchange is generally characterized by what Sahlins called "general

6. This applies in the first instance to the position of the man in a society. Women have quite different chances to realize their need for self-assertion. The crucial importance of the husband-wife relationship is most understandable if seen in relation to the exchange situation. Direct exchange is found in any marriage bond, but particularly in a sexual one. The woman always gets the chance to assert herself through her husband, for she can make him dependent on her. Simone de Beauvoir has illustrated this situation lucidly in *The Second Sex.*

reciprocity," where "the counter is not stipulated by time, quantity or quality" (Sahlins, 1964:147).[7]

Proceeding from the thought that interchangeability of the partners is a requisite of a system to warrant that both components of the ambivalence can be emphasized at every moment, it is not surprising that Berndt concludes that in fact no kinship relationships can be regarded as dominant. For the emphatic attachment of importance to one specific kinsman or kinswoman will cross the direct and reciprocal exchange. The great significance of marriage relationships in the system of reciprocal exchanges is emphasized by the influence arising from the relationships with those within the kinship group through whom a marriage partner can be obtained.

It might be said in conclusion that in these societies the extremely simple social structure of the real ambivalence of man's social existence is to a large extent bound up with (and based on) an undeveloped economic basic structure that excludes all but direct exchange.[8]

II.

If this elementary level is broken through, the social structure of the ambivalence will certainly be affected. Sahlins (and many others) distinguished between vice versa movements—or reciprocity—and "centralized movements: collection from members of a group, often under one hand, and redivision within this group" (Sahlins, 1965:141), pooling and redistributive reciprocity. Lévi-Strauss makes a similar distinction when he regards marriage by exchange as the most simple form of reciprocity, and bride-price marriage as a "modality of the marriage by exchange" (Lévi-Strauss, 1949:178). For a bride-price marriage the members of a group pool their resources in order to obtain a wife for one of the members.

In cultures with a more developed economic basic structure, pooling and redistribution are the modalities (complications) of direct exchange. This will have consequences for the social structure and the social structure of the fundamental ambivalence.

> Cooperative food production, rank and chieftainship, collective political and ceremonial action, these are some of the ordinary contexts of pooling in primitive communities. . . . Goods collectively produced are distributed through the collectivity. Rights of call on the produce of the underlying population, as well as obligations of generosity, are everywhere associated with chieftainship. The organized exercise of these rights and obligations is redistribution. [Sahlins, 1965:142]

7. Sahlins' interpretation of "generalized reciprocity" shows essential differences from the one proposed here.

8. Generally speaking, in simple societies there also will be forms of indirect exchange.

In this short compass it is impossible to discuss the causes for the development of these more complicated economic structures.[9] Every culture has special features which contributed to these complications. It is sufficient to point out the socially institutionalized opportunity which these societies offer to certain individuals and/or groups for an accentuation of their need for self-assertion. The chief *is* more important than his followers.

The chief and persons of high social status may demonstrate their need for self-assertion within the framework of social norms (their dependence of others as well, because their "noblesse obliges" them). However, the starting point of this analysis is the fundamentally ambivalent basis of all social actions. This means that, apart from the social demonstration of dependency to the chief, the followers should also have opportunities to satisfy their own need for self-assertion. Such an opportunity is offered when the follower in his turn can make the chief dependent, since there exist relationships of *direct* exchange between chief and follower.

As was discussed above, "the gift" has a very special significance and function. By his gift or service the follower can put his chief under an obligation. But the chief is the personification and representation of more than his own interests. It was Malinowski who said, "Deprive the chief of his privileges and financial benefits and who suffers most but the whole tribe?" In this respect the chief is much more important than his followers, but they can assert themselves through the services rendered in connection with the chief. The followers enable the chief to be a real chief. Seen in this light the personal involvement of the followers in the pride and glory of "their chief" is quite understandable.

Since in these societies also the need for self-assertion is accentuated through another person (for the chief through his followers and for the followers through their chief), it will be clear that in such a structure a kind of dichotomy will occur. The chief is in the first place the representative of importance and this position is emphasized as such in accordance with the social norms. The follower is primarily a representative of dependence, and in accordance with the social norms this dependence on the chief receives the greater emphasis.

The system of direct exchange between chief and follower, which involves an indirect realization of the two components, will naturally cause a discrepancy between norm and reality.

Unlike the situation in the discussed Australian (and comparable) societies, in the economically higher developed societies the members of a group do not participate equally in community life. When marked differences exist as to status, the opportunities for a relationship of direct exchange between a man of high social status and a man of low social status

9. Cf. Sahlins (1958) for an attempt to explain the differences in the social stratification of the Polynesian islands, two of which will be discussed here.

are of great importance. Such a direct relationship may be based on kinship relationships which automatically comprise relationships of direct exchange. Or institutionalized relationships may exist between individual "important men" and "common men": the patron-client relationships—which indeed are often characterized by pseudo-kin relationships (see Wolf, 1966).

Some societies are characterized by a sharp division between "important men" and "common men"; in others the difference is less marked. Striking cases in point are the differences between the social structures of the Rotuman and Fijian as described by Howard:

> While the Fijian chief exercised a genuine dominance, in the psychological sense, over his subjects, the Rotuman chief did not. To put this another way, in Fiji the powers of the office were conceived as being embodied in the proper individual. They were personalized. In Rotuma, the powers belonged to the office alone (see p. 104).

The implications of these differences for the dominance of certain kinship relationships can be explained on the strength of the hypotheses stated here. In Rotuma—and comparable societies—the chiefs, and/or the persons who have the greatest opportunity to accentuate their need for assertion, are only slightly different from others. Moreover the chiefs are still in an uncomplicated relation of direct exchange with their followers.

> Chiefs in Rotuma cannot readily inflict their will on their subjects. Instead of acting as authorities, and offering their opinions as to courses of action, they tend to stay out of discussions until a consensus has been reached. At district meetings their role is to sum up arguments and put into action decisions arrived at by others (see p. 104).

Some persons, in Rotuma the chief, are permanently slightly more important than others, but the others still have direct access to him.

It will be clear that this same aspect is expressed by the intrinsic attributes of the relationship between an elder brother and a younger brother. The elder brother is more important than the younger brother, but otherwise they are more or less equal, and because of the position they have equally in the kinship system as a whole, the younger brother has direct access to his elder brother. This may seem all too easy a reversal of the arguments advanced by Howard:

> It is not difficult to conceive of both Fijian and Rotuman societies as constituting variations on a single structural plan, one in which the father-son link was emphasized, the other in which it was de-emphasized. In Fiji, father-son dominance can be hypothesized to have led to continuity in social units, . . . reliance upon authority in decision-making, and a generally apolitical society. In Rotuma, a de-emphasized father-son relationship can be

hypothesized to have led to discontinuity in social units, . . . rivalry for power and influence, and a generally political social orientation (see p. 104).

Howard in particular indicates the elder brother-younger brother relationship as important. However, the consideration that a general structure of the fundamental ambivalence is basic to the dominant kinship relationships seems to be confirmed by the material on Nzakara society gathered by de Dampierre. In this society "The ancient, egalitarian lineage system has given way to a differentiated system where one lineage is no longer equal to another and where one clan is no longer equal to another" (see p. 247). Proceeding from an analysis of the kinship terminology and from the general content of the kinship system, de Dampierre arrives at the conclusion that in the Nzakara society the original marriage system of sister-exchange has been replaced by another system. Here too, a deviation from the established pattern of direct exchange and perforce the accentuation of the "equal vulnerability of all members."

> The following analysis will deal with the system of kinship in . . . the Nzakara kingdom. . . . It explores the extensions of this privileged relationship between elder and younger, and more particularly . . . its metastases in the domain of authority (see p. 247).

In this society where, through the effect of a number of historically determined factors, direct exchange has been replaced by a system comprising groups that are "more important" than others, the kinship relationship between elder and younger brother also appears to be of crucial importance.

Kopytoff's interpretation of the dominance of kinship relationships in Suku society seems to confirm our arguments.

> [Suku] subsistence rests on horticulture, done exclusively by women, and on hunting and fishing, done mainly by men. Traditionally, they were organized into a kingdom of typical Central African pattern, with the king standing at the apex of a pyramid of regional chiefs and sub-chiefs. Complementing this formal political organization was another system in which conflicts were often resolved through self-help, hostage-taking, armed fighting, and the use of mediators (see p. 69).

In Suku society kingship and the pyramidal structure of regional chiefs, whose "position duplicated that of the king, but on a smaller scale," have given occasion to a dichotomy of the fundamental ambivalence. Within the framework of social norms some individuals have greater opportunities to assert themselves than others. To offer the others equal opportunities to assert themselves, relationships of direct exchange are more or less essential. In Suku society such relationships are usually based on kinship relationships, since the corporate lineage has a dominating effect on the whole system.

> On the one hand there were the politically quasi-independent lineages, maintaining relations among themselves by means of techniques that are generally associated with stateless societies. On the other hand, there was the formal political organization, built on a hierarchical model and imposed from the top, which functioned well within certain limits. The two systems are not so much contradictory as they are complementary.

And within the lineage "the principle of sharing (direct exchange), deriving from the conception of lineage unity, operates in conjunction with another, that of seniority, upon which the hierarchical organization of the lineage rests" (Kopytoff, 1964:94). Notwithstanding an accentuation of seniority, direct exchange between kin is possible. Kinship means right of access to other kin. This right is very ambivalent; it is having a right to the other's dependence, but equally as much having a right to his support and protection. And this last implies that both the supporter and the protector have opportunities to assert themselves. The generalized reciprocity within a kin-group implies a continual relationship with the principal feature that the dependence-relationships are capable of being reversed in the course of time. The son, who in his youth was dependent on his father, makes his old father dependent on him when he grows up.

Against this background Kopytoff's tendency to interpret the MoBr-SiSo relationship as the dominant kinship relationship in Suku society is rather striking. Although the son is reared by his own father, the Fa-So relationship is *not* dominant.

> Suku marriage . . . is virilocal: The husband is the sponsor of the couple's residence. As to inter-generational residence, sons live with their father at least until the father's death; they move with him when he moves (for example, upon *his* father's death. When the father dies, a son has several choices open to him. He may remain with his father's living brothers (and perhaps move with them when they move), or he may join one of his lineage elders (see p. 71).

Very rightly Kopytoff says, "The Suku attributes of the mother's brother relationship derive not from any other dyadic relationship, nor are they its own attributes *sui generis*. Rather they are correlates of the Suku relationship of person to lineage, that is to the group."

However, we would like to rephrase this statement slightly. The mother's brother-sister's son relationship is so important because, on a smaller scale, it duplicates the way in which the fundamental ambivalence is socially structured. To his sister's son the mother's brother is the exponent of authority and entitled to express his need for assertion. On the other hand, the sister's son has direct access to his mother's brother because he is his kin. This relationship of direct exchange is characterized by "mutual legal dependence and mutual distrust" (see p. 74). This also applies to the father-son relationship in the patrilineal hierarchical society of the Fijians as described by Howard.

The structure of the fundamental ambivalence as a whole is not contingent on the existence of a patrilineal or a matrilineal kinship organization. But the nature of the lineage has a direct effect on the nature of the ambivalence in kin relationship such as Fa-So, MoBr-SiSo and Br-Br.

In Suku as well as in Fiji, father and son live together. Both societies have a hierarchical structure, but in Fiji the father-son relationship is a replica of the social structure of the fundamental ambivalence, and in Suku it is the mother's brother-sister's son relationship. The different nature of the lineage gives the ambivalence inherent to these relationships a different color. In either society, Fijian or Suku, the hierarchy is not yet absolute; the division of the two components in the social structure is not yet complete. In these societies the great significance of kin relationships and, as such, relationships of direct exchange, is still very important.

In some societies, though, the two components are clearly distinct. This implies that within the framework of ideal social norms hardly any direct exchange relationships can exist between personifications of dependence and personifications of authority over others. "The premise of inequality" (Maquet, 1954) provides the blueprint for an ideology which gives some individuals the right to emphasize their self-assertion and others the obligation to be dependent. The Mexican society of San Juan, studied by Hunt, is a typical example. In this peasant society the caste-like class distinctions play a considerable role. Hunt speaks of "el'te families" with large estates and ample opportunities for education in technological fields such as law, medicine, accounting, engineering, who form a sharp contrast with the majority of the poor. In this (and comparable) societies the economic gap between the important men and the common men is intensified by an enormous cultural distance. Here, the contrasts are much more fundamental than in Suku or Fiji societies, which are essentially based on kin relationships.

Such great contrasts between "important men" and "common men" generally impede the relationships of direct exchange between *all* important men and *all* common men. Yet, such relationships are institutionalized mostly in the form of dyadic patron-client relationships, the personal relationships between a patron and his client (in which a patron can have several clients). These are often forms of pseudo-kin relationships (the godfather-relationships in Mexico).

The ideology underlines the dichotomous interpretation of the society. The important man is only allowed to command, and the common man must only obey. Hunt's lucid description of "the difficulty with achieving a satisfactory male ego idea" is illustrative. The wide gap between the cultural ideal of what a man should be and what the man himself is psychologically prepared to do, is difficult to span, for the reality is ambivalent.

Within the group of close kin the dichotomous structure of the fundamental ambivalence has far-reaching consequences. Ideally, the father-son relationship is stressed. And ideally, the son's obligation of absolute dependence on his father is strongly accentuated.[10]

> The father-son relationship is ideally one of dominance of the father throughout their lives. Even if a son is married, living in a separate household, and financially independent, informants agree he should still obey and "respect" his father's desires (see p. 114).

Ideally, the son cannot realize his need for self-assertion as long as his father lives; "people say a son should obey a father *all* his life even when both are old" (see p. 114). The son has no access to his father; he cannot even enter into a relationship of direct exchange with his father. Hunt argues that fundamentally the above ideal "is primarily a function of . . . the amount of property that is involved. If there is a large estate, the inheritance of it will be in doubt, and this induces many sons to be obedient . . . at least until the heirs are apparent" (see p. 114). In this situation the positions of father and son cannot be reversed. The father remains in possession of his property, even in old age; he does not become a non-productive member of the community who is dependent on his son, like old people in other, less complicated societies.

The patron-client relationship has already been mentioned as a social means to realize the need for self-assertion. Through relationships with "important men," the common man can have recourse to a direct relationship with a person who participates in the world of the mighty. A similar situation may be seen within the group of close kin. The son has no access to his father, but can be in a relationship of direct exchange with his mother, while she is in a relationship of *direct* exchange with his father.

In accordance with the premise of inequality, women are inherently inferior to men (Hunt). The ideology introduces a dichotomy—the man should assert himself and the woman is expected only to be dependent.[11]

Such a division is, however, difficult to realize in the husband-wife relationship, since it comprises a sexual relationship implying direct exchange (here, too, the ideology has introduced a dichotomy; ideally the woman is not allowed to take any initiative or to be emotionally involved; the sexual relationship is thus interpreted as an expression of dependence on the part of the woman).

Despite suggestions to the contrary, the husband-wife relationship is always one of direct exchange, even when there is no sexual intercourse.

10. The wider the social gap between the two components of the ambivalence, the greater the discrepancy between the ideal and the actual situation. Hunt describes this clearly. For the sake of conciseness only the ideal situation will be considered here.

11. This holds true for many societies; the difference between man and woman could be the first step towards a dichotomy.

This is true at any rate for communities such as San Juan which forbids certain activities to men. Hunt describes this clearly:

> . . . in San Juan, females are considered inherently inferior. But they are also the dispensers of much of the comfort of life. It is the right and duty of women to provide these comforts for the men associated with the families with which they are at the moment residing. . . . Feelings of being . . . dependent on a woman are not significant for these particular aspects of interactions, because the women can be relied upon to be responsible and the culture dictates this as their duty and privilege. Men can, of course, take care of themselves, and sometimes have to. But doing so seems to evoke none of the feelings of independence from mother which is a characteristic of American middle-class males. On the contrary, a man who is not able to find a woman to care for him is seen as effeminate and a failure as a man[12] (see p. 125).

From this point of view the mother might be seen as a mediator between father and son. Consequent upon her direct relationship with the father she can be regarded as a patron; the person who can look after the son's interests and also the person to whom the son has direct access.

> . . . [the mother] is the intermediary between the son and the husband. She is often the only parental figure who is with the children continuously and is available to them, not being a distant, authoritarian, cold, or feared person [see p. 137].

Hunt rightly points to the opportunity for the mother to "maneuver herself into a position of power behind the scene, by manipulating information between them."

The social structure of the fundamental ambivalence strongly stresses dichotomy; some persons are important, others should only be dependent on the important ones. But both groups have an indirect way of realizing the other component of the ambivalence. It is the stress laid in the ideology on the expression of one component which necessitates an indirect realization of the other component.

Within the set of kinship relationships the position of the father is obviously the replica of the position of the "important ones." But the son is the "heir apparent" of the father and should therefore share to some extent the importance of the "important ones." In this respect the mother plays a significant role, which becomes more important as the ideology renders the father more inaccessible. The importance of the mother-son relationship in San Juan (also in Japan, for example) is thus, despite the formal stress laid on the father-son relationship, perfectly comprehensible.

It will be obvious that in these societies the social structure of the am-

12. Ideally, feelings of being dependent upon women are considered and phrased as unimportant. But in fact this real dependence will have consequences. The unconscious aspects of the mother-son relationship, as discussed by Hunt, are indicative in this respect.

bivalence is complex. But here too, the fact that a person can only assert himself through another person is fundamental.

III.

In some societies—notably Western-American society—the necessity to assert oneself through another person no longer prevails. An intricate techno-economic development has introduced the importance of impersonal media which can satisfy the need for assertion; first, money which, as an impersonal standard of value, permits the expression of a need to assertion without the "help" of another person. A man might do this by buying a bathtub of solid gold or by subscribing to a society for the advancement of the fine arts. (This does not imply that people cannot do these things just because they like the color of gold, or are interested in the fine arts.) The personal relationships of direct exchange are often no longer recognizable. Money is a key factor in the system of exchange, and people are prepared to go to great lengths to get it. In his discussion of the forms of reciprocity, Sahlins considers the most characteristic form of exchange in Western society to be a "negative reciprocity, the unsociable extreme . . . the attempt to get something for nothing" (Sahlins, 1965: 481), but in our opinion this is only partly true. Many Western people are prepared to exert themselves for their "opposite numbers." In the Western world this opposite number is not another person, but money, an impersonal quantity.

This situation has important consequences for the structure of the fundamental ambivalence. The possibility to deny the other person to a high degree has, in Western society, narrowed down the expression of the individual need for assertion to the experience of independence. Not without reason, Hunt states that "dependence, like manipulation [of human relationships], is a red herring of considerable stench to Americans. Like manipulation, it is a complex word, highly ambiguous" (see p. 121).

In these circumstances the "premise of inequality" is no longer of any significance, since its key point is that via a relationship of direct exchange personifications of importance remain more or less within the reach of the "dependent," the "common men." The impersonal media (such as money, but also "social security laws" excluding patriarchical relationships) have ousted the institutionalized forms of direct exchange between personifications of importance and the common men. Moreover, the stress on independence requires, of all parties, the avoidance as much as possible of *institutionalized* personal relationships which automatically comprise mutual obligations. Only *self-desired* relationships of dependence are justified.

An all-embracing ideology of equality is the logical consequence of such stress on independence. When the realization of the individual need for assertion has found a social structure in the form of, primarily,[13] the manipulation of the environment, the dependent persons are also able to satisfy their self-assertion need in a direct and personal relationship of exchange with a person of importance. Where this opportunity has ceased to exist the presupposition of equal opportunities for all becomes a *conditio sine qua non* for the social realization of the individual self-assertion urge.

This equality greatly differs from the equality discussed in regard to the Australian Aborigines. There, to be equal meant to be "equally vulnerable," to be willing to accept alternative and intermittent expressions of both aspects of the fundamental ambivalence—the dependence as well as the need for assertion—in a relationship of direct exchange with another person.

In Western-American society, however, the ideal of equality is *equal independence for all men.* It will be obvious on account of this stress on independence that discrepancies will arise between the ideal and the actual situation. All the same, the ideal of "equal independence" is pursued in the norms as well as in social organization.

Another consequence of the stress on independence is that, ideally, the expression of dependence is possible only when the dependence is self-desired. In Western societies this comes most to the fore in the syndrome of "romantic love." Ideally, such an unmistakable relationship of direct and reciprocal exchange as a marriage bond is acceptable only if based on a romantic love which only later should develop into "real love." Characteristic of romantic love is that the chosen object turns out to be the (illusory) representative of the very individual desires of the one who loves. In this sense "independence" is central, despite a stress on an ideal dependent—love. In Western society many other institutions can be pointed out in which a stress on independence is also central.[14]

The above structure of the fundamental ambivalence makes it clear why Hsu characterized the husband-wife relationship as the dominant relationship in Western-American society (Hsu, 1963). For solely in the husband-wife relationship is a free choice implicit. All the other kinship relationships are uninvited—a son cannot choose his father, nor his mother, brother, or sister. (It is not without significance that, in particular in Western society, so much is done to wipe out the "bad lucks" that are a result of this "injustice.")

13. In Western societies such realizations of individual need for self-assertion are still important. There is of course a continuum, but only a number of types come under discussion here.

14. In my preliminary paper the expression of the need for self-assertion was linked only to a striving after independence. This erroneous interpretation is presumably due to an ethnocentric way of thinking; in Western thought a person can only actually assert himself when he is independent. After discussions at Burg Wartenstein and later with Professor Köbben of Amsterdam University it was possible for me to drop this premise.

In Western society the way in which the fundamental ambivalence is socially structured duplicates most clearly the husband-wife relationship. The experience of dependence can only agree with the ideal of independence if it is self-desired.

Examples of Discongruent Social Structuring of Human Ambivalence

Having discussed the three main types of structure of the interrelationships, attention will now be focused on two societies where special circumstances have complicated the structure of the ambivalence of interhuman relationships, namely the Iroquois and the Hindu societies as discussed by Wallace and Hsu. Special socioeconomic circumstances allow the Iroquois an emphasis on non-dependence which in fact does not seem to be in accordance with the degree of organizational development of their society.

In Hindu society the emphasis on non-dependence is presumably connected with a brilliantly rational solution for the interpretation of the ambivalent relationship between man and the supernatural. The relationship between this structure and the dominant kinship relationship will be discussed for both societies.

The great stress on independence (as the expression of an individual need for assertion) is characteristic of Western-American society. But other societies also show this feature, as illustrated in Wallace's description of the Iroquois. On the basis of a unique socioeconomic situation in Iroquois society, the ideal of independence, particularly for men, was greatly stressed.

> The Iroquois during the classic two centuries of the colonial period were a population of *sedentary females and nomadic males.* The men, frequently absent in small or large groups for prolonged periods of time on hunting, trading, war, and diplomatic expeditions, simultaneously protected the women from foreign attack and produced a cash crop of skins, furs, and scalps which they exchanged for hardware and dry goods. These activities, peripheral in a geographical sense, were central to the economic and political welfare of the Six Nations. The preoccupation of Iroquois men with these tasks, and the pride they took in their successful pursuit, cannot be overestimated. But the system depended on a complementary role for *women,* who *had to be economically self-sufficient, through horticulture,* during prolonged absences of men, and who maintained a genealogical and political continuity in a matrilineal system in which the primary kin relationship (not necessarily the primary social relationship) was that between mother and daughter (see p. 374; my italics).

It will be clear that this "independent economic structure" of a society offers possibilities for over-accentuation of independence. Ethnographic records from the seventeenth and eighteenth centuries show that this was certainly true for men, who were expected to behave with extreme independence (the men were not even allowed to express dependence of physical pain). In his paper "Dreams and the Wishes of the Soul," Wallace has linked the ideal of the Iroquois men as "brave, active, self-reliant, and autonomous; [who] cringed to no one and begged for nothing," and the reality of ambivalence. For the typical Iroquois male, who in his daily life was a brave, generous, active, and independent spirit, nevertheless "cherished some strong, if unconscious, wishes to be passive, to beg, to be cared for" (Wallace, 1958:247).

"This unallowable passive tendency, so threatening to a man's sense of self-esteem" can, as Wallace explains, find an institutionalized expression (that is, sanctioned by social norms) in dreams. The desires advanced in such a dream often serve the purpose of guidance in social activities. "The Iroquois have, properly speaking, only one single Divinity, the Dream. To it they render their submission, and follow all its orders with the utmost exactness" (Wallace, 1958:235, quoting Father Fremin).

Wallace states that particularly the dreams in which the need to be passive becomes manifest were realized according to the institutionalized systems of dream-fulfillment.

> This unallowable passive tendency, so threatening to a man's sense of self-esteem, could not appear easily even in a dream; when it did, it was either experienced as an intolerable painful episode of torture or was put in terms of a meeting with a supernatural protector. However, the Iroquois themselves unwittingly make the translation: an active manifest dream is fulfilled by a passive, receiving action. The arrangement of the dream guessing rites raises this dependency to an exquisite degree: the dreamer cannot even ask for his wish; like a baby he must content himself with cryptic signs and symbols until someone guesses what he wants and gives it to him. [Wallace, 1958:247]

For all men the stress on independence was virtually alike. In the eighteenth and nineteenth centuries the circumstances of life for the Iroquois underwent a fundamental change. In the period from 1783 to 1797 the Iroquois were confined to reservations. And then "no longer were females sedentary and males nomadic; both males and females were sedentary. The system—under encouragement from whites—shifted to a family farm economy, with the man as the major farm worker, with the nuclear family replacing the matrilineage as the effective socioeconomic unit for the sedentary population, and with the husband-wife replacing the mother-daughter relationship in kinship primacy" (see p. 375).

This change in the socioeconomic basis of the Iroquois society made the stress on independence no longer possible. The limited knowledge and technical equipment of the Iroquois necessitated a strong and direct interdependence. The former tendency to deny a dependence on women could no longer be upheld, and the actual economic independence of women also became impossible. In the old days women had been economically self-sufficient, not dependent on men.

By emphasizing the husband-wife relationship (including the importance of emotional involvement and virtually free mate selection) the ideal of independence could to some extent be maintained. Connected with a free mate selection, the husband-wife relationship offers the opportunity to realize the individual need for assertion as a form of independence which will be a self-chosen dependence.

The pronouncements of the prophet Handsome Lake, cited by Wallace, are illustrations of determinate attempts at eliminating the discrepancy between the ideal and a new reality. With good reason Wallace speaks of "the Iroquois (who, far from copying the Europeans) were creatively developing potentialities inherent in their own kinship system to their new technological and political circumstances" (see p. 375).

In the examples discussed we have strongly emphasized that the type of structure of the fundamental ambivalence differs with the degree of technological and economic development of the societies. This, however, is by no means intended as a contribution to a new economic determinism. The relation between techno-economic circumstances and ideology is not easy to establish, and certainly not monocausal.

By stressing the essential ambivalent nature of every individual and social structure of human possibilities, monocausality in any form is precluded. In theoretical analysis it is possible only to attempt a more specific determination of the nature of the *interdependence* of the basic components; and only in theoretical analysis are the two basic components separable. Although our descriptions may have suggested the reverse, in the reality of social life the need for assertion is inseparably bound up with the need to be interdependent with another person.

A similarly complicated interdependence occurs in the relationship of man to the humanly uncontrollable supernatural powers. This situation is also ambivalent: Man is obviously dependent on these powers (disease, death, and so on) but on the other hand he wants to control and be independent of them. Man's actions, which are determined by his interpretation of the supernatural, are socially structured within the framework of religious practices and values of each culture. Another ambivalent situation: There is a need to express dependence and at the same time a need to control; to be God's humble servant as well as to be one's own master even in the face of powers greater than any human ones. Since the *human* interpretation of the supernatural is central in religion, the eventual realization of non-dependence is a very important component.

It is remarkable that the types of action in relation to the supernatural can be divided in a way that corresponds exactly with the tripartite division discussed. Parsons distinguished between: 1. ritual—which depends on the conception of the relevant aspects of the supernatural as contributing an order, the "laws" of which can be understood and adapted to, in a way that is essentially analogous to instrumental manipulation of the empirical world. The problem is to do the "right thing" in order to bring about the desired goal state (magical rituals); 2. supplication—which depends on the conception of the relevant supernatural entity as an actor who must make a decision about what to do in relation to Ego. Ego's "technique," then, is to influence the decision in a direction favorable to the realization of his goal (prayer, sacrifice, and so on); 3. contemplation —which operates on the actor's own state of mind in such a way as to make him "receptive" to the supernatural influences (Buddhism) (Parsons, 1964:375–76).

These different religious "techniques" also occur side by side in the same social system. In *ritual* the "direct exchange" between man and man's interpretation of the supernatural powers is obvious. The dependence on a supernatural power is overtly acknowledged. But at the same time there is a possibility of controlling this supernatural power by forcing it in some way into dependence. For the performance of ritual *X* will keep illness away, while ritual *Y* guarantees a successful hunt. Man and the powers he tries to manipulate with his magic rituals are therefore "equally vulnerable." In this respect the structure of the ambivalence between man and the supernatural powers resembles the structure of the interpersonal relationships of, for instance, the Australian Aborigines.

In the cases of *supplication* the threatening supernatural powers are more or less pooled. Like the chief in "redistributive reciprocity" and "centralized reciprocity," the supernatural power is infinitely more important than its followers. God, as a representative of the infinite powers, cannot be seen as "equally vulnerable." Still, between God and man a relationship of direct exchange exists. The relationship between the supernatural powers and man can be seen as a patron-client relationship (Foster, 1965: 1286–94, and Kenny, 1960:14–23).[15] The structure is dichotomous; the supernatural powers are inexpressibly powerful, but through a relationship of direct exchange mortals can acquire some sort of control. A complete dependence on God will take man to an ultimate state of bliss. In reaching heaven, man attains immortality and independence of the miseries which befell him in his earthly existence.

In *contemplation* even dependence on God is denied. In such religious systems man himself should control the supernatural powers, or better still, he should achieve independence during his earthly existence. He can set about it in various ways. Such a way is found in the obligatory denial

15. A striking analogy appears to exist between the ever-increasing significance of the position of the Virgin Mary in medieval Christianity and the important position of the mother (as discussed on p. 394) in societies where, due to an extreme dichotomization of the fundamental ambivalence, relationships of direct exchange are blocked. The Calvinistic interpretation of God, as an absolute God who cannot be influenced, would seem the ultimate stage of a dichotomy between "absolute control" and "absolute dependence."

of any form of desire in Buddhism, but also in the development and application of scientific thought which makes man less dependent on supernatural powers.

The latter is closely connected with the development of Western culture and the technical and economic advancement of Western society. In some cultures, particularly the Hindu-Buddhistic culture, the religious conception of the ambivalent relationship between man and the supernatural powers is *not* convergent with the social structure of the interpersonal relationships. This confirms the view that no simple relation (economic deterministic) exists between the technical and economical circumstances in a society and the prevalent ideology.

Hindu society is illustrative in this respect, since it clearly demonstrates how both ideology and techno-economic circumstances may influence the kinship system. Hsu considers the mother-son relationship to be the dominant kinship relationship in Hindu society (Hsu, 1963:162 *ff.*). He relates this dominance to the way in which man's social existence is shaped in cultural norms and systems.

In Hinduism the ambivalent relationship between God and man is solved by greatly stressing the idea that man can control his own existence. Weber says that according to the Hindu conception of life, "it depends only on a man's behavior whether he will be born as a God or as a worm in the intestines of a dog. . . . Man is his own and sole savior" (Weber, 1964:145–47). The essence of Hindu society, the hierarchical caste-structure with the Brahmans at the top, is closely related to this ideology. The fact that the over-accentuation of independence consequent upon this ideology is applied only to the Brahmans, is the strength of Hinduism. Manifestations of dependence are not only allowed but even prescribed for members of all the other castes; only Brahmans should be "gods on earth." But even for the Brahmans the accentuation of independence is prescribed only for the final stage of life (*sanyasi ashrama*). During this stage the Brahman ideally should renounce the world and live as an ascetic, subsist on roots and fruits which he gathers himself, and walk alone (see Manu VI; 1, 2, 25, 50, 53, 56, 57, 58).

The techno-economic development of the world, in which the question of the relationship between man and the supernatural was rationally solved by denying the gods, was very uncomplicated. As a result the only way to experience independence of the world was to renounce this world. Such non-attachment is, however, only asked of the Brahmans, but according to the idea of reincarnation, every man can attain the Brahman stage. Not all members of the society are confronted with the discrepancy between the ideal of non-attachment (independence) and the need of interdependence with both supernatural powers and other humans. But inherent in the logic of the doctrine, this stage may come for all members of the society. The influence of these ideas in daily life in India should not be overestimated. It will, however, be clear that this rational solution did not cause any acute tension between ideal and actual actions. Only the Brahmans had to renounce life and not submit to an ambivalence of feelings.

The great variety of creeds and ritual activities in Hinduism arise from the omnivalent appreciation of man's actions. In Hinduism this omnivalence is allowed, but hierarchized. The hierarchy is crucial, each stage having its own value. In the actuality of social life this means that all sorts of functional groupings (such as occupational, racial, political) occupy their own distinct place. The Brahmans are unquestionably the apex of this system. They can be gods on earth. This is very important. The Brahman example, that is to say the actions of the "ideal Brahman" as defined in the sacred books, determines the actions of all others. Srinivas' description of the occurrence of "sanskritization" or "brahmanization" is illustrative. Notwithstanding the definite actions which the ideology prescribes for each special group (varna-caste, sub-caste, and even sub-sub-caste in the Indian society) the actual situation is not static. This means that some groups (castes) want to better their positions. In most cases these claims are based on an improvement in their economic positions (Srinivas, 1966: 1–46; Hsu, 1963:97). The claims are mostly substantiated by "brahmanization," i.e., the adoption of vegetarianism, teetotalism, preference for dowry marriages, denial of commensality, and the rigorous obligation of endogamy.[16] The underlying rationality of all these actions is one of non-attachment, or, as Hsu calls it, unilaterality. According to Hsu this unilaterality arises from the dominant kinship relationship in Hindu society, namely the mother-son relationship. "The basic attribute which characterizes the [mother-son] relationship is unilateral dependence" (Hsu, 1963: 51–52), and "unilateral dependence is the basic idea in the Hindu way of life" (*ibid.*, p. 182).

By commenting critically on two of Hsu's arguments we shall try to substantiate our hypothesis: it is the content of the structure of the ambivalence of the need for interdependence and the need for non-dependence which determines the dominance of certain kinship relationships and the content of interpersonal relationships in a specific culture as a whole. We shall also attempt to illustrate the unique position of Hindu society as one in which the ambivalence in religious terms is structured as one of human independence (independence of supernatural powers), while in social terms it had to be structured as one of interdependence (because of the rather uncomplicated socioeconomic development of the society).

In defining unilaterality Hsu states that "unilateral dependence is one-sided dependence. It means that the individual need not feel resentment against being a recipient nor need he feel obliged to reciprocate what he

16. It would not come within the scope of this paper to give a detailed description, since the process of interdependent influences and actions is very complex. For more information cf. Srinivas, 1966.

has received,[17] . . . "but if human relations must, in the final analysis, be based upon balancing of obligations, however long delayed, how does the Hindu social system maintain and continue itself?" This question is answered by Hsu with a reference to the supernatural orientation of the Hindu way of life, as expressed by S. Radakrishnan.

> If the fundamental form of the supreme is *nirguna*, qualityless, and *acintya*, inconceivable, the world is an appearance which cannot be logically related to the Absolute. In the unalterable eternity of Brahman, all that moves and evolves is founded. By It they exist, they cannot be without It, though It causes nothing, does nothing, determines nothing. While the world is dependent on Brahman, the latter is not dependent on the world. This one-sided dependence and the logical inconceivability of the relation between the Ultimate Reality and the world are brought out of the word "Māyā."

Hsu says that since the ultimate responsibility of their actions is found in dharma or the sacred laws, givers and receivers need have no direct reference to each other. "If givers give because of dharma and recipients take also because of dharma, then human beings need not be indebted to each other at all" (Hsu, 1963:4–5).

In our opinion this does not sufficiently answer the question of how in actual life the obligations are balanced. Radakrishnan's description of the Māyā concept certainly does not explain its appeal to the Hindu, nor the reason for the acceptance of the rationalization of the attempts to deny reciprocity.

The same objection seems more or less to apply to another of Hsu's points of departure; that is, the reason why in Hindu society the mother-son relationship is dominant. In answering this question Hsu again refers to a "supernatural orientation."

To account for the importance of the mother-son relationship—an importance which in our opinion is beyond doubt in the Brahmanized part of Hindu society—Hsu provides the following arguments:

> In Hindu society adult males and females are [extremely] segregated. The higher the caste [the more in conformity with Brahman ideals!], the more the family tends to appropriate complete segregation. Male children before puberty or adolescence tend therefore to be under the protective and guiding hands more of females such as mothers and grandmothers and other females than of fathers, grandfathers and other males.
>
> The relationship between Hindu fathers and their sons is not close then because of that segregational pattern and because Hindu males' strong aversion of pollution (which makes it impossible for him to carry his own infant) and because Hindu fathers are also likely to be preoccupied with some

17. For a more detailed description of the importance of the intricate reciprocity in Hindu society, and of the efforts to deny it, see Heesterman, 1963, and van der Veen: a forthcoming publication on dowry-marriage in a Brahman caste.

aspect of the ritual activities such as pilgrimage, designed to bring them closer to their Deities of Truth. [Hsu, 1963:48–49]

In the last two arguments particularly, there is a direct reference to a supernatural orientation as a causal factor. A thing that is essential to Hsu's arguments is thus explained, but only partly. Hsu does not solve the question of why this supernatural orientation is so important in Hindu society, for he does not relate his solution to inherently human needs.

It would seem possible to arrive at a more universally based cue by giving attention to the specific way in which the inherently human ambivalence is structured in Hindu society. As was said above, the Brahmans, by virtue of the special Hindu interpretation of the relationship between man and the supernatural, need to express independence. We cannot account for the fact that in Hindu society this rational solution for a universal human problem was found. Here again there seem to have been uniquely historical processes which led to the merging of the concepts of rebirth and expiation of guilt into one logically consistent conception. This conception, however, resulted in a stress on independence in a society that otherwise offered little scope to the idea that man could be independent of other *men*. The expression of independence had to be realized in a world in which man was still exceptionally dependent. This meant—and to a great extent still means in India—that the most evident relationships of human dependence had to be virtually dismissed, even though these relationships of emotional dependence are inescapable because they result from man's ambivalent needs.

It is therefore a man's *duty* to look after his wife and children, but not his right to express openly his emotional attachment (interdependence) as regards them. Wife and children are of necessity bracketed together with the husband—at any rate in the technically and economically little developed Hindu society in which the ideal rules of living were initially set up.

In India, being dependent on other men is unavoidable, and perhaps for that very reason it must be denied in a most extreme form. In the Western world dependence can be accepted only if it is self-chosen. In India it has to be denied altogether, if the ideal of independence is to be realized. As a Brahman informant of Carstairs said, "Of course a man loves his wife and son, but there is some limit to his love. He has affection for them and he regards it as his duty to bring up his son and love him, and give him money for his education. He will be dutiful to his wife also, but not as much attached to them as a worldly man, who is affectionate without limits, and who suffers without restraint if they die" (Carstairs, 1959:231).

The worldly men (that is, the non-Brahmans) may express their ambivalent needs in a direct way. But the Brahman-ideal is the ideal for all Hindus. Though all other expressions of human possibilities are accepted, non-attachment is the ultimate goal.

This stress on the denial of interdependence is prevalent in many aspects of Hindu society, as was clearly demonstrated by Hsu in his analysis of Hindu social systems (Hsu, 1963). The denial of interdependence also explains why the mother-son relationship is the one kinship relationship in Hindu society that ever could be so important. To put it hypothetically, the mother-son relationship is by far the most suitable relationship in which the need for "interdependence" can be realized without violating the strong emphasis which is placed in Brahman ideology on the need for "independence."

According to the Hindu concepts of life and society, which are essentially hierarchical, the woman is definitely a "lower incarnation"; like the Sudra (the lower caste) her only occupation is to "serve meekly." Ideally therefore, there is no question of reciprocity in the relationship between a man and a woman (see also Hunt's remarks on dependence on women in Mexico society). Man and woman are not partners of the same order. Thus, in the relationship with his mother the son can give expression to his feelings of interdependence (especially in the emotional sense) without constraint. Ideally his mother is there to serve him. Besides, between a mother and her son there is no relationship of direct exchange such as between husband and wife.

Here we find a striking resemblance to the situation in Mexican society already discussed. However, there is an important difference. Hsu has clearly stated that in Hindu social ideology the father-son relationship is not stressed (Hsu, 1963:50 *ff.*). This will be understandable on the basis of the following hypothesis. In Mexican society the father-son relationship is a replica of the patron-client relationship. It is an expression of the way in which the fundamental ambivalence of human existence is solved in this society: accentuation of one component (interdependence, even dependence) for one group, and accentuation of the other component (non-dependence, even independence) for another group in the society.

Because of accentuation of independence based on religion, it is, ideally, undesirable for a Brahman in Hindu society to have any relationship. It is a father's duty to look after his children, but is also his duty to leave his family in the final stage of his life and to withdraw completely from the world (cf. Hsu, 1963:35–37). The ideal denial of one component (interdependence) is valid for all Brahmans. Due to the impossibility of a static society, the Brahmanic ideal is an example for all the other non-Brahman members of the society, and the ideal of non-attachment is a general principle in Hindu society.

In the "sacred books," which are a guide for the way in which non-dependence may be reached according to Hindu ideology, the father-son relationship is not given much attention. Hsu explains that it is the relationship with the guru that is particularly accentuated (Hsu, 1963:30). The proposed hypothesis accounts for such an accentuation. Just as in Western society, where the realization of independence for all members of the group is stressed, so in Hindu society is the relationship of dependence stressed which concerns a self-chosen dependence; for the pupil is free to choose his own guru.

It will be clear that in practice the ideology of non-attachment and the reality of extreme interdependence will give rise to a very complex situation of relative balance. The need for dependence has to be realized, so an accentuation of the mother-son relationship is most appropriate. The brother-sister relationship also complies with the requirements and is therefore highly institutionalized in Hindu society. Feelings of mutual attachment may be openly demonstrated.

The relationship between spouses is also a relationship between a man and a woman, and as such it could also comply with the requirement that dependence should be manifest as little as possible. But the husband-wife relationship is always one of *direct* exchange, which constitutes a much greater threat to the ideal of non-attachment. It is easier to preserve the illusion that the woman should "serve meekly" in relation to a mother or a sister than to a wife. The ideology of non-attachment is only compatible with an ideology which interprets the husband-wife relationship as an absolutely unilaterial relationship. According to Hindu ideology the woman (the bride) is a gift [Manu, III:29]).

Against this background it is understandable why a woman should follow her husband in death. She may do this either directly by "sutee," or indirectly by submitting to the role of the widow prescribed by the (Brahmanic) norms—a life of severe aloofness. The threat to non-attachment inherent in the husband-wife relationship can only be neutralized by an over-accentuation of the role of the wife as servant.

In Western society stress on independence is compatible with stress on self-chosen dependencies. The enormous organizational and technical development always offers the possibility of largely denying the "inevitability" of the dependencies. In Hindu society the stress on independence was formulated as an ideal in a society where denial of "inevitable dependence" was next to impossible. In this society the ideal could only be attained by the rejection of any form of dependence.

Conclusion

The complexity of the social interdependencies naturally requires a far more elaborate substantiation of the advanced hypotheses. Social phenomena can, however, be interpreted unequivocally by paying attention to a fundamental and universally human aspect—the ambivalence of man's social existence.

The dominance of specific relationships, recognized and substantiated by Hsu, can thus be related to the content of cultures in general. The structure of the fundamental ambivalence is determinant for the general content of cultures. And the nature of the structure is governed by a number of relatively simple components. The way in which these components are interrelated in the different cultures has complicated consequences which can, however, be analyzed because of their inherently logical consistency.

Such an analysis should start from three premises: first, the two components of the fundamental ambivalence are both realized within the framework of social norms; second, the tendency toward an ideological separation of the two components within the framework of social norms; third, the tendency in social norms to accentuate the non-dependence component in particular as the socio-technical development grows. The third premise is in agreement with the material here presented, but is not necessarily generally valid.

The hypotheses advanced in this paper would appear to answer the requirement of "explaining more and more facts with fewer and fewer theories." The question why in a specific society specific kinship relationships are dominant, and why—as found by Hsu—kin and non-kin behavior are highly convergent, may be answered by referring to one and the same central theme in the structure of man's social behavior.

EIGHTEEN TALCOTT PARSONS

Kinship and the Associational Aspect of Social Structure

This paper is a highly speculative attempt to delineate a theme in the development of social organization that I think is of special importance in modern society—and hence to all comparative studies of social structure. This structural theme is the associational aspect of social relationships, involving particularly the voluntary principle with respect to membership and certain major patterns of equality in the relations among members. The institutions of citizenship, as crystallized in the principal "democratic" societies of the modern world, comprise its largest-scale form. However, it also permeates the immense network of modern private voluntary associations and, in modified form, the modern professional world (cf. Parsons, 1968).

The principal manifestations I have in mind occur in fields well removed from considerations of kinship. Yet we know that the primordial matrix of all social organization is kinship. Hence anything so important as the associational complex should at least have certain roots in the kinship system, perhaps roots that have evolved from the most primitive levels of social organization through a long succession of developments while displaying certain continuities throughout.

It is in this context that I wish to consider Francis Hsu's hypotheses about primacy-relations among different structural elements in the kinship complex, notably dyadic pairs. I should like to select, not one category of dyad, but a special relation between two categories of dyads which are inherent in all kinship systems: the marital relation of man and woman who generally share a common household and constitute the socially responsible parents of offspring; and the relations of siblings of opposite sex (brothers and sisters) among the offspring of the parental couple. I wish to suggest that there is a vital relation between these two categories of relational dyads which under certain circumstances can become critical in the development of social structures.

It is generally agreed that the rules prohibiting incest, or, more generally, regulating endogamy and exogamy, are central to all kinship systems. Among the negative rules that enjoin marriage among relatives and particularly concern the nuclear family, however, the one which has probably received least adequate attention is the prohibition of brother-sister incest.[1] It is striking that, among the possibilities within the nuclear family, only in the sibling case do we find instances of positive institutionalization of intrafamilial incest, most notably in the brother-sister marriages of the Pharoahs of Ancient Egypt and the Incas of Peru. To my knowledge there are no cases of the requirement of incestuous relations between parents and children for the propagation of legitimate heirs.[2]

Some preoccupation with the case of Ancient Egypt has yielded the conviction that the cases of institutionalized brother-sister incest—always confined to high elite groups if not to royal families (Middleton, 1962)—are closely linked with a strong hierarchical emphasis in the general social structure. Indeed, characterizing the society of Ancient Egypt as strongly hierarchical can scarcely be challenged. I would also like to suggest the converse, that in societies where the incest taboo among siblings is strongly sanctioned, a more egalitarian trend is likely to prevail in the social structure.

Insofar as equality across the sex line exists at all, surely brother and sister are as equal as it is possible to be. The question is whether and in what sense their equality is contained within a kinship unit which is much "more equal than others" with reference to the wider population.[3] The

1. This stricture certainly applies to my own paper, "The Incest Taboo in Relation to the Social Structure and the Socialization of the Child" in my collection of papers, *Social Structure and Personality* (New York: Free Press, 1964).

2. It must be recognized, of course, that it would be simply impossible to establish such incestuous institutions for any number of generations. Biologically as well as socially, no family system could survive for long once the generational axis of its boundaries and internal differentiation had been collapsed in favor of parent-child incest. It is particularly interesting, however, that the religious system of Ancient Egypt utilized the theme of mother-son incest in grounding the symbolic meaning of the institutions of Pharaonic succession, even though it was brother-sister incest that was actually practiced. See my *Societies: Evolutionary and Comparative Perspectives* (Englewood Cliffs: Prentice-Hall, 1966) p. 60; and Henri Frankfort: *Kingship and the Gods*, Part II (Chicago: University of Chicago Press, 1948).

3. Two qualifications must be made about the equality of siblings. The first concerns birth order where the siblings have both parents in common. Here such patterns as primogeniture can introduce drastic inequalities, yet in our broader context comprise

extreme case of this is a royal family—the "purity" of the royal line was surely critical in the Egyptian system. This type of case must be distinguished from that of an aristocracy in which the hereditary upper group is to some degree a "company of equals" whose basic equality is symbolized by their eligibility to intermarry while intermarriage with non-aristocrats is forbidden. Such an aristocracy is "laterally extended" through a network of affinal relationships. Indeed, the intermarrying lineages constitute an affinal collectivity,[4] having not only eligibility to intermarry, but also various other social privileges, such as being received at court, as common badges of membership.[5]

The prevalence of prescriptive marriage systems among the most primitive societies has been an important finding of anthropological research (cf. Lévi-Strauss, 1949; Needham, 1960). It seems to be associated with the egalitarian emphasis which once aroused a good deal of attention in ideas about "primitive communism"—for example, in Morgan, Marx and Engels, and indeed Veblen. It may be suggested that a first major step of differentiation from this "base" of social evolution involved the differentiation from "commoners" of a set of lineages constituting an "upper class." The closure of an upper class through endogamy breaks the affinal collectivity of the society as a whole. Such a process might lead to segmentation into distinct societies, but it might also be compatible with the continuing inclusion of both classes in the same society, which would then require a basis of common solidarity other than ones which can be institutionalized through affinal relationships. When this is established, I should speak of "aristocracy" as an institution. As such it is not incompatible with chieftainship and, at a more advanced stage, monarchy, so long as the top lineage, and individual, is *primus inter pares* rather than, like the divine Pharoah, unequivocally elevated above all others.[6]

This general type of aristocratic pattern, having a relatively "flat" top on the stratification structure, seems to have been particularly important in the ancient civilizations on the northern shore of the Mediterranean and in

---

secondary variations that depend on other factors such as a strong lineal emphasis. The second concerns plural marriages, especially polygyny, and the relations of children who have one parent in common, the other parent of each differing in relative status. It is notable that the connections we find most important have occurred in societies with institutionalized monogamy, so that relative "seniority" of mothers, for example, could not affect the relative status of a father's sons.

4. It is particularly important that long after the segmentation of European society into territorial—more or less "national"—states, common ties were established by royal marriages. The fact that Kaiser Wilhelm II was a grandson of Queen Victoria presumably put some kind of brake on the genesis of hostility between Britain and Imperial Germany. The classic instance of consolidating political jurisdictions through royal intermarriages was the marriage policy of the Hapsburg Emperor Maximilian.

5. For my use of the concept of the affinal collectivity, I am indebted to the work of Charles D. Ackerman, in particular his Harvard Ph.D. thesis entitled "Three Studies of the Affinal Collectivity," and to extensive discussions with him.

6. See my *Societies* (1966), Chaps. 3 and 4. On the divinity of the Pharaoh and the hierarchical emphasis of the Egyptian case, see Frankfort, 1948.

the Mesopotamian area. The societal units were localized, the most important type being the "city-state," the top of which consisted of a confederated set of aristocratic lineages. Greece, from the Mycenean Age on, was the premier example, but early Rome was of the same general type. The main unit of these city-states was the patrilineage, with the status of the nuclear family relative to the lineage presenting a complex problem.[7]

The society of classical antiquity had developed a three-class—rather than two-class—system. Aristocratic lineages seem typically to have been the "patrons" of what in Rome were called "client" groups, who by virtue of this patronage were much more definitely included in the societal community than were the two other crucial population elements, namely slaves and what in Greece were called "metics," the "resident aliens" who remained "alien" even if resident for an indefinite number of generations. The sharpness of the line excluding aliens indicated that what evolved into the "citizen" community of a Greek polis was also an affinal collectivity, since clearly clients could marry each other, if not with aristocrats and not in general with outsiders (cf. Fowler, 1921; Ehrenberg, 1964). There was no mechanism like modern "naturalization" for acquiring a new citizenship.

These communities developed, as the crucial process underlying their "classical" form, a kind of obverse of the differentiation between the aristocracy and the common people. This involved the "extension" of many of the status-characteristics of the aristocracy to the client elements by processes which I call inclusion and upgrading (see my *System of Modern Societies*, Chapter II). Classical "democracy" was the outcome of these processes, that is of the establishment of a basic equality of status, concerned especially with political rights, for all adult males within the "citizenship" body. In Rome the old aristocracy were the "patricians," and the "plebeians" were newly included. The same basic developmental pattern was crucial in Greece, most saliently in Athens (Fowler, *op. cit.;* Ehrenberg, *op. cit.*). Metics and slaves continued to be drastically excluded, and active participation was limited to adult males.

Perhaps this can be regarded as a crucial stage, in societal evolution, in the development of the nuclear family toward something like its modern form. The inclusion of adult males as equal citizens precluded the continuation of the previous order of diffuse salience of the lineage *within* the citizen body, which had included drastic discriminations of formal power by class membership of lineage and of status by birth order within the lineage (Fowler, *op. cit.*; Ehrenberg, *op. cit.*). The citizen body remained a stratified affinal collectivity, however, with much political influence and opportunity to attain high office accruing only to those having honored

7. One major benefit I got from the Burg Wartenstein Conference was a better appreciation of the problematical status of the nuclear family in the more primitive kinship systems, and of the extent to which its sharp institutionalization is a late development particularly relevant to Western society.

ancestral and affinal lineages (Syme, 1939). It is notable that a high premium was placed on having honorable citizen ancestry on *both* sides of a family. Although women were for the most part denied the participatory rights of citizenship, they were at the same time the wives, daughters, sisters, and mothers of citizens. Hence they were in a critical sense included. To our modern consciousness, this is perhaps best exemplified by the status dignity of the Roman matron of the late Republic and early Empire.[8]

In the processes of expansion into the Hellenistic and Imperial forms, the Greek and Roman patterns of citizenship were not only vastly extended, but also greatly diluted, above all in political content and in defining an effective affinal collectivity (Syme). These same influences, however, created the framework of the "individualism" of Roman Imperial society, especially in the Eastern areas, which became the matrix for the formation of the Christian synthesis between Judaic and "classical" components of culture.

The long and complex process of the institutionalization of the Christian cultural pattern involved the symbolic—and, I suggest, eventually substantive—interrelation of the two main "lateral" components of the nuclear family. The early Christian church was in sociological form an association, a "community" of believers. It has long been emphasized that, however much the church sanctioned many types of inequality, including the status of slavery, all souls were equal on the spiritual level, i.e. equally sinful and/or equally eligible for salvation. The sole primary exception has concerned the doctrine of predestination, which was accepted only for a comparatively brief phase and did not come very close to attaining thorough societal institutionalization.

In the social setting of the Roman Empire, the Christian communities did not constitute a social reform movement, but essentially a movement of withdrawal from "normal" commitments to social participation (Troeltsch, 1960); they were "in the world, but not of it." This clearly meant devaluation of secular life as then structured, including marriage and the family; St. Paul's dictum that "it is better to marry than to burn" seems unduly grim to most moderns. Christianity never institutionalized the drastic pattern of withdrawal which characterized early "pure" Buddhism, however. It organized not only local communities, but a vast system of "lay" members who lived within ordinary worldly affairs, earning their livings by the "sweat of their brows" and marrying and procreating children, as well as increasingly involving themselves in the political processes of secular society.

8. An illuminating account of the transition from the class system of aristocratic lineages and clients to the equality as citizens of all adult males and their "families" is given in C. R. Noyes, *The Institution of Property* (New York: Longmans, Greene, and Co., 1936). It should be remembered that in early Roman law the *familia* was not, in our sense, a "family" but the aristocratic lineage *plus* its clients. The *pater-familias,* the only "individual" who was *sui juris,* was the male head of the total unit, kinship lineage, *and* clientele.

The church also developed a stratification system, the upper group of which had certain resemblances to the aristocracies of antiquity, including a functional equivalent of endogamy. This "aristocracy" crystallized in the form of the monastic orders, withdrawn subcommunities devoted to the "religious life," the achievement of "perfection" in this sense. They were, however, organized associational communities, in a sense patterned on the model of the early church communities (Troeltsch), although their withdrawal from the world was clearly signalized by the institutionalization of celibacy.

Here I take very seriously the version of the Christian familial symbolism which came strongly to the fore. It has frequently been pointed out that the Hebrews referred to their God much less as "Father" than as "Lord." But the Christian God was from the beginning Father, and Christ was His "only begotten Son." [9] This symbolic pattern was extended so that Christians were "brothers" and "sisters." The sibling terminology then became constitutive for the orders, the brotherhoods and sisterhoods "in Christ," who in a symbolic sense was their "elder brother." Indeed, Christian salvation was symbolically "identification" with Christ, meaning essentially achievement of membership in the community in which He was at the same time "head"—qualitatively different in his "charisma" from all other members—and participating member, in His humanity as distinguished from His divinity (Troeltsch).[10]

The fact that the Christian "religious" were symbolically siblings while making a central point of their celibacy, suggests a symbolic linkage between their celibacy and the incest taboo among siblings, which, parenthetically, included homosexual as well as heterosexual references. In psychoanalytic terms, monasticism, with its involvement of "repression," was institutionalized "latency." This repression served the symbolic assertion that religious interests were higher than any of "this world," of which not just "sexual" but marital interests were taken as a prototype. Parallel considerations apply to the other two basic renunciations of monastic status, namely of organizational independence through the vow of "obedience" and of personal economic interests through the vow of "poverty."

The symbolic involvement with latency suggests that, for the long run, the societal significance of the model of renunciation, in all three respects, did not lie in eliminating worldly involvements from the action system, but in achieving new levels of control over them. Latency children are gen-

9. The implications of the severity with which early Christianity reorganized the principal symbols and patterns of meaning that it inherited from Judaism and Hellenistic culture have been essayed by Arthur Darby Nock in his *Early Gentile Christianity* (New York: Harper Torchbooks, 1964). Of particular interest is his analysis of how stronger and more generalized meaning was obtained partly by the radical symbolic redifferentiation of using such terms as "father" and "son" in a sharply transcendental context.

10. See also Hans Lietzmann *A History of the Early Church* (Cleveland: Meridian, 1961), especially the discussion of the controversies leading up to the Nicene Creed.

erally expected to eventually achieve adult "genitality," not to remain celibate. Siblings eventually come to marry, but not each other. The effect of the sibling incest taboo is to force *lateral* extension of the affinal collectivity. The institutionalization of this extension involves enforcing the "discipline" of latency celibacy and the taboo on increasingly broad sectors of the social structure.

The recent revival in discussion of the celibacy of the secular priesthood reminds us that this institution has not been fundamental dogma of the church, but a matter of organizational policy or "discipline." It was not fully established until the papacy of Gregory VII in the eleventh century on the eve of the High Middle Ages. From the point of view of institutionalization of the religious values, this constituted an upgrading of the secular—including the parish—priesthood, giving the priests a status, roughly, of "brothers" of the religious, and including them in the associational collectivity at the "upper" level of the church.

However that may be, the basic medieval social system, as its rationale was formulated above all by Thomas Aquinas, involved three interpenetrating two-class systems. The first was that of church and state itself, with the church clearly being the higher in evaluative terms. The second, within the church, was that of religious and laity, with the secular clergy standing in between, although tending to gain approximate equality with the religious—celibacy comprising at least one principal common symbolic boundary. The third, within the "state" (that is, secular society), gradually crystallized, in and out of the feudal structure, between aristocracy and the common people.

The crystallization of the medieval system, which Troeltsch (*op. cit.*) called the first "Christian society," involved perhaps the first really unequivocal Christian legitimation of marriage, as one focus of the legitimation of secular society more generally. In a sense, it thereby symbolized ("defined the situation") that church and state were differentiated *parts* of the same system, a position very different from that of the early church, even in the period after Constantine's conversion.

European aristocracy came to be the upper-level manifestation of the significance of the hereditary principle for secular social organization (cf. Bloch, 1961). This was both one of the most important aspects of the societal regression which had taken place with the fall of the Western Roman Empire and the structural base from which a new society had to be built. My suggestion is that its primary structure was very similar in fundamentals to that of the pre-democratic *polis* of antiquity, but with two critical exceptions. One was the presence of a structurally *differentiated* church, having a celibate clergy, both religious and secular, as a cardinal structural feature, but also an organized laity that articulated with the clergy through a basic, although "second class," membership status. The second was the differentiation between the urban sectors and the sectors having potential for wider political organization in territorial terms. The landed aristocracy was grounded in the rural community sector, with its wealth generated mainly by the agricultural production of manorial serfs. The urban sector was continuous with the *polis* of antiquity, via the Roman *municipia,* but, with certain important qualifications, had been deprived of political independence.[11] Monarchy and aristocracy were to become the main sources of higher-order political integration in the modern system.

European aristocracy was broadly a loose confederation of patrilineages, with monarchs on the whole in the position of *primus inter pares.* One of its primary characteristics was a wide extension of intermarriage ties and a lateral openness in establishing them. With the segmentation into territorial states, only gradually was this open "market" constricted—and then less at the top than farther down. Royal marriages across "state" lines continued to be important into the present century, even though the Reformation introduced a major rift because of objections to interfaith marriages.

The "clients" were most importantly the peasantry who were placed, starting with feudal bases, in dependency relations to particular aristocratic lineages, prototypically to "lords of a manor." Only at high levels in the feudal-aristocratic hierarchy could "bourgeois" elements gain the status of clients. Yet the possibility was crucially important because some eventually became strong enough politically to assert their claims to inclusion.

This general form of society established, relative to Christian values, the status of the "genital" maturity of the Christian laity—to be sure, watchfully supervised by those who were symbolically "married" to Christ, namely the religious. Surely this is like the older generation's permission for their offspring to assume the adult role, including marriage. In terms of the structure of the society as a whole, however, the aristocracy was the original focus of this new religious permissiveness, since it was the *responsible* class of secular society. In regard to responsibility, the symbolism of the priesthood, as in the role of "fathers" relative to all laymen, was also significant.

In another respect, however, the celibate community of the priesthood served as a special model of social structure. Erotic relations of the sort involved in marriage are inherently "particularistic." The "latency" pattern could more closely approach universalistic standards in that brothers and sisters are in a certain sense each others' equals and can be expected to associate with each other and love one another without particularistic discrimination, whereas a spouse in a sense belongs "with" if not "to" the other spouse. Hence we may suggest a "dialectic" relation between the hereditary emphasis of aristocratic institutions, which accentuates the lin-

11. The importance of the urban sector in mediating the associational political patterns of antiquity into modern European society was suggested by Max Weber in *The City* (Glencoe: Free Press, 1958).

eage, and the associational emphasis of affinal relations, since men who may marry each others' sisters are in some sense symbolically "brothers." [12]

The affinal relation could, however, be differentiated from that in which the relation among the symbolic "brothers" was abstracted from the kinship nexus and based upon common membership in a political associational collectivity—the transition from fraternity to common citizenship. This transition constituted the establishment of a line of differentiation *within* the role-participation structures of individuals, in the first instance adult males, between their capacities as lineage members and as citizens. This role structure then came under pressure to become a line of differentiation in the structure of the community itself. This concept of citizenship, basically continuous in structure with that of antiquity, was essential to the transition from the feudal basis of political organization to a "state" basis in the more or less modern sense (see my *System of Modern Societies*, 1970).

Again in a symbolic and psychodynamic sense, this constituted a reversal in the prestige-order of the stages of psychosexual maturation. The role-complex which we have labeled citizenship was desexualized and given a higher order of prestige than that of lineage membership, which was above all institutionalized about kinship, including marriage. Thus citizen bodies, or more generally a very large category of associational relationships, were "celibate" in the sense *not* that their members abstained totally from erotic relationships, but that, through differentiation of the social structure at the *role* level, internalized in the typical personality, the component of erotic attachment, with its particularism and diffuseness, was excluded from the expectations and motivational complexes which governed the behavior of "citizens."

This process may be regarded as the most important aspect—along with its political and economic counterparts which related to the principles of obedience and poverty in the monastic tradition—of the post-medieval institutionalization of the Christian pattern. It first took firm hold through the Reformation, and was symbolized by the marriage of the Protestant clergy, the example being set by Luther himself, a former monk whose wife was a former nun. As Weber (1958) so sharply emphasized, the basic "Puritan" conception was that *every* Christian should become a monk, symbolically, in terms of the seriousness of his commitment to the Christian mission. At the same time, it came to be taken for granted that all religious men should marry, but should *control* the erotic component of their personalities in the interest of their higher obligation to contribute to the Kingdom of God on Earth.

As in classical antiquity, in post-medieval European aristocracy, but also in the peasantry and to a degree in the "bourgeoisie," the incorporation of

12. In the modern languages we use the term "brothers-in-law" when this has actually occurred.

the nuclear family in the lineage structure conflicted with the potentials of the social and erotic composition of the nuclear family. It prevented the individual citizen from coming into his own, because the lineage rather than the individual was the main unit of participation and, as with the Roman pater-familias, only heads of lineages were, as individuals, full "members." Given the fact that the system was one of patrilineages, it is understandable that the process of inclusion tended to proceed from heads of lineages, to their younger brothers and sons, and to the adult males among their clients. The general pattern in both societies has been the emancipation into the status of citizens—persons free to engage in associational memberships—of the adult male groups.

As the adult male becomes emancipated from lineage solidarities, not only is the nuclear family differentiated out as the primary kinship unit, but there ensues a profound change in the character of the marriage relationship and eventually the relationships between parents and children. The main early index of this change is freedom in the choice of marriage partner, in the first instance for the male, as distinguished from the arrangement of marriages by the elders in the interest of the lineage. This type of choice operates within a wider affinal collectivity than the arrangement system could admit, and shifts the criteria of appropriateness in a "personal" direction. The very fact that the marriage agreement comes to be more between "individuals" than between lineages means that motives which appeal to individuals *independently* of their respective lineage memberships become increasingly prominent. Since social status and economic considerations are closely bound up with the lineage system, it is perhaps not surprising that mutual erotic attraction should come increasingly to the fore. The end of this road is the "romantic love complex" (see Goode, 1963).

It seems that this constellation defines the main phenomenon of differentiation which we are considering. From the point of view of the structure of *secular* society, a more universalistic and affectively-neutral associational sector emerges from the lineage-dominated aristocratic upper sector. This new sector eventually comes to a certain culmination in the pattern of political citizenship—that is, in the societal community—but is by no means confined to it. Indeed, it may be suggested that the development of the male role-structure in occupational situations is just as important, the sector for achievement complementing that of citizenship. In a sense male occupational associates are symbolically "brothers," as are fellow citizens. These developments have involved the concomitant differentiation of a "private" sphere, which increasingly has come to center on the nuclear family complex. Moreover, in a sense not previously the case, the "personal" relation between marriage partners has become the constitutive structural element of the nuclear family, and this personal element has become in a newly crucial respect an erotic relationship; hence the tendency for sexual compatibility to become a criterion of whether a marriage should even continue, to say nothing of being considered satisfactory.

We have stressed the similarity of pattern in the processes of differentiation, extension, inclusion, and upgrading which occurred in the world of antiquity and in post-medieval Europe. But the differences are at least as important. The first crucial one was that incipiently modern secular society has been secularized in a sense not true of the ancient world. Above all, this has meant that the secular society was set free to differentiate *on its own terms* without directly involving the integrity of the main religious system. This outcome is most dramatically formulated in Weber's analysis of the Protestant conception of the calling (Weber, 1958). Not only did it erase the basic line between religious and laity, thus between married and celibate as categories of concrete persons, but, in the most strictly religious terms, *all* honorable callings came to be of basically equal religious worth. The spiritual equality of membership in the church became institutionalized into the societal equality of callings and, by implication on some level, of individuals.

This development also provided the basis upon which religion has been "privatized," so that, with the separation of church and state, religious toleration, and denominational pluralism, concrete religious bodies have become voluntary associations, clearly differentiated from the status of their members as citizens in the societal community (Parsons, 1960). The private religious sphere may then be considered another "layer," which in value terms stands higher than the societal community itself and which also is in some sense "celibate" for its participants. Clearly, the differentiation from secular society is matched within the personalities of individual participants. All the laity of the various religious groups are expected to be free to marry, and most of them do, as well as the Protestant and Jewish clergy. The current discussion of the status of celibacy for the Catholic secular priesthood seems to fit in this situation. Indeed, our time may see the question of permitting even the Catholic religious to marry raised as a fully serious question, not one of the simple abandonment of religious commitments.

Another very basic trend of modern society has been the "emancipation" of women. The "traditional" woman in the European tradition, we may say, was "totally" encompassed by her familial role, while men had already become citizens who were only partially incorporated into the kinship system.[13] The essential process here, following by some time the corresponding differentiation of the masculine role, has been the involve-

13. My daughter, the late Anne Parsons, in connection with her studies of South Italian kinship, once remarked that for the traditional Neapolitan girl there were only three possibilities, namely the conventional role of wife and mother, or to secede drastically from this role, either "upward" by becoming a nun, or "downward" by becoming a prostitute. All three were "total" statuses not permitting differentiation in the sense of the above discussion. See her *Belief, Magic and Anomie* (New York: Free Press, 1969).

ment in spheres outside the family and its symbolic representation in "social" contexts (Giele, 1961). Occupation has been one primary field of participation; the other, symbolically more crucial, has been the franchise—women's suffrage has now been institutionalized almost throughout the modern world (Switzerland still holds out).

These processes have clearly resulted in the extensive, though not yet complete, inclusion of women, particularly educated women, in the "celibate" community of citizenship. It is a striking fact that many of the female pioneers in the struggle for inclusion, the first generations of professional women and the suffragist leaders, were celibate—and often made it a virtue, as one aspect of their "dedication." Indeed, these women may reasonably be compared to members of celibate religious orders, although they functioned "in the world" instead of withdrawing from it.

The differentiation of the sphere of citizenship from kinship, with both its marital and sibling references, does not exhaust the differentiation of the personality types or of the role types of either sex, nor their significant modes of interrelation. While the adult masculine role was the only substantial focus of citizenship, the nuclear family was in a sense segregated, as was the lineage when it was the primary unit of the upper societal community. We have suggested that free choice of marriage partners on "personal" grounds undermines the segregation of the family. A force going much farther in this direction is the universal formal education which, from about their Oedipal periods on, incorporates children in the school as well as the family. Another development in the Western world, which has advanced farthest in the United States, has made formal education increasingly coeducational. This clearly enforces, and is a function of, the inclusion of both sexes in the citizenship community, above all by encouraging children of both sexes to internalize achievement motivation.

This development has also created the cross-sex "peer group," which interestingly is strongly resisted by children during the latency period, but emerges with dramatic force in adolescence. It carries a patent significance as a "marriage market" in circumstances of the free choice of marriage partners and of the many associated complications. In our symbolic terminology, peers in this sense are "brothers" and "sisters" who, being legitimately eligible to agree on marriages, may eventually "pair off." At a certain level of ideal type conceptualization such "pairing off" should require a very clear, possibly rigid, boundary between the two patterns of non-erotic siblingship and erotically "sealed" marriage. In modern, "free" relationship systems among age-peers of opposite sex, this is a situation of considerable strain which has been undergoing important change.

There is no doubt that the school situation serves as an agency of differentiation, both of the class as a social system and of the personalities of its individual members (cf. Talcott Parsons, "The School Class as a Social System," 1960). In the former context, it is the new upper class of achievers which tends to become differentiated. In the latter context, the part of the personality which is oriented to the impersonal, universalistically oriented values and activities of "task performance" is differentiated from that oriented to the diffuse status of "child." It is particularly noteworthy that, even for the lower socioeconomic groups, this focuses on predominantly intellectual achievement. On the whole, practical applications become serious concerns later, either in the occupational world as such or at higher levels of education.

The scholastic achievement complex introduces an hierarchical element into the system of age-graded peer groups and classes that is relatively dissociated from the statuses of families of orientation. However, the degree of this dissociation is lessened by the relative homogeneity of residential neighborhoods and of the social origin of pupils in a given school, especially an elementary school. This situation is now very tense because of its relation to racial segregation. At the same time, however, age-peers constitute extrafamilial groups of the associative type having a wide variety. Coeducation encourages their crystallization across the sex line. The peer-group context is also a focus of emancipation from dependence on the family of orientation. Furthermore, as distinguished from the formal school system, peers are groups of "friends" rather than competing associates.

The situation of peer-group formation involves a parallel to the emancipation of marriage choice from lineage considerations in that it also makes possible an emphasis on "personal" attraction. This includes a certain disposition to hostility toward parental discipline and expectations, as well as to the assertion of the legitimacy of interest and modes of behavior on the borderline of adult approval, if not beyond it. This is a well-known pattern of modern "youth culture."

It is important to understand what may go on psychologically regarding the institutionalization of universalistically structured derivatives of the motivational components that are so important in the earlier stages of socialization when they are rather tightly bound into particularistic relational systems, notably the nuclear family. In earlier stages of societal development, these components have been institutionalized in the structure of major particularistic groupings such as lineages. The associational type of system requires considerably more emancipation from particularism and particularistic motivational supports, however, and, in general, more than do hierarchical social groupings.

The psychoanalytic account of the socialization process emphasizes two analytically distinct motivational components: erotic interests, which dominate the "pleasure principle," and "cathexis" and affective attachment, which at the appropriate stages certainly focuses on the "reality" principle and ego-development, perhaps especially during the more or less immediately pre-Oedipal stage in which attachment to the mother predominates.

Members of the adolescent peer group may be considered symbolic siblings, entering into a sibling-like relation extending far beyond the range of kinship involvements. When of opposite sex, they are even potential marriage partners. Hence, they are engaged in establishing adult heterosexual erotic interests, not only genital in the anatomic sense, but also to same-generation persons of the opposite sex. In all three of these respects, the "genital" complex is different from the eroticism of childhood, and can be attained by the individual only through a far-reaching reorganization of the latter. Nevertheless, it was one of Freud's most important insights that they are fundamentally continuous with each other.

From very early in the development of human personality, erotic motives stand in a relation of complex interdependence with affective relations, which involve diffuse attachments and loyalties to persons and collectivities (cf. Talcott Parsons, "Social Structure and the Development of Personality," 1960). Solidarity motivated by strong affect, and sometimes producing passionate loyalties, is a well-known feature of adolescent peer groups. This may certainly be interpreted as involving a generalization of the affective ties which are generated in the individual during his socialization experience in the family. In particular, such generalization becomes increasingly prominent in the parent-child relationship as the latter tends to become de-eroticized from latency on. However, it is also particularly important to sibling relationships, especially during and after the latency period, because it is with sexual maturation that the sibling incest taboo becomes salient.

My suggestion is that the old "dialectic" relationship between the two lateral types of relation, that of marriage and that of siblingship, the one erotic, the other prohibiting eroticism, is coming to play a new role in modern youth culture and to constitute a new motivational and structural basis for associative patterns. In the background of this process, certainly the "emancipation" of women, the restructuring of the nuclear family that stresses equality in the marriage relationship and reduces "authoritariansim" in the treatment of children, and the prevalence of coeducation throughout the educational system, all play a paramount part.

The foregoing suggests a particularly important involvement of the feminine role in processes of restructuring. In the past, it has not only been more fully encompassed in the family than the masculine role, but also particularly central to the socialization of the child. Childhood erotic and affective attachments have both been more to the mother than to the father, although the latter has certainly been much involved, too. In earlier systems, women have been relatively excluded from the peer group experience by their more immediate transition from encompassment in the family or lineage of orientation to encompassment in the family or lineage of procreation through their marriage. They have also been more excluded until recently from the "celibate" spheres of adult, predominantly masculine, occupational and political concern. Men, though exposed to many more associational contexts, have participated mainly on a same-sex basis.

Given the context of adolescent "emancipation" from adult control and diffuse solidarity, it is understandable that the lines of solidarity generally extend laterally in age-grade terms. Given the importance of heterosexuality for the incipient adult, it is understandable that erotic themes are prominantly involved, and that they are predominantly heterosexual, although homosexuality is by no means absent. Given the much greater emancipation of women, but also their continuing involvement with family and especially child care, it is not surprising that certain leadership roles in the youth culture—and in its extensions upward in the age range—should be taken by girls. It is said that the diminution in the fear of pregnancy due to "the pill" has greatly accentuated this in the erotic context.

It seems likely that there is now occurring something of a "sexual revolution" which may well involve considerably more overt "sexual freedom" than indulged in even by the "flaming youth" of the 1920's generation. However, subgroups which act upon a full development of the "free love" pattern seem to represent rather "sectarian" minorities, not the introducers of a pattern that will become general in society. The main reason for this judgment concerns the intimate interrelation between eroticism and affect in the socialization process, and the enormous importance of affectual ties, independently of erotic gratification, for the solidarity of kinship and other groups. If the modern peer-group phenomenon is an extension of kinship solidarity in a certain direction, as we have argued, the logic of the role of the incest taboo in kinship systems should prove relevant.

It is suggestive that, in the most recent phase, a primary slogan of radical youth culture has focused upon the importance of "love," evidently not a love which implies or requires complete freedom of mutual sexual access. It seems likely that one function of the current involvement with drugs is to de-eroticize cross-sex peer relations by stressing another kind of freedom from the sense of inhibition.

Whatever the case with these complex issues, it does seem that the broad process of differentiation of a new set of associational structures, both from the family and from the more impersonally "celibate" world of citizenship and occupation, may prove very important for modern society. This may come to provide networks of solidarity on much more highly universalistic bases than kinship and the older sort of friendship, yet at levels which tap the kind of motivational complexes which have been central to them.

I suggest that a new focus of universalistically structured solidarity is in process of development, one which is parallel to, but differentiated from, the complex which we have called citizenship in reference to a matrix from which much of the more universalistically structured part of modern society has evolved. A critical reference point for the analysis of this new development lies in the fact that sibling groups comprise members of *two* sexes, not one.

The processes of differentiation and inclusion within the structure of

Western society, which we sketched above, concerned in the first instance the masculine role, departing above all from the relations among brothers and centering on the masculine role in its "lateral" involvement in social structure. Thus, we have had a development from literal to symbolic "brotherhood" and then to "citizenship" as a prototype of associational membership, which approaches Nelson's category of "universal otherhood" (Nelson, 1949). It would seem that there should be a parallel series of steps of differentiation and inclusion centering in the feminine role in the context of siblingship, namely the relations among sisters, and in the generalization of this pattern outside the kinship nexus on increasingly universalistic bases.

The structural isolation of the nuclear family, which we believe to be one primary consequence of the gradual break-up of lineages through the process of social differentiation, should probably be treated as the central point of reference. Its main immediate consequence was the isolation of women in the "wife and mother" role and a sharpening of the contrast with the masculine role. The narrowing of the lives of "bourgeois" women compared to what they had been in the heyday of aristocracy was very conspicuous. The "Victorian" version of the "good woman" pattern may be considered a parallel of monasticism for men.

Is it too fantastic to suggest that the parallel to the celibacy of the secular priesthood has been the "drawing" of husbands and fathers into the family? This started with romantic love and its implication of diffuse, more or less "total" mutual commitment, including above all the expectation and indeed obligation of parenthood. Since men have typically been anchored in the occupational world, only a "sectarian" minority could entirely sacrifice the differentiation of roles and personality in favor of being a "totalistic" family man, but undoubtedly the claims of the family on the "normal" adult man have come to be firmly established. We may regard this as the complement of the "emancipation" of women from the family in favor of participation in the labor force and citizenship.

The mere "drawing in" of the individual man to the diffusely affectional context of his family of procreation is not, however, a stable terminus for the general process of inclusion of men in a domain of predominantly feminine concerns, any more than the inclusion of the secular clergy was a stable stopping point in the process of inclusion of larger circles of the population in the higher-order pattern of citizenship. The obvious direction of change has been the extension of familial-type affectional relations to wider groups, forming something like universalistic "sisterhoods," which could eventually include men on the basis of personality differentiation.

If, in symbolic and psychological terms, the prototype of Western religious celibacy has been latency, the prototype of this new development may well be the adolescent phase. Since the family is again the primary point of reference in the development itself, the generalization from sibling status within the family to the adolescent peer group seems to be crucial. Its emergence might even be called the "Reformation" of the evolution of the feminine complex in Western social structure, for it has brought a much broader collectivity system, not only the strictly "religious"—that is, the family—into the "affectional community."

It should not be surprising that such a development is fraught with severe conflicts. In an earlier phase, members of the two sex groups have faced each other with severe anxiety and pointedly funneled their tentative approaches into the marriage context, for example, through the "rating and dating" pattern. It may well be that we are now seeing the emergence of two primary sectarian extremes, each involving an exaggerated symbolization of one of the sex roles.

On the one hand, there are clear manifestations of a "cult of masculinity" emphasizing toughness and physical prowess, merging into violence, as primary symbols of being "really" men. The motorcycle is a particularly interesting symbol in this context, perhaps in part because the ordinary automobile is symbolically the "family" car and can connote subservience to women. The girl on the rear seat of the motorcycle is safe, being totally under the control of the "rider." On the other hand, we have the recently emerging "hippie" groups, which symbolically accentuate the assimilation of sex roles to each other, but in a form which is much more feminine than masculine—for example, the adoption of long hair by males.[14]

The Victorian "good woman," precisely as distinguished from her aristocratic predecessors, was not only confined within the family, but was also expected not to be strongly interested in the erotic side of marriage, if not to be fully frigid.[15] Insofar as she had erotic interests, they were to be channeled mainly into the mother role. The connection of this complex with the assertiveness of women in claiming inclusion in the "celibate" community of citizenship and occupations may be important, since the step to a fully celibate role was rather easy.

The general process of "emancipation" of women, however, has entailed recurrent waves of expression, both overt and symbolic, of their rights to be erotic in the adult genital sense. Indeed, it may be argued that the erotic complex has come to center far more in the feminine than in the masculine role. Thus, with all its variations, feminine dress on the whole plays up erotic assets whereas masculine dress plays them down—for example, the increasing tolerance of exposure of the female body.

The focus on the adolescent phase of psychosexual development, as suggested above, may be given a special significance. Adolescence is the period of the maturation and first arousability of genital erotic interests for both sexes. Yet it is also a period in which, particularly in modern soci-

14. In this connection, it is not unimportant that the Christ figure, through much of the history of European art, has been portrayed with a strong feminine cast and in terms which are ambiguous with respect to sex role.

15. The pattern of the "child wife," who was too young and "innocent" to be erotically engaged in the role of wife, was perhaps only an extreme form.

eties, most of the fundamental personal commitments have not yet been made, but in which a tentative and competitive situation is maintained.

From the point of view of the functioning of modern society, there can be no doubt that the family is of critical, and in certain respects of increasing, importance in that it has become much more differentiated and functionally specialized than before. Equally clearly, the feminine role is particularly central to the modern "isolated" nuclear family, especially in that the wife-mother has a near monopoly with respect to influence on her children, especially in the crucial pre-Oedipal phases. She also has a very special relation to the psychological security of her husband, since typically he also has made a heavy "investment" in both his marital and parental relationships.

It is perhaps Freud's greatest insight that erotic motivation is the most important single point of leverage for the early socialization of the human child. Because it is a category or *generalized* motivational energy, it can be mobilized in the interest of initially undefined functions in developing the truly human personality. It is one of the principal "plasticities" of the human organism which make society and culture possible.

The erotic component is basically organic, however, being neither cultural in the sense of a fully "symbolic" medium, nor social in the sense of being transmissible through the communication processes of social interaction. However, it is on the boundary of these potentials, erotic stimulation being susceptible to *mutual* interaction, even though the pleasure which is its output remains private to each organism—the famous orgasm is particular to the individual organism and cannot be shared in the sense in which common values or knowledge can be shared.

It is well known that the erotic complex is highly vulnerable to exploitation and other processes destructive of solidarity.[16] Because of its organic character, it cannot provide the main basis of stable social relationships, especially since this stability is inherently threatened by the intrusion of "aggressive" drives, the psychological counterpart of Hobbes' "passions" which can lead to the war of all against all.

Very generally, the organic particularism of erotic motivation is "bound in" by a series of cybernetically higher-order media in which personalities and, through them, social systems gain motivational investments in Freud's sense. The most immediately important of these media is what the psychoanalytic tradition, developing Freud's concept of an economy of cathexes, has come to call *affect*. Affective ties actually bind individuals to one another through the fundamental motivational dispositions of each, but also upon a diffuse basis of *sharing* which is not involved in the erotic mechanism. Seen in this light, affective ties are the principal psychological substratum of social solidarity; they are "dynamically" linked with erotic

16. A number of the recently published and publicized "underground" novels dwell upon this potential of the erotic complex.

interests, but must be clearly distinguished from them analytically. A basic functional reason for the importance of the incest taboo is the necessity of "raising" motivations of solidarity to a higher level than primacy of erotic interests will permit (cf. Talcott Parsons, "The Incest Taboo," 1964). Marriage may then be regarded as the prototype of the integration of the affective and erotic levels, being a relation of social solidarity which is a "community of fate" for the partners as well as a focus of mutual erotic gratification. Above all, this community is involved in the sharing of the functions of parenthood, for the institution of marriage is incomprehensible without the expectation that the *typical* couple will have children, though not all will.[17]

At this point, we must utilize the paradigm of the generalized medium of societal or action interchange.[18] We suggest that erotic motivation is the "security base" of the affect medium. Precisely in that the individual's security can no longer rest in his lineage, a demand is generated that the basis of affective security should be "purely personal," a demand which readily translates into erotic terms. Here homosexual eroticism is well known to be more regressive than heterosexual; hence the least secure elements "go in" more for homosexual than heterosexual relations. More generally, however, it is crucial that the modern preoccupation with eroticism has to do with the process of establishing new bases of solidarity centering about the mechanism of affect, not only with erotic gratification as such. There is a parallel to the gold standard preoccupation of monetary development until very recently. The line of argument is that if two people really "mean it" with respect to their mutual attraction and common solidarity, they will "put it on the line" in organically erotic terms, the "real" basis of "authentically" belonging together. The difficulty in generalizing this argument is that erotic involvement has an extremely limited potential for generalization at the societal and cultural levels. Too sharp insistence on its importance is radically "deflationary" in that it greatly restricts the bases of personal involvement in social relationships.

If the erotic component is the "base" of a generalized medium, it must belong to a larger category in the sense that precious metals belong to the

17. This complex of integration of the erotic and affective levels of cultural "definitions" for American kinship has been admirably analyzed by David M. Schneider in *American Kinship: A Cultural Approach* (Englewood Cliffs, N. J. Prentice-Hall, 1968), which has appeared since the draft of this paper was written. In particular, Schneider shows that sexual intercourse, within marriage, is the primary symbol of the "diffuse enduring solidarity" which, by cultural definition, should characterize not only the relation of spouses to each other, but the family as a whole, including both the parent-child and the sibling relationships. Schneider's analysis is based on a study of a sample of American families, but, to an approximation, the patterns he elucidates are increasingly characteristic of modern, industrial type, societies.

18. This paradigm has been developed in my papers "On the Concept of Political Power," reprinted in R. Bendix and S. M. Lipset (eds.): *Class, Status and Power* (New York: Free Press, 2nd ed. 1964), and "On the Concept of Influence," in *Public Opinion Quarterly*, Spring, 1963.

larger category of physical goods or commodities. Gold is appropriate as a monetary base because of certain well-known characteristics, namely durability, scarcity, and high value in small bulk, considerable non-monetary instrumental usefulness (what economists call the industrial value of gold), and high "expressive" valuation in the general context of decoration, for example, for jewelry and decoration of buildings or statues. For this combination of reasons, its acceptability transcends narrow particularistic limits.

I suggest that the larger category to which erotic pleasure belongs is that of the valued intrinsic and relational properties of human individuals which refer especially to the body. We will call these properties, from the point of view of others' access to them, "intimacies." Different cultures draw different lines of access and evaluation of intimacy. However, there is a central complex of privacy that seems to exist everywhere, which consists of the sharing of "residence" in the sense of premises of daily living, perhaps above all sleeping, and of commensality—that is, the privilege of eating (and sometimes drinking) in company with others, including a sharing in food tastes and/or taboos. Similarly, lines are drawn between clothing appropriate for public contexts and dress appropriate only to intimate occasions and company. Most societies have important rules about full exposure of the body to non-intimates.

Within the general category of intimacies, the properties of erotic pleasure which correspond to the high value in small bulk and the durability of gold are evidently the intensity of pleasurable experience—as compared to eating, for example—and the access to *mutuality* of stimulation, especially between *pairs* of persons. The fact that mutuality of pleasure can be optimized in the genital heterosexual relationship is undoubtedly organically grounded—homosexual and autoerotic gratification are by and large "second bests." Beyond these central characteristics, the connection of the erotic component with other elements in the intimacy complex establishes both an "instrumental" aspect, by which kinds of "attractiveness" are generally associated with suggestions of erotic capacity, and a value aspect, by which expectations of erotic "prowess" comprise a part of individual "self conception" or a component of identity. This is a potent combination, so it should not be surprising that preoccupation with erotic matters is at least as strong as the historic *auri sacra fames* of the economic sphere.

In all known societies, the institutionalization of intimacies has centered about kinship groups. We explain this broadly by the relation of kinship to the socialization function, which requires high levels of intimacy between the children being socialized and a relatively small number of adults. The broad evolutionary trend has been to differentiate from kinship units a progressively larger proportion of the functions which do not intrinsically involve intimacies, notably political and economic functions, though also religious and educational functions—the latter two raising some special problems, however. This process has increased the concentration of the kinship system on the area of intimacies, a fact which raises new questions about the relation of kinship to the rest of the social structure.

A critical juncture in this evolutionary process was reached with the stage that we have called the "isolation" of the nuclear family, which involves by far the highest known levels of concentration of focal intimacies in one small unit of society. Like any other product of structural differentiation in society, however, the isolation of the nuclear family has given rise to a new set of interchanges between the newly differentiated units and other units with which they stand in complex transactional relations. Political and cultural relations are undoubtedly relevant here, but the most obvious comparative reference is to the economic sphere. The famous "loss of function" of the family emerged through the differentiation of the economy, with the resulting dependence of families on the occupational earnings of their members, but with the opening for family members of opportunities for achievement that had been precluded under older conditions.

This phase in a sense culminated general progress in the differentiation of the economy, from the institutionalization of markets for particular products to the institutionalization of markets for the primary factors of production, labor being a primary factor. If labor was to be "marketable"—hence, as often put these days, "alienated"—there had to be a reorganization of the conditions under which commitments to labor contributions could be generated. This reorganization focused in the first instance in the new type of family, but has spread from there in various ways.

We have already discussed the isolating effect of the new family system upon the feminine role of wife-mother, as well as the tendency to mitigate the resultant strain by drawing the husband more fully into the family and lessening the rigidity of the lines of sex-role differentiation within the family so that, for example, it should not be regarded as basically unmasculine for a man to participate in household chores or child care. The obverse of this has been increased feminine participation in the extrafamilial world of occupation, citizenship, and the like. The more general tendency has been toward an increasing differentiation in the personality structure of *both* sex types, with marriage serving as the focal point of integration for a four-fold structure that has instrumental and expressive primacies in both masculine and feminine roles, but with differential emphasis in each. Here, the increased concern with the erotic component of the marriage relation is connected with its being a "ritual" symbolization of *both* the solidarity of the couple and the differentiation of their roles. The erotic relation in marriage is the "intimacy" par excellence (cf. Schneider, 1968).

The process of differentiation of which the development of a labor market is a principal outcome, as a phase in social evolution, has involved a process of upgrading in adaptive capacity. The upgrading process has entailed the propagation of the differentiation between kinship and employing units upward in the scale of social stratification. In the early phase, as reflected in the writings of the classical economists—and Marx—the employed person was typically the "laborer," whereas the higher echelon of the economy consisted of employer-proprietors in the format of the "family firm," whether commercial farmers or industrialists. Larger and larger proportions of the higher echelons of the labor force have gradually become "employed," so that they work in *occupational* roles, rather than ascriptive or independent "proprietary" roles. The most crucial development has been the involvement of both managerial or "bureaucratic" and technical or professional personnel in occupational roles.[19]

This upgrading process has been one primary impetus behind another major impact on family structure, namely the enormous development of the system of formal education. It is highly significant that the Educational Revolution, which will probably prove even more important than either the Industrial or the Democratic Revolutions, is occurring *after* the other two. On the "demand" side, it has been the need for educated personnel in occupational roles which, as much as anything else, has stimulated the enormous expansion, though the backing of deep-seated values is also of vital importance.

Formal education has plunged an increasing proportion of children above the age of about six into extrafamilial roles in some respects analogous to the occupational roles of their fathers. The expectations of performance, and the evaluation of performance, have become structurally independent of the familial setting and have exerted a pressure in some respects parallel to that exerted by the development of the labor market. In the first instance, these pressures operated on sons, but through them the rest of the family. In particular, boys could regard their schooling as rather direct preparation for their occupational careers. This tendency was importantly enhanced by the massive educational upgrading of the whole population, which, starting from approximate universal primary education, has almost attained universality at the secondary level and has been vastly and rapidly increasing the proportion of age cohorts in the system of higher education.

It might seem that this development would accentuate the asymmetry of sex roles within the family as well as elsewhere. However, in American society in particular, and increasingly in the rest of the modern world, the main pattern of formal education has come to be *coeducational*, subjecting girls as well as boys to achievement standards framed in terms of *common* patterns centering around the cognitive culture of modern civilization. This has become a powerful source of leverage for inclusion in the feminine personality of a prominent "achievement" component feeding

19. I have discussed the relations between these changes and the modern form of bureaucracy or formal organization in several of the essays included in *Structure and Process in Modern Societies* (Glencoe: Free Press, 1960).

directly into the "celibate" system of the society. It is very important that the foundations of this aspect of feminine, as well as masculine, personality are laid in the "latency" period of psycho-sexual development.

In modern society, the differentiation of sex roles continues to be as crucial as their assimilation to each other. Clearly, the importance of this differentiation is rooted in the structure and functions of the "isolated" nuclear family. The implications of this structural situation are made salient to the members of the maturing age-cohort during adolescence. Not only do the great majority of youth now remain within the educational system through secondary school and to ages of reasonable marriageability, but rapidly increasing proportions of them continue into college and beyond.

Precisely because the adolescent girl is in some ways blocked from full participation in the "masculine" world of occupation and occupation-oriented education much as her mother was, yet is strongly expected to participate in them in some other ways, she is under strong pressure to find a sphere for herself in which femininity has primacy in "symbolic" terms, but which is free of the particularistically restrictive confines of the nuclear family in its "Victorian" form. Moreover, given the important relation to the status of coeducation, this cannot meaningfully take the form of sex-segregated associational patterns.

In Western society the main associational structure which was rooted in the egalitarian transcending of lineage hierarchy was grounded, more than in any other form of organization, in the masculine religious orders. The "brotherhoods," though they long maintained a "distance" from primary involvements in secular society, succeeded in providing the basic model for the democratic association of the modern world, for the complex of "citizenship" in its extension first to all adult males, then to all adults regardless of sex. The element of "celibacy" in their model for the associational system was symbolically if not literally crucial, because associational relations comprise the field of the severest involvement of universalistic standards which must also be in the strictest sense "affectively neutral." Within this context, the celibate model is the pattern which symbolically stressed *equality* among peers by contrast with the hierarchical structure of the parent-child relationship, in this case especially the father-son relation.

For at least two centuries, there has been a strong tendency for opinion in the Western world to hold that the "impersonality" of this pattern has systematically undermined the motivational foundations of any "good society." We suggest that this malaise has been related in a certain sense to the "undue" neutralization of the feminine component of the more general normative-motivational structure, in the first instance rooting in the isolation of the nuclear family. In the last few pages we have outlined a series of steps by which, we think, a certain redressing of balance has begun to take place. It has involved a restructuring of the various roles within the family, as well as their modes of involvement outside. In particular, the feminine role in the adolescent peer group has become a focal reference for the development of a new pattern of "laterally" structured associational community.

We have argued that the differentiation between the household and the employing organization was the primary source of the isolation of the nuclear family. On the side of employment, this differentiation involved the development and institutionalization of a labor market, by virtue of which households and jobs are linked through the former's output of labor commitments and the latter's output of consumers' goods, with money mediating the relations of exchange. For the economy, this constitutes the mobility of a crucial *factor* of production. Of course, both labor and consumers' markets must be institutionalized, but the former is particularly crucial to the economy. Here, the key institutional complex is contract, especially its "non-contractual" components (cf. Durkheim, 1933, especially Book I, Chapter VII). This institutional structure is also part of the primary structure of the normative component of the societal community.

Just as occupational and job choice have become basically voluntary for the individual, so has the choice of marriage partners. In an important sense, then, what we have been discussing is the institutionalization of the marriage market as the set of voluntary arrangements which center on affective attachments. There is a certain parallel in that both "markets" imply high levels of commitment, even though they are not equal. A person generally has a full-time job, doing justice to which is incompatible with too much "moonlighting." Similarly, he has a single marriage partner to whom he is committed in sharing daily household life.

Furthermore, both nexus are flanked by wider complexes of voluntary relationships. On the side of the economy are the consumers' markets, the markets for the factors of production other than labor, and the ramified network of financial markets. The system of contract, then, ramifies into the property system, as well as into the norms governing employment, varying from the simple types of hiring unskilled labor to academic tenure. In a somewhat similar way, we suggest, the "marriage market" is flanked by other components of a nexus of affectively-toned voluntary relationships. This network has its own distinctive institutional structures, for example, of kinship, friendship, private association, and recreation, which constitute the framework of what may be called "affective community." These structures follow a major pattern of differentiation, and the differentiated components are linked by generalized media of interchange. Affect constitutes the core medium of these interchanges, as money does for the economic market system, but links with a variety of other media.

At the analytical level of the general system of action, which interrelates the behavioral organism, personality, social and cultural systems with each other, affect is the generalized medium most closely involved with the social system. Its primary articulation with the organic level is the one we have sketched to its erotic security base. It is the capacity of erotic motives to serve as a basis of attachment to another person which makes erotic pleasure socially relevant. Only, however, when the motivational basis of attachment is generalized beyond the erotic level can there emerge, as Schneider so clearly shows, a basis of solidarity for the family as a whole, to say nothing of beyond it. This is the level which we are calling affect, which in some contexts may legitimately be called "love." It may be surmised that religious celibacy, as its role in the historical background of our society has been discussed, as well as the more general negativism of the early Christians to erotic motives, has had something to do with institutionalizing the medium of affect in broader circumstances.[20]

Like other generalized media, affect operates both as a reward and as a facility. If it is to function as a "cement" of solidary relational systems of any considerable extensiveness, rewards cannot consist only of "intrinsically" valuable inputs. Sexual intercourse is a case of the "barter" of pleasurable stimulations which are indeed intrinsically valuable. The genesis of affective capacity is, we consider, an essential condition of the wider solidarities, a thesis which has an obvious bearing on the problem of significance of the incest taboo. Beyond that, however, it is necessary for affective attachments to articulate satisfactorily with the other generalized media of the action level. Without attempting to elaborate, we may suggest in particular with the functions of performance capacity through the *recognition* (in Thomas' sense) of achievements as valued performances, and through what I have called—in the paper referred to above—the "moral sanction of association" as a form of the definition of the situation. These interchanges at the level of the general system of action constitute a substratum of symbolic processes at the social system level which are particularly important to the motivational integration of individuals in social systems.

Along lines we have already sketched, the "economy" of affect operates in the first instance within the family. For the child, the first primary step in the generalization of affect seems to center in the latency period. In order to be rewarded adequately for learning effectively, the post-latency child no longer has to receive the "gold" of erotic stimulation, having developed the capacity to be satisfied with "love"—that this is not easy is

20. The decision to place affect in the primarily social system position among the generalized media at the general action level has been reached since the first draft of the present paper was written, and will be published in an article entitled "Some Considerations about General Theory in Sociology," in a symposium edited by John C. McKinney and Edward A. Tiryakian. This article treats *performance capacity* as the medium focusing on the personality system, *intelligence* as that focusing on the *behavioral organism*, and the *definition of the situation* that of the cultural system. The most important reference for this scheme is the paradigm of W. I. Thomas of the "four wishes" and the "definition of the situation." See W. I. Thomas, *Social Behavior and Personality*, Edmund H. Volkart, ed. (New York: Social Science Research Community, 1951.)

the whole point of Freud's treatment of the Oedipal problem and its precarious resolution. The repression of childhood eroticism in latency constitutes a kind of "embargo on gold" that forces investment in "narcissistic" forms to develop a capacity to enter genital attachments later. In psychoanalytic terms, the original objects of erotic attachment, the parents and secondarily siblings, become "lost objects." Erotic capacity is differentiated from the affective component of the complex, both becoming capable of "investment" in new objects of the same generation and opposite sex.

The next main step of differentiation occurs with the formation of the adolescent peer group, which is a function of exposure to secondary education and the continuing pattern of coeducation, as well as of the age of genital erotic maturation. The peer group and its members remain linked to the wider society through the importance of the recognition medium. However, it is a doubly competitive context, through competition for preferment along occupational lines, especially through college admission, and through the marriage market in the "rating and dating" involvements. Yet functional imperatives maintain certain bases of solidarity that underpin these competitive strains in a manner analogous to the institutions of contract, property, and employment in the economic context.

These general processes seem to comprise an extension beyond the family of the affective component of family solidarity, with the implication that new elements will gain inclusion in more or less family-like affectional solidarities. The "core" of family solidarity is the affectional component of the marriage relation in the romantic love ideal, which, through the socialization of the couple into their parental roles, can be extended to the family as a whole. Relatively mature children may be particularly appropriate agents of extension outside the family because they have been deprived of childhood eroticism but are excluded from the special intimacies of their parents. The girl may be especially strongly motivated in this direction through sex-role identification with her mother, who has been the primary manager of the affective economy of the family.

The fact that adolescence introduces the "child" into much broader circles of social participation than he has experienced before becomes highly significant to him. The senior high school is much larger and more variegated, in the composition of its population and in its activities, than either elementary or junior high schools. It is, in short, a much more pluralistic subsociety than those previously experienced. Hence, it is natural that the new foci of solidarity should be relatively broad, extending at least to "our school" and perhaps beyond. The primary keynote is group loyalty based on a diffuse cathexis to the group as a whole and to its members, a well-known emphasis of youth culture.

Considerable strain over the relation between affect and eroticism would seem to be inherent to such a situation. Modern marriage is characterized by the enhanced importance of the erotic component, but also by the imperative of enforcing latency and the incest taboo on children. The peer group is also a "marriage market," with the consequences we have sketched. The extension of affect to wider groups, then, raises the question of the exchangeability of this medium for its security base of eroticism—indeed not only heterosexually but also homosexually. It seems that, with progressive extension of the institutionalization of affective solidarity, the demand for "gold" will decline; indeed, its universalization is manifestly impossible because of the inherent limitations of erotic capacity and generalizability. However, each movement of extension seems likely to reopen and redefine the erotic question.

Exactly how far the affective basis of more universalistic, generalized "community" solidarity is being—or is capable of being—extended in modern society remains problematical. In modern youth culture, and particularly in its recent manifestations, however, there has begun to be institutionalized a series of differentiations and generalizations which have been propagated from the marriage pattern of the isolated nuclear family and which must be stabilized, if at all, around the affectional, rather than the erotic, element of the solidary tie; like monetary metal, the erotic element is too limited a base on which to ground sufficiently extensive and viable universalistic solidarities under modern conditions.[21]

Before the differentiation of the isolated nuclear family, the affective component of the family relational system was severely restricted by the operative exigencies of the lineage as a unit of generalized social status, particularly in a broad political context. As can be discerned in the case of European aristocracies, this situation forced concern with the erotic-affective component largely outside the familial context, especially into the area of the erotic experimentalism of aristocratic circles. To a degree, the "Puritanism" of the Victorian family ideal was a reaction against this. However, this ideal could not successfully mediate the adolescent transition from childhood latency status to adult marital-parental status without receiving strong reinforcement from motivational components other than fulfillment of what passed as adult expectations. What seems to have emerged is the partial institutionalization of a basis of solidarity, integrated through a generalized medium, which is *intermediate* between the erotic base of solidarity and the "celibate" basis of primarily morally-oriented relationships that operate in the world of occupation and citizenship, a relational pattern which had its roots in the incest taboo, especially that of brother and sister.

A somewhat parallel process of differentiation has evidently developed with reference to the other motivational component of participation in the associational-achievement complex of modern society. This concerns the developing status of the generalized medium, operating at the general action level, which is based in the social system, articulating it with the

21. This development bears a striking resemblance to a variety of utopian communities and religious sects of the past. Perhaps the new element is a close involvement with the main structure of the society and a claim not to be forced into self-isolation from it.

personality of the individual on the one hand, the cultural system on the other.

It would seem to follow from the above analysis that the interplay between the affective complex, to which primary attention has been paid, and that of achievement, rooted in valuation of the performance capacity of individuals and its effective utilization, is a particularly important feature of the social, cultural, and psychological conflicts of the modern world. Where there is more or less "alienation" from the success complex and the recognition of performance, we would expect that there would be not only a tendency to shift over to the affective "love" complex, and to pursue it to emphasize its erotic security base, but there would also be "regression" to the security base of the performance medium. For reasons that cannot be gone into here, I should argue that this base lies in *moral* commitments which, in the present terms should be treated as involving the definition of the situation. These would be "simplified" moral commitments which refused to take account of the exigencies of effective implementation in concrete societies.[22]

If this is the case, as a corollary, this asocial element can give rise to an assertion of nearly absolute autonomy on the part of the individual in this crucial respect, backing his refusal to give way to "pressure to conform" with social expectations. It does not seem far-fetched to suggest that Existentialism, which has been so prominent in Europe in the last generation, is an assertion of the overwhelming importance of this security base. Those who nearly absolutize its importance are the "fundamentalists" of a modern moralism in a sense parallel to that in which the cult of the erotic is the fundamentalism of the modern need for affection and "love."[23]

We suggest that this form of "fundamentalism" is a response to a complex process of evolution by virtue of which an increasingly associational societal community is emerging from ascriptive fusion with two basic structures of the antecedent society, namely political authoritarianism and ascriptive social stratification. Of course, the societal community is not isolated; there is a ramifying network of other associational structures, both subsocietal and intersocietal. Its position is critical, however, perhaps as a special harbinger of the completion of the Democratic Revolution. It is not fortuitous that the center of Existentialism has been in France, in the wake of the traumatic defeats and humiliations of World War II. France, after all, was the special home of the "Great Revolution," but also the country in which its incompleteness remained particularly salient through the first half of the present century. Moreover, the French process of democratization has centered about the movement to liquidate aristocracy

22. This is essentially what Max Weber referred to as *Wertrationalität,* which underlay what he called *Gesinnungsethik,* the ethic of "absolute" value.

23. In a certain sense Existentialism is a "neo-Protestant" movement in that, at the next level "down," it repeats the protest of Protestantism against the institutional requirements of Catholicism, but its equivalent of the church is secular society, especially the political aspects.

rather than political authoritarianism as such—which, for example, partly explains the rather romantic evaluation of the Soviet Union by French Existentialists.[24]

We suggest that these two processes of differentiation and integration have been converging on a new consolidation of two main features of the modern societal order, immature as it may be. Both involve the theme of "reconciling" the individual, on the one hand his deepest motivational interests and on the other hand his moral responsibilities, with his membership in a going society. Thus they are both facets of the problem of placing individualism in a new setting.

We suggest that the "dialectic" of Existentialism concerns the institutionalization of associational structures in society at the *collective* level, where integration of the autonomous responsibility of the individual with the collective interest can perhaps be approached. Here the "fundamentalist" view is that without an approach to absolute autonomy, men cannot act responsibly at all. The "institutionalized" position is to further full development of the pattern of democratic association, in which individual responsibility can be exercised *within* a framework of collective structure.

The other reference is to the ultimate individuality of the sources of motivation, but also to the possibilities and conditions of their integration in *role* structures of social systems. The cult of the erotic is the assertion that "real" personal gratification must occur outside the context of institutionalized social relationships; that is, it allegedly must ultimately rest on an organic basis. However, we have argued that a mediating mechanism between this erotic base of motivation and social solidarity is affect, as analyzed here. Through generalization of the medium of affect, it is possible to integrate much wider social systems than previously, avoiding the scylla of fixation on erotic concerns and the charybdis of "political" integration of the lineage type.

On the present basis, it is not possible to say what order of integration between these two newly structured patterns may now be developing or may comprise a future possibility. However, it does appear that a kind of integration, perhaps a "crossing-over" of the two original "associational" components with which our analysis started, may be under way. On the one hand, the originally highly particularistic confinement of the erotic relationship to the marital pair may have been generalized, through upgrading to the status of affect. Generalization of the affect mechanism can then lead to a basis of solidarity far transcending the original narrow limits. Thus, members of the new "peer" groups could consider themselves as non-erotic siblings, across the sex line, without sacrificing the basic affectional ties which have characterized families at the ideal level. On the other hand, the "celibate" associational types of higher-order derivation

24. On the post-War French intellectual scene, see the suggestive article by Michael Crozier in *Daedalus*, Winter 1964, entitled "The Cultural Revolution: Notes on the Changes in the Intellectual Climate of France."

may have become somewhat "familized," so that contact with the affectional mechanism is not tabooed, nor is doing justice to the moral commitments made by the individual.

In any case it seems essential, in considering these subtle and complicated problems of modern society, to keep in mind the possible substantive and symbolic associations with the structure of the kinship system, in particular the marriage relation and the relations of siblingship including those between persons of both sexes.

NINETEEN FRANCIS L. K. HSU

Eros, Affect, *and* Pao

In the preceding chapter Parsons has introduced an illuminating analogy. He compares the role of the erotic element in kinship and its ramifications in human relations at large with that of gold (or some other precious metal) in economy.

If eros in human relations is comparable to the metal gold in economic relations, affect is in my view comparable to the legal tender money. In the economic arena gold is the crude material; money is what most societies have made of it. The reality (and value) of the former can be cross-societal even without prior agreement and negotiation between the societies concerned, but the reality (and value) of the latter is strictly dependent upon the politico-economic power and ability of each society that issues it, and can only be used cross-societally through agreement, negotiation, the flow of goods, confidence, or even cultural direction (for example, some societies want to join a regional common market, while others do not).

Until gold (or silver or cowrie shells) is transformed through legal fiction into money, its circulation is limited. Even traditional Chinese type of commercial and industrial differentiation, and certainly large scale transactions of the modern world on regular bases, would be difficult if not impossible. In other words, the crude metal gold (or silver or whatever) cannot serve as the agent to bind large numbers of people or peoples together for common goals intrasocietally and intersocietally.

This is precisely the role of affect with reference to eros.[1] The crude sex urge will remain important on the personal level, but it can at best unite a few individuals (two lovers, a man and his harem, several men and their common wife, and the children of such unions). When it is transformed into affect, it is then more heavily regulated by law and custom and channeled into common expressions by culture (for example, rules concerning marital fidelity and incest), and may eventually even serve as an agent to bind different societies together (matrimonial alliance between two or more tribes or castes; or the spread of the Western pattern of equality between the sexes in many societies which have gone about changing their laws and customs accordingly).

The economy of every society has to have some gold (or silver or cowrie shells), as a valuable and a medium of exchange. Some societies have confined themselves to such basic materials as the medium of exchange; but the network of exchange spreads more widely in societies where money or some sort of legal tender exists. These societies are more likely and able to participate in international trade than others. The societies which stick to some basic valuable such as gold do not go far in social, economic, and political development.

The human network (kinship and beyond) composing every society has to have some eros as the commodity for binding some people together and for its continuation. While all presently known human societies transform eros in some degree into affect (that is to say, no society exists where sex and its immediate consequences [infant children] are the sole agent for joining individuals together), some societies have transformed this basic commodity into affect more than others, and some have even moved affect still farther so that it operates independently of eros. The question of how eros, affect, the network of human relationships, and culture patterns are linked with each other awaits clarification.

Four Ways of Eros and Affect

The parallel between gold-eros and money-affect is not a straightforward one. We must deal with the complexities of each culture separately. In our present exercise we shall examine how the differential relationships between eros and affect are linked with differences in kinship. Here we do not speak of the primeval origin, but simply regard kinship as the human "factory" which manufactures in each new generation of individuals the psychological elements or orientations by means of which they examine their traditions (past), problems (present), and solutions (future).

One basic channel of expression for every culture is its religious symbo-

1. According to Western usage the terms eros and sex are often distinguished. This is rooted in a Western cultural peculiarity which we shall attempt to clarify. For the time being the reader is asked to treat these two terms synonymously.

lism. If we compare those of Chinese, Hindu, Japanese, and Western cultures we obtain the following: A. China—eros is irrelevant to affect (no need for active attempt to separate eros from affect; eros and affect each have separate areas of relevance as a matter of course); B. Japan—eros enters into some aspects of affect, but often does so in disguise; C. Hindu India—eros and affect mingled; D. West—eros is actively separated from affect.

This four-way comparison may be graphically illustrated by the following four reproductions of religious symbolism: Plates A, B, C, and D.

Plate A is a common Chinese representation of the God of Longevity. It is found in numerous Chinese books and paintings. It adorns the ceremonial wall of Chinese homes whenever the birthday of an old man or old lady is being celebrated. Plate B is a common Japanese representation of the same god. The most unusual feature in the Japanese version, from the Chinese point of view, is the enormous elongation of the god's bald head.[2]

Plate C is a Hindu representation of the *Lingam* (phallis), or the god Shiva. This is the form found in Gudimallam, Madras, first century B.C. (according to Basham, 1954: plate facing p. 105). Later representations of the *lingam* in Hindu temples are not usually so realistic, except in the great Shiva temple in Banaras. They tend to be simple rod-like forms on top, similar to the Japanese God of Longevity's head. But as a rule each also has the female sexual organ (*yoni*) at its base, so that the two elements together are supposed to symbolize male and female principles in congress. The Nativity scene represented in Plate D is familiar to all Christians. It symbolizes the Virgin Birth.

To the Chinese, whose kinship system is marked by the absence of the attribute of sexuality or of libidinality, the sexual element is not a point of contention, to be glorified, denied, or disguised. Consequently it has either no place in religious representations (as in Plate A) or is present as a matter of course, as when some gods have spouses. The Chinese Kitchen God is usually associated with his wife, and both are objects of worship. But many Chinese gods (of war, of literature, of wealth, etc.) have no spouses.

The Japanese, Hindu, and American symbols increasingly concern themselves with the erotic element. In the Japanese kinship system libidinality is only a subordinate attribute (Hsu, 1969); the Japanese phallic

2. In China this deity is one of the household gods together with the Kitchen God, Gate Gods, God of Joy and Bliss, etc. I am not aware of any special temple dedicated to him. In Japan this deity is commonly known as Fukurokuju or Fukurojin (old man of blessing) and as one of the Shichi Fuku Jin (or Seven Gods of Blessing). The other six are Daikoku, Ebisu, Bisamon, Benten (the only female in the group), Hotei, Jurojin. I am also not aware of any shrine especially dedicated to Fukurojin. On the other hand Daikoku, and especially Ebisu, are honored in many shrines. The latter is variously thought to be God of Prosperity, of Trade, of Sailors, of Fishing, etc. One of the largest shrines dedicated to this god is the Ebisu Jinja in Nishinomiya, near Osaka. A set of statues of Shichi Fuku Jin is placed next to the Butsudan in many households.

symbol is but the elongated head of an old god borrowed from China, who cannot by any stretch of the imagination be associated with sexual prowess (as in Plate B). In the Hindu kinship system libidinality is a dominant attribute; the sexual reference in the Hindu representation is obvious or even glorified but not complete (as in Plate C). The *lingam* is a symbol. Even when the *lingam* and the *yoni* are given together, they are but two principles in interaction, and bear no indication of the consequences of the union.

The Western representation (as in Plate D) signifies not only Western preoccupation with sex, but also its result.[3]

A most interesting point which emerges from this comparison is the fact that, while the Chinese God of Longevity and Japanese God of Blessing grant pure blessing without further complication, the *lingam* and the Virgin Birth are associated in India and in the West with destruction as well.

In the Hindu case Shiva is not only known as the Creator and the Destroyer at the same time, but he also suffers from obvious aggression from his wife, the Mata of Mother Worshippers. When Shiva's consort appears in the ferocious form of Kali, the latter has a black face, a garland of human skulls around her neck, and her husband's naked body under one of her feet. Hindus say that is why Kali is invariably also represented as having her tongue hanging out, for she was astonished by what she had mistakenly done (stepping on her husband).

The West has gone much further in this association. Virgin Birth is not enough; Christ has to be destroyed for Him to atone for the sin associated with the birth of all men.

EROS IN THE WEST

The husband-wife dominated Western kinship embodies, in my hypothesis (Hsu, 1965), the attributes of discontinuity, exclusiveness, volition (freedom), and sexuality. Exclusiveness leads to the all or none approach, either one or the other (with reference to eros, this attribute exposes itself in Virgin Birth and celibacy of clergy, or orgy and Existentialism, etc.). When affect is thus lifted from eros, the probability is very high for nationalistic solidarity (within each society) or for universalistic solidarity (at least in ideals). But it also contains the seeds of perpetual disruption of that unity (intrasocietally or intersocietally). This is because exclusiveness tends to separate those who want only affect versus those who want only eros, and those who want affect to combine with eros versus those who want one or the other alone to triumph.

3. The central theme of the Virgin Birth is, of course, a denial of both. But the psychological link between explicit denial of and preoccupation with the same object may be amply illustrated by the following Chinese tale. A poor farmer suddenly came to a fortune of 300 ounces of silver. There being no banks or safety deposit boxes in the village, he dug a deep hole in his backyard and buried it. Still fearing that someone would discover the treasure, he put this sign beside the hole: "There are no 300 ounces of silver here."

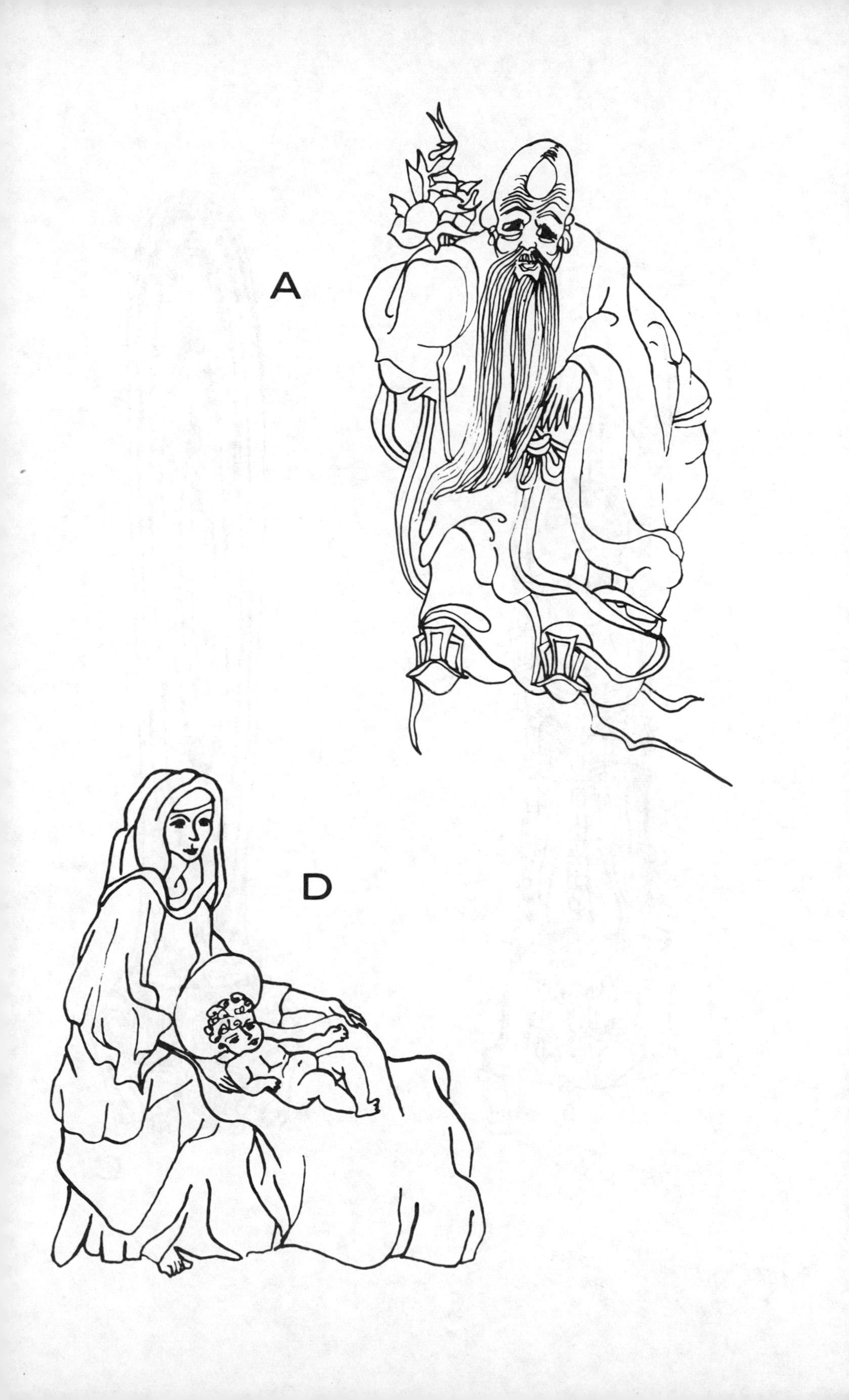
A
D

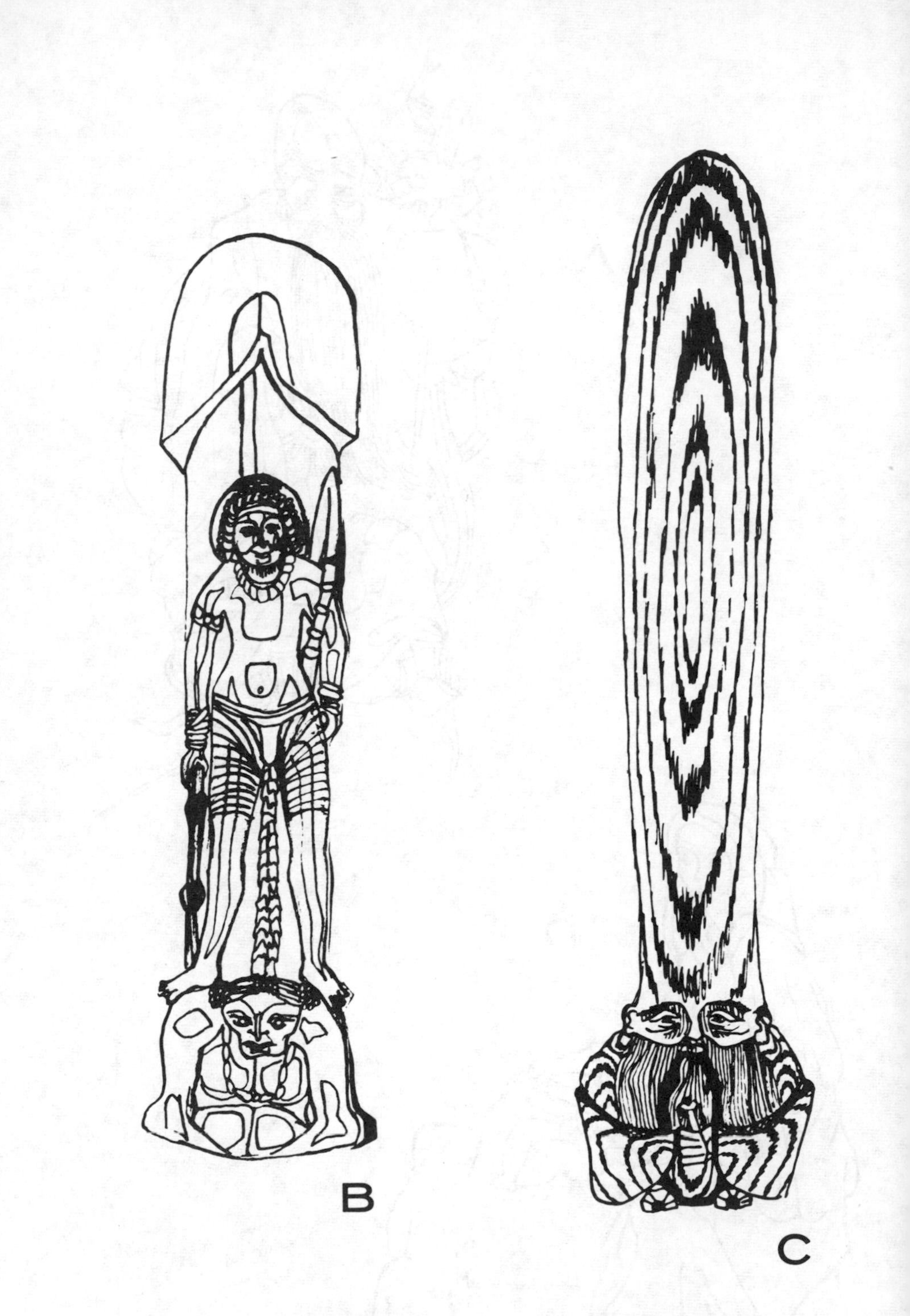
B
C

This process of constant disruption is greatly aided by the attributes of volition and discontinuity. Volition means the individual is encouraged to value the status of making his own decisions and being his own master (individuation, the need for every individual to find himself, high value of privacy, etc.). Discontinuity means that he has less worry about deviation from the past, if his own will dictates it. He must, of course, find justifications for his deviating ways (inefficiency of the old methods, "it's time for a change," or the incongruency of the results with the overall social framework—for example, "In a free society we must have more sex education"). But all the justifications will be based on ideas in line with the attributes of volition and discontinuity.

The separation of eros from affect forces eros into two divergent expressions. The first is its restriction to marital relations. The attributes of discontinuity but especially of volition and exclusiveness make strict monogamy the only legally accepted form of marriage. Therefore, though mistress-keeping and other forms of extramarital liaisons were common and accepted among European aristocracy and the upper crust before modern times, concubinage was never included within the definition of marriage and was never legalized in the West. This was why Henry VIII had no other recourse than execution of his wives. This condition is in sharp contrast to China where, though not a majority occurrence, concubinage was until recently a legalized institution, and where a concubine was a secondary wife and her offspring were legal (albeit second-class) children of her husband. Plurality of wives was legal in Japan and India.

It is this fact, that eros is customarily and legally restricted to a single marital bond, that made the Western husband-wife dyad so qualitatively different from other husband-wife relationships and from all other Western human ties. That relationship involves eros, maximum affect, intimacy, and commitment.

Under the dominant husband-wife dyad the attributes exclusiveness and discontinuity foster in the Western parent-child relationship a high degree of affect, intimacy, and commitment, second only to those in the husband-wife relationship. However, the effects of these attributes on the parents and on their children are asymmetrical, because while the parents are already mature and in full control of their powers, the children are immature and not yet well developed in their powers. Consequently, parents have complete control of their children, but children have to regard their parents as the ultimate source of reward and punishment.

Under such circumstances the effective functioning of the sphere of kinship as kinship tends to be perpetually small. Since eros is restricted to the husband-wife relationship, other genetically related persons tend to merge with a vast majority of individuals to whom one is either bound by affect or not. And just as exclusiveness and discontinuity have separated parents from parents, so they will also separate children from their elders. As the children grow this separation becomes more and more apparent; and it is in the West and not in China, Japan, or India that we find laws declaring the legal and economic (and by implication social) independence of the children at around the age of twenty. This makes what Parsons speaks of in the preceding chapter as the "concentration of the kinship system on the area of intimacies" inevitable.

The effects of this separation between parents and their growing children are also asymmetrical: Now the grown children tend to be less interested in (and in need of) their parents than their parents are in them. Under the influence of the attributes exclusiveness and discontinuity, children have been the private possession of their parents, and the parent-child intimacy is only second to that between spouses. There are several factors that make this separation harder for the parents than for the children. It is an observable fact that humans do not easily give up their exclusive possessions. To do so at a time when the parents are getting to middle age or beyond is even more arduous. Also, since eros is restricted to the marital relationship and since minor children are such an intimate part of that relationship, parents are likely to be tempted to find compensatory sources of erotic gratification in their children of the opposite sex for any significant deficiency in its satisfaction from their married partners. This is an aspect of Oedipus complex. Adding to this strain is the attribute of sexuality which undoubtedly renders the resolution of this inverse Oedipus complex more difficult.

However, with the attributes exclusiveness and discontinuity, growing children will only hasten their separation from their parents. And if the parents seem to retard or refuse the inevitable, the children must reject the elders. At a time when the children are blooming physically and mentally, meeting all kinds of new people in an ever widening horizon, this process of separation from parents becomes for them more and more natural. Here the attribute of sexuality will increase the urgency of the youngsters' need for members of the opposite sex far beyond what Freud saw as normal development after resolution of the Oedipus complex (Freud, 1943:295). Here the attraction of a peer of the opposite sex is both the more realistic love-object and the more desirable one than a parent of the opposite sex.

In an earlier paragraph we observed that the separation of eros from affect forces eros into two divergent lines of expression. We have so far analyzed its role in the marital relationship and its consequences. The other expression of eros is its diffusion throughout Western culture. While every society to a certain extent separates eros from affect, and more or less depends upon affect but not eros for cementing social relations in general, Western society, with its attributes of exclusiveness and discontinuity, makes this separation absolute and relies heavily upon affect for cementing social relations. Reaction to this absolute separation is aggravated by the attribute sexuality, which makes it impossible for Westerners to treat eros as a mere biological need in a class with food. Therefore the tendency to its complete denial tends to be countered by the tendency to its complete indulgence. It is this combination, and not merely the "process of establishing new bases of solidarity centering on the mechanism of affect" that has given rise to the "modern preoccupation with things erotic" (Parsons, Chapter 18), which includes also such fads as sex education, prize-winning movies such as "Blow Up," "A Man and a Woman," "Georgy Girl," "Chelsea Girl," and countless others, and the ever increasing demand for enjoyment of sensuality and sex quite apart from moral rules or the marital bond. The word "modern" in Parsons' statement above seems therefore to be misplaced. It should be replaced by the word "Western" to conform to the facts.

This Western configuration of human problems and their solutions is characteristic of Western civilization from time immemorial. Even the dominance of the husband-wife dyad in the Western kinship system was as old. For example, when Noah learned of the impending flood from God as a punishment for the wickedness of his men, his solution was to pack up his wife, his three sons and their wives, and pairs of all animals in a ship to escape the disaster. When the flood subsided they landed on Ararat. After thanking the Lord by appropriate rituals, Noah and his wife apparently lived for a while with his sons and their wives together. Then Noah drank the wine he made and, while under the influence of liquor, masturbated in his tent. Ham, seeing his father engaged in self-eroticism, told his two brothers about it. They were disgusted with Noah, and some kind of quarrel ensued. Noah then played favoritism by blessing Shem and Japheth and cursing Ham and condemning Ham's son Canaan to be their slave.[4]

This Western treatment of this legend provides us with the most clear indication of dominance of the husband-wife dyad, with all its attributes. When the flood came Noah was 600 years old and his own father Lamech had died five years before. But Noah merely took his wife and three sons and their wives to the ark, and we have no indication as to what happened to his widowed mother. In those legendary times people lived long. Lamech died when he was 777 and Noah did not die until he was 950. Is it not reasonable to suggest that Noah's mother might have survived his father for a little over five years. The fact is that neither he nor the narrator of the legend concerned themselves with her.

Noah and his group did not remain in the soil where they were born and lived till the flood came. Instead they emigrated to some totally new place (Ararat) by means of the ark. If they did not intend to emigrate they would have at least tried to return to their old home. But they did not

4. The passage concerning Noah's self-eroticism is generally deleted or changed into more neutral statements in the modern versions of the Bible containing such expressions as "and became drunk and lay uncovered in his tent," "And Ham . . . saw the nakedness of his father, and told his two brothers outside." If these newer statements were correct, we should be greatly puzzled as to why the brothers should be so very ashamed of their father's naked body and why Noah should be so very angry with Ham, who merely told his two brothers about his nakedness, which they covered with a garment.

even make any gesture in that direction. Noah and his sons did not remain together long. They quarreled and each son then went his own way with his wife. These are clearest expressions of discontinuity, exclusiveness, and volition (on the part of the sons) as well. And the source of trouble which caused their dispersion was sexuality.

The legend of Noah's approach to the flood and its aftermath thus inevitably set the tone of the husband-wife dominated kinship system of the Western man.

Eros in Chinese Society

Here we must also begin with the Chinese father-son dominated kinship system. And this is also an old, old pattern, the psychocultural stage having been set long before the First Emperor of Ch'in politically consolidated the country into one empire at 221 B.C. For the Chinese legendary treatment of the primeval flood was in sharp contrast to its Western counterpart.

The Chinese account is briefly as follows: Emperors Yao and Shun (said respectively to have reigned 2357–2258 B.C. and 2258–2206 B.C.) were great and moral rulers. In Yao's old age a terrible flood devastated the country. Yao appointed an official to control the flood, but the official was unsuccessful. Yao decided to appoint the able and popular man Shun as his successor to the throne. Emperor Shun exiled the official who failed to control the flood and appointed the exile's son Yu in his place. Yu worked for many years, going all over the country, and succeeded finally in eradicating the flood. During his many years of duty he passed by his own house three different times (during the first year of his absence his wife gave birth to a son) but he was so mindful of his duty that he did not enter it even once. After his success, Yu was appointed the next emperor by a grateful Shun, obviously also in response to the people's will.

We can see at once how the Chinese approach is different from the Western one and how it is commensurate with the attributes of the father-son dyad: continuity, inclusiveness, authority, and asexuality. The Chinese legend did not name any chosen person (as Noah was) to be favored by God and spared from the disaster; instead all Chinese were to be saved from it (inclusiveness). The Chinese legend did not carry the theme that the Chinese (or some part of them) should take refuge in a boat or flee the country; instead they remained where they were born and lived (continuity). There was no question of sons going in different directions from their fathers; instead Yu worked hardest to succeed in what his father failed, thus vindicating his father's name (authority, continuity, and inclusiveness). Finally, Yu did not even once visit his wife during his many years of work even though he could conveniently have done so three times (asexuality).

In the Chinese configuration eros is merely a reality to be dealt with, like man's need for fire or food. Man has to take precautions so that it is used properly, and he is protected from its destructive effects. It may be bought; it may be used for material or other gains; it gives pleasure; it is part of the marital relationship; it is necessary for continuation of the patrilineal ancestral line. It may be combined with a particular kind of affect (that between a man and his wife or concubine or mistress), but it has no intrinsic relationship with affect in other areas or in general. For example, in the Chinese concept of *hsiao*, or filial piety, a man is enjoined to devote his all to his parents, for their wishes and pleasures, at the expense of his marital and other relationships. If there is a conflict between his wife and his mother or father, there is no question about whose side he should take to make himself respectable in the eyes of society (albeit he may do so unwillingly, or he may decide to be bad and not follow the socially acceptable way). There is no doubt that many Chinese took the side of their parents, even to the extent of divorcing their wives in consequence. Some great stories and poems have been left to posterity on this.

In my paper "Suppression Versus Repression: A Limited Interpretation of Four Cultures" (1949), I analyzed the differences between two basic ways of dealing with sex. For the Chinese, sex, like everything else, has its place, time, and partners with whom it can be resorted to. In the wrong place, at the wrong time, and with wrong partners, it is absolutely forbidden. Thus between a Chinese father and his son sex as a subject cannot be touched upon at all, just as the business spirit, expressed by the American phrase "business is business," is inapplicable to Chinese parent-child, sibling, and teacher-pupil relationships; among these one should "give" and maybe later accept "gifts" or "favors," but one should not be calculating at all.

Eros can combine with affect in whole (rare for men, more common for women) or in part; eros and affect can be irrelevant to each other; or affect (a particular kind) can reign so supreme that it eliminates everything else, including eros. But there is no need to *deny* the existence of eros in order to mobilize affect, any more than there is need to deny the existence of business in order to mobilize friendship, or to deny the existence of filial piety to parents in order to mobilize loyalty to the emperor. Each kind of commodity (or joiner or element) is relevant to a particular human configuration and not to others. In terms of the gold-money analogy, the Chinese situation can be described as gold-money parallelism. There is no need for *protestation* in favor of pure gold or pure money. With this pattern the dominant attributes continuity, inclusiveness, authority, and asexuality originating from the Chinese kinship system articulate well.

Inclusiveness makes it unnecessary for the Chinese to approach the world in terms of all or none, absolutely black or absolutely white. Even in philosophical ideals the Chinese have never had the conception of the absolute virtue as opposed to the absolute evil. Instead the Chinese have developed the complementary principles of *yin* and *yang* (darkness and light, or female and male). The attribute continuity makes sharp breaks difficult. In this it finds additional support in the attribute inclusiveness as well. Since what has begun tends always to exist anyhow, its denial will do no good. Instead a more workable solution is either complete incorporation by designing a scheme large or vague enough to tolerate all, or situation-centeredness (the positive side of suppression) in which the prominent element in one human setting is not that in another one. The same actor can be involved in different settings at different times where different (or opposing) dramatic roles and emotions are required of him.

That this situation-centered approach was the socially accepted norm in China is partially indicated by the very low status (in fact, a sort of outcast status) traditionally assigned to Buddhist monks. Monks were men who left their families of origin, remained celibate, and never for the rest of their lives used the first or last names they used before entering monkhood. Chinese monks, in contrast to their Western counterparts, were always treated like the scum of the society. The famous *Chu Tze Chih Chia Ke Yen* (or *Precepts for Administration of the Family*) by the leader of the Neo-Confucianist, Chu Hsi of Sung dynasty, contains an injunction against inviting monks and priests into one's home. Even today the author of an article in the *Central Daily News* published in Taiwan (1967) begins his general statement about different classes of human beings by lumping monks and priests together with prostitutes, actors and actresses, roaming traders, and porters.

Chinese Buddhist monks completely discarded eros and even affect following the doctrine of non-attachment in Chinese terms. Conceptually they were extreme in their abstention and negation. But instead of being respected and adored for it, they were objects of contempt and had no active or effective role in the society. The clergy never was at any time of Chinese history in a position to contend even mildly for political power.

As we pointed out above, in the Chinese conception eros can be combined with affect in whole or in part. When the daughter of a wealthy nobleman ran away with a lowly foot soldier, eros and affect indeed operated wholly together. When many a filial son tried to please both his wife and his father, the two were combined in part. But many rich old men married young girls for gratification or for sons, and the girls lived out their part of the bargain because their poverty-stricken parents need the fat brideprice for existence. And a few times in Chinese history powerful empress-dowagers had male consorts who were not treated as husbands or even sweethearts. These were examples of eros without affect. The same was even more true with prostitution. The latter was such a legally and socially accepted institution in traditional China that prostitutes could be summoned into the homes of wealthy merchants for entertainment by song and dance, conversation, or spending the night. It was not unusual for a local official to offer a prostitute to a house guest whom he wanted to please, as part of his hospitality. Some members of the literati might frown upon this, but even a majority of them would not (and did not) condemn it. If they did not do it and did not approve of it themselves they certainly realized it was not uncommon among wealthy merchants and bureaucrats. Most of them would not (and did not) strenuously object to being at the receiving end of such hospitality.

Prostitution and the marriage of a rich old man to a young concubine for gratification or for sons also exemplify how eros can be obtained for money. A girl born to poor parents would be lucky if she got to marry a rich husband as concubine. The extreme of this pattern was when a eunuch, after achieving power and wealth in the court, retired from service and "married" a wife. This happened more than once in Chinese history. As a matter of fact, a number of wealthy eunuchs, after the fall of the Manchu dynasty in 1912 and their discharge from the palace, married. Between 1934 and 1936, as medical social worker in the Peking Union Medical College Hospital, I met quite a few of these eunuchs and their wives. Some had adopted children.

Finally, the central concern among traditional Chinese with reference to proposed marriage was not "love" (eros, or eros and affect) of the prospective partners but non-romantic qualifications such as ability, money, health, family reputation, severity or kindness of the boy's mother, and so on. Physical defects which would prevent either spouse from functioning sexually were part of this package, but only a part. That was why some girls in traditional China insisted (and the society encouraged them in this) on "marrying" their dead fiancés by going through all the wedding rituals after which they became full-fledged members of their dead husbands' clans.

Previously we noted that traditional Chinese society had a case of gold-money parallelism. There is in this pattern no inseparable relationship between the two, and effective functioning of one is not necessarily dependent upon the other. Money could be based on gold, but it does not have to be, if faith in the government which issued it is strong. The Chinese confidence in the collective Chinese way of life was so great that an overwhelming majority of its members did not wish to pull out or take actions to jeopardize it.

For this reason, the society could afford to assume a relatively rational posture about eros, since it is not considered to be its foundation or root. So on the one hand the time-honored Chinese philosophy expressly states that sexual congress in marriage is one of the major relationships (*lun*) of mankind (the term *lun* is the same one used in designating the Five Cardinal Relationships, *Wu lun*). In fact Mencius went farther and even simply spoke of sex and food as two *ta yü*, or great desires, of all human beings. On the other hand, the Chinese society is replete with proverbs and stories and aphorisms on the bad consequences of overindulgence for the individual and his kin group or for the society as a whole. At least two traditional operas and many popular stories and novels are based on the theme of reward to or reverence for men who were able to resist the temptation of eros and keep their minds on weightier matters, such as passing the imperial examinations. A good Chinese young man is one who concentrates on his career tasks at the expense of eros. In fact the previously recounted story of the Chinese mythological hero who conquered the primeval deluge bears this theme. A Chinese husband who works hard at his office or in his school room does not have to worry about neglecting his wife at home.

That the Chinese culture only looks askance at sex if it is resorted to improperly, but not at sex itself, is indicated by the fact, already explained before, that it considered celibacy to be no virtue. On the contrary, avowed celibates had exceptionally low status in Chinese society.

In this light we can say that the Chinese culture makes it possible for affect to function without eros. Here the Chinese culture truly distinguishes itself. One can observe without the fear of exaggeration that the Chinese culture was most highly developed in affect just as Western culture as a whole is today most highly developed industrially. My criterion for "development" is, in either case, the degree of differentiation of the central substance involved (means for joining humans together in the case of China versus means for production in the case of the West, and the productivity of this differentiation (different kinds of human relationships in the case of China versus different kinds of goods in the West).

THE FIVE CARDINAL RELATIONSHIPS *(Wu Lun)*

The five cardinal relationships in Confucian China were lord and subject, father and son, husband and wife, brother and brother, and friend and friend. It is at once apparent that four of the five pertain to affect and not eros. Lest it be said that the father-son may not be entirely free from eros (Freud), we have to note that the Chinese traditional justification for marital relations is filial piety. For Mencius said that of the three unfilial acts, lack of heir is the worst. Thus even eros is pressed into the service of filial piety.

However, the Chinese emphasis on affect at the expense of eros is not merely expressed in the five cardinal relationships. The same relationships are also recognized in the Western culture, though not seen in that order. The truly Chinese characteristic is that four of the five relationships have each a specific variety of virtue assigned to it. To the father-son relationship is assigned the virtue of filial piety (*hsiao*); to the brother-brother relationship, fraternalness (*ti*); to the lord-subject relationship, loyalty (*chung*); to the relationship between friends, faithfulness (*hsin*). These are four of the much extolled Eight Virtues, the others being courtesy, or propriety (*li*), righteousness (*yi*), integrity, or clear discrimination (*lien*), and self-consciousness, or sense of shame (*ch'ih*). It is of note that the virtue of harmony, normally assigned to the relationship of husband and wife, did not make the list.[5] Nor did it make another list of five virtues, which combined two others—kindness (*jen*) and wisdom (*chih*) with righteousness, propriety, and faithfulness.

We must note three features peculiar to the Chinese situation. First, all of these virtues have as their primary objectives the cementing of interpersonal relations, but not such virtues as bravery and creativity, which center only in the individual. Second, in contrast to the Western world, an overwhelming amount of Chinese literary and moral energy was spent in discussing, analyzing, amplifying, and exemplifying them. In the United States a few famous essayists dwelt on self-reliance (Emerson), solitude (Thoreau), or frugality (Franklin). But all of these American virtues discussed are individual-centered. Third, many Chinese virtues are so specific to particular relationships that they even tend to be non-transferable to other relationships.

The Chinese sages recognized that fraternalness can support filial piety (a man who is brotherly toward his siblings is likely to be filial toward his parents), and the Chinese classics often speak of "yi hsiao cho chung" (transfer filial piety to parents into loyalty to the emperor, as when a man sacrificed his life for the throne). But filial piety is inapplicable to the relationship between friends, and fraternalness is not applicable to the relationship between lord and subject. Finally, eros is irrelevant to all these. It is particular to the marital relationship and certain well-defined extramarital situations such as prostitution, and to nothing else.

If we think of two of the basic characteristics of industrial development as differentiation and productivity, we must observe that the Chinese have achieved a high degree of development in affect through differentiation, which in turn was linked with high productivity in human relationships in quality and quantity.

Previously we mentioned how eros was mobilized according to Chinese precepts in support of affect (marital relations were part of one's filial duty to parents). But there were two other ways that signified separation between eros and affect much more clearly.

One of these was the fact that where there was a conflict, eros must be sacrificed in favor of affect within the primary kinship grouping. We already noted that if a man's wife was in disharmony with his parents there was no question as to whose side he should take. One of the traditional Chinese grounds for divorce was the displeasure of the husband's parents. One of the famous *Precepts for the Administration of the Family* already cited was that a good man would not allow his wife to instigate quarrels with his brothers.

5. Two even more restricted virtues are *chen* and *chieh*. Both of these are virtues specific of a wife to her husband, but not vice versa. The former concept refers to a woman's faithfulness to her husband; the latter to a widow who will not remarry.

The other way of separation between eros and affect was to be found in the marital bond itself. The usual phrase for marital harmony was "the husband sings and the wife harmonizes." But a somewhat less common phrase was for them "to show respect to each other as guest and host." These were high ideals, but there were men and women who not only lived up to but exaggerated them. According to the biography of Liang Hung, in the *Book of Later Han Dynasty (Hou Han Shu)*, Liang was a wage laborer, hulling rice from house to house. "When he returned home every day his wife gave him dinner. [She respected him so much that] she did not dare to raise her eyes in front of his face. She raised the tray containing the dishes and bowls to the level of her eyebrows." Ever since then the phrase *chu an ch'i mei* (raising the tray containing dishes and bowls to a level with the eyebrows) has been used to eulogize utmost respect between married partners.

Later in the Yuan (Mongol) dynasty a rags-to-riches opera was composed which greatly embellished this fact. According to the opera a girl Meng Kuang was betrothed to Liang. Before they were married Liang's family became poor and the girl's father planned to select a different husband for her. She insisted, and her father reluctantly accepted Liang as a son-in-law into his house on a matrilocal basis since he was so poor. Later the father-in-law chased both her and her husband out. So the dispossessed couple found refuge in the house of a Mr. Wu. The girl Meng Kuang respected her husband so much that she "raised the tray with dishes and bowls to the level of her eyebrows" before serving it to him. When her father heard about this he "realized" that Liang was "not an ordinary man" (meaning that he really had "class"). (Here the text does not clearly indicate whether or not the father-in-law thought both his daughter and son-in-law were "not ordinary.") So he secretly sent his daughter's wet nurse to give his son-in-law some traveling funds and to encourage him to take the imperial examinations. The opera ended with Liang achieving the highest honor.

The pattern of marital adjustment between Liang and his wife in Han times was even more graphically exaggerated by a high official in Hupei province and his wife in the last century. This couple lived in separate parts of the same family courtyard. Before he visited her he would first send a messenger boy with his calling card. And when they met they sat on opposite sides of a low tea table (Chen, 1935).

Reverting to our previous observation that the Chinese culture had a case of gold-money parallelism, we may now go one step further and say that gold (eros) was used very little in the Chinese human economy. But money (affect) was the main instrument for its very high level of development. The development was so high that some of the tools (affect) were highly differentiated and not always easily transferable (the Eight Virtues, the Five Cardinal Relationships, and so on). We are, in this regard, reminded of the differences between primitive workshops and modern industrial enterprises. In the former not only the processes of manufacture but also the sale of the products are likely to be in the hands of only one or a few persons. In the latter, the division of labor is likely to be high, and tools and techniques appropriate to one part of the process cannot easily be adapted to fill the requirements of another part in the same factory without more or less drastic rearrangement and reorientation. This same limitation also applies to changing over from one industry to another. For example, sales personnel will have great difficulty in switching over to manufacturing; textile mills cannot easily be used for auto production.

CREDIT INSTRUMENT AND RECIPROCITY

However, we have not quite exhausted our analysis. Money is more efficient than gold in economic development because it fits a greater variety of requirements, both industrial and commercial, and also because it can circulate more widely with less encumbrance. But an even more efficient tool which can link even larger circles of producers, manufacturers, traders, and consumers is some sort of credit instrument. Through this instrument we are able to carry on industrial and commercial transactions without the trouble of counting dollars and cents, of worrying about the authenticity and quality of the coins and notes, of the problem of physically transporting the coins and notes, of the risks of theft and embezzlement, and so forth.

If gold and money in economies are respectively likened to eros and affect in human relations, what is the element in the latter which may conceivably correspond to some sort of credit instrument in the former? I submit that in Chinese society that element is the concept of *pao* or, roughly, reciprocity.

Some sort of reciprocity is indispensable for the continuation of all human societies. Its importance was long ago demonstrated by Malinowski (1922) and by Mauss (1922–23). But the Chinese culture has given it such a special place that it has become an active motivator in Chinese behavior. It may be regarded as the most generalized ingredient undergirding even relation-specific virtues such as *hsiao* (filial piety) and *chung* (loyalty).

The most comprehensive statement of the properties of the concept of *pao* is to be found in Lien-Sheng Yang's *The Concept of* Pao *As a Basis for Social Relations in China* (Yang, 1957).

According to Yang, although the term *pao* has a wide range of meanings, that which is most relevant to social relations in China is "response" or "return."

> The Chinese believe that reciprocity of actions (favor and hatred, reward and punishment) between man and man, and indeed between men and supernatural beings, should be as certain as a cause-and-effect relationship, and, therefore, when a Chinese acts, he normally anticipates a response or return. Favors done for others are often considered what may be termed

"social investments," for which handsome returns are expected . . . in China the principle is marked by its long history, the high degree of consciousness of its existence, and its wide application and tremendous influence in social institutions. [Yang, 1957:291]

Yang sees the concept of *pao* as expressing itself in Chinese society in two major forms. For a majority of *hsiao jen*, the common men, the central expectation is equivalence in time: The doer of a favor will be recompensed by a return from the recipient later, or the inflictor of injury can be sure that retaliation awaits him in time. Fearing endless chains of retaliation, wise men and government often spoke against revenge or blood feuds.[6]

On a higher level stand the *chun-tsu* or gentlemen who will extend their help without seeking reward and give to others without regretting or begrudging their liability (Yang, 1957:305). Yang explicates Mencius on this subject:

> As for a gentleman, in the words of Mencius, "If he treats others politely and they do not return his politeness, let him turn inward to examine his own [feeling of] respect," in other words, to make sure whether his own outward politeness came from true respect. For this inward examination, Mencius gives a lengthy illustration which may be summarized as follows: If a gentleman who is benevolent and observant of propriety is treated by a man in a perverse and unreasonable manner, the gentleman will first reflect upon himself, asking whether he himself has been wanting in benevolence or propriety, and also whether he has been failing to do his utmost. After he is satisfied with himself, if the man still repeats his perversity and unreasonableness, the gentleman will say, "This is a man utterly lost indeed! Since he conducts himself so, what is there to choose between him and a brute? Why should I go to contend with a brute?" [Yang, 1957:305]

Yang is of the opinion that the two approaches outlined here are quite different, but contends that since "in any period of Chinese history there were more small men than gentlemen," "reciprocity" was "the normal standard" for Chinese behavior as a whole (Yang, 1957:309). This contrast in approach between the gentlemen and the common men does not negate the fact that for both, the concept *pao* was basic to all human relations. Filial piety was usually spoken of as repayment to parents for their pains in giving their children life and raising them. In fact one of the spurious Buddhist scriptures of Chinese origin is *Ta Pao Fu Mu En Teh Ching* (*Scripture on the Repayment of Parents' Kindness*). Loyalty to the emperor was invariably couched in terms of repayment of the latter's

6. A Chinese saying is: "If injury is recompensed with injury, when will mutual retaliation come to an end?" (Quoted by Yang, 1957:293)

7. Besides these two forms there is the approach of what Yang describes as knights-errant (*yu hsia*) who, amongst other characteristics, may "even reject" any reward for favors given. But these knights-errant were generally outside the mainstream of Chinese society.

benevolence. The psychology was so deep-seated that quite a few eulogies of animals (for example, dogs who saved their masters from drowning) centered in the anthropomorphizing theme of how the beasts gave their lives to repay their masters' kindness.

The difference in approach to *pao* or reciprocity between the common men and the gentlemen is nevertheless of great consequence. This difference was two-fold. The gentlemen would not "seek" (but not reject) reward for favors done, or "regret" or "begrudge" his liability "if he had benefited an ungrateful or wicked man" (Yang, 1957:305). At the same time, the gentleman would seek to benefit others more than he was recompensed in return. This approach applies not only to those who are actually gentlemen according to Chinese custom, but also to those who aspire to that status. As I observed elsewhere:

> Whether we look at China, India or other societies in the world, including the Apollonian Zuni described by Ruth Benedict and the "effeminate" and cooperative Arapesh documented by Margaret Mead, we find some ambitious individuals who wish in some ways to excel over or differ from their fellow human beings. In the Chinese way of life the ambitious ones strive to become the most illustrious "sons" of the family and the clan, and, in so doing, make their clan more illustrious than other clans. The primary way of doing this is to upset the balance of long-run equality between obligations and rewards, by making one's obligations much bigger than one's rewards. In the same sense as a departed ancestor shading his descendants like a tree, a living man who can spread his personal shade to cover a large number of clansmen (and others if he is in a position to do so) is a more important man in the kinship group than another man who is unable to do so. [Hsu, 1963:167]

As we shall later see, this tendency on the part of aspiring gentlemen has become quite a problem in Chinese society today.

EROS AND *Pao*

The Chinese pattern of a highly differentiated affect without eros, and the extension of this differentiation by means of the concept of *pao* or reciprocity so that eros is even further removed from it, has found ample expression in Chinese philosophy, art, novels, and poetry. In a previous publication (Hsu, 1953) I demonstrated the contrast between Western and Chinese art and fiction in terms of the individual-centered versus situation-centered dichotomy. The locus of the former is the individual himself: his anxieties and fears, desires and aspirations, loves and hates, all of this leading either to the triumph of the individual or his destruction. The locus of the latter is the social situation in which the individual finds himself: he is a filial or unfilial son; he is an upright or corrupt official; He is rewarded with success in imperial examinations because he refused the advances of another man's wife; he fails in business because he usually short-changes his customers; and so forth. It is not his own impulses which he can follow. It is the social group or groups of which he is a part that he must come to terms with.

We can now see how *pao* or reciprocity is intrinsic to the Chinese situation-centered orientation as eros is to the American (Western) individual-centered orientation. The more the emphasis is placed on the individual, the larger role eros is bound to have, for the social life is always close to its organic base. In such circumstances affect will have to be strenuously promoted, in the process of which eros will have to be strenuously excluded (repressed) to make larger groupings possible and durable. Eros by its very nature is exclusive and invariably will tie a few people together. It stands ready to pull the larger groupings asunder. But the individual-centered emphasis unavoidably encourages the individual to place individual satisfaction above the requirements of the group. That means the eternal danger of ascendance of eros over affect.

On the other hand, the more the emphasis is placed on the social situation of the individual, the more eros can be relegated to its restricted area of operation, for the commodity most required in social life is not so close to the organic base. The important criteria of correct behavior reside in the nature of the interpersonal link, not the desires and wishes of the individual. In this case affect can be effectively utilized for joining human beings together without the ever threatening spectre of eros. Eros and affect each has its own sphere of direct relevance. Each needs not impinge upon the other, and the situations most relevant to each one tend to be well defined. Even affect is also greatly differentiated according to the situational requirements. This line of development leads to the concept of *pao* or reciprocity, which is the group basis of affect, as contrasted to eros, which is its individual basis.

In this chart the two patterns are seen as forming a continuum, with the Westerners always returning to the individual, which view is inevitably tied to the organic base of man (eros), and the Chinese always emphasizing the place of the individual in a human network, which view is inseparable from the duties and obligations characteristic of the group (*pao*). Both societies need affect: in the case of the West for joining more than a few members together; and in the case of the Chinese for differential cohesion and solidarity within the larger and more impersonal framework of *pao*.

In the former, the individual is trained and encouraged to make his own life and to feel that he is free to make his own arrangements for it. The expressions most commensurate with his approach to the world are: "I love to . . ."; "It is exciting . . ."; or "This interests me . . ." His ideals will include such values as freedom, progress, initiative, independence, and struggle against authority, all of which can be grouped together under the term autonomy in Western psychiatry.

In the Chinese situation, the individual is trained and encouraged to follow the established order of things and to feel that he will do best for

The relationship among eros, affect, and *pao* may be seen in the following scheme:

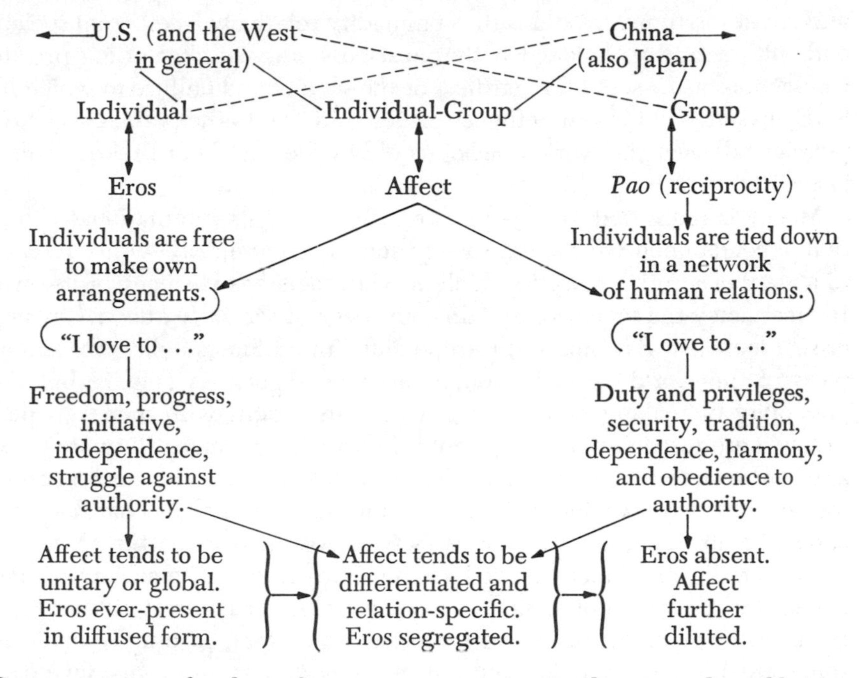

himself if he follows authority. The reasons he most frequently gives himself for acting or not acting are: "I owe to . . ."; "I can't face my ancestors . . ."; "My parents will be pleased . . ." His ideals will include such values as duty and privileges, security, tradition, dependence, harmony with fellow human beings, and obedience to authority.

Probably this contrast is why Freud, a Western sage, thought that libido is behind all human motivations and activities, and that civilization means serious obstruction of individual psyche,[8] while Confucius, a Chinese sage, laid so much emphasis upon *li* or propriety and said: "If the meat is cut improperly one should not eat it" (*ke pu cheng pu shih*).[9]

8. Some Western psychiatrists and analysts have considered Freud to be wrong in this.

9. Confucius made very little reference to sex and never said anything positive about it. His most famous disciple, Mencius, who paid much more attention to "human nature" (*hsing*), stated in a formal interview that food and sex are perfectly natural tastes. For this and other reasons I. A. Richards comments that "it is possible that Mencius anticipates some of the educative prescriptions of Freud" (Richards, 1932:75). Creel reports having heard a "practicing psychiatrist comment, after reading some of Mencius' psychological passages, that he seemed to have anticipated some of the theory of modern psychiatry" (Creel, 1953:89). I can confirm the latter from the views of several psychiatrists. However, even Mencius' main thrust was fundamentally different from that of Freud. Mencius believed in the goodness of human nature. And he laid great emphasis upon the proper relationship between ethics and psychology.

It is also interesting that these last characteristics in the relationship among eros, affect, and *pao* are still analogous to that among gold, money, and credit instrument. Gold is the commodity relatively freest from society and culture, and its holder has the most possibility of concluding private transactions as he sees fit, regardless of the society and culture in which he finds himself. That is why refugees prefer gold (and other valuables), and peasants all over the world consider gold as the best hoard if they suffer insecurity.

Money is more tied to a particular society, and its international valuation depends upon where that society stands economically with reference to a number of other societies, each of which also has currency of its own. In emergency the money of certain countries not seriously affected by any crisis (such as Swiss francs in Europe and United States dollars in various parts of the world) may be sought after as eagerly as gold is, but the possibility of making absolutely private transactions with money is definitely more restricted than with gold. For one thing, many illiterate peasants can recognize gold but not United States dollars. The conversion of money into gold inevitably involves some institutional mechanism, and cannot be done, in the final analysis, between two private parties alone.

Any credit instrument is tied to some institutional mechanism, and cannot be made use of without reference to it. In contrast to money, a credit instrument (such as drafts, letters of credit), is usually made in some sizeable denomination and not in a few dollars and cents. One cannot as a rule use it to pay retail shops. Even personal checks, which are halfway between money and full credit instruments, cannot be freely used except when secured by personal acquaintances, check cashing agencies, or certification. In other words credit-instrument users are least free to engage in private two-party transactions. One cannot run away with it and use it with any one at will.

DIFFERENCES BETWEEN *Pao* AND CREDIT INSTRUMENTS

However, here the parallel between eros-affect-*pao* on the one hand and gold-money-credit instrument on the other ends. The superiority of the credit instrument over gold and even money is that it can with efficiency link large groups of mankind economically. Its full use is both generative and an expression of a high degree of active economic unity within a society, and also among a group of participating societies in some larger economic structure (the most advanced results of which are such things as the Sterling Area and the European Common Market). If our analogy holds completely we should expect the Chinese, with their concept of *pao*, to show a much higher degree of unity and solidarity than Westerners, among whom no corresponding concept ever achieved such philosophical and ideological importance.

From one point of view this expectation is fulfilled. For example, compared with Hindu India, the Chinese society has achieved and maintained an impressive degree of political unity and solidarity through historical times (Hsu, 1963:72–78). Furthermore, if we contrast the histories of the continent of Western Europe and of the continent of China, we find the latter to be marked by long periods of political unity and solidarity, while the former reveals disunity and internecine wars. This contrast is especially notable when we reflect on the fact that the racial and ethnic origins of what we call the Chinese today were probably at least as diverse as those of their present-day European brethren.

However, there are some drastic differences between the Chinese and the Westerners which cannot be accounted for by the factors discussed so far. For one thing, the relationship between Chinese emperors and their subjects was always a negative one. When the emperor went anywhere, all windows along his route had to be shut tight, and no one except those in his entourage could appear on the street. To a lesser extent this calculated distance prevailed in a graded way between higher and lower officials, and between all officials and the people. This contrasts sharply with the kind of highly positive and emotional relationship between the rulers and their subjects in the West. I simply cannot think of any single ruler in Chinese history who had the kind of triumphal return that Richard the Lion Hearted enjoyed in front of his adulating subjects, men, women, and children; nor of one who was ever criticized by his official as was Queen Victoria at the hands of Gladstone, after the death of Prince Albert, for not appearing in public. There were few outstanding instances of officials who were devoted to their rulers to such an extent that they defended a falling dynasty to the death: Wen T'ien-hsiang at the end of Sung and Shih K'e-fa at the end of Ming are two most famous examples. But there were many more who simply became high instruments for the new dynasty or retired from active work altogether. And once a dynasty or leadership seemed to be on the verge of collapse a majority of the contenders for power or supporters of the existing regime tended to throw in their lot with the emerging new dynasty or leadership in order to be assured of a place under the sun. I regard this as strong evidence of lack of positive solidarity. This tendency was also helped by the fact that the new leaders usually ruled in the same way as the old; the personnel of the administration changed from time to time, but the nature of the administration did not. For this reason, I think, before 1912 China had no revolution, only revolt.

Along with this tendency was the fact that the Chinese never developed any significant cause-oriented groups or movements. Nearly all of their non-kinship groupings were local in nature. This included the most numerous *hui kuan*, which Ping-ti Ho terms *landsmanns* organizations (Ho, 1966). The only real exception is the organization of gangsters, such as the *Hung Pang* (Red Group) or the *Ch'ing Pang* (Blue Group). Occasionally these had been joined or formed by the *yu-hsia* or knights-errant mentioned before, and occasionally they worked toward the restoration of a fallen dynasty. Dr. Sun Yat-sen's 1912 revolution was materially helped by some of these groups in China and in the United States. But more often their purpose was no more than gangsterism, and they sometimes protected their vested interests with violence. The T'ang wars of the early twentieth century were known in the United States predominantly for the latter.

The gangster or knight-errant organizations shared the next characteristic of all Chinese non-kinship groupings: lack of missionary zeal. None of these organizations was ever primarily interested in improving some part of the society or of the traditional way of life. The knights-errant righted some individual wrongs from time to time. Some gangster organizations did side with rebels or revolutionaries. But none had developed a central philosophy or an ideology that it wanted to see prevail in all China or all the world. At best it was a restoring or holding operation. Usually it was not even that. And these were always outside the mainstream of Chinese society.

Finally, even when the scholar-officials banded themselves they hardly did better. The Tung-Lin movement of the late Ming dynasty was just such an example. It was dissatisfied with the government but it did not have any clear-cut program (Hucker, 1957:157). It discussed and objected. But above all it lasted less than twenty years (counting from 1604 A.D.). Only two other somewhat more clearly formulated but less short-lived movements or controversies existed in Chinese history; each centered around an outstanding personality: Fan Chung-Yen (989–1052) (Liu, 1957) and Wang An-Shih (1021–86), both of Sung dynasty.

Much has been written about Chinese religion in Western terms: so many Buddhists, Taoists, and Confucianists, so many sects of Buddhism. In fact a majority of Chinese cannot be described, for they "belong" to no formal religious organization or temple. They will visit different places of worship or sacred spots as they feel the need to do so. The "sects" of Buddhism have no meaning to them, for they hardly make any theological or even ritualistic differentiation when they do worship. The only religion that is common to all Chinese (except the small group of Christians, but including most Moslems) is ancestor worship, membership of which is naturally limited to those related by patrilineal kinship. The few instances of religious persecution in China were different from their counterparts in the West both in quality and quantity (Hsu, 1968). The fact is that few Chinese ever cared to die for such extra-kinship affiliations or causes and few Chinese in power found them relevant enough to the maintenance of their authority. Here again some esoteric religious practitioners, like the knights-errant, found it convenient at times to join in some rebellion. The Boxer Uprising which lasted less than one year was an outstanding example.

Contrast this picture with that of the West, with its Christian movement, Protestant movement, seven Crusades, the nursing movement initiated by Florence Nightingale, the Inquisition and witchhunting and burning, the democratic movement beginning with Magna Carta, Nazi and Fascist movements, communist movement, anti-vivisection movement, feminist movement, abolition movement, nationalistic movement, etc. All of them have spanned over long periods of time, and most of them can claim numerous martyrs and memberships of a magnitude no historical Chinese movement could even remotely match. Furthermore, sorcerers (sometimes designated witches, as in Witches Sabbath) were known to be organized with the express purpose of destroying orthodox creed and church, mostly Christianity. Is there any explanation for this enormous contrast?

DIFFUSION OF EROS

I submit that one basic factor for this contrast is to be found in a fact already mentioned previously, that, though affect has to be lifted from its erotic base for purposes of joining larger numbers of members in the Western society, eros cannot but be diffused in it. The extreme attempt to eliminate eros to the extent of its complete denial through the unnatural Virgin Birth is aimed at affect without eros. This is commensurate with a kinship content with exclusiveness as one of its dominant attributes. However, as we noted before, this complete denial is incompatible with a pattern of social life which is so close to the organic base because it centers in the individual. So what complete denial has done is to drive eros underground so that the latter appears in disguise everywhere: in art, in literature, in drama, in social intercourse, in the leader-follower relationship: "I am crazy about my boss"; "I love Kennedy." Even in the stronghold of this complete denial, namely the Christian church, nuns are said to be "married" to Jesus.

However, under the same impetus of the dominant kinship attribute of exclusiveness, eros is not likely to remain underground. In human relations no less than in relations among elements of the physical world, action generates reaction. The counter-movement of eros without affect has only in recent decades begun to erupt. A wholly new kind of sex-for-sex's-sake movie and play and literature has now taken over the markets. We noted that this trend is more than the desire to establish "new bases of solidarity centering on the mechanism of affect." In this configuration the role of the dominant attribute of sexuality in the Western kinship system has reinforced in each new generation of Westerners the Western preoccupation with eros. The attributes of volition and discontinuity facilitate the self-seeking activities of the individual, especially when he attempts to negate or break with the past. A host of positive and related cultural values such as creativity, initiative, and independence provide this orientation with ample support.

The Chinese dominant kinship attribute of inclusiveness never was commensurate with absolute denial of eros in favor of affect. What it encouraged was proper human contexts for eros and for affect. In the prostitute-patron relationship naked eros is "natural." In the concubine-husband relationship naked eros may have a shared role with affect. In the wife-husband relationship naked eros tends to be overshadowed by affect, since the relationship between the married couple and his parents is more important in the Chinese scheme of things than all else.

Given its proper places where it can operate, in excess if the individuals choose to do so, eros has no necessity to go underground, nor to stage strong reactions toward a pattern of eros without affect. The Chinese dominant kinship attributes of authority and continuity do not encourage initiative, creativity, independence, or a break with the past whether with reference to eros or to economic enterprise. And the attribute of asexuality has made it easier for the Chinese not to be troubled by sexuality where it is irrelevant. The Chinese "respect" their superiors, are "filial" to their parents, and do not consider eros to be an impediment to a normal relationship with the supernatural.[10] The question of "love" simply did not arise. Their gods did not "love" them, nor did they "love" their gods. "Marriage" to a god even in a symbolic sense was so absolutely incongruous in Chinese thought that such a suggestion would be ludicrous. Confucius' reply to a disciple who asked him to comment about gods and spirits was that one should "respect gods and spirits, but keep them at a distance."

Thus, for the Western man diffused eros is likely to be involved in any relationship however remote from it. The presence of diffused eros disables him from ever completely weaning affect from it. Consequently, affect in the Western world has remained global and not well differentiated because it is always more or less tied to its organic root. In the Chinese world, affect has differentiated itself so greatly that in its extreme form, affect is thinned into pure *pao*, because the Chinese have been able to separate eros from it through the clear structuring of human relationships. Their affect tends to be much more removed from its organic root.

However, differentiation has its drawbacks. It can lead to specializations that are irreversible or at least difficult to interchange with each other. In biological evolution many species became extinct because they had painted themselves into a corner, so to speak, by being overspecialized in some direction so that they were no longer able to deal with changes in the physical environment or challenges of rival species. Although one cannot always speak with assurance of extinction or survival in the psycho-cultural sphere, in my view the relationship-specific differen-

10. Women are not supposed to go to a temple of worship during their monthly period. Many women wash themselves from head to toe before going for such an occasion. During a cholera epidemic, when the help of all gods is urgently prayed for, the whole village or community is supposed to abstain from sex, meat, and entertainment. But all this either has to do with cleanliness or with impressing the supernatural with the sincerity of the immediate request.

tiation of affect and further separation of affect into *pao* in the Chinese system possibly represents just such an example.

Since affect tends to be global and since eros is ever present, affect in the Western configuration can be more readily mobilized in any direction, and the diffused eros can always provide its direction with strong tendency to attachment and commitment. The global or unspecialized nature of affect enables the individual more readily to cross or to be freed from existing boundaries, and the ever-present eros propels him, once he has decided on his goal, with great emotional force. Therefore, he tends to be free to champion new causes, or to find new ways of championing old causes in or outside of his own society, with determination and a singularity of purpose that is truly astonishing to the non-Western man. If he cannot find utopia he is likely to try to mold the world in his image, which means to build his own utopia. This was why an aristocratic Beatrice Webb could decide to serve a period of apprenticeship in the squalor of East London, why a high-born Florence Nightingale could decide to face the hazards of the battlefield to care for the wounded in Crimea, why so many old Spanish settlers in Mexico could decide to join forces with the Indians to fight Spanish newcomers in a war of independence from their own society of origin, and why so many Westerners could decide, before steamships and planes made their travels easy and Western armed might secured their safety, to become missionaries in faraway, hostile lands and convert heathens to their God. I cannot help but see the tremendous hand of eros in the following account of St. Francis Xavier's arrival in Goa:

> The Society of Jesus has generally been noted for the erudition of its members, but it was founded by two men, Loyola and Xavier, who were essentially ecstatics, men of tremendous emotional force, for whom vision had a much greater value than learning. Both of them had been through a spiritual crisis, after which they abandoned the life of hunting, society, and war to which, the one as a Spaniard, and the other as a Basque aristocrat, they had been born, and conceiving of the idea of the regeneration of Catholicism, menaced by its own internal weaknesses, the rise of the new learning, and the appearance of new heresies, they founded in 1540 the Society of Jesus, thereafter dividing the work, Loyola selecting Europe as his field, and Xavier Asia. The conversion of the whole Orient was Xavier's ambition, and he felt within him a sufficient force of soul to accomplish this miracle. . . . As Papal Nuncio he disembarked at the wharf of Goa in 1542. Many diginitaries of the Church were there to meet him, and a large crowd. As he stepped ashore it was noticed that he was barefoot, that his gown was ragged and his hood of the coarsest stuff. Refusing to enter a palanquin and go in procession to the lodging prepared for him in the Archbishop's Palace, he desired them to point out the direction of the then hospital, a primitive institution compared to the later Jesuit hospital. Then motioning them to follow, he led the way on foot, his face turned up to Heaven, his lips moving in prayer. He had black eyes and a black beard and an air of wild happiness.

> When he came to the hospital, he began at once to wash the sores of the lepers. [Collis, 1943:28–29]

The Chinese have produced no great religious man like St. Francis Xavier, nor any comparable to lesser Western missionaries and religious martyrs. In fact, the Chinese for their great numbers and their long history of wars, conquests, expansion, turmoils, enormous influence, and philosophical productivity, are spectacular for their complete absence of missionaries. Even their martyrs, for any cause whatever, were few and far between. In modern sociological jargon one might say that if in Western history the yield of missionaries and martyrs was at a rate of 100 per 100,000 population per year, the yield of missionaries in Chinese history would be at a rate of zero at any time, and its yield of martyrs would be at a near zero rate.

Since affect tends to be differentiated and since eros tends to be absent in most of its operating spheres, affect cannot be so readily mobilized in any direction, and the absence of eros tends to moderate any energy even after it is mobilized, so that attachment and commitment to non-traditional objectives (such as in non-kinship groupings and causes) will be mild. The relationship-specific affect simply cannot be easily conducted into channels in which they did not flow before. The absence of eros in such areas deprives the individual of the necessary emotional energy for urgency, and he tends to be cautious and therefore more rational. Large groupings can be formed by rulers and by force of territorial contiguity or livelihood, and the dominant kinship attributes of continuity (which favors prolongation of any relationship once it has begun), inclusiveness (which favors multiple affiliations), and authority (which favors no sharp break with the past) keep the society supplied with men who agree to play their part. But there is not likely to be great solidarity within such large groupings, because the affect is not diffused with eros and therefore not so highly emotionally charged as it is in the West.

The individual under such circumstances is much less free to champion new causes, or to find new ways of championing old causes, or to seek utopia by leaving his own society. He will not have the urge to make the world in his own image. Instead he will try to find his best place in it. He would treat non-Chinese with respect if their conduct measured up to Chinese standards. But he is not likely to treat them with obvious contempt even if they do not, for why should he bother with people whom he does not want to know better? In his relation-specific affect he is not much concerned with those who are very different from him. Not having rejected his parents, he does not have to avoid vertical relationships and seek only peers. He can view those lower than him with no urgency for their uplift in the same way he is seen by those whose station is above him. There is little personal involvement in others not covered by relation-specific affect.

This is why so few Chinese ever were seafarers and ever emigrated.[11] This is why Chinese rulers and public officials and heroes did not have to possess sex appeal, and were as a rule poor public speakers. This is why the age-old Chinese motto was "each man should only sweep the snow from in front of his own house." This is why the Chinese have never been known for missionary activities for the spread of Chinese religious creeds or of the Chinese way of life.

The network of *pao* or reciprocity can extend itself widely over large territories and sizable populations as well as between societies. But it tends to become more and more a matter of pure business: exchange without sentiment. The central focus will be the correct thing to do since *pao* is socially required and its standard is culturally determined. It is inevitable that, in time, the correct thing to do tends to substitute for true sentiment on the part of the individual. The result is tremendous numbers and varieties of motion of exchange motivated by *pao*, but little or no real involvement or zeal among the parties to the exchange. Lacking diffused eros the Chinese individual tends to confine his most intense involvement to kinship and a few other core relations. The following essay entitled "Drama and Human Life" from a recent issue of a major Taiwan newspaper confirms this analysis and even goes beyond it.

> Last week at an evening party in honor of the delegates of the National Assembly, Delegate Yen Hsi-chen and her husband Mr. Hou Ch'ung-hsiu performed together the drama of Wu Chia P'o. [This is part of an opera which features prominently a hero who, after eighteen years of absence from home, returned to his patiently waiting wife. It is one of the most popular operas in China.] Miss Yen acted as the wife Wang, and Mr. Hou played the role of her husband Hsueh. The acting and singing were good and correct, and they became objects of much favorable comment afterwards.
>
> After seeing this performance, many friends talked about it in the following vein: The acting of a husband and wife in real life, performing the roles of a husband and wife on stage, naturally would be good because the stage roles are identical to their real roles. These friends considered that this was the most important reason why their performance was such a great success. At that time I only listened to these comments, but I did not enter into the discussion. Long afterwards, however, I reflected on this matter on several occasions.
>
> If we look at it in abstraction, drama on the stage is life, and life is also drama on the stage. The actual situation is that drama is compressed life, while life is drama prolongated. I have often seen movies recording track races. If the movie is run at a higher speed, the human beings participating in the race run as fast as horses; but if the same movie is run at a slower

11. Superficially this statement seems questionable, since the Chinese populations in Malaya, Thailand, Indonesia, Philippines, and Vietnam are considerable. However, when we measure the number of Chinese abroad in terms of Chinese in China we find the ratio of the former very small indeed. On the other hand, the number of Europeans outside Europe is larger than in Europe.

speed, the human beings in the race look like snails. One is fast and one is slow, but this difference in speed is no more than that difference between drama on the stage and life as we actually live it from birth to death.

In the drama we have different roles: there are the roles of *sheng* [the male role], *dan* [the female role], *ching* [various kinds of warrior or petty official roles], *me* [auxiliary roles], and *ts'ou* [clown roles]. Among the various roles in actual life we find *chun* [emperor, head-of-state, or chief administrator-of-organization], *ch'en* [subordinate official and secretary], *fu* [father], *tsu* [son], *hsiung* [older brother], *ti* [younger brother], *fu* [husband], *fu* [wife], and *p'eng yu* [friend]. The stage for performing drama is found in a theater. The stage for the performance of life is on the earth. The time span for a drama is usually one evening. The time span for the human drama of each man is one life. Actors and actresses describe what they do on stage as acting. Human beings describe what they do in life as reality. However, if we raise our sights and look at the world from a higher level, what real differences are there between the various roles of actual human life and the various roles of a drama? Is there a real difference between the earth and a theater? Is there any real difference between one lifetime and one evening? Is there any real difference between living and play-acting? Therefore, when I say that human living is play-acting, I think I have not made a big mistake.

If you want to make the drama good, you must have good actors and actresses who will each play male, female, military, auxiliary, or clown roles according to the requirements of his or her role. The singing and the acting must all be done exactly according to the requirements of the stage-craft and the song-craft. The beat and the rhythm and the rhyme must all be exactly correct. In the same way if you want harmony in human life, you must have the head administrator, the subordinate officials, the father, the son, the older brother, the younger brother, the husband, the wife, and the friends each acting according to his duties and obligations, and each expressing his sentiments as required by custom. It is said in the classic *Chung Yung* [often translated as the doctrine of the mean, but E. R. Hughes, the English student of Chinese philosophy, objected to it and prefers the title "the mean-in-action" (Hughes, 1943:1)]: "To have emotions of pleasure and anger and sorrow and joy surging up, this is to be described as being in a state of equilibrium. To have these emotions surging up, but all in tune, this is to be described as a state of harmony. This state of equilibrium is the supreme foundation, this state of harmony the highway, of the Great Society, [civilization]. Once equilibrium and harmony are achieved, heaven and earth maintain their proper positions, and all living things are nourished" [Hughes, 1943:106]. This shows that even in the wider universe all heaven and earth and a myriad of things will be in their proper places and be productive if each part will act according to its role and the accepted rhythms and rules. How can a relatively small matter of a drama and a relatively short matter of a human life compare with these great events that occur in the entire universe?

Since human life is a drama, birth is then like the lifting of the stage curtain, and death is just like the closing of the stage curtain. In every drama, after the curtain is lifted, all the performers must act according to the theme of the drama and in harmony with the rhythm and the beat—each acting his or her part out to the best of his or her ability as dictated by the dramatic role. No performer can be out of tune or out of step with the other performers or with the orchestra and go on his own. Also, each performer does not have to worry about what he physically cannot do or intellectually cannot reach. All each performer has to do is to carry out what he is supposed to do, according to the pre-arranged emerging drama. When he has done his best in this capacity, he is a great success and can bow to the audience and retreat behind the curtain with no regret.

The attention of a really good performer will be most concentrated on how he can do his best on the stage. He will not become pessimistic because of the tragic theme or tragic turn of events in the drama. His whole attention is on how in his performance he will execute just the required harmony, make just the expected gestures, and take just the correct steps according to the plan of the drama, but he will not become sorrowful just because the play is about to terminate. That kind of pessimism is misplaced. Those people who, in daily life, constantly worry about life and death not only do not understand human life, but they do not even understand drama. [Shih Huan (pen name), in *Chiung Yang Jih Pao* (*Central Daily News*), Taipei, Taiwan, March 7, 1965]

The Western counterpart of this Chinese development is the continuous proliferation of closed groupings side by side with the great popularity of universalistic philosophies and creeds. Superficially these two are contradictory to each other. In fact they spring from the same source: affect underlined by diffused eros. This kind of affect ties the Western man to a romantic view of life in which the world must be all good or all bad. He must ally himself with all those who feel like him against all those who feel against him. He is happiest therefore when he participates in large, universalistic movements. But as his grouping grows larger and larger, he will be dissatisfied with its impersonality because he desires the personal touch (eros). So he seeks out some of those within the larger association with whom he can achieve a more intimate rapport. The result is a situation marked by perpetual fissionary tendencies and struggles in which all causes do not lack promoters with personal involvement or zeal. The Western man prizes himself on "living," or "giving his all" to, whatever cause he is promoting. Having no kinship base where he can relax in security, he finds new "homes" as he moves along. The extraordinary popularity of counsellors and psychoanalysts in the West for individuals who cannot find personal fulfillment in life or in work bears witness not only to the large number of people who fail to find "homes," but also to the large number who never had an opportunity to develop a talent for close personal attention (eros). All societies, especially ones made up of millions of people, must be organized in terms of broad structures and functions which inevitably put its members into broad categories. The latter can never satisfy the needs of all or most individuals whose orientation is always close to the organically based self.

RUNAWAY EROS AND RUNAWAY *Pao*

The present trend in the West of indulgence in erotic thoughts and things is a reaction against its complete denial under Western Christian thought in general and the puritanical strain in particular. Such a countermovement is but one facet of an essential and recurring Western phenomenon: Orthodoxy has always been countered by anti-orthodoxy in whatever field. In the present instance it may be properly described as a situation in which eros has run away. It has run away not because "of the process of establishing new bases of solidarity centering on the mechanism of affect" (Parsons, Chapter 18), but because of the desire for eros *without* affect.

For a number of years the age for dating and going steady and marriage has been progressively lowered in the United States. A combination of factors has produced this phenomenon, chief of which is the need for the security of having a group of one's own by giving one's declaration of independence from parents some subsistence. In a husband-wife dominated kinship, where the attributes exclusiveness and discontinuity combine to make parents more intimate with each other than with either their own parents or their children, the latter are forced to find human security of their own and, in so doing, they cannot but be heavily influenced by the examples of how their parents have treated their grandparents.

The attribute of sexuality assures the continued importance of eros in their interaction; but that the recent "preoccupation with things erotic" is not due to "the process of establishing new bases of solidarity centering on the mechanism of affect" is clear from several points. First, as already noted, in Western thought, especially Western Christian thought, solidarity through affect has always expressed itself in terms of denial of eros. Second, solidarity is not central to the recent trend of preoccupation with things erotic, because the propagators and the practitioners of the new trend want *individualized experiences*, not group solidarity. Their extreme representatives are the hippies who look for experiences or happenings, whether via sex or LSD, unrelated to other experiences and happenings or individuals. The fact that often these people congregate together and seem to form some kind of group is an artifact of the non-hippies (including law enforcement agents) who usually see and treat them as a group.

Finally, it is highly inefficient to seek the maximization of eros through affect. Affect inevitably leads to larger social involvements, so that other responsibilities (not the least of which are children and respectability) will inevitably curtail eros. Those who are preoccupied with eros, ancient or modern, have never been known for their devotion to marital or family life.

In Western history mistress-keeping and other forms of extramarital erotic activity (for example, those of Boswell as depicted in *Boswell's*

London Journal) were by and large the privilege of the leisurely upper crust.[12] Some of the less fortunate might frequent cheap houses of prostitution now and then, but they had not the time, the *savoir-faire*, and the financial means for achieving such erotic sophistication as drinking wine out of a cup inserted in ballerinas' slippers. In modern times we read about the activities of the international jet set and of well-known characters in the world of show people. But the democratic process means that whatever once were the prerogatives of the few tend to diffuse among the many, by way of imitation and of demand, especially since the majority has become so affluent. Eros has seemed to run away because the majority now feels that they should enjoy some of the things once limited to the few, and they also have the time, the *savoir-faire* (thanks to mass media), and the economic wherewithal to make it possible.

The Chinese counterpart of runaway eros is runaway *pao* or reciprocity. The Chinese have always prided themselves on giving high value to *jen ch'ing wer* (human feelings). What they actually practice may not, as we have seen before, be calculated to satisfy individual human feelings, but rather the requirements of *pao* or reciprocity. We also noted that those who aspire to higher status usually try to outdo others by getting more people obligated to them and/or by more ample return gifts so that the recipients of their gifts become more obligated to them than they are to the recipients.

In traditional times those who were able to do this were limited to a minority of Chinese: those who fitted the gentleman class and a few others who were in a position to aspire to that status. Under the Western type of democratizing process the Chinese trend will inevitably be one of escalation of the circles and especially the burden of *pao* or reciprocity.

Political accidents have created, at least for the time being, two different Chinese societies: one on the Chinese mainland and the other in Taiwan. As yet we cannot say too much about the development in mainland China in this regard because it is new and because we have insufficient access to it. But what little we know about it indicates that the overwhelming effort in the field of social reorganization centers in the direction of eliminating all forms of private *pao* (for example, by reduction or elimination of wedding, funeral, birthday, and new year celebrations and of kinship duties and obligations; by making promotion through individual ties difficult) in favor of one form of public *pao*, first to the Communist Party and then to Chairman Mao Tse-tung (Hsu, 1968). I make no claim that this hypothesis of what is developing in China is the only truth. I merely emphasize that if we make this hypothetical assumption we shall find the profuse public homage to Mao and the near sacred importance accorded his little red book more understandable.

In Taiwan, a similar form of public *pao* is first claimed for the Kuomin-

12. It may be, of course, that they were also the only ones who kept journals.

tang or Nationalist Party and then to President Chiang Kai-shek. It is not generally realized by Westerners that whenever Chiang is mentioned in newspapers and magazines he is not referred to by his full name but always as "President Chiang" or the "President" or the "Leader" and this designation is always given an elevation in the text. Furthermore, Chiang's birthday and his late mother's birthday are both occasions for national celebration. All of this is in line with traditional Chinese homage accorded to the emperor.

One problem is that the social organization as a whole in Taiwan has not been under the kind of attack or drastic reorganization as it has been on the mainland. The public *pao* therefore goes hand in hand with myriad forms of private *pao* among the individual citizens.

A degree of democratization inevitably goes on in every country of the post-World War II world, regardless of the form of its government.[13] With it more individual citizens in any society tend to want more of whatever the upper crust of that society enjoyed before the process began. Some of these rising demands may be totally contrary to democratic ideals, or uneconomical. For example, in Hindu India lower castes that used to take widow remarriage as a matter of course have been known to forbid such remarriage as a caste-raising device. Other low castes that had not practiced the crushing dowry system for their daughters (instead some of them used to require bride-prices from the families of the grooms) have now decided to institute this practice which was the economic downfall of many a Brahman family (Hsu, 1963:20–22). So more Chinese in Taiwan today aspire either to a wider personal circle of *pao* or to having others more obligated to them than they are to the others.

On top of all this, the latter process is aggravated by the fact that two million or more mainland evacuees who came to Taiwan after 1949 have left most of their relatives and others in their *pao* circles behind, so that they tend to look for substitutes for these vacant roles.

The combined result of these factors is an enormous escalation of the burden of *pao*, as expressed in the following essay entitled "*Li* [Propriety] Means Reciprocity" from Taiwan's *Central Daily News*:

> Recently we have a new term in our society: "*hung huo*" [red disaster]. Every inhabitant in the metropolis as a rule receives several red invitations every month. Some receive more, and others receive less. In particular the white collar workers and bureaucrats in large organizations often have to expend their entire monthly salaries on *ying ts'ou* [maintenance of propriety]. This is most likely true during an astrologically propitious month when all kinds of happy events take place. Of course, those who are on the receiving end of gifts must invoke the old Chinese saying "*ch'ueh tzu pu*

13. Here I am speaking strictly in comparative terms. For example, the Russian society under the Communist regime is much more democratic than under the Czarist regime, though the former is not as democratic as United States society under either major party.

kung" [it is impolite to refuse]; but those who are at the giving end often have to act according to the Chinese proverb "*yin ch'ih mao liang*" [spending salary not yet earned]. For the wealthy this is not serious. The old Chinese proverb is, "One becomes enamored of propriety after getting wealthy." But for those who are not so affluent this is disastrous. What else can they do except to go around declaring how they love to be hit on the head?

Formerly, although people were in the habit of sending many invitations for numerous purposes, they still observed some rules. Now the situation has developed in such a way that invitations are dispatched to those with whom the sender has spoken only once upon a time a few words somewhere by chance. Furthermore, if a man is getting married himself and he sends out the invitations, this is still excusable even to those whom he has met briefly just once. But invitations are now sent on the pretext of the marriage of one's sister's daughter, or of one's mother's brother's son. Even worse are those invitations for tea which will take place in Kao Hsiung to people located in Taipei [a distance of about 200 miles]. The addresses of old acquaintances who have not been seen for ten years will be tracked down, and invitations sent. In truth, one gets the feeling that between Heaven and Earth there is literally no escape. For those who have received the invitations, the dilemma is a bad one. They do not really want to send a gift. On the other hand they also are afraid of offending the senders by not doing so. After long deliberation, what they must do is eat less food so that they can manage a small gift even when they know that they cannot enjoy the dinner or tea that is indicated on the invitation because it is given so far away.

The Chinese people are well known for their propriety (*li*). They like to talk about it. They also love face. Especially if a man wants to operate successfully in the society and being much in demand he must maintain this propriety everywhere. Superficially, exchange of congratulatory and condolence gifts is certainly in accordance with traditional custom, a custom which indicates that human beings feel deeply for each other. In reality, those whose sole income is supplied by salaries cannot bear the burden and must go outside of their regular sources for supplementary cash. This then imperceptibly becomes a major stumbling block to the abolition of corruption in bureaucracy. The result is that instead of being a custom symbolizing strong human feelings, the human feelings get thinner every day.

The ancients say, "Propriety means reciprocity—when you only receive and do not give this is not propriety; when you only give and do not receive, this is also not propriety." There is no question that those who have received gifts in the past must reciprocate with gifts when future occasions arise. Among close relatives and very dear friends, it is reasonable to reciprocate with money. Also, in the case of friends who are really poor—who need, for example, money for the funerals of their parents or money to help out with their daughters' dowries—gifts are not only reasonable, but also necessary. Outside of such circumstances, we really should follow the Confucian dictum that, "in the matter of propriety, extravagance is not as good as frugality.

Our Ministry of Interior once proposed a kind of "form letter of propriety" for precisely the purpose of taking the place of the gifts on such occasions, since gifts have become such a difficult problem to so many people. But it never worked. It has not checked the tide of this terrible custom. Maybe many people feel that their face is much more important and that therefore they do not want to appear to be so cheap as to respond to such invitations merely with a letter of propriety expressing their congratulatory or condolence sentiments, but with no gift. We might actually follow the example of the Americans. Let us manufacture many different kinds of beautiful cards which can be used for marriages, for funerals, for birthdays, for promotions, for births of babies, for graduation, for a variety of expressions of sympathy, etc. We can have all kinds of cards printed. What we should do in the case of all those people who have no special relations with us is to respond with a card. In this way we shall not have to suffer from economic wounds, and we shall also have taken care of the Chinese custom of "propriety means reciprocity."

Those who want to dazzle other people by the size of their circles of social intercourse can put these cards into albums. They can also show everybody those albums whenever they have an occasion to do so. Those who want merely to exchange greetings with friends, such cards can show that they are both well. To deal with those who want to use such occasions for collecting money, these cards can express the respondent's sentiment that "my heart is willing, but my flesh is weak." Even those who want to use such occasions for conspicuous consumption may be satisfied. After mailing the card, the respondent and his entire family can descend upon the celebrant's house for a feast. I am sure that they will all be pleased.

In this way maybe we can keep the "red disaster" somewhat in check. I hope that the Ministry of Interior and the printing merchants will give this suggestion some earnest thought. [*Central Daily News*, June 11, 1965]

This writer speaks only about what escalation of *pao* does to the individual economically and barely alludes to its link with bureaucratic corruption. The latter is but a part of a larger configuration of its consequences in which valuable time and energy are expended on unproductive ends, while all kinds of private and public needs (not the least of which is efficiency in governmental machinery) remain unmet.

INTERNAL IMPETUS TO CHANGE

So democratization of eros has led to the profuse and widespread preoccupation with things erotic and demand for pornography, near-pornography, and for such self-gratification devices as LSD in the name of depicting reality or of expanding inner freedom. But democratization of *pao* has led to the suffocating of social relationship with their endless rounds of feasting, gift-making, courtesy calls, which run the danger of stifling all initiative in the name of propriety or the concern for human feelings (*jen ch'ing wer*). In each case the end results follow the initial premise, and no amount of attack on the latter is liable to change the course of its development unless something is also done about the former.

However, social reform is outside the scope of our analysis. One last point that may be of interest to the reform-minded concerns differential implications of the eros orientation versus the *pao* orientation with reference to social-cultural change. Over the centuries every society or culture has undergone more or less change. The differences among them in this regard are: (1) some societies and cultures have changed at a faster pace than others; (2) some societies and cultures have responded to external pressures by adaptation more expeditiously than others; and (3) some societies and cultures have exhibited more internal impetus to change than others. What concerns us here is the third of these differences.

While all societies and cultures must rely upon affect as the chief agent for social solidarity to deal with stability or change, we have seen that Western society tends to press it toward the eros end of the spectrum, while Chinese society tends to press it toward the *pao* end of it.

If Parsons' Freudian-based main thesis is on the right track, as we have good reason to think it is—that the role of erotic impulse in socialization and the brother-sister incest tabu are the two basic ingredients at the very origin of human society and culture—then those societies and cultures that are closer to the eros end cannot but possess greater internal potentiality for reform and change than those which are closer to the *pao* end.

Organized power or tyranny may be able to initiate large projects and movements and force the outward compliance of sizable populations, but the execution, continuance, and especially expansion of such projects and movements must depend upon the willing skill and wholehearted commitment on the part of a majority of the individuals in their support. Otherwise the projects and movements will inevitably dwindle and disappear as happened to those begun by many a despot in world history.

A society and culture with an affective base of solidarity leaning toward eros will not only produce more individuals ready for active and zealous involvement in projects and movements begun by others, but will produce even more individuals who will initiate with determination such projects and movements themselves. In this process the husband-wife dominated kinship system is a suitable human machinery to produce and reinforce the psychological orientation for it generation after generation. This kinship system perpetually ejects the individual from his family of origin, so that he has to find new groups for his social needs.

The father-son dominated kinship system of the Chinese is equally suitable for producing and reinforcing the psychological orientation for a society and culture with an affective base of solidarity leaning toward *pao*. While this system will supply more individuals ready and willing to maintain the status quo and to intensify whatever maintenance of that status quo requires, it will not produce many dissidents, and even fewer who have new ways to offer and are willing to go to extreme lengths to fight for their realization.

Escalation of eros may generate violence, crime, and dislocation, but also continuous pressures for reform and change. Being extremely strong by nature and having been nursed in a kinship system with exclusiveness and discontinuity as two of its dominant attributes, these pressures will lead to authoritarian tendencies and thereby generate authoritarian tendencies in its opponents for self-defense.

Escalation of *pao* may impress outsiders by its flurry of ostentatious courtesy and gestures of conspicuous solicitude, but also lead to stultifying intensification of existing customs with little opportunity for true innovation. Being imbued with no eros and having been associated with a kinship system with inclusiveness and continuity as two of its dominant attributes, the intensification merely generates a similar intensification all around.

Eros, since it is at the very core of the human psyche, can be counted on to be a fountainhead for new demands for continuous evolution of culture. There will not be many dull moments. In the last analysis the human psyche must be regarded as the origin of all human culture in the first place.

On the other hand *pao*, since it is far removed from eros, is not the center of human creativity. It can serve to maintain the status quo, to intensify it, or to proliferate it, but not to change its course. Probably this is why so many elements in the patterns of life of the eros-oriented culture of the West have been so attractive to so many individuals reared in cultures not so oriented, including the *pao*-oriented ones of China and Japan. Of course Western power of conquest has had a great deal to do with this attraction since the latter part of the seventeenth century. But when the colonizer-colonized relationship is terminated, the fascinating thing is that many Western cultural elements have diffused so widely. In this picture we are not merely speaking of material products such as automobiles, electric appliances, box-spring beds, and central heating, although these also have made the lives of many (the organic base) in the non-Western world more comfortable than have the items provided by their own culture. Even more impressive is the spread of universal education (which gives more people a chance of getting what was available before only to the few), the ideas of freedom and equality (which enable the underdogs to stand up to their superiors), the folk-rock music, chaotic and individualistic dances from the old "twist" to the newer dances, and of course the fashion of self-choice in marriage.

With reference to the last point one anthropologist observes:

> Very few societies leave it to individuals who are to be married to decide for themselves. The near-anarchy of American practice in this regard is most exceptional, although it represents a discernibly *increasing trend* in many parts of the world, as the acids of "modernity" corrode the "old kinship bonds." [Hoebel, 1966:344; italics mine]

In the light of our analysis, the most important element in that nebulous complex "modernity" is probably eros, and the most important element in that well-known anthropological complex "kinship bonds" is *pao* or some sort of reciprocity. When *pao* meets eros, there is a good probability that eros will win in the long run.

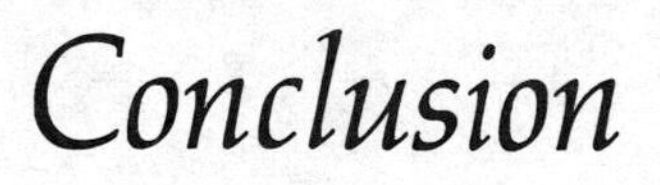

Kinship, Society, and Culture

The task of the contributors to this volume was to discuss, develop, revise, or challenge my hypothesis, stated in Chapter 1, from different angles. Some of the significant points which emerged from this exercise are:

1. The hypothesis holds a great deal of promise both for intensification of our understanding of one single society and culture and for the comparative study of different societies and cultures.

2. The concepts of dominant kinship dyad and dominant attribute can help us to assess the relevance of one human relationship to another by examining the pressures and restraints that such relationships put on each other in terms of behavior. There is a great deal of evidence that attributes occur in much the same way in interpersonal relationships inside and outside the core kinship group. These concepts may prove particularly important in opening a new way of viewing the socialization process.

3. The distinction between structure as organization of dyads and content as organization of attributes presents certain analytical advantages over the approach in which the concentration is on structure alone and in which all facts are seen as matters of structure. This distinction can enable students to ascertain more refined, and in many ways more significant, differences between kinship systems which have often escaped attention.

4. The idea of dominant dyad and dominant attributes may lead to a new perspective in describing and explaining certain processes of social evolution. For example, the Handsome Lake cult among the Iroquois is an attempt to shift Iroquois life from mother-daughter dominance to hus-

band-wife dominance. The reasons Handsome Lake gives for the need to shift are entirely consonant with the respective attributes of these two dyads. Similarly, the Anglo-American husband-wife dominance may be seen as a significant emergent form in kinship almost comparable to the emergence of mammals in the biological realm.

5. The idea of attributes proposed in this hypothesis is one way of reducing human relationship to comparable units cross-culturally. It is in the same direction as the concept of elements in chemistry, of phonemes and morphemes in linguistics, and of the more recently proposed emic unit in human behavior (Pike, 1964). The difference between our attributes and emic units is that the former deal exclusively with interrelationships between individuals while the latter are not so restricted.

Problems of Theory and of Application

In the course of this joint venture the contributors have made many other points supporting, criticizing, or extending the hypothesis, on theoretical grounds or with reference to application.[1]

Although agreeing that there are good reasons to begin with an analysis of the relationship between kinship and behavior, Levy feels the need for systematic attention to demographic possibilities and probabilities in human situations. He is of the opinion that such a step would permit a radical simplification, reduction and clarification of the hypothesis and/or its component hypotheses.

Bohannan thinks that, in order for such hypotheses to be useful in investigating the problem of dissolution of marriages and households, we must not start with the dyads but with a series of "givens" (which he calls "problems") which the analyst himself must decide, and find out what happens when each of the givens is affected by the same rule; how is it transformed? The rule is also something the analyst makes. It may not be an ethnographic rule, although it may be. The analyst can use one of the rules drawn from the culture of a particular people, or he can derive rules from other sources. This procedure allows one first to figure out principles of how household groups are built up. Then, through the expectations that are added to and/or derived from the structure as well as those of the same rules which allowed the groups to build up, one can examine how they disintegrate and appreciate the problems created by the disintegration. One does both by exactly the same method: by considering the superimposition either of actual dispositions of people on the ground or of their values about their social commitments.

1. The bulk of the statements in this section attributed to various contributors was first made at the concluding session of the symposium and later published as part of our report on the symposium in *Current Anthropology* 8 (5) 512–17 (Dec. 1967). They are incorporated here with slight revisions. Their scope is, in some instances, not confined to materials presented in the preceding chapters.

Kopytoff is impressed by the paradox that the standard functional analysis of a single society (all too often a statement of assumed covariation on the basis of a single case) is widely accepted in anthropology although its validity is hard to check. When the same approach is used with three or four societies, the analysis is more open to criticism precisely because the covariations are more visible and more checkable. Hsu at least has four cases of covariation, and this makes a critique easier than in the numerous single-case analyses that have been made. Multiple-case analyses also reveal more clearly the observational biases in reporting. Contrasting his own with Robert Hunt's description, Kopytoff was reminded of his note-taking in the field on a Suku fishing party; he noted down its composition had nothing to do with lineage structure and he stopped there. For Hunt, facing the same event in Mesoamerica, this would only have been the beginning of investigation. Given the total structure of Suku society, Kopytoff's lapse is peripheral; in Hunt's society, the lapse would be inconceivable. The bias is not the observer's alone; the societies themselves impose descriptive and eventually analytical priorities. Hunt has, inevitably, to be more "subtle" in his perception of variables since so many of them are not formally structured in his culture (nor, significantly, in the present "culture" of anthropological theory with its tribally-biased sample).

Such different cultural emphases in different cultural areas demand further clarification of Hsu's terminology. For example, for most African societies "dominance" must be differentiated as to whether it is meant to be jural or to refer to sentiments only, but both aspects are important in analyzing the family. In Euroamerica, jural considerations have generally been left out of the analysis of parent-child relations—a matter perhaps of ethnocentric bias in social science that Hsu has so often shown to exist. We take our jural framework for granted and deal with the residual emotional framework as if it were a closed system. Yet, the Euroamerican family is sovereign in far fewer of its functions than is the Suku kin-group; the larger society thus impinges more on it. It is perhaps this stripping of so many functions from the Euroamerican family that makes the relationships in it so amenable to being analyzed in such "purely" psychological terms.

The stereotyped "modern Western family" is a unique historical emergent, similar to evolutionary emergents in biology, rooted in the last half-millennium of Western culture-history; yet in other respects, it is part of the emergent that we call "industrial society," a phenomenon as unique in the universe of societies as mammals and reptiles are unique in the biological universe. The problems of comparison become no less complex than those facing comparative anatomists who must radically shift their frames of reference and their variables when comparing mammals with reptiles as opposed to a primate with other primates. Our single structural-functional frame of reference is not adequate for comparing the Americans, the Chinese, the Suku, and the Tiv. Culture-historical factors as well as varieties of institutional complexity are no less relevant here than phylogenetic relations and evolutionary emergence are in biology.

Barth tested the hypothesis of a dominant kinship relationship in two groups: the Pathans in Pakistan, where he did his field work, and the Cyrenaica Bedouins, from the literature. He finds that this concept enables him to bring out certain regular patterns in the empirical material, and thus has great descriptive utility. However, the concept entails no analytical framework for understanding and explaining these patterns. Barth utilized the general mechanisms of role formation to remedy the latter weakness. He showed how general values regarding descent, masculinity, and sexuality are relevant to the behavior of males in a variety of situations in Middle Eastern societies, and that these values are such as to give a permanence to the father-son dyad that may legitimately be characterized as dominance, while other dyads such as that of husband-wife are strongly modified and in part suppressed. He found that while the father-son dyad is dominant in both, different behavioral solutions are generated in the two different societies.

Howard finds the most value in taking Hsu's position as a starting point because it seems to lead right to the heart of important ethnographic material. In examining social relationships with a view to ascertaining which one of them is most significant for cultural and behavioral outcomes, he feels he is dealing with an approach that can help to clarify the relationship between aspects of culture and the social system. Howard thinks that the concept of dominant kinship dyads is of primary importance. He reported that he shifted in his thinking about it throughout the conference. There were times when he wanted to throw it out completely because it masked all kinds of important differences. But later he came to the view that the very attempt to evaluate the significance of dyads with regard to their effect forced him to look at the kinds of pressures and restraints that they put upon behavior. This attempt to evaluate significance was one of the most valuable exercises we went through together. He is still convinced that in most cases one can't find a single dominant dyad, but that the exercise of looking for it has highlighted many of the important issues, such as the significance of domestic groups and the matricentric family. When we ask ourselves, dominant for what, how are the dyads important, how do you evaluate their importance, we are really getting very close to the key problems in the study of interpersonal relations. On the negative side, Howard had reinforced in the conference his bias that it is very difficult to compare whole societies as societies. According to him, we would be, for most purposes, comparing quite disparate units when we compare nations like the United States with Rotuma. This suggested to him the great need we have for better typologies of aspects of culture, of institutions, of activity systems—so that we are clear about what we are comparing. Only when we have constructed typologies suitable for the purpose will the attempt to find relationships between such phenomena as social relations within the domestic group and aspects of religion, political institutions, and so on become feasible.

Hunt finds the Hsu model inadequate for explaining his Mexican data. For example, he can locate not one, but two dominant relationships within the family. However, the application of the hypothesis has enabled him to see more in his Mexican material than before. To the question, "What is the nature of the compatibility between larger institutions and the core group?" Hunt was able to generate a fair number of propositions in specified ways. Hunt and Parsons note the comparability of the attributes in the Hsu hypothesis with the elements which constitute the periodic table in chemistry. The trouble is that the social sciences don't have their periodic table as yet. Many "compounds" have been described, but they overlap. Whenever typologies are set up that work for any large number of types of societies, over-granulation is the result. The basic units in terms of which we can describe human behavior simply do not as yet exist. We have some such basic units for the biological recruitment principles in kinship and they work very well—age, sex, generation, and the like. Hsu's attributes are a start toward isolating some behavioral units, but much more work needs to be done.

Rohlen emphasizes the interplay of dyads, the distinction between affective and jural ties, and the fact that they constitute partially independent systems. Although noting that his analysis of the Tikopia data supports the Hsu hypothesis, Rohlen finds some attributes (such as asexuality and inclusiveness) impossible to apply because of the lack of clear and workable definitions.

Concentrating on the two Australian "tribes," Berndt shows the interplay between certain elements emphasized in the kinship subsystem and certain cultural foci relevant to the behavioral patterns. He does not regard these two as being representative of all Australian aboriginal societies, but considers that analysis of these might help us to distinguish the broad types, of which there are probably about a dozen or so.

Berndt holds that, in dealing with kinship and culture, we must take into account what can be called the "quality of interaction" (Hsu's "content") between persons—whether those involved are juveniles or adults. In kin-oriented societies—and this, of course, applies to aboriginal Australia—a different quality is involved in all forms of interaction from that which obtains in societies not oriented predominantly in those terms. There is also the matter of interplay between public and private, or formal and informal interaction. Berndt takes up the question of whether, and why, certain dyads can be regarded as more dominant than others: for example, the Gunwinggu sister-brother relationship and the Murngin mother's mother's brother-sister's daughter's son relationship. These are discussed fairly systematically. Additionally, Berndt contrasts reliance and cooperation among Gunwinggu brothers with rivalry among Murngin brothers. However, he demonstrated that the four types of dominance elaborated in Hsu's hypothesis do not fit the two aboriginal societies he treats. The Hsu categories, he contends, are too culture-bound; they represent shorthand descriptions of specific societies (Chinese, Indian, Western European, for instance). They have not that wide sense of relevance, in general and abstract terms, that is essential to anthropological theory. In his opinion, we cannot simply single out one paired kin relationship or dyad and classify it as being dominant. For this purpose, we must think in terms of clusters of specific relationships. Berndt's main emphasis is on how one relationship influences another and, he says, it is imperative that in considering this problem we keep in mind the total range of acknowledged kin relationships in any one society. He is satisfied that sufficient empirical material is presented in his paper to provide, if necessary, a restatement in Hsu's terms of a "type"—if one wanted to do this. We have to take into account systems which emphasize, say, the sister-brother relationship, or a cluster of relationships. If we seek universalistic statements (as Hsu would seem to do), these could be so broad that our powers of prediction will be considerably lowered; but if we conceive of groups of similarly constituted societies and cultures and derive from them generalizations of a limited range of validity (for example, taking a few Australian aboriginal societies and cultures), then we can make some general statements about them. They will, of course, be general statements of a relatively narrow range, statements about what they hold in common—and what they don't. If we do this, Berndt suggests, we can make some headway. In other words, Berndt does not think that we can speak of a Hsu hypothesis—but we might very well be able to speak later of a number of Hsu hypotheses.

De Dampierre finds that, as far as the kinship of the Nzakara of Central Africa are concerned, one could neither compare interactions nor societies, but only schemes of interactions and models of societies. He thinks that in order to avoid confusion we must adhere to either or both of these distinctions.

Newell finds the hypothesis broadly convincing as it applies to China, less easily to India, but not so easily to the more heterogeneous African societies analyzed. He suggests one kind of project that will enable us to prove or disprove parts of the hypothesis, thus building up a more massive foundation for it. For example, in some border areas of India there is a sort of clan system. There is also some evidence that where the land is poor or the population is increasing, the number of castes is few. Could it be that where the land is poor or the population increasing, the caste system is less diversified so that the clan has a more real existence? If one could show that the basic relationships of the kinship content of the culture area (father-son in China and allegedly mother-son in India) applied even where one had a caste system in China (among certain border people in Sinkiang) or clan system in India, then we would be able to isolate more easily the mechanisms of kinship content in the wider society.

Sofue stresses that Hsu's hypothesis has shed a new light on those aspects which the traditional "kinship algebra" had mostly neglected in the past. At the same time, however, he thinks that Hsu's intuitive and literary method seems to suffer from one weak point—oversimplification. Japanese kinship, for example, is interpreted by Hsu simply as father-son dominated. But from the psychological viewpoint the mother-son relationship is also very important in Japan. He proposes the distinction between the overt (or structural) dominance and covert (or affective) dominance in each society.

Experimental results by Strodtbeck among the sailors at Great Lakes Naval Base indicate a link between identification with mother and femininity. Strodtbeck suggests that this link might conceivably be regarded as a sort of confirmation of the dominance of the mother-son dyad in the Hindu kinship as postulated in the Hsu hypothesis. However, he sees difficulties, some of which have to do with the fact that evidence for mother-son dominance is not clear in the literature on India. One of the exciting problems for him in the intersection of social psychology and anthropology is the explanation in a given society of the emergence of an expression of needs which in turn reshaped other institutions. He thinks that dream materials or even certain kinds of gossip may reach back fundamentally to recurrent dyadic relationships and at the same time embody the slight modification of metaphors that are the precursors of change. The locus for such innovation would not be the same in all cultures. He finds Hsu's analysis of Chinese, Indian, and United States cultures to suffer from a gap that is functionally related to the lesser explication of what he spoke of as the "subinstitutional social-psychological processes." For example, Hsu does not deal effectively with the phenomenon of stratification within the societies or the perspective of the woman in the process. These oversights are those which have a morphological parallel to the lesser concern for the way in which roles become differentiated and ranked in subinstitutional social interaction. Had we constructed a more explicit paradigm for thinking about parallels between the process within small groups and within the larger societies, according to Strodtbeck, it would more definitely structure the search for certain constancies that could be crucial to explicating the way in which dominant dyads make their mark on institutions.

Edgerton examined Hsu's brother-brother dominance hypothesis as it applied to four East African societies: the Sebei of Uganda, the Pokot and Kamba of Kenya, and the Hehe of Tanzania. He scrutinized series of responses by the four African groups to a whole set of questions that would seem to bear on certain features of the brother-brother dominance hypothesis (chiefly pertaining to authority and rivalry) and found both confirming and disconfirming results. At a more general level, he points to three weaknesses of the Hsu formulation; first, the problem of variability, both in the sense of what the individual actor actually does and in the sense of the normative structures that exist in any given social system. He does not think the question of variability has been addressed sufficiently. He thinks variability affects centrally the question of dominance—of whether or not one can find dominance, statistically or normatively.

The second problem is that Hsu's hypothesis does not take into account the reciprocation or interaction between systems, or between subsets of a system. Due to the interaction between kin and extra-kin systems, and of course between the personnel in these systems, questions of causality become immensely difficult.

Finally, there is an ecological criticism—which is to say that we may very well find covariation between kin systems and extra-kin systems for the very good reason that both of these systems are "determined" by a more basic system, which could very well be an economic variable or a technological one or some kind of historical process. He thinks "chicken and egg" problems are *real* problems, because there are different kinds of hen houses and different kinds of chicken feed, and that these may be the essential questions for this ecological dilemma.

Fernandez finds the Hsu hypothesis and its propositions valuable in viewing his Bantu materials. He thinks that he can reinterpret Fang-Zulu complaints about their situation, their feeling of malaise in their social and cultural life, etc., in terms of a sense of imbalance in dyadic relationships. Fernandez is interested in the notion of counterbalance or symmetry and asymmetry among the constellations of dyads. He regards this problem to be crucial in the socialization process.

With Berndt, Fernandez emphasizes the necessity of looking for the content in terms of interaction, but he sees it differently. What we are or should be trying to do in locating dominance, according to Fernandez, is not only to find a relationship of intense interaction, but one in which the cultural substance of that interaction is crucial in forming the images by reference to which individuals develop their adult strategies. We may have strong interaction without significant change in the image of the world held by the participants in that interaction. Dominance from this point of view is understood as that relationship which presents or transfers the most significant image of the world upon which the adult will act. What are the metaphors, the representational devices, of the socialization process which pass from one pole of the dyad to the other and with which at later stages the world will be understood? Here the distinction between culture and society as it has been put forward is crucial to any understanding of dominance. Social dominance is not necessarily cultured dominance.

Wallace thinks that the hypothesis promises to suggest a whole family of ways (of which this hypothesis is just one) of increasing the depth to which an individual society can be investigated. He finds this to be true in thinking about the Handsome Lake cult and the decline of the Iroquois "matriarchy." The ways in which one would carry out an investigation of an individual society from this point of view—whether by direct translations or by transformations of other kinds—is unsettled. But he does not think it arguable that it is possible to find a kind of code internal and particular to an individual society by which characteristics of the kinship system are transformable into characteristics of other kinds of social organization. The principle is not contestable at all. He thinks it deserves to be taken as an article of faith, that there is a relationship between the kinship system and other aspects of the society. This investigation will not prove or disprove that, of course. The question is, just how does it work? To what extent can one write intra-cultural and cross-cultural laws? And to what extent, apart from that, can we design programs of analysis and investigation that will sharpen the understanding of individual societies?

Van der Veen sees the ambivalence inherent in man's need for independence (non-dependence) as being more fundamental than kinship dominance. The latter is a form of structuration of the conflicting needs. People everywhere have to interact on the basis of these ambivalent needs. And in every culture both needs have been given an ideological as well as a structural form. Since there is a question of ambivalence, there always will be a relative balance between each of these two needs. That means that in one society the interdependence component may be stressed and in another the non-dependence component. The different kinship dyads also differ in this respect. In the father-son dyad, for instance, the dichotomization of the two needs will be more outspoken than in the brother-brother dyad. The father-son dyad is characterized as one between a non-dependent father and a dependent son, while in the brother-brother dyad both brothers are equally interdependent. He sees an ideological accentuation of "non-dependence" in Anglo-American as well as Hindu society. In both societies the ideology is essentially the same, but the structural contexts differ so that in Anglo-American society the husband-wife dyad is stressed and in Hindu society, the mother-son dyad. He thinks that compatibility between a specific type of structuration of the fundamental ambivalence and the dominance of certain kinship dyads can be demonstrated. Once we acknowledge this ambivalence we shall be able to see that the question of dominant dyads is especially important in more complicated societies. In such societies, the possibility and the need to separate the two components, and consequently to give more stress to one component, is greater than in very uncomplicated societies where both components are so tightly related that over-accentuation of one is impossible.

Parsons's initial basis of interest in this symposium was rather instrumental, namely the attempt to analyze complex societies as systems, knowing that one had to come back to the place of kinship even when one was dealing with the largest of systems. His primary focus is on modern society and particularly its American variant. (He thinks it terribly important to place the latter in a context of variation.) It is very clear to him that modern society emerged as a special, and in certain respects an extreme, type. It is not in the middle of some spectrum. He is inclined to agree with Igor Kopytoff that modern American society is an evolutionary emergent, and therefore not a typical kind of society. He regards the evolutionary perspective as of enormous importance in comparative work; and simply cannot see sociology or anthropology getting very far without it. Outside of the question of evolution he finds a great deal of clarification of the nuclear family problem, and can now see much more clearly some of the limitations of using the nuclear family as an analytical tool by distinguishing between its analytical position and its empirical position in particular kinds of systems. He emphasizes the fact that if sociology and anthropology are to go beyond certain levels in attempting to explain mechanisms, they have to be among other things psychologists, just as the attempt of psychology to go it alone, without the structural and cultural frameworks that the social scientists could provide, has been uniformly disastrous. He noted Durkheim's personal intellectual history as an excellent illustration of this. As Durkheim went along he became very much of a social psychologist, which was the last thing that he was going to be when he began.

Hsu's chapter on "Eros, Affect, and *Pao*" was written after the symposium. It was inspired by the other papers and especially by the interchanges. The main concern is to intensify our analysis of the Dominant Dyad in Kinship hypothesis by seeking to define and delineate a new basis for affect in addition to eros.

Arensberg[2] sees the real value of the hypotheses ("Hsu's is a family of hypotheses") lying in their daring, in their suggesting a large number of possible linkages, and in their spelling out the hypothetically possible form of such linkages—between kinship customs, socialization experience of individuals in them, and other institutions, or rubrics of custom, in society. The value of such hypotheses lies in their existence, but not yet in their proof. We need many hypotheses for trial in moving toward generalization in cultural and social science and we need them in quantity, in complex statements or guesses as to the interconnectedness of many variables, and of many ethnographic and psychological data, so that we can deploy before us the whole range of such possible interconnections, and work with them as comparable and contrastable systems. He wants less to discard, reject, or confirm the Hsu hypotheses than to show how they need to be augmented or expanded to do their job of modeling the fit-together of the ethnographic facts of the spectrum of the world's cultures. He thinks that first of all it is necessary that we learn better how to identify and characterize any putative common element—a structural principle, or a bit of culture content, common to both kinship and extra-kinship rubrics of culture in any given society. We need to be more definite as to how such a common element ought to be identified and compared—found sim-

2. Arensberg participated in the Wenner-Gren symposium, but was not able to complete his paper for the present volume.

ilar or different—*both* for its form within the kinship and for its form within the extra-kinship institution (caste, club, monarchy, empire). We need *common terms of ethnographic description* if a connection is to be tested for in any way. It is not enough to say that one kinship dyad is dominant over another—mother-son over brother-brother—(except as a very rough shorthand mnemonic for initial comparison of the family and kinship systems), nor that one dyad is of greater or lesser importance in the socialization of the young than is another. The whole matrix of the essential relationships of kinship of most frequent involvement in the life-events, first of the child undergoing socialization, later of the adults acting out the customary roles for which they were socialized, must be compared system by system; and within each the actual interactional form of the putatively dominant (that is, most frequent, or most durable, or most "important" by any other definition) interpersonal relationship must be identified, isolated, and put into shape for further identification in its occurrence in extra-kinship institutions. If a value "emphasis" is to be identified in other terms than those of the symbolism of the people themselves ("The cow is the mother of us all," "Filial piety is owed also the emperor"), then a value operating in common between a kinship system and an extra-kinship institution must be connected with something else common to both.

Of course, the functional considerations internal to each kinship system are relevant, as Hsu's instance of the "suppression" (to infrequency and hidden position) of the husband-wife dyad in favor of the father-son dyad in the Chinese joint-family (a parallel to Barth's Bedouin data), but they must be related *not only* to their putative effect upon an individual's learning the culture maze, *but also* to the structural emergence, persistence, and effect upon other rubrics of the social organization and cultural system in question. One cannot leave unchallenged the old and well-discarded Kardnerian projectionism, holding that individual learning somehow creates or forms adult culture. One must cope with the facts which show institutional history and the functions of preserving the forms of extra-kinship institutions to have as much force in shaping *what* individuals learn as does what individuals learn in childhood condition their adjustment to adult conditions and usages. The connection we seek between kinship and institutions of the non-kinship kind lies not in gross institutional differences alone (caste or club), but also in the local adaptation of common institutions (the use and form of monasteries, for example, or variants of Buddhism).

Some Areas for Future Work

Foremost among the areas needing future efforts is how to determine the dominant dyad, or dyads, in a given society. Of course, a kinship system may be dominated by (1) a single dyad; (2) two dyads simultaneously; (3) two dyads alternatively (depending upon the situation); (4) two dyads, one of which is subordinate to the other; (5) multiple dyads; (6) no dyad; or (7) one dyad jurally and a second dyad in matters of affect. Some of the contributors have even suggested the possibility of a dominant relationship between a man and his lineage, or between a man and his land.

In general there seem to be three sources for determining kinship dominance: that kinship dyad which (a) takes precedence over others in the value emphasis of the society, or (b) takes precedence over others in the maintenance of the social and cultural system, or (c) has greater importance than others in the socialization of the young. The three sources may converge and reinforce each other, or they may differ and undercut each other. The convergence or divergence among the three sources leads to a higher or lower degree of dominance of a relationship in a given kinship system. If no dyad can fulfill the criteria, then there is a lack of dominance in that kinship system.

Dominant dyad in value emphasis is found in verbal or written expressions (specific statements by authoritative individuals, classics that enjoy protracted popularity), projective tests (for example, frequency of appearance of certain dyads or intensity of feeling associated with them). Dominant dyad according to requirements for maintenance of the social and cultural system is seen in decision-making with reference to conflict resolution (for example, to maintain the Chinese type of joint family the husband-wife dyad has to be suppressed in favor of the father-son dyad) or to steps taken by the individual toward the successful life (to be a successful American wife the woman must necessarily adhere more to her husband than to her parents) or to the overall interest of the society (every revolutionary regime or major religious movement tries to do something to change or reorient some aspects of the kinship relationships; the Iroquois under their modern chief who promoted the husband-wife dyad at the expense of the mother-daughter dyad, as reported by Wallace, was an example in a non-literate society.) This dyad can also be seen in terms of the difficulty with which it is or can be broken (for example, filial piety, divorce laws, or amount of effort to repair or solidify it).

Dominant dyad as a result of socialization can best be ascertained by examining the dyad (or dyads) in the kinship system which centrally bear on or are most influential (instrumental or in affect) in the bringing up and maturation of the individual (for example, the Nuer way of driving little boys away from their mothers' huts toward the common byre, where they will sleep from seven or eight years of age—yet the boys in later life retain their membership in their mothers' huts, but this is followed by severe initiation and age set, and so on).

A second area requiring future attention is the origin of the attributes of each dyad. For the time being, these are derived from logical and empirical grounds. The justification for using these attributes even though their origins remain unsystematic is that the value of any concept is how intellectually productive it can be, rather than where it comes from.

A third area deserving our attention is whether the identification of structural principles, or the comparison of kinship and socialization content and adult culture, can or cannot confine itself to treating social relationships, enculturation, or culture as in any way exclusively or even preponderantly grounded in the personal experience of *dyadic relationships.* Ethnographic facts show that frequently *one-many* relationships (leadership, command, authority) and *many-many* relationships (segmentary opposition, solidarity-antagonism, ethnocentricism) also shape the events of cultural behavior and are needed by us both for internal analysis of any one culture and for comparison of cultural system with cultural system. Maybe the matrices we need to describe both kinship and non-kinship relationships and "content" must be more than reductions to simple dyads.

The fourth question is: Is it possible that dominance of some dyad is more likely to occur in a literate and more complex society than a non-literate and simpler society? If so, the Hsu hypothesis is more relevant for investigating the former type of societies than the latter type.

Finally, different aspects of the main hypothesis need to be broken up systematically into a number of more restricted but interlinked hypotheses (some of these are already given in the preceding chapters) to expedite separate investigations.

The contributions gathered here have demonstrated, as a whole, that the hypothesis is indeed helpful in stimulating new lines of inquiry regarding links between specific kinship dyads and the kinship systems of which they are a part as well as those between kinship systems and the psychocultural contexts of which they are a part. This is not a global hypothesis aimed at explaining everything by kinship, but one intended to pinpoint the link between certain elements of kinship and other elements in the larger human arena. However, even with this limited objective in mind, we realize that ours are but the results of a first approximation which we hope will spur more efforts in the same direction. In this way we may reach new understanding of the linkage between kinship and culture.

Bibliography

Ackerman, Nathan. 1958. *The Psychodynamics of Family Life.* New York: Basic Books.

Alexander, Franz. 1952. Development of the fundamental concepts of psychoanalysis, in Franz Alexander and Helen Ross (eds.), *Dynamic Psychiatry.* Chicago: University of Chicago Press.

Aramoni, Aniceto. 1961. *Psicoanalisis de la Dinamica de un Pueblo.* Mexico: Universidad Nacional Autonomo de Mexico.

Bales, Robert F. 1950. *Interaction Process Analysis, A Method for the Study of Small Groups.* Cambridge, Mass.: Addison-Wesley Press.

———. 1953. The equilibrium problem in small groups, in Talcott Parsons, Robert F. Bales, and E. A. Shils, *Working Papers.* New York: Free Press.

Bales, R. F., and P. E. Slater. 1955. Role differentiation in small decision-making groups, in Talcott Parsons and Robert F. Bales (eds.), *Family, Socialization, and Interaction Process.* New York: Free Press. Pp. 259–306.

Bandura, A. 1962. Social learning through imitation, in M. R. Jones (ed.), *Nebraska Symposium on Motivation: 1962.* Lincoln, Neb.: University of Nebraska Press. Pp. 211–269.

Barth, F. 1959. *Political Leadership among Swat Pathans.* London: Humanities Press.

———. 1966. Models of social organization. *Royal Anthropological Institute: Occasional Paper No. 23.*

Bateson, Gregory. 1936. *Naven.* Palo Alto: Stanford University Press (2nd ed., 1958).

———. 1943. Cultural and thematic analysis of fictional films. *Trans., New York Academy of Sciences* II, 5:72–78.

———. 1952. End linkage, in Margaret Mead and Rhoda Metraux (eds.), *The Study of Culture at a Distance.* Chicago: University of Chicago Press.

Bateson, Gregory, and Margaret Mead. 1942. *Balinese Character.* New York: New York Academy of Sciences.

Batt, Carl. 1965. *Mexican National Character and the Inferiority Complex.* Unpublished Ms.

Beauvoir, Simone de. 1953. *The Second Sex.* New York: Bantam.

Befu, Harumi. 1966. Duolocal residence in Shirakawa, Central Japan. Paper read at the Pacific Science Congress, Tokyo.

Belshaw, C. B. 1965. *Traditional Exchange and Modern Markets.* Englewood Cliffs, N. J.: Prentice-Hall.

Benedict, Ruth. 1934. *Patterns of Culture.* New York: New American Library.

Bermudez, Maria Elvira. 1955. La vida familiar del Mexicano. *Mexico y lo Mexicano*, No. 20. Mexico: Antigua Libreria Robredo.

Berndt, C. H. (forthcoming). *Marriage and Family Life in Western Arnhem Land.* (ms. volume.)

———. 1970. Prolegomena to a study of genealogies in north-eastern Arnhem Land, in R. M. Berndt (ed.), *Australian Aboriginal Anthropology.* Perth: University of Western Australia Press.

Berndt, R. M. 1951. *Kunapipi.* Melbourne: Cheshire.

———. 1952. *Djanggawul.* London: Routledge and Kegan Paul.

———. 1955. "Murngin" (Wulamba) social organization. *Amer. Anthro.* 57:84–106.

———. 1959. The Concept of "the Tribe" in the Western Desert of Australia. *Oceania* 30, No. 2. (Also in I. Hogbin and L. R. Hiatt (eds.), *Readings in Australian and Pacific Anthropology.* Melbourne: Melbourne University Press, 1966.)

———. 1964. The Gove Dispute: the Question of Australian Aboriginal Land and the Preservation of Sacred Sites. *Anthropological Forum* I, No. 2.

———. 1965. Marriage and the family in north-eastern Arnhem Land, in M. F. Nimkoff (ed.), *Comparative Family Systems.* Boston: Houghton Mifflin. Chapter 5.

———, ed. 1970. *Australian Aboriginal Anthropology.* Perth: University of Western Australia Press.

Berndt, R. M., and C. H. Berndt. 1951. *Sexual Behaviour in Western Arnhem Land.* New York: Viking Fund Publications in Anthropology, No. 16.

———. 1964/68. *The World of the First Australians.* Sydney: Ure Smith; Chicago: University of Chicago Press.

———. 1970. *Man, Land and Myth in North Australia: the Gunwinggu People.* Sydney: Ure Smith.

Berreman, Gerald D. 1965. *Himalayan Village.* Berkeley: University of California Press.

Bettelheim, Bruno. 1965. Lecture, Child therapy: the hiers of little Hans. The University of Chicago.

Blanchard, W. H. 1959. The group process in gang rape. *J. Soc. Psych.* 49: 259–266.

Blau, P. M., and W. R. Scott. 1962. *Formal Organizations.* San Francisco: Chandler.

Bloch, M. 1961. *Feudal Society.* Chicago: University of Chicago Press.

Bohannan, Laura, and Paul Bohannan. 1954. *The Tiv of Central Nigeria.* London: International African Institute.

———. 1968. *Tiv Economy.* Evanston, Ill.: Northwestern University Press.

Bohannan, P. J. 1963. *Social Anthropology.* New York: Holt, Rinehart & Winston.

Brown, Roger. 1965. *Social Psychology.* New York: Free Press.

Bryant, A. T. 1929. *Olden Times in Zululand and Natal.* London: Longmans, Green.

Burton, Roger V., and John W. M. Whiting. 1961. The absent father and cross-sex identity. *Merrill-Palmer Quarterly* 7:85–95.

Carstairs, G. M. 1959. *The Twice Born.* London: Hogarth.

Caudill, William. 1963. Sibling rank and style of life among Japanese psychiatric patients. *Proceedings of the Joint Meeting of the Japanese Society of Psychiatry and Neurology and the American Psychiatric Association*, 35–40.

Caudill, William, and David Plath. 1966. Who sleeps by whom? Parent-child involvement in urban Japanese families. *Psychiatry* 29 (4):344–366.

Chapple, E. D., and C. M. Arensberg. 1940. Measuring human relations: an introduction to the study of the interaction of individuals. *Genetic Psychology* Monograph 22:3–147.

Ch'en, Kung lu. 1935. *Chung Kuo Chin Tai Shih* (*Recent History of China*). Shanghai: Commercial Press (2 vols.).

Cohen, Yehudi. 1964. The establishment of identity in a social nexus: the special case of initiation ceremonies and their relation to value and legal systems. *Amer. Anthro.* 66:529–552.

Collis, Maurice. 1943. *The Land of the Great Image* (*Being Experiences of Friar Maurique in Arakan*). New York: Alfred A. Knopf.

Count, Earl. 1967. The lactation complex. *Homo* 18:38–54.

Creel, Herlee G. 1953. *Chinese Thought from Confucius to Mao Tse-tung*. Chicago: University of Chicago Press.

Davenport, William. 1965. Sexual patterns and their regulation in a society of the southwest Pacific, in Frank A. Beach (ed.), *Sex and Behavior*. New York: Wiley.

Diaz, May. 1965. *Tonala*. Berkeley and Los Angeles: University of California Press.

Diaz-Guerrero, Rogelio. 1955. Neurosis and the Mexican family structure. *Amer. J. Psychiat.* 112:411–417.

———. 1961. *Estudios de Psicologia del Mexicano*. Mexico: Ed. Porrua y Obregon.

Doi, Takeo. 1956. Japanese language as an expression of Japanese psychology. *Western Speech* 20:90–96.

———. 1960. Jibun to amae no seischinbyori (Psychopathology of jibun andamae). *Psychiatria et Neurologia Japonica* 60:733–744

———. 1962. Amae: a key concept for understanding Japanese personality structure, in R. J. Smith and R. K. Beardsley (eds.), *Japanese Culture: Its Development and Characteristics*. Chicago: Aldine.

———. 1963. Some thoughts on helplessness and the desire to be loved. *Psychiatry* 26:266–272.

Doke, C. M. 1954. *The Southern Bantu Languages*. London: Dawson's of Pall Mall.

Durkheim, E. 1933. *The Division of Labor in Society*. New York: Macmillan.

———. 1966. *The Division of Labor in Society*, 2nd ed. New York: Free Press.

Easton, David. 1958. The perception of authority and political change, in Carl Friedrich (ed.), *Authority*. Cambridge: Harvard University Press. Pp. 170–196.

Eberhard, Wolfram. 1952. *Chinese Festivals*. New York: Henry Schuman.

Edgerton, R., and F. Conant. 1964. Kilapat: the shaming party among the Pokot of East Africa. *Southwestern J. Anthro.* 20:404–418.

Eggan, Fred. 1950. *Social Organization of the Western Pueblos*. Chicago: University of Chicago Press.

Ehrenberg, V. 1964. *The Greek State*. New York: W. W. Norton.

Eissenstadt, S. N. 1965. *Essays on Comparative Institutions*. New York: Wiley.

Elkin, A. P. 1950. The complexity of social organization in Arnhem Land. *Southwestern J. Anthro.* 6 (1):1–20.

Elkin, A. P. 1954/64. *The Australian Aborigines: How to Understand Them.* Sydney: Angus and Robertson (1st ed. 1938).
Elkin, A. P., R. Berndt, and C. H. Berndt. 1951. Social organization of Arnhem Land, I. Western Arnhem Land, *Oceania* 21 (4):253–301.
Ema, Myeko. 1940. *Hida no onna-tachi (Women in Hida area, Central Japan).* Tokyo: Miluni-Shobo.
Erikson, E. H. 1950. *Childhood and Society.* New York: W. W. Norton.
Evans-Pritchard, E. E. 1957a. The origins of the ruling clan of the Azande. *Southwestern J. Anthro.* 13:322–343.
———. 1957b. The Zandé royal court. *Zaire* 11:361 ff., 713.
———. 1957c. Zandé kings and princes. *Anthro. Quarterly* 30:61–90.
———. 1960. The organization of a Zandé kingdom. *Cahiers d'Etudes Africaines* 1:5–37.
———. 1963. The Zandé state. *J. Royal Anthro. Inst.* 43:134–154.
Fernandez, J. W. 1962a. Folklore as an agent of nationalism. *African Studies Bulletin* V (2):3–8.
———. 1962b. Fang witchcraft and Christian acculturation. *Cahiers d'Etudes Africaines* I (6): 244–270.
———. 1966. Principles of opposition and vitality in Fang aesthetics. *J. of Aesthetics and Art Criticism* 33 (4): 53–63.
Firth, Raymond. 1940. *The Work of the Gods in Tikopia.* London: The London School of Economics and Political Science Monographs on Social Anthropology No. 2.
———. 1954. The sociology of "magic" in Tikopia. *Sociologus* 4:97–116.
———. 1955a. Privilege ceremonials in Tikopia: a further note. *Oceania* 26 (1): 1–13.
———. 1955b. The fate of the soul, in Charles Leske (ed.), *Anthropology of Folk Religion.* New York: Vintage.
———. 1957. *We, the Tikopia,* 2nd ed., abridged. Boston: Beacon.
———. 1959a. *Social Change in Tikopia.* London: George Allen and Unwin.
———. 1959b. *Economics of the New Zealand Maori.* Wellington, New Zealand: R. Owen.
Fortes, M. 1959. *Oedipus and Job in West African Religion.* Cambridge: The University Press.
Fortune, Reo. 1935. *Manus Religion.* Philadelphia: American Philosophical Society.
Foster, G. M. 1963. The dyadic contract. *Amer. Anthro.* 65:1280–1295.
Fowler, W. W. 1921. *The City-State of the Greeks and the Romans.* London: Macmillan.
Franck, K., and E. A. Rosen. 1945. A projective test of masculinity-femininity. *J. Consulting Psych.* 13:247–256.
Freedman, Maurice. 1966. *Chinese Lineage and Society.* L. S. E. Monograph No. 33. London: Athlone.
Freud, Sigmund. 1943. *A General Introduction to Psychoanalysis.* Authorized English translation by Joan Riviere of the revised edition. Garden City, New York: Garden City Publishing.
———. 1952. *A General Introduction to Psychoanalysis.* New York: Washington Square Press.
Friedrich, Carl (ed.). 1958. *Authority.* Cambridge: Harvard University Press.
Fromm, Erich. 1941. *Escape from Freedom.* New York: Holt, Rinehart & Winston.
———. 1951. *The Forgotten Language.* New York: Evergreen Press.

Geddes, W. R. 1959. Fijian social structure in a period of transition, in J. D. Freeman and W. R. Geddes (eds.), *Anthropology in the South Seas*. New Plymouth, New Zealand: Thomas Avery & Sons.

Giele, J. 1961. *Social Change in the Feminine Role: A Comparison of Woman's Suffrage and Woman's Temperance, 1870–1920*. Unpublished Ph.D. dissertation, Radcliffe College.

Gluckman, Max. 1950. Kinship and marriage among the Lozi of Rhodesia and the Zulu of Natal, in A. R. Radcliffe-Brown and D. Fortes, (eds.), *African Systems of Kinship and Marriage*. London: Oxford University Press.

———. 1955. *Custom and Conflict in Africa*. New York: Free Press.

———. 1960. The rise of the Zulu empire. *Scientific American* 202 (4):152–169.

———. 1964. *Custom and Conflict in Africa*. New York: Free Press (2nd ed.).

Goffman, E. 1959. *The Presentation of Self in Everyday Life*. New York: Doubleday.

Goldschmidt, W. 1960. *Understanding Human Society*. London: Routledge and Kegan Paul.

Goode, W. J. 1963. *World Revolution and Family Patterns*. New York: Free Press.

Gough, Harrison. 1952. Identifying psychological femininity. *Ed. Psych. Measurement* 12:427–439.

Gouldner, A. W., and H. P. Gouldner. 1963. *Modern Sociology*. New York: Harcourt, Brace & World.

Guthrie, Malcolm. 1953. *The Bantu Languages of Western Equatorial Africa*. London: William Dawson.

Guttman, David. 1965. Women and the concept of ego strength. *Merrill-Palmer Quarterly* 11 (3):229–240.

Hagen, Everett. 1962. *On the Theory of Social Change*. Homewood, Ill.: Dorsey.

Heesterman, J. C. 1964. Brahmin, ritual and renouncer. *Wiener Zeitschrift für die Kunde Süd-und Ostasiens* VII:1–31.

Herskovits, Melville. 1948. *Man and His Work*. New York: Alfred A. Knopf.

Herskovits, Melville, and Frances Herskovits. 1959. Sibling rivalry, the Oedipus complex and myth. *J. Amer. Folklore* 72:1–15.

Heston, J. C. 1948. A comparison of four masculinity-femininity scales. *Ed. Psych. Measurement* 7:375–387.

Hetherington, E. Mavis. 1965. A developmental study of the effects of sex of the dominant parent on sex-role preference, identification, and imitation in children. *J. Personality and Soc. Psych.* 2 (2):188–194.

Hetherington, E. Mavis, and Yvonne Brackbill. 1963. Etiology and covariation of obstinacy, orderliness, and parsimony in young children. *Child Development* 34:919–944.

Hewes, Gordon W. 1954. Mexicans in search of the "Mexican": notes on Mexican national character studies. *Amer. J. Econ. Soc.* 13:209–223.

Hiatt, L. R. 1965. *Kinship and Conflict: A Study of an Aboriginal Community in Northern Arnhem Land*. Canberra: The Australian National University.

Hitchcock, J. T. and Leigh Minturn Triandis. 1963. The Rajputs of Khalapur, India, in Beatrice Whiting (ed.), *Six Cultures*. New York: Wiley. Pp. 202–362.

Ho, Ping-ti. 1966. *Chung Kuo Hui Kuan Shih Lueh (An Historical Survey of Landsmannschaften in China)*. Taipei, Taiwan: Student Publishing.

Hoebel, E. Adamson. 1966. *Anthropology: The Study of Man*. New York: McGraw-Hill.

Holy Bible. 1946. New Testament Section. New York: Thomas Nelson and Sons.

———. 1952. Old Testament Section. New York: Thomas Nelson and Sons.

Homans, G. C. 1962. *Sentiments and Activities*. New York: Free Press.

Howard, Alan. 1966. Plasticity, achievement, and adaptation in developing economies. *Human Organization* 25:265–272.

Hsu, Francis L. K. 1943. Myth of Chinese family size. *Amer. J. Soc.* 18 (2): 555–562.

———. 1948. *Under the Ancestors' Shadow*. New York: Columbia University Press.

———. 1949. Suppression versus repression. *Psychiatry* 12:223–42.

———. 1953. *Americans and Chinese: Two Ways of Life*. New York: Henry Schuman.

———. 1959. Structure, function, content and process. *Amer. Anthro.* 61:790–805.

———. 1961. Kinship and ways of life: an exploration, in Francis L. K. Hsu (ed.), *Psychological Anthropology: Approaches to Culture and Personality*. Homewood, Ill.: Dorsey Press.

———. 1963. *Clan, Caste, and Club*. Princeton, N.J.: Van Nostrand.

———. 1964. Rethinking the concept "primitive." *Current Anthro.* 5 (3): 169–178.

———. 1965. The effect of dominant kinship relationships on kin and non-kin behavior: a hypothesis. *Amer. Anthro.* 67:638–61.

———. 1966. Rejoinder: a link between kinship structure and psychological anthropology. *Amer. Anthro.* (Brief communication) 68:999–1004.

———. 1968. Chinese kinship and Chinese behavior, in Ping-ti Ho and Tang Tsou (eds.), *China in Crisis: China's Heritage and the Communist Political System* Vol. 1, 579–608. Chicago: University of Chicago Press.

———. 1969. Japanese Kinship and Iemoto. Chapters XI, XII, and XIII in the Japanese translation of *Clan, Caste, and Club* (1963). Tokyo: Baifukan.

Hucker, Charles O. 1957. The Tung-lin movement of the late Ming dynasty, in John K. Fairbank (ed.), *Chinese Thought and Institutions*. Chicago: University of Chicago Press. Pp. 132–162.

Hunt, Eva. 1969. Kinship in San Juan: genealogical and social models. *Ethnology* 8:37–53.

Hunt, Robert. 1965a. *A History of the British and American Anthropological Study of National Character*. Unpublished Ph.D. dissertation, Northwestern University.

———. 1965b. The developmental cycle of the family business in rural Mexico, in June Helm (ed.), *Essays in Economic Anthropology*. Proc. 1965 Annual Spring Meeting, American Ethnological Society. Seattle: University of Washington Press. Pp. 54–79.

———. 1967a. Introduction, in R. Hunt (ed.), *Personalities and Cultures*. New York: Natural History Press. Pp. ix-xxi.

———. 1967b. *Toward a Componential Analysis of Interaction*. Paper presented to Annual Meeting. Central States Anthropological Society, Chicago, Illinois.

———. 1968. Agentes culturales mestizos: estabilidad y cambio en Oaxaca. *America Indigena* 28:595–609.

Ibbetson, Sir Denzil C. J. 1883. *Report on the Revision of the Panipat Taksil and Karnal Parganah of the Karnal District 1872–80*. Allahabad: Government Printing Office.

Institute for Research, Indiana University. 1953. *Sexual Behavior in the Human Female*. Philadelphia: Saunders.

Iturriaga, Jose E. 1951. *La Estructura Social y Cultural de Mexico*. Mexico: Fondo de Cultura Economica.

Kahn, R. L., and D. Katz. 1960. Leadership practices in relation to productivity and morale, in D. Cartwright and A. Zander (eds.), *Group Dynamics*. Evanston, Ill.: Harper & Row.

Kelman, H. C. 1961. Processes of opinion change. *Public Opinion Quarterly* 25:57–78.

Kenny, H. 1960. Patterns of patronage in Spain. *Anthro. Quarterly* 33:14–23.

Kinsey, Alfred, Wardell B. Pomeroy, and Clyde E. Martin. 1948. *Sexual Behavior in the Human Male*. Philadelphia: Saunders.

Kirk, H. David. 1964. *Shared Fate: A Theory of Adoption and Mental Health*. New York: Free Press.

Klineberg, O. 1954. *Social Psychology*. 2nd ed. New York: Holt, Rinehart & Winston.

Kopytoff, Igor. 1961. Extension of conflict as a method of conflict resolution among the Suku of the Congo. *J. Conflict Resolution* 5:61–69.

———. 1964. Family and lineage among the Suku of the Congo, in R. F. Gray and P. H. Gulliver (eds.), *The Family Estate in Africa*. London: Routledge and Kegan Paul.

———. 1965. The Suku of southwestern Congo, in James L. Gibbs, Jr. (ed.), *Peoples of Africa*. New York: Holt, Rinehart & Winston.

Koyama, Takashi. 1954. Daikazokusei (Extended family system), in Japanese Society of Ethnology (eds.), *Nippon shakaiminzoku jiten (Dictionary of Japanese Folk-Society and Culture)* Vol. 2. Tokyo: Seibundo-Shinkosha Co.

———. 1960. *Study of the Contemporary Family* (in Japanese). Tokyo: Kobundo.

Lawrence, W. E., and G. P. Murdock. 1949. Murngin social organization. *Amer. Anthro.* 51 (1): 58–65.

Leach, E. R. 1951. The structural implications of matrilateral cross-cousin marriage. *J. Royal Anthro. Inst.* 81:23–55.

LeBarre, Weston. 1954. *The Human Animal*. Chicago: University of Chicago Press.

Lévi-Strauss, C. 1949. Les structures élémentaires de la parenté. Paris: Presses Universitaires.

———. 1953. Social structure, in A. L. Kroeber (ed.), *Anthropology Today*. Chicago: University of Chicago Press.

———. 1958. *Anthropologie Structurale*. Paris: Libraire Plon.

Lewis, Oscar. 1951. *Life in a Mexican Village: Tepoztlan Restudied*. Urbana: University of Illinois Press.

———. 1959. *Five Families*. New York: Basic Books.

———. 1961. *The Children of Sánchez*. New York: Random House.

Lipsitt, P. D. 1965. *Defensiveness in Decision Making as a Function of Sex Role Identification*. Unpublished Ph.D. dissertation, University of Chicago.

Liu, James T. C. 1957. An early Sung reformer: Fan Chung Yen, in John K. Fairbank (ed.), *Chinese Thought and Institutions*. Chicago: University of Chicago Press. Pp. 105–131.

Lounsbury, Floyd. 1964. The structural analysis of kinship semantics, in Horace G. Lunt (ed.), *Proceedings of the Ninth International Congress of Linguists*. The Hague: Mouton. Pp. 1073–1093.

Maccoby, Michael. 1964. Love and authority: a study of Mexican villagers. *The Atlantic* 213:121–126.

Maccoby, Michael. 1967. On Mexican national culture, in Martindale (ed.), *National Character in the Perspective of the Social Sciences. Annals Amer. Acad. Pol. Soc. Sci.* 370:63–130.

Maccoby, Michael, N. Modiano, and P. Lander. 1964. Games and social character in a Mexican village. *Psychiatry* 27:150–162.

Malinowski, Bronislaw. 1922. *Argonauts of the Western Pacific.* London: Routledge and Kegan Paul.

———. 1927. *Sex and Repression in Savage Society.* London: Routledge and Kegan Paul.

———. 1929. *The Sexual Life of Savages.* London: Routledge and Kegan Paul.

Manu, The Laws of. 1886. *The Laws of Manu,* in F. Max Miller (ed.), *The Sacred Books of the East,* Vol. XXV. Oxford: Oxford University Press.

Maquet, J. J. 1961. *The Premise of Inequality in Ruanda.* Oxford: Oxford University Press.

Marcus, P. M. 1960. Expressive and instrumental groups: toward a theory of group structure. *Amer. J. Soc.* 66:54–59.

Mauss, Marcel. 1923–24. Essai sur le don, forme archaïque de l'echange. *Année Sociologique* Vol. 1.

———. 1954. *The Gift: Forms and Functions of Exchange in Archaic Societies.* English translation by I. Cunnison. New York: Free Press; London: Cohen and West.

McClelland, D. C. 1961. *The Achieving Society.* Princeton, N. J.: Van Nostrand.

McDavid, J. W. 1959. Imitative behavior in pre-school children. *Psychological Monographs 73* (16, whole number, 486).

Mead, Margaret. 1930. *Growing Up in New Guinea.* New York: William Morrow.

———. 1942. The comparative study of culture and the purposive cultivation of democratic values, in Bryson and Finklestein (eds.), *Science, Philosophy and Religion,* 2nd symposium. New York: Conference on Science, Philosophy and Religion. Pp. 56–69.

Meggitt, M. J. 1962. *Desert People.* Sydney: Angus and Robertson.

———. 1965. Indigenous forms of government among the Australian aborigines. *Bijdragen tot de Taal, Land- en Volkenkunde* 120:163–181.

Middleton, Russell. 1962. Brother-sister and father-daughter marriage in ancient Egypt. *Amer. Soc. Rev.* 27:603–611.

Miller, D., and G. E. Swanson (eds.). 1960. *Inner Conflict and Defense.* New York: Holt, Rinehart & Winston.

Minturn, Leigh and W. W. Lambert. 1964. *Mothers of Six Cultures.* New York: Wiley.

Mofolo, Thomas. 1931. *Chaka—An Historical Romance.* London: Oxford University Press.

Morgan, Lewis H. 1871. *Systems of Consanguinity and Affinity of the Human Family.* Smithsonian Contributions to Knowledge, Vol. XVII. Washington: Smithsonian Institution.

Mulder, Mauk. 1959. Power and satisfaction in task oriented groups. *Acta Psychologica* 16:178–225.

———. 1960. The power variable in communication experiments. *Human Relations* 13:241–57.

Mulder, Mauk, Rob van Dijk, et al. 1965. Non-instrumental liking tendencies toward powerful group members. *Acta Psychologica* 22:367–386.

Mussen, P., and L. Distler. 1959. Masculinity, identification and father-son relationships. *J. Abnormal Social Psych.* 59:350–356.

Murdock, G. P. 1949. *Social Structure.* New York: Macmillan.
———. 1957. World ethnographic sample. *Amer. Anthro.* 59:664–687.
———. 1959. *Africa: Its People and Their Cultural History.* New York: McGraw-Hill.
———. 1962. Ethnographic Atlas. *Ethnology* 1:113–134.
Nakane, Chie. 1965. Towards a theory of Japanese social structure. *Economic Weekly*, Bombay (February). Pp. 197–215.
Naroll, Raoul. 1956. Social development index. *Amer. Anthro.* 58:687–715.
Needham, R. 1960. *Structure and Sentiment.* Chicago: University of Chicago Press.
Nelson, B. 1949. *The Idea of Usury, from Tribal Brotherhood to Universal Otherhood.* Princeton, N. J.: Princeton University Press.
Newell, W. H. 1952. Gaddi kinship and affinal terms. *Man in India* (April).
———. 1960. A Himalayan village, in M. N. Srinivas (ed.), *India's Villages.* London: Asia Publishing House.
———. 1962. Submerged descent line among the Gaddi people of North India. *J. Royal Anthro. Inst.* 92 (1):13–21.
———. 1963. Inter-caste marriage in Kugti village, Note 59. *Man*, London (April). Pp. 55–56.
———. 1966. Scheduled tribes and castes of Himachel Pradesh, Census of India. Also published in Ishwaran (ed.), *Social Change in India.* Leiden: E. J. Brill, in press.
Nimkoff, M. F. (ed.). 1965. *Comparative Family Systems.* Boston: Houghton Mifflin.
Nkrumah, K. 1956. *Ghana: The Autobiography of Kwame Nkrumah.* Edinburgh: Nelson.
Parker, Arthur C. 1913. *The Code of Handsome Lake, The Seneca Prophet.* Albany: New York State Museum Bulletin No. 163.
Parkman, Margaret A. 1965. *Identity, Role and Family Functioning.* Unpublished Ph.D. dissertation, The University of Chicago.
Parsons, Anne. 1964. Is the Oedipus complex universal? The Jones-Malinowski debate revisited and a South Italian "Nuclear Complex," in Muensterberger and Axelrad (eds.), *The Psychoanalytic Study of Society,* Vol. III, 278–328. New York: International Universities Press.
Parsons, Talcott. 1952. *The Social System.* New York: Free Press.
———. 1960. *Structure and Process in Modern Societies.* New York: Free Press.
———. 1964a. *The Social System.* New York: Free Press.
———. 1964b. The incest taboo in relation to the social structure and the socialization of the child, in *Social Structure and Personality.* New York: Free Press.
———. 1968. Professions, in David L. Sills (ed.), *International Encyclopedia of the Social Sciences.* New York: Macmillan.
———. 1970. *System of Modern Societies.* Englewood Cliffs, N. J.: Prentice-Hall.
Parsons, T. and R. F. Bales. 1955. *Family, Socialization and Interaction Process.* New York: Free Press.
———. 1956. *Family, Socialization and Interaction Process.* London: Routledge and Kegan Paul.
Paz, Octavio. 1959. *El Labertino de la Soledad.* Mexico: Fondo de Cultura Economica.
Peter, Prince of Greece and Denmark. 1963. *A Study of Polyandry.* The Hague: Mouton.
Peters, E. 1965. Aspects of the family among the Bedouin of Cyrenaica, in M. F. Nimkoff (ed.), *Comparative Family Systems.* Boston: Houghton Mifflin.

Pike, K. L. 1964. Towards a theory of the structure of human behavior, in Dell Hymes (ed.), *Language in Culture and Society*. New York: Harper & Row. Pp. 54–62.

Radcliffe-Brown, A. R. 1924. The mother's brother in South Africa. *South African J. Science* 21:542–555. Reprinted in *Structure and Function in Primitive Society*. New York: Free Press, 1952.

———. 1951. Murngin social organization. *Amer. Anthro.* 53 (1):37–55.

———. 1952. *Structure and Function in Primitive Society*. London: Macmillan.

Ramirez, Santiago. 1966. El Mexicano—psicologia de sus motivaciones. Cuarto, Ed. Mexico: Editorial Pax-Mexico.

Ramirez, Santiago, and R. Parres. 1957. Some dynamic patterns in the organization of the Mexican family. *Int. J. Soc. Psychiat.* 3:18–21.

Ramos, Samuel. 1934. *El Perfil de Hombre y la Cultura en Mexico*. Mexico: Imprenta Mundial.

Rapaport, Anatol. 1964. *Strategy and Conscience*. New York: Harper & Row.

Raven, B. H., and J. R. French Jr. 1958. Legitimate power, coercive power, and observability in social influence. *J. Personality* 26:400–409.

Richards, I. A. 1932. *Mencius on the Mind: Experiments in Multiple Definition*. New York: Harcourt, Brace & World.

Ritter, E. A. 1955. *Shaka Zulu*. London: Panther.

Roheim, Geza. 1932. Psycho-analysis of primitive cultural types. *Int. J. Psychoanalysis* 13:1–224.

Romney, K., and R. D'Andrade. 1964. Cognitive aspects of English kin terms. *Amer. Anthro.* 66 (3):146–70.

Rubel, Arthur. 1965. The Mexican-American palomilla. *Anthro. Ling.* 7:92–97.

Sahlins, M. D. 1958. *Social Stratification in Polynesia*. Seattle: University of Washington Press.

———. 1962. *Moala*. Ann Arbor: University of Michigan Press.

———. 1965. On the sociology of primitive exchange, in *The Relevance of Models for Social Anthropology*. A. S. A. Monographs 1. London: Tavistock; New York: Praeger.

Schneider, David M. 1961. Introduction: the distinctive features of matrilineal descent groups, in David M. Schneider and Kathleen Gough (eds.), *Matrilineal Kinship*. Berkeley and Los Angeles: University of California Press.

———. 1968. *American Kinship: A Cultural Approach*. Englewood Cliffs, N. J.: Prentice-Hall.

Schooler, Carmi and William Caudill. 1964. Sympatology in Japanese and American schizophrenia. *Ethnology* 3:172–178.

Sears, R. R. 1957. Identification as a form of behavioral development, in *The Concept of Development*. Minneapolis: University of Minnesota Press.

Seeley, John R., Alexander Sim, and Elizabeth W. Loosely. 1956. Differentiation of values in a modern community, in *Crestwood Heights*. New York: Basic Books. Reprinted in Norman W. Bell and Ezra F. Vogel (eds.), *A Modern Introduction to the Family*. New York: Free Press, 1964. Pp. 453–464.

———. 1965. *Crestwood Heights*. New York: Science Editions.

Shepler, B. 1951. A comparison of masculinity-femininity measures. *J. Consulting Psych.* 15:484–486.

Simon, Anne W. 1964. *Stepchild in the Family: A View of Children in Remarriage*. New York: Odyssey.

Slater, P. E. 1961. Toward a dualistic theory of identification. *Merrill-Palmer Quarterly* 7 (2):113–126.

Smith, William Carlson. 1953. *The Stepchild.* Chicago: University of Chicago Press.

Sofue, Takao. 1964. Tokyo no daigakusei ni okeru tekio no ichi bunseki (An analysis of the degree of adjustment in Tokyo college students). *Japanese Annals of Social Psychology* 5:133–160.

———. 1965. *Regional Variations of Japanese Personality: An Analysis by the Aid of the Sentence Completion Test (Preliminary Report).* Paper read at the Annual Joint Meeting of the Anthropological Society of Nippon and the Japanese Society of Ethnology, Sendai.

Spencer, P. 1965. *The Samburu: A Study of Gerontocracy in a Nomadic Tribe.* Berkeley: University of California Press.

Srinivas, M. N. 1966. *Social Change in Modern India.* Berkeley: University of California Press.

Stephens, W. 1962. *The Oedipus Complex: Cross Cultural Evidence.* New York: Free Press.

Strathern, Andrew and Marilyn Strathern. 1966. Dominant kin relationships and ideas. *Amer. Anthro.* (Brief Communication) 68:997–999.

Syme, R. 1939. *The Roman Revolution.* London: Oxford University Press.

Tannenbaum, Frank. 1950. *Mexico, The Struggle for Peace and Bread.* New York: Alfred A. Knopf.

Tatje, Terrence A., and Francis L. K. Hsu. 1969. "Variations in Ancestor Worship Beliefs and Their Relation to Kinship." *Southwestern J. of Anthro.* 25:153–172.

Troeltsch, E. 1960. *The Social Teachings of the Christian Churches.* New York: Harper Torchbooks.

Turner, V. W. 1957. *Schism and Continuity in an African Society: A Study of Ndembu Village Life.* Manchester: Manchester University Press.

Vogel, Ezra. 1963. *Japan's New Middle Class.* Berkeley: University of California Press.

Wallace, A. F. C. 1958. Dreams and the wishes of the soul: a type of psychoanalytic theory among the seventeenth century Iroquois. *Amer. Anthro.* 60:234–248.

———. 1965. The problem of the psychological validity of componential analyses, in E. A. Hammel (ed.), *Formal Semantic Analysis. Amer. Anthro.* (Special Publication) 67 (5,2): 229–248.

Wallace, Anthony, and John Atkins. 1960. The meaning of kinship terms. *Amer. Anthro.* 62:58–79.

Warner, W. L. 1937–58. *A Black Civilization.* New York: Harper & Row.

Weber, M. 1958. *The Protestant Ethic and the Spirit of Capitalism.* New York: Scribner's Paperback.

———. 1964. *The Sociology of Religion.* Boston: Beacon Press.

White, Harrison C. 1963. *An Anatomy of Kinship, Mathematical Models for Structures of Cumulated Roles.* Englewood Cliffs, N. J.: Prentice-Hall.

Whiting, John W. M. 1959. Sorcery, sin and the superego, in M. R. Jones (ed.), *Nebraska Symposium on Motivation: 1959.* Lincoln, Neb.: University of Nebraska Press. Pp. 174–195.

———. 1960. Resource mediation and learning by identification, in I. Iscoe and H. W. Stevensen (eds.), *Personality Development in Children.* Austin: University of Texas Press. Pp. 112–126.

Whiting, John, and I. L. Child. 1953. *Child Training and Personality.* New Haven, Conn.: Yale University Press.

Whiting, John, Richard Kluckhohn and Albert Anthony. 1958. The function of male initiation ceremonies at puberty, in E. Maccoby, T. M. Newcomb, and

E. L. Hartley (eds.), *Readings in Social Psychology*. New York: Holt, Rinehart & Winston. Pp. 359–370.

Wolf, Erik. 1959. *Sons of the Shaking Earth*. Chicago: University of Chicago Press.

———. 1966. Kinship, friendship and patron-client relations in complex societies, in *The Social Anthropology of Complex Societies*. A. S. A. Monographs 4. London: Tavistock; New York: Praeger.

Yang, Lien-sheng. 1957. The concept of Pao as a basis for social relations in China, in John K. Fairbank (ed.), *Chinese Thought and Institutions*. Chicago: University of Chicago Press. Pp. 291–309.

Young, Frank. 1962. The function of male initiation ceremonies: a cross cultural test of an alternative hypothesis. *Amer. J. Soc.* 67:380.

Zelditch, Morris. 1955. Role differentiation in the nuclear family—a comparative study, in Talcott Parsons and Robert Bales (eds.), *Family, Socialization and Interaction Process*. New York: Free Press. Pp. 307–351.

Index